Sea and Land

Sea and Land

An Environmental History of the Caribbean

PHILIP D. MORGAN, J. R. MCNEILL,
MATTHEW MULCAHY, AND STUART B. SCHWARTZ

OXFORD
UNIVERSITY PRESS

OXFORD
UNIVERSITY PRESS

Oxford University Press is a department of the University of Oxford. It furthers
the University's objective of excellence in research, scholarship, and education
by publishing worldwide. Oxford is a registered trade mark of Oxford University
Press in the UK and certain other countries.

Published in the United States of America by Oxford University Press
198 Madison Avenue, New York, NY 10016, United States of America.

CIP data is on file at the Library of Congress

ISBN 978–0–19–755545–3 (pbk.)
ISBN 978–0–19–755544–6 (hbk.)

DOI: 10.1093/oso/9780197555446.001.0001

1 3 5 7 9 8 6 4 2

Paperback printed by LSC communications, United States of America
Hardback printed by Bridgeport National Bindery, Inc., United States of America

CONTENTS

PREFACE AND ACKNOWLEDGMENTS

The origins of this book began with an invitation extended to Philip Morgan in 2012 by Bernard Bailyn, then director of Harvard University's International Seminar on the History of the Atlantic World, 1500–1825. Professor Bailyn said he would like to hold a one-day workshop, on the integration of the Atlantic world, the "densely woven networks of social, economic, and political ties," and to center it on the Caribbean. He was hoping for a discussion of the Caribbean as the focal point for understanding the Atlantic as a region, with some attention to ocean regions as such, pointing to comparisons with other ocean-regional areas. However wide-ranging the discussion might be, the core should be the multinational, polylingual, polycultural Caribbean, with its filiations reaching throughout four continents. He promised a small but savvy audience and five sharp commentators: Peter Coclanis, Malick Ghachem, Jane Landers, Peter Miller, and Stuart Schwartz. The event proved to be the last meeting of Bailyn's International Seminar. It would be nice to think it ended on a high note, with a bang, not a whimper, but that may be wishful thinking on Morgan's part.

Rather than explore the integration of the Atlantic world via the Caribbean, Morgan decided that he would concentrate on a single theme, the Caribbean environment, although he tried to think capaciously about that subject. He did not then, and does not now, consider himself an environmental historian, but he believes that it is vitally important to consider what they and others— climatologists, marine biologists, biogeographers, paleotempestologists, and the like—have to tell us about this pivotal region. In his original paper, he suggested a number of themes and went into great detail on a number of issues. A few early reactions from friends to whom he circulated his manuscript suggested that he had not gone far enough. John McNeill thought he should do more with soils; Matt Mulcahy said that he must devote more space to insects; David Geggus, somewhat tongue in cheek, but only just, said, "Frankly, I was hoping for a little more on the history of the Solenodon, and you clearly neglected the political thought of the gecko." Jeff Bolster, who has written perhaps the best environ-mental study of a part of the Atlantic Ocean, wondered whether sections of the paper really constituted history. He raised the issue, because he sensed for years, rightly or wrongly, that his colleagues imagined that he had gone "off the deep end" when he turned from writing African American history (real history in their eyes), to counting fish (which is not what they imagined historians do). At times, Morgan mused that he, like Bolster, had gone off the deep end.

When he began thinking about publication, Morgan toyed with the idea of a short book with at least two other essays. Of the commentators, Schwartz, who was then completing a book on hurricanes, was an obvious choice for an essay on natural disasters. Schwartz invited Matthew Mulcahy, who had written his own book on hurricanes and had participated as a member of the audience in Bailyn's International Seminar, to team with him on the essay. In April 2013 John McNeill invited Morgan to circulate a version of his paper to the Georgetown University Environmental History Seminar. After this stimulating and challenging event, McNeill agreed to contribute the third essay of the projected volume on the changing disease environments of the Caribbean. This is a short account of how this book came together. With the help of his co-authors, Morgan wrote the in-troduction; and all four of us contributed to the concluding chapter.

Morgan would like to thank a number of people who read earlier versions of this essay and made useful suggestions, including most of all his co-authors—John, Matt, and Stuart. Particularly helpful readers of early versions of this essay include Bernard Bailyn, Jane Landers, Malick Ghachem, David Geggus, Peter Coclanis, and especially Jeff Bolster, who was most encouraging. Kate Murphy was extremely generous in pointing him toward natural history material. As the essay developed, he received useful feedback from Stuart McCook, Bertie Mandelblatt, and Molly Warsh. One constant provider of key information has been Bill Keegan.

McNeill thanks Trevor Burnard, Jeff Cimmino, Cam Elliott, Monica Green, Kyle Harper, Emily Mendenhall, Andrew Meshnick, Phil Morgan, Matt Mulcahy, Tim Newfield, Philip Rotz, Eleanora Rohland, Stuart Schwartz, and Molly Warsh.

Mulcahy and Schwartz recognize several individuals who read all or parts of their chapter and offered helpful feedback on matters historical and scientific. They are grateful to Michael Chenoweth, Clint Conrad, Anya Zilberstein, Bertie Mandelblatt, Susan Ferber, Louis Gerdelan, Reinaldo Funes Monzote, Phoebe Labat, Philip Morgan, and John McNeill, and the anonymous reviewers of the manuscript at Oxford. David Turnham and Catherine Savell helped with the translation of some French materials. A number of people shared references with us, including Phil Morgan, Malick Ghachem, Bridget Brereton, Diogo de Carvallo Cabral, Wim Klooster, Patrick Barker, and Christopher Church.

Zachary Gahs-Buccheri at the Loyola-Notre Dame library helped track down a variety of materials via interlibrary loan.

Portions of this chapter appeared in somewhat different form in "Nature's Battalions: Insects as Agricultural Pests in the Early Modern Caribbean," *William and Mary Quarterly*, 75, no. 3 (July 2018), 433–64; and in "Miserably Scorched: Drought in Plantation Colonies of the British Greater Caribbean," in *Atlantic Environments and the American South*, ed. Thomas Blake Earle and D. Andrew Johnson (Athens: University of Georgia Press, 2020), and are used with permission.

All dates are as they appear in the documents; except for English/British sources prior to 1752, the new year is dated January 1. The English/British colonies remained on the Julian calendar until September 1752.

Sea and Land

THE GREATER CARIBBEAN, c.1790

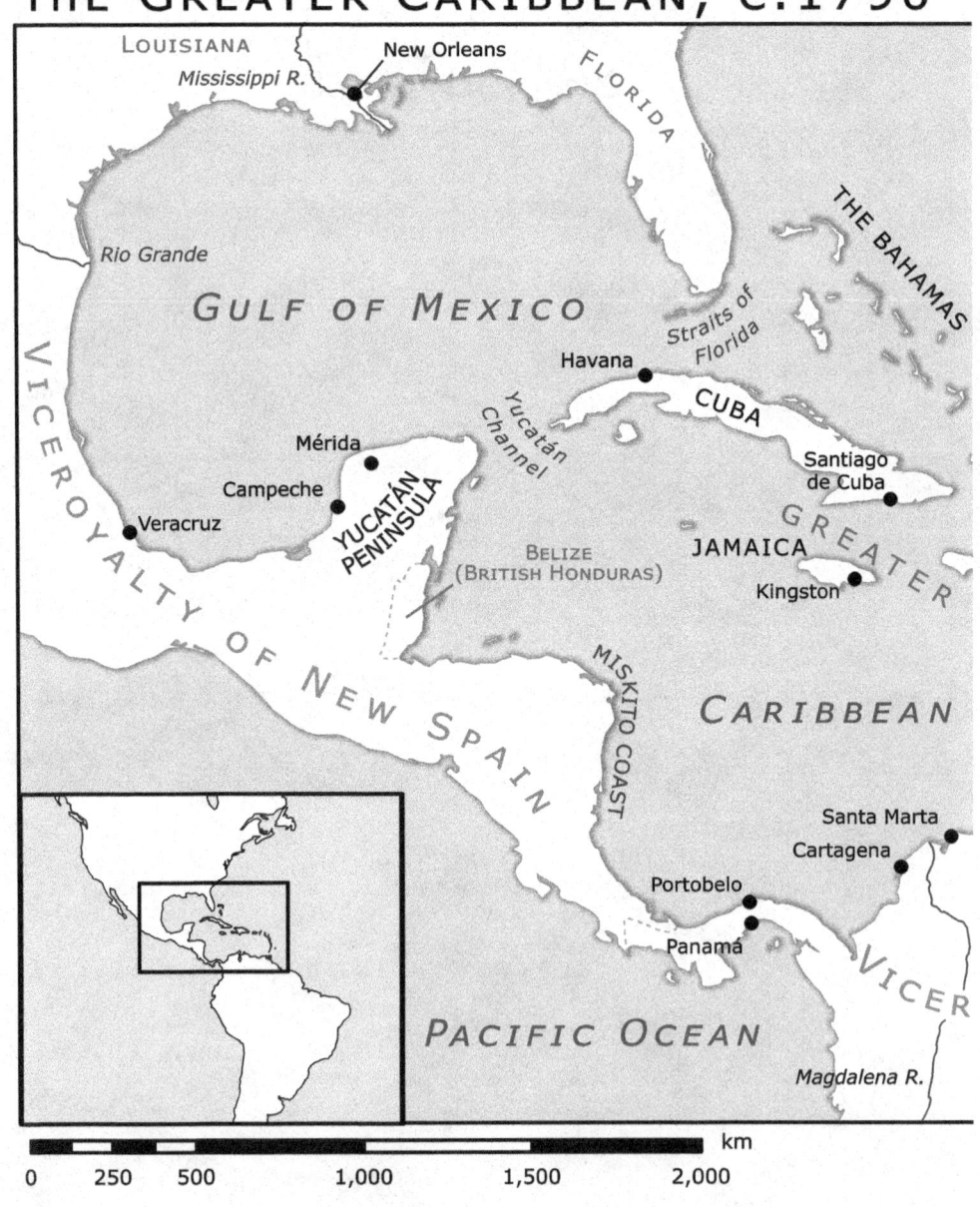

LOUISIANA
New Orleans
Mississippi R.

FLORIDA

THE BAHAMAS

Rio Grande

GULF OF MEXICO

Straits of Florida

Havana

Yucatán Channel

CUBA

Mérida

Campeche

Santiago de Cuba

Veracruz

YUCATÁN PENINSULA

BELIZE
(BRITISH HONDURAS)

JAMAICA

GREATER

Kingston

VICEROYALTY OF NEW SPAIN

MISKITO COAST

CARIBBEAN

Santa Marta

Cartagena

Portobelo

Panamá

VICER

PACIFIC OCEAN

Magdalena R.

km

0   250   500   1,000   1,500   2,000

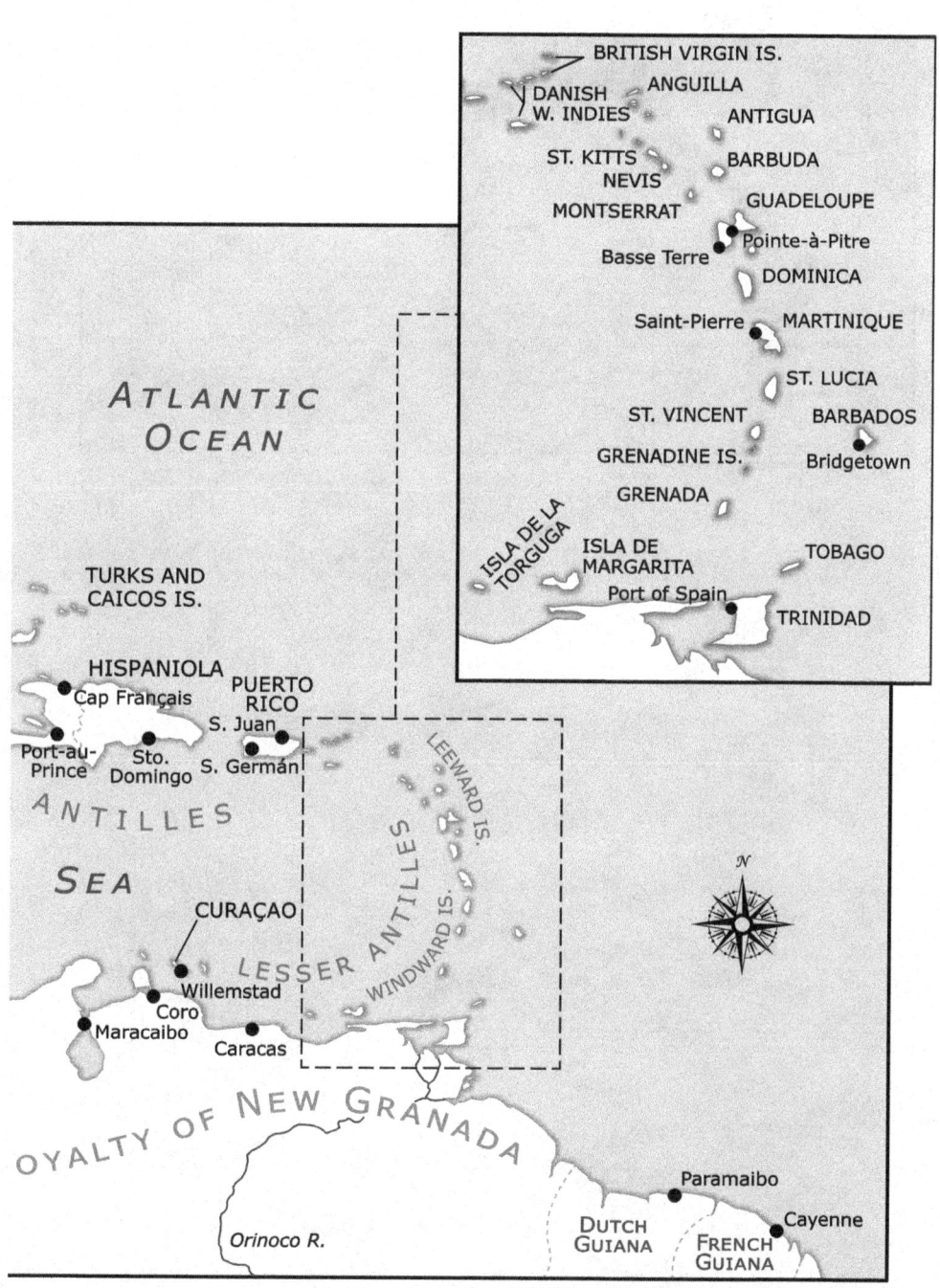

BRITISH VIRGIN IS.

DANISH W. INDIES

ANGUILLA

ANTIGUA

ST. KITTS

BARBUDA

NEVIS

MONTSERRAT

GUADELOUPE

Pointe-à-Pitre

Basse Terre

DOMINICA

Saint-Pierre

MARTINIQUE

ST. LUCIA

ST. VINCENT

BARBADOS

GRENADINE IS.

Bridgetown

GRENADA

ISLA DE LA TORGUGA

ISLA DE MARGARITA

TOBAGO

Port of Spain

TRINIDAD

ATLANTIC OCEAN

TURKS AND CAICOS IS.

HISPANIOLA

Cap Français

PUERTO RICO

S. Juan

Port-au-Prince

Sto. Domingo

S. Germán

ANTILLES

LEEWARD IS.

SEA

CURAÇAO

WINDWARD IS.

LESSER ANTILLES

Willemstad

Coro

Maracaibo

Caracas

N

OYALTY OF NEW GRANADA

Paramaibo

Cayenne

Orinoco R.

DUTCH GUIANA

FRENCH GUIANA

© 2021 G. Wallace Cartography & GIS
Cartography by Geoffrey Wallace

The Western Caribbean, c.1790

FLORIDA

GRAND
BAHAMA

GREAT ABACO

Atlantic Ocean

GULF OF MEXICO

NASSAU

ELEUTHERA

Straits of Florida

CAT ISLAND

ANDROS
ISLAND

LONG ISLAND

San Juan
River

Havana

Matanzas

CROOKED ISLAND

MAYAGUANA

CUBA

LITTLE INAGUA

Caicos Passage

TURKS AND CAICOS ISLANDS

YUCATÁN

Yucatán Channel

ISLA DE PINOS

GREAT INAGUA

SIERRA
MAESTRA

TORTUGA

HISPANIOLA

COZUMEL

Cap Français

STO. DOMINGO

CORDILLERA
CENTRAL

Santiago
de Cuba

S. DOMINGUE

CAYMAN ISLANDS

Saint Marc

PUERTO
RICO

San Juan

JAMAICA

Les Cayes

Port-au-Prince

Santo
Domingo

San Germán

VIEQUES

L. Enriquillo

ISLA DE MONA

Newcastle Barracks

BLUE MOUNTAINS

Spanish Town

Kingston

Port
Royal

Caribbean Sea

© 2021 G. Wallace Cartography & GIS
Cartography by Geoffrey Wallace

km

0   100 200   400   600   800   1,000

THE EASTERN & SOUTHERN CARIBBEAN, C.1790

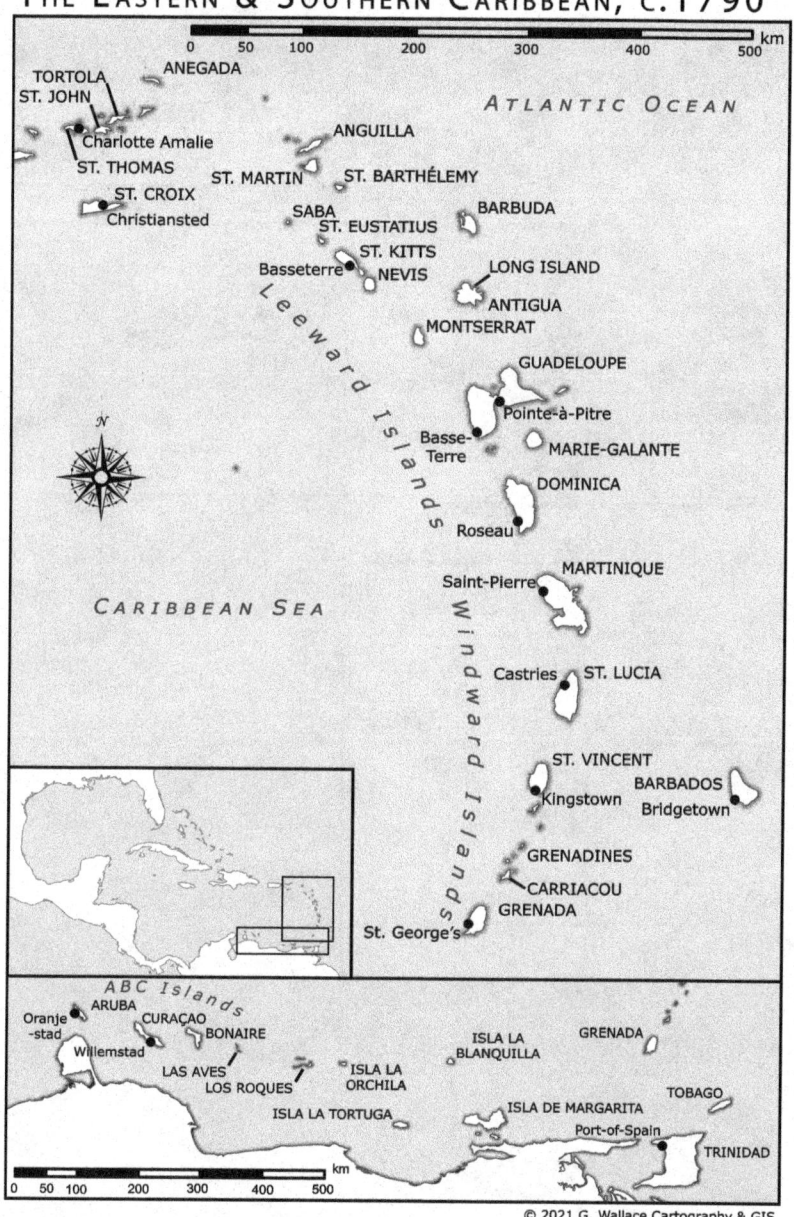

ATLANTIC OCEAN

ANEGADA
TORTOLA
ST. JOHN
Charlotte Amalie
ST. THOMAS
ST. CROIX
Christiansted

ANGUILLA
ST. MARTIN   ST. BARTHÉLEMY
SABA   BARBUDA
ST. EUSTATIUS
ST. KITTS
Basseterre NEVIS   LONG ISLAND
                          ANTIGUA
             MONTSERRAT

Leeward Islands

GUADELOUPE
Pointe-à-Pitre
Basse-
Terre   MARIE-GALANTE

DOMINICA
Roseau

CARIBBEAN SEA

MARTINIQUE
Saint-Pierre

Castries   ST. LUCIA

ST. VINCENT
Kingstown   BARBADOS
              Bridgetown

GRENADINES
CARRIACOU
GRENADA
St. George's

Windward Islands

ABC Islands
ARUBA
Oranje   CURAÇAO
-stad   BONAIRE
Willemstad   ISLA LA   GRENADA
                                  BLANQUILLA
            LAS AVES   ISLA LA
            LOS ROQUES   ORCHILA
                    ISLA LA TORTUGA   ISLA DE MARGARITA   TOBAGO
                                          Port-of-Spain
                                                              TRINIDAD

km
0 50 100 200 300 400 500

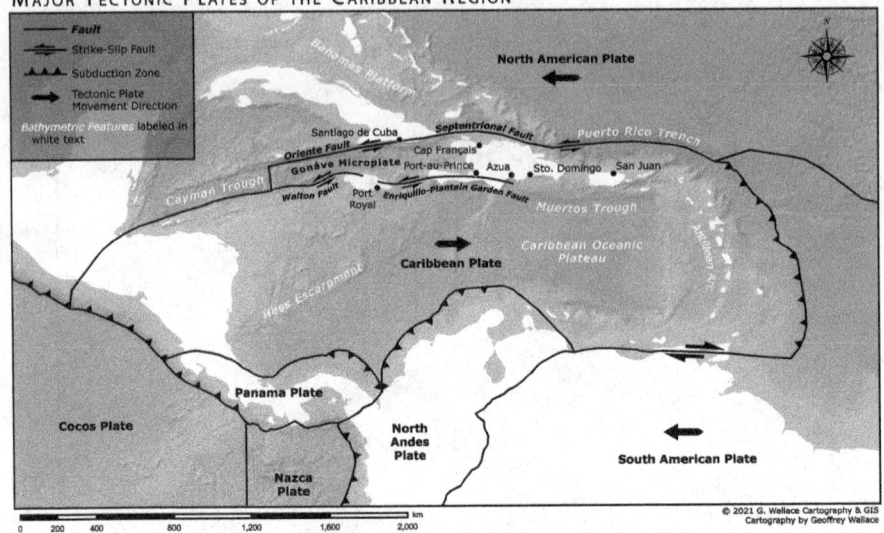

MAJOR TECTONIC PLATES OF THE CARIBBEAN REGION

Fault
Strike-Slip Fault
Subduction Zone
Tectonic Plate Movement Direction
Bathymetric Features labeled in white text

North American Plate

Bahamas Platform

Santiago de Cuba
Cap Français
Septentrional Fault
Puerto Rico Trench

Oriente Fault
Gonâve Microplate
Port-au-Prince
Azua
Sto. Domingo
San Juan

Cayman Trough

Walton Fault
Port Royal
Enriquillo-Plantain Garden Fault
Muertos Trough

Caribbean Plate

Caribbean Oceanic Plateau

Hess Escarpment

Panama Plate

Cocos Plate

North Andes Plate

Nazca Plate

South American Plate

© 2021 G. Wallace Cartography & GIS
Cartography by Geoffrey Wallace

km
0   200   400   800   1,200   1,600   2,000

Volcanoes of the Lesser Antilles

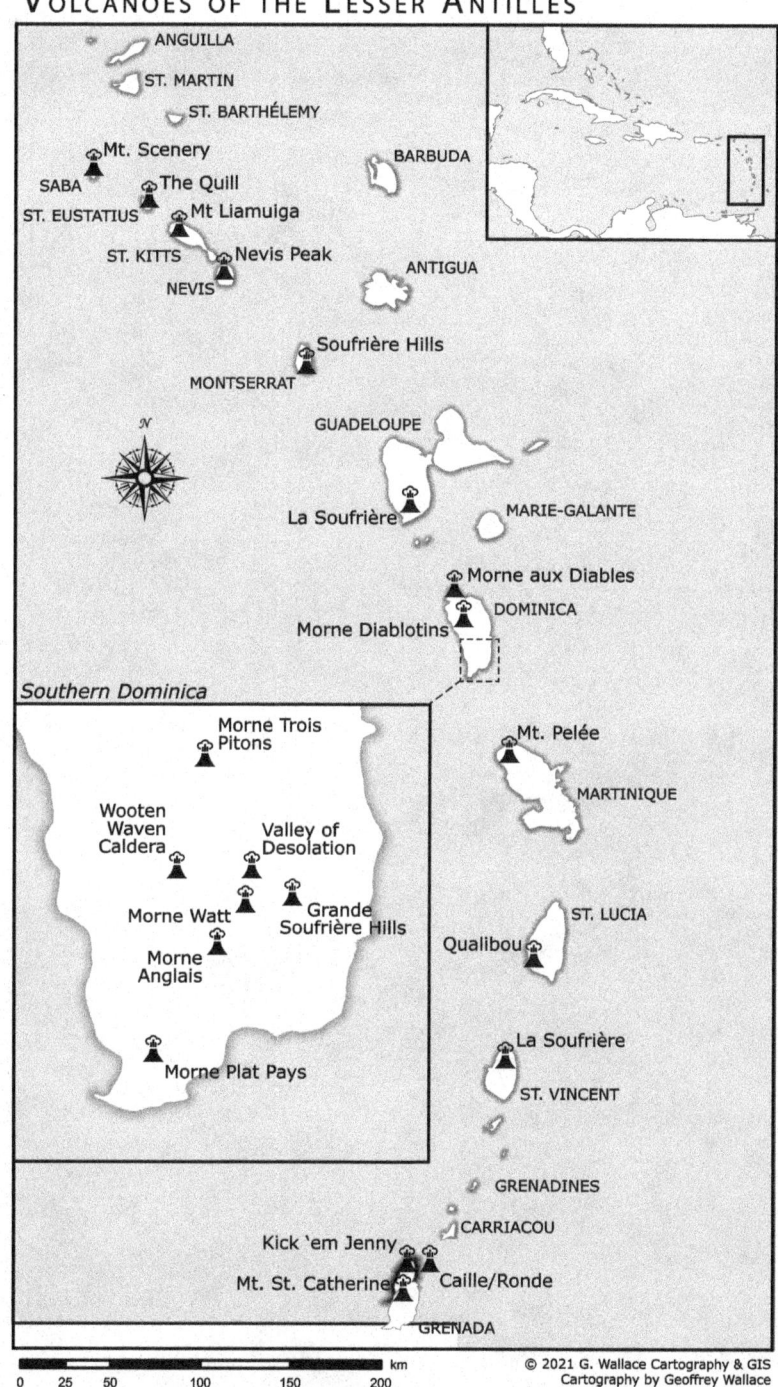

ANGUILLA

ST. MARTIN

ST. BARTHÉLEMY

Mt. Scenery

SABA

The Quill

ST. EUSTATIUS

Mt Liamuiga

ST. KITTS

Nevis Peak

NEVIS

BARBUDA

ANTIGUA

Soufrière Hills

MONTSERRAT

GUADELOUPE

La Soufrière

MARIE-GALANTE

Morne aux Diables

DOMINICA

Morne Diablotins

N

Southern Dominica

Morne Trois Pitons

Wooten Waven Caldera

Valley of Desolation

Morne Watt

Grande Soufrière Hills

Morne Anglais

Morne Plat Pays

Mt. Pelée

MARTINIQUE

ST. LUCIA

Qualibou

La Soufrière

ST. VINCENT

GRENADINES

CARRIACOU

Kick 'em Jenny

Mt. St. Catherine

Caille/Ronde

GRENADA

km

0   25   50   100   150   200

© 2021 G. Wallace Cartography & GIS
Cartography by Geoffrey Wallace

Introduction

PHILIP D. MORGAN

German naturalist Alexander von Humboldt (1769–1859) knew the Caribbean well. In the last year of the eighteenth century and first four years of the nineteenth, he spent many months in the circum-Caribbean region. The first island he saw in the Americas was "extremely picturesque . . . skillfully cultivated" Tobago, "the dazzling whiteness of the rocks" contrasting with "the green of the scattered trees," and the "high cylindrical cacti crown[ing] the mountain tops." His first port of call was Cumaná, the capital of New Andalusia, a province within the Captaincy General of Venezuela, where he lived for about a year and which he described as "a very hot but dry place." From Cumaná, he explored Venezuela's Caribbean coast, visiting Caracas and going as far west as Lake Valencia. He spent time in Cartagena and Veracruz, ports with extensive Caribbean connections. He twice visited the largest island in the region, Cuba, where he lived for four and a half months. He wrote of an "Antillean Mediterranean," the rimland extending from Mexico south and east to the Guianas.[1]

Humboldt left the Caribbean in 1804, but he continued to write about the region for the rest of his life. His *Personal Narrative of Travels in the Equinoctial Regions of the New Continent*, published in many volumes between 1814 and 1829, details his vivid experiences in the circum-Caribbean region, and his *Political Essay on the Island of Cuba* (1826) combines dense statistical data about, and lyrical evocations of, the island. According to the distinguished Cuban anthropologist Fernando Ortiz, Humboldt was a "bold inventor" of the island of Cuba, promoting its importance, which he saw stemming from its size, soil fertility, naval bases, character of its population ("three-fifths of which are free men"), and, above all, the advantages of Havana's geographical position, commanding the outlets of the Caribbean Sea.[2]

Sea and Land. Philip D. Morgan, J. R. McNeill, Matthew Mulcahy, and Stuart B. Schwartz, Oxford University Press.
© Oxford University Press 2022. DOI: 10.1093/oso/9780197555446.003.0001

Humboldt's observations and wide-ranging interests prefigure many of the themes of this book. His writings highlight how beauty and violence, promise and degradation went hand in hand in the early modern Caribbean. The lush tropical scenery of the Caribbean region, for example, thoroughly captivated Humboldt. His elation knew no bounds, as evident in his July 16, 1799, letter to his brother Wilhelm, documenting his first delirious impressions of the tropics, obtained on the coasts of Venezuela. "What trees! Coco palms, 50 to 60 feet high! Poinciana pulcherrima, with foot-tall bushes of the most magnificent bright red blossoms; Pisange, and a cluster of trees with huge leaves and aromatic blossoms the size of a hand. . . . And what colors the birds have, and the fish, even the crabs (sky-blue and yellow)!" Almost every sentence ends in an exclamation point. He and his companion, a young French scientist, Aimé Bonpland, ran "around like fools; in the first three days, we could not categorize anything because we would always toss aside one object in order to pick up another." Bonpland assured Humboldt "that he will lose his mind if the wonders do not soon cease." Even "more beautiful than these individual marvels," Humboldt concluded, "is the impression of the entirety of potent, profuse, and yet also so light, uplifting, mild nature of the plants." His first encounter with the tropics was the most memorable, vivid, and long-lasting. "In my imagination," he wrote, "I shall see Cumaná and its dusty ground more intensely than all the marvels of the Andes."[3]

The "organic vigor typical of the Torrid Zone" was evident, Humboldt thought, in the first people he encountered from the deck of the corvette *Pizarro* that had conveyed him across the Atlantic in 41 days (including a stopover in the Canary Islands). They were 36 Guaiquerí Indians divided into two groups of 18 in two "pirogues," or canoes, each fashioned from one tree trunk, who had ventured out to the ship. They were "naked to the waist and very tall." They "looked very muscular, with a skin colour between brown and coppery red." From afar, they looked like "bronze statues." They were nothing like the feeble, weak natives described by previous travelers. These Indians offered the Europeans fresh coconuts and "stunningly coloured fish." Their pirogues contained other "riches": huge leaves covering bunches of bananas, the scaly armor of an armadillo, cups made from the fruit of the calabash tree. The chief of one of the canoes stayed on board the *Pizarro* to act as a coastal pilot, guiding it past the Caribbean islands of Coche, Margarita, and Cubagua before landing at the harbor of Cumaná. Humboldt recorded the name of the pilot, Carlos del Pino, a "most trustworthy" Guaiquerí, "a keen observer, and led by a genuine thirst for learning he had studied the produce of the sea and land around him." Enlightenment ideals, it seemed, were not limited to Europeans, at least in Humboldt's eyes. He recognized his good fortune that the first native he encountered was "a man whose knowledge was to prove extremely helpful" accompanying him "for sixteen months up and down the coast, and into the interior." On their last night on deck before disembarking at Cumaná, the "Indian pilot" entertained the ship's complement with "stories about the plants and animals of his land," mentioning a mountain range not far from the coast and plains inhabited by two kinds of crocodiles, boas, electric eels, and various species of jaguars.[4]

The Caribbean Sea features prominently in Humboldt's travelogues. He first saw Tobago because the captain of the *Pizarro*, fearing the south wind and the approach to the Boca del Dragón (the outlet of the Gulf of Paria), thought that the safest entrance to the sea was through the channel separating Trinidad from Tobago. Humboldt regularly traversed parts of the sea. Just to mention a few journeys: a narrow pirogue, overloaded with sugar cane, bananas, and coconuts, conveyed him and his scientific instruments across the Gulf of Cariaco, a body of water he crossed three times; he traveled from Cumaná to La Guaira on one of the thirty-foot sailboats common in these waters, none of which "has been lost at sea in a storm," due to the "skill of the Guaiquerí pilots"; in Nueva Barcelona he hired a *lancha* (sloop or shallop) that usually smuggled cocoa to the island of Trinidad to take him to Cumaná; in Cumaná he boarded an American ship loaded with salt for Cuba; and he secured passage on a Catalonian sloop anchored at Batabanó in southern Cuba for Porto Bello or Cartagena, "depending on how the Santa Marta gales might blow." He conducted experiments at sea, paid attention to channels, currents, depths, and water colors, and knew well the importance of the Gulf Stream. For his map of Cuba, he used "the astronomical observations of the most experienced Spanish seafarers." For him, Cuba dominated "the northern Caribbean Sea, known as the Gulf of Mexico," which was "a Mediterranean with two outlets." The channels meet at Havana, he declared, "the opposing direction of the currents and the atmospheric disturbances—quite violent at the beginning of winter—lend these waters at the edge of the tropics a peculiar character."[5]

For Humboldt, the terrestrial and maritime wonders of the Caribbean region abounded. The profusion of the sensual impressions almost overwhelmed him: the size and abundance of the plant life, the vivid colors of the flora, the intense heat, dazzling light, and the "exquisite honey and flower aroma that characterizes Cuba's anchorages." The sensory overload from the flora was matched by the faunal marvels. Huge spiders devoured hummingbirds. An enormous boa had antlers stuck in its throat after swallowing a stag. The Cuban crocodile was "said to be very daring and even climbs into boats when it can. It often wanders a league inland just to devour pigs. It reaches some 15 feet long and even chases (so they say) men on horseback." Cuban Indians tied a line to the tails of remora or suckerfish that would then attach themselves to the shells of sea turtles allowing them to reel in huge specimens. On the southern coast of Cuba, Humboldt saw more fireflies, "signposts in the dark," than anywhere else in the Americas and analogized that "the firmament's starry vault had lowered itself onto the savanna." In a nice domestic touch, he noted that in poor homes, 15 of these insects in a perforated gourd sufficed as a torch during the night. A young woman in Trinidad de Cuba told Humboldt "that she had relied on the cocuyos' [fireflies'] phosphorescence every time she breastfed her child at night during a long and difficult crossing to the Tierra Firme. The ship's captain did not want to have any other light on board, out of fear of pirates."[6]

Of course, insects were an irritant (or worse) as well as a boon. The mouth of the San Juan River on the southern shores of Cuba, Humboldt reported, was "a place sailors fear because of its countless *mosquites* and *zancudos* [crane flies]." Botanizing walks in the forests near Cartagena would have been a delight in this fertile marshy soil, noted Humboldt, "if we had not been devoured by mosquitoes, *zancudos*, chigoes and numberless [other] insects." Some insects could be dangerous. Also near Cartagena, Humboldt observed a thick acacia bush "infamous for a deplorable event." This acacia "is armed with very sharp thorns, and extraordinarily large ants live on it. A woman, annoyed by her husband's well-founded jealousy, planned a barbarous revenge. With the help of her lover, she tied her husband up with rope, and at night chucked him into this *Acacia cornigera* bush. The more violently he struggled the more the sharp thorns tore his skin. His screams were heard by some passersby who found him after several hours covered with blood and dreadfully stung by ants." Humboldt ascribed the violence of this crime's passion to the "coarseness of manners," not the tropics, thereby undermining a standard trope about the effects of a hot climate. In Cumaná the "persistent destructive activity of the termites, the white ants," meant no documents older than 150 years survived. "Only those who have seen the quantity of ants that infest the countries of the torrid zone," declared Humboldt, "can picture the destruction and the sinking of the ground caused by these insects." Their excavations resembled underground canals, which flood with water during the rains and undermine buildings. When troops of ants ravaged the fine plains of La Vega on the island of Santo Domingo, Humboldt reported, the monks tried to burn the ant larvae and fumigate the nests. They then told the inhabitants to choose a saint by lot; the choice fell on Saint Saturnin, and the ants disappeared as soon as the saint's festival was celebrated. Humboldt passed no judgment on this tale.[7]

Likewise, an incident at Cay Bonito (Lovely Cay) off the southern coast of Cuba, which Humboldt declared "worthy of its name because of its abundant vegetation," captured the danger and violence that existed amid the region's natural wonders. While Humboldt and his companions "were busy gathering herbs," the sailors manning his ship "looked for spiny lobsters." Irritated at not finding any, they compensated for their disappointment "by climbing the Mangroves, and inflicting terrible carnage on the young *Alcatraz* [brown pelicans] grouped by twos in their nests. . . . The young birds valiantly defended themselves with

their enormous 6 to 7 inch beaks. The adult birds hovered above our heads, let-
ting out hoarse and plaintive cries. Blood dripped from tree tops, for the sailors
were armed with clubs and *machetes.*" Although Humboldt remonstrated with
the sailors for their "lack of empathy and for their pointless cruelties," they would
not desist. His explanation was that, "condemned to long obedience on the sol-
itary seas, sailors are more than pleased to impose a cruel dominion on animals
as soon as the opportunity arises." Thus, "the ground was covered with wounded
birds, in the throes of death." Before their arrival, "a deep calm had reigned in this
little corner of the earth. Now, everything seemed to cry out: Man was here."[8]

Humboldt's view of nature, confirmed and elaborated by his tropical sojourn,
was that it was a web, in which all elements were connected. It was a living whole,
a unified ecosystem. Pull one thread and the whole tapestry would unravel. At
the Venezuelan coast, Humboldt noted how excessive pearl fishing had completely destroyed oyster stocks. Similarly, indigo plantations at Lake Valencia,
near Caracas, impoverished the soil. For Humboldt, monoculture led to the import of food, dependency, and the horrors of slavery. Deforestation made the
land barren, water levels fall, and soils leach. He believed in the forest's ability to
enrich the atmosphere with moisture; trees stored water, protected the soil, and
had a cooling effect. Thus

> when forests are destroyed, as they are everywhere in the Americas,
> by European planters, with imprudent haste, the springs dry up com-
> pletely, or merely trickle. River beds remain dry part of the year, and are
> then turned into torrents, whenever it rains heavily on the heights. As
> grass and moss disappear with the brushwood from the mountainsides,
> so rainwater is unchecked in its course. Instead of slowly raising the
> river level by filtrations, the heavy rains dig channels into the hillsides,
> dragging down loose soil, and forming sudden, destructive floods.
> Thus, the clearing of forests, the absence of permanent springs, and
> torrents are three closely connected phenomena.

Humboldt understood ecological chain reactions.[9]

Humboldt was also well aware of the impact of disease in the Caribbean. As
the *Pizarro* approached the region in July 1799, a "malignant fever" broke out
among crew and passengers, threatening to turn into an epidemic. In Humboldt's
view, the captain failed to apply the simplest remedies. He did not fumigate, and
he had forgotten to bring "an ounce of quinine." Who would have predicted,
Humboldt mused, "that a Spanish ship would be without this Peruvian bark feb-
rifuge"? An "ignorant" surgeon on board prescribed bleedings, "attributing the
fever to what he called the heat and corruption of blood." One sailor, close to
death, began to recover only when transferred from an "asphyxiating, noxious,

and humid atmosphere" below decks to the open air near a hatchway. One passenger died within three days of contracting the fever. Even yellow fever, or
"black vomit, as it is called at Veracruz," noted Humboldt, "does not carry off the
sick so frighteningly quickly." Fortunate to disembark at Cumaná, a "dry place
celebrated for its salubrity," he enjoyed good health, particularly during those
first dangerous months when "Europeans are exposed to the burning heat of the
Tropics." At La Guaira, the port of Caracas, he felt suitably acclimatized to stand
hatless in the sun taking temperature readings, prompting a doctor to offer him
a potion to ward off "an attack of yellow fever" that would occur that very night.
Amused, Humboldt obliged the doctor. When yellow fever raged in Havana,
he observed, residents of Havana take to the hills "where the air is purer."
Acknowledging that cramped, overcrowded Caribbean cities had high death
rates, he nevertheless thought that yellow fever "has had far less of an impact on
mortality rates than is popularly believed." From his statistical reckonings, births
almost equaled deaths at times. Extreme fluctuations owed much to the varying
influxes of "poorly acclimated foreigners," both black and white.[10]

Humboldt experienced and learned about natural disasters characteristic of
the region. Beginning 4.12 in the afternoon of November 4, 1799—less than
four months after his arrival in Cumaná—he felt two successive seismic shocks,
15 seconds apart. "Everybody ran out into the streets screaming," he observed.
He described the "great impression" that this first earthquake made on him,
causing him to mistrust the very ground on which he walked. He tried to make
sense of the warning signs—a reddish mist on the horizon, the absence of a sea
breeze, stifling heat, thunderclaps, and electrical discharges—but ultimately dis-
counted meteorological associations. He consulted people's memories and the
surviving historical record. The "direction of the earthquake was from north to
south," he noted, "rare in Cumaná." Two years earlier a severe earthquake had
almost destroyed the city, and some of the same "ill omens" had presaged that
event. He saw "traces of that terrible catastrophe everywhere; new buildings
rose over the ruins of the old." He delved deeper into the past. In the fifteenth
century, apparently, Native Americans preserved memories of a "powerful cat-
aclysm" that formed the Gulf of Cariaco. In 1530 "the inhabitants of the Paria
and Cumaná coasts were terrified by new shocks" that caused coastal flooding.
At the end of the sixteenth century, "earthquakes were very common and, according to tradition, the sea flooded the shore several times, rising some 90 to
100 feet above normal." And then on October 21, 1766, the city was "completely
destroyed." The Indians "celebrated with dances of joy, following an ancient su-
·perstition about the destruction of the old world and the birth of a new one."
He concluded that great earthquakes do not happen regularly at Cumaná, that
shocks follow the shoreline, and that mainland earthquakes were linked to volcanic activity on Caribbean islands. Thus, Humboldt conjectured that a volcanic

eruption on Guadeloupe on September 27, 1797, was connected by some form of "underground communication" to the Cumaná earthquake less than three months later. Similarly, the great earthquake of Caracas in 1812 preceded the volcanic explosion on St. Vincent by just a month. Humboldt thought every-thing was connected.[11]

In part because of where he resided in the Caribbean, Humboldt's experiences of hurricanes were less frequent than earthquakes. The Venezuelan coast, where Humboldt spent the bulk of his time in the Caribbean, was located outside the main hurricane zone, while nearby Trinidad and Tobago experienced fewer storms than the islands farther north in the Leewards. He described a violent storm that destroyed the saltworks on the Araya peninsula in 1726 as a very "rare event" and added (perhaps too confidently for a recent arrival) that "no one in the Antilles believes anymore that hurricanes come in predictable patterns." Likewise, Humboldt's time on Cuba fell outside of hurricane season. When he first visited Cuba in December 1800 to March 1801, he stated that "there had not been a proper hurricane since August of 1794; the storm of November 2, 1796 was fairly weak." Given his location in Havana, he may not have known about a storm that struck the eastern part of the island in early November 1800. Humboldt claimed that Cuba experienced fewer hurricanes than Saint-Domingue, Jamaica, and the Lesser Antilles, and that, overall, "hurricanes are rarer at the two ends of the long chain of the Antilles (at the SE and NW extremities)," although, in reality, Cuba's size meant that hurricanes struck the is-land frequently. Notwithstanding his lack of direct experience and observation, Humboldt appreciated the central place of the great storms in the Caribbean environment. Ironically, when Humboldt was leaving the Caribbean in May 1804—too early for the hurricane season—on a ship from Cuba bound for the United States, he spent a week battling a raging storm, presumably one produced by the "extremely violent northeasterly winds (*los nortes*)" that he knew well. During this storm, he felt closer to death than at any other time in his life.[12]

Humboldt recognized the power of not just wind, water, and earth, but also fire. From the mountains overlooking Cumaná harbor, he observed, "several parts of the vast forests that surround the mountains were on fire." The "reddish flames, half-hidden by clouds of smoke, stunned" Humboldt and his companions. "The inhabitants set fire to the forests," he continued, "to improve their pasturage and to destroy the shrubs that choke the scant grass." At the same time, he added, "enormous forest fires are also caused by the carelessness of the Indians who forget to put out their camp fires." As a result, "these accidents have diminished the old trees along the Cumaná-Cumanacoa road, and inhabitants have justly noticed that aridity has increased all over the province [of New Andalusia], not only because the land has more crevices from earthquakes, but also because it is less forested than it was before the conquest." In the two months he stayed in Caracas—during the dry season—he could see the leafy fields of the Guaire Valley surrounded by a curtain of mountains. "To improve the land," he noted, "the savannah and grass on the rocks were set on fire." Seen from afar, "these great fires created surprising light effects." Where "the savannah climbed up the slopes and filled the gorges cut by torrential waters," he analogized, "these strips of land on fire seemed at night like lava hanging above the valley." His other mention of fire concerned the dangers of overcrowded Caribbean cities. On April 25, 1802, a major fire broke out in a suburb of Havana City resulting in almost 200 houses burning to the ground and 10,000 or so of the mostly poor inhabitants seeking shelter in an adjacent neighborhood.[13]

Preoccupied with precise measurement, Humboldt thought that the study of nature and society should be more than impressions and evocations, but rather grounded in quantitative data. His *Political Essay on the Island of Cuba* contains a raft of statistical information about the population, climate, trade, agriculture, and ports of the island. He was an assiduous cartographer, determining the exact geographical positions of Cuba's towns and cities and charting its coastline with unprecedented meticulousness. He invented isotherm and isobar mapping, connecting regions that shared the same average temperature and atmospheric pressure. His book contains, among other things, censuses; marriage, birth, and death rates; information on surface areas and geological structures; rainfall and wind directions; accounts of various crops; imports and exports; and shipping returns. He determined that "the mortality of blacks varies widely on the island of Cuba, as it does throughout the Antilles, depending on the type of work, the humanity of masters and overseers, and the number of female blacks who can care for the sick." He calculated that only about a quarter of Cuba's slaves were involved in sugar production. Few topics evaded Humboldt's statistical eye.[14]

For Humboldt, "slavery is possibly the greatest evil ever to have afflicted humanity," but he also recognized "degrees of suffering and deprivation." He saw a great difference "between a slave who works in a rich man's house in Kingston or Havana, or who works for himself and gives his master only a daily amount, and a slave who labors in a sugar factory [or plantation]." The masters' attempts at discipline revealed a hierarchy of suffering and "degrees of human depravity": the coachman is threatened with being reduced to a coffee plantation, while the coffee worker is threatened with a sugar estate. Every "drop of sugarcane juice cost blood and groans," Humboldt averred, but the lot of a sugar plantation slave "who has a wife and lives in his own cabin, finds comfort after work in the midst of an impoverished family," cannot be compared "to that of a slave who is isolated and lost in the crowd." Slavery was tyranny, Humboldt was convinced, but it was not a monolithic institution.[15]

A keen booster, Humboldt was convinced that the circum-Caribbean region had a great future. For him, the "Torrid Zone" or "equinoctial region" was the very heart of America. Venezuela's coastline had major advantages over that of the United States, he claimed, "thanks to the beauty of its ports, the tranquility of the sea, and its superb timber forests." Nowhere were the "anchorages so close, nor ports so conducive to the establishment of military settlements," he added. Furthermore, storms and hurricanes "never reach" the mainland coast. The destruction of Saint-Domingue's sugar industry during the Haitian Revolution (1791–1804) propelled Cuba onto the international economic stage as the world's foremost sugar producer. Its geostrategic importance waxed rather than waned. He extolled the agricultural potential of the torrid zone, the "immense fertility" of its soil, which "corresponds to the heat and humidity." Plants "yield more abundant harvests more quickly." Thus, an acre planted with bananas, he explained, "produces nearly twenty times as much food as the same space sown with cereals." A large population, he claimed, "can be fed from a small plot of land covered with banana, cassava, yams and maize." His optimism was boundless.[16]

Humboldt was neither the first nor the last European to be captivated by the Caribbean's physical environment, but his observations and musings anticipate many of the issues and forces examined in this work. He explores the binaries of land and sea, humans and animals (including insects), promise and peril, bewitching beauty and nightmarish horrors, efflorescence and degradation, exuberance and menace, utopian visions and dystopian realities, health and sickness, qualitative and quantitative assessments that are at the center of this book. With his modern conception of nature as an integrated ecosystem, he was attuned to the dangers of environmental destruction, deforestation, and climatic shocks. When nature is seen as an interconnected web, its vulnerabilities become all the more apparent. This book, we hope, will do justice to Humboldt's passion for the region, its extravagances, exuberances, and Edenic nature, as well as its dangers, diseases, and disasters.

* * *

With Humboldt as inspiration, *Sea and Land* provides an overview of the environmental history of the Caribbean and a detailed examination of some of the central environmental forces and characteristics that defined the region. It addresses four key questions. The first is the most fundamental: why focus on this part of the world, specifically? Second, who are the pioneers of Caribbean environmental history, on whose preceding work we build? Third, how is the region defined geographically? Where are the region's limits? Finally, what are the chronological markers? When should we begin and end?

From today's perspective, the Caribbean region's low global profile—"a scattering of insignificant, small, and not particularly well-off mini-states, accidents of history and geography," as one historian puts it—helps to explain its relative neglect by scholars. For the late V. S. Naipaul, the Trinidadian novelist, Caribbean territories lacked "their own internal reverences"; they were "manufactured societies, labor camps, creations of empire, and for a long time they were dependent on empire for law, language, institutions, culture." For Naipaul, "history is built around achievement and creation" and "nothing was generated locally" in the Caribbean. Jamaica during the times of slavery, according to another native son, sociologist Orlando Patterson, was "a monstrous distortion of human society." Distaste has bred disregard. Even the more positive assessment by historian Eric Hobsbawm nevertheless focused on rupture and fragmentation. For him, the Caribbean region is "a curious terrestrial spacestation from which the fragments of various races, torn from the worlds of their ancestors and aware both of their origins and of the impossibility of returning to them, can watch the remainder of the globe with unaccustomed detachment."[17]

These judgments notwithstanding, the Caribbean deserves attention for being both last and first. The region was about the last place in the Americas to be settled by the first Americans, the so-called Indians. Its youthful, latecomer status helped account for its dynamic evolution and shaped its history. It was also the first place in the New World to encounter the full force of European colonial development. Furthermore, although the Antilles produced the first black republic and second independent nation of the Americas—Haiti—colonialism lasted longer in the Caribbean than in most regions of the world. In contrast to the American mainlands, in 1850, just two insular societies—Haiti and the Dominican Republic—were independent. "No part of the so-called Third World," declares anthropologist Sidney W. Mintz, "was hammered so thoroughly or at such length into a colonial amalgam of European design." The most dramatic aspect of this battering was the virtual extirpation of the indigenous populations and their replacement by outsiders. The destruction of aboriginal populations occurred earlier and more nearly completely in this region than anywhere else in the Americas. Moreover, the region owns the dubious distinction of being the first in the Americas to be introduced to black slavery, sugar cane, and the plantation system, which rapidly and thoroughly transformed the region's demographic and physical landscapes. Nowhere was the influence of this unholy trinity more systematically and intensely felt: the Caribbean received more African slaves over a longer period of time, produced more sugar, and developed the most regimented plantation system of any region in the Americas, although Bahia, in present-day Brazil, was not far behind.[18]

The Caribbean was a vital site in the creation of the modern western world. "Almost from the very first," Mintz observes, "the Caribbean was a key region in the growth of overseas capitalism." The Antillean islands were, he continues, "Europe's first economic bridgehead outside itself. Nor were these islands mere ports of entry, ports of trade, or ports of call; in fact they were Europe's first overseas colonies," although historians of Ireland, Madeira, the Canaries, and several African outposts might dispute this. They were also a launching pad for expansion into mainland America. Spaniards transferred—and modified—the institutions, practices, and templates that they forged on the islands as they moved onto the continental landmasses. No other part of the Americas was more diverse and international, with greater mixing and interaction of peoples, than the Caribbean. This region, Mintz declares, "has been one of the truly great arenas for the interpenetration of African, European, Amerind, Asian, and other traditions, and the values, life-styles, attitudes, and behaviors of its peoples reflect that fact." The mixing, movement, and displacement of peoples led to intense sociocultural interaction and hybridity, and, as this book emphasizes, a parallel ecological mixing of ingredients—animals, plants, microbes—from Africa, Europe, elsewhere in the Americas, and indeed Asia.[19]

The term for this moving and mixing is *creole*, which designates any person or thing born or created in the Caribbean, with an ancestry external to the region. A creole can be anything from a chicken to a language to a form of knowledge. In environmental terms, it can refer to a "motley assemblage of indigenous and invading species, jostling one another in unstable ecosystems." A creole ecology emerged from the constant arrival, dispersal, and mingling of new plants and animals. Caribbean gardens blended mounding techniques of pre-Columbian *conucos* (plots of land), the ridging of plantation cane fields, the short-handled hoe of African provenance, and a crop repertoire that included aboriginal domesticates as well as European, African, and Asian imports. Similarly, throughout the region, a kind of creole knowledge arose concerning various aspects of the physical environment, including phenomena like hurricanes. As Stuart Schwartz and Matthew Mulcahy point out in Chapter 3, knowledge about hurricanes and the signs for approaching storms "drew on indigenous wisdom, traditional European ideas about weather and astrology, limited reference to classical authorities, but mostly on maritime and local experience." Finally, as John McNeill notes in Chapter 2, in the early modern period, Caribbean populations "quickly mixed and merged, producing creoles who were, genetically speaking, among the most global citizens on earth."[20]

Despite its vital role in modern history, and the allure its natural history held for Humboldt and earlier generations, the Caribbean has attracted scant attention from environmental historians. To some extent the historical cultural, linguistic, and imperial divisions of the region long undercut both the ability and the desire of its inhabitants or visitors to write about the region as a whole. Early European visitors, chroniclers, and observers found its flora, fauna, and "nature" fascinating. The Spanish official Fernández de Oviedo in the sixteenth century, the French missionary Father Jean Baptiste Labat in the seventeenth century, and the Jamaican planter-historian Edward Long in the eighteenth century gave considerable attention to aspects of the region's characteristics that would today be considered environmental, but they tended to write about only their own linguistic or cultural areas. By the late eighteenth century, organizations with an interest in science in places such as Le Cap in St. Domingue or Havana began to discuss environmental issues. Naturalists applied the new methods and technologies of study to the area. Moreau de Saint-Méry (1750–1819), the Martinican polymath, published his most notable work, *Description topographique, physique, civile, politique et historique de la partie française de l'isle Saint-Domingue* in 1789. Another eminent figure was the Spanish priest Jose Celestino Mutis (1732–1808), who lived most of his life in New Granada (Colombia). Interested in astronomy, entomology, mathematics, and botany, he corresponded with European savants such as Linnaeus and Humboldt and promoted natural science. Later, an occasional individual like the Cuban-born and French-educated Andrés Poey (1825–1919), who became first director of the Havana observatory, went beyond studying only his particular island to examine phenomena such as hurricanes, earthquakes, cloud formations, and climate across the region as a whole. By the twentieth century, some historians, geographers, and social and physical scientists involved in the study of subjects from Caribbean agriculture and animal husbandry to politics and literature made environmental concerns central to their work, but usually in studies limited to their own home island or cultural-linguistic community.[21]

Even today, there are no general syntheses. The nearest equivalent is David Watts's *The West Indies: Patterns of Development, Culture and Environmental Change since 1492* (1987), which is in the best traditions of British historical geography. It covers most of the bases—geology, climate, vegetation, soils, and fauna—but with a pronounced tilt toward the British Caribbean. The chapter on aboriginal peoples arguably paints too rosy a portrait of how "a large population was maintained, especially in [Island] Arawak terrain, in some comfort and style and over a long period." The strength of the book lies in its account of how "Northwest Europeans" developed plantation agriculture, focusing on the environmental impact of sugar estates. A broader work that pays some attention to the Caribbean is Shawn William Miller's *An Environmental History of Latin America* (2007). Miller examines the role of pestilence, biodiversity's gains, the ecological niche of large livestock, sugar's transformative influence, natural disasters, and the rise of the conservation movement. His estimate of 3 to 7 million for the pre-Columbian population of the islands is toward the high end of the spectrum of expert opinion, but his linking of the Caribbean to South America is noteworthy.[22]

Alfred Crosby never wrote solely about the Caribbean, but his *Columbian Exchange* (1972) has much to say about the region. He was one of the first to note and explain why no massive smallpox epidemic occurred among the Indians of the Antilles for a quarter century after Columbus's pioneering voyage. One of his signature observations was that "the Antilles were less than a perfect base camp" for European horticulturalists. European grains, grapevines, and olive trees all failed. But many European garden crops prospered; Iberians learned to like or tolerate American foods—bread made from manioc flour, pumpkins, beans, potatoes—and they could "always dessert on such familiar fruits as oranges, lemons, pomegranates, citrons, and figs" that did well in the Caribbean. Another important addition in the early years was the banana brought from the Canaries in 1516. Watching the Caribbean islands "from outer space during the years from 1492 to 1550," Crosby mused, the intention seemed to be a sensationally spectacular replacement of people by pigs, dogs, and cattle. Riding on horses bred in the Antilles, war dogs from the same islands at their side, their saddlebags packed with cakes of Caribbean cassava, followed by herds of swine, cattle, and goats, "a commissariat on the hoof," all raised on the islands, the Spaniards ventured onto the continental landmass, having "created in the Caribbean the wherewithal to conquer half a world."[23]

Three other works are also worthy of mention as touchstone texts for Caribbean environmental history. Carl Sauer's *The Early Spanish Main* (1966) explored not just human actions, but the impact of those acts on the natural world, through 1519. Sauer greatly admired pre-Columbian peoples, who in his estimation, "suffered no want" and "lived in peace and amity." He notes when the Caribbean Sea became standard on maps; he describes the "natural history of the islands" as "mainly a reduced extension of adjacent South America"; and he examines the littoral in painstaking detail. Bonham Richardson, also a geographer, synthesized half a millennium of Caribbean historical geography in his brief *The Caribbean in the Wider World, 1492–1992* (1992), substantially focusing on the twentieth-century study. Historian Richard Grove takes a broad view of the history of environmentalism, by focusing on tropical islands across the globe in his *Green Imperialism* (1995). He argues that in the seventeenth and eighteenth centuries on small islands, including some in the Caribbean, a "coherent and wide-ranging critique of environmental degradation first emerged."[24]

These influential works that prefigured or touched on Caribbean environmental history are part of a larger scientific literature. In this century, with the international growth of interest in the environment and its history, a new generation of scholars in the region and beyond it have intensified research, integrating studies from the natural sciences and other disciplines and often employing a broad regional and comparative framework. Studies of issues such as natural resources, conservation, epidemiology, and climate have now made the environment and ecology of the Caribbean a central historical concern. This volume is an effort to integrate this recent surge of interest and research in a new general environmental history of the region.[25]

Islands are the heart of the Caribbean region. About 3,700 of them—those that are at least 1 square kilometer in size (another 3,300 or so are cays, reefs, and exposed offshore banks)—constitute the core of this broad geographic area. Almost a half of the 3,700 islands are named, but a majority are so small they remain anonymous. The key Caribbean islands form an overall archipelago (which can be subdivided into a number of smaller archipelagos), a group or cluster, arranged in the shape of a half-moon arc or chain that extends from Cuba in the northwest to Trinidad in the southeast. One popular writer has even likened this chain to Michelangelo's arm of God on the Sistine Chapel. A more prosaic way of conceptualizing the chain is to see the Antilles as an island bridge connecting North and South America. The arc, in this way of thinking, has a continental focus, sometimes meriting the term "continent of islands," and—in addition to the islands already mentioned—encompassing the Bahamian islands to the north and the islands off the Venezuelan coast—Aruba, Bonaire, Curaçao—to the south. Cuban scholar Antonio Benítez-Rojo described the Caribbean as no common archipelago but rather a "meta-archipelago," possessing "neither a boundary nor a center." The Caribbean, he continued, "flows outward past the limits of its own sea," connecting it to the Gulf of Mexico and the Atlantic Ocean.[26]

Emphasizing islands as the core of Caribbean history can easily lead to notions of fragmentation, insularity, and isolationism. For the people living in "a small place," writes novelist Jamaica Kincaid of her native Antigua, "every event is a domestic event; the people in a small place cannot see themselves in a larger picture, they cannot see that they might be part of a chain of something, anything." Even within small islands, archaeologist Basil A. Reid observes, "myriad microenvironments such as river valleys, forested areas, grasslands, coastlines, plains, hills, and mountains often pose significant challenges" to insular unity. This stress on microenvironments, island localism, and isolationism is real but should not be exaggerated. There is a long history of mobility among islanders, almost all of whom lived near the sea and many of whom sailed and paddled freely.[27]

Equally worthy of emphasis is the connectivity between islands as well as to neighboring continental landmasses. This way of thinking views the Caribbean Sea as a bridge rather than barrier and puts the sea at the heart of the region. Oceanic islands are not necessarily "bounded environments," notes archaeologist Scott Fitzpatrick, just "because they are surrounded water and separated from other places physically as well as mentally." Indeed, one distinctive feature of the Caribbean archipelago is that it is possible to move from one island to the next almost entirely within view of one another, virtually without a break, throughout the entire chain. From this perspective, as archaeologists Joshua M. Torres and Reniel Rodríguez Ramos underline, the Caribbean can be considered "a continent divided by water." Another distinctive feature is the emergence of interaction spheres, the processes that occurred between islands and that were extensions of developments within them. Apparently, for example, the Taínos of western Puerto Rico and eastern Hispaniola visited each other almost daily, evidence of their strong ties, whereas the native Hispaniolan term for the peninsula that led from their island to Jamaica was *Guanacabibe*, meaning "back of the island," an indication of the attenuated linkages between those two places. Another example of interaction spheres is the various inter-island cooperative responses to natural disasters that occurred frequently in the region. Equally, port cities on many islands of the colonial Caribbean functioned as a unified disease environment thanks to the volume of shipping among them—as noted in Chapter 3. Thus Caribbean insularity and fragmentation, while sometimes valid, should be interrogated, not simply assumed.[28]

In addition to the archipelagic model, there are at least two more capacious frameworks for thinking about the region. The first posits a Caribbean basin approach. It simply suggests that the region include not just the islands, but rather all the lands that the Caribbean Sea touches, physically and/or culturally. Thus, the Venezuelan and Colombian coasts, the Guianas and Suriname, and the entire coast of Central America from Panama to the Yucatan can be considered part of a Caribbean basin or rimland. Simple as this framework is to propose, very few broad-gauged examples exist. Another even larger entity is the so-called Greater Caribbean, generally understood as the plantation zone stretching from, say, Virginia in the north to Bahia in the south. But, as historian B. W. Higman notes, "these larger regional conceptions have validity for some periods and patterns of development but not for all." Broadly sympathetic to both of these frameworks, which follow in the tradition of Humboldt, this book touches on related mainland territories, depending on the issue, such as trade, plantations, disease, or hurricanes, but accepts that confining attention largely to the islands sets useful limits and provides a stronger "ecological coherence" to any study of the region. In short, as Sauer noted in his classic study, the Caribbean is "a natural region" but one that is "fuzzy about the edges."[29]

Environmental history often takes a long perspective, and this study is no exception. The chapters that follow span the pre-Columbian era through the first decades of the nineteenth century. When does the story begin? There are a number of possible starting points. The earliest record of human habitation on the continental portion of the Caribbean basin dates to roughly 14,000 BP (before the present) in what is now Colombia and Venezuela. About 10,000 BP, bands of hunters and foragers frequented what became Trinidad, prior to the island's separation from the mainland by rising sea level. The earliest known settlement site, located along the west coast of Trinidad, dates to ca. 7700 BP. The impact of subsequent waves of migrants and their colonization of the islands over many thousands of years forms an important part of this story. The shift from foraging to farming, the evolution of fishing techniques, the rise of pottery-making, the intensification of agriculture and fishing, the subsequent spectacular demographic collapse, and rise of Indian slavery are some of the key developments explored in the following pages.[30]

Another kind of colonization began after 1492 CE with the arrival of Europeans and Africans in the region. While pre-Columbian people had a significant impact on the region's environment, these newcomers unleashed a series of forces with unprecedented environmental consequences. As a result, the bulk of each chapter concerns those forces and their effects during the long early modern period—stretching across the sixteenth, seventeenth, and eighteenth centuries, and into the early nineteenth. Among the changes over this long period were: the development of plantation agriculture, the accelerated pace of deforestation, the impact of introduced livestock, the extinctions and extirpations of fauna, biodiversity's gains as well as losses, the transformative role of sugar, diversification into secondary and minor crops, the rise of urbanization, the emergence of conservation, the encounter with new natural disasters such as hurricanes and the more frequent and intense experience of known hazards like earthquakes, the impact of introduced diseases, changes in health regimes, and demographic collapses and evolutions.

Chapters 1, 2, and 3 conclude at various points during the first half of the nineteenth century, reflecting the specific focus of each study. Certainly, the 1830s and 1840s represent a period of significant transition in the region. By then slavery was ending in most places in the Caribbean, other than Cuba and Puerto Rico. Indentured servants from India, Africa, and China began taking the place of slaves. Furthermore, partly due to changes in patterns of infectious disease, the end of slavery roughly coincided with a transformation from a demographic regime of negative natural growth, sustained only by forced immigration, to one of natural increase. Plantations were still important institutions, but the sugar industry was poised for decline—even if, paradoxically, the end of slavery for a time accelerated the industry's growth as planters embraced industrialization in the face of labor shortages—and peasantries were on the rise. Technological changes, particularly the use of steam machinery on land and at sea, had a marked effect on the environment. Likewise, the arrival of the telegraph and changes in the collection of weather data helped improve understanding of tropical storms and cyclonic activity from the 1840s onward. Natural disasters were as destructive as ever, and in some places seemed to be worsening, but the context in which such events occurred, especially in the case of hurricanes, changed significantly by the middle of the nineteenth century. So in several respects, the middle of the nineteenth century in Caribbean environmental history marked the end of an era.[31]

This book consists of three chapters devoted to periods before about 1850 and a fourth that carries the story to the present. Morgan offers a general account of the early Caribbean environment, covering all the elements—earth, fire, water, and wind. His chapter ranges across many centuries, pays attention to animals as well as to humans, and most of all brings seascapes and landscapes into the same frame. It also introduces and explores briefly the topics of the next two chapters, disease and disaster. McNeill's chapter outlines the story of human health and disease in the region. He begins with the original settlement of the region but emphasizes the post-Columbian catastrophe and the disastrous disease regime of plantation slavery. He calls each of these a "syndemic," a term borrowed from medical anthropology to refer to the simultaneous swirl of multiple infections and exacerbating social stresses. Schwartz and Mulcahy trace the impact of various disasters—hurricanes, earthquakes, tsunamis, droughts, floods, insect infestations—that routinely struck colonies and their effects across time. The frequency and ferocity of disasters, they argue, helped define the region in the eyes of its inhabitants and did much to shape life there throughout the long early modern period. The final chapter treats the last 170 years of Caribbean environmental, disease, and disaster history, a period in which new influences and forces came into play. The disappearance of plantation slavery altered the character of the region, as did decolonization. Hurricane winds still blew, marlins still swam, and mahogany still grew. But the Caribbean's linkages changed, so that Africa played a smaller role and the United States a bigger one in the region's environmental history. The economy evolved, bringing greater reliance on smallholder farming, tourism, and in places industries such oil refining—each with its own set of environmental implications.

Each chapter highlights recent scholarship that has explored the Caribbean environment and points to areas for further research. Moreover, this book probes new evidence generated in the natural sciences and incorporates related work in half a dozen disciplines, from archaeology to zoology, relevant to the subject.

The Caribbean region has been central to one of the great achievements of historians in the past half century, the illumination of the world of plantation slavery and its central role in the creation of the modern world. But it has lagged behind most other regions of the globe when it comes to environmental history, another historiographical achievement of recent decades. This book aims to redress that situation and make environmental perspectives more accessible and more indispensable, to scholars and students alike, to foster both a fuller appreciation of the extent to which environmental factors shaped historical developments in the Caribbean and the extent to which human actions have transformed the biophysical environment of the region over time.

If the Caribbean has generated less environmental history than other regions, the current scientific literature on topics such as hurricanes, deforestation, tropical diseases, ocean environments, and coral reefs is robust and expanding rapidly. Concerns about climate change prompt further investigations into such topics. Anthropologists, sociologists, and literary scholars have focused increasingly on environmental themes and issues in the region. The notes for this book cite some of this recent scientific and social scientific work. In short, it seems an appropriate moment to synthesize—with caution—this material and to highlight topics that require more research, with a focus on the transformations of the early modern period.

The environmental study of the Caribbean has languished for many reasons: its fragmentation, heterogeneity, and diversity, to name just a few. It contains about 50 insular societies of various kinds, 24 distinct polities—one more than the total in the rest of the Americas—and 13 sovereign states, scattered over more than 4,000 kilometers. In addition, at least 10 mainland states have coasts that are usually considered part of the Caribbean. Environments range in scale from sizable Cuba to tiny Saba, from low-lying Anegada to the highest mountain peak in the Dominican Republic, from Bonaire's arid shrub to Hispaniola's giant Ceiba trees. By any measure, from island size to elevations to vegetation, the region is as differentiated as it is complex. Any attempt to encapsulate the experience of Caribbean people in a few, pithy observations comes at the cost of oversimplification. Risking it, the Caribbean environment can be summarized in a creole proverb: "Me lickle but me tallawah," which means, "I may be small but I am strong, tough, even dangerous, and should not be underestimated."[32]

The Caribbean Environment to 1850

PHILIP D. MORGAN

Thinking about the early Caribbean environment raises a series of dichotomies. One of the most significant concerns the relationship of land and sea. The Caribbean Sea comprises over 90 percent of the region's area. The islands are minuscule by comparison. The sea was not just a passive backdrop, or a corridor for exploration and exchange, but a powerful agent, continuously shaping human affairs. Early naturalists understood this lesson well. The Royal Society's first directions to mariners venturing to the West Indies were to explore such matters as the declination of the compass, regional tidal patterns, the shapes of foreign coastlines, the nature of the sea floor, maritime weather patterns, the relative gravity of salt and fresh water, and the weight of sea water at different latitudes. French naturalist, Charles Plumier, who visited the Caribbean on three occasions between 1689 and 1697 and spent, in his words, "several years wandering about the Islands," made drawings of about 600 mollusks, 350 fishes, and many representations of a crocodile and of turtles—most or all of which were Antillean in origin. Yet, in general, the marine environment has been much less well studied than the terrestrial. This chapter aims to redress this balance by paying as much attention to the sea as to the land.[1]

Although agriculture was transformative in the early Caribbean, fishing should be equally acknowledged. After all, as archaeologist Brian Fagan pithily notes, fishing "fed civilization." There were "three ancient ways of obtaining food—hunting, plant foraging, and fishing"; and "only the last remained important after the development of agriculture." With one foot in their *canoa* (dugout canoes) and the other in their *conucos* (agricultural plots), Caribbean fishermen-farmers symbolized the union of water and soil. They revered Jocahu or Yucahu, the supreme Taíno deity, "lord of cassava *and* the sea." Sea turtles and frogs emerged as avatars, central motifs in their art and religion. Many of

Sea and Land. Philip D. Morgan, J. R. McNeill, Matthew Mulcahy, and Stuart B. Schwartz, Oxford University Press.
© Oxford University Press 2022. DOI: 10.1093/oso/9780197555446.003.0002

the Europeans and Africans who arrived in the Caribbean were also maritime, island, or coastal peoples.[2]

A second dichotomy is the relationship between the region's natural bounty and its vulnerability. The Caribbean is an extraordinarily rich, diverse environment; at the same time, it is extremely fragile and volatile. Island ecosystems were easily alterable because of their small size and their comparative isolation. The Caribbean is also famously in the tropics, which made it, in European eyes, simultaneously an earthly paradise and a place of nightmarish menace. On the eve of the Seven Years' War when Jean-Antoine Riqueti, chevalier de Mirabeau, assumed the governorship of Guadeloupe, he found the island at once a "promised land" of immense fertility and a terrifying nest of "rascality," of disorder. Naturalists visiting the region alternately praised its sumptuousness and barely disguised their fear at its perils. In comparison to cooler climes, the tropics seemed to teem with noxious, dangerous, and threatening creatures. Hans Sloane's images accompanying his *Natural History of Jamaica* highlighted arresting conjunctions: he paired Native American pots in which slaves boiled their meals and land crabs, good to eat, but sometimes poisonous, thereby touching on hidden dangers; another drew on a verbal pun, African "lutes" and the Jamaican "luteus," connecting the vitality of slave music and a plant that was used to bind their limbs. Attention to climate, natural disasters, and disease illustrate a double-edged theme of bounty and vulnerability, of ecosystems to disturbance and of newcomers to threats.[3]

The combination of exuberance and menace applies equally well to plants and animals, a third theme. The Caribbean exhibits a remarkable efflorescence of fauna and flora. It is a place of great evolutionary richness, a biodiversity hotspot, the home to giants, dwarfs, and oddities of all kinds. Some of the surprises are absences—there are few large snakes, carnivores, or mid- to large-sized mammals. It is also the site of many extinctions and enormous degradation, beginning well before the twentieth century. "More faunal species," noted David Watts, one of the region's preeminent geographers, "have become extinct in the West Indies within the last century than in any other part of the world except Antarctica." The extinctions began well before the twentieth century. Simultaneous richness and impoverishment represent another central contradiction.[4]

The last part of the chapter focuses more explicitly on the human relationship with the environment. Once again a contradictory mix of creativity and loss must be confronted—a fourth leitmotif—with attention turning first to the earliest settlers, the Amerindians, and then pivoting to Europeans and Africans. Humans brought about vast changes—improvements in some cases, deteriorations in others. Amerindians certainly shaped the environment in fundamental ways. For the last 14,000 years in the Caribbean basin, there has been no "pristine" landscape; humans have been constantly modifying it.[5] There was no static state or climax ecosystem; all was in flux, susceptible to human agency. Through the plants and the animals they introduced, as well as their profit-seeking mentality, Europeans molded the environment in newly dramatic and intensive ways. Many of the results involved depletion, but they, along with Africans, introduced much new fauna and flora to the region, planting the seeds of environmental renewal in some cases and conservation in others. Contemplation of environmental change in the Caribbean can easily give rise to an apocalyptic view of generalized, continuous degradation, but there are also signs of reinvigoration.

Along the way, this chapter notes some of the ways in which the Caribbean was both backward and a leading edge of development in the years 1492–ca. 1850—another dichotomy. An exotic location to Europeans fostered an empirical and experimental approach to medicine, based on observation and experience, informing new theories of disease causation and courses of treatment. The vulnerability of island environments underscored rarity and heightened concerns about conservation. Living in a multinational world in close proximity to one another facilitated cooperation as well as conflict, emulation as well as rivalry, borrowings as well as repudiations across imperial lines. The agricultural revolution that occurred in the Caribbean was one of the most radical and intense anywhere in the modern world, with the region's plantations producing highly regimented, quality-controlled, mass-produced agricultural products. Deforestation occurred earlier, perhaps more intensively, here than anywhere else in the Americas. Whether it was the search for gold, pearls, mahogany, turtle shell, or sugar, such commodities generated a "boom" or "Wild West" mentality. A short life expectancy sharpened the "get rich quick" mentality. Science, botany, and estate mapping were all avant garde in the Caribbean. A precocious modernity characterizes the region in general. In these—and no doubt other—ways, the Caribbean was in the vanguard of change.

A final underlying theme is an attempt to capture the diversity of the Caribbean. Depictions of the Caribbean region often oversimplify opposed pairings—Arawak versus Carib, wet versus dry season, crab versus shell cultures, colonizer versus colonized, buccaneer versus settler, planter versus peasant, absentee versus resident, master versus slave, settlement versus exploitation colony. But such juxtapositions seem unlikely to capture fully the region's extraordinarily rich mosaic of landscapes and seascapes, exuberance and vulnerability, fauna and flora, traditions and customs.

* * *

The Caribbean Sea is the world's second largest, behind the South China Sea, at about 1,063,000 square miles. It stretches approximately 1,060 miles north to south from Florida to Panama and 1,400 miles east-west from Barbados to the Yucatán. The broad arc of islands from western Cuba to southeastern Trinidad extends over 1,850 miles; including the Bahamas adds another 600 miles to its length. The Caribbean Sea is as large as Alaska, Texas, and California put together, and is larger than Hudson Bay and the North, Red, and Baltic Seas combined. It is connected to the Gulf of Mexico, the fifth largest sea in the world, making these combined bodies of water the largest connected seas in the world. The Gulf of Mexico contains more shallow than deep water, but the Caribbean is almost twice as deep as the Mediterranean. Even more than the Mediterranean, because of size, depth, and partially enclosed character, the Caribbean is an arm of the Atlantic Ocean.[6]

As such, the Caribbean Sea plays a key role in the ocean conveyor belt that transports equatorial waters to higher latitudes, just as it receives colder waters from farther north. Thus the North Equatorial Current, an 800-mile-wide, sluggish, westward-flowing body of water that forms the southern component of the North Atlantic gyre—the huge clockwise swirl of water—is the primary current flowing into the Caribbean Sea. The North Equatorial Current is joined by warm waters pushing up from Africa past northeastern Brazil in the South Atlantic, most notably the Guiana Current. These combined Atlantic waters penetrate the various Lesser Antillean passages and continue westward as the Caribbean Current, which eventually surges through the Yucatan Channel, before intruding into the Gulf of Mexico, where it bifurcates, the more forceful flow moving east by the northern coast of Cuba, the weaker arm initially moving west and circulating clockwise around the Gulf of Mexico. The Florida Current feeds into the mightiest flow of them all, the Gulf Stream, pushing more water than all world's rivers combined. The direction of water and wind in the Caribbean is largely westward, helping to explain why people, fauna, and flora tended to move from south to north, east to west in the Caribbean.[7]

The Caribbean is a semi-enclosed sea, with many ingresses and one major outflow. The Antillean chain has nine major passages through which Atlantic waters enter the Caribbean Sea. They are conventionally grouped into three: moving from south to north, they are the three so-called Windward Island Passages south of Martinique (Grenada, St. Vincent, and St. Lucia), the four Leeward Island Passages between Martinique and the Virgin Islands (Dominica, Guadeloupe, Antigua, and Anegada); and the two Greater Antillean Passages (Windward and Mona). A major trough, the Anegada trench, separates the northern Lesser Antilles from the Virgin Islands; it is one of a few water gaps in the Caribbean basin across which land is not visible. The three major groupings of passages contribute about equal amounts of Atlantic water to the Caribbean Sea. As this prevailing westward thrust of water and wind hits the continental shelf off the coast of Honduras and Nicaragua, one part moves in a counterclockwise fashion southward into the Gulf of Mosquitos, and onto Panama and Colombia. The other part, the major egress for all this Atlantic water, is the Yucatan Channel, where Caribbean Sea waters move into the Gulf of Mexico.[8]

Humans adapted to the constraints and possibilities posed by these winds and currents. The gyre or circular wind and current systems of the North Atlantic help explain why Europeans venturing west ended up in the Caribbean basin; why the natural route from European ports to North America traced a great arc to the southward; why most shipping entered through the Windward Islands; why Spaniards had a major advantage in settling the Caribbean; why Havana, viewed as the "gateway" of the Americas by early modern contemporaries, was so well located for shipping leaving the Caribbean and Gulf of Mexico; and why the Bahamas were strategically important and navigationally dangerous. In an age of sail, the Atlantic wind and current system helps explain why the Caribbean became the key to European overseas expansion. The Caribbean was the first transoceanic sphere of European power.[9]

Within the Caribbean itself, there are further ramifications of the dominant winds and currents. One obvious implication of the strong westward flow is how much harder it is to sail or canoe in the opposite direction. The perils of trying to sail east are illustrated by the tragic story of the *Zong*, the slave ship that overshot Jamaica in 1781 and then had to backtrack, but not before forcing overboard 132 captive Africans. Given the direction of winds and currents, there is unsurprisingly little evidence of North American indigenous peoples moving southward; instead native peoples tended to migrate out of South America into the Caribbean. Finally, rather than island-hopping up the Lesser Antillean chain, Native American migrants from South America apparently ventured out to sea in a direct canoe route from what is now the Venezuelan coast to Puerto Rico. Seemingly, they did so because this route was less hazardous, avoiding the dangerous crosscurrents and bottleneck effects of fast-moving waters being pushed through narrow inter-island passes by the northeast trades. Bypassing islands in the chain rather than using them as stepping stones made sense. Traveling directly to Puerto Rico from South America was also quicker than island-hopping—a crew of eight in a moderate-sized canoe could make the journey in about a week. Long before the Europeans arrived, Native Americans knew much about the Caribbean Sea's winds and currents.[10]

Native Americans were adept canoeists and capable seafarers. Employing fire and shell or stone tools, they hollowed their dugouts from a single log (often from the ceiba or silk cotton tree, one of the region's largest and most lightweight trees). The largest canoes, perhaps 20 meters in length, could contain scores of people as well as trade goods used in inter-island commerce. Smaller canoes were more commonplace in nearshore fishing. Miniature canoes and paddles (Taíno term *nahe*) were parts of burial offerings—an indication of their prestige value. Native canoeists paddled at a speed of about three knots per hour and did not use sails until introduced to them by Europeans. Based on wind and current patterns, computer modeling suggests canoe pathways that connected various parts of the Caribbean. In the Archaic Age (4000–2500 BP), a number of islands—from Antigua in the south to Anguilla in the north—in the northern Lesser Antilles formed an active exchange network, in which flint, found in particular on Long Island off the northeast coast of Antigua, was a key item of trade. While neighboring islands were always visible in the Northern Lesser Antilles, the more than 100- kilometer open-seas Anegada Passage was a challenging trip. While crossing it, canoeists lost sight of land and had to rely on mental maps, celestial navigation, and movements of clouds and birds to guide them. The canoe trip from Saba or Anguilla to eastern Puerto Rico across the Anegada Passage would have taken two full days and nights.[11]

Due in part to oceanographic conditions and seafaring technology, prehistoric settlers in the Ceramic Age first left from the Venezuelan coast and traveled directly to the Greater Antilles and northern Lesser Antilles. Only after colonizing these northerly islands did they later move southward through the Lesser Antilles, in the face of the prevailing winds and currents. Still, the passages between islands were short and land was always visible. The northerly Antillean islands, according to radiocarbon datings, were settled before those in the Windward chain—Dominica to Grenada—by at least a few centuries. In any case, people probably did not move in only one direction, following the alignment of islands in a series of short hops, even if, overall, colonization seems to have occurred in a "big jump" to the northward first, followed by "small hops" in a southward direction down the chain of the Lesser Antilles.[12]

Islands form just 8 percent of the Caribbean region, but they can be subdivided in many ways. In terms of landmass they are usually grouped into five archipelagos: Greater Antilles (89 percent of the insular land area), the Bahamas (5 percent), the Lesser Antilles (3 percent), Trinidad and Tobago (2 percent), and the islands just north of the Venezuelan coast, sometimes called simply the Southern Caribbean (1 percent) (see Table 1.1). These groupings can be further subdivided: the Lesser Antilles, for example, into inner and outer arcs or into Windward (south of Dominica) and Leeward (north of Guadeloupe) chains; the islands just north of the Venezuelan coast can be arranged into at least three clusters: Aruba, Bonaire, and Curacao, often referred to as the ABC islands, is one; the Los Roques archipelago, another; and Margarita, Cubagua, and Coche is a third. Adding the Virgin and Cayman Islands to the Greater Antilles is a common practice—geology unites them—but there is not much that is "Greater" about either grouping. Some classifications exclude the Bahama archipelago altogether, since these islands do not border the Caribbean Sea. Rather, they are situated in the southern North Atlantic, the northernmost of which fall outside the tropical zone. Still, this chain of islands stretching over 600 miles so

Table 1.1 **Size and Elevation of Caribbean Islands**

Island Group	Area (sq miles)	Maximum Altitude (feet)
Southern Caribbean	**846**	
1% land area		
Margarita	444	3,018
Curaçao	171	1,230
Bonaire	111	348
Aruba	75	620
Coche	21	197
Los Roques archipelago	16	407
Cubagua	8	105
Trinidad and Tobago	**1,980**	
2% land area		
Trinidad	1,864	3,087
Tobago	116	1,877
Lesser Antilles	**2,615**	
3% land area		
Guadeloupe	657	4,813
Martinique	421	4,583
Dominica	305	4,672
St. Lucia	233	3,120
Barbados	166	1,109
St. Vincent	150	4,048
Grenada	133	2,756
Antigua	108	1,319
St. Croix	83	1,165
St. Kitts	65	3,793
Barbuda	62	125
Nevis	36	3,232
Anguilla	35	240
Montserrat	39	3,002
St. Thomas	32	1,555

(*continued*)

Table 1.1 **Continued**

Island Group	Area (sq miles)	Maximum Altitude (feet)
Tortola	22	1,739
St. John	20	1,276
Anegada	15	28
St. Martin	13	1,358
St. Eustatius	8	1,969
Carriacou	7	955
Saba	5	2,877
Greater Antilles and Caymans	**80,094**	
89% land area		
Cuba	42,827	6,470
Hispaniola	29,321	10,417
Santo Domingo	18,680	10,417
St. Domingue/Haiti	10,641	8,793
Jamaica	4,411	7,402
Puerto Rico	3,435	4,390
Cayman Islands	100	165
Bahama Archipelago	**5,560**	
5% land area		
The Bahamas	5,399	207
Turks and Caicos Islands	161	161

closely linked, culturally as well as physically, to other Caribbean islands, Cuba and Hispaniola in particular, that the five-archipelago division makes sense.[13]

Another way of classifying Caribbean islands, by type and origin, is tripartite: land-bridge, continental, and oceanic. Land-bridge islands—once connected to each other or to a larger island at times of lower sea level—include most of the Virgin Islands, which were once part of a much larger Puerto Rican landmass; the fringing islands around Cuba and Hispaniola; and many Bahamian islands formerly parts of larger banks, the largest of which, Great Bahama Bank, once formed a landmass greater than Hispaniola. A second group, continental islands, are those once connected to a mainland. Trinidad and Tobago are the most obvious exemplars, as are the other islands north of the Venezuelan coast. Finally, one last broad group, oceanic islands, are those that never had a connection to a larger continental landmass. The chain of islands stretching from Sombrero and Anguilla in the north to Grenada in the south is the prime example.[14]

Geologically, the Caribbean islands are also often divided into three groups, based on age and mode of formation. The Greater Antilles are the oldest part of the Caribbean, essentially fragments of continental crust, formed in the Pacific Ocean, pushed eastward by plate movements. A second major group of islands consists of the Bahamas. The shallow oceanic platform on which these islands rest is also old, a block of crystalline rocks, but it has been fairly stable, retaining its position close to North America. The 2,000 cays and 700 islands that comprise the Bahamas took modern shape only a few million years ago as reduced sea levels during Pleistocene glacial periods exposed them. Finally, the youngest group, the islands of the contemporary Lesser Antilles, primarily comprises a volcanic arc, the eastern edge of the eastward-moving Caribbean plate. Today the Lesser Antilles contain 21 live volcanoes distributed among 11 volcanically active islands, although the most frequently active is the aptly named Kick 'Em Jenny, just north of Grenada.[15]

This triangular view of the Caribbean islands—whether by origin or age—leaves much out. The Lesser Antilles consist of a double arc of islands, not just an inner volcanic, but also an outer limestone, group, often labeled the "Limestone Caribbees," which was uplifted in the front of the advancing Caribbean plate. This latter, to the east of the main volcanic arc of the Lesser Antilles, comprises several young, low-lying islands consisting of coral limestone, developed on an older volcanic or crystalline base, and includes Marie Galante, the eastern half of Guadeloupe (known as Grand-Terre), Antigua, Barbuda, and Anguilla. Often rising only a few meters above sea level, these islands tend to be arid. In addition, the group of islands north of the Venezuela coast—including Aruba, Bonaire, Curaçao, Margarita, and Cubagua—are also mainly low-lying, with surface features comparable to those of the outer arc of the Lesser Antilles. A third group comprises Trinidad, Tobago, and Barbados, where Andean crystalline rocks form the northern coast of the first, much of the second, and part of the third—although Barbados's reef limestones make it more akin to the Limestone Caribbees. Finally, Jamaica's geological history is unlike the rest of the Greater Antilles. Jamaica was connected to Central America until about 50 million years ago, when it broke off and moved eastward to its rather isolated position. Unlike the other Greater Antillean islands, it was completely submerged until about 12 million years ago. With these qualifications and modifications, a simple tripartite division becomes a sevenfold one.[16]

Another way of dividing the Antilles is to think about the interface of land and sea and to split it into areas with major banks and extensive reef systems and those without. The bank systems around Cuba and Hispaniola are particularly rich and enhance the biological diversity of those two islands. With complex shorelines, large offshore cays, embayments, and surface water resources, both Cuba and Hispaniola have extremely productive coastal wetland and estuarine environments. Jamaica and the Cayman Islands, on the other hand, have few of those features. This absence may help to explain why the former was not settled by Native Americans until ca. 600 CE and the Caymans never were. Their relative isolation no doubt is also part of the reason, as is the lack of water on the Caymans, but their size should have proved attractive. The Cayman trench separating Jamaica and the Caymans is the deepest part of the Caribbean, making northern and western Jamaica and the whole of the Caymans inhospitable to a fringing reef.[17] The truly immense bank-island system is in the Bahamas. This entire archipelago includes about 85,541 square miles of shallow-water marine habitats, a larger bank system than all the other Caribbean islands combined, and 10 times the size of the ground area. The Lesser Antilles, in general, has least productive reefs, but with some notable exceptions. In the northern part of the chain, Saba Bank supports extensive shallow-water habitats, as does Anguilla Bank. In the south, the shallow banks of the Grenadine chain, between Grenada and St. Vincent, especially around the island of Carriacou, the name meaning the "land of many reefs," was the other most notable exception. Small islands with extensive reef systems proved particularly attractive to Native American newcomers who often settled on them before occupying larger islands nearby.[18]

In short, the Antilles, an overall archipelago of more than 7,000 large and small islands, cays, reefs, and exposed offshore banks, is extremely diverse. The islands originated in a variety of ways—volcanism, uplifted island arcs, exposed coral banks, movements of major plates, changes in sea levels—and over time pieces of islands, as well as whole islands, became attached and unattached, submerged and reemerged. This dynamic geological history has produced a remarkably varied region. Its physical contrasts are striking. Pico Duarte (10,146 feet) in the Central Mountains of the Dominican Republic is the highest mountain peak east of the Mississippi River and the Andes, whereas the same country's Lake Enriquillo is 147 feet below sea level. Some islands—the Caymans, Barbuda, and Anguilla, most notably—hardly rise above the sea; other islands feature mountains that soar majestically into the sky. Cuba is a giant, the seventeenth largest island in the world; Saba, at 8 square miles and St. Eustatius at 13 square miles, are pocket size. Some islands are surrounded by shallow banks, others by deep-water passages. Vegetation ranges from tropical rainforest to arid desert, from huge mahogany trees to shrubs stunted by wind and salt spray. The region's contrasts are breathtaking.

The contrasts become even greater when the surrounding mainland is taken into account. The lands touched by the Caribbean Sea are obviously part of

Figure 1.1 The bounty of the sea, reflected in an array of fish caught in a net, flanked by two Native Americans, atop of which is Neptune and his trident. Apparently, the display was part of an early natural history cabinet in Havana. This image appeared in the first Cuban book illustrated by a Cuban. Antonio Parra, *Descripción de diferentes piezas de historia natural las más del ramo marítimo* (Havana, 1787). Ink on paper. John Carter Brown Library.

the region; this rimland provides the southern and western boundaries of the Caribbean basin, stretching from the Yucatan Peninsula to the Amazon. Distinguishing New Grenada from Venezuela, or the Mosquito Shore from Belize, are important markers. Quite how far this Greater Caribbean region extends is not easily answered. For some, the Caribbean should be demarcated from Greater Amazonia, which is seen as comprising the tropical forest and savanna regions of northeastern South America, and so encompassing the Amazon and Orinoco river basins, the Guianas, and the coastal region south of the

Amazon. For others, the circum-Caribbean encompasses tropical and subtropical America ranging from Mexico to South America, given the environmental similarities and strong cultural affiliations connecting the insular Caribbean and these tropical forest lowlands. From the perspective of marine biodiversity, the distribution of shore fish species—about 1,600 overall, twice as many as inhabit Brazilian waters—suggests a Greater Caribbean region extending south to at least the Guianas and north to the Carolinas. Most of the Caribbean falls within the North Atlantic hurricane belt, although the northernmost and southernmost islands generally experience tropical storms, not hurricanes. Another way of thinking of this part of the ecological Atlantic is a giant plantation region, stretching from the Chesapeake to Bahia. It can be subdivided into the Lowcountry and the Wild Coast, Florida and northeastern Brazil, and so on— but, in one historian's words, "the whole region featured a broad unity in its orientation to export agriculture based on slave plantations."[19]

For all its variations, the Caribbean region shares some dominant features—above all, water. This is a world where dry land is not readily available. Appropriately, Guiana's name comes from the Amerindian term for "land of water." The Taíno name for Jamaica, Xaymaca, supposedly means "land of springs." The sea comprises nine-tenths of the region. Persistent trade winds and powerful currents unify and shape the region. Unsurprisingly, a Jamaican priest/ amateur scientist printed three works in the 1780s with many accompanying drawings as he sought to explain the origins of water spouts. The Caribbean is a driving force in the North Atlantic climate system, helping power the Gulf Stream. All but the northernmost Bahamas are part of the tropics. The hurricane track affects all except the southernmost islands and southern rimland. Most Native Americans lived by coasts; many settlements were fishing villages; and they gained almost all of their protein from the sea. When the Europeans and Africans arrived, the infamous trinity of sugar, slavery, and the plantation brought another kind of unity to the region.[20]

Utopia and Dystopia

Nowhere in the New World was the disjuncture between natural bounty and vulnerability so marked as in the Caribbean. Famously part of the torrid zone, the Caribbean, in European eyes, was both an earthly paradise and a place of nightmarish menace. The region inspired wonder and anxiety in roughly equal measure. A place of extraordinary exuberance, the Caribbean region is also particularly precarious, not just because of its many small and fragile islands, but also because of its susceptibility to earthquakes, volcanic eruptions, hurricanes, droughts, pests, and disease. A visitor to the French Caribbean in the nineteenth century counted 67 disasters between 1657 and 1858, a catastrophe every three years, leading him to opine, "Perpetual suffering, continual panic. The sword suspended by a thread over the head of Damocles was less terrifying."[21]

Although constancy is usually said to characterize the Caribbean tropical climate—hot and wet supposedly encapsulates it—there was and is considerable variation. The major exceptions to uniformly hot temperatures are primarily the northern Bahamas and northern parts of the Greater Antilles, which can be affected by frontal weather systems from North America during winter, and the higher elevations of mountains in the Greater Antilles and to a lesser extent in the Lesser Antilles. Frost has been recorded on the highest peaks of the Cordillera Central in Hispaniola. Still, despite local variability and many island microclimates, the warm waters of the Caribbean Sea produce a stable regional temperature range between 59 and 86 degrees Fahrenheit.[22]

Furthermore, the region is swept by the northeasterly trade winds. Blowing for most of the year, these are among the most constant and energy-rich winds on earth and bring in moisture from the Atlantic. They account for much of the humidity and control most weather. Their cooling accounts for the rainfall the region receives. Precipitation is moderate throughout much of the Caribbean, but heavy at mid-elevations on the windward sides of the higher islands and sparse on the leeward sides, through the moist air lifted over hills and mountains (the orographic effect). Thus most hill or mountain land on Caribbean islands can expect to receive between 60 and 100 inches of rain, sometimes considerably more, over the course of the year, depending on leeward or windward exposure. By contrast, annual precipitation on low-lying islands can be as little as between 30 and 40 inches—also true of the smallest volcanic islands such as St. Eustatius and Saba. The lowest rainfall is on small, especially low-relief islands such as the Turks and Caicos and the Netherlands Antilles, where average annual rainfall is generally between 8 and 30 inches. These rainfall differentials had a major impact on the spread of sugar plantations, since the crop required at least 40 inches of rain a year and grows best with 60 to 70 inches.[23]

Guadeloupe and Dominica present interesting cases of the variations possible on a single island. Guadeloupe's eastern, windward side (Grande-Terre) is fairly flat, low-lying, and made of limestone. Because of the lack of orographic uplift, its annual precipitation is as little as 47 inches. Conversely, the western, downwind part of the island is volcanic and dominated by the mountain of Basse-Terre. Its windward eastern slopes experience a remarkable 430 inches of rainfall annually at highest elevation, while the coast on the leeward side receives less than 55 inches. Thus the small surface area of this one island presents dramatic rainfall contrasts. Rugged, largely mountainous Dominica receives considerable rainfall overall (350 inches annually in some places) and boasts 365 rivers and streams, but experiences scarcity of water. Precipitation varies significantly.

The leeward slopes are in rain shadow for most of the year and receive much less rainfall than windward regions. Groundwater also varies in quality. Wells dug close to the shoreline could become brackish in high tide, and many springs are hot and contain impurities. Dominicans used various methods to capture rainfall—cisterns, upturned conches, and ceramic pots. Sugar planters depended on rivers, wells, canals, and ponds to supply water for people, animals, and factories. They had their slaves build and maintain a system of aqueducts, dikes, and trenches to control water levels. Even on an island with as much rainfall as Dominica, it exhibits a wide variety of microclimates and much attention has to be paid to the management of water.[24]

Most Caribbean islands experience distinctive wet and dry seasons. The rainy season generally lasts from April or May through November, with peaks in the spring and fall and something of a midsummer drought, but significant variations occur throughout the region. Based on this seasonality, five major climates have been identified in the Caribbean. A humid, rainforest type, with only 0–2 dry months, is evident in much of the inner arc of the Lesser Antilles, most of Puerto Rico, Hispaniola, eastern Cuba, the Blue Mountains of Jamaica, and the northern Bahamas. A second type, with roughly 2–5 dry months, applies to much of the western half of the region—most of Cuba, Jamaica, parts of Hispaniola, southern Puerto Rico, and most of the Bahamas. A third climate, which is confined to a few rain shadow districts of Hispaniola and Jamaica as well as parts of the Turks and Caicos Islands and parts of the coast of Venezuela, has 6–7 dry months. A fourth, with 8–10 dry months, is restricted to most of the islands north of Venezuela from Margarita to Curaçao. Here, in the southern Caribbean, the rainy season is the reverse of the general pattern and takes place in winter (November to January). Finally, a dry desert or semi-desert type, with 11–12 dry months, applies to Aruba and the nearby Venezuelan coast.[25]

This description of the Caribbean climate suggests stability, but it has been marked by change. Rainfall fluctuations, especially the frequency and severity of storms, droughts, and floods, are related to atmospheric and oceanic circulations. Shifts in North Atlantic air currents (the North Atlantic Oscillation, or NAO) affect the amount of annual rainfall in the Caribbean. El Niño events (warmings of the ocean surface in the eastern equatorial Pacific) also typically bring heavy rains to the northwestern Caribbean, but with variations. Thus Cuba experiences increased rainfall early in the season (January to March) following a warm El Niño–Southern Oscillation (ENSO) event, whereas in Jamaica the heavier than usual rainfall comes somewhat later, in May and July. Conversely, El Niño years typically bring intensified drought to the southern Caribbean.[26]

Long-term climatic changes have profoundly affected the region. Over the course of the pre-Columbian occupation of the region, a significant rise in sea level—amounting to over 16 feet—created coastal flooding and transformations in coastal ecology. The loss of landmass has been estimated at over 15 percent overall. For example, during the past 6,000 years, an estimated 27 percent of Cuba has been submerged under water. Around 7000–6000 BCE a rising sea level created the island of Trinidad by submerging the land bridges between it and the South American mainland. Remnants of those bridges form the westward-extending peninsulas of the island. Its fauna and flora reflect the mainland connection. Some of the earliest pre-Columbian settlements are probably now under water. Relative sea level rise was not uniform or constant. A sharp reduction in the speed of relative sea level rise, circa 6000 BP, seems to have accompanied an increase in pre-Columbian colonization of the islands.[27]

Alternating wet and dry, cooling and warming periods characterize the long-term Caribbean climate. In broad terms, climatologists describe a warmer, wetter early to mid-Holocene, ca. 7000–4000 BP; followed by a drier mid- to late Holocene, ca. 3500 to 2300 BP; and then a wetter era, 2300 to 1200 BP. A closer look at more recent times reveals short-term fluctuations. Thus, from roughly 1 to 550 CE warm, wet conditions prevailed. A period of cooling then lasted from about 500 to 900 CE. Warming began again ca. 850 CE and reached a peak in 1000 CE that continued until about 1100 CE. This last cycle roughly coincides with the drier, so-called Medieval Climate Anomaly, ca. 900–1300 CE. Droughts are particularly pronounced in the Caribbean from about 700 to 1000 CE, as they were in Central America. The Little Ice Age, an era of cooling, began to take hold at least by 1300 CE, and reached its height in the seventeenth century. After 1850, dramatic warming occurred, and has increased through the present day.[28]

The impact of climate change can be measured on macro- and micro-scales. The earliest period of human habitation in the Caribbean coincided with a warming period and a large rise in sea level. As archaeologist Isabel C. Rivera-Collazo notes, "the areas we see as coasts today were far inland at the time of early migration"; the evidence of the earliest colonization of the islands is almost certainly now submerged under water. About 2,000 years ago, Jamaica's climate experienced a shift from wet, humid to drier, cooler conditions, which undoubtedly affected forest habitats. Human occupation of the island began about 1,200 years ago. Based on a newly dated fossil record, an island species of monkey went extinct about a 1,000 years ago—much later than originally thought. The shift from moist to dry forest may have made life difficult for them, but extinction was likely driven by humans. On Carriacou, the increased aridity and warmer sea surface temperatures from ca. 900–1300 CE seem to have produced declines in the fish catch and a growing reliance on large or easily acquired mollusks. Similarly, on St. Martin, an increase in land crabs appears to coincide in part with wet phases, and bivalves mostly surface in archaeological sites during dry phases. An investigation of Antigua reveals that the years

1776–80 represented one of the longest continuous episodes of below-average rainfall levels ever recorded on the island and directly led to a decline in the island economy.[29]

Europeans ventured to the Caribbean during the period now known as the Little Ice Age, lasting roughly 1300 to 1850, which reduced average temperatures by about 1 degree Celsius in the Northern Hemisphere. The coldest decades on average were the 1590s, 1600s, 1640s, 1690s, 1700s, 1780s, and 1810s. From Thomas Thistlewood's temperature records in Jamaica between 1764 and 1776, the average temperature was 3.4 degrees Fahrenheit lower than the mean of temperatures between 1951 and 1980. Jamaica in the eighteenth century was undoubtedly cooler and moister than in the twenty-first century. During the Little Ice Age, then, a substantial cooling occurred in the tropics, equal to or greater than in the higher latitudes. Furthermore, wet and dry seasons were probably more pronounced in the seventeenth and eighteenth centuries than today.[30]

As a result of cooler sea surface temperatures, hurricanes might have been fewer and weaker during the Little Ice Age, but apparently they were not. From 1690 to 2008, a total of 258 hurricanes and 292 tropical storms passed through the Lesser Antilles, with no discernible trends in frequency or intensity. If anything, hurricanes were less frequent in the twentieth century than in the cooler previous centuries, although it may be too early to calculate the full effects of global warming. Nevertheless, the most active hurricane periods were the 1770s, early 1780s, and 1806–16—perhaps with warming trends beginning to increase—whereas some of the least active were 1716–25, 1755–64, and 1793–1805 (the last is hard to explain if warming trends were real toward the end of the Little Ice Age). The sheer unpredictability of hurricanes and the rapid shifts from intense to less intense activity are impressive. Apparently, the eighteenth century saw intervals comprising the most and the fewest hurricanes.[31] Geological and biological data shows that strong hurricanes occurred in the eleventh and twelfth, the early fifteenth, early eighteenth, and especially early nineteenth centuries. In the late eighteenth century, a waning Little Ice Age saw increased hurricanes and, additionally, better conditions for mosquitoes and yellow fever epidemics. The first systematic investigation of coastal geomorphology in the region—of an Atlantic coast sand dune on Long Island in the Bahamas—reveals that it was quite stable during and after Lucayan occupation, which began about 1,000 years ago. However, in three days in 2015, the storm surge of Joaquin, a Category 4 hurricane, stripped about 30 feet from the dune face. Such a remarkable transformation in such a short period of time is the result of more intense hurricanes associated with global warming.[32]

There were geographical variations too. In the south, Barbados seemed to be located outside of the hurricane zone, because for the first three decades of settlement no major storm struck the island, until a major one hit in 1675.

Conversely, in 1670 a ship captain thought a "great many" Antiguans would willingly depart that island to escape the "terrible Hurry Caines that doth everie yeare distroye their Houses and crops." Grenada avoided hurricanes for the most part. The same was largely true of Trinidad and Tobago and the islands off the Venezuelan coast. For St. Vincent, the expected frequency of a Category 1 hurricane is about once every 15 years; but a century or more can separate Category 3 hurricanes. In the north, the Bahamas missed most hurricanes. For a time, the English on Jamaica boasted that their island was hurricane-free until five hit between 1712 and 1751. Then again, the 1760s and 1770s might have lulled Jamaicans into another sense of false security because during those two decades the island escaped the full impact of major hurricanes, only for five to hit the island from 1780 to 1786.[33]

Atlantic hurricane frequency is now known to be linked to the cycle of warming (El Niño) or cooling (La Niña) of the waters in the equatorial eastern Pacific. The former tends to decrease hurricane activity and precipitation in the Atlantic basin, thus causing droughts; the latter causes an increase in tropical storms. Native Americans reported that the decades prior to Columbus's arrival were a period of low hurricane frequency. The period from approximately 1498 to 1510 saw an increase in hurricane activity characteristic of unusually frequent La Niñas. Then, from roughly the 1520s to the 1650s—the period of Spain's virtually exclusive control of the Caribbean region—La Niña activity was frequent and intense. The following epoch, from the 1650s to 1720, when the English, French, and Dutch began to establish their own settlements, was one of decreased hurricane activity, a factor that facilitated the successful development of plantation agriculture. Finally, from about 1750 to about 1805, most years were marked by the effects of an intensified El Niño and La Niña cycle. Historian Sherry Johnson connects the warming anomaly to many of the political and military crises of the time: for example, she attributes (in an example of likely overstretch) the British occupation of Cuba in 1762 to "the cumulative effects of a decade of environmental stress" and the liberalization of Caribbean trade to the ecological crisis generated by the hurricanes of 1766. In these five decades, she emphasizes, misery and deprivation seemingly stalked the Cuban landscape almost unremittingly; starvation and famine supposedly were never far away.[34]

If the quintessential Caribbean disaster is the tropical cyclone, it was not the only hazard that early modern inhabitants of the region faced. A more mundane problem—lack of water—accounted for more lives. This occurrence was especially acute in the so-called Limestone Caribbees, the low-lying outer arc of the Lesser Antilles, as well as in the Dutch and Spanish islands off the Venezuelan coast. Antigua suffered constant droughts. In 1721, after a four-year drought, the legislature acted to preserve public ponds. Five years later, Antiguans imported fresh water from Guadeloupe and Montserrat, amid reports that cattle and slaves were dying. The island held regular fasts to induce rain and frequent thanksgivings to celebrate their return. In the second half of the eighteenth century, the most severe drought on the island of Jamaica occurred in the late 1760s and early 1770s. It was a circum-Caribbean phenomenon, as newspaper accounts from the Yucatan Peninsula of Mexico, coastal Belize, and the Bay of Honduras confirmed; one estimate was that 80,000 Indians had died from famine. According to medical reports from Cruzian doctors, the weather on the island of St. Croix in the early nineteenth century was unusually dry: 11 of 26 years were drought years. For the doctors, the droughts prevented the decomposition of the fallen leaves and therefore reduced the disease-producing miasmas. A drier atmosphere was healthier, they argued.[35]

Dry weather increased the chance of fires. Of all the elements in the early modern era, fire was the most dangerous. Native Americans had used fire to clear land, and Europeans followed suit, in part because they believed fire would cleanse the air and dissipate unhealthy "vapors." But during the period of extreme climatic variations associated with the Little Ice Age, fires became both more frequent and more destructive. In the mid-seventeenth century, rains followed by an "extraordinary drought" produced wildfires that raged throughout the Yucatán, causing havoc. In 1650, French settlers, thinking St. Croix covered with too many "old trees, that prevented the circulation of air," set fire to the woods, which then burned for months. On Jamaica in the dry season, bushfires—ignited by lightning strikes, Maroon encampments, or slaves clearing new provision grounds—raged for weeks. Thomas Thistlewood, the Jamaican overseer and diarist, noted in April 1754, "many of the Mountains on fire, you shall hear the Crash of great Trees falling very frequently." Fire as catalyst, encapsulated in the sugar boiling house where dried crushed cane was burned, could easily become a threat, as most dramatically demonstrated by slaves on Saint-Domingue in 1791 when they torched almost the whole northern plain. Eighteenth-century sugar planters imported "fire engines" to douse fires and took out fire insurance on their most valuable buildings. Large forest fires, lasting for a month or more—largely caused by humans, inadvertently or purposely, and perhaps by lightning too—occurred about every 17 years on average in Suriname in the second half of the eighteenth and early parts of the nineteenth century. Even without a slave accidentally dropping a lighted pipe or a master unwittingly knocking over an oil lamp, strong winds and dry conditions made a tinderbox of the tightly packed, wooden buildings in Caribbean towns. Fires raged in Bridgetown in 1666, 1766, and 1845. Augustín Crame's 1779 plan of Panama City contains empty white spaces to indicate the loss of streets, blocks, and homes caused by devastating fires of 1737 and 1756; two years after the map was drawn another fire broke out, leaving only 50 houses intact. In 1769, St. John's, the capital of Antigua—always a dry island but particularly so in that year—lost two-thirds of its buildings, including 260 houses. Seven years later, Basseterre, St. Kitts, went up in flames. In 1808 a huge conflagration consumed most of Port of Spain, Trinidad.[36]

In addition to droughts, floods, and fires, the Caribbean was and is prone to volcanic activity. There have been at least 34 eruptions of Lesser Antillean volcanoes during the past 400 years, of which about a third occurred before 1840. According to radiocarbon dating and one historically documented case, three happened in the seventeenth century: Soufrière Hills in Montserrat had a dome-forming eruption in ca. 1667, Mt. Scenery on Saba in ca. 1670, and La Soufrière on Guadeloupe in 1690. In the eighteenth and early nineteenth centuries, another eight occurred: the Soufrière on St. Vincent in 1718, 1780 [1784], and 1812–14; Soufrière on St. Lucia in 1766; Montagne Pelée on Martinique in 1792; and La Soufrière on Guadeloupe in 1797–98, 1812, and 1836–37. The bigger islands of Guadeloupe, Martinique, and St. Vincent have been the most active, whereas the smaller islands from Montserrat to Saba comprise lower-altitude volcanoes that produce smaller eruptions. Twenty-one of the historic eruptions have occurred since 1900, perhaps indicating growing volcanism or better reporting.[37]

As a distinguished archaeologist notes, "the list of phenomena associated with Lesser Antillean volcanism is a terrifying litany: ashfalls, ballistic projectiles, debris avalanches, earthquakes and seismic tremors, laharic mudflows, lateral blasts, unstable lava dome formations, lava flows, lightning strikes (probably a major cause of natural fires), pyroclastic flows and surges, tsunamis, and deadly hot volcanic gases." Most of these frightening events had local impacts, but ash clouds in particular could reach neighboring islands. They collapsed buildings, destroyed vegetation, and affected the health of humans and animals. Interestingly, Père Breton's famous dictionary of 1665 listed many Kalinago words revealing perceptions of natural risk—for example, different types and strengths of storms, hurricanes, floods, sea swells, earthquakes, landslides—but nothing specifically about volcanic activity. After all, living in the Caribbean for a while taught that hurricanes were to be expected. It was also possible to mitigate the risk. But volcanic disasters happened infrequently, were unpredictable, and tended to occur at intervals that exceeded the limits of intergenerational memory. Perhaps for those reasons, the Kalinago failed to develop a vocabulary for such possibilities, suggesting how terrifying they were.[38]

The impact of the 1812 volcanic eruption on St. Vincent has been assessed in rigorous fashion. Contemporary estimates suggest that it reduced gross domestic output by about 14 percent and destroyed about 7 percent of the infrastructure of sugar estates. It killed few people, in part because less than 5 percent of slaves resided in the most hazardous zone and many were relocated prior to the eruption. Most of the island escaped unscathed. Prompt assistance from neighboring island, Barbados, averted the immediate threat of famine, and the British

Parliament provided significant relief aid. Although properties on the Leeward side of the island did not equal their pre-1812 output in the immediately succeeding years, estates on the Windward side nearly doubled production in the same period. Recovery thus proved quick and strong in the most dynamic part of the island. A contemporary sketch of the eruption inspired J. M. W. Turner, the famous painter, to produce his sublime version, contrasting the tranquility of the sea and the violence of the volcano, light and dark.[39]

While volcanic activity is absent in the Greater Antilles, earthquakes have been more frequent there and more devastating than in the Lesser Antilles. For some early modern Europeans, hurricanes and earthquakes were linked: both were disturbances of air, one above ground and one below. The dominant tectonic process in the Caribbean is subduction, an underthrusting of the Caribbean plate, which is moving eastward relative to the North American and South American plates at the rate of almost an inch a year. This movement creates faults, and Hispaniola is rather unusual in having two major faults running in parallel throughout the island. Movements along these two faults and others in the Lesser Antilles have created well over a hundred registered earthquakes in the region between 1500 and 1800. A partial count for the sixteenth century is possibly 5, for the seventeenth 19, and for the eighteenth 91 (of which 85 were 1750 onward). The apparent rise in incidence reflects better reporting over time. About 56 percent of the earthquakes occurred in the Greater Antilles; three-quarters of Lesser Antillean earthquakes were in the Windward chain, Martinique being most prone. Counting only major earthquakes of about 7.0 or more on the Richter scale (there is obviously much imprecision) would reduce the count to 2 for the sixteenth, 6 for the seventeenth, and 9 for the eighteenth—again suggestive of underreporting in earliest times; and only two of these occurred in the Lesser Antilles.[40]

The most famously devastating Caribbean earthquake in the early modern period occurred on June 7, 1692, when half of the richest and most important trading center in British America, Port Royal, Jamaica, sank into the harbor in one of the Atlantic world's greatest disasters (2,000 people died in this horrifying event, and perhaps another 2,000 or so from dysentery and other diseases in its aftermath). Thereafter, June 7 was a fast day on the island. In the wake of the disaster, local officials planned a new town—Kingston—at a supposedly more secure site across the harbor. Abandoning one town and building another was an "antiseismic strategy," and the very planning of Kingston—its wide streets, limitations on heights of buildings, and large plazas—owed some inspiration to the traumatic experience. Apparently, erecting low buildings with foundations buried deep into the ground was one localized subterranean Jamaican response. The earthquake also inspired much debate about its causes: whether the result of divine punishment or natural phenomena, attributable to floating gas clouds or underground chemical combustion, how locally or globally connected. Between 1667 and 1799, Jamaica was subject to about 30 earthquakes; most were minor. None were on the scale of 1692—and it would not be till 1907 before another major earthquake happened.[41]

Important as Jamaica is to the story of earthquakes in the region, the island of Hispaniola is the centerpiece because of movements along its two parallel faults. The earliest historically documented earthquake on the island occurred in 1562 along the northerly fault. The towns of Concepcion de la Vega and Santiago de los Cabelleros, which were then insignificant places in the northern part of what is now the Dominican Republic, were both destroyed. From paleo-seismic evidence (excavations along the fault), a more serious rupture occurred about the early thirteenth century (perhaps suggesting a recurrence interval of about 300+ years, since another earthquake happened along the fault in 1842). Other serious earthquakes on the island have been confined to the south. They occurred in 1615, possibly 1673 and 1684, certainly in 1691, and perhaps 1761. In Saint-Domingue, near Port-au-Prince, four significant earthquakes have occurred— November 9, 1701 (calculated as a 6.8 quake by modern seismologists); a series of large earthquakes migrating from east to west starting with an October 18, 1751 (estimated 7.5) quake near the eastern end of the fault in what is now the Dominican Republic and ending with the November 21, 1751 quake (6.7) near Port-au-Prince; and again near Port-au-Prince on June 3, 1770, probably the most devastating of all (7.5)—indicating that the January 12, 2010 earthquake, however tragic, was nothing new in geological terms. The 1770 earthquake reportedly led to the deaths of 30,000 people, mainly from starvation and disease caused by the chaos after the event. Indeed, the post-earthquake epidemic may be an example of intestinal anthrax, associated with the consumption of uncooked—smoked or salted—beef. The havoc and loss of life it caused easily outstripped the more famous Port Royal, Jamaica, earthquake. Indeed, it is the most devastating earthquake in the history of the Caribbean—until January 12, 2010.[42]

About 30 tsunamis hit the Caribbean between 1498 and 1798. Two of them were teletsunamis—generated more than 1,000 kilometers away. About nine hours after the huge Lisbon earthquake in 1755, a tidal wave, perhaps as high as 5 to 6 meters, moving at an approximate speed of 600 kilometers per hour, reached Antigua. Santiago de Cuba was almost completely inundated. Contemporaries described "agitated," "roaring" seas, advances and retreats, and a "sudden flux and reflux," as well as a coloring "as black as ink." The second event occurred six years later due to another powerful earthquake off the Iberian coast, and this teletsunami traversed the Atlantic Ocean, reaching Barbados more than 5,800 kilometers from Portugal in 8.5 hours, arriving at 4:30 p.m. Most of the others were tectonic tsunamis, caused by the movement of oceanic plates, the earliest of which in the colonial era occurred along the Venezuelan coast in 1498 and again in 1530, and occurred infrequently thereafter. Altogether, the Caribbean appears to have experienced 1 tsunami in the fifteenth, 5 in the sixteenth, 4 in the seventeenth, and 23 in the eighteenth century. Better reporting over time no doubt accounts for much of the increase.[43]

Another dimension of Caribbean vulnerability was the disease environment. Proximity to Europe and Africa introduced alien diseases earlier and more frequently here than elsewhere; furthermore, there was no escaping the effects on islands. When exposed to European "crowd diseases" such as smallpox, measles, mumps, whooping cough, and influenza, isolated Amerindians, lacking the immunities that derived from childhood infections, were at their mercy. The first known New World pandemic, one of smallpox, began in Hispaniola in December 1518 and then moved westward to Cuba and the Central American mainland the following year, before reaching Mexico in 1520. When forced migrants from Africa arrived in great numbers, they brought with them new, virulent strains of disease such as malaria and especially yellow fever. The destruction wrought on Amerindians was almost total. Because the region came to host a range of tropical diseases and because it was such a hub of trade, its microbiotic traffic was particularly intense. The Caribbean was a crossroads of contagion, a notably lethal place, where the velocity of infection was swift.[44]

Despite some of their immunities to yellow fever and resistance to malaria, many Africans exposed to a new disease environment and thrust into the sugar fields typically died off within their first year or so on the islands; but for Europeans, the Caribbean was a fearsome charnel house, killing them off at rates exceeding even those of Africans. Newly arrived young European adults died at about four times the rate of their African counterparts. Garrison mortality averaged about 20 percent annually, but the worst casualties were among the unseasoned expeditionary forces. About three-quarters of various European armies sent to the Caribbean died in a matter of months of arriving in the region. Such was the experience for the 29,000 men, "possibly the largest amphibious assault force yet assembled in world history," sent to the West Indies during the War of the Austrian Succession (or its local equivalent, the War of Jenkins' Ear). In seizing Havana during the Seven Years' War, more British soldiers and sailors died in two months than died in North America during the entire war. Spain's ability to hang onto its Caribbean islands owed much to its disease-experienced troops—through a policy of permanent garrisons in which survivors carried immunities to yellow fever and by reliance on locally recruited militias also with immunities to yellow fever and resistant to malaria—and to the invaders' lack of immunities. Just as the Russians relied on "General Winter" to destroy invaders, the Spanish in the Caribbean depended on the "black vomit" to hold onto their Caribbean possessions. Approximately 180,000 British, French, and

Spanish soldiers and sailors lost their lives, mostly from disease, in trying to put down the slave rebellion in Saint-Domingue in the 1790s and early 1800s. The British decision in 1795 to create the so-called West India Regiments, essentially an Africanization of part of their army, was a response to the region's lethality to those born and raised in the British Isles. Medical practitioners began to promote the idea that men of African descent were immune, or at least highly resistant, to tropical diseases. Supposedly, black bodies were able to withstand physical challenges well beyond the capacities of their white counterparts.[45]

Caribbean warfare was therefore highly influenced by experiences of disease. The reason expeditionary forces were so large is that strategists learned that disease, particularly yellow fever, was more destructive than the enemy in Caribbean siege warfare. A battle of attrition ensued: attackers had to be willing to withstand enormous losses, and defenders had to hope they could wait long enough (usually about six weeks) before yellow fever began mowing down the non-immune invaders. Generally, the defenders, by possessing some immunities through spending their childhoods in the Caribbean, had the upper hand, although one should not minimize how an epidemic, once begun, could affect all; but still the urgency of offensive strategists is all the more understandable when they possessed a predominance of raw recruits. Military planners, primarily from the experience of the War of Jenkins' Ear onward, assumed that men "seasoned" in the Americas were less susceptible to tropical disease than recruits from Europe. They were right about West Indians, though less so about North Americans, and they were right too about Africans who largely came from regions of the continent where yellow fever and malaria were endemic. They did not know the etiology of yellow fever—in order to survive, the virus that causes yellow fever generally needs to have access to a sizable population of non-immune individuals and to be carried from the blood of one to another by the female mosquito *Aedes aegypti*—but they knew that newcomers were more vulnerable than natives. Not for nothing did the Spaniards, who had far more creoles among their ranks than any others in the Caribbean, nickname yellow fever the "patriotic fever." They also knew the symptoms—about a week of fever, headache, jaundice, and bloody vomit—and the usual outcome, that is, about 85 percent of infected individuals died. After the establishment of yellow fever, as McNeill notes, a "new eco-military regime" had emerged in the Caribbean.[46]

Differentials in resistance to malaria and yellow fever helped make African slavery in the plantation zone the most economic labor regime. Many West Africans were resistant or immune to falciparum malaria; they carried the so-called sickle-cell trait, a genetic adaptation to the world's most highly malarial environment, which confers resistance and sometimes full immunity to the deadliest form of the disease. West Africans in particular, and West-Central Africans to some degree, also suffered less acutely from yellow fever than did other populations because they grew up in a yellow fever environment, which conferred immunity at low risk. Europeans, if born and raised in temperate climes, proved highly susceptible to both yellow fever and malaria. Europeans born in the Caribbean, on the other hand, if they survived childhood were also likely immune to yellow fever, and resistant, although not as much so as West Africans, to malaria. As McNeill points out, "It is among Atlantic history's crueler ironies that in their bodies slaves brought new infections—yellow fever, falciparum malaria, and hookworm among them—to which they also carried (inherited or acquired) resistance or immunity, which in turn raised the value of slaves against other forms of labor."[47]

Such a disease environment made it extremely difficult for Europeans to establish settler colonies in the Caribbean. There were some spectacular failures. In 1697–98, a Scottish effort to colonize Darien, in Panama, came to grief amid gruesome epidemics, which killed about 80 percent of those who had sailed to the isthmus. In 1763–65, the "most spectacularly deadly colonization effort in the history of the Americas" occurred at Kourou in French Guyana. Of the 13,000 to 14,000 Europeans who arrived at Cayenne, the death rate was about 90 percent. More humdrum failures occurred in other places. British and French settlers had a difficult job creating self-sustaining white populations in their respective imperial spheres. Only the Spanish were truly successful. In 1750, 165,000 white people lived in the Spanish Caribbean, almost two-thirds of all the whites in the region. By 1830, their numbers had more than tripled, and comprised about 86 percent of the whites in the region. The Spanish had no inherent advantages; they simply established fairly large populations, before yellow fever arrived, and their children born in the Caribbean were immune to the disease by adulthood.[48]

Precisely because the disease environment was so virulent, medical practitioners, much like botanists (often one and the same person), flocked to the islands. In Antigua there was 1 doctor for every 163 whites and 1,068 blacks in 1730; in Jamaica a half century later 1 for every 241 whites and 3,286 blacks. Indeed, one contemporary noted in 1740 that Jamaica was "crowded with raw unexperienced youths" seeking medical work. The Spanish Caribbean, with its healthier reputation, attracted fewer physicians; in the 1790s Cuba had about 100 doctors. In the British sphere they were often Scots, or trained in Scottish universities, quite often working for the army; many saw themselves as agents of empire. As army surgeon John Bell put it, "The preservation . . . of any number of lives must be of important benefit to the state; for if five hundred men either die, or are so weakened by disease as to be unfit for actual service, that number must be replaced, at a great expence to the nation. But independent of the expence occasioned by the death of a soldier on foreign service, it ought to be considered that success in every military operation must, in great measure, depend on the

health and vigour of the troops." Because health issues played such a significant role in the military history of the West Indies, medical practitioners had
much on which to reflect and wrote far more books and pamphlets than their
counterparts in North America. Particularly in the last quarter of the eighteenth
century, literature on island diseases ballooned and the colonies began to play an
important role in the production of knowledge. A growing international community of European physicians and scientists, for example, began to take an
interest in leprosy and conflate it with so-called African diseases such as yaws.
Military and naval hospitals provided much scope for clinical observation, dissection, and therapeutic trials. An 1801 review in a New York journal, *The Medical
Assistant*, by Jamaican resident Dr. Thomas Dancer, noted how much medicine
was "indebted to physicians of the West Indies for many valuable publications,"
arising "not only from their importance in relation to the enterprises of agriculture, commerce and war, but also, in a great degree, from the bold and decisive
features they assume, by which they are calculated to arrest attention, and to
throw light upon the whole circle of medical principles."[49]

West Indian medical practitioners read works about the East Indies and
the standard European authorities, but they also drew upon the personal
experiences of fellow doctors, sometimes in neighboring islands, and often
across imperial lines. Thus Antoine Poissonnier-Desperrières, who published a
treatise on the fevers he had observed in Saint-Domingue from 1749 to 1751,
followed four years later by a work that explored a range of diseases that struck
sailors, cited Scotsman James Lind's work on scurvy liberally and positively as
well as his ideas about the putrefaction of European bodies in warm climates.
Similarly, Benjamin Moseley's *Treatise on Tropical Diseases* (1787), based
on over a decade's experiences in Jamaica, cited the work of Chévalier on the
French West Indies and Rouppe on the Dutch Caribbean. Hector M'Lean's *An
Enquiry into the Nature, and Causes of the Great Mortality among the Troops at
St. Domingo* (1797) contrasted the lifestyles of British and French residents
in the Caribbean to make the case that proper seasoning and acclimatization
could ward off disease. Saint-Dominguean exiles—men such as Jean Deveze,
Felix Pascalis-Ouviére, and Louis Valentin—circulated their medical knowledge drawn from the Greater Caribbean (both French and English sources)
around the Atlantic basin. In 1804 a former resident of St. Thomas, a Danish
island, used a New York periodical, the *Medical Repository*, to rebut Dr. Colin
Chisholm's account of the yellow fever outbreak in Grenada. Perhaps the most
interesting figure is José Agustín Tomás Domínguez, formerly John Holliday
from Scotland, who in 1792 arrived with his University of Edinburgh medical
degree in Havana, where he adopted the Catholic faith and a Spanish alias in
order to obtain a license to practice medicine. In 1794 he produced studies in
both Spanish and English on yellow fever, explored common local therapeutics,

and acted as an influential medical intermediary across English-speaking and Spanish-speaking populations. When the practice of cowpox inoculation arrived in the Caribbean at the turn of the nineteenth century, it rapidly spread across imperial boundaries. In the early nineteenth century, French physician Nicholas Chervin visited a number of British West Indian islands collecting testimony intended to prove that yellow fever was not contagious. Sometimes, through time lags or differing circumstances, a practice losing popularity in one imperial sphere gained credence in another, or vice versa. Proximity led to borrowings and shared knowledge.[50]

Caribbean practitioners also took note of and sometimes incorporated the remedies of enslaved doctors who possessed knowledge of African medical traditions. African (and Amerindian) cures for fevers often involved bathing, alternating hot and cold, which influenced some Europeans, who recognized the power of some slaves' herbal remedies. The most famous and successful medical practitioner of African descent, Doctor Gramman (or Great Man) Quacy (also Kwasi or Quassi) in Surinam, gained renown for the efficacy of his herbal roots. Born in West Africa in the 1690s, he discovered a special bark useful in reducing fevers. Described as a diviner, sorcerer, healer, and creator of obía (charms or amulets), he and others like him straddled the porous early modern boundary separating the magical from the medicinal. Individuals such as James Thompson in Jamaica experimented with herbal remedies suggested by slave informants. In Saint-Domingue, Nicolas Bourgeois was impressed by Africans' ingenuity "in the art of procuring health," especially their herbal knowledge and their repudiation for bleeding and purging. Edward Long said of Jamaica's medical practitioners, "what can be more reproachful than to have it said, and with truth, that many of the Negroes are well acquainted with the healing virtues of several herbs and plants, which a regular physician tramples under foot." For Long, "Negro cures" worked "wonderfully" where European medicines failed. Perhaps enslaved Africans first introduced the technique of smallpox variolation into the Caribbean. Working among slaves enabled doctors to observe certain diseases—such as yaws and elephantiasis—which were entirely new to them and seemed to affect Africans almost exclusively. Some European doctors experimented on these diseases—borrowing from Gold Coast Africans the practice of inoculating against yaws. In a backhanded compliment, army surgeon George Pinckard in 1806 noted that on Barbados "the very *negro doctors* of the estates too justly vie with [white doctors] in medical knowledge." His assessment of those white doctors, however, was that they are "only pre-eminent in ignorance" and are "more illiterate than you can believe." Most Europeans were disdainful, if not downright contemptuous, of African medical skill, which they regarded as little more than superstition. The confluence of non-European bodies and pathogens in the Caribbean created conditions for Europeans to develop ideas about difference, transforming the Caribbean into an important arena in the history of modern racial classification.[51]

Some enslaved medical practitioners, feared by both slaveholders and slaves alike, and empowered by powerful knowledge, emerged as central figures in hundreds of court trials across the Greater Caribbean, where they stood accused of administering poison. From 1680 to 1850, more than 500 enslaved people of African descent appeared in the tribunals of Virginia, Martinique, Surinam, and Bahia accused of this crime. In the trials, ideas about health, healing, benign therapeutics, and malevolent powers clashed. The two most famous cases of alleged poisoning—Macandal in Saint-Domingue in 1758 and Tacky's Rebellion in Jamaica in 1760—raised issues of magical powers, and unfolded at a time of crisis, during the Seven Years' War. In Saint-Domingue, the timing and scale of deaths attributed to poison may have resulted from the circulation of mycotoxins from spoiled flour. In the 1780s a group of colonial doctors promoted the idea that most deaths ascribed to poison were in fact caused by epizootic livestock diseases. Although the largest single poison crisis occurred in Martinique in the 1820s, overall poisoning cases declined from circa 1760 onward, suggesting that fears of sorcery's power diminished over time.[52]

Dirt-eating—variously called pica, geophagy, or mal d'estomac—was an ailment particularly associated with the tropics (although it occurs in many parts of the world). In early sixteenth-century Cuba, Spaniards claimed that Taínos ate earth as a means of deliberate self-harming. Fearful of the loss of labor threatened by widespread suicide, Spaniards punished the alleged culprits by forcing them to eat their genitals covered in mud or scalded their mouths before burning them to death as a terrifying example to others. As Africans replaced Indians in the work force, geophagy became associated with the newcomers, sometimes with particular African ethnic groups, and went by the term *Cachexia Africana*. Some said that dirt-eating caused nearly half of all deaths among slaves on individual plantations. For some interpreters, the disease was a mental disorder, a racial pathology, perhaps linked to the trauma of the slave trade. In the seventeenth-century Spanish Caribbean, a black ritual practitioner despaired of curing a woman sick from eating soil. On the other hand, Jamaican physician Thomas Dancer believed dirt-eating was no different from the cravings of pregnant women. Others thought it a form of resistance and blamed spiritual healers and obeah practitioners for promoting it. For yet others, it was a sign of poor nutrition. In the late eighteenth century, competing views of Cachexia Africana became part of the abolitionist debate, with antislavery advocates attributing it to malnourishment and starvation while proslavery advocates described it as a pernicious African custom or addiction.[53]

In the seventeenth and early eighteenth centuries, the notion that hot climates altered human bodies was widespread. The tropics were, it came to be thought, a distinct disease zone. After all, most newcomers underwent a seasoning fever, a rite of passage, through which their bodies became inured to the climate. In 1793 a New England migrant to Jamaica observed of her son that a "six months fever" has made "a perfect creole of him." Furthermore, by the eighteenth century, most commentators insisted on the peculiarities of warm climates and their associated diseases. Bodily putrefaction, according to naval surgeon James Lind, could be attributed in most cases to exposure to putrid effluvia, or pernicious vapors or miasmas, resulting in malignant fevers. It was not just heat, but the air—particularly humid, stagnant, corrupt air—that adversely affected human health; so, not surprisingly, the meteorology of the tropics was a subject of systematic investigation from Edmund Halley onward. In 1787, just before emigrating from England to Maine, Benjamin Vaughan, the Jamaican-born diplomat, wrote his friend Thomas Jefferson about how European philosophers accounted for the humidity of the atmosphere of eastern North America. A key reason, Vaughan, noted, was "the cultivated parts of the West Indies (a supposed appendage of the part of America in question) being divided into small islands exposed to the sea air." West Indian sea air, apparently, had widespread effects.[54]

Debates about the effects of climate on human bodies are captured well in the late eighteenth-century attempt to settle almost 600 Jamaican Maroons in Nova Scotia. Suffering from severe winters, the deportees hankered for their island's tropical fruits and vegetables; they wanted to hunt wild hogs; and they demanded the signature Caribbean products of rum, coffee, sugar, and cacao. Other commentators insisted that the Maroons might be tempered by a cooler climate, which would subdue their fiery temperaments. A knowledgeable few pointed out that the Trelawny Maroons came largely from Jamaica's mountainous highlands, where temperatures were much cooler than the island's lowlands, thus supposedly easing their transformation into industrious, reliable subjects—if only they would relinquish their profligate and traditional ways, by not overheating their houses, and dressing inappropriately. In 1800, after four years in Nova Scotia, the allure of a hot climate—in Sierra Leone— saw the Maroons relocate once more. Their critics anticipated that the African heat would inflame their innate volatility. The competing explanations for the Maroons' inability or unwillingness to "acclimatize" raised old notions of climatic determinism and new Enlightenment ideals of human malleability. The debates also revealed that climate was much more than an atmospheric phenomenon; it was a cultural construction.[55]

By the late eighteenth century, fever, it was being argued, was a product of an individual's nervous temperament. Some progressive physicians in the Caribbean, drawing on a nervous theory of fevers emerging from a number of European medical schools, began to argue that endemic fevers showed no symptoms of putrefaction of the humors and were rooted in the nervous rather than in the digestive system. A growing number of Caribbean doctors attributed disease not, say, to accumulations of bile but to depleted energy. For some, the nervous system, perhaps overstimulated by excessive heat, was the cause of yellow fever. Corresponding shifts also occurred in treatments—essentially away from bloodletting to vomits and purges and eventually to chemical and botanical preparations. Powder from the bark of the cinchona tree, often referred to as "Peruvian" (from its Andean habitat) or "Jesuit bark," first came to be used extensively and promoted in the colonies for fevers."[56]

A robust drug trade emerged in the eighteenth century. Bioprospecters sought new drugs to adopt into the European materia medica, and in a short space of time medicines went from being luxuries to staples in a competitive marketplace. The idea of a "specific," a medicine that would theoretically have the same effect on anybody in any location suffering the same ailment, undergirded this development. The old understanding that individual imbalance led to disease conflicted with a growing opinion that diseases had essential qualities. No longer was illness simply an internal matter; disease became an entity that threatened the body from without. Caribbean customers bought preparations of ipecac, opium, cinchona, jalap, rhubarb, sarsaparilla, and the like, purported to cure many common illnesses. Each medicine could be procured and applied regardless of a patient's particular circumstance. Jamaica became the prime destination for London's medicinal trade. On the eve of the American Revolution, the island received five times more medicines (in weight) than Virginia and Maryland.[57]

These shifts in paradigms were not uniform. By the end of the eighteenth century, some physicians on the islands recommended bloodletting in fevers, adapting an old practice to new ideas about the body. The liberal use of calomel in hot climates was also justified on grounds that tropical diseases required more drastic treatments than those in temperate regions. There was no unanimity on whether yellow fever was contagious or not, or whether quarantine was justified or not; debates raged on whether the disease was locally inspired or imported. Nevertheless, gradually many West Indian physicians came to favor restorative treatments, such as in bathing in warm and particularly cold water, which, as one claimed, excited "the tone and vigour" of the body. Once the alleviation of the causes and symptoms of nervous debility became the primary aim, there was growing resistance to strong purgatives and greater reliance on exposure to airs and waters of different temperatures as ways to stimulate the nervous system. For this reason, bathing and carriage rides came into vogue.[58]

Moving within the Caribbean, some doctors believed, had a deleterious impact on health. James Grainger, for example, thought that, once "accustomed to one island," slaves "run no small risk of their lives when transported to another," even if it was "equally healthy." He further noted that "it has often been observed that slaves carried from one plantation to another, though on the same island, are apt for some time to droop and be sickly." Contemporaries were well aware of different microclimates and their impact on health. Fresh air and drinkable water signified a salubrious setting; a marshy lowland likely bred miasmas and noxious vapors. Higher elevations and coastal locales invited cooling breezes; morasses and stagnant water produced pestilential fevers. Lowland planters built highland retreats; military planners situated barracks and hospitals on hillsides, mountaintops, and dry sandbanks. When eighteenth-century Jamaicans debated the merits of moving the capital 12 miles from Spanish Town to Kingston, they made extravagant claims about the relative healthiness of the two locales. In the eighteenth century, people believed that local environments exhibited marked climatic variations, which in turn affected human bodies, shaping individual and collective health.[59]

Given the emphasis on the importance of climate and air, however, doctors often recommended a change of scene as a way to restore health. Doctors regularly advocated a movement from lowlands to highlands or a sea voyage as especially restorative. Sailors referred to sea breezes as "the doctor." In 1787 a Scottish doctor sent his enslaved bricklayer on a coasting vessel around Jamaica to see if the six-week jaunt would restore him to full health. Ironically, he suffered from seasickness, vomited violently, and spent much time below deck—in "very bad air"—but returned, seemingly purged and cured. Examples of West Indians moving from the disease-ridden tropical zone to more temperate locales in a bid to save their lives are legion. One account of Charleston, South Carolina, in the 1780s, pointed to the presence of "a great number of valetudinarians from the West-Indies, seeking for the renovation of health, exhausted by the debilitating nature of their sun, air, and modes of living." Counterintuitively, there was also considerable traffic from mainland to islands. Although many emphasized the fierce malevolence of the torrid zone and the extreme virulence of the region's diseases, a belief in the tropics as an Eden encouraged others to move to a warm climate as a cure for many ailments.[60]

The most famous eighteenth-century American medical tourist was 19-year-old George Washington, who in 1751 accompanied his older half-brother Lawrence—who had been in poor health ever since a Caribbean military expedition a decade earlier—to Barbados. Lawrence had a pulmonary complaint, and the warm air of Barbados was supposed to prove restorative. The renown of Dr. William Hillary, the Bridgetown physician, was an additional inducement for the journey. While acknowledging Barbados as "the finest island of the West Indies," Lawrence explained to his father-in-law that "this climate has not afforded the relief I expected from it." From Francis Le Jau, the Anglican missionary, to Henry "Light Horse Harry" Lee, the Virginia-born cavalry officer, a constant trickle of people went from North America to the Caribbean in hopes that the sun would restore them to health. In the early nineteenth century, St.

Croix and Cuba in particular gained reputations as sanatoriums for tuberculosis patients. Vice President William Rufus King took the oath of office on March 24, 1853, in Cuba, where he had gone for "the cure." He died shortly after returning to the United States.[61]

Certainly, some parts of the Caribbean were seen as healthier than others. In the early eighteenth century, Mark Catesby noted that the Bahamas "are blessed with a most serene Air . . . more healthy than most other Countries in the same Latitude." Indeed, he maintained that they were even healthier than some more northerly colonies, so that "many of the sickly Inhabitants of Carolina retire to them for the Recovery of their Health." The northern coast of Cuba was also seen as particularly wholesome, because of its prevailing trade winds. Promoters of the conquest of that island cited its salubriousness. Barbados was usually considered healthier than Jamaica, although gradually the mountainous areas of the larger island had its proponents. Wide open spaces had many advocates. In 1759 Dr. William Hillary, Lawrence Washington's physician, believed that Barbados was free of the "intermitting fevers" that plagued the rest of the West Indies, in large part because deforestation allowed the air to circulate freely and made the island less prone to miasmas. In 1774, when Nicholas Cresswell visited Barbados, he described it as "a high rocky Island, and reckoned the most healthy in the West Indies." In the same year, Edward Long thought that the "healthy air of Barbados is owing to the island's being entirely cleared of wood." Indeed, Barbados was not malarial.[62]

The Caribbean was in the vanguard of medical reform. Exotic locations fostered an empirical and experimental approach, leading to new therapeutic possibilities. Some of the most important centers were the medical establishments of the armed forces, where cadavers were widely available and experiments could take place. Medical practitioners in the Caribbean colonies routinely challenged the received wisdom of European medical circles. They tended to argue that fevers were the product of local conditions and intimately connected with climate, and they developed a distinct branch of medicine— one devoted to warm or hot climates. Their most decisive break with European authorities was their shift away from bloodletting, their faith in various chemical and botanical preparations, and their increasingly pathological investigations and observations. Fevers, they believed, were distinct entities, possibly imported, that affected certain parts of the body. The decline of bleeding went hand in hand with an increasing use of emetics, antimonial vomits, and drugs in the treatment of fevers.[63]

Medical empiricism also encompassed black healers, who probably saw more clients than any other medical specialists. They were creative yet pragmatic, inventive yet authoritative, experimental yet tradition-bound. These cosmopolitan healers of African descent drew on diverse sources of therapeutic knowledge, to which their often extensive travels had exposed them. They drew inspiration from their relation with animals, whether controlling the movement of snakes or placing a patient's "dead" arm inside a freshly killed bull; or from natural objects, such as three polished stones, tied to a specialist's feet, or the seashells that decorated an altar in a Portobelo home; or from chewing herbs and roots that were then applied to patients' wounds. Their remedies—in some cases claiming to command hurricane-strength winds and rains—harnessed the power of nature. Inquisition records in the seventeenth-century Spanish Caribbean reveal over a hundred healers and ritual practitioners. The Caribbean was a site of medical innovation, experimentation, and knowledge production in large part because the medicine practiced by enslaved Africans on Caribbean plantations drew on a variety of medical, religious, and cultural traditions, including Amerindian, African, and European ones.[64]

Caribbean cartography was also cutting edge. A notable feature of the earliest European maps of the Caribbean was the speed with which the Spanish drew the outline of the islands. A sketch of the north coast of Hispaniola, perhaps produced by Columbus himself in 1492, identifying (La) Natividad, Monte Christi, and Tortuga Island, is the first surviving European map of part of the region. By the turn of the sixteenth century, world maps depicted the discoveries of Columbus in the Antilles. One beautiful world map, known as the Alberto Cantino portolan of 1502, depicts a recognizable Caribbean chain of islands. As early as the mid-sixteenth century, cosmographer Alonso de Santa Cruz could produce a masterpiece, his map of Cuba, remarkable for its detailed coastal outline, based on information he gleaned from pilots.[65]

Native collaboration was essential to early European mapping. The use of Indian names on maps is in part an index of the Indian contribution to cartographic knowledge and in part a measure of European appropriation and control. Lucayan people living in what became the Bahamas explained to Columbus the position of adjacent islands using sand drawings. Later, in Europe, two of them were able to set out the general position of the islands using beans. Over a century later, a French Jesuit who encountered Caribs in Saint Vincent marveled at the attention they paid to the stars. He also noted that they "content themselves in their navigation to make certain marks on wooden planks they rely on to travel," an indigenous kind of map. Furthermore, natives shaped maps, literally by the sheer force of their presence. A 1716 map of the eastern province of the Audiencia of Guatemala uses white, largely blank space (dotted with settlements) to show the Spanish civil domain, and dense vegetative green to demarcate the realm of Afro-Amerindian dominion where "zambos," or Mosquitos, held sway.[66]

The greatest shift in Caribbean mapmaking over the course of the early modern period involved a transition from littorals to interiors, from coastal outlines to mountains, from hydrography to topography. This was hardly a wholesale transformation—navigation was still the primary purpose of most maps, and maritime charts were fundamental—nor was it confined only to the Caribbean. The French were in the vanguard, establishing the first official hydrographical bureau in 1720, before the British did in 1795. Jacques-Nicholas Bellin's (1703–72) *Neptune françois*, published in 1753, was the best compilation of coastlines, maritime towns, and harbors of its time.[67]

Nevertheless, over time attention began turning to the land and to interiors—the source of all plantation wealth. Estate maps—detailed internal layouts of large agricultural units—began to appear on large sugar islands by the mid-eighteenth century. Caribbean islands supported a large population of surveyors, reflecting the demand for their services from a wealthy plantocracy. State-sponsored topographical maps, as distinct from an estate plan commissioned by a private proprietor, also began to be produced. Not long after Surinam became a Dutch colony (1667), a survey of all plantations became a priority. In the 1680s a local surveyor forwarded *leggerkaarten*, or land surveys, of different parts of the colony to Amsterdam so that an engraved generalized map could be produced. It was published in 1688. Another notable example is the map of St. Croix produced by Johannes Crononberg in 1750. It reflects a regular rectangular grid of plantation lots, which is how the land had been laid out when the Danes bought the island from the French. The map did more than reflect a grid; it added windmills, horse- or ox-driven mills, plantation houses, slave quarters, and detailed land use, distinguishing most particularly among sugar, cotton, provisions and pasture, forest and bush. It even depicts fields as small as 300 by 500 feet. This map is a remarkably detailed image of the island's development at mid-century, far more advanced than institutional cartography at the time.[68]

Still, all other Europeans lagged behind the French in the production of sophisticated topographic maps. In 1732, for example, a military officer produced a plan of Grande-Terre (the eastern wing of the island of Guadeloupe) according to a rectangular grid, listing the size of the lots and the names of the proprietors. In the 1760s French geographer-engineers produced remarkably detailed topographic maps of Martinique and Guadeloupe by use of triangulation. The map of Martinique is complete and is about 13 square meters in size (2.7 by 4.85 meters). The map of Guadeloupe consists of 16 parts and covers a space almost double the size of the Martinique map, if pieced together. The map shows hills, valleys, vegetation, plantations, fields, settlements (seemingly a precise count of buildings), towns, rivers, and a network of roads.[69]

Living in a multinational world in close proximity facilitated exchanges of all kinds. In the case of maps, some were state secrets, but others aimed at propaganda. Generally, most borrowed from one another, usually across imperial boundaries. Similarly, an intricate network of naturalists were often in touch with one another across Caribbean territories, read each other's works, and drew on a wide range of informants. The Spanish Caribbean—the earliest settled, and home to the biggest and richest islands and most of the mainland rim—earned most attention.[70]

Efflorescence and Degradation

The Caribbean region forms a spectacular natural laboratory, a biodiversity hotspot, its evolutionary exuberance taking many forms. The luxuriance and beauty of tropical nature is a well-worn theme, but still the global dimensions are staggering. The islands, representing just 0.15 percent of the world's land surface, are home to over 2 percent of the world's endemic plant species, 3 percent of the world's amphibians, 5 percent of the world's land snails, and 6 percent of the world's reptiles. Of the approximately 13,000 plants presently found in the Caribbean, about half are indigenous and unique to the region. The two continental islands of Trinidad and Tobago, sharing much with the mainland, harbor almost 7,000 plant species. Cuba, the largest island in the Caribbean, has the richest flora and about half of its approximately 6,000 species of flowering plants are unique to the island. The lushness of Caribbean plants—gigantic leaves and flowers, towering trees, dense vegetation—amazed European visitors, who were intoxicated by the flora's extravagance and overpowering smells. Even attending to plants and vertebrates does not begin to capture the true level of species diversity on the islands, which resides in its invertebrates. Cuba's highest level of species diversity (discounting microbial life) is its insects. Despite its small land surface, then, the Caribbean islands host a remarkably rich fauna and flora.[71]

The vegetation of the Antilles consists of about 13,000 species of plants. Formed over millions of years, a remarkable variety of forms owes much to a complex geological history, separation from and proximity to continental landmasses, and dispersal across water and through air. The most widespread plant formation in the Antilles is not the iconic tropical mountain rainforest, so associated with the region, but rather the dry forest, characterized by thorn woodlands and desert-like scrub. In general, trees in dry forests are smaller, simple in structure, and less varied than wetter forest formations. Temperate forests are dominated by one or a few key species; tropical forests are characterized by diversity. No one species dominates. As one natural scientist has noted, the "island of Jamaica, with an area of about 6,000 square miles, about that of Connecticut, furnishes approximately four-fifths as many species of flowering plants as are to be found in the United States east of the Mississippi river." For most groups of plants, more member species inhabit the tropics than temperate zones.[72]

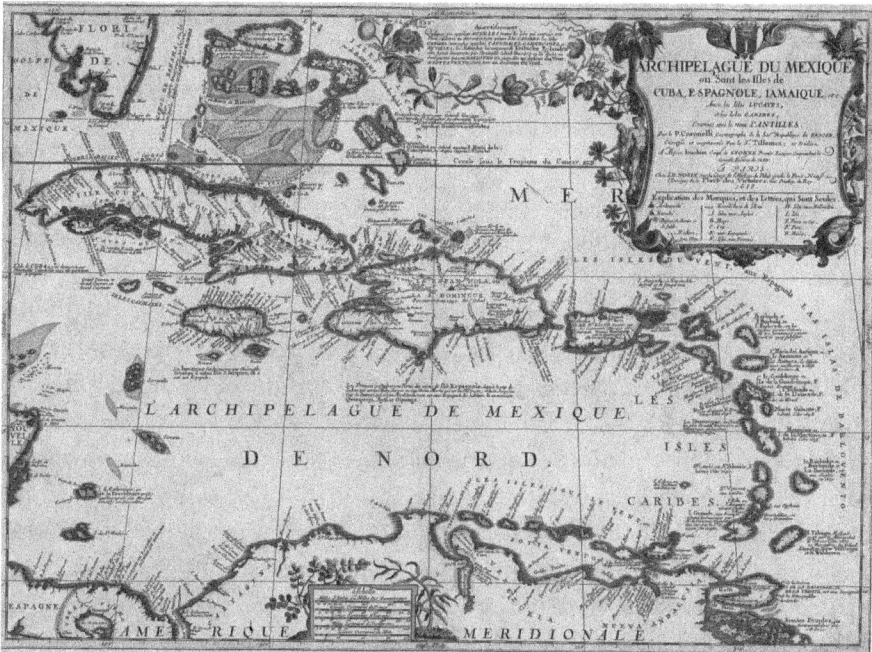

Figure 1.2 Archipelague du Mexique, ou sont les Isles de Cuba, Espagnole, Jamaique, etc. Avec les Isles Lacayes, et les Isles Caribes, connües sous le nom d'Antilles. By Vincenzo Coronelli, 1688. The map depicts the Caribbean islands as well as parts of Florida, Honduras, Nicaragua, Costa Rica, and the northernmost part of South America, with historical notes on the antiquity of the settlement and ownership. It is engraved with a Caribbean cornucopia of fauna and flora—passion fruits, flowers, figs, mamey, manioc, acajou, pineapple, indigo, ginger, flying fish, and a turtle—as well as human figures. Engraved map. John Carter Brown Library.

The vegetation of the Antilles has a long and varied history of human use. More than 60 types of wood have been identified from prehistoric archaeological sites in the Greater Antilles. Black ironwood, found in the Bahamas, is one of the hardest and densest woods in the world. Other hard dense woods such as lignum vitae ("wood of life") and mahogany excelled as fuelwood and for construction of tools and building materials. The ceiba, one of the largest trees of tropical America, yields strong, lightweight wood that made good canoes. Mangrove trees, estimated at covering almost 4,600 square miles in the Caribbean, which grow at the water's edge in land unsuitable for crop production, regenerate quickly, and are a good source of high-quality fuelwood and charcoal. The calabash tree produces large, hard container fruits that can serve as bowls, scoops, and fishnet floats. Palms are multipurpose plants, providing in some cases edible fruit, but also wood, thatch, and fiber. Cordage and plant fibers were useful in clothing, basketry, netting, hammocks, ropes, and fishing lines. Trees supplied edible fruits such as soursop, guava, and star apple as well as gums, tannins, resins, and dyes. Tobacco was important as a medicine; and a narcotic snuff made from the pulverized seeds of the cojóbana or cojobilla tree was vital in Amerindian religious rites. The Taíno regularly used three types of pepper, observed Las Casas, two domesticated and one wild. From South America, migrants brought home garden fruits, such as yellow sapote, wild avocado, and perhaps sapodilla; and introduced trees such as papaya, genip, and the Panama tree.[73]

The anonymous authors/illustrators of the "Histoire Naturelle des Indes," probably created in the 1590s, focused most of their energies on the plants of the circum-Caribbean and their uses. They began with garlic of the Indies, "sweeter than that of France," which the Indians roast "on the fire like a pear and eat." They then depicted an array of nourishing fruits: soursop, caco plum, avocado, mamee (or mamey) apple, agave, guava, coconut, watermelon, and wild fig, with the pineapple highlighted as "exquisite," tasting like a raspberry, and "eaten raw with salt only to relieve the Indians of stomach pains." Other attractions included sweet potatoes, eggplants, tomatoes, beans, squash, and plantains. One herb, bregele, softened iron; another, lacique, alleviated pain; a third, roumerre, was "very good for bad air"; but most important was tobacco, or *petun*, "a special herb which the Indians use for food as well as an extremely beneficial medicine." Trees supplied resins and barks, or as in the cabuya tree, the material to "make ropes and nets for fishing"; the cotton shrub also doubled as "hedges to close off their gardens." Staple foods were important. Maize "is a grain, which the Indians use for baking bread; after being ground in a wooden mortar, it yields a very white and very good flour." The root that was most critical to subsistence was cassava: "when eaten before the sun sends its rays upon it, puts [the Indians] in mortal danger" but solar power "purifies" and removes the threat. They knew promise and peril went hand in hand, although they ascribed too much to the power of the sun, instead of human endeavor.[74]

The manchineel tree is emblematic of the promise and perils of Caribbean vegetation. Found in coastal areas, it is superficially attractive—bright green leaves, a sweet-scented blossom, and an apple-like fruit—but this appearance belies its lethality. The Spanish named it *manzanilla de la morte*, or "little apple of death." When Nicholas Creswell visited Barbados in 1774, he heard that one manchineel apple "is sufficient to kill 20 people," and the "poison is of such a malignant nature that a single drop of rain or dew that falls from the tree upon your skin will immediately raise a blister." Coming into contact with its sap or simply looking up at it, some people went temporarily blind, an experience suffered by the buccaneer Alexander Exquemelin; others "change[d] colors, [went] mad, and then die[d]." Eating land crabs or fish that had ingested manchineel was also said to be perilous. When Saint Barthélemy became a Swedish colony in 1785,

Figure 1.3 Pyne Frute. By John White, 1585. En route to Roanoke, naturalist John White spent time in the Caribbean. Like many visitors, he was impressed by the pineapple. Lauded for its exquisite taste, it even became a decorative emblem in household decoration, and one European landowner constructed a folly as homage to the fruit. Watercolor over graphite. British Museum.

the new governor called for the eradication of "this very beautiful but highly toxic" tree, an indication of the menace manchineel evoked. The indigenous people of the Caribbean used the caustic latex from manchineel as a poison to tip darts and arrows. When Ponce de León visited Florida in 1521, an Indian managed to project a dart, laced with manchineel poison, into his thigh. He was dead within days of retreating to Cuba.[75]

Edward Long, the historian of Jamaica, came to manchineel's defense. The stories about its deadliness were "vulgar errors," he claimed, "romantic tales" told by "early voyagers and travelers," who were seduced by the fruit's "lovely" appearance, which was rather like an English crab apple. Newly arrived sailors, taking refuge from the rain under the tree's branches, would suffer terrible blisters—a likely story, Long implied. Instead, he offered practical observation. Manchineel's "wood makes very handsome furniture, resembling in appearance the English oak." The sawyers and carpenters "generally cover their mouths and nostrils with crape, in order to exclude the finer particles from getting down their throats." Inquiring "among the Negroes," Long "could not learn that they suffered any inconvenience from drops of the juice, which were accidentally spurted upon their skin." Long also reported the dissection experiments of "a gentleman" and consulted the botanical writings of Patrick Browne, Henry Barham, and Hans Sloane—all to disprove lethality. Long concluded that these "fictions" at least served to warn "straggling sailors . . . against smarting for the rash indulgence of a liquorish appetite" by eating "any fruit that falls in their way." Science, however, does not side with Long.[76]

In the tropics, organic material quickly decomposes and is rapidly recycled into tree and plant growth. Accordingly, most nutrient storage is in the vegetation, not the soil. Burning trees releases a big nutrient windfall, but this was infrequently repeated in the same spot. On a rather uninviting island such as Barbuda—low and flat, and made of largely limestone, with thin soils and limited fresh surface water—the Amerindians cleared land through regular burnings. In addition to the nutrient bonanzas for their fields, they exploited lignum vitae, a drought-resistant hardwood species, and greenheart and torchwood, for fuel and house construction. They engaged in these practices for 14 centuries before abandoning their homeland ca. 1300 CE. When Europeans arrived a few centuries later, the vegetation had rebounded. What seemed untouched and unoccupied was in fact secondary growth and a modified landscape. Compared to soils in temperate latitudes, the tropical soils of sterile volcanic ash were transformed naturally into fertile soil in a remarkably short time—perhaps within a decade. The strong trade winds distributed not just volcanic ash but also African dust, the clay minerals of which increased the nutrient-holding abilities of Caribbean soils. At the same time, however, most Caribbean soils were extremely vulnerable to considerable erosion, especially where the protective cover of natural vegetation has been removed.[77]

Alluvial soils are rare in the Caribbean, particularly on its islands. To the north, the Gulf of Mexico is one of the largest estuarine regions in the world; to the south, the Orinoco and Amazon Rivers form the world's largest drainage basins. By contrast, floodplains are not common in the Caribbean—Trinidad and parts of Hispaniola and Cuba are the insular exceptions. The rimland has extensive lowlands fed, in some cases, by large rivers such as the Magdalena in present-day Colombia, but nothing on the scale of the Mississippi. In French Guiana, raised fields—building mounds above the water level to secure dry location for cultivation and concentrate fertile material—date to the eleventh century. To control variations in water level, the Indians cut canals and ditches, actively molding the aquatic landscape. Apparently, this intensive agricultural land use allowed population density to reach between 50 to 100 persons per square kilometer. In most parts of the Caribbean, however, the rarity of alluvial soils helps explain their general lack of fertility and low durability.[78]

Not on the scale of the Guianas and not generally in swampland, Native Americans in other parts of the Caribbean engaged in *conuco* agriculture—constructing mounds, some as high as a meter and about 3 meters in circumference, in which they planted a mixture of crops—which helped preserve soil fertility and protected against erosion. Arranged in regular rows, the mounds improved drainage, permitted more lengthy storage of mature tubers in the ground, and made it easier to weed and harvest the crops. Even in places where soils were shallow and the limestone bedrock lay close to the surface, indigenous farmers enhanced their gardens and plots on which they grew cotton and food crops by adding nutrient-rich red clays and mixing it with organic materials to increase fertility. Also Amerindian farmers allowed their lands to regenerate after a fairly short period of cultivation.[79]

Following the Amerindian example, Europeans cleared land by burning the vegetation, but they did so on a massive scale. One early observer noted that "all the earth is black with cinders." The resulting rich soil was of course deceiving. The assumption was that fertility was boundless, infinite, or, as one early visitor put it, "a most rich soil allwayes greene [growing] and baring fruit." Contemporaries occasionally expressed disquiet at the rapidity and extent of the destruction. Compared to the Caribs, "who wisely left shady groves standing in the midst of their fields," an observer on St. Kitts in 1625 noted, "the French cut and slashed right and left, intent on only clearing the ground as rapidly as possible, and without a thought of future protection against the sun." He claimed that the French "tore up the earth, which loosened for the first time, gave forth an unhealthy exhalation, which was often fatal to the labourers in their weakened conditions." Europeans engaged in commercial monoculture that quickly exhausted soils; their sugar boiling houses introduced lead and mercury into the ground; increased mining, coal combustion, and waste incineration gave rise to emissions of metals into the atmosphere to which bats were exposed. In 1661, the first official recognition of declining soil fertility came when the president and council of Barbados recorded that "the land is much poorer, and makes much less sugar than heretofore." Introducing livestock into a region with no previous history of large mammals, allowing them to roam and breed at will, led to soil compaction and considerable soil runoff.[80]

If the land largely seemed inexhaustible, so did the sea. The Caribbean contains the greatest concentration of marine species—over 12,000 and counting—in the Atlantic Ocean. Its extensive coral reefs, the most structurally complex and taxonomically diverse marine ecosystems on earth, as well as vast seagrass beds covering bays, lagoons, and continental shelves, together with mangrove swamps and marshes, provide rich habitats for a range of marine creatures. More than 3,000 mollusks, just under 3,000 crustaceans, and over 1,300 fish inhabit the Caribbean Sea. Invertebrate animals include echinoderms, primarily sea urchins; crustaceans, crabs and lobster; and mollusks, both bivales and gastropods. One of the oldest living creatures on earth, stromatolites, estimated at 2,000 years old, have been found in the waters near the Bahamas, which have also been described as "Shark Eden," because of its rich tropical waters, where 40 shark species can be found. Native Americans used shark teeth as tools and laced their vertebrae into necklaces. At least 25 species of whales regularly visit Caribbean waters; the Bay of Samaná in eastern Hispaniola is a favorite wintering ground of the humpback whale. A new species of medium-sized baleen whale, known as Rice's whale, has been recently discovered in the Gulf of Mexico, with sightings in Caribbean waters; it has been immediately declared endangered. The presence of the Caribbean monk seal, known as "lobos de mar" (sea wolves) by the Spaniards, is recognized in the many rookeries—"cayo lobos" or "seal cay"—dotted throughout the Caribbean. The West Indian manatee, or giant sea-cow, specimens of which could weigh over 600 kilograms, is the most widely distributed of the three existing species of that mammal, more so than its Amazonian and West African counterparts. Amerindians consumed its fatty flesh, made leather from its thick skin, and created tools and musical instruments from its bones. Apparently, a cacique in Hispaniola adopted a young manatee as a pet and trained it to like human companionship. That manatees appear in Antillean ceramic iconography but not at all in that of South America, points to how fully maritime the islanders had become. Six of the seven species of sea turtles in existence today inhabit the Caribbean; they were a prime target for Amerindian and later European hunters. When observers claim that there are "no large game" in the Caribbean, they are thinking in terrestrial rather than in marine terms.[81]

Europeans were astonished at the marine life they encountered in the tropics. Christopher Columbus described fish "of the brightest colors in the world— blue, yellow, red, multi-colored, colored to a thousand ways" and "so unlike ours that it is amazing." Gonzalo Fernández de Oviedo was astounded at the "many other fishes which have no names in our language." Mark Catesby thought "the shallow seas encompassing" the Bahamas "remarkable for their abundance and variety of its watery inhabitants, exceeding in number of species, and excelling in the elegance of their colors and marks, but inferior in wholesomeness and goodness of taste to the fish in more northern latitudes." Catesby was clearly ambivalent in his admiration for tropical abundance, but emphatic that the "nearer the torrid zone" the "more numerous" the marine species, an assessment that is correct. Reverend John Lindsay thought the parrot- or soapfish, "the most lovely little fish I have ever seen," declaring, "Nature seems here to wanton in brilliance of fancy." The two archaeologists who have surveyed most comprehensively the

Figure 1.4 The West Indian Manatee. By James Stewart, ca. 1837. There is an anthropomorphizing quality to this depiction. Watercolor, graphite, pen and gray ink on thick, smooth, cream, wove paper, Yale Center for British Art, Paul Mellon Collection, B1981.25.2313.

marine remains throughout the neotropics declare that "the diversity of faunal assemblages in the Bahamas is startling," with reef fishes accounting for the vast majority.[82]

Northern and Southern Antillean marine environments had much in common. The claim of abundance may seem incongruous, since both areas, particularly the small, low-lying, arid islands of the Bahamas in the north and their offshore Venezuelan counterparts in the south appear uninviting, compared to larger, more ecologically diverse landmasses. But their maritime orientation is where their wealth of resources reside. An incredible array of marine invertebrates—most importantly queen conch—as well as sea turtles, close-to-shore reef fishes such as parrotfish, grunts, and jacks, and more offshore, deepwater fish such as snappers and groupers, and true blue-water pelagic fish such as tuna, made these two polar extremes of the Caribbean particularly attractive for fishing and mollusk collecting. In addition, salt was readily available in both these parts of the Caribbean, enabling the preservation of marine food.[83]

The shores, mangrove swamps, and waterways of the Caribbean teemed with aquatic birds—tens of millions, it has been estimated, but home to fewer than 2 million today. Large flocks populated the region, including the ibis in Trinidad and the long-legged flamingo on Bonaire. More generally, herons, egrets, gulls, boobies, ducks, terns, noddies, and ospreys—to mention just a few species— were commonplace. For Amerindians, as ceramic art expert Lawrence Waldron notes, maritime birds seemed to unite "the living earth, the watery underworld, and celestial spirit realms." They were "among the shaman's paramount avian associates" and "featured on the most sacred of surviving Antillian artifacts." Although representations of wading birds and ducks appeared widely on native pottery, the pelican commanded most attention. Possessed of an enormous bill, the brown pelican of the Caribbean is one of the largest birds in the world, standing over 3 feet tall, with a wingspan that can reach 6 feet. Their kamikaze dives into the sea are spectacular; their single-file flight formation may have seemed akin to Amerindian men paddling in unison in their canoes. A distinctive Caribbean competitor to the pelican, with an even wider wingspan and greater acrobatic skill, was the magnificent frigate bird, known as a remote presence and majestic fliers. But in terms of aquatic birds, the pelican, followed by herons, ibises, flamingos, and ducks, were the species that captivated the imagination of island artists.[84]

Native Americans consumed maritime birds as well as revered them. The native inhabitants of the islands of the Venezuelan Caribbean ca. 1000 to 1500 CE, for example, consistently targeted just a few families of birds for food or feathers or both, and used their bones for fashioning tools and adornments. Ground-nesting brown boobies and mangrove-dwelling red-footed boobies were the birds of choice, followed at some distance by brown pelicans. The Los Roques archipelago reports 95 species of birds; just 7 percent appear in the archaeozoological samples. Over time in the Bahamas, the indigenous inhabitants shifted from the "low hanging fruit" of ground-nesting boobies and flightless Key West quail doves to open grassland thick-knees. At one site in Puerto Rico, natives ate 14 species of birds, since none had the plumage that would signal ceremonial use. At a site on tiny Saba in the Archaic era, natives settled to exploit a high-ranked animal—the bird known as Audubon's shearwater—that became available in a single season of the year. In all these and other sites, natives did not depend on birds for their food supply; they supplemented a diet heavily based on marine resources.[85]

Other than the maritime environment, the next richest faunal locales in the Caribbean were the forest canopies. There, the many birds, bats, and insects contrasted with the much fewer species on the ground floor where rodents dominated. Lush rainforest canopies must have been noisy places, a cacophony of birdsong and beating wings. Pigeons, doves, songbirds, hummingbirds, and parrots were especially numerous. The island chain forms part of the major flyway route of migratory species between North and South America, adding to the seasonal avian diversity. In general, the largest islands, with a greater range of habitats, possess the most bird species. Thus, 250 land birds and 190 aquatic birds are present on Cuba. More hummingbird species are typically found on islands with the most diverse habitats, but there are anomalies. The greatest number of hummingbird species on any Caribbean oceanic island is the five found on the fourth largest island, Puerto Rico, followed by the four species found on two smaller islands, Dominica and Martinique. Cuba, the largest island, has only two species. Noted for its diminutive size, speed, and ravenousness, the humming-bird is unique in its management of energy, alternating between wing speeds of up to 90 beats per second and periods of torpor, short bouts of quasi-hiber-nation when their heart rate and breathing slow to a standstill in response to falling temperatures or limited food supplies. This alternate freneticism and slug-gishness became, for some eighteenth-century observers, a metaphor for creole degeneracy, a descent into lethargy, claims that creole Americans denied—and an indication of the "intertwined histories of hummingbirds and humans," as historian of science Iris Montero Sobrevilla notes. The forest bird that appeared most prominently in Antillean iconography was the owl. Nine species—in-cluding a Puerto Rican screech owl, Cuban pygmy owl, Hispaniolan ashy-faced owl, and Jamaican owl exist on the islands, along with other large-eyed, owl-like, nocturnal avian species, such as nightjars, nighthawks, and oilbirds. Absent from South American visual art, nocturnal birds, according to Waldron, were seen by Amerindians as "messengers from the underworld presaging deaths and births."[86]

Almost half of the world's 360 species of parrots, that iconic Caribbean bird, renowned for their ability to mimic human speech, inhabit the lowland forests of the neotropics. In October 1492 Columbus saw large flocks darken the sky. Europeans traded for native-tamed parrots, one of the earliest items in the Columbian Exchange, no doubt building on an inter-island indigenous commerce in these birds. Mark Catesby painted *The Parrot of Paradise of Cuba* from a specimen "shot by an *Indian*, on the Island [of] Cuba." That natives in-corporated parrots into their households and adopted them as fictive kin may have encouraged Europeans to see them as family pets. Parrots are strong fliers, capable of crossing large expanses of water to reach distant islands. As a result, island archipelagos often have one or two representatives from a group of closely related species with nonoverlapping ranges. The St. Vincent Amazon, with its green plumage, dominates one side of the island, and a yellow-brown variety dominates the other side. Parrots' feeding habits have a marked effect on the landscape. By consuming tree seeds before they have a chance to be dispersed by the wind, they help to prevent any single tree species from dominating a forest. These brightly colored birds have long attracted humans, who preyed on them for food and feathers, as well as for companionship. Extinctions occurred early. On Grand Turk in the Bahamas, parrot remains are not found in deposits after 1200 BC. Since 1500 CE, about half of the 20 or so known extinctions of parrots worldwide—birds such as the Cuban macaw, Guadeloupe parakeet, and Martinique Amazon—have occurred in the Caribbean. No macaws are native to the Caribbean region today, but perhaps as many as 13 species have been observed there in recent centuries. At least three species of macaws were present in eighteenth-century Jamaica, but a 1765 painting by Reverend John Lindsay, executed on the island, is of a scarlet macaw, previously not thought to have been present on the island. The largest and most colorful of the West Indian parrots, macaws had great prestige and value in the Antilles and would doubtless have been traded far and wide.[87]

Bats are the most numerous mammals in the Caribbean. Fifty-seven species are extant on the islands, of which a half are unique. In the Dominican Republic, for example, 90 percent of native terrestrial mammal species are bats. Caribbean bat species have suffered significant extinctions—about 25 percent—since the onset of the Holocene ca. 11,700 BP, but that reduction pales into insignificance when compared to the 80 percent decline in land mammals, most notably sloths, shrews, rodents, and primates. The bats' ability to fit particular ecological niches, avoid predation, and travel long distances quickly accounts at least in part for their resilience. Some species, such as the Antillean fruit bat, can venture so widely in their nightly feeding that they can eat on one island and roost on another. Most Caribbean bats eat insects and are active at dusk; others are entirely nocturnal and focus on fruit, pollen, and nectar; a few target fish; and the rarest, a Trinidad species, sucks blood. A number are omnivorous. For ancient Antilleans, bats and night birds were closely related. In Taíno art, skull-like images portending death meld with images of bats and owls, animals of nocturnal habits and ominous associations.[88]

In contrast to their usual extravagance, the islands lacked large, even midsized, land mammals. The prime reason is that the vast majority of Caribbean fauna reached the islands from South America and some species encountered difficulties in crossing large bodies of water. The most notable exception is Trinidad, separated from the mainland by the narrow Straits of Paria, and thereby easily colonized. Of land mammals, the sloth, two species of anteater, ocelot, pine marten, raccoon, two species of howler monkey, and many species of bat inhabit this continental island. On islands more distant from the mainland, land mammals are restricted to a few insectivores, rodents, and a smaller range of bats. Still, it is curious that there are no carnivorous mammals known from the Greater Antilles. Perhaps the predatory birds of the Caribbean, including owls, eagles, and vultures, filled this gap.[89]

Lacking large mammals, the Caribbean environment hosted a range of rodents—from spiny rats or rice rats to agoutis and pacas—as well as other small mammals. The Antilles have been home to over 60 species of rodents, only 13 of which have survived to modern times. South American groups migrating to the islands, particularly from the Ceramic Age onward (500 BCE), brought small animals with them. Accompanying the migrants were agouti, opossum,

Figure 1.5 Cartagena. By Jan van Kessel. Ca. 1666. An intriguing juxtaposition of bats, in various stages of life, and a fortified Cartagena, dominated by a church and port. It conveys the dystopian and exotic perceptions of the Caribbean, as well as its urban character. Oil painting. Alte Pinakothek, Munich, and Sotheby's Lot 124f.

dog, guinea pig, peccary, and armadillo. Dog and guinea pig were the only introduced domestic mammals, but possibly some wild species, such as agouti and hutia, were managed in captivity. DNA analysis of guinea pigs indicates that Ceramic Age Indians first introduced them into Puerto Rico from modern-day Colombia, and from that Greater Antillean island, they radiated westward, eastward, and southward. One scholar has raised the question of whether there was "a prehistoric pet trade in the Greater Antilles" of hutias, guinea pigs, parrots, and perhaps monkeys, "as well as the inevitable dog." Apparently, Lucayans introduced hutia as a food source, and the hutia that appear in the Turks and Caicos were larger than modern specimens.[90]

Among introduced mammals, dogs stand apart. In archaeological deposits, they are found as fragmented, burned bone, indicating that Amerindians ate them, but they also appear in burials, both alone and associated with human remains. At one site in Guadeloupe, 16 dogs were found buried among 30 humans: 4 were interred at an individual's feet; 1 was buried with 4 shell beads around its neck; another with a Queen Conch shell on the pelvis; and almost all of the dogs were buried with their legs pulled together, as if bound. Many dogs were not from the island in which they were buried; and their diet was not dissimilar from humans, suggesting they fed on scraps and leftovers. In contrast to those found in burials, specimens found in middens are larger in stature, suggesting the possibility of distinct dog types that served dedicated purposes—some as hunting companions, others as food. Columbus during his first voyage reported two types of dogs in the Bahamas: one akin to a larger mastiff, the other to a smaller terrier. He also encountered "dogs that never barked" on the north coast of Cuba. The Spaniards thought that this small, yellow, nonbarking canine was useless as a sentry, but had no hesitation in eating it, following Amerindian practice. Images of prehistoric dogs appear in rock paintings, petroglyphs, woodcarvings, and pottery across the circum-Caribbean region. Island peoples traded among themselves for dog teeth that they fashioned into objects of personal adornment. Archaeologists have noted the frequent absence of the fourth mandibular premolar in Caribbean dogs, which may represent the intentional removal of teeth to facilitate tethering by the mouth. The dog obviously played a major role in the prehistoric Caribbean as hunter, companion, status symbol, guardian, trade object, food item, and sacrificial offering, sometimes accompanying human burials. According to Fray Ramón Pané, the Taíno revered a canine zemi, Opiyelguobirán, the guardian spirit of the dead, their guide to the underworld.[91]

The Caribbean's most numerous and diverse small to midsized animals were reptiles and amphibians. Images of turtles and frogs abound in the region's visual art. There were lacunae, however, both in art and nature. Few large snakes have inhabited the Caribbean, no doubt due to the lack of medium-sized and large mammals on which they might have preyed. Once again, Trinidad is the exception, because of its proximity to the mainland and its diverse mammalian prey, so it is able to support boas, anacondas, and coral snakes. An archaeological study of Guadeloupean snakes indicates little or no consumption of them by Amerindians. In the early seventeenth century, Caribs on neighboring Martinique and Dominica claimed that they did not catch or eat eels because they were "sisters of snakes." The kin recognition is noteworthy, as is the apparent dietary taboo. Visitors to the French Caribbean in the nineteenth century obsessed about the dangers of the "dreaded" or "terrible" Martinican pit viper, whose bites were "nearly always fatal." Caimans and crocodiles occur fairly widely in the Caribbean. Four crocodile species are extant: Southern Cuba and the nearby Isla de Juventud are presently home to a crocodile that once ranged widely in the Greater Antilles; the American crocodile is the most widespread, present on three of the four Greater Antillean islands; and two other species inhabit the greater Caribbean region. Carried by storms and currents, aided by expert swimming, able to tolerate saltwater, and clinging to flotsam, the Trinidadian and Venezuelan spectacled caiman and the Orinoco crocodile sometimes washed up in Grenada, the Grenadines, and even Barbados.[92]

Although most families of frogs are absent in the Caribbean, the region hosts more than 170 species of one particular frog genus (*Eleutherodactylus*), which breeds out of water and lays eggs on land. Frogs in this genus sing in response to rain; though tiny in size, they are large of voice. Camping at the foot of Mount Diablo in Jamaica in the late seventeenth century, physician and naturalist Hans Sloane had his sleep "very much interrupted by the Croaking of a sort of Tree Frogs." The most recognizable animal of Puerto Rico is the coqui, a small endemic frog. Like bats, frogs and toads mostly feed on insects and therefore are most active at dusk and by night. A favorite haunt is the bromeliads that grow on mossy trunks and branches, the funneled interior of which, when filled with rainwater, makes a perfect nest. Singing frogs do not exhaust the order Anura. A recently discovered species of brightly colored "poison arrow" frogs from Martinique point to expanding diversity, as does one edible "mountain chicken" (or giant ditch frog, or *chapeaux*) endemic to the Antilles, and vulnerable to predation because of its size and sedentary nature. True tree frogs and a commonly encountered marine toad were probably human introductions from South America. Rivaled only by turtles and bats, frogs are the animals most commonly represented in Antillean visual art. The famous flexed leg motif of the frog was ubiquitous.[93]

The Antilles are home to many varieties of lizards of widely ranging sizes and colors, including geckos, iguanas, skinks, and anoles. Perhaps no land animal is more emblematic of the diversity of Caribbean fauna than one of the region's evolutionary marvels, the *anole*, known for its dewlap (an extensible structure located on the throat), expanded toepads, and a remarkable ability to change color, chameleon-like. Only one such species inhabits the southeastern United States, but Cuba boasts 63. The adjoining Central American and South American mainland has more anole species (210) than the islands (151), but the presence of over 40 percent of all anole species on the small land area of the Caribbean islands is remarkable. Notable for their incredible variety in color, size, shape, habitat use, and behavior, some have adapted to water, even consuming crayfish, others to eating snails and fruit, while most rely on insects; some occupy treetops, others the ground, and yet others caves; some move extremely quickly, others in more labored fashion. No other reptile—indeed few other animals, perhaps only a type of frog and the hummingbird—comes close to this number of species and such ecomorphological diversity. No anole has gone extinct except possibly one (*Anolis Roosevelti*), and *Anolis* fossils in amber from the island of Hispaniola demonstrate the antiquity of the island radiation.[94]

The anole attracts attention because of its variety and adaptability, but its history raises broader issues. Island size clearly matters for species size and variation. Given their restricted space, islands generally support fewer species than continents—true of anoles, but not by much. Furthermore, the adage—the larger the island, the greater the number of species—usually, though not al-ways, holds true. Cuba and Hispaniola contain the most species of this lizard (104); but some rather large islands (such as Dominica and Guadeloupe) in the Lesser Antilles contain only one species, despite having much habitat diversity, whereas a small island such as Isla Juventud (just north of Cuba) boasts 11 species. The difference between an oceanic island (Dominica and Guadeloupe) and a land-bridge island (Juventad) helps explain this discrepancy. The reduced competition and predation that occur on islands can produce high local densities of fauna, a remarkable diversity of forms, and broad distribution across environments. Thus, islands, which can be species-poor overall, can also be rich in unique forms, that is, those endemic to an island or archipelago. Thus a specific family of geckos has radiated into more than 85 species in the Caribbean. There are some remarkable efflorescences, in other words, as niche opportunities and lack of predation facilitate particular adaptive radiation As a result, small islands can be extraordinarily abundant environments.[95]

The last reptile to be considered is perhaps the islands' most iconic animal—the sea turtle. Six marine turtle species frequent the Caribbean. The green turtle, averaging 440 pounds, was the most common, highly valued for its meat and eggs. A decline in the size and number of green turtles has been documented at prehistoric archaeological sites in the Bahamas. The Cayman Islands likely hosted the "largest green turtle rookery that ever existed." The leatherback is the largest living turtle, averaging 1,212 pounds, and with a carapace about 6 feet long; it is a deep sea species, ranging widely, conserving heat because of its massive size. The loggerhead is also large, averaging 1,000 pounds; it often enters estuaries and the lower reaches of freshwater streams. The hawksbill, averaging 130 pounds, is famous for its shell. Rounding out the array were the Atlantic ridley and the olive ridley, both about 120 pounds. The shape of the turtle's carapace is reflected in many vessels made by Amerindian potters; and the oval outlines of Amerindian houses, it has been suggested, also evoke turtles. Turtle shells are present in human burials and also served as a form of griddle for cooking. In their traditional narratives, as Waldron notes, "pre-Columbian Antilleans saw themselves as 'Children of the Turtle.'"[96]

Insects are by far the most numerous Caribbean creatures. They have fascinated humans for mundane as well as divine reasons. They could be troublesome, as in the bedbug disturbing sleep or locusts destroying crops; but they were also the keys unlocking human society, whether bees serving as models of human behavior or brightly colored butterflies reflecting the divinely inspired beauty of nature. The representation of insects in pre-Columbian Caribbean art is almost nonexistent, so what appear to be a series of butterflies or moths carved by stone sculptors on St. Vincent suggests that these delicate and colorful creatures captured the imagination of at least one group of Windward Island

Figure 1.6 Turtle. By Reverend John Lindsay. Ca. 1770. At sea, the green turtle, the most common of the six species indigenous to the Caribbean, was an adept air-breathing, migratory, marine herbivore; on land, slow and clumsy, it was easily immobilized by being turned on its back. Watercolor on paper. Bristol Museums, Galleries & Archives / Bridgeman Images.

artists. For Hans Sloane, the wisdom of God manifested itself nowhere more powerfully than in "the smallest animals, called insects" because it was possible to have a complete catalogue of them. Still, insects were challenging to collect, preserve, and represent. No better illustration of the problem is the image of mosquitoes in the late sixteenth-century *Histoire Naturelle des Indes*: hundreds of dots, representing a swarm of mosquitoes, "so small that one cannot see them." In calm conditions, "they come in droves attacking people, stinging them in such a manner that one would take them for lepers." Netting helped, as did smoky fires. Interestingly, the only known Taíno terms for an insect are *jejen* or *maye*, meaning mosquito.[97]

Many other Caribbean insects inspired wonder. One of the questions Governor Thomas Lynch took with him to Jamaica in 1670–71 was: did fireflies stay bright after they died? Some insects, such as the cochineal beetle, used to make a red dye, were much in demand in the Caribbean, since it could make fortunes. On the other hand, the cotton-tree worm, or *Cossus* (a delicacy sought by slaves), could devour imperial fortunes by burrowing through the hulls of European ships. Other kinds of worms attacked humans. One of Sloane's African female slaves, "a queen in her own country," removed what she said was "a chego" from his foot. Sloane mentioned capturing a great house spider in Jamaica. One wonders if it is the same species on display in Pierre Eugene Du Simitière's Philadelphia museum, which opened in 1782. He described it as "the largest of all the Spiders known," the size of a crab and like a crab in "burrowing and living under ground. It comes out at night especially when the moon shines . . . it comes into the houses to seize its prey which are cockroaches and other insects. It is found in the mountains as in the plains and in hoeing ground you are almost sure to meet with some, its bite is said to be dangerous." He says it is not to be found in Sloane's natural history of the island. Insects are important nutrients for many people in the neotropics. Yet, so far, research on insects and their contribution to human nutrition, as revealed in archaeological deposits, has not taken place in the Caribbean.[98]

The harvesting of beeswax in the early colonial Yucatán Peninsula reveals how one human-insect relationship in the Americas changed dramatically without direct intervention by Europeans. The Spanish demand for beeswax to make candles for religious and domestic purposes certainly played a critical role in its production, but this was an extractive industry carried out entirely by indigenous people interacting with New World bee species—stingless varieties—not European imports. As early as 1514 when a large piece of beeswax washed up on the shores of Cuba, Bartolomé de Las Casas thought it must have come from the nearby Yucatán Peninsula where honey and beeswax were "very abundant." From the mid-sixteenth to the early eighteenth century, beeswax became a key export product for the Spanish colonial province of Yucatán. Candles made from *cera de Campeche* (as the local beeswax was known) illuminated church interiors, religious ceremonies, and private homes. The indigenous people of the Yucatán Peninsula responded to the rising demand for beeswax by expanding their foraging to lowland forests that teemed with wild honeybees. As historical geographer Geoffrey Wallace notes, "Before it found its way into Spanish hands, beeswax passed through a complex commodity chain of collection, transportation, and trade that lay . . . for the most part beyond Spanish control."[99]

In the sixteenth century, Cuba was the first place in the Caribbean where Spanish settlers succeeded in relocating the European honeybee. Beekeeping flourished as a source of wax during the eighteenth and nineteenth centuries. The Spanish Crown protected Cuban beekeepers; and the island had a privileged role in the trading of beeswax for candles over other parts of the Caribbean. By the nineteenth century, Cuban beeswax had the reputation of being one of the best in the Americas. It was made with the European honeybee, *Apis mellifera*, and its wax was easier to bleach, while the beeswax from native bees was darker. Catholic celebrations required white beeswax candles.[100]

Island biota, Robert MacArthur and Edward Wilson argued in their landmark 1967 book, *The Theory of Island Biogeography*, assume a dynamic steady state in which species continually disappear from islands only to be replaced at an equal rate by new colonists. A rough balance, it is claimed, existed between the addition of new species by colonization and the loss of established species by extinction. Essential processes of dispersal, invasion, competition, adaptation, and extinction need to be disentangled. Continual change is the norm. The attainment of equilibrium can depend on the organism. After a hurricane, spiders, which disperse mainly by ballooning, can recover equilibrium quickly, whereas lizards, which disperse by rafting or floating, may take much longer. Unsurprisingly, birds exhibit higher rates of colonization than, say, reptiles. Equilibrium, then, operates at different speeds. Another implication of the dynamic steady state theory is the relationship between species number and area. Within-island multiplication of species is greater for larger islands; conversely, the rate of extinction is higher on smaller islands. Birds invading the Lesser Antilles from the north penetrated the island chain farther than species coming from the south. Perhaps Greater Antillean birds were already successful colonists and had negotiated a large water gap, giving them an advantage.[101]

Islands are havens and breeding grounds for anomalies. They are, in science writer David Quammen's words, "natural laboratories of extravagant evolutionary experimentation." The potential for speedy divergent evolution in small populations explains why so many prodigious or diminutive species exist on islands. The limited resource base on islands sometimes led to reductions in body mass and metabolism rates. Thus some capromyid rodents found on small, flat islands in the Bahamas are much smaller than their relatives on larger, higher islands in the Greater Antilles. Perhaps hummingbirds do so well in the Caribbean for the same reason; Cuba boasts the smallest hummingbird in the world. Similarly, the smallest member of an order of passerine birds, the "San Pedrito," or Puerto Rican Tody (*Todus mexicanus*), is endemic to that island. Furthermore, the smallest snake (a Lesser Antillean threadsnake), the smallest constrictor (from Cuba) and many of the smallest lizards are insular endemics in the Caribbean. Conversely, resource abundance may occur, which, along with a lack of natural predators, could allow a species to grow in size. Jamaica, for example, has an unusually big anguid lizard; the extinct caproymid rodent on St. Martin was the size of a black bear, perhaps because it was the only browsing herbivore on the island.[102]

Islands may be havens, but they are also typically vulnerable, and extinctions happen there more than on continents. The greatest loss in the Caribbean has been among the non-flying mammals: only 1 in 10 of the land mammals once present on the islands still survives. All of at least 17 species of megalonychid sloths are extinct; only 2 of 12 insectivores have survived; almost 80 percent of the 61 species of rodents have disappeared; and about a half of the 57 species of Caribbean bats are extinct or have been locally extirpated. A notable extinction concerns one of the most iconic groups of land birds on tropical islands, namely parrots. The West Indies was home to about 50 to 60 endemic species, represented by macaws, parakeets, and parrots. Now only 12 remain: all 15 known species of macaws, all Lesser Antillean parakeets, and parrots between Puerto

Rico and Dominica no longer exist. Twelve of the 13 flightless species of birds
in the Caribbean were extinct when the Europeans arrived, including a Jamaican
ibis and the Cuban giant owl, the largest known owl species. Sometimes the
extinctions can be dated fairly precisely: when Sir Francis Drake passed through
the Caribbean in the late sixteenth century, the saltwater crocodiles that gave the
Cayman Islands their name were widespread; just over a half century later, when
an English visitor arrived, they were gone.[103]

There are success stories. For example, 43 island populations of doves,
hummingbirds, and songbirds have been reported from fossil deposits on a
number of small islands in the northern Lesser Antilles, but only 6 of these species are missing today. Losses are few compared to the more than 450 species of
birds present in the modern Lesser Antilles. The native avifauna of the Lesser
Antilles is "largely intact"; extinction has been "a minor factor for small land-bird
populations" in the archipelago. Extinction rates are inversely related to island
size, but even in that regard, anomalies occur. Thus Montserrat has a low extinction rate in its bird population, despite its small size; perhaps its proximity
to a much larger island, Guadeloupe, has resulted in frequent recolonizations.
Conversely, the seventh largest Lesser Antillean island, Grenada, has a high
apparent extinction rate; perhaps its relative proximity to the South American
mainland encouraged immigrations of birds, which then caused or encouraged
local extinctions. In general, tropical island birds tend to have lower turnover
rates than those in temperate regions. Fossil records demonstrate that butterflies
have had the lowest rates of extinction in the Caribbean. Anole lizards introduced
to even the smallest islands in the Bahamas have surprisingly survived, even
thrived at least for a while; but from time to time a hurricane will wipe them
out. Spiders, on the other hand, rebound extremely quickly; within a year after
a hurricane, the average number of species on some small Bahamian islands was
the same as before. The process of extinction is extremely varied and depends
on many factors.[104]

If the basic storyline of Caribbean fauna and flora is one of efflorescence and
degradation, a couple of spatial variations are worth highlighting. One is the role
of small islands. A small island with many habitats can have greater faunal diversity than a larger island with less varied ecology. An island's proximity to a
mainland is also a factor. Thus, among small islands, Grenada, with a diverse
ecology but far from the mainland, has almost twice as many bat species as
sparsely forested Curaçao, just off South America. Seemingly unprepossessing,
tiny islands have much to tell us about faunal and floral development. Mona,
located about equidistant from Hispaniola to the west and Puerto Rico to the
east, shares a number of butterfly subspecies with Puerto Rico and none with
the much larger Hispaniola. The constant winds from Puerto Rico to Hispaniola
help explain this pattern. One of the most cavernous places on earth, Mona is

home to large numbers of bats. These flying animals have deposited guano over millennia throughout all areas of the cave systems, giving rise to extensive reserves of the mineral phosphorite, which was mined for industrial and agricultural purposes in the nineteenth century. Long before then—as early as 2800 BCE—Amerindians began using the caves. They took full advantage of the island's flora, forming paints from phosphorites, charcoal, and ochers from the cave floors, sometimes mixing them with plant gums as a binding agent, to draw human-animal-plant figures on the cave walls. Mona was a hub of interaction. From roughly 1300–1500 CE, its subterranean spaces were a major attraction; the islanders built two stone-lined plazas in the interior of the island as ceremonial centers. On his second voyage in 1494, Columbus briefly stopped at Mona to recover his health, perhaps indicating that the island appeared salubrious; and in the early sixteenth century its small population supplied cassava for the gold-mining enterprises of its neighboring islands. Today, Mona supports the largest hawksbill sea turtle nesting ground in the Caribbean.[105]

A second spatial variation is the existence of buffer zones or frontiers. The Mona Passage has been seen as an important marine boundary between two distinct human colonizations of the archipelago, which, if true, undoubtedly had faunal and floral implications. The almost complete absence of agouti remains north of the Anegada Passage suggests there were obstacles to supporting those animals in captivity. A similar barrier impeded the transportation of Antillean hutias, which reached remote parts of the Virgin Islands but were not taken north to the Bahamas or south into the Lesser Antilles. Proximity to the source of diverse animal species probably influenced the success of introductions. For example, South American mammals such as the armadillo and opossum are found on Grenada and St. Lucia, but not farther up the island chain. Visual representations of terrestrial mammals are confined to the Windward Islands, which are the only places where mammal motifs vie with those of birds and reptiles. Mammals native to the mainland such as the opossum, armadillo, and anteater appear in the Caribbean's visual art with declining frequency, moving northward up the Lesser Antillean chain.[106]

Impact of the Early Settlers

The Caribbean basin was the last major region in the Americas to be settled. The earliest record of human habitation on the continental portion of the Caribbean basin dates to 16,000–14,000 BP in what is now Colombia and Venezuela, and 13,000–10,000 BP elsewhere. The colonization of this last major unoccupied region in the hemisphere began, most scholars say, about 7,000 to 8,000 years ago, but the process took about twice as long.[107]

About 10,000 BP bands of hunters and foragers frequented what became Trinidad prior to the island's separation from the mainland following sea-level increases. The earliest known settlement site is located along the west coast and dates to ca. 7700 BP, when the island was still attached to the mainland. The early occupation of Trinidad—relative to the rest of the insular region—can be attributed to its size, its proximity to the mainland, and its lack of hurricane destruction, since it lies on the margins of the tropical hurricane belt. These three factors help explain Trinidad's strikingly high biodiversity, which served as another inducement to colonization.[108]

About 7000 to 6000 BP, other migrants left Central America and settled in Cuba and Hispaniola. Cuba is of course the largest island in the region—covering almost a half of the landmass of the Caribbean archipelago—and its location made it accessible from the mainland by several possible routes. The most likely pathway was not the Yucatan Channel to western Cuba due to facing strong ocean currents, but via the longer Isthmo-Colombian area of Central America to southern Cuba. Belize was probably one jumping-off point.[109]

How should one characterize these earliest settlers, and their chronological evolution? Paleo-Indian is one term (17,000–7,000 BP) to describe the first Antilleans, followed by Meso-Indian (7,000–3,000 BP), and then Neo-Indian (3,000–500 BP). Another overlapping classification scheme focuses on consecutive "ages": the Lithic (6000–4000 BP), Archaic (4000–2500 BP), and Ceramic (2500–500 BP). Thus, the Paleo-Indians of the Lithic Age are defined primarily by their flaked-stone blades used in hunting. The Meso-Indians of the Archaic Age were renowned for their ground-stone technology and their reliance on plant gathering, pursuit of small game, and exploitation of marine environments. Lithic and Archaic Age cultures are usually described as aceramic or pre-ceramic, but pottery and evidence of farming have now been found in their sites. Since the assumption was that Arawak speakers from South America introduced pottery to the islands, the terms "Pre-Arawak" and "Pre-Arawak Pottery Horizon" came into use to describe Archaic Age sites that exhibited pottery. Some argue that Lithic and Archaic ages overlap. So one last classification scheme favored by some archaeologists is to label the whole period as the Holocene and subdivide it into three intervals: Early (11,700–8200 BP), Middle (8200–4200 BP) and Late (after 4200 BP). Finally, some scholars substitute Anthropocene for the epoch of Earth's history known as the Holocene, on the grounds that humans should be recognized as a major geological force, although whether the starting point should be the first use of fire around 1.8 million years ago or the beginning of agriculture around 8,000 years ago or some other baseline is a moot question.[110]

Early human migration into the Caribbean was initially two-pronged and occurred at opposite ends of the archipelago. The first flank proceeded from the south into Trinidad; the other moved into Cuba from the west and south about a millennium later. The Trinidadian-bound migration stalled for about 2,000 years before moving northward into Tobago; the Cuban-bound migration, while occurring later, moved rapidly eastward into Hispaniola, Puerto Rico, and elsewhere. This last migration from Central America into the Greater Antilles, seemingly more consequential and purposeful, marks the true onset of Caribbean colonization. How the migration happened is largely a mystery, but one can infer long-distance scouting, followed by the establishment of seasonal camps, founding communities, further exploration, local expansion and settlement, and additional island hopping. Movements would have been south as well as north, east as well as west. Colonists continued to communicate with their homeland and with other settlements. The idea of waves of migrants, if implying regularity, not infrequency, seems apt. Initial colonization led to population infilling, and in some cases to abandonment and relocations. All the while, the people engaged in opportunistic foraging, hunting, some farming, and above all, mollusk-collecting and fishing.[111]

The motives of migrants—some local, others universal; some personal, others general—are hard to decipher. Population pressure, lack of food, limited carrying capacity, drastic environmental change, and conflict situations may have played a role but do not seem pivotal. More likely, the islands were attractive for settlement. Available land could support tropical agriculture. Abundant marine life more than compensated for the lack of terrestrial fauna. Natives already exchanged commodities, plants, and animals; they now expanded their commercial networks. The earliest migrants pursued high-quality flints; they immediately targeted siliceous rock formations in Antigua, Puerto Rico, Hispaniola, and Cuba; and they bypassed islands devoid of chert.[112]

Archaic Age colonization occurred at different tempos in different places. One set of movements in the northern Caribbean was from west to east, from Puerto Rico to the Virgin Islands and northern Lesser Antilles, not from south to north, from Trinidad and Tobago moving up the Antillean chain, as once was believed. A prominent reason for this claim is that, to date, no definite Archaic Age sites have been found in the Windward Islands of the southern Lesser Antilles. If there were northward movements, they largely bypassed the Windward Islands altogether, a pattern that seems implausible. A second example concerns the enigma of Jamaica, which, despite being the third largest Caribbean island and replete with resources, was not settled until about 600–700 CE). The answer to why such a large island did not attract Lithic and Archaic Age occupations seems to lie in its location, well south of Cuba and far west of Hispaniola, its position outside typical voyaging corridors, its invisibility from other shores, its high seas, and its unfavorable wind and current patterns. Moreover, when Jamaica was settled—despite its late date—its earliest immigrants were not Ceramic

Age Arawaks, but rather pre-Arawak forager-farmers from Hispaniola. One last example concerns the islands of Aruba, Bonaire, and Curaçao, which, lying close to the South American continent, presumably would have been settled early, but were not. The first people to live on Curaçao arrived about 4500 BP, Bonaire about a thousand years later, and Aruba not until about 2400 BP. A lack of land animals and low rainfall seemingly inhibited settlement. Furthermore, four significant tsunamis, occurring at approximately 4200, 3500, 1500, and 500 BP, directly affected these southern islands, causing large-scale destruction of mangroves and reefs, depleting food supplies, and encouraging new adaptations to altered environments, such as moving to leeward-side inland bays. As the third major event roughly coincided with the arrival of Ceramic Age people, followed by departures directly to the western Greater Antilles, the tsunami of 1500 BP apparently stimulated much mobility and flux.[113]

This mention of the arrival of Ceramic Age people, despite the prior evidence of pottery making in the region, marks another significant divide in Caribbean history. Beginning about 2500 BP, these new Arawak-speaking peoples represented a second major phase of migration into the islands. They came from the tropical forests of the Orinoco and other river basins of lowland South America. In their earliest incarnation, they have been dubbed the Saladoids, referring to their distinctive pottery. In addition to making pottery, they practiced agriculture and lived in circular plaza villages. Bypassing the Windward Islands, Saladoid horticulturalists first settled the Virgin Islands, the northern Lesser Antilles, and Puerto Rico. There never was a single Saladoid migration, and their dispersal diversified them even further. After reaching Puerto Rico, expansion westward ceased, for unknown reasons. Perhaps the putative Archaic Age groups resisted the Saladoid advance. Whatever the cause, the result supposedly was a 1,000-year pause, during which the varied Saladoid cultures flourished on Puerto Rico and islands to the east and south, but not west. Furthermore, purported "Archaic Age" populations were still present in the insular Caribbean at a much later date—1,000 years later—than the movements of Early Ceramic/Saladoid populations out of northeastern South America.[114]

The Late Ceramic Age (500–1500 CE) saw the emergence of a variety of distinct and complex societies in the Caribbean. Populations grew, inward migration continued, settlements spread, agriculture intensified, fishing became even more central to subsistence, social stratification deepened, chiefdoms arose, and expansion into new areas such as the Bahamas and Jamaica occurred. Hispaniola and Puerto Rico were the most developed of these elaborate societies, the heartland of the Taíno, a label derived from the natives' language meaning "noble" or "good," but Jamaica, much of Cuba, the Bahamas, the Virgin Islands, and the northern Lesser Antilles (as far south as Montserrat) were also part of the Taíno world. The Taíno lived in villages, usually arranged in circular or oval fashion;

their houses were also predominantly circular; they cultivated large fields or *conucos* as well as house gardens, but their main animal protein came from the sea; they engaged in extensive inter-island trade; they formed chiefdoms as their preferred polities; they built ceremonial plazas and ball courts; they practiced forms of matrilineal descent; and they established links to the spirit world through rituals such as *areyto* (communal song), the use of *cojoba* (an hallucinogenic drug), intermediaries such as shamans (*behiques*), and objects such as cemis or zemis (often three-pointed stones or shells). Above all, one historian claims, the Taíno did not become a "people of the sea, venturing out to trade or seek resources" like their Pacific Ocean contemporaries; rather, they were an "island people, most at home on land." But why were they not both?[115]

Furthermore, as with the culture of the Saladoids, the Taíno version was no monolith. Even the "Classic Taíno" of Hispaniola and Puerto Rico, the central core, were markedly different. The two islands developed from distinct types of ancestral societies and through divergent processes. Just to take one example, the stone-lined plazas that began appearing around 900 CE were unique to Puerto Rico. The variations were even greater at the margins—western Cuba, Jamaica, the Bahamas, and the northern Lesser Antilles. Cuba in particular stands apart. Scientific studies of the Cuban population show that it likely moved from the west, probably Central America, and not from South America, like the other islands' Taíno population.[116]

In a provocative new finding, about 700/800 CE a separate migration of Caribs took place in the circum-Caribbean. They left what is now Colombia, ventured across the Caribbean Sea, and arrived in the Greater Antilles. This was not the same Carib migration into the Lesser Antilles from eastern South America, but an earlier movement that left from much farther west. A comparison of the facial characteristics of skulls across the circum-Caribbean reveals three distinct clusters: Cuba/Yucatan (probably Archaic); Puerto Rico/Venezuela (Arawaks); and Hispaniola/Jamaica/Bahamas (associated with a pottery style known as Meillacoid). This last cluster suggests a third migration. Native Lucayans more closely resembled groups from Hispaniola and Jamaica than Cuban inhabitants. Meillacoid pottery is also identical to that associated with the Carib expansion across South America that began around 500 CE. This finding may help to explain why Columbus said that he encountered Caribs in the Bahamas and north coasts of Cuba and Hispaniola. It contradicts the long-accepted verity that Caribs never advanced farther than Guadeloupe in the Lesser Antilles. And it makes the name Caribbean even more accurate.[117]

Genome data provides further insights into the peopling of the Caribbean. One study finds evidence for two dispersals into the western Caribbean during the Archaic Age. In short, successive populations, originating on the American mainland, settled and resettled the Caribbean. Another study found that an

Archaic ancestry profile, derived from a single source, spread throughout the Greater Antilles, and persisted with generally little mixture well into the Ceramic Age. Then, at least 1,800 years ago, a ceramic-using population most likely originating in northeastern South America and related to present-day Arawak-speaking groups moved throughout the Caribbean. Hispaniola's history in particular is enriched by this new evidence: some related male individuals were buried 50 miles apart, an indication of considerable mobility; long-term population continuity along the southeastern coast differentiated this region from the rest of the island; and the island's population at pre-contact is projected to have been no more than 10,000–20,000 people, far less than previous estimates.[118]

The Taíno's influence never extended in a major way to the Windward Islands in the southern part of the Lesser Antilles and, from about 1300 CE onward, became tenuous in the Leeward Islands in the northern section. In the fourteenth and fifteenth centuries, several of the islands in the northern Lesser Antilles— from Saba to Nevis—were abandoned. It is not clear why. Perhaps climatic change was partly to blame. Another theory is the encroachments of an aggressive northward intrusion, a wave of warlike, marauding, supposedly cannibalistic Caribs, originating in mainland South America. Rather than experiencing a migration wave, the Windward Island societies were more likely engaged in an intensified interaction with the mainland. The Island Caribs, who called themselves Kallinago or Kallipuna, intermarried with the local Igneri (the indigenous inhabitants of the southern Lesser Antilles). They were more mobile than the Taíno, lived in small settlements, preferred fertile coastal plains and valleys, situated their villages by rivers, and were less hierarchical. Island Caribs gravitated to the Windward coast of islands, facing the Atlantic, where rough seas and steep cliffs aided defense. They moved south as well as north, but were primarily local, not necessarily a major migrant wave.[119]

How did these peoples of the precolonial Caribbean interact with their environment? At the risk of oversimplification, three periods will be explored: the so-called Lithic and Archaic phases (ca. 6,000 to 2500 BP), then the Early Ceramic period (2500 to 1500 BP), and finally the Late Ceramic period (1500 to 500 BP).

Archaic Antilleans are usually portrayed as small, mobile bands of hunter-gatherers and foragers. This characterization is indisputably true in one sense: their flaked-stone blades and ground-stone spears and axes were effective killing weapons. More than 40 Archaic Age settlements arose on Antigua, in large part to produce the high-quality flint blades unavailable elsewhere in the Lesser Antilles. With these formidable assets at their disposal, Archaic Age Indians caused local extirpations of the largest mammals, such as sloths, peccary, and manatees. Shortly after their arrival in the Greater Antilles, the vast majority of the terrestrial fauna—particularly the larger species such as giant flightless owls, large tortoises, and iguanas—became extinct. At an Archaic Age Trinidad site, two shifts occurred: a decline in the hunting of primarily terrestrial game—red howler monkeys, opossums, armadillos, and red brocket deer—and a growth in fishing, together with a decrease in the gathering of freshwater and estuarine mollusks and an increase in mangrove marine species such as oysters and crown conch. Green turtles provided the best return in both calories and protein; and their remains appear in many Archaic Age sites, particularly early in their existence. The best understood Archaic Age site in Anguilla reveals the overwhelming presence of marine gastropods—queen conch, milk conch, king helmet, and so on—in the subsistence regime of its inhabitants. Moreover, analysis of Archaic Age skeletons indicate a diet dominated by marine species from coral reef and seagrass habitats.[120]

In another sense, Archaic Antilleans were more than mobile hunters. Some communities set down roots and became sedentary. Archaic Age Indians made pots long before the beginning of the so-called Ceramic Age. As early as 4600 BP, Archaic Age communities in Cuba began using pottery in small quantities. In addition, an array of plants, grains, and fruit trees—sapodilla, wild avocado, yellow sapote, primrose, and palms—have been identified in Archaic Age deposits. These earliest Antilleans also cultivated maize. They used tools, often made of shell, to fell trees, dig heavy soils, and process plants. Since at least 3300 BP in Puerto Rico, as one scholar notes, "the Antillean botanical trinity of manioc, sweet potatoes, and maize" existed. Finally, when humans first arrived in the Caribbean, the climate was turning warmer and moister. When conditions were getting wetter, there was intensive burning of large tracts of land to create savannas, or grasslands, to facilitate hunting and gathering of fruits. The Archaic Age Indians' footprint may have been light compared to their successors, but they modified their natural habitats in significant ways.[121]

Originating in the tropical forest beside the Orinoco River, Early Ceramic Age colonists making for the Antilles were presumably likely to head for the interiors of islands, to replicate what they knew. But the majority of their settlements, particularly early on, were located close to the coast, which helped the newcomers keep in touch with others by canoe. They also gravitated toward small islands, another surprising choice, since they generally support fewer and less diverse terrestrial animals than large islands. Only early in the Ceramic era did land animals play much of a role in subsistence. Thus at Trants, Montserrat, one of the earliest Ceramic Age sites in the Antilles, marine and terrestrial animals comprised roughly equal shares of the protein diet. Marine sources of protein grew more important over time. At the Early Ceramic site known as Golden Rock on St. Eustatius, over 50 different mollusk species have been identified and most of the diet came from marine sources. Another benefit of a small island was that it was often located on marine banks teeming with fish—that was especially true of Carriacou, Saba, Anguilla, the Turks and Caicos, and the Bahamas. Furthermore, it has been estimated that a small island even as tiny as Saba (5 square miles) could support a population of about 400 people. A circumscribed catchment area had advantages in terms of energy expenditure, and a small island often sufficed for most needs. Finally, small island locations were readily defended, even if particular settlements seem not to have been located with defense as their priority. For all these reasons, smaller islands were often settled first.[122]

While the characteristic pattern of Early Ceramic Age settlements combined horticulture, pottery making, hunting of land animals, fishing, and mollusk collecting, plants were key. After all, Ceramic Age peoples introduced a wide range of fruit-bearing plants—papaya, guava, mamey, soursop, cherimoya, and pineapple—as well as tobacco, pepper, peanut, probably the sweet potato, and cojoba into the Antilles. If the Arawaken-speaking Saladoids did not carry manioc there, they expanded its use to become the foundation of subsistence in the region. Perhaps no other plant equals it in the amount of food that can be produced in a given area; its caloric yield is ordinarily three times that of maize and requires much less effort to tend. It is also fairly drought-resistant. It could be harvested year round, left in the ground until required, and its bread kept indefinitely. The plant's qualities can be summarized as "no harvest season, no storage season, no short season."[123]

Nevertheless, the bitter variety had to be processed carefully and arduously to remove the poisonous hydrocyanic acid that it contained; and the resulting product is almost pure starch, providing a high caloric content, but deficient in protein, fats, and many other kinds of nutrition necessary for human survival. In 1707 Hans Sloane marveled at how so many people "should come to venture to eat Bread, made only by baking the Root of Cassada, which is one of the rankest Poisons in the World, both to Man and Beast, when Raw." To compensate, Caribbean Indians also grew several types of sweet potatoes, cocoyams, beans, gourds, chili peppers, guava, avocado, soursop, peanut, pineapple, papaya, and more. The range of tuberous and seed plants grown by indigenous peoples counters the Spanish colonial insistence that the Native American staples were just manioc and sweet potato. At least three-quarters of the indigenous diet came from plant foods.[124]

Was manioc's introduction into the Caribbean transformative, even revolutionary? One distinguished scholar of the region describes it as "the most important food plant introduced intentionally before 1492." Paleobotanical studies, however, have questioned whether the foundations of the pre-Columbian agricultural economy rested so heavily on a single staple. The diversity of large islands in particular encouraged the inhabitants to cultivate a range of crops. The hallmark of tropical agriculture is a reliance on diverse suites of crops.

Pre-Columbian farmers cultivated scores of herbs, spices such as chili peppers, medicinal plants such as tobacco, fish poison, thatch, and fruit trees such as mamey and papaya.[125]

During the Late Ceramic Age a more intensive agriculture undoubtedly emerged. Settlements tended to shift from coastal to interior hilltops sites, with a premium being placed on access to arable land. River terraces were considered desired locations. Villagers built large fields (*conucos*) and mounded the soil in which to produce their most important crops. They constructed earthworks, causeways, and roads. Water procurement and management became priorities, especially as droughts became more severe. Late Ceramic Age Antilleans dug ditches and devised pot stacks and various types of containers to capture water. They engaged in rudimentary forms of irrigation. In some places, the natives enhanced the soil, using such techniques as adding nutrient-rich red clays and then mixing them with organic materials to increase fertility.[126]

Contrary to earlier conceptions, maize was present in the indigenous Caribbean diet. Unlike manioc, it contains large amounts of protein, but requires more soil nutrients and more labor and is less tolerant of high rainfall and humidity. As a result, native groups in the Caribbean consumed it while still green or immature, often roasting the kernels. It was present in the Bahamas, for example, by 800 CE, and was fairly widely cultivated. Apparently, maize was part of a broad-based diet, commonly used with other plants. Maize, too, was part of the regular diet of high-status people on the Greater Antilles, which might explain why it was offered often to Europeans.[127]

Amerindians used fire to modify their environment and did so almost from the moment they arrived in the Caribbean. Evidence of charcoal suggests an early (Archaic Age) human occupation for a number of Lesser Antillean islands. On Barbuda, an increase in the sustained use of fire began as Ceramic Age (ca. 2100 BP or 100 BCE) peoples settled on the island to clear vegetation for their settlements and gardens and ended when they abandoned those settlements around 1300 CE or 700 BP. About the same time, dramatic changes in vegetation due to human-induced burning took place in in the Oropuche Lagoon area, Trinidad, suggesting extensive landscape modifications by Ceramic Age people. If the motives for setting fires are hard to gauge—to facilitate hunting, or to engage in horticulture—the impacts are a little more obvious. Thus in southwestern Jamaica around 800 CE, the first Amerindian settlers began to clear land that produced greater sediment buildup on the coast, transforming Bluefields Bay from free-circulating seagrass into a muddy mangrove habitat. An estimated 90 percent of pre-Columbian Cuba was in forest, with tropical forest dominant (at least 75 percent), and pinewoods representing only about 5 percent of the land. Apparently, Savanna grasslands, the term originating from the Taíno word *sabana*, were unusual, accounting for no more than about 6 percent of the Cuban archipelago. Indigenous Cubans cleared woodland but not on a huge scale. European claims that the island was almost entirely wooded or, as one resident opined, that it was "entirely covered with a continuous forest," are exaggerated. They were probably witnessing a significant reforestation, as Native Americans suffered a demographic collapse. Landscapes previously burned were going unburned. Still, Native American savannas and tilled fields were scattered throughout the island, and it probably was not possible to walk from one end of an island to another under trees.[128]

Since the last Ice Age glaciation, otherwise known as the Holocene epoch (11,700 years ago to the present), the Caribbean has experienced more mammalian extinctions than any other global region. Before humans arrived, the Antilles contained a remarkable 130–40 terrestrial species, including sloths, insectivores, primates, rodents and bats, but only 73, just over a half, have survived. The big questions are what caused this drastic decline and when did it happen. The end of the last glaciation produced significant environmental change—flooding of low-lying caves by rising seas, reduced island area, and habitat loss and transformation. But correlating the dates of extinction of native mammals and the presence of humans demonstrates a widespread overlap. On Hispaniola and Cuba, humans and sloths likely coexisted for more than 1,000 years. On Jamaica, a species of monkey persisted into the period of human occupation, making it likely that its extinction was anthropogenically driven. Humans, it would appear, were the primary agents of the fauna's demise. Body mass is also an important predictor of extinction risk. Larger-bodied species are typically more vulnerable to environmental changes, and to disproportionate exploitation by humans. Conversely, smaller mammals, while more numerous, would have been increasingly vulnerable to competition. The proposed "Goldilocks hypothesis" suggests that the surviving members of the Caribbean land mammal fauna are neither too large nor too small, but instead are "just right." Compared to Archaic Age Indians, those of the Ceramic Age exploited a wider range of smaller or medium-sized mammals—amphibians, reptiles, seabirds, rodents, and hutias in the Greater Antilles and rice rats in the Lesser Antilles—but extirpated none of them before the Europeans arrived. Humans did not settle the Bahamian islands for much of the Holocene, only arriving ca. 700 CE. The Lucayans preyed on hutias, but the rodents survived into the historic period, whereas the so-called Cuban crocodile and tortoises were extirpated within a few centuries of human arrival, thereby confirming the difference between a large population of herbivorous small rodents compared to a smaller population of bigger-bodied crocodiles and tortoises.[129]

Native Americans in the Caribbean are often said to have lacked animal husbandry; they certainly had no pack animals. But when South American groups migrated to the islands during the Ceramic Age (2500–500 BP), they brought along two domesticated species—dogs and guinea pigs—and seemingly some other mammals such as the armadillo and opossum. The latter got no farther north than Grenada and Saint Lucia. The guinea pig arrived in the Caribbean around 600 CE. They appear earliest in Puerto Rico; from there, whether as trade items or accompanying their owners, they radiated out to the rest of the Caribbean. Thus far, over 200 guinea pig fragments have been reported from 18 Ceramic Age sites on 10 Caribbean islands—not a huge number, but enough to indicate that they were a source of food. Some guinea pigs of Colombian origin were found in Puerto Rico and Carriacou, at opposite ends of the Caribbean basin. Hutias were much more abundant and native to the Greater Antilles, the Bahamas, and Virgin Islands—there are at least 45 reported extinct and extant species. Endemic to Jamaica, hutia were the preferred terrestrial source of meat for that island's Taíno population. The Taíno of Hispaniola used dogs to help hunt hutias and constructed corrals to contain them. Hutia exploitation was part of the subsistence economy. Native Americans clearly domesticated, exploited, and managed animals.[130]

Caribbean natives had terms, *iegue or Nhamácachi*, for tamed animals that should not be killed. This attitude toward some animals is captured well in the story of a Taíno man in the mid-sixteenth century who survived in the mountains of Hispaniola by hunting "wild" pigs, aided by his three tamed pigs. He also foraged for plants and roots, which he shared with his three porcine companions. When Spanish soldiers inadvertently killed his three domesticated pigs, the Indian lamented, "Those pigs gave me life and maintained me as I maintained them; they were my friends and good company." He gave them individual names (unfortunately not recorded). Conquistador-turned-chronicler Gonzalo Fernández de Oviedo y Valdés, who wrote a history of the West Indies and related this tale, was astonished that an Indian could convert the hunted into hunters, but also disparaged the man's excessive familiarity with his animals. In the neotropics, Native Americans thought that in addition to peccaries, parrots, monkeys, tapirs, and sloths were prime candidates for taming.[131]

Early in the colonization of the Antilles, Native Americans tended to eat the most easily available land animals such as iguana and the land crab. On Guadeloupe, for instance, pre-Columbian populations hunted the well-named *Iguana delicatissima* for more than 2,000 years before the arrival of Europeans. Using a noose slipped over the animal's neck, they targeted only large individuals. After capture, the iguanas were sometimes corralled, before being skinned, cooked, and consumed. At the Coralie site on Grand Turk, on the other hand, which was occupied from about 700 CE onward, the earliest settlers captured giant iguanas at first but then the iguanas' size diminished over time. In Archaic and early Saladoid middens, land crabs were common, so much so that one archaeologist labeled the Early Ceramic Age a "Crab Culture." However, the

Saladoids never relied entirely on crabs or other terrestrial animals for their pro-tein, nor did they necessarily overexploit them. Apparently, some communities (mostly Saladoids) preferred land crabs, while others favored mollusks.[132]

The main supply of protein in the Native American diet came from the sea—mainly from fish but also mollusks. Mollusk collecting defines the Archaic Age; from their shells, the natives fashioned a wide variety of tools (gouges, blades, scrapers) necessary for their existence. The queen conch was preferred: it was abundant, supplied a large amount of meat for a mollusk, and was suitable for making a wide variety of tools. As a result, shell heaps dotted most Archaic Age settlements. In the Ceramic Age, if anything, the indigenous diet became even more reliant on the bounty of the sea. Fish comprised an overwhelming ma-jority of vertebrates consumed at Ceramic Age sites and provided a major por-tion of dietary protein, along with a complement of marine invertebrates. Less than 10 percent of the prehistoric Bahamian diet derived from mollusks. So, although a number of Ceramic Age archaeological sites have produced an as-tonishing array of these marine invertebrates—tens of thousands of specimens and anywhere from 50 to 70 species, dominated by the queen conch and West Indian top snail or whelk—they can be considered akin to a garnish or flavoring in stews. The innumerable gastropods and bivalves were a supplement. Fish constituted the foundation of the indigenous diet, and their variety was remark-able. They came from a range of habitats—coral reefs, seagrass beds, estuaries, rocky banks, mangrove swamps, and the deep sea. The most numerous in-shore fish were grunts, parrotfish, triggerfish and surgeonfish; farther offshore, groupers and snappers were widespread; while jacks, tuna, flying fish, and sharks tended to inhabit deeper waters. Marine turtles, monk seals, manatees, dolphins, and whales were other marine sources that could be exploited.[133]

Archaeological comparisons of "early" and "late" prehistoric settlements on a series of islands reveal evidence of overfishing, particularly with respect to large fish and turtles. Within 200 years of settling on a site in Grand Turk (ca. 700 to 900 CE), the Amerindians had extirpated mature breeding turtles and turned to capturing juveniles. At a Saint Lucia site in the Windward Islands, settled from ca. 900 to 1500 CE, sea turtles were evident early on, but small fishes soon replaced them. At many sites on a range of islands, average fish weight declined at least by half, sometimes as much as 80 percent, from roughly the eighth to the fifteenth century. Apparently, over time, Native Americans captured a larger number of juveniles, fish that had not reached their full growth potential. Furthermore, a growing Native American population led to declines of nearshore marine fauna and growing exploitation of offshore species, including tuna, large jacks, flying fishes, and mackerel. In addition, Native Americans increasingly caught fewer predatory fish such as groupers and snappers and more omnivores and herbivores, mostly parrotfish and surgeonfish. The supposition is that aggressive

Figure 1.7 Von seltzamer Fischeren der Indianer. Harvesting the Sea. Various methods of fishing in the Caribbean, ranging from the use of nets to a novel way of catching whales. In Wolffgang Richter, *Neundter und Letzter Theil Americae* (Frankfurt am Main, 1601). Ink on paper. John Carter Brown Library.

carnivores were captured first, leading to a shift for fish lower in the food chain. Finally, in some places shellfish species such as queen conch were overexploited, as were West Indian top snails, evident in a decrease in size over time among those harvested. In all these ways, overfishing occurred in the pre-Columbian Caribbean.[134]

At the same time, pre-Columbian peoples almost certainly did not have the capability to deplete offshore and deep-sea stocks; and not all places were affected by overfishing. Indeed, small islands, particularly those adjacent to productive marine banks, reveal sustainable fishing regimes. In Anguilla, where the number of significant Amerindian sites rose from about 3 to 14 from "early" (ca. 500/600 CE) to "late" (ca. 1000 CE) periods—it has been estimated that perhaps 10,000 people lived on the island in 1000–1200 CE, much the same size as the population today—there was no evidence of overharvesting. There was no decreased body size in the harvested fish population; reef fishes dominated diets throughout, even though there was a rise in the capture of mackerel and tuna, a result perhaps of changes in fishing strategies. Seemingly, the Anguilla Bank, an especially productive reef system, could support the growing demand without depletion. Similarly, on a Carriacou site explored for a millennium (400–1400 CE), coral reef fish increased in relative abundance over time, while the exploitation of offshore fish, most notably a well-developed tuna fishery, remained steady. On a St. Thomas site in the Early Ceramic Age, an astonishing array of mollusks revealed no decrease in size over time; apparently, intense predation was sustainable. At a Late Ceramic Age site on Nevis, a study of a large mollusk assemblage of 58,000 items showed no signs of overharvesting despite intensified exploitation of some species. In fact, there was an increase in the average individual weight of the three main species. The Native American population in the Caribbean, some argue, was too small and too technologically unsophisticated to have had much impact on fish breeding stocks. Furthermore, declines of some species shifted growing attention to others. Thus, on Grand Turk, a decline in birds, reef carnivores, and green turtles was offset by an increase in abundance of conches. Individual daily catches seem to have ranged from about 120 to 300 conches a day.[135]

Over time, specialized settlements arose devoted purely to the exploitation of marine sources. Occupied from ca. 900 to 1500 CE, Île à Rat, a tiny island located off the northwest coast of Hispaniola, supplied fish and shellfish for the large villages upriver and away from the coast. The fish were small and the conches were not adults, an indication that severe depletion had already occurred. Similarly, some coastal villages in southern Cuba specialized in fishing, and supplied more inland settlements. Fishing villages in the southern Bahamas exported fresh and preserved fish to Hispaniola. Communities in Hispaniola found it rewarding to travel by canoe to exploit the abundant marine resources surrounding Grand Turk. Fishing villages arose in the southern Bahamas that seem to have exported fresh and preserved fish to Hispaniola. Nowhere else in the Caribbean are sea turtle remains found in such abundance. Within 200 years, mature breeding turtles had been extirpated and fishing focused on juveniles. The earliest settlements on Jamaica, dating from about 700 CE, also seem to have focused initially on sea turtles, suggesting that they were extensions of Cuba, more like short-term base camps. Residents on Saba, the smallest island of the Lesser Antilles, perhaps an outpost of a Puerto Rican polity, exploited the substantial fishing grounds of Saba Bank. Apparently, Native Americans on the island were drying and salting conch meat for future food, trade, and tribute. This was not just subsistence fishing.[136]

What is most striking about the prehistoric Caribbean fishery is its remarkable diversity. The dominant resource varied among sites as a reflection of preferences and local availability, which often changed seasonally and over time. On Middle Caicos, the most common food item was bonefish, probably because of proximity to the flats and shallows that this fish inhabited as well as its lean, white meat, which made it a good candidate for salting. In Archaic Age Trinidad almost half of the fish caught belonged to the sea catfish family. Even on a small island such as Anguilla, fishing was highly localized. Some communities specialized in doctorfish, reflecting their proximity to extensive nearshore seagrass beds; others caught more parrotfish and tunas because they were closer to reef habitats. Similarly, while two fishing villages on Carriacou shared a focus on reef fish, one settlement caught far more tuna than the other. The difference is attributable to the proximity of the reef slope, which allowed Amerindians at one site access to deeper open waters and enabled them to take advantage of tuna migration.[137]

The marine animals that most caught the attention of the Taíno were sharks and rays, although visual representations of these menacing creatures were rare. The late sixteenth-century authors of *Histoire Naturelle des Indies* said of the "tiberon," or shark, that it was "very vicious," able to rip off an arm or leg and eat it. The Taíno had at least five names for types of sharks and two for rays. The tiger shark (*carite*) was a fierce predator. Indeed, on the north coast of Puerto Rico a skeleton of a 29-year-old man, dated to 1000 CE, shows the loss of one arm and the marks of a tiger shark attack, presumably the cause of his death. Another burial at the same site revealed an individual with a stingray spine lodged in his rib cage, a wound that apparently caused his demise. Stingrays provided the material for spear tips and their skins were useful to process manioc. In 1627 on St. Christopher, the Kalinago killed just over 30 Europeans (and 3 of their native allies) with arrows tipped with poisoned stingray tails. Sharks provided meat and raw materials for tools and decorative items; their skin could serve as an abrasive. The indigenous people of the Caribbean made necklaces and amulets from vertebrae and teeth of sharks.[138]

Just as the Native Americans in the region intensified food production through mounding, terracing, and some rudimentary irrigation, along with partial domestication of animals, so, too, they gradually elaborated a full range of fishing technologies. They developed many capture techniques, including bows and arrows, harpoons, spears, hooks and lines, basket traps, fish pots, seine nets, fish poisoning, and weirs. They built dams across the mouths of tidal creeks to trap fish, and corrals to keep them alive until needed. Lagoons could act as natural traps. At Spanish Water, Curaçao, the remains of at least 41 dolphins from at least 4 species, hunted within the lagoon and butchered on the banks, have been discovered. Communities even on the same island tended to focus on offshore, line fishing in deep water, whereas others specialized in trapping and netting close to shore. They deployed seine nets of different mesh, made from palm fiber cordage and cotton, with gourd floats and heavy stone or shell sinkers. An archaeological discovery of small, thin, flat aerodynamic weights at a Hispaniolan fishing village is the first indication that Antilleans used cast nets—a finding confirmed by the remains of small, bait-size, schooling fish. Natives even used remora, suckerfish named *pez reverse* by the Spanish, as a way of attaching a line to a larger fish or turtle that could then be reeled into welcoming arms. As the Native Americans' evolving fishing techniques indicate, they managed as well as hunted their prey. Their lack of pack animals constrained their lives only a little because they lived near the water and had canoes.[139]

Because fish spoiled quickly in a tropical climate, Antilleans employed three main preservation techniques: drying, smoking, and salting. The wooden lattice on which they dried and smoked their fish, a *barbacoa*, gave its name to an American pastime. Native Americans likely viewed salt ambivalently. Apparently, Caribs avoided it, although they ate clay. On the other hand, natives would have known that salt intrusions, as with rising sea levels, compromised fresh water, and that airborne salts transported by persistent trade winds generally hampered plant cultivation. But salt's main positive attribute was as a preservative. Amerindians took advantage of certain islands—Middle Caicos in the Bahamas archipelago, Bonaire off the coast of Venezuela, and Anegada in the Virgin Islands—to produce salt, as places where the "white gold" was harvested. But at coastal sites in Puerto Rico and Hispaniola in particular, fish were processed (heads removed) and preserved by salting, so that the fillets could be sent to interior settlements. At one site on Middle Caicos, the Lucayan Taíno engaged in a year-round cycle of catching, processing, salting, and transporting their marine products primarily to Hispaniola. They built earthen embankments and a road system leading to a natural solar-distilled salt pond; they raked the salt and put it into woven baskets or cotton sacks. As soon as the pond became salt-producing, people arrived to take advantage of its bounty, which involved significant investments of time in building infrastructure.[140]

The abundance of animal protein, primarily in the form of marine resources, was a key element of the indigenous Antillean diet and probably explains why some Caribbean Indians did not cultivate as much maize as their South American counterparts. At one site in Guadeloupe half of the diet was marine based, and human bones analyzed to date generally show little evidence of nutritional disorders. Most Native Americans in the region seemingly enjoyed good health. Breastfeeding lasted at least two years. The natives' teeth often reveal extreme wear, perhaps attributable to a starchy and gritty diet. European visitors to the Caribbean describe the Indians as a "fine shaped people" or as possessing a "fine stature." They were probably taller than their distant cousins in eastern North America, with the exception of the Calusa of Florida, who had a similar diet to Caribbean natives and were exceptionally tall. One intriguing finding from a burial site in inland Puerto Rico, 5 miles from the sea, is of an individual with auditory exostosis ("surfer's ear"), a typical affliction of people who regularly dive.[141]

Overall, then, while Native Americans certainly modified their environment, the levels of exploitation were limited. Their impact on the three major marine mammals of the region—the manatee, monk seal, and humpback whale—seem to have been modest. Native Americans may have butchered carcasses near the shore, taking only lighter and consumable parts to their villages. But that no manatee skull has been found at a Native American site seems telling. Similarly, evidence of seals are absent from most archaeological sites in the Lesser Antilles, indicating they played at most a small role in Native American subsistence. Finally, modern estimates of the numbers of turtles and seals in the Caribbean as the Europeans arrived suggest that Amerindians hardly overexploited them. The lowest estimate of green turtles in the pre-Columbian Caribbean is 30 million, and monk seals perhaps numbered a quarter of a million. The biomass of reef fishes and invertebrates required to support such populations suggests that reefs were about six times more productive in the immediate pre-Columbian Caribbean than they are today. Only remote Pacific reefs are as productive as Caribbean reefs once were. Just as reforestation occurred in the sixteenth century because fewer natives were burning trees, so the drastic decline of the native population provided some respite to the marine environment, allowing stocks of fish, turtle, and seals to rebound.[142]

The indigenous peoples of the Caribbean were farmer-fishermen. They cultivated as many as a hundred or so plants, and they caught hundreds of varieties of fish and mollusks. Their diet was evenly divided between the two. It is fair to describe them as a maritime people, but there were probably few specialist fishermen. Women and children were active foragers, even if men did most of the fishing. This was also largely subsistence fishing. Over time, some settlements became special-purpose fishing villages; and indications of commodity fishing began to emerge. Social networks extended well beyond a single village. In some areas, settlements took the form of pairs, suggesting cooperation between socially allied communities. Overfishing occurred in some places, but generally aquatic resources were sustainable. Like other fishing societies, the Antilleans enjoyed a complex, communal ritual life. One Lucayan male on Eleuthera was buried with an Atlantic trumpet triton in front of his thorax, parts of a sea turtle at his foot, and 29 sunrise tellin shells, a clump of red ocher, and a fish bone scarifier behind his shoulder. Maritime products were valued in trade and exchange relationships. Beads and shells regularly passed from hand to hand. The red jewel box shell disk beads, manufactured throughout the Lucayan Islands, were an important trade good. The spectacular queen conch shell served as both status symbol and ritual trumpet, endowed with intense symbolic power.[143]

Native Americans were a major presence in the Caribbean long after the conquest, and much of their experience revolved around slavery. From the beginning, Spaniards distinguished between Indians who were *guatiao*, or friendly, and those who were Caribs (*caribes*) and resisted Spanish authority. Labeling the latter savages and cannibals, Spaniards justified their enslavement. In 1494, at the end of his second voyage, Columbus transported about 500 Native American slaves to Seville and dreamed of a profitable slave trade of American "Indians" to Iberia, Italy, Sicily, and the Atlantic islands. On Hispaniola, the most densely populated native island, and the one that Spaniards initially targeted, relations between Taínos and the Spanish quickly moved from barter to mandatory labor in the gold washings. The Spaniards in the early Caribbean developed a form of Indian vassalage, the *encomienda*, a system of labor and tribute extraction that was meant to be distinct from slavery, but that in its essence was a form of forced labor. The demographic collapse of Native Americans first on Hispaniola and then on the other Greater Antillean islands encouraged a slave trade from other islands and mainland regions elsewhere in the Caribbean into Hispaniola. As early as the 1520s, colonists on that island petitioned to bring natives from other islands because there were none left. Early in the sixteenth century, Bahamians or Lucayans were one source for slaves among Spaniards on the Greater Antilles; somewhat later in the century a major trade from Central America into the Caribbean ensued. In sixteenth-century Central America, conquistadores branded Indian slaves and shipped hundreds of thousands to Panama, the Caribbean, and other parts of Spanish America. From 1515 to 1542 slave-raiding expeditions to Nicaragua captured an estimated 200,000 Indians in Nicaragua alone, who were transported to the Antilles. During the second quarter of the sixteenth century, the Indian slave trade was the principal economic activity of parts of the circum-Caribbean mainland.[144]

In the beginning, Indians were the primary labor force in the sugar economy. Indian slaves cultivated the first sugar grown in the Caribbean. In early sixteenth-century Hispaniola, at least 10,000 imported Indian slaves, along with the native inhabitants, formed the labor force of the early sugar industry. Enslaved Indians provided the initial labor and, through their sale, the preliminary capital that made plantation agriculture possible. Indians and Africans worked alongside one another as forced laborers in Hispaniola's fields, homes, and gold mines. One spectacular clue to their intimate associations is a cotton cemí, representing an ancestral spirit or deity, a Janusesque figure, one side human, the other a bat. It is a recognizably Taíno artifact, which dates to the early sixteenth century, but is a synthesis of many styles and materials. It combines over 20,000 indigenous shell beads; European glass beads, mirrors, and wooden base; and an African rhinoceros horn from which is carved the human face. The Taíno, or possibly mixed-race, craftsman who fabricated this object, must have known Africans and Europeans well.[145]

Throughout the extended Caribbean, many indigenous communities believed that gold grew like a plant and should be gathered at particular times and seasons. Lucayans told Columbus that they collected gold at night by candlelight. In various metalworking communities of the Caribbean, refiners added herbs to molten mixtures of gold and copper to enhance the sensory experience. Guanín metals (gold-copper alloys) were sacred objects, fashioned to honor nature's bounty. As literary scholar Allison Bigelow notes, "Taíno metalworking traditions were [not] ecologically innocuous; after all, they demanded substantial amounts of water and charcoal to wash minerals and fuel fires."[146]

Adapting indigenous slaving practices to the new realities of the colonial world, Indians responded both to Europeans' demand for slaves and to the broader economic transformations wrought by colonial trade. Doing so led some natives to redirect their energies toward slaving for Europeans. In other cases, the Kalinago (or Caribs) of the Lesser Antilles, for example, signed treaties with Europeans to create zones of mutually respected sovereignty. In 1660 French, English, and fifteen Kalinago representatives signed the first international intra-Caribbean treaty that recognized Dominica and St. Vincent as Kalinago territory. Thereafter, these refuges attracted African slaves escaping French or British zones. In the late seventeenth century, then, the Kalinago welcomed an increasing number of slaves who escaped to their territories, rather than returning them to the Europeans.[147]

In the seventeenth and eighteenth centuries, as the import of African slaves into the Caribbean became a flood, there was always a trickle of Indian slaves coming into the region, increasingly from farther afield. Beginning in the late sixteenth century, ship captains occasionally marketed and sold Brazilian Indians as slaves in various Caribbean ports. In the aftermath of King Philip's War (1675–76), New Englanders shipped hundreds of defeated Indians to the Caribbean as slaves. The largest slave trade from British North America to the Caribbean came from South Carolina involving hundreds if not thousands of Native Americans. One of the most notable Indian slave trades in the eighteenth century concerns that from New France to the French Caribbean. Canadian settlers actively traded Indian slaves—"panis" was the common term, but they might be Pawnee, Fox, Sioux, or Apache. Canadians soon realized that an Indian slave bought in Montreal or Quebec for 300 or 400 livres could yield a thousand livres or more in Martinique. How many Indians blended into the massive population of enslaved African is impossible to say; from the early eighteenth century onward, French Caribbean censuses that once recorded "mulatto, Negro, and Indian slaves" collapsed those categories into a single group, labeled "Negro" or "Negress," other times merely "slaves." Nevertheless, an indigenous slave system, operating deep in the North American interior, supplied slaves for the distant Caribbean.[148]

Another stream entered the Spanish Greater Antilles. They included Yucatecan Mayans, Chichimecas or "mecas" (referring to any nomadic Indians), Apaches, and *Guachinango*, an umbrella term, which referred to *castas* with a recognizable indigenous ancestry, usually from central New Spain or Mexico. In 1768, for example, 300 *Guachinango* Indians arrived in Cuba from Mexico. These Indians often worked as domestics, in the shipyards, and on fortifications. When the British invaded Havana in 1762, *Guachinangos* were staunch defenders of the city. Some Indian deportees in the nineteenth century even worked on sugar plantations. In their appeals to the Crown and the Council of the Indies, white Cubans often lamented that their island was "without Indians," but the reality was more complicated. There were *indios* present in all the Spanish Greater Antilles. Even as some Cubans requested Indian laborers for their homes, the escape of native captives and their collaboration with runaway slaves of African descent eventually led local magistrates and the governor in Havana to demand that no more Indians be sent. In 1800 one fugitive Indian armed with bow and arrows and reputed to be a cannibal, allegedly terrorized plantations in central Cuba. The story of Indian diasporas illustrates how histories of slavery include multifarious groups from far-flung places.[149]

Indian slavery in the Caribbean rose and then fell dramatically, but did not disappear entirely. In pre-Columbian times, indigenous slavery became more widespread as Taíno society developed more hierarchical and stratified chiefdoms. Carib society was somewhat more egalitarian than that of the Taíno, but depended heavily on raiding for captives. Nevertheless, under both systems, indigenous slavery was not commodified; Taíno and Carib alike generally incorporated slaves into their kinship structures. Europeans then adapted Indian slavery and transformed it. Before the early seventeenth century, Europeans enslaved more Indians than Africans. Native Americans responded to the European invaders by selling them slaves; indigenous enslavement expanded. But the appalling demographic disaster that befell Native Americans meant that the European reliance on Indian labor did not last long in the Antilles. Thereafter, Indian slaves continued to trickle into the region as a small stream compared to the much larger flood of African arrivals. These Indian newcomers were often put to work as hunters, fishermen, and domestic servants, sometimes on the forts and fortifications, and even in sugar mills, but for the most part they were marginal to the emerging system of slavery that came to overwhelmingly depend on African labor. The natives became largely invisible.[150]

* * *

Impact of Europeans and Africans

While Native Americans modified the Caribbean environment, Europeans and Africans transformed it. Native Americans transferred some animals, usually small and most not fully domesticated, into and throughout the Caribbean; Europeans imported large domesticated mammals, notably horses, donkeys, cattle, sheep, goats, pigs, even camels (as well as chickens and stowaway rats). Although these animals provided new sources of protein and new means of transportation, they trampled soils and disrupted native horticulture. The compacting of soils led to erosion and gullying. Spanish colonization resulted in an explosive growth of secondary vegetation; with a decline in indigenous attention to *conucos*, native and introduced weeds, grasses, herbs, and shrubs spread, with the help of grazing animals; and they in turn helped destroy soils. Given the huge decline of the native population in the early Caribbean, these animals ran free, forming enormous wild herds. The term *cimarrones* initially described feral animals before human Maroons. As early as 1514—just three years after the Spanish arrived in numbers—a reported 30,000 hogs ran wild on Cuba. In the 1520s, herds of as many as 8,000 cattle roamed the Hispaniolan countryside, after their initial introduction in 1493. The Spaniards developed ranches on the big islands. Mounted herders, or *vaqueros*, chased feral herds with dogs and pikes, in pursuit of hides and tallow. The buccaneers, too, got their living—and their name, from *boucan*, the wooden grating on which they grilled their meat—by hunting these feral livestock. Their popularizer, Alexander Exquemelin, claimed that they killed 1,500 wild swine every day on Hispaniola, but "there is still an incredible quantity of wild pigs on the island." As historian Alfred Crosby noted, the Spanish pig, once ashore in the Caribbean, "became a fast, tough, lean, self-sufficient greyhound of a hog," rather like a wild boar, as depicted on an early seventeenth-century Bermudian shilling.[151]

Europeans came to the Caribbean accompanied by their so-called vassal animals—primarily horses and dogs—as well as livestock. The terrorizing effect of horses on foot soldiers defies exaggeration. Enlisted as partners in colonization, horses carried Spanish soldiers into battle, while dogs served as their scouts, and cattle, sheep, swine, and goats their sustenance. Twenty hunting dogs accompanied Columbus on his second expedition of 1493. Specialists in tracking, harassing, and killing, they were formidable adversaries, and deployed to attack deer, peccaries, and hutias, which they soon drove to extinction in many places. Spaniards even ate the Indians' dogs when supplies ran short. Infamously, the Spaniards also used their dogs to attack natives—first in Jamaica in 1494, then Hispaniola the following year, and in most subsequent campaigns. In Vasco Nuñez de Balboa's invasion of Panama in 1513, Leoncico, a mastiff/greyhound mix, was the lead dog, celebrated for retrieving runaways. The willingness to let loose the "dogs of war" points to how some Europeans viewed Indians—as near beasts themselves.[152]

An inadvertent part of the Columbian Exchange, European rats arrived in the Caribbean, where they multiplied prodigiously. Their introduction is thought responsible for the extinction of an insectivore on the Greater Antilles. They posed an even greater threat to young canes than plant diseases or insects. One knowledgeable observer claimed that rats destroyed 5 percent of the sugar crop each year. He reported that over 39,000 of these rodents were killed on a single plantation during a six-month period. Thus one remedy was to employ slaves to catch rats. According to James Knight, a historian of Jamaica, "Mundinga Negroes are very expert" at hunting vermin; every plantation had two or more enslaved hunters dedicated to the task. Hans Sloane reported that the sugar-fattened rats were a delicacy in Jamaica and were sold by the dozen. Another more drastic solution was to burn the infested fields from the edges inward or to abandon them temporarily, as happened in Grenada in the mid-1790s. The poet James Grainger recommended that Leeward Island planters breed "savage cats" or import mongooses from the East Indies, a natural predator, as a means of battling rats (the latter suggestion was adopted in the nineteenth century). By the early nineteenth century, planters in Barbados, and then elsewhere, imported cane toads from Demerara to battle rats. In sum, "the whisker'd vermine race," in poet Grainger's words, caused considerable economic damage, prompting a variety of attempted solutions.[153]

Weighing up the Columbian Exchange in terms of the impact on animals is a mixed bag. From the perspective of imported domestic animals, pigs and cattle did spectacularly well; horses were slower to adapt but soon thrived. Some native fauna suffered habitat extinction. One Spanish commentator wrote in passing of doomed toads in Panama, when trees were cleared for pasture to support livestock. As one example of the problems invasive species wrought, rabbits multiplied fast and damaged native and colonists' gardens. The rat, probably the black rat, arrived as a stowaway that carried disease and then honeycombed the earth with its burrows. A few native fauna benefited from the new animal arrivals; alligators preyed on dogs, and opossum on chickens. Others fared less well. Indians had long captured wild birds, sometimes for food, or for plumage, or as pets, but, with the arrival of parrot-obsessed Europeans, increasingly as trade goods. In the early Columbian encounters, parrots were a prime item of exchange. Scarlet macaws were the most popular parrots among Parisian nobility during the eighteenth century. Europeans prized the bird.[154]

Animals and humans remained closely entangled during the era of slavery. The means of domesticating animals—whipping, chaining, branding, castration, hobbling, shackling, ear-cropping, the use of collars and prods—were regularly applied to captive humans. Aristotle was on the mark when he said the ox was the poor man's slave. The ease of association between slave and domestic animal, the repeated equation of the two, the inextricable coupling, was a feature of Caribbean slavery. As one sugar planter put it, slaves and livestock were the "sinews of a plantation." A sugar estate, an attorney declared, was hardly worth the name unless "animated," by which he meant by human and animal labor. Beans were considered suitable provender for horses because they were well known to be "a nourishing food for the negroes." The term "driver," later used to describe an enslaved foreman, originally meant one who caught wild horses; the word "Maroon" (deriving from the Spanish word for feral livestock) was early applied to a hunter of wild cattle. Slaves sometimes shared names with horses and cows. "Spanish marks" on donkeys usually meant they had been imported from Cuba, while "country marks" on humans signified African origins. The etymological origins of the term "mulatto" seemingly derives from the Spanish and Portuguese word for mule.[155]

Animals were regularly instruments of domination and occasionally tools of subversion. Thus slaveholders used horses to establish their dominion; they rode around their estates, not just to monitor but to intimidate their enslaved people, who in return occasionally turned the tables by riding horses at night or fleeing on horseback. In 1730 an Ibo woman in Jamaica took a "young bay horse" to aid her escape. Richard Ligon's mid-seventeenth-century map of Barbados depicts a more likely scene: a mounted white man, perhaps a patroller, firing a gun at two enslaved people fleeing on foot; the only other enslaved man is on foot following a camel. A running footman often accompanied his master when out riding, holding onto the horse's tail, a symbol of subjection; but the horse's tail was an important status symbol in West Africa and featured in ritual events among plantation slaves. Cattle powered the machinery of sugar cane processing, but a hierarchy of enslaved workers arose to drive and direct them. Toussaint Louverture was an enslaved coachman and horse handler before becoming one of Saint-Domingue's most accomplished horsemen and the colony's revolutionary leader, earning the soubriquet "Centaur of the Savanna." Large livestock generally buttressed the plantation regime, whether as beasts of burden or by providing fertilizer; small livestock, such as chickens, pigs, and goats that some slaves possessed, could be sold in the Sunday markets to earn cash. Cuban bloodhounds were bred specifically to track and terrorize Maroons and rebels; slaves possessed their own dogs to aid them in hunting.[156]

Ranching, a significant agricultural activity throughout much of the Spanish Caribbean for more than three centuries after colonization, did not immediately lead to a large degree of deforestation. Ranchers cleared land for pasture, which in turn soon diminished in quality, but they also relied on the forests for feed for cattle and pigs, especially during the dry winter season. During the summer wet

season in the Veracruz lowlands, ranchers would graze their cattle on the pied-
mont shrublands. To some extent, then, ranchers were interested in the maintenance of the forests. In any case, ranching was lightly populated in the Spanish
Caribbean. On Hispaniola and Cuba in the early seventeenth century, the average *hato* (of which there were not more than 200 on Hispaniola) employed
two to three slaves.[157]

Farmers cleared more land than ranchers. On early seventeenth-century
Hispaniola, farms or *estancias* outnumbered *hatos* by more than two to one. They
also employed more slaves: two-thirds of the roughly 10,000 enslaved people on
Hispaniola in the first decade of the century worked on farms growing primarily
cassava, maize, and vegetables, along with some tobacco and ginger. A quarter
of the estancias specialized in the cultivation of ginger, while half of the slaves
worked in producing food crops. Since these units averaged 16 slaves, the extent
of land clearance was more than that involved in ranching. In addition, a free
black peasantry began to emerge on the outskirts of Spanish Caribbean towns
and cities in the late sixteenth and early seventeenth centuries. Nineteen free
people of color owned estancias in early seventeenth-century Hispaniola. Their
farms typically consisted of anywhere from 3,000 to 10,000 mounds of yucca, as
little as a half to as much as 500 *fanegas* (about 300 hectares) of maize, and perhaps a plot of vegetables or a grove of plantains or other fruits.[158]

On Cuba, shipbuilding had a greater impact on the forests than ranching.
Because Cuban hardwoods proved so durable and valuable, local officials soon
developed an interest in conserving them. As early as 1550 in what has been
dubbed Cuba's "first conservationist regulation," the Havana city council prohibited enslaved blacks from cutting mahogany and cedar within a radius of 2
leagues around the city. Two years later, they banned nonresidents and ships
of foreign flags from felling and exporting trees. Then, in the early seventeenth
century, to the annoyance of Cuban residents, the Spanish Crown placed large
forest tracts off limits to the local populace in order to ensure the navy's long-
term timber supply. By the early eighteenth century, when Havana was Spain's
most important shipyard, royal edicts reserved the best woodlands for shipbuilding. Once again, a measure of conservation was built into the early Cuban
reliance on its forests.[159]

Other islands followed Spanish Cuba's lead. Bermuda, not in the Caribbean
but closely connected to it, developed a vibrant shipbuilding industry that specialized in building fast sloops out of its native cedar, which proved excellent for
seagoing vessels. Finding their local trees insufficient, Bermudians sought cedar
and other hardwoods from surrounding islands and the Bay of Honduras. At
home, the Bermuda Assembly enacted some of the earliest forest conservation
laws in British America. In 1693, for example, it passed an act to prevent the destruction of young cedar trees. Furthermore, Bermudians began replanting trees

as they cut them on a 20- to 30-year maturation cycle; in the eighteenth century nine-tenths of Bermuda's land was in timber reserves for shipbuilding. Similarly, in the Bahamas, the colonial assembly in 1729 passed several forest conservation measures designed to protect its shipbuilding industry. They forbade destruction "by Fire of all Timber Trees growing on these Islands," levied fines for damage "done by Cattle running loose," and prohibited all timber exports.[160]

Deforestation in the Caribbean occurred for other reasons as well. There were of course many practical purposes for tropical timber: a number of hardwoods such as cedar, ebony, and bulletwood were used in house or fort construction; the European clothing industry valued dyewoods such as brazilwood, fustic, and logwood; less valued woods such as balsam could serve as fuel; many used the bark or roots of shrubs or vines such as sarsaparilla for their medicinal properties; and eventually mahogany became highly valued by furniture makers. Fear drove tree-felling too: trees were the source of miasmas, many thought, the cause of fevers; and much lumber was simply cut down and left rotting in the fields. Conversely, burning trees liberated the nitrogen and potassium stored in the "giant nutrient towers" that the wood and bark represented, temporarily raising the organic levels of the soil, as much of this stockpile entered the ground among the ashes. No wonder farmers preferred to cut and burn. In addition, forests harbored escaped slaves, giving planters security reasons for felling trees. Ideals were also part of it: reshaping the land fulfilled pastoral ideals and notions of improvement. To some people, cutting down trees and replacing them with tended and bounded fields created order. One late seventeenth-century settler in Jamaica spoke of loving the country more and more as "the negroes goe tumbling down the trees" to make way for sugar cane and cacao plantings.[161]

In the seventeenth century, rudimentary environmental protection began in piecemeal fashion. In the 1680s, for example, Jamaican legislators forbade the killing of those "harmless" birds known as carrion crows or vultures, "which are soe usefull in devouring carrion carcases, which otherwise by their stinck and noisom smell would infect the air and so breed foul and contagious distempers." The effects of deforestation also merited attention. A 1683 law for clearing "the River called *Rio Cobre*, or the Town River that passeth by *St Jago De La Vega* [Spanish Town]" noted that the river had already "wholly lost its Old Channel by means of the extraordinary Floods, and by the abundance of Trees and great quantities of Rubbish that fall into the same." Neighboring sugar plantations were at risk even with "small Floods"; good "Manurable Land now will be turned into mere Bog and Morass." A new drainage commission was set up to dredge and, if necessary, redirect the river's course. But the threats of flooding and soil erosion waxed rather than waned.[162]

Mahogany's popularity as a luxury wood began in the early eighteenth century. Jamaica was the main supplier initially, and by the 1720s it was the leading

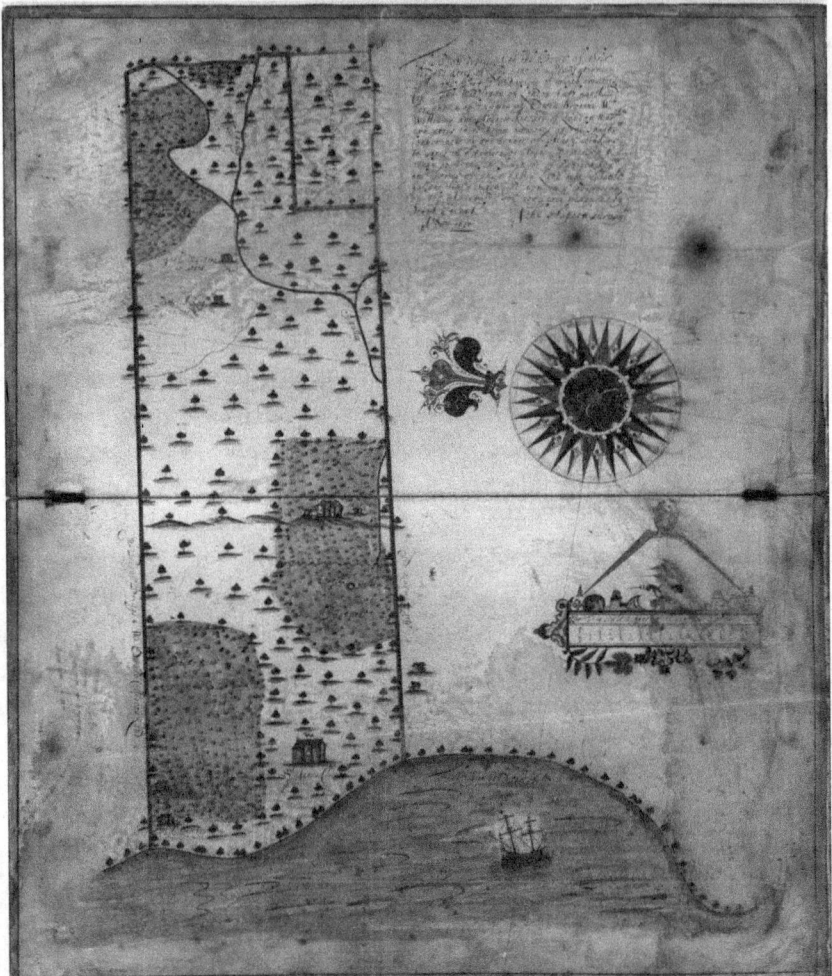

Figure 1.8 John Hapcott, survey of 300 acres, part of Fort Plantation that Captain Thomas Middleton purchased in 1646. This plan of an estate near Jamestown, or present-day Holetown, Barbados, includes a church, ship, saltpeter house, mill, and dwellings. Land use is indicated by "Fallen land," referring to areas cleared for agriculture, specifically sugar cane, and "Potato peece" noting an important food source. The legend refers to Mr. Wright's plantation "taken too farr into this land," suggesting a neighbor's encroachment before the establishment of recognized boundary lines. The survey depicts land clearance, although much woodland remains. Ms. Map. John Carter Brown Library.

exporter of West Indian mahogany. At mid-century, when the island supplied about 90 percent of England's imports of this "fancy wood," accessible mahogany trees were rapidly disappearing on the island, and by the late eighteenth century they were essentially all gone. In the meantime, the search was on for other sources. The most desirable species, the short-leaf West Indian

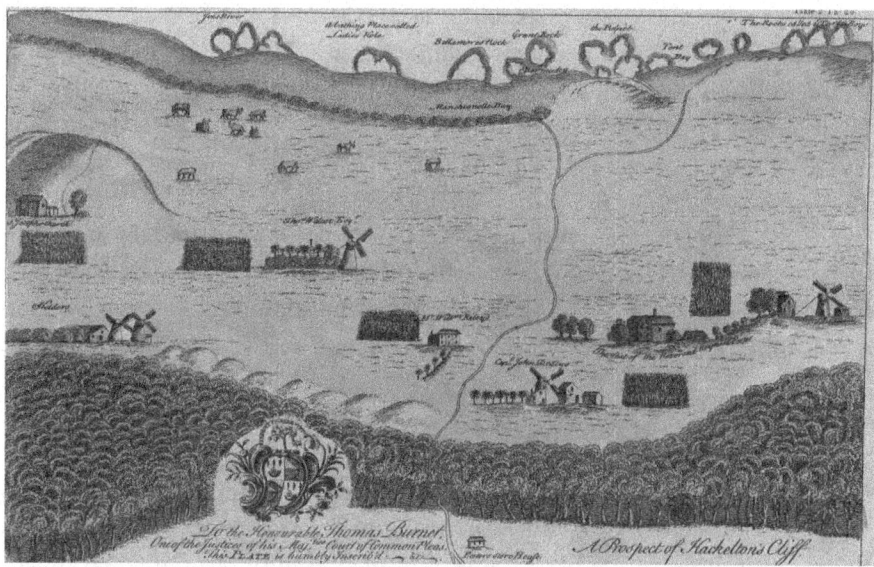

Figure 1.9 A prospect of Hackelton's Cliff, Barbados. Reverend Griffith Hughes, *Natural History of Barbados*, 1750. Drawn a century after Hapcott's survey, this prospect reveals a largely cleared landscape, dotted with windmills, dwellings, cattle, and sugar cane fields, with forest remnants in the foreground and coastal landslips caused by deforestation in the background. Engraving and colors. John Carter Brown Library.

mahogany, was available only in the north-central Caribbean, Cuba, Hispaniola, and the Bahamas (as well as smaller islands such as the Turks and Caicos and the Caymans), all of which were tapped. By the late eighteenth century, "St. Domingo wood" gained a reputation for excellence, and later on Cuban mahogany came to dominate the world market. But the big-leaf Honduran species, initially thought of as inferior to the West Indian variety, had a broader territory, and the race to find the best mahogany stands generated intense geopolitical rivalries, or timber wars, in places such as the Bay of Honduras (now Belize) and the Mosquito Shore (now Nicaragua and Honduras). Desirable for its lustrous, highly polished surface, mahogany is found only in small clusters, grows slowly, and is difficult to regenerate.[163]

With other trees and in other places, attempts at sustainable forestry methods had more success. The French were one of the first to engage in significant replanting—on Martinique, in part because it suffered the most acute and earliest deforestation of any French Caribbean island. West Indian planters in general began to see the virtues of creating hedges as windbreaks and as sources of shade. They also recognized the profits to be made from dyewoods such as fustic or logwood, or from spices such as pimento, or from the medicinal properties of a shrub such as physic nut—leading them to create small stands,

walks, or hedges of them. Eighteenth-century commentators began extolling the
aesthetic contribution of hedges, claiming they added beauty to the landscape.
By the end of the century, a new, much more positive view of trees and their use-
fulness began to take hold. Their presence could enhance rainfall, it was argued,
and their loss encouraged aridity. The older view that trees were responsible for
miasmas was beginning to change.[164]

Other parts of the Caribbean saw little deforestation. Well into the twentieth
century, over 90 percent of Suriname's total surface area was in forest, mainly
tropical rainforest, inhabited by Amerindians and Maroons. A low population
density spared much of the forest cover. Limited soil fertility in the interior
and difficulties in transporting lumber farther encouraged concentration on
the coast and riverbanks. The kind of timber Suriname had to offer—snake-
wood, gums, honey, wax, beefwood, redwood, fustic—was also not much in demand in Europe, so it was exported in fairly small amounts. Suriname *quassia*
or bitterwood (*Quassia amara*), used to reduce fevers, became an export in
the eighteenth century. Overall, however, deforestation was minimal in this
Caribbean colony.[165]

The true ecological maelstrom to hit the Caribbean involved the transformation to sugar. Barbados's rapid conversion to a fully commercial sugar economy
destroyed its forest cover within a generation; the speed was "almost without
parallel in an agricultural area," notes one authority. Sugar cultivation began
in earnest in Barbados in the 1640s, and toward the end of the decade about
40 percent of the island's forests were gone; by the next decade, alarmed island
authorities began to restrict timber cutting; by then, it was too late. By the late
seventeenth century, the island's open landscape reverberated to the sound of
turning windmill sails rather than to birdsong. Today, Barbados has the fewest
breeding seabirds of any territory in the Caribbean. The sugar industry, historical geographer J. H. Galloway observes, "supported the densest concentrations
of rural population in the Americas." Exhausted soils, eroded landforms, and
the spread of many alien plant species, particularly shrub weeds, replaced the
lush, native vegetation. Soil erosion was such that one heavy downpour in 1668
carried hundreds of coffins from a local churchyard out to sea.[166]

The Barbadian model occurred in other places at varying rates. By the mid-
eighteenth century, Cuba had a growing sugar industry, and sugar planters
saw the Royal Forest Reserves as a significant obstacle. Conversely, naval
commanders wanted cedar, often used in ship hulls, banned in the construction of sugar mills. By the late eighteenth century, Cuba still had 80 percent
forest cover, but sugar's voracious demands began to encroach markedly. A late
eighteenth-century *ingenio* could not be built with fewer than 500 to 600 trees;
a mill burned the equivalent of one large tree per hour; and Cuba's sugar plantations collectively felled, according to one estimate, about 360 square kilometers

of woodlands annually as firewood. By the end of the eighteenth century, Cuba's sugar producers were succeeding in overcoming the navy's preservationist concerns. In 1815 a royal edict gave private property owners the right to fell trees with complete impunity. By the early twentieth century, Cuba's forests covered about a sixth of the island.[167]

Sugar plantations were revolutionary enterprises not just because of the demands they placed on resources but because they were famously "factories in the field," proto-industrial enterprises relying on processing equipment and indoor labor to an unparalleled degree in agriculture. Precise timing was paramount in early modern sugar production. Once cut, canes had to be harvested immediately or the juice would deteriorate. During the harvest, sugar mills and boiling houses ran late into the night and sometimes around the clock. Slaves would toil in the field from sunup to sundown and then continue their labors through the night, working in shifts. Although sugar could be planted or harvested at any time of the year, the wet season made the crop difficult to harvest and the onset of the hurricane season always threatened to impede shipping. Until the introduction of a new variety of cane in the 1790s, sugar took over a year to mature so planters had to pay close attention to the sequence of harvesting and planting their fields. Planters also became attentive to standardized, clock-based units of time in their management. They constructed elaborate work logs and reduced people to interchangeable units of production.[168]

Sugar planters inscribed their attitude toward space on island landscapes; they emphasized geometric order, defined precisely plantation boundaries, and demarcated fields by straight lines. One Jamaican overseer directed his slaves in "cutting down trees abt the Negroes houses," to follow the customary practice of building slave housing "in strait lines, constructed with some degree of uniformity and strength, but totally divested of all trees and shrubs." The aim was to permit surveillance of the occupants. Planters had surveyors provide lovingly detailed estate maps, which were always more highly developed in the sugar colonies than in any other part of the New World.[169]

Innovative sugar planters experimented with various methods to reduce the detrimental aspects of growing cane. Their laborers used mill trash (cane tops) as a fuel in order to minimize further deforestation; they manured to restore soil fertility; they planted provisions amid canes to maintain soils; they tested different cane varieties, adopting strains that would reduce the lengthy growing cycle; and they developed the widespread practice of cane holing to minimize erosion. The planters' primary aim was to make profits as well as drive their labor force in ever more "efficient" ways, but an element of conservation (of labor as well as resources) was involved as well. Enlightenment faith in the practical and moral utility of progress encouraged planters to think of their actions as both benevolent and profitable.[170]

Figure 1.10 Plantation and Slave Settlement, St. Lucia. By unknown artist. Ca. 1830.
Notable are the towered church, mansion house, irregularly situated slave houses
with garden plots, and a score or more presumably enslaved persons in motion on the
landscape. Watercolor on paper. *Slavery Images: A Visual Record of the African Slave Trade and
Slave Life in the Early African Diaspora*, accessed August 23, 2021, http://www.slaveryimages.org/s/
slaveryimages/item/1430

For some, the humble plantation hoe, the primary agricultural implement
in the Caribbean, is a symbol of the region's regressive, backward character.
Purportedly, Antillean agriculture—characterized by no more than a handheld
digging stick—had not advanced much since biblical times. In fact, this "specifically Atlantic commodity" was "as alien to Africans as to Europeans." The
plantation hoe's blades had to be strengthened to cope with cane holing, the
most demanding task on a sugar plantation, as field gangs broke the rock-hard,
compacted soil in the dry season. Even though produced in huge numbers, hoes
were bespoke goods. Makers offered a staggering array of hoes—designed for
men or women, adults or children, for specific tasks, with different finishes, for
particular islands or territories, for specific crops, and even for individual plantations. Those Caribbean planters who turned to the plow found that furrowed
land experienced higher moisture loss and was far more vulnerable to soil erosion than land that was hoed. As befits an agricultural tool, the environmental
adaptation of the hoe was crucial to its success.[171]

Slaves almost certainly influenced the evolution of the hoe as part of the everyday labor negotiations in which they were involved. In recent decades, a central assumption in the study of Caribbean slavery has been that enslaved people
were determined to achieve freedom. A heroic resistance paradigm reigned

Figure 1.11 Parham Hill House and Sugar Plantation, Antigua. By Thomas Hearne. 1779. Cane harvesting is taking place, overseen by a man on horseback, and carters are taking the cane to the mill. A cart moving barrels is also depicted, as well as three individuals: perhaps a female market vendor, child, and armed man. Another windmill is located on a distant hill, surrounded by mountains, and the coast is also nearby. Pen and gray ink and water color. British Museum, London.

supreme. Plumbing "the single largest archive of first-person testimony from and about enslaved people in the Americas"—the legal records of early nineteenth-century Berbice, the last frontier of slavery in the British Caribbean—historian Randy Browne argues that the vast majority of enslaved people recognized that escaping slavery was unlikely and were therefore preoccupied with the challenge of survival. They struggled against not only their owners but also their environment and one another. When they negotiated for reduced workloads with managers and drivers, went to court to protest domestic violence, stole food from their neighbors, claimed basic customary rights such as access to provision grounds and the protection of property, or used spiritual powers to treat epidemic disease, their most urgent goal was to stay alive. In some cases their survival strategies tested the limits of the slave system, while in others they reinforced the hierarchies and internal divisions that allowed masters to maintain the upper hand. A central aim of this new slavery scholarship is to avoid the simplistic binary of structure versus agency. The coercive power of the slave system was real, but the institution was not so hegemonic that individuals had no choices or room to maneuver. A sophisticated understanding of the slave system requires sidestepping polarized views of freedom versus slavery or oppression versus resistance.[172]

As much as sugar drove the ecological transformation of the Caribbean, it was far from the only significant crop. Indeed, at the end of the eighteenth century—the peak of the Atlantic slave trade to the region—only about half of the region's slaves worked on sugar estates. In 1790, about 1.6 million slaves lived in the Caribbean; approximately 800,000 worked in industries other than sugar. This was very definitely, as the title of one book has noted, Caribbean slavery without sugar. The range across imperial lines was particularly impressive: in the Spanish Caribbean in 1790, three-quarters of the slaves worked outside the sugar sector; in the French Caribbean in the same year, it was close to two-thirds; in the British Caribbean the majority—about 65 percent—worked on sugar estates. Within the British sector, Jamaica was the major outlier, with only about half its slaves on sugar plantations, while the proportion of sugar slaves on the Leeward Islands and some of the Ceded Islands was a remarkable four out of every five.[173] These variations suggest that at least three factors shaped the extent of monoculture.

The first, most obviously, was the imperial sector itself. The Spanish Caribbean did not develop a fully sugar-based economy until late in the eighteenth century, in part because Spain had its own sugar sector between Malaga and Motril, and controlled the Canary Islands. Cuba was a late bloomer as a sugar economy, as were Puerto Rico and Santo Domingo. Slaves therefore living in the early Spanish Caribbean worked in the most economically diverse ways. Slaves lived on farms and ranches in the Spanish Caribbean. Many were cowboys, spending their days on horseback, herding livestock. Yet others cleared fields, chopped timber, harvested plantains, produced cassava, marketed food, boiled water to extract salt, and paddled canoes to move goods from one place to another. In the early seventeenth century, the main cash crop on Hispaniola was ginger. Hides, tobacco, resins, and timber, along with ginger, were the main exports. Tobacco farms, with fairly small slave populations, were commonplace. The main purpose of agricultural labor was to sustain the local populations and to provide for the fleets. Plantains, fresh beef, dried beef, turtle, salted pork, butter, maize, and other foodstuffs were the key products on early Spanish Caribbean farms.[174]

A second factor affecting the extent of diversification was topography. The larger islands were always much more varied economically than the small islands. The best example is the French colony of Saint-Domingue, occupying the western third of Hispaniola. On the eve of its revolution, there were approximately 8,000 plantations in the colony. Only about 1 in 10 of these units were sugar estates, and they employed only about one-third of the colony's slaves. By far the most numerous economic units were the over 6,000 indigo and coffee plantations. There were another 700 cotton estates, a small number of cacao walks, and perhaps 500 or so independent market gardens. In Saint-Domingue, indigo and coffee together employed more slaves than sugar.[175]

The indigo plantations are particularly notable. In the early eighteenth century, they employed more of the colony's enslaved laborers than any other activity. In 1720 the average workforce on a Saint-Dominguean indigo plantation was only about 14 slaves, while sugar plantations averaged 60 slaves. Considered difficult and fickle to grow, indigo required constant weeding, but, unlike sugar, demanded no night work, much less heavy lifting, and no extensive land preparation. Still, the constant paddling of the liquid indigo in the vats was more onerous than coffee, cacao, and cotton processing. Indigo grew well at high elevations, in remote regions, and given its high unit value, was cheaper than a bulk commodity such as sugar to transport overland. In the eighteenth century, Saint-Domingue supplanted India as Europe's chief supplier of indigo. By the late eighteenth century, the colony's indigo plantations averaged 80 slaves, much fewer than the average of 200 on sugar plantations, but larger than the average of 50 on coffee estates. Indigo estates typically contained more children than sugar plantations, suggesting higher fertility, lower infant mortality, and perhaps different purchasing patterns. Saint-Dominguean sugar planters expressed a preference for Africans from the Bight of Benin; indigo planters had to make do with more Africans from west-central Africa.[176]

Jamaica boasted the second largest slave population in the late eighteenth-century Caribbean. Not as diversified as Saint-Domingue, Jamaica was nevertheless much less fixated on sugar than most of the other British Caribbean islands. In 1768, less than a third of Jamaica's settlements were sugar plantations; 7 out of 10 establishments comprised cattle pens, provisioning farms, cacaao walks, and cotton, indigo, coffee, indigo, and pimento plantations. By the late eighteenth century, the island's major secondary crop was coffee. Its production usually combined daily individual quotas in picking and group work in sorting the beans. The majority of plantations were small, with fewer than 50 enslaved workers. Coffee, like indigo, grew well at higher elevations. Coffee slaves lived more secluded but generally healthier lives than their sugar counterparts, with slave fertility higher and mortality lower.[177]

The third factor was temporal. Early in any Caribbean society's development, there was an initial highly diversified period when capital was scarce and slaves were put to growing a wide range of crops such as cassava, tobacco, or cotton, all crops that could be produced on a small scale. In general, when a society turned to sugar, the early phase of this development was heavily monocultural. Almost everything was sacrificed to producing as much of the lucrative staple as possible. Over time, as the advantage of virgin soils was lost, plantations usually shifted to a wider range of cash crops and other income-generating activities. Caribbean sugar planting has been likened to a relay race with one island successively passing the baton to another. Once an initial boom period was over, sugar planters had to adapt, and further price fluctuations tended to provide impetus to increased diversification. Some planters turned to further processing of the staple crop. Over time, for example, Barbadian sugar planters changed from exporting raw muscovado sugar (a brown sugar with a strong molasses flavor) to a whiter, more refined, clayed sugar. Slave work routines changed accordingly. Another strategy was to allocate more slaves to provisioning over time. Wars, with their accompanying disruptions in the supply of salted fish and foodstuffs, spurred this shift to greater self-provisioning over time. Yet another strategy was to add complementary crops to the primary staple or to branch out into other crops entirely. The most obvious development was the rise of coffee, but Sea Island cotton boomed, too, for a time in the late eighteenth-century Caribbean. Finally, slaves could be put to fishing, timber cutting, raising livestock, supplying provisions, or engaging in skilled work as ways of generating more income. Dedicated livestock pens emerged. By the mid-eighteenth century, open-range cattle ranching—along with pens and watering holes—managed by enslaved herders, was well established on Barbuda. The incorporation of new grasses—Guinea or Scotch grass—improved pasture for livestock. More cattle helped with replenishing the soils of sugar estates. Some planters also turned to the plow and greater use of animal power in transportation. So diversification generally happened early, as well as late, in a Caribbean society's development.[178]

The short-lived cotton boom in the second half of the eighteenth century was rooted in increased demand from the European textile industry, particularly England's (or more especially Lancashire's) rapidly growing spinning mills. Between 1750 and 1800 West Indian cotton plantations supplied two-thirds of that industry's raw material, growing a variety of strains. Local factors were also at play. On the Danish island of St. Croix, cotton plantations came to occupy the drier eastern end of the island, enjoying a period of prosperity from roughly 1740 to 1770, and providing fairly healthy working conditions for the sector's slaves. In Barbados, cotton production was greatest after the devastating hurricane of 1780. The loss of major sugar works encouraged planters to turn to cotton, because the crop matured faster, yielded quicker returns, and was less labor intensive; but it was difficult to juggle the labor demands of each crop if the two were grown on the same plantation. Still, the combination of sugar and cotton particularly suited a creolized labor force, such as that of Barbados, with more young and old slaves (who could be assigned to cotton) than a predominantly adult African labor force (who could be delegated to sugar). Other parts of the Caribbean less suited to sugar, such as the Bahamas, turned almost entirely to cotton in the 1780s. From 1785 to 1790, Bahamian cotton production rose from 124 to 442 tons and cotton acreage from about 2,500 to 12,000 acres. Bahamian Loyalist Joseph Eve's invention of a wind-powered version of the mechanical cotton gin aided productivity; and production peaked in 1810 at over 600 tons of cotton. By the last quarter of the eighteenth century, on Carriacou, in the Grenadines, almost all the approximately 50 farms grew cotton. In the 1790s this small island, only 8,000 acres in size, accounted for about a seventh of total British West Indian production. Cotton farming on Carriacou involved some large-scale planters: the median number of slaves per cotton farm in 1790 was 47, and the top quartile of planters owned 60 percent of the island's slaves, each of them possessing an average of 164 slaves. But Eli Whitney's cotton gin and the expansion of cotton into the US southwestern interior, as well as competition from other parts of the globe, ended large-scale cotton farming in the Caribbean."[179]

By the late eighteenth century, even on dedicated sugar plantations, then, slaves spent less and less time on the major staple. The best evidence comes from Barbados. In the 1790s, some Barbadian sugar slaves devoted only one-third of their time to sugar, dividing the rest between cotton and provisions. On Barbados, the supply of provisions came via estate labor, but on larger islands, the dominant practice was to reserve provisions grounds, often in hilly interiors, for the enslaved so that they could produce their own food on their own time. The average size of the allotment per slave also rose over the course of the eighteenth century. Reflecting the slaves' African background, the provision grounds tended to be irregular rather than angular.[180]

The Haitian Revolution of 1791–1804 changed everything. It was the slaveholders' worst nightmare, a stark reminder of the dangers of slave resistance. The void left by the demise of Saint-Domingue's powerhouse economy prompted a huge boom in plantation agriculture elsewhere, leading to what historians now term "the second slavery." France re-established and reinvested in slavery in 1802. The first nation to abolish slavery in its Atlantic empire in 1793–94, France was unique in subsequently re-enslaving most of its black citizens. Thus the Haitian Revolution was not the beginning of the end of slavery in the French empire, but the beginning of a renewal and expansion of enslaved labor in France's remaining tropical colonies. A new generation of elite slaveholders in the Caribbean broadly adapted European industrial technologies, particularly the steam engine, to the processing and transportation of agricultural commodities. In the 1830s Cuban planters built the first railroad network in the circum-Caribbean region. They ensured that the apparatus of the state protected their interests; they consolidated their authority by driving out small landowners so as to capture markets no longer supplied by the slaves of Saint-Domingue. With the help of experts immersed in the Industrial Revolution, they engaged in chemical experiments to discover a whiter sugar. They reinvented the technologies of slavery, pursuing ever more regimented systems of plantation labor and ever more sophisticated accounting techniques. Rather than declining in the early nineteenth century, slavery found a new lease of life.[181]

To borrow a term from a historian of Bermuda, there was a Caribbean commons that also deserves recognition. It was a zone, a set of maritime and terrestrial spaces, where resources were generally available, could be exploited by many, and generated considerable wealth. Slaves engaged in a wide range of activities in the Caribbean commons. They extracted pearls, raked salt, fished, pursued whales, turtles, and manatees, salvaged shipwrecks, and engaged in privateering. Salt compounds existed in many places, particularly parts of the Venezuelan coast, Bonaire, and the Turks and Caicos Islands. Turtling was another activity that occupied many slaves, who used nets and harpoons at sea, and the simple method of flipping the animals onto their backs on land as means of capturing them. The hunting grounds were bars, banks, and cays throughout the region, linking places such as the Cayman Islands, Miskito Cays (Nicaragua), Tortuguero (Costa Rica), and San Andrés and Providencia Islands (Colombia). Some slaves even specialized in diving for sponges. A forest commons also existed in the Caribbean. Slaves extracted a whole range of tropical woods, resins, and dyes. Braziletto, fustic, and lignum vitae were common attractions, and timber camps, employing slaves, formed on many parts of the Caribbean rimland. Finding stands of mahogany required a huntsman, considered an highly skilled individual. Gangs of 10 to 12 men, usually divided into pairs, swinging heavy axes on a springy platform about 12 feet above the ground, engaged in the extremely dangerous work of felling huge mahogany trees. They were accompanied by less skilled enslaved men who trimmed the trees and squared the trunks, and cattlemen who trucked the trunks to various shipping points. Bermudian slaves, who regularly resorted to the Caribbean commons, seem to have earned for their masters as much money from salt raking, tropical wood harvesting, and wrecking as they did from the more conventional shipping and shipbuilding sectors of that island's economy.[182]

Diversification mattered. For one thing, it helps explains much about the varied demographic performance of the region's slaves (see Table 1.2). A number of features stand out. From 1715 to 1750, in particular, the slave population of the Spanish Caribbean grew spectacularly fast—at a natural rate of about 3 percent per annum. Since early Cuban, Hispaniolan, and Puerto Rican slaves were largely engaged in mixed farming, this rate of natural increase, one of the highest recorded in the world at the time, should not be so surprising. By the second half of the eighteenth century, as sugar took off, especially in Cuba, so the rate of natural increase of the Spanish Caribbean's slave population dropped significantly, although it was still almost 1 percent a year—well above the global average for

Table 1.2 **Growth of Caribbean Slave Populations (in 000s), 1715–90**

	Beginning Population	*Ending Population*	*Net In-Migration*	*Annual Rate of Natural Increase/Decrease*
1715–50				
British	167	279	367	−3.4%
French	85	325	270	−0.5%
Spanish	30	121	23	+3.0%
Dutch	34	74	84	−2.4%
Danish	4	13	7	+0.6%
Subtotal	320	812	751	−1.5%
1750–90				
British	279	473	804	−4.2%
French	325	693	603	−1.2%
Spanish	121	270	110	+0.5%
Dutch	74	128	133	−2.0%
Danish	13	30	32	−1.7%
Subtotal	812	1,594	1,682	−2.0%

Source: Adapted from David Eltis and Paul Lachance, "The Demographic Decline of Caribbean Slave Populations: New Evidence from the Transatlantic and Intra-American Slave Trades," in David Eltis and David Richardson, eds., *Extending the Frontiers: Essays on the New Transatlantic Slave Trade Database* (New Haven, CT: Yale University Press, 2008), 335–63. Updated with latest in-migration figures, supplied by David Eltis, to whom I am greatly indebted for his generosity.

the time. The British slave population experienced the steepest rate of natural decrease—minus 3 percent per annum in the first half of the eighteenth century, rising to minus 4 percent per annum in the second half of the century. The concentration on sugar and a surging African slave trade account for this poor performance. The experience of the French Caribbean slave population sat between these two extremes. Its rate of natural decrease was about a third less than its British counterpart. The difference is mainly attributable to the highly diversified nature of the French Caribbean economy. As an illustration, by 1790 Saint-Domingue had imported about as many Africans as Jamaica, yet its slave population was twice as large. The main difference is the degree to which the French colony grew coffee and cotton, its main growth sectors after 1750, both of which were considerably less demanding on their workforces than sugar. In short, Caribbean rural slavery was far from all about sugar, even if it was the main

driver of the overall economy; and the extent of diversification explains much
about the varied demographic performance of the region's slaves.[183]

An important aspect of Caribbean diversification was the introduction of
African food plants and animals into the region. In the drought-prone areas of
the Caribbean, for example, the enslaved grew varieties of millet and sorghum,
often referred to as guinea corn, which survived better than European cereals.
Similarly, they cultivated African tubers, such as yams, plantains, and taro, in
their provision grounds and subsistence plots because they withstood hurricane
damage better than most crops, required little attention, were high yielding, and
were readily prepared as food. In their gardens they valued the banana plant for
the shade it provided as well as for its fruit. The enslaved "Africanized" the food
systems of Caribbean plantation societies by tending ground nuts, okra, pigeon
peas, watermelon, sesame, and many other African cultigens. They raised guinea
fowl and African woolless sheep for their meat. Africans also recognized many
New World plants by their likeness to the tropical flora of their homelands and
they gave them African names. In 1756 the naturalist Daniel Rolander observed
how Surinamese "black slaves are the only ones that avidly follow the examples
of the Indians in this land. . . . They have greatly benefited from eating the
capsules and mature seeds of Amomum. When the white residents saw that the
consumption of this plant was beneficial to the Blacks and Indians, they finally
thought it would be worthwhile to try it as well." Now known as "masusa," this
plant's name derives from Kikongo. Unlike Europeans who remained fearful of
malarial mangroves (the name is another African loanword—in this case from
Wolof), Africans gravitated to them as familiar and productive environments,
supplying firewood, fish, and shellfish.[184]

The Caribbean was not just much more diversified than the conventional
picture allows; it was also more urbanized. From the beginning, the Spanish
established a series of secondary and small port towns, as well as major administrative centers, on the islands and surrounding rimland. Changing sites was
typical. There was an experimental, fluid character to the early port towns, given
their vulnerability to internal and external attack and the environmental hazards
they faced (disease, hurricanes, fires, mosquito infestations, and depredations of
insects). Known as the "tomb of the Spaniards," Veracruz shifted location three
times in the sixteenth century. However unstable, poorly defended, and inad-
equately supplied, these towns were the gateway, the key to the Indies. Most
Spanish Caribbean towns followed the grid-iron design of southern Spanish
cities, built checkerboard fashion around a central plaza. Dutch and even British
empires followed suit to a degree, but what was true for the French Caribbean,
namely the small size of its towns but the huge scale of their commerce, was a
fairly general phenomenon.[185]

In most parts of the eighteenth-century Caribbean, towns comprised at least 10 percent, often more, of the population. There was a distinct urban hierarchy (see Table 1.3). The largest city in the region was Havana, Cuba, the third most populous city in the Americas (behind Lima and Mexico City), and which at the end of the eighteenth century stood at about 50,000 people, larger than Philadelphia. At a bit more than half Havana's size, Kingston, Jamaica, was a second ranked urban place, as was Saint Pierre, Martinique, with populations of 27,000 and 20,000 respectively. In a third tier were a number of towns, ranging from 10,000 to 15,000 people each, such as Cap Français in Saint-Domingue; Cartegena on the mainland; Bridgetown, Barbados, the most important town in the early British Caribbean, until superseded by Kingston; Willemstad, Curaçao; and Paramaribo, Surinam. By the late eighteenth century, the proportion of slaves who lived in urban places ranged from about 1 in 20 on French Saint-Domingue to almost 1 in 2 on small non-plantation islands such as Danish St. Thomas or Dutch St. Eustatius. In between these extremes, about 1 in 10 slaves lived in towns on most British islands, and 1 in 5 in most Spanish and Dutch territories. In the eighteenth century, the Caribbean was far more urbanized than North America. In 1790 about 250,000 enslaved individuals, or about 1 in 6 of all Caribbean slaves, lived in urban places.

Why some towns developed more than others owed much to natural resources and geopolitics. Founded in 1519 on the northwest coast of Cuba (after originally being established as San Cristobal on the southern coast), Havana commanded the exit from the Caribbean Sea. Situated at the entrance to the Straits of Florida and the Bahamas Channels, it provided access to the Gulf Stream, the fastest route back to Europe. It became the way station for Spain's treasure fleets. In addition, the magnificent harbor of Carenas, as Havana's deepwater bay was initially known, easily accommodated hundreds of ships that could readily be defended. Still, Havana's progress to becoming the richest and largest city in the Caribbean was not inevitable. In 1555 a French corsair sacked the town. As late as the 1570s, Bayamo, an inland southern town, outranked Havana. Benefiting from its location in the fertile valley of the Cauto River, Bayamo had easy access to the sea and was a naturally defended site that proved ideal for contraband trade. "In contrast to other port cities that grew to serve the commercial need of a vibrant agricultural or mining hinterland," historian Alejandro de la Fuentes notes, "in Havana it was the port that made the hinterland." In the late eighteenth century, Jamaican towns assumed new municipal powers to "police" the threats from restive slaves and disorderly poor whites, whether through nightly watches, liquor licensing, market regulation, fire prevention, slave curfews, traffic control, street maintenance, or even a 1794 act empowering the town of Montego Bay to drain a local swamp so as to remove "the evil effects from noxious vapour."[186]

Table 1.3 **Circum-Caribbean Cities and Towns, ca. 1790**

Town, Colony, or Region	Total Population	% Slaves	% Free	% Whites	% Society	Tier
Havana, Cuba	51,000	34	19	47	19	First
Caracas, Venezuela	28,000	22	49#	29		Second
Kingston, Jamaica	27,000	62	12	26	9	
Coro, Venezuela	26,000	11	75#	14		
Santiago de Cuba, Cuba	21,000	29	31	40	8	
Saint-Pierre, Martinique	20,000					
Vera Cruz, New Spain	16,000*					Third
Cartagena de Indias, New Granada	16,000	19	50#	31	12	
Cap Français, Saint Domingue	15,000	66	10	24	3	
Bridgetown, Barbados	14,000					
Merida, Yucatan	14,000	28	50#	22		
Willemstad, Curaçao	12,000	47	23	30	55	
Paramaribo, Suriname	12,000					
Santo Domingo, Santo Domingo	11,000					
San German, Puerto Rico	11,000	20	45#	34	10	
Maracaibo, Venezuela	10,000*					
Campeche, Yucatan	9,000	44	33	23		Fourth
Port-au-Prince, Saint-Domingue	6,000	65	6	29	1	
San Juan, Puerto Rico	6,000	18	48	35	6	
Matanzas, Cuba	6,000	31	14	55	2	
Christiansted, Saint Croix	5,000	62	16	22	21	
Les Cayes, Saint-Domingue	4,600	66	7	27	1	
Point-à-Pitre, Guadeloupe	4,500	59	14	27	4	
Basse-Terre, Guadeloupe	4,500	56	12	32	4	

Table 1.3 **Continued**

Town, Colony, or Region	Total Population	% Slaves	% Free	% Whites	% Society	Tier
Santa Marta, New Granada	4,000*	15	69#	14	9	
Oranjestad, St. Eustatius	3,000*					Fifth
Roseau, Dominica	3,000*	61	8	31	13	
Spanish Town, Jamaica	2,500*	65	15	20	13	
Stabroek (Georgetown), Demerera	2,500	68	13	19	6	
Charlotte Amalia, St. Thomas	2,200	70	12	18	39	
Kingstown, St. Vincent	2,000*					
Port of Spain, Trinidad	2,000*					
Saint Marc, Saint-Domingue	1,500	65	12	23		
Rio Hacha, New Granada	1,500	11	80#	9		
Fredricksted, St. Croix	1,100	56	15	28	4	

Note: All numbers are rounded. Asterisk reflects an especially flimsy estimate. % free refers to the percentage of the town comprised of free coloreds. # contains fairly high proportion of Indians.

Sources: Havana, Santiago de Cuba, and Matanzas: Ramon de la Sagra, *Historia de la Isla de Cuba economico-politica y estadistica* (Havana: Imprenta de las viudas de Arazoza y Soler, 1831), 4 (courtesy of Elena Andrea Schneider). Caracas: John Lombardi, *People and Places in Colonial Venezuela* (Bloomington: Indiana University Press, 1976), 62, 133; and P. Michael McKinley, *Pre-Revolutionary Caracas: Politics, Economy, and Society, 1777–1811* (Cambridge: Cambridge University Press, 1985), 10, 23 (courtesy of Jesse Cromwell). Kingston, Jamaica: Trevor Burnard, "A Crucible of Modernity: Kingston, Jamaica and its Black Inhabitants, 1745–1780," in *The Black Urban Atlantic in the Age of the Slave Trade*, ed. Jorge Cañizares-Esguerra, Matt D. Childs, and James Sidbury (Philadelphia: University of Pennsylvania Press, 2013), 122–44. Coro and Willemstad: Rupert, *Creolization and Contraband*, 134 and 195; and see also Wim Klooster, *Illicit Riches: Dutch Trade in the Caribbean, 1648–1795* (Leiden: KITLV Press, 1998), 61. Saint-Pierre, Basse-Terre, and Point-à-Pitre: Anne Pérotin-Dumon, *La ville aux îles, la ville dans l'île: Basse-Terre et Pointe-à-Pitre, Guadeloupe, 1650–1820* (Paris: Karthala, 2000), 78, 292, 329–31. Campeche: Adriana Delfina Rocher Salas, "Religiosidad e identidad en San Francisco de Campeche. Siglos XVI y XVII," *Anuario de Estudios Americanos*, 63 (2006), 27–47, 44 n. 39. Cap Français, Port-au-Prince, Les Cayes, and Saint Marc: David Geggus, "The Slaves and Free People of Color of Cap Français," in Cañizares-Esguerra, Childs, and Sidbury, *Black Urban Atlantic*, 101–21; Geggus, "Urban Development in Eighteenth Century Saint Domingue," *Bulletin du Centre d'Histoire des Espaces Atlantiques*, 5 (1990), 197–228; and Geggus, "The Major Port Towns of Saint Domingue in the Later Eighteenth Century," in *Atlantic Port Cities: Economy, Culture, and Society in the Atlantic World, 1650–1850*, ed. Franklin W. Knight and Peggy K. Liss (Baltimore: Johns Hopkins University Press, 1991), 87–116. Cartagena de Indias, Santa Marta, and Rio Hacha: Anthony McFarlane, *Colombia before Independence: Economy, Society, and Politics under Bourbon Rule* (Cambridge: Cambridge University

(continued)

Table 1.3 **Continued**

Press, 1993), 353–55; Aline Helg, *Liberty and Equality in Caribbean Colombia, 1770–1835* (Chapel Hill: University of North Carolina Press, 2004), 80–88; and Ernesto Bassi Arévalo, "Race, Class, and Political Allegiances in the Provinces of Cartagena and Santa Marta (Colombia) during the Independence Wars" (MA thesis, Institute of Latin American Studies, University of London, 2004), appendix B (courtesy of Ernesto Bassi). Bridgetown: Pedro L. V. Welch, *Slave Society in the City: Bridgetown, Barbados, 1680–1834* (Kingston, Jamaica: Ian Randle; Oxford: James Currey, 2003), 53. Paramaribo: Cornelis Ch. Goslinga, *The Dutch in the Caribbean and in the Guianas 1680–1791* (Assen, Maastricht, Netherlands: Van Gorcum, 1985), 519. Santo Domingo: María Rosario Sevilla Soler, *Santo Domingo tierra de frontera (1750–1800)* (Sevilla: Escuela de Estudios Hispano-Americanos, 1980), 35. San German and San Juan: "Estado general que comprehende el numero de vecinos y habitantes que existen en Ysla de S, Juan de Puerto Rico, con inclusion de los parvulos de ambos sexos y distincion de clases, estados y casta por fin del ano de 1790," figures kindly supplied by David Stark; see also Bibiano Torres Ramírez, *La isla de Puerto Rico (1765–1800)* (San Juan, Puerto Rico: Instituto de Cultura Puertorriqueña, 1968), 16. Maracaibo: Manuel Lucena Giraldo, *A los cuatro vientes: Las ciudades de la América hispánica* (Madrid: Fundación Carolina Centro de Estudios Hispánicos e Iberoamericanos, Marcial Pons Historia, 2006), 141–42. Christiansted, Charlotte Amalia, and Fredericksted: Neville A. T. Hall, *Slave Society in the Danish West Indies: St. Thomas, St. John, and St. Croix* (Mona, Jamaica: University of the West Indies Press, 1992), 5, 87–88. Oranjestad: Richard Grant Gilmore, "Urban Transformation and Upheaval in the West Indies: The Case of Oranjestad, St. Eustatius, Netherlands Antilles," in *Cities in the World 1500–2000,* ed. Adrian Green and Roger Leech (London: Maney, 2006), 83–96. Roseau: information supplied by Nick Radburn. Spanish Town: James Robertson, *Gone Is the Ancient Glory: Spanish Town, Jamaica, 1534–2000* (Kingston, Jamaica: Ian Randle, 2005), 91. Georgetown, Demerera: The National Archives (hereafter TNA), C.O. 111/3, "General State of the Colony of Demerera," 1798, information kindly supplied by Katherine Smoak; TNA, C.O. 260/11, "Return of the White Inhabitants and Slaves with Sugar Estates in the Government of St. Vincent," 1791, information and subsequent extrapolations generously offered by Simon D. Smith. Port of Spain, Trinidad: Kit Candlin, *The Last Caribbean Frontier, 1795–1815* (Basingstoke, UK: Macmillan, 2012), 52.

As in Cuba, the larger Antillean colonies boasted a number of port towns, even if one dominated. Thus, in the late eighteenth century, Saint-Domingue had 13 port towns, of which Cap Français was the largest and most important. Founded in the late seventeenth century, Cap Français—or Le Cap, as it was known—gained a reputation as the "Paris of the Antilles," with its tree-lined squares, mostly stone dwellings, barracks, hospital, cafes, billiard halls, and a theater that seated 1,500 people, the largest in the Caribbean. Situated on the edge of the northern plain, it was a point of transshipment and a market for the richest agricultural hinterland, not just in the colony but in the Western Hemisphere. Nevertheless, so diverse and fragmented was the colony that Le Cap handled only about a third of the colony's export trade and had less than a half of the urban population. A key reason that Port-au-Prince, despite being the colonial capital, never approached Le Cap's rank was its late development—founded in 1749—and its susceptibility to disasters. Earthquakes in 1751 and 1770 leveled the city, and a fire in 1784 destroyed its commercial section. In the early nineteenth century, Jamaica had even more—16—port towns than Saint-Domingue.

Figure 1.12 The Piazza at Havana. By Dominic Serres. Ca. 1765–70. The largest city in the Caribbean, Havana boasted an imposing central plaza. Here it is shown under occupation, with British sailors in the foreground and a platoon of soldiers in red jackets drilling in the distance. It is one of a series of 11 paintings of military engagements and scenes of the city by Serres, a sailor, who seemingly spent time in Havana as a prisoner of war. Oil on canvas. National Maritime Museum, Greenwich, London.

Kingston dominated the southern coast of Jamaica; most of the outports were located on the northern coast of the island. From its founding in 1692 until the abolition of the slave trade in 1807, Kingston imported about a million Africans, making it the leading slave port in the Caribbean.[187]

Small islands generally hosted a single port town—or at least one major entrepôt. Thus Willemstad arose on Curacao's southern coast as an excellent base for trading with and raiding the Spanish Main, just 70 miles away. A regional transshipment center and the only urban settlement, it drove the entire island economy. In peak years, over a thousand vessels called at Willemstad harbor. By the end of the eighteenth century, Willemstad had become one of the largest and most cosmopolitan ports in the Caribbean. Located in the midst of English and French islands in the Leeward Island chain, Oranjestad in St. Eustatius was Willemstad's northern counterpart. Oranjestad was not a natural harbor, so lading had to be done offshore with canoes and launches. This drawback did not seem to matter much, for by the 1740s more than 1,200 vessels called there, growing to over 2,000 vessels annually by the early 1770s, and reaching its apogee of 3,500 in 1779. It was the busiest port in the Caribbean and earned the nickname the "Golden Rock." St. Thomas possessed one of the best natural harbors in the Caribbean, with a large protected bay that gave rise to the town of Charlotte Amalie, a major center of shipping and trade. When Admiral George Rodney sacked Oranjestad in 1781, Charlotte Amalie quickly replaced it as the Caribbean's premier neutral entrepôt. Still Oranjestad rebounded. In 1787 more than 2,700 ships dropped anchor and over 2,800 departed. Ships hailed from almost 100 different ports. Oranjestad, Charlotte Amalie, and later Gustavia, St. Barthélemy, in the northern Caribbean and Willemstad in the southern were the Caribbean's primary emporia or, in traveler Janet Schaw's words, places "of vast traffick from every quarter of the globe."[188]

The connections between ports and across empires—interaction zones—deserve explication. Envisioning Caribbean history from the northern shores of New Granada, from such ports as Portobelo, Cartagena, Santa Marta, and Riohacha during the age of revolutions, uncovers dense and thick connections to Jamaica, Hispaniola, Curaçao, Saint Thomas, and the United States—a transimperial Greater Caribbean, in other words. These were the key nodal points linking people who operated in interstitial spaces. A 1786 map drawn by New Granada's head of the coast guard inverts the usual northward orientation of cartographic representation to focus on South America's coast as if seen from Jamaica and Hispaniola, thereby confirming the existence of a transimperial space. Frequently crisscrossing political borders in Caribbean and Atlantic waters, sailors gathered and spread information obtained at ports and on the high seas. This was a world of dynamic movement, porous borders, and vibrant networks of mariners, indigenous (Cuna and Wayuu) traders, and itinerant merchants. These Caribbean peoples inhabited a space that, in historian Ernesto Bassi's words, "was not exclusively Spanish, British, or French but simultaneously Spanish, British, French, as well as Dutch, Danish, Anglo-American, African . . . and indigenous." Bullion, cotton, cattle, hides, timber, dyewood, and tortoiseshell went out, and in return came dry goods, flour, liquors, iron, earthenware, and slaves. Of particular interest are the cosmopolitan Wayuu and Cuna natives, who deployed seaborne mobility and multilingualism to maintain a measure of autonomy.[189]

The Caribbean urban landscape also encompassed a place such as Jodensavanne, which the governor of Suriname in 1748 described as "the only town in the whole world where only Jews live." Founded in 1685 and situated 30 miles south of Paramaribo on the upper reaches of the Suriname River, it was often depicted as an idyllic, healthy haven, a place of Edenic abundance. It was home to the most privileged Jewish community in the Americas, where Jews enjoyed religious liberty, administered their own tribunal, and conjured utopian thoughts of a New World Zion, a revived Jerusalem. In reality, however, Jodensavanne was also sparsely populated, its soils infertile, a hamlet rather than a town, the poor outnumbering the rich, enslaved Africans forming a majority of its residents, more a holiday resort than a place of residential stability, and an embattled military outpost.[190]

Garrisons were a prominent feature of the Caribbean built environment. The fabled Morro fortress, constructed in large part by enslaved labor (as was true for most Caribbean forts) and located on a promontory that stood at the entrance to Havana's harbor, was said to be impregnable. By the mid-eighteenth century, part of a network of three forts and string of signal towers, it defended the largest and most strategic naval base in the Americas. Typical of a Lesser Antillean fort was Cabrits, situated on a naturally defensible headland on northwestern Dominica. Located on an inner hill measuring about 500 feet above sea level and surrounded by an outer hill rising to about 630 feet above the sea, the site was the result of volcanic activity. Brimstone Hill, about 700 feet in height, was another fortification situated on a volcanic extrusion located along the northwest coast of an island—in this case, St. Kitts in the Leeward chain. Between 1790 and 1815, from 50 to 200 enslaved Africans lived and worked there. As an indication that all was not military labor, some of the slaves made Afro-Caribbean pottery, fashioned with clay from the island's southeast peninsula. Tiny Nevis boasted 12 forts in the early eighteenth century, although none were too imposing. Still, engineers produced some of the most detailed plans of any Caribbean space in the early modern period when they represented military installations, whether bastioned traces, ramparts, gun platforms, batteries, round towers, signal stations, dockyards, arsenals, powder magazines, hospitals, and barracks. The most haunting fortress in the Caribbean was the massive La Citadelle Laferrière built in the northern mountains of Haiti at the instigation of Henri Christophe. Constructed over many years in the early nineteenth century, it was a place of retreat in case of invasion, a symbol of the new nation's fortitude, and a brutal folly, built by forced labor at a terrible price in human lives.[191]

Many Caribbean domestic houses exhibited a dual aspect, at once concerned about military defense, but also exuding openness and hospitality. Often erected on fortified masonry foundations, with corner towers and loopholes or portholes for musketry, these castellated houses were strongholds, asserting dominance over a contested landscape, reflecting fear of Maroons, foreign invaders, and rebellious slaves. At the same time, domestic dwellings tended to be low to the ground, committed to single-story living, dominated by a central hall, flanked by smaller chambers, and above all surrounded by airy piazzas, galleries, and porticoes, in which low compass-backed Windsor chairs, Campeche chairs, and hammocks were available. The emphasis was on fluidity, circulation, and receptivity, although single-story living, low-hipped roofs, and broad, raised masonry foundations were a response to hurricanes and earthquakes.[192]

Europeans not only reshaped landscapes, but also seascapes. The novelty and abundance of the tropical marine environment captivated Europeans. They expressed astonishment—whether it was oysters growing on mangrove trees, the brilliant hues of many fish, the flying fish, the slow-moving sea cow or manatee that could be mistaken for a mermaid, or the sheer number and variety of turtles. But once they had overcome their awe, they soon made a growing impact on marine resources, outdoing the depredations of Native Americans.[193]

The earliest and most dramatic inroad occurred in the early sixteenth century when Spaniards devastated pearl beds near Cubagua (an arid island, about 10 miles from the Venezuelan mainland). Between ca. 1510 and 1540, they harvested approximately 40 million oysters a year (only about 1 in 10 oysters produced a pearl), for a total of well over 1 billion oysters. The hunt for pearls took a huge toll on the environment. For one thing, the dominant pearl-producing mollusk of the western Atlantic will produce a pearl only after four years and its life span is just five years. For another, oysters feed by "particle suspension," and all the water disturbance created by many canoes and divers diluted the food particles they eat, making it harder for them to reproduce. Finally, oysters filter the water, so removing them in such large numbers degraded water quality. Both the Spanish Crown and local inhabitants were aware of the danger of overharvesting and of the need to protect a precious resource, but then again there was the allure of glittering profits. Thus the Spanish Crown licensed various mechanical devices—from dredges to diving bells—that, if they had worked, would have increased pearl harvests. The locals largely resisted such novelties, arguing for the expertise of humans and the value of vernacular knowledge—to distinguish between mature and young oysters, for example, or to limit dredges to depths beyond which human divers could not go. Such knowledge extended to the Taíno term *xaguey*, which referred to the underwater depressions where good pearl-bearing oysters were found.

The Spanish Crown took its stewardship role seriously, even if sustainability was not achieved. In the early 1530s it prohibited pearl diving outside of the months of February through April to protect breeding oysters. The Crown also banned big boats able to carry six or more divers; declared a maximum four-hour workday; and limited diving depths to 5 fathoms or 30 feet. Despite the imposed constraints, overharvesting and a tropical storm almost ended pearl fishing on Cubagua at mid-century. Although there was a partial recovery in the 1570s and 1580s and further growth at the neighboring islands of Margarita and Coche, pearl fishing moved westward along the Venezuelan coast to Colombia and Panama. There the delicate balance between exploitation and cultivation would be repeated all over again—and with no better results.[194]

Another approach to the long sixteenth century is to take the notion of the commons seriously and search for the ways people of American, African, and

European heritage divided and distributed the means of subsistence, profit, and power. Popular struggles over shared resources and collective property need to be connected to processes of dispossession, accumulation, slaving, and marronage. The negotiations and arrangements that occurred over communal resources—whether fisheries, forests, or grazing grounds—illuminate empire making in the early Atlantic. How Iberian mariners organized harvests of fish from Caribbean waters can be linked to how Maroons capitalized on feral livestock roaming the forested pathways of the Greater Antilles. Focusing on the early period of sea-borne ventures, when all was in flux, reveals the tentative nature of actions and claims. The early Atlantic was a scene of self-invention by all kinds of people who found themselves in novel circumstances in which opportunities beckoned and dangers loomed. All of the institutional constructs within which later generations worked, or against which they rebelled, grew out of these early provisional arrangements. The usual account of early Iberian colonies is that they were the products of systems of rule and of law adapted from the Reconquest. Highlighting the resources of the Atlantic and Caribbean commons is to emphasize how it attracted uneven and episodic forms of exploitation, and to show how these practices gave rise to imperial institutions—not the other way around. This approach blends environmental history and socio-legal analysis, revealing how imperial agents creatively combined legal repertoires and customary practices to commercialize and privatize commonly held resources.[195]

Once the shift to sugar happened, European fishing in the Caribbean aimed largely at local markets. Many a plantation employed an enslaved fisherman, but his catch was to supply his master's family, not the larger enslaved population. Still, a growing commodification of marine animals increasingly targeted regional and international markets. Thus over time Europeans intensively hunted monk seals primarily for oil (used to grease machinery on sugar plantations), turtles for shell and meat, whales for their oil and other products, and seabirds for their plumes and eggs. Europeans sought monk seal skins to make trunk coverings, caps, belts, straps, and bags, even a girdle designed to relieve lower back pain; sailors prized its fur for weather forecasting, claiming that its hairs became erect as rough seas threatened, but remained flat when calm seas prevailed. As early as the late seventeenth century, Hans Sloane described the manatee population around Jamaica as "destroyed"—he also noted that "Manati straps," whips made from their hides, had been banned for being too "cruel"—and William Dampier said the same was true of green turtles. The disappearance of these "keystone species" had deleterious effects on grass beds, reefs, and the food chain. By the early eighteenth century, local legislatures began passing laws to regulate, for example, net mesh size, indicating concern about overfishing.[196]

No steady baseline marine system has ever existed. A sea is an extraordinarily changeable environment; fluctuations are normal. Yet each generation tends to imagine that its first experience of a marine environment is the norm, making it difficult to determine the numbers of any species at any particular time. Furthermore, human impacts on any marine system must also be assessed against constantly occurring natural change, even though natural fluctuations are hard to measure, particularly when they are underwater.[197] Two examples—how to estimate the numbers of turtles and monk seals and the scale of European impact—will suffice to make the point.

The green (*Chelonia mydas*) and hawksbill (*Eretmochelys imbricate*) turtles are iconic Caribbean marine animals. One estimate of the pre-Columbian number of green turtles, based on extrapolations of early hunting estimates, ranges from 33 million to 39 million; another calculates the population at 91 million adults; and a third, based on the carrying capacity of seagrass beds, is a startling 661 million. If these numbers seem exaggerated, recall that early Europeans spoke of seas being "thick" with turtles and ships "bathing in them." For hawksbills, the pre-Columbian estimates are from half a million to 11 million. The present-day numbers for green and hawksbill turtles in the Caribbean are 300,000 and 30,000, respectively. The scale of the loss is staggering. One foundation for these estimates is the number of historic nesting beaches: 59 for green turtles, 9 of which were major; 55 for hawksbills, 7 of which were major. Early nautical charts noted particularly dense concentrations of them. The green turtle rookery on the Cayman Islands was, by all accounts, astounding in its scope. One seventeenth-century estimate was that as many as 50 nesting females could be taken in less than three hours. In the seventeenth century, according to one modern estimate, the Cayman Island rookery hosted approximately 6.5 million adults. Another basis is the size of major nesting sites in the twentieth century, giving some indication of what was possible in the past. A site of green turtles on the Costa Rican Caribbean littoral and of hawksbill turtles on the Panamanian Caribbean coast supported 130,000 and 135,000 adults, respectively.[198]

By 1800 turtles had grown scarce in many parts of the Caribbean. Green turtles provided 200–300 pounds of lean, high-protein meat, as well as their calipee fat, which came increasingly to be seen as a delicacy. They were an ideal cargo for transatlantic or inter-American ships, occupying little space, requiring minimal maintenance, and living many months in captivity. Hawksbill turtles took up even less room, because they were killed for the 5–10 pounds of high-quality motley-colored shell they yielded, which was then converted into jewelry, combs, and brushes by European artisans. Turtles were most easily caught on land when nesting; but they were also captured in nets and kept alive in corrals, or harpooned so that their meat could be salted. Cayman "turtle rangers" imitated the Native American method of nighttime hunting from boats, using torches to attract and harpoon turtles. The removal of these two species changed reef ecologies in fundamental ways. Green turtles are herbivores and feed on seagrasses; hawksbill turtles feed primarily on sponges. A rise in seagrass disease and coral overgrowth can be attributed in part to the relative absence of large-scale grazing turtles.[199]

Monk seals were also fairly common in the Caribbean, if not on the scale of turtles. One estimate puts their number at about a quarter of a million in pre-Columbian times. At least 13 breeding colonies existed in the region—from the Dry Tortugas in the north to Guyana in the south, from Veracruz in the west to Guadeloupe in the east. The seals' range contracted over time as European settlers began hunting them vigorously. By 1700, few monk seals were present in the eastern Caribbean, with known breeding colonies on Curaçao and Guadeloupe already eliminated. During the eighteenth century, the northeastern Caribbean range of the monk seal—waters off the islands of Hispaniola, Puerto Rico, and the Bahamas—suffered serious depletion. Jamaican hunting parties, for example, ventured north to the Bahamas, where they apparently killed hundreds of seals nightly during winter when female seals came ashore to breed and nurse their pups. Caribbean settlers sought seal oil, used as a lubricant in the sugar industry, as a coating for boats, and for domestic lighting and cooking purposes. By the twentieth century, monk seals were confined to the western Caribbean and southern Gulf of Mexico. The last known breeding colony was on the Serrano Bank, southwest of Jamaica, and it came to an end in the 1950s. The Caribbean monk seal is the one marine mammal to be driven extinct by humans in tropical seas, a process that occurred over centuries of depletion.[200]

The extent of the environmental damage to reefs, seabeds, and various marine species was so obvious that attempts to arrest it were present almost from the first. Spanish authorities tried vainly to stop the degradation of the pearl beds, even as they contributed it by licensing more efficient pearl-harvesting methods. One of the first acts passed by the Bermuda assembly in 1620 was an attempt to prevent the killing of young turtles. Forty-one years later, the Bermuda Council banned oversized nets. In 1691 they passed an act against "Fish Hawling," which attempted to address the "great destruction of fish" by limiting net sizes in length, protecting certain fish species, and prosecuting fishermen who caught "excessive quantities tending toward waste." The intention was for violators to lose fishing rights and pay fines. In the 1680s Jamaican legislators prohibited the use of dogwood bark, tobacco, or other substances to poison fish in rivers, lakes, and ponds. In 1711 they again banned the practice of taking fish by poison or "intoxication" as well as the use of a seine with less mesh than 1¼ inches "from knot to knot," except in the case of shrimp nets, in order to avoid excessive kills and the capture of young fish.[201]

On tropical islands, as environmental historian Richard Grove puts it, "a coherent and wide-ranging critique of environmental degradation first emerged." In part this development owed something to the projection of Edenic or paradisal properties onto islands, ideals that inevitably fell short. Colonial expansion also promoted the rapid diffusion of new scientific ideas among island colonies, and between center and periphery. The need to understand the unfamiliar led the state to employ experts (usually physicians, sometimes surgeons on ships) as proto-scientists long before Europe did. The isolated oceanic island also promoted, in Grove's words, a "detached self-consciousness and a critical view" of European behavior. In addition, the combination of unusual flora and rapid deforestation on fragile tropical islands helped develop concepts of rarity and fears of extinction. Tropical islands became the location for some of the earliest experiments in systematic forest conservation, water-pollution control, and fisheries protection anywhere in the world. Spanish Cuba was the first place in the Caribbean to pioneer forest reserves (in 1748), but other islands soon followed suit. In 1764 systems of forest reserves were quickly put into effect on newly acquired British territories in the Caribbean. Despite the distance from metropolitan authority, the colonies had a significant impact on the history of environmentalism. Colonial networks of botanical exchange encouraged the slow development of an environmental consciousness. The Caribbean's settlers and imperial officials tried to offset the enormous costs of the environmental revolution in which they participated.[202]

The colonial botanical garden formed the basis for a new kind of learning, information collecting, and networking in the tropical environment. The Dutch developed the concept in the Cape Colony. By encouraging the development of horticultural expertise, they were instrumental in transferring, among other things, precious spices from the East to the West Indies. Some time prior to 1707, the French government sponsored two royal botanists, the Lignon brothers, on Guadeloupe, whose efforts might technically be called the first botanic garden in the Caribbean. Nine years later, the Paris Academy of Sciences sought to form a botanical establishment on Martinique. In 1722 Pierre Barrère served as royal botanist at Cayenne. Not until the later 1770s, however, were formal royal gardens established in Saint-Domingue—the first at Port-au-Prince in 1777. Twelve years earlier, the British established their first state-sponsored botanic garden in the Americas at St. Vincent. In 1775 a group of wealthy Jamaican planters voted in their legislature to establish two botanic gardens and to provide public funds to support a full-time botanist. In 1793 the Economic Society of Havana proposed the creation of a botanical garden, although it did not open until 1817. Botanical gardens played an increasingly important role in the intercontinental spread of flora.[203]

Often accompanying botanic gardens were scientific societies, clubs, and official organizations. In the late eighteenth-century, Spanish Caribbean royal officials sponsored attempts to stimulate agricultural production. They sent 12 technicians to Venezuela's easternmost province, for example, to grow linen;

Figure 1.13 One of the first botanic gardens in the Western Hemisphere, its foundation on the island of Saint Vincent, dating to 1765, was significant in the development of early environmentalism. Reverend Landsdown Guilding, *An Account of the Botanic Garden in the Island of St. Vincent* (Glasgow, 1825). Google Books Project, courtesy of the British Library.

established experimental plots devoted to exotic crops such as cinnamon, mangoes, and cloves; and conducted a soil survey to pinpoint the best sites for tobacco production. In 1781 the Society for the Encouragement of Natural History and of Useful Arts, one of the first learned institutions to be founded in a British colony, was established in Barbados. Three years later, the Cercle des Philadelphes, a major scientific body, formed in Saint-Domingue. In 1791 a Physico-Medical Society with an attached botanic garden was founded in Grenada. Few had scientists from neighboring Caribbean islands as foreign members, although informal contacts certainly occurred.[204]

Besides the botanic garden and local societies, an intricate network of naturalists existed in the various Caribbean islands. They were often in touch with one another and their respective metropolitan authorities, read each other's works, and drew on a wide range of informants. In the early eighteenth century, Jamaican surgeon and naturalist Henry Barham, one of Hans Sloane's most active correspondents and collectors, noted that he would "sett forth the Known Vertues and experienced Qualitys" of plants, information supplied by Spaniards. After studying in Paris and Leiden and spending almost a decade in Jamaica, Dr. Patrick Browne published his *Civil and Natural History of Jamaica*

(1756), which was, in the opinion of one authority, "scientifically speaking, the most up-to-date treatment of the natural history of any of the British colonies." Browne was the first British or American contributor in print to follow Linnean principles. When in 1763, Nicolai Jacquin, a Leiden botanist who spent four years in the West Indies, published his comprehensive natural history, he extensively cited Browne. In the late eighteenth century, William Urban Buée, a French resident of Dominica, reported on the techniques he used to cultivate clove trees, sent Joseph Banks clove saplings to be cultivated in Kew Garden and promised to send samples of the cinnamon plants on which he was currently engaged "in some trials." Similarly, Alexander Anderson, the second director of the St. Vincent botanical garden, relied on exchange and correspondence with foreign naturalists. His "most valuable correspondents" were those in the French colonies. From these acquaintances Anderson received seeds and news about recent botanical arrivals. In 1789 he reported "that it is not the true Bread Fruit they have got in Martinico." The following year he hoped to obtain cochineal from Saint-Domingue or from "a French gentleman of considerable property & corrispondent of science" in St. Lucia. Anderson's French correspondents provided valuable specimens and intelligence about the recent botanical acquisitions of Britain's rival.[205]

Cross-imperial exchanges were not always amicable; they might proceed via illicit smuggling, theft, or outright military force. Thus the Jamaican planters Hinton East and his neighbor Matthew Wallen acquired the mango tree, mangostan, walking cane, cinnamon, bohea, and green tea for their gardens as a result of naval engagements during the American Revolution. Governor Robert Melville of St. Vincent sent "a man to the Spanish Main to bring the more valuable plants of that country" back to his colony; he was indifferent to the niceties of how he procured them. Alexander Anderson, too, was willing to steal plants. In 1790 he suggested that cochineal might be obtained by "any one of a scientific turn among our Logwood cutters" in the Bay of Campeche. The Bay's proximity to Oaxaca, the region of New Spain where the best cochineal was produced, Anderson reasoned, would make it easy for a logwood cutter to obtain the valuable dye "thro the medicum of the Indians." He was also happy to acquire natural curiosities through the spoils of war. In 1793 he declared that he "hope[d] we shall now be able to take Martinico and the other French Islands, as they have many valuable plants of the E. Indies that we yet want, among them the Nutmeg. Hostilities having commenced I am cut off from any correspondence with them, & can procure nothing in a friendly way as heretofore."[206]

European botanists in the Caribbean relied on Native American and African informants to a greater degree than their counterparts in North America. At the turn of the eighteenth century, Maria Sibylla Merien found Africans and Amerindians more useful as collectors and informants than Europeans: a black slave woman brought her a maggot; Indians supplied lantern flies; and slaves gathered shells for her from the sea. In 1715 Henry Barham sent an "Indian slave" to the Bay of Campeche to cut logwood and secure seeds for transplanting to Jamaica. He endorsed the use of ambergris as an antidote to poisons, a practice of Florida Indians. Similarly, he recommended the medicinal use of arrowroot, pilewort, ragwort, sassafras, and tacamahac based on Native American customs. The following year, James Petiver requested that a ship captain lend flycatchers to some of his "blacks" on Jamaica so that they could "take & kill whatever butterflies & Moths they meet." Hans Sloane mentioned that a European gentleman had observed the native Indians' use of arrowroot as an antidote to poisoned arrows, and acknowledged getting information from "Inhabitants, either Europeans, Indians, or Blacks." In 1725, Mark Catesby was in the house of the governor of the Bahamas viewing "chegoes," taken from his host's feet, through a microscope, when the official "produced an oddity on the point of his needle." Catesby first "showed it to the Negroes and [then] others," although "none of them had seen the like." In the 1770s in the Virgin Islands, William Thornton learned about African poisons by talking to "a very intelligent mundingo negro" and a "negro of Sierra Leone." He also met another "ingenious . . . Mundingo" who tanned goat skins using mangrove bark and thereby made perfect water carriers. He also witnessed other blacks "practice various devices for taking fish," including intoxicating them with root bark. In 1778, Henry de Ponthieu reported that the French "have long accustom'd to avail themselves in [Caribbean] plants in Physic and surgery being instructed by the new Negroes that arrive from the different parts of the African continent." In St. Vincent, Alexander Anderson "often viewed the negro gardens with surprise, being filled with all kinds of vegetables in the greatest perfection, while their master's garden was a bed of dry earth." The reason, Anderson soon discovered, was that blacks did not clear their plots but left trees to shelter their crops, while whites did the opposite. European naturalists believed that blacks and Amerindians had special knowledge about the natural world, which made them both valuable and threatening in about equal measure.[207]

Some remarkably accomplished botanical descriptions emerged from these collaborations. In the early sixteenth century, Gonzalo Fernández de Oviedo, who was governor of Cartagena and Santo Domingo and lived in the Caribbean for many decades, was a pioneering observer of the fauna and flora of the region. Franciscan Charles Plumier ventured to the French Antilles between 1689 and 1697 as a member of three botanizing expeditions. His *Description des Plantes de l'Amerique* (1693) and its more than 100 plates are especially notable, as are his many unpublished illustrations of Caribbean fishes and birds. Hans Sloane got his start in 1687 when he left for Jamaica for two years of observing its plants, animals, and peoples; his account of the island's fauna and especially flora made his name. No botanist is more remarkable than the German-born Maria Sibylla Merian, who in 1699, at age 52, boarded a ship for Suriname, where she spent just under two years depicting the plants and particularly insects and butterflies of that colony. Enterprising and adventurous, she raised the artistic standards of natural history illustration and helped transform the field of entomology. Her *Metamorphosis of the Insects of Suriname* (1705), with its 60 copperplates of vivid butterflies, voracious caterpillars, and menacing reptiles, is striking for its crystalline accuracy, vibrant colors, and electrifying intensity. A lesser figure, but impressive nonetheless, is the Scottish illustrator John Lindsay, who has left 121 drawings of Jamaican plants, birds, and animals, some of which are captivating. Similarly, Dr. Anthony Robinson's 163 large-scale drawings of Jamaican birds and eggs point to his exceptional abilities. Especially notable is Charlotte Dugée, a mulatto from Saint-Domingue, who produced more than 600 sketches of plants in the forests of Guiana in 1764–67.[208]

As a vital hub of traffic, the Caribbean was the locus of other important scientific endeavors in the early modern period. In 1671 Richard Bohun claimed that a barometer could be helpful in predicting a coming hurricane. The year after Barbados was hit by two successive hurricanes, in 1674 and 1675, the Royal Society provided the first barometers to overseas correspondents and naturally sent them to Barbados. In 1680 Colonel William Sharpe, governor of the island, was the first person in the Americas to make daily observations of the weather using a meteorological instrument (other than a wind vane) and made the first known measurements of barometric pressure within the circulation of a hurricane. His record contributed to Edmund Halley's understanding of the distinctions between tropical and temperate zones. Two years later a French expedition to Guadeloupe and Martinique was sponsored by the French Académie Royale des Sciences to map longitude, make solar observations near the equator, plot variations of the compass, and take daily barometer and thermometer readings. In fact, the astronomers took their instruments on to a slave ship, which transported them, along with 250 African captives, from Gorée (in modern Senegal) to Guadeloupe. When George Washington visited Barbados in 1751, he had dinner with Thomas Stevenson, who had studied lunar eclipses and would later record some observations of Halley's comet. By the late eighteenth century, apparently, harbor pilots and ship captains in the Spanish Caribbean used barometers widely to predict bad weather. When German naturalist Alexander von Humboldt traveled through much of the Spanish Caribbean, he went with a large collection of scientific instruments, collecting thousands of measurements and hoping to discover broad patterns in the natural world.[209]

The proximity of Caribbean territories inspired emulation. Scientists both cooperated, but more often competed, across imperial boundaries. English naturalist James Petiver's herbal, which he published in 1715, included a translated and abridged text of a French traveler to Spanish America. Others entered via smuggling or the asiento contract (the exclusive right to provide slaves to Spanish dominions), which facilitated exchanges. Thus William Houstoun, a South Sea Company surgeon, resident in Vera Cruz, introduced many plants into the English orbit. For instance, he transplanted seeds of jalop, a popular purgative, into Jamaica. In the 1730s, his replacement, Robert Millar, was charged with collecting natural specimens in Jamaica, Cuba, and elsewhere in Spanish America. English botanists also tended to be in awe of the French. In 1785 an Antiguan observed that "The French have certainly supply'd all the plants which grow in the English islands" and noted admiringly that Guadeloupe had several clove trees and black pepper from Cayenne and cinnamon from India. Alexander Anderson followed innovations not just of the French, but of the Spanish colony of Trinidad and the Dutch colonies of Demerara and Essequibo. For botanical information, the Tortolan-born William Thornton relied in part on French books and his friend Julius Philip Benjamin Von Rohr, born in Saxony, who lived in the Caribbean for about 40 years, visited Surinam and Cayenne, and practiced medicine on St. Croix. In the late 1780s, Hippolyte Nectoux, the director of the Port-au-Prince gardens in Saint-Domingue, and Thomas Clarke, the director of the Jamaican garden, became friends and correspondents. In 1788 and 1789 Nectoux visited the British island and received from Clarke almost 40 plants, including the tea plant and others with medicinal value. Clarke's gift prompted Charles Mozard, editor of Saint-Domingue's official newspaper *Affiches Américaines*, to comment, "The time has passed where nations try to monopolize certain of nature's riches. The flame of philosophy has dispelled the obscurantism that produces this antisocial system [of monopolies]." He predicted that the exchange of rare plants would continue in both directions and that "Everything rare in the gardens in Port-au-Prince will be speedily conveyed to our neighbors." Mozard, like Joseph Banks, evoked the Enlightenment ideal that intellectual fraternity trumped national rivalries.[210]

What emerged in the Caribbean, reflected in the botanical interchange, is best described, to borrow a term from John McNeill, as a "creole ecology." It was a "motley assemblage of indigenous and invading species, jostling one another in unstable ecosystems." Much was lost in the process, flux was constant, but gradually a new mosaic took shape. Caribbean gardens blended mounding techniques of pre-Columbian *conucos*, the ridging of plantation cane fields, the short-handled hoe of African provenience, and a crop repertoire that included aboriginal domesticates as well as European, African, and Asian imports. There was a constant arrival, dispersal, and mingling of new plants and animals. To Native American crops such as cassava, maize, sweet potatoes, and tomatoes, Europeans added their own vegetables and grains and even more importantly bananas, citrus fruits, and sugar cane, all originally from South or Southeast Asia.

African slaving vessels introduced guinea corn, yam, rice, the ackee tree, and okra. Local experimentation produced hybrids such as the grapefruit, a cross between the sweet orange and pomelo or shaddock, originating in Barbados. Local place names—Whitey Pond Piece, Burnt Mangrove, Slippery Gut, Fat Hog Quarter—often convey past land uses and environmental information in creole form.[211]

Sometimes the arrivals can be dated fairly precisely. African yams arrived early—by 1510. The banana tree came in 1516 from the Canaries and was called *guineo* on some islands, due to its immediate origins in the African zone of the same name, although it can be traced to South East Asia originally. Asian coconut had reached Pacific American coasts in pre-Columbian times, but entered the Caribbean about 1525. Ginger, also either from Asia or the Atlantic islands, arrived around the middle of the sixteenth century. In the seventeenth century Colonel James Walker brought arrowroot from Dominica to Barbados, before it went to Jamaica. The Portuguese brought mango to Bahia in about 1700, and it is mentioned in Puerto Rico after 1740; Edwin Lascelles is said to have imported a mango tree into Barbados in 1742. Guinea grass apparently arrived in Jamaica from Africa in 1745; the ackee tree made the same migration in 1778. Admiral Rodney captured a French ship bound from Mauritius to Saint-Domingue in 1782 and, as a result, cloves, cinnamon, nutmeg, and mangoes arrived in Jamaica. Captain Bligh famously introduced breadfruit to St. Vincent and Jamaica in 1793.[212]

But with many other crops—humble eddos, cocos, and plantains, for example—and animals, origins are much less precise. We know that European livestock arrived early and formed the most consequential imports. Africa supplied sheep and guinea fowl. Even camels were tried for a while. The origins of the green monkeys in Barbados, St. Kitts, and Nevis were probably heterogeneous—not just from Senegambia, but probably also from the Gold Coast, and perhaps other African coastal regions, perhaps even from Cape Verde. Different strains seem to have mixed on the islands to form slightly different groups.[213]

* * *

A classic way to think about the Caribbean is to deploy the concept of creolization, and it applies equally well to the environment as to much else about the region. The term itself derives from the Spanish *criollo* and Portuguese *crioulo*, meaning someone or something usually of foreign derivation that becomes native to a new locality. Creolization thus refers to processes of exchange and adaptation "by which people, animals, ideas, and institutions with roots in the Old World are born, grow, and prosper in the New." Whether Spanish or Portuguese in origin, the term derives from the same root, Latin *creare*, to make something or someone new. One of the first appearances of the term in English was the

1604 translation of Jesuit naturalist José de Acosta's *Natural and Moral History of the Indies* (1590), which referred to "Crollos" as "Spaniards borne at the Indies." Thereafter, the term was often associated with Spanish Americans; but whites and blacks more generally in the West Indies also merited it and, over time, they largely embraced the ascription. William Dampier was one of the first British authors to use the term—in 1698—to refer to an "English Native of St. Christophers, a Criole, as we call all born of European Parents in the West Indies." According to an early history of Barbados, "Creolian Negroes" despised "saltwater Negroes" and began to "value themselves much on being born" on the island.[214]

The designation *creole* applied not just to people but to animals, plants, and artifacts. In 1756 Patrick Browne in his *Civil and Natural History of Jamaica* described a "larger hairy Creole-Crab with prickly claws"; the local bread, made from unripe plantains, became creole bread; European fruit that underwent adaptations in the Caribbean became creole fruit; in the Hispanophone islands, a *pollo criollo* is a chicken raised from local, not imported, stock; *ron criollo* is illegal, bootleg rum; when new varieties of sugar cane became widely available, local planters referred to the older strain as "creole cane." Haitians use the word kreyòl (*Créole* in standard French) to refer to their national language; and linguists use the term to describe mixed or nonstandard languages that began life as pidgins and became mother tongues, of which there are many in the Caribbean. Among the Saramaka, *kióo* (creole) describes the lifestyle expected of young men, not the hidebound ways of their elders. Ships sporting some variation of the term—*Amiable Creole, Deux Créoles, La Belle Creole, Favourite Creole, Jean Creole*, or simply *La Creole*—docked at Caribbean ports in the eighteenth century. Creole can refer to almost anything, from crops to cuisine, from music to art that arises in the Caribbean—and some would argue elsewhere too.[215]

Just like the Caribbean environment itself, creoles tended to be viewed ambivalently at best, negatively at worst. Most often the characterization of British creoles in the Caribbean was pejorative, a view that intensified greatly during the Stamp Act crisis. North Americans described the stamped paper that came from the Caribbean as the "marks of Creole Slavery." West Indians were "mean spirited, cowardly, dastardly Creoles" because of their failure to resist the act. Naturally, Edward Long's *History of Jamaica* (1774) offered a more positive assessment, particularly of the physical character of "Creoles," a term he readily used, of native-born Jamaicans, who he saw as "stamped" by the climate and local environment. Thus, they were in general "tall and well-shaped," with "keen and penetrating" sight; they were surprisingly agile, graceful dancers; their cheeks were "remarkably high-boned." In addition to being "sensible, . . . brave, good-natured, affable, generous," he acknowledged their many faults: supineness, indolence, haughtiness, "fits of rage," and fickleness. Similarly, a newspaper article, "A Character of the Creoles of St. Domingo," published in 1788, began from the premise that "the burning heat of the sun in the torrid zone" so affected the "organs of the inhabitants" as to make them very different from those of temperate climes. A scorching sun was usually thought to debilitate, but, in this case, the argument went, creoles were "generally well made and of an elegant shape." Not swaddled in infancy, "their limbs rarely suffer any deformity, but receive from the temperature of the climate an activity and suppleness." Lauded for their ease of movement, their "majestic walk," the women's "delicacy of features," creoles also had "a lively imagination and a quick apprehension, occasioned by the rapid development of their physical powers." But, even in play, a creole child is trained to be a tyrant. The passions reign uncontrolled: imperious, inconstant, reckless. Nevertheless, the essay ended by returning to the creoles' "good qualities"—openness, generosity, bravery, and trust—which overall outweighed the negative stereotypes of indolence and intemperance. Interestingly, the term *creole* when applied to slaves was more uniformly positive than when used of whites. Mention of creole in conjunction with a slave generally conjured up connotations of good sense, hardiness, and fidelity, compared to the putative backwardness and alien character of an African.[216]

Creolization as a process incorporates notions of mixture, blending, and hybridity as much as it does the foreign becoming local. Creolization denotes the international character of the Caribbean. Scores of Native American societies existed in the region on the eve of European contact and continued to exist for some time thereafter. Settlers from Spain, France, Britain, the Netherlands, Sweden, and Denmark occupied territories often in close proximity, sometimes the same islands at the same time, and sometimes sequentially as many islands changed hands. Joining these diverse Europeans and their enforced intimacy with Native Americans were coerced African migrants from literally hundreds of states and stateless societies. The heterogeneity of Africans far surpassed that of Europeans. Even a few Chinese arrived in Trinidad in the early nineteenth century, harbingers of a much larger Asian migration later in the century. The hybrid nature of the peopling of the Antilles is one of its most distinctive characteristics, and it is reflected in the environment's rich mixture of plants, animals, and peoples. The Caribbean became one of most varied social mosaics anywhere, notable for its jostling and blending of peoples, plants, and products. Out of the Caribbean region emerged a new, thoroughly dynamic, creolized creation.[217]

Finally, a creole ecology must address the complexity and importance of the region. In giving primacy to the sea over the land of the Caribbean, this chapter has highlighted the contrast between large and small islands, oceanic and continental islands, volcanic and limestone areas, islands and rimlands, coasts and hinterlands, and fluid maritime spaces and bounded terrestrial landscapes.[218] However broadly or narrowly conceived, the Caribbean was no marginal, peripheral region. The environmental changes it witnessed were emblematic of those happening elsewhere in the New World. It just experienced them more intensely and precociously than most other places. In this period, to offer one illustration, sugar overtook grain "as the most valuable single commodity entering world trade." In the early modern era the Antillean region boasted the most valuable, dynamic, and volatile colonies in the Americas, perhaps the world. As Abbé Raynal, the great popularizer of the Enlightenment, noted in 1770, when reflecting on the significance of the Caribbean colonies: "The labours of the people settled in those islands are the sole basis of the African trade: they extend the fisheries and the cultures of North America, afford a good market for the manufactures of Asia, and double, perhaps treble, the activity of all Europe. They may be considered as the principle cause of the rapid motion which now agitates the universe."[219]

2

Disease Environments in the Caribbean to 1850

J. R. MCNEILL

On his third voyage to the Caribbean, in 1498, Columbus reckoned he had stumbled on an earthly paradise.[1] Among the promising indications that he was close to the Garden of Eden, he thought, were that the people he encountered seemed without guile or disease. Those people soon suffered as grievously from a panoply of diseases as any people in world history. Millions more who arrived in the Caribbean in Columbus's wake found the region a living hell, rife with deadly infections. By global standards, disease played an unusually powerful role in Caribbean history from 1492 to 1850.

This chapter consists of three main parts. The first deals with the—necessarily sketchy—health history of the Caribbean peoples from their first arrival roughly 7,500 years ago until the arrival of Columbus in 1492. The region's health and disease history after 1492 makes sense only in light of what came before. The second part considers the disease experience of the indigenous population of the Caribbean between 1492 and about 1650, one of the grimmer chapters in world history. The third, hardly more cheerful, focuses on the disease regime of Caribbean plantation society between about 1650 and 1850. Each part will focus more on lethal diseases that affected demographic history—typically acute infections such as measles, smallpox,[2] yellow fever, and malaria—than on chronic conditions.

The chapter concerns changing disease environments rather than the history of medicine. Before 1850, ecological change, demographic trends, migration patterns, nutrition, and linkages to the rest of the Atlantic world all did more than medicine to shape Caribbean disease history—despite the occasional practice of quarantine and the advent of smallpox vaccination in 1804. In the best

Sea and Land. Philip D. Morgan, J. R. McNeill, Matthew Mulcahy, and Stuart B. Schwartz, Oxford University Press.
© Oxford University Press 2022. DOI: 10.1093/oso/9780197555446.003.0003

of circumstances, medical intervention relieved some of the sufferings of sick people. In the worst, it killed them.[3]

This chapter will show that the disease environment of the Caribbean, especially after 1492, was a built environment. Hurricanes, earthquakes, and (in most cases) drought are genuinely natural phenomena. They occurred in the Caribbean before humankind ventured there, and will occur long after humankind disappears from the face of the earth. But disease disasters are always partly caused by human behavior. Smallpox, influenza, malaria, and all the rest did not circulate in the Caribbean before people arrived. Human diseases required humans, and some diseases required humans to live in certain ways. Disease history must be about humans in their changing ecological contexts, and in the Caribbean, particularly after Columbus, human action dramatically changed the ecological contexts that affected health, most consequentially by introducing pathogens from afar and by installing a plantation economy. Almost all that ecological change was the unexpected consequence of actions taken in near complete ignorance of any implications for disease ecology. This is normal in world history before 1850, although the ferocity of the Caribbean disease environment after 1492 was not at all normal.

The Caribbean region—typically warm and humid and therefore hospitable to many pathogens—was a comparatively easy place to build, by accident, a ferocious disease environment. That unhappy accident required the introduction and frequent reintroduction of a wide range of pathogens from other continents, which began after 1492. It also required the dismal social condition of Caribbean populations, which after 1492 often included severe stresses that made diseases harder to withstand. Stresses such as malnutrition or extreme anxiety can in effect make certain pathogens more potent by compromising human immune response. All this, and more, contributed to the making of the cauldron of contagion that was the Caribbean—after 1492.

The first nine-tenths of the roughly 7,500 years of human occupation in the Caribbean were by global standards agreeably healthy, but beginning in 1492–93, two disastrous chapters in global health history unfolded in the Caribbean, each one a part—and likely the worst part—of a larger story in the Americas. To crystallize understanding of these twinned disasters, I borrow a new concept from medical anthropology, the notion of "syndemics." A syndemic occurs when two or more diseases form a cluster, simultaneously affecting a given population in social, political, or environmental contexts that sharpen the effects of that disease cluster. The notion combines biological and social variables into a single concept. Although invented to make sense of HIV/AIDS and used by medical anthropologists to describe contemporary (and possible future) situations, it helps to illuminate the distinctively bleak health history of the Caribbean after 1492.[4]

Evidence

The evidence from which one can piece together Caribbean disease history is scattered, inconsistent, and often problematic. For the centuries after 1492, archives in two dozen countries contain fragments of the story, providing local data on disease outbreaks, hospital expenditures, medical hypotheses, and much else. In addition, literate visitors to, or residents of, the Caribbean published several dozen books devoted to the region's natural history. These texts offer extensive remarks on health and disease, normally couched in the conceptual framework of Hippocratic medicine—which no longer carries any weight in medical circles. These books exist in English, French, Spanish, Dutch, and, in at least one case, Swedish.[5] These textual sources are indispensable for the period after 1492. However, neither they nor any other texts shed any light on earlier periods. Caribbean island peoples before 1492 did not use writing; while nearby mainland coastal cultures such as the Maya did, their surviving texts focus on other matters than health and disease.

Some of the evidence for periods both before and after 1492 is not textual but bioarchaeological. Dozens of digs in the Caribbean have yielded human remains, and in some cases they have undergone analysis yielding information about certain diseases. Tuberculosis, leprosy, and syphilis, for example, leave signatures in their victims' bones, as, less reliably, do some forms of anemia and malnutrition and perhaps malaria.[6] Mummified remains of tissues are rare in the Caribbean because its warmth and humidity speed the decay of organic material. So the analyzed human remains in the Caribbean are few, and it is unwise to draw any but the most tentative conclusions about the *prevalence* of diseases across the islands and over time. Bioarchaeological evidence is extremely useful, however, for establishing the *presence* of a specific infection.[7]

Finally, some of the evidence is genetic. It is possible to isolate old genetic material from human remains. Remnants of the pathogens that cause plague, malaria, relapsing fever, smallpox, tuberculosis and typhus, among others, have been pulled from old European bones. The sample size of available human remains is small for the Caribbean, but nonetheless, fossil DNA evidence—the young science of paleogenomics—is an essential tool in prying into the 7,500 years of disease ecology in the Caribbean.[8]

A second variety of genetic evidence about disease history is drawn from the current population of the region. But only a few diseases, malaria being the best example, exert strong selective pressure on human genomes over long periods of time, producing discernible genetic variation among different populations based on their ancestors' disease experience.

The body of evidence concerning Caribbean disease history is far from stable, so some data and evidence will need revision before long. The available texts do not change much, but new information trickles out every year from bioarchaeological and paleogenomic work. In practice, this mainly affects conclusions pertaining to the period before 1492. But paleogenomic evidence recently resolved debates about the origin of yellow fever, a disease that came to the region only after Columbus. The fact that yellow fever was African, rather than American, in origin was suggested as early as 1796, but proven beyond reasonable doubt only thanks to twenty-first-century genetic research.[9]

The perils of relying on any of this evidence include retrospective diagnosis. Identification of any disease, whether from texts, archaeology, or genetic evidence, can often be tricky.[10] The plague of Athens, the symptoms of which Thucydides detailed, has been diagnosed as at least 15 different diseases. Today's doctors often misdiagnose infections even with the luxury of clinical examinations of patients, something historians are not afforded. So every diagnosis in this chapter should be regarded as provisional. Moreover, the presence of telltale lesions or pathogen DNA in human remains does not necessarily indicate an epidemic. Bioarchaeological evidence provides strong support for the presence of certain diseases, but only weak support for conclusions about the prevalence of any disease.

Epidemics, Populations, and Disease Resistance

The human body is susceptible to hundreds of different disease-causing pathogens. Dozens of ways exist to classify pathogens based on symptoms provoked, means by which they are communicated, their genetic structure, and so on. This chapter will refer to vector-borne diseases, such as malaria, yellow fever, and dengue, all of which travel from human to human via mosquitoes. Lice convey typhus from one human host to another. Snails, flies, and many other small creatures may serve as vectors of human disease. The pervasiveness of these diseases depends in large part on ecological conditions for their vectors. The chapter will also refer to crowd diseases, such as measles, smallpox, mumps, influenza, rubella (German measles), and pertussis (whooping cough). These spread human to human with no vector and, except for influenza, no animal reservoirs. These acute infections make people sick for a week or three, and, except for influenza, either kill them or leave them resistant, perhaps fully immune, for life.[11]

Healthy human immune systems fight infection in two main ways. First, they operate protective mechanisms, collectively called "innate immunity," that attack invading cells. Second, they have special cells that detect and assault specific pathogens, and in effect have a memory that allows them to maintain the capacity to mass-produce antigens so fast as to overwhelm any familiar pathogen later in life. This is called "acquired immunity," "conferred immunity," or "adaptive immunity," and is important to understand. Acquired immunity is not heritable from parent to child (although a mother's breast milk may loan specific immunities to her infant). It is not a result of biological superiority on anyone's part. It is a result of the fact that all mammals' immune systems can calibrate themselves to combat specific pathogens.

Crowd diseases can sustain themselves indefinitely only in large populations. They require enough non-immune babies or in-migrants to serve as hosts among whom the pathogens may circulate. In large enough populations, an acute infection may become "endemic," or ever-present. In smaller populations, however, crowd diseases burn through the available hosts quickly, killing some and leaving only immunes behind, in whose bodies these pathogens cannot survive. The size of the population required for the indefinite circulation of infection varies from pathogen to pathogen and with population density. Diseases that are extremely infectious, such as measles, require larger populations (at least 250,000 to 500,000) in regular contact to stay in circulation and avoid "burn-out" or "fade-out." Others, such as smallpox, which do not spread as readily from person to person, require smaller populations (at least 100,000 to 200,000) because they do not immunize or kill everyone so quickly.[12]

Broadly speaking, until the arrival of modern medicine and public health programs, small populations experienced disease differently than did large populations. Bands of hunters and foragers, for example, which typically contained dozens of people, or isolated farming villagers whose communities numbered only in the hundreds or low thousands, could suffer regularly from pathogens with animal reservoirs (such as the yellow fever virus); from pathogens that produce incomplete immunity and allow victims to serve as hosts time and time again (such as malarial plasmodia); and from pathogens that linger in human bodies in infectious stages for years rather than days or weeks (such as those that cause Chagas' disease). Because they could not sustain the crowd diseases, smaller populations hosted a thinner roster of diseases overall, did not lose as many babies and toddlers to endemic disease, and stood at acute risk of searing epidemics when any of the crowd diseases reached them. Larger populations, on the other hand, hosted a wider variety of diseases, lost roughly half of all children to disease before age six, and consisted, in their adult ranks, of survivors of the crowd diseases generally immune to reinfection except by influenza.

Crowd diseases are in effect herd diseases. Human communities and herd animals have been swapping infections for millennia. Since the advent of domesticated herds some 10,000 years ago, the pace of this exchange has accelerated, as humans have come to live cheek by jowl with cattle, sheep, pigs, chickens, camels, and numerous other species.[13] This particular feature of the crowd diseases is important for the history of the Caribbean and the early Americas generally, because there herd animals were comparatively rare and domesticable herd animals rarer still. The number of human infections acquired from herd animals native to the Americas is likely only one: a form of tuberculosis derived from a pathogen previously confined to Pacific fur seals on the coast of Peru.[14] All this helps to explain the happily impoverished disease environment of the pre-Columbian Americas and the Caribbean region. Of the two dozen or so most important diseases in human history, at most three existed in the Americas before 1492: Chagas' disease, tuberculosis, and possibly syphilis, none of which kills swiftly.

Freedom from the greater part of the burden of human disease resulted from legacies of the deep history of the Americas. First, the Americas had no apes, the creatures from which pathogen transfer to humans was likeliest to occur. Moreover, the monkey species in the Americas were much more distant in evolutionary terms from humans than were monkeys native to Africa and Asia. Thus primate-to-human pathogen transfers were many times less likely in the Americas than in Afro-Eurasia. Second, when the ancestors of the first Americans left Siberia via the Bering land bridge some 15,000 to 33,000 years ago,[15] they did so before any animals other than dogs had been domesticated anywhere in the world, which meant that crowd diseases had had little opportunity to take root among them in their Siberian homeland. And, as far as we know, they carried none with them into the Americas. Third, when crossing from Siberia to America, they came in small groups, unable to sustain much infection among them, and passed through extreme cold, which is hostile to many pathogens and vectors. Fourth, after people arrived in the Americas, there wasn't much time, compared to other continents, for animal-to-human pathogen transfers to take place. And fifth, the first Americans and their descendants domesticated only a few animal species, and only one herd animal, llamas. This kept the odds low, compared to Afro-Eurasia, of a crowd disease evolving and sustaining itself in the Americas. So the founding generations of Native Americans brought little in the way of disease with them, and found an environment in the Americas with few primates or herd animals able to pass infections to them. That legacy of good fortune lasted until 1492.[16]

The Pre-Columbian Disease Regime
of the Caribbean

Linguistic, genetic, archaeological, and zooarchaeological evidence agrees that the first settlers on Caribbean islands came from the South American coast adjacent to Trinidad—the lower Orinoco basin.[17] The first people to colonize Trinidad, after rising sea levels had made it into an island 7 miles offshore, probably arrived about 7,800 years ago.[18] Just where they went next is uncertain, but the most recent work suggests paddlers made it to Cuba and Puerto Rico, around 5,500 to 4,000 years ago, before venturing to the smaller islands of the eastern Caribbean.[19] In the meantime, intrepid voyagers from Central America probably also paddled to Cuba, over 100 miles as the seagull flies. All these early colonists were fisher-hunter-gatherer peoples, although they may have dabbled in horticulture. The paucity of archaeological sites suggests their numbers were small.[20]

Like others arriving on previously uninhabited islands around the globe, they initially found a bounty of edible creatures, including sloths the size of sumo wrestlers and large flightless owls.[21] Tasty animals that could not reproduce fast enough to withstand the efficiency of human hunting soon went extinct, perhaps as much as 90 percent of the islands' fauna.[22] (Initial settlement of scores of other islands around the world brought similar consequences.)[23] Consequently, by the time agricultural peoples arrived in the West Indies, no sizable land animals remained. This matters for Caribbean disease history given that most of the important human infections came from large land animals.

Some 2,800 years ago, a new stream of migrants from the Orinoco basin trickled into the Caribbean. They practiced horticulture and brought manioc (cassava), maize, beans, sweet potato, and cocoyam, as well as pottery skills, with them. Manioc, their main crop, allowed Caribbean people to store surplus food for the first time, and therefore they could develop social hierarchies based on the ability to accumulate food and provide or deny it to others. Archaeologists generally call the hierarchical society that appeared by 500 CE *Taíno culture*, a term that encompasses considerable local variety. Genomic evidence implies that the Taíno mixed very little with the earlier inhabitants of the Caribbean before about 500 CE.[24] These new settlers, like their hunter-fisher-gatherer predecessors, chose some islands over others. They did not occupy Jamaica, the third largest of all Caribbean islands, until about 600 CE, making it among the last sizable places on earth to acquire a permanent human population. For reasons unknown, complex, hierarchical society after 600 CE blossomed mainly on Hispaniola and Puerto Rico. Cuba and Jamaica, and the smaller islands of the Lesser Antilles, developed much less in the way of dense settlement, political organization, and specialization of labor. But on Hispaniola and Puerto Rico, chiefdoms and federations of villages evolved, and manioc cultivation spread widely over both islands.

The Caribbean is distinctive in world history for developing social complexity and political hierarchies based on manioc. Elsewhere, rice, wheat, potatoes, or maize generally served as the caloric and nutritional basis of complex, hierarchical society. Although manioc provides more calories per unit of cultivated area than any of these other staple foods, is more resistant to drought, and tolerates poor soils, it is very low in protein and in many nutrients essential to human health such as iron, magnesium, phosphorus, and niacin.

No one lived by manioc alone. Caribbean peoples supplemented their diets with a wide variety of fruits. They also hunted turtles, monk seals, and manatees on some islands, gathered shellfish, and, where possible, exploited the many species of reef fish. In most places at most times, their diet apparently was a good one, with sufficient protein and calories to sustain health.[25] Theoretically it is possible that ancient Caribbean populations hosted all manner of diseases that we cannot detect, conceivably some that no longer exist. But given the connections between human disease, animal diseases, and population density, it is safe to say that ancient Caribbean peoples likely suffered little from infectious disease.

Fragmentary bioarchaeological evidence, which meshes well with the more abundant data from North America, indicates they had tuberculosis and treponemal infections such as yaws and syphilis, as well as arthritis and bad teeth.[26] Treponemal infections are slow-acting, chronic conditions rather than acute infections—although often fatal after many years. They spread by direct human contact. Both yaws and syphilis were likely present on many islands after 500 CE. A sample of 536 skeletons from five different sites in today's Dominican Republic, on Hispaniola, from 800 and 1500 showed apparent syphilis infection in 6–14 percent of cases. Skeletons from before 1200 BCE, however, show no signs of syphilis.[27] Studies on other islands also indicate syphilis was present, as do many skeletons from elsewhere in the Americas, but only after about 500 CE.[28] Some scholars doubt syphilis existed in the Americas before 1492, and insist that from the skeletal evidence one cannot definitively tell the difference between syphilis and other treponemal infections. A cautious conclusion is that pre-Columbian Caribbean populations after 500 CE hosted some treponemal infections, perhaps including syphilis.[29]

The presence of tuberculosis (TB) in the pre-Columbian Caribbean provokes less scholarly controversy. TB is also a bacterial infection, spread directly from human to human via coughs and sneezes.[30] Like syphilis, it is often fatal but only after years of infection. It exists in both human and animal populations; in the Americas the pre-Columbian roster of TB hosts includes turkeys, llamas, dogs, bison, and seals. TB, too, can leave skeletal lesions, and paleopathologists have

DELL'HISTORIE DEL
le lor fefte ui mettono d·lle gioie. L'habito loro fi è
che la maggior parte portano vna camifcia fenza
maniche, altri uanno tutti nudi , & alcune uolte fi
tingono tutto il corpo di negro.

**Il modo di pefcare , & nauigare nel
mare di Mezzo giorno.**

I n tutta quefta cofta della marina, gli Indiani fo-
no grandiſſimi peſcatori , le barche che uſano tan-
to per peſcare , come per nauigare , ſono a modo di
*   zattare*

Figure 2.1 Illustration from Girolamo Benzoni's *La historia del Mondo Nuovo* (*History of the New World*; Venice, 1565). This image, by a European artist of the 1560s, represents the indigenous people of the eastern Caribbean, often called Caribs, on a fishing expedition. Expert fishermen, according to Benzoni, they were seafarers and paddled regularly among the islands of the Lesser Antilles. Library of Congress, Washington, D.C., LC-USZ62-97211.

found plenty of examples in human remains in the Americas from 700 CE onward. It shows up less frequently in Mesoamerica than in either North or South America, and only occasionally in Caribbean island archaeology. But excavations in both the Bahamas and the Dominican Republic have yielded ancient tuberculosis cases.[31] Aside from the archaeological finds suggesting syphilis and tuberculosis, no good evidence exists for other infectious diseases in the Caribbean before 1492.

This does not mean that pre-Columbian peoples of the Caribbean were always healthy. There is bioarchaeological evidence for parasitic diseases, such as hookworm, elsewhere in the Americas before 1492.[32] Hookworm might or might not also have lurked in the Caribbean, where warm soils and sedentary populations would have suited it nicely. Skeletons from northwestern Cuba, dated to roughly 4500–2700 BC, indicate that about half of all children died by age 11, and that anemia and parasitism were widespread. People were small: adult males stood on average 1.57 meters (5'2") tall and females 1.43 meters (4'8").[33] Evidence from skeletons in Puerto Rico implies the presence of severe anemia and iron deficiency among children, probably a result of nematode (worm) parasites.[34] Given that most Caribbean populations after about 600 CE farmed in permanent settlements, it would be surprising if they did not carry a hefty load of parasites.

Whatever health challenges ancient Caribbean peoples faced, they were occasionally complicated by malnutrition. Skeletons from throughout the islands (as in most places in the world) show lesions commonly resulting from malnutrition in children, a reflection presumably of periodic drought and crop failure— although many other things might also result in children going hungry. Evidence from teeth suggests nutrition and health both slowly deteriorated across the region between 500 BC and 1400 CE.[35]

Skeletal remains indicate that ancient Caribbean peoples did not live notably longer, if at all, than other populations around the world. Famine and warfare took their toll. But lethal infections were mercifully underrepresented in the ancient Caribbean.

The reasons for this good fortune, similar to that of the Americas as a whole, lie in the deeper ecological history of the region. The people who settled in the Caribbean, like those who first came to the Americas, had little in the way of disease to bring with them. Their arrival about 7,500 years ago gave the resident microbes of the Caribbean little time in which to adapt to the opportunity presented by human bodies and jump from their old hosts to new, human, ones. But the most important reasons for the freedom from pestilence in the pre-Columbian Caribbean were the paucity of domesticated animals and the low density of human populations for most of the pre-Columbian era. Caribbean peoples had dogs and, after about 500 CE, guinea pigs, but no other domesticated animals.[36] Caribbean peoples did not have any of the domesticated animals used elsewhere in the Americas, such as turkeys, llamas, or alpacas (although the Muscovy duck may have existed on Trinidad). And the human populations remained sparse until the final centuries before Columbus.

The (apparently) complete absence of the common crowd diseases of Eurasia and Africa helps to explain the catastrophe that befell indigenous Caribbean peoples after 1492. When those infections arrived, they met a population in which no one was a survivor of a childhood bout of smallpox, measles, or any crowd diseases, and no one's immune system was primed to recognize the viruses and bacteria behind these diseases. Caribbean indigenous people, as individuals, had immune systems calibrated to the range of infections each had encountered so far in life (like everyone else on Earth), but none of them had an immune system calibrated for any of the crowd diseases that sailors, soldiers, slaves, merchants, and priests carried across the Atlantic after 1492.[37]

The Columbian Syndemic, 1492–1650

World history includes a handful of fairly well documented extreme population catastrophes. Some are notable for their scale. The Second World War cost some 60 million lives, the 1918–19 influenza epidemic perhaps 50 million, and the famine associated with China's Great Leap Forward in 1958–61 killed about 35 million. These terrible calamities reduced human population by less than 2 percent on each occasion. Other population catastrophes are notable for their intensity. Violence, starvation, or disease (or some combination of them) occasionally obliterated small populations entirely. This fate befell many indigenous peoples in modern times, such as the original Tasmanians. These terrible calamities, and many others like them, killed at most a few million people in each case.

Two population catastrophes in world history are notable for both their scale and their intensity. The first of these was the plague pandemic of 1346–52. In those places where the record is most reliable, it seems to have killed 40 percent or more of the population. It ravaged dense populations in Southwest Asia, Egypt, and Europe, and quite possibly in China, India, and West Africa as well. It did not reach the Americas, and missed many pockets of population elsewhere. But its global toll likely exceeded 100 million at a time when only about 450 million people strode the earth.

The second was the catastrophe that befell Amerindians in the first few generations after 1492. Its scholarly study is fraught with (mostly) respectful disagreement. The first bone of contention in the debates is the size of the American hemisphere's population in 1492.[38] The earliest published estimate, by a seventeenth-century Jesuit, Giovanni Battista Riccioli, was 200 million.[39] Modern scholarly attempts began almost a century ago, and those who considered the matter initially preferred figures in the 40–75 million range. By the 1930s and 1940s, lower numbers seemed more plausible. But in the 1960s, estimates ballooned. The highest, that of anthropologist Henry Dobyns, came in at 90–112 million. Since then efforts to address the issue have settled on a range of 30–60 million people (see Table 2.1).

Table 2.1 **Estimates of the Population of the Americas in 1492 (in chronological order)**

Sapper (1924)	40–50 million
Spinden (1928)	50–75 million
Willcox (1931)	13 million
Kroeber (1939)	8 million
Steward (1949)	15 million
Rosenblat (1954)	13 million
Borah (1964)	100 million
Dobyns (1966)	90–112 million
Mörner (1967)	33 million
Thornton (1987)	72+ million
Denevan (1992)	54 million
Alchon (2003)	47–54 million
Newson (2006)	50–60 million
Livi-Bacci (2008)	30–40 million

Sources: Ángel Rosenblat, *La población indígena y el mestizaje en América* (Buenos Aires: Editorial Nova, 1954), 2 vols.; Russell Thornton, *American Indian Holocaust and Survival* (Norman: University of Oklahoma Press, 1987), 23; William Denevan, ed., *The Native Population of the Americas in 1492* (Madison: University of Wisconsin Press, 1992); Linda Newson, "The Demographic Impact of Colonization," in Victor Bulmer-Thomas, John Coatsworth, and Roberto Contés Conde, eds., *The Cambridge Economic History of Latin America*, (Cambridge: Cambridge University Press, 2006), 143; Massimo Livi-Bacci, *The Destruction of the American Indios* (Cambridge, UK: Polity, 2008), 6.

Different methods brought different results. By and large the highest of the high counters, as they were dubbed, worked from estimates of carrying capacity.[40] Other high counters worked backward from the first available population counts, or from counts of tribute payers to Spanish authorities, using a depopulation ratio to reach an estimated population size for 1492. The low counters also worked backward from the earliest population counts, but applied a more modest depopulation ratio. Low counters were more inclined to discount the guesses of eyewitnesses, on the grounds that they lacked the ability to estimate large human numbers accurately. Recent archaeological work seems to support larger estimates. (I regard the work of Linda Newson as the best available and prefer her hemispheric estimate of 50–60 million.) The debate over the size of the population of the Americas in 1492, although no longer as sharp as it was between 1965 and 1995, will continue, perhaps enlivened by paleogenomic studies and new archaeological techniques.[41]

The entire debate carries political overtones. Low figures imply lesser social complexity, technology, and productive skills among Amerindians. Higher figures are more compatible with an image of agriculturally skilled and economically sophisticated populations. Such contrasting images of pre-Columbian Amerindian society have served any number of ideological agendas.

The population debate carries major significance for the disease history of the Americas. The larger the estimates, the larger the disease catastrophe that befell Amerindians. The smaller the estimates, the more plausible it is to suppose that diseases played only a modest role and that violence, starvation, and other causes of death mattered more. Low counters often reject the notion that pathogens might have run ahead of contact and killed large numbers of people who had never seen Europeans or Africans.

The size of the indigenous population of the West Indies as of Columbus's arrival is no clearer than that of the hemisphere as a whole. While no one before Ricciardi in 1672 attempted to estimate the entire population of the pre-Columbian Americas, for the Caribbean the first Europeans to see it guessed about indigenous population size. Columbus hoped his guesses would convince Spaniards of how bountiful the newly discovered lands were. The Spanish churchman Bartolomé de Las Casas offered guesses calculated to show how wicked and brutal Spaniards were in their Caribbean conquests. The earliest newcomers to the Caribbean typically offered totals that strike modern scholars as suspiciously high and intended to serve political agendas. Modern estimates span about one order of magnitude. The low counters from the mid-twentieth century typically preferred 200,000 or 300,000 for the island Caribbean as whole.[42] More recently, higher estimates have prevailed—around 2–4 million.[43]

Hispaniola had the largest population in 1492, but just how large is in dispute. Las Casas at one point wrote 3–4 million and at another 1 million for Hispaniola alone. Other early visitors guessed half a million. The range of modern scholarly estimates for Hispaniola is from 60,000 to 8 million, lately centering around 300,000 to 600,000.[44] As always, different methods bring different results. Archaeologists often prefer higher estimates based on projections from inferred populations of unearthed settlements.[45] Historians, who are typically uncomfortable with estimates not directly supported by documents, tend to prefer lower figures.[46] Geneticists, for their part, now offer the lowest estimates.[47] These disputes over Hispaniola's pre-Columbian population are characteristic of the Caribbean as a whole.

Whatever Hispaniola's population in 1492, it fell quickly. Authorities undertook counts of the native population as it dwindled before their eyes. Whatever the imperfections of their methods, the trend they revealed is not in dispute. In round numbers, they estimated a population of 60,000 in 1508, falling to 34,000 in 1510, to 26,000 in 1514, to 18,000 by 1518–19 and to less than 2,000 in 1542.

Other Spanish observers thought few to none survived. In 1528, two officials of the Spanish Crown on Hispaniola wrote to Madrid that the Taíno, "once so numerous, became extinct." Another Spanish eyewitness on Hispaniola wrote in 1542 that "the Indians are extinct."[48] Gonzalo Fernández de Oviedo, an official in charge of gold smelting on Hispaniola from 1514 to 1523, and one of the most important authors on the Spanish conquest of that island, maintained in the 1530s that only a "few hundred" survived.[49] In 1550, a Spaniard wrote to the Crown that only 150 remained. Around 1570, the chronicler López de Velasco wrote that fewer than 100 still lived on Hispaniola.[50]

The catastrophic decline in native population probably started later on the other big islands, but was just as thorough as on Hispaniola. On Puerto Rico, Spanish efforts at colonization began in earnest in 1508. By 1530 the indigenous population, whether it was a few tens of thousands or half a million in 1492, had sunk to about 2,000; by 1540 only 50 indigenous individuals remained. On Cuba, where the 1492 population probably stood at about 150,000, Spaniards arrived in force in 1511. The native population by 1531 had fallen to 4,000, and by 1542 only 2,000 remained, according to Spanish estimates. In Jamaica, where Spanish settlers arrived in 1509, by 1542 probably even fewer Amerindians survived than on Cuba.[51] A 1611 count made by Spanish authorities found 74 "*Indios*," and no subsequent document mentions any on Jamaica. Even the smaller islands, visited but not settled by Spaniards, lost almost all their population. The Bahamas, which probably had at least 40,000 people in 1492, had zero by 1513.[52] Martinique in 1555 had only about 100 people in all. Guadeloupe in 1523 was apparently entirely depopulated, although just how that happened is unclear. Modern scholars, echoing some of the early Spanish authors, often write that the native population of the island Caribbean was extinct by the middle of the sixteenth century.[53]

That is exaggeration: the indigenous population of the island Caribbean is not extinct.[54] Sixteenth-century observers missed many who fled to forests or mountains. The genetic makeup of today's Caribbean population shows enduring indigenous ancestry. On Puerto Rico that proportion is higher than on the other big islands, about 10–15 percent—compared to 8 percent on Cuba.[55] So the indigenous population of the Caribbean lives on biologically.[56] The survival of indigenous genes in the modern Caribbean population is roughly analogous to the survival of Taíno words, such as hammock, barbecue, canoe, or tobacco, in modern languages: they survived, but are vastly outnumbered in their new contexts. Probably no fully Taíno person, culturally or biologically speaking, remained after 1600. But a few who were substantially Taíno did.

The Columbian syndemic reached the mainland coasts of the Caribbean soon after hammering the big islands. In the hinterland of Veracruz, Mexico, indigenous population fell by 96 percent between 1519 and 1599. In the nearby

Tabasco region, where an estimated 130,000 to 200,000 people lived in 1500, only 10 percent remained by 1600, and only 2–3 percent by 1650. In the Yucatan peninsula, the Maya population fell by 90 percent, from roughly 2 million in 1500 to 200,000 in 1550. In the Petén Lowlands of Guatemala, population fell by 94 percent between 1520 and 1620. In Honduras, the losses were comparable in areas where Spaniards settled: 96 percent decline in the sixteenth century. In areas of Honduras without Spanish settlement, most of which were on the Caribbean side of the country, the losses came to 50–67 percent. In Nicaragua, indigenous population fell by about half between 1492 and 1587 on the Caribbean coast, where little settlement effort occurred, and about 95 percent in other districts where the Spanish presence was more pervasive. In Panama, according to Oviedo, some 2 million Amerindians lost their lives between 1514 and 1530. A Spaniard who crossed Panama in 1548, Pedro Cieza de León, reported that "the natives are few because wiped out."[57] The population catastrophe that began on Caribbean islands spread to the mainland coasts, and, in time, to the far corners of the Americas.

From the sixteenth century, two main explanations for the population catastrophe of the Caribbean and the Americas more broadly have competed for adherents: violence and epidemics. Both are correct, but in what proportion?[58] Again, political overtones animate the scholarly discussion. Since the time of Las Casas, observers and historians have found in the fate of Amerindians an opportunity to indict Spaniards for their violent cruelty and inhumanity. Modern historians have taken the opportunity to inculpate or exculpate conquistadors, or Europeans generally, or simply imperialism itself. Some authors present the story as an inevitable outcome of the encounter of diverse disease pools and attribute virtually all Amerindian misfortune to infections. Others maintain the role of diseases is easily exaggerated and that violence, dispossession, and enslavement account for the larger share of the demographic disaster.[59] The concept of syndemics may help focus these debates.

Evidence for Spanish violence in the sixteenth-century Caribbean is irrefutable.[60] For those historians comfortable only with interpretations that carry a proper weight of documentation behind them, and suspicious of inferences, Spanish violence is the most convincing explanation for the depopulation in the Caribbean, at least until 1518, because multiple written records attest to it.[61] Those records probably contain exaggerations, as most of them were produced in order to achieve policy changes on the part of the Spanish Crown. The emphasis on Spanish barbarity served the propaganda purposes of Spain's enemies for centuries. But even so, the written record leaves no doubt that violence contributed to the vast loss of life in the Caribbean.

Enslavement and forced migrations within the Caribbean basin, also well documented in Spanish archives, added to the syndemic beginning in the 1490s.

Seizing, keeping, and exchanging captives had been part of the pre-Columbian tradition in the region. When Spaniards arrived, they soon began bartering with local elites for captives and conducting their own slaving raids. Soon, pearl fisheries off the coast of Venezuela and gold mining on Hispaniola each employed enslaved Amerindians, captured both on Caribbean islands and in the hinterlands of Caribbean coasts.[62] In 1503, the Spanish Crown legalized the use of Amerindian slave labor and the scale of both capture and barter grew. The rapid decline in Amerindian population ensured perpetual labor shortage and motivated further slaving. Raids focused on the Bahamas, the Lesser Antilles, the northern coast of South America, and Hispaniola. The Crown encouraged enslavement of any Amerindians designated as "Caribs," a term applied originally by Taíno to their enemies, and used mainly for inhabitants of the Windward and southern Leeward Islands but also almost anyone who resisted Spanish authority with marked success. The scale of enslavement was considerable, reaching its peak between 1514 and 1540. The Crown illegalized it in 1542, but the practice continued, if on smaller scales, and by mid-century its geographical reach extended as far afield as Brazil.[63]

The slave trade in the early Spanish Caribbean raised the risk of death for hundreds of thousands. In effect, the region reproduced an established pattern in world history in which centers of population and production required forced in-migration to offset elevated mortality. Societies in ancient Mesopotamia and the ancient Mediterranean (among other places) maintained active slaving frontiers to keep their fields, workshops, and palaces fully staffed. As in the early Spanish Caribbean, their disease environments, combined with harsh treatment of the enslaved, killed people so fast that the quest for new labor kept expanding to new lands.

Another plausible explanation for the Columbian catastrophe is lowered birth rates. In their quest for gold, early Spanish authorities on Hispaniola and other islands dragooned males into mining work. They thereby sundered families, lowering fertility among indigenous Caribbean peoples. In addition, malnourished women were less likely to conceive than well-fed women. Moreover, in times of extreme disruption, people are reluctant to bring children into a terrifying world. There is minimal evidence one way or another concerning birth rates among Caribbean people either before or soon after Columbus,[64] but extreme societal disruption has lowered fertility sharply in other times and places, and therefore might well have done so in this case.[65]

Starvation brought on by climate shocks might also have played a role. Malnutrition, particularly of certain key micronutrients, makes several diseases more dangerous, including most respiratory infections, diarrheal diseases, malaria, and measles.[66] (Mortality rates for smallpox, plague, and yellow fever are not much affected by malnutrition.) Droughts, common enough in the

Caribbean, might coincidentally have become more frequent or more severe. The worst are typically associated with El Niño years, when (usually) both the Lesser and Greater Antilles are drier than normal (the Central American coast of the Caribbean, on the other hand, is often wetter than normal during an El Niño). The imperfect record of El Niños in the sixteenth century indicates that the Caribbean might have been subject to killing drought in 1500, 1525–26, 1531–32, 1535, 1539–41, 1544, 1546–47, 1552–53, 1558–61, 1565, 1567–68, 1574, 1578–79, 1581–82, 1585, 1587–89, and 1596. The El Niño of 1531–32 coincided with a calamitous measles epidemic, and could easily have exacerbated the toll if it entailed harvest failures and widespread hunger. However, not all El Niño events produced drought and not all droughts were deadly. Moreover, the sixteenth-century record of El Niños appears unexceptional compared to that of more recent centuries, in which widespread killing famine was rare in the Caribbean. So starvation alone likely killed comparatively few. But drought leading to hunger, combined with other stresses in a syndemic, could easily have raised disease mortality and thus contributed to the catastrophe.[67]

Violence and starvation together could not account for population losses on the scale witnessed in the Caribbean between 1492 and 1550. Only a few thousand Spaniards settled in the Caribbean, and many of them were genteel priests or sedentary merchants rather than men of violence.[68] Even with steel-edged weapons, horses, and attack dogs, it is far-fetched to suppose Spaniards could actually have killed more than a small proportion of Caribbean peoples, even if one accepts the lowest estimates of Caribbean indigenous population in 1492.[69] For what it is worth, the bioarchaeological evidence for cranial trauma among Amerindian populations in the Americas generally shows no increase at the time of contact and colonization.[70] Sustained or frequent killing droughts would have caused suffering among Spaniards as well, and therefore would be featured prominently in the written record. But they do not feature prominently, so it is reasonable to conclude that drought and starvation played small supporting roles and were far from dominant variables behind the population catastrophe.

Slaving, however, likely played a larger role. Not only did it tear families apart and reduce fertility, but it raised mortality indirectly. Slave raids, whether conducted by Spaniards or Amerindians, led to violent deaths, even if the slavers' intent was to keep their quarry alive. Probably more important demographically, slave raiding brought thousands of people from all around the Caribbean into ships, ports, mines, and labor camps and exposed them to all manner of infections. After 1518, when smallpox was on the loose in the Caribbean, the toll among those transported and gathered together by the Spanish slave trade climbed mercilessly. As thousands died, the hunt for Amerindian captives quickened, creating a spiral of death motivated by labor demand but executed mainly by microbes.[71]

Newly introduced diseases, abetted by the effects of slaving, surely account for the largest part of the Columbian syndemic. But how large was it? The textual evidence is thin, indeed sketchy enough that some historians have concluded that diseases played no role in the grisly fate of Caribbean native populations prior to a well-attested smallpox outbreak in 1518. No surviving Spanish text mentions any specific disease before 1518. So a few modern scholars have concluded, along with the geographer David Watts, that "Very little of the demographic disaster can be ascribed to the effects of European diseases."[72] (By "European diseases," Watts meant the crowd diseases common in Europe, Asia, and Africa.) That skeptical judgment finds some support with respect to two of the deadliest crowd diseases, smallpox and measles.

Consider transatlantic travel from the perspective of the smallpox virus. To get across the Atlantic required some unlikely coincidences: first, at least one infected sailor or passenger, showing no symptoms had to embark (symptomatic cases would hardly be allowed on shipboard). Second, several other people capable of hosting the virus had to be on board. Only a small proportion of adult Africans and Europeans were non-immunes, and—given the routines of sailors' lives—probably an even smaller share of African and European sailors.[73] On those rare voyages when both these unlikely conditions were met, the original infected individual had to come in contact with at least one other susceptible, who in turn had to convey the virus to a third susceptible and so on. Transatlantic voyages in the sixteenth century took 6–7 weeks, often longer, while infected bodies remained infectious for only a week or 10 days in the case of smallpox. The probability of smallpox making it along a chain of susceptible hosts lengthy enough to arrive in the West Indies was low and a successful transatlantic voyage required a lot of luck.[74]

It was even harder for measles to leap the Atlantic. It spreads more easily and faster than smallpox and exhausts the supply of available hosts more quickly. Its victims remain infectious more briefly than smallpox sufferers, only 5 or 6 days on average. As with smallpox, just about every sailor and passenger in the early sixteenth century would have been a survivor of a childhood bout, and unable to host the virus.

So it is no surprise that the first good evidence of a smallpox epidemic in the West Indies comes from 1518, some 26 years after Columbus first set foot in the Americas. Nor should it be a mystery that the first likely epidemic of measles in the Caribbean came only in the early 1530s. These two highly lethal viruses probably do not explain any of the catastrophe that befell Caribbean populations between 1492 and 1518.

Influenza was another matter, however. Its many strains mutate constantly, so people may acquire immunity to one strain but remain vulnerable to new ones. Thus the average ship's crew, although immune to smallpox and measles, could much more easily transmit influenza to the Americas. Moreover, most flu viruses flourish in pigs, ducks, and chickens as well as human bodies. Thus, when Spanish expeditions began to carry pigs and fowl with them in 1493, they raised the odds of successful transmission of influenza.

As time went on, the probability of imported pathogens making a successful Atlantic crossing improved. The sheer number of voyages across the ocean increased. The size of ships, and of crews, also grew, raising the odds of a sufficient number of susceptibles embarking on any given voyage. As trade and shipping expanded, more Spaniards took to the sea, and presumably more young ones, and some from isolated hamlets, less likely to be immune to all the crowd diseases than were veterans of the teeming disease pools of Seville. In addition, the average duration of transatlantic voyages declined slightly, so fewer non-immune bodies were required for a virus to make the trip intact.[75]

Somehow, within the first 500 or so transatlantic voyages, all the major crowd diseases made it to the Americas—which did not ensure that they would stay there. It is likely that several times pathogens made the crossing, infected all the people within reach (perhaps the population of a small island), and then died out by killing the last body available, or being extinguished by immune response. It might have taken multiple successful crossings for any given crowd disease to wreak large-scale havoc in the Americas.

However, once the crowd diseases reached the large, dense populations in Mexico (1521) and the Andes (late 1520s), their "domestication" in the Americas began. Although those dense populations fell precipitously, they still produced enough babies to keep the crowd diseases in circulation, gradually converting epidemic infections into endemic ones. Whether already endemic by 1580 or so, or spreading in the form of periodic epidemics, viruses such as measles, smallpox, or influenza circulating in Mexico ensured frequent reinfection of almost everywhere else in the Caribbean, even out-of-the-way islands. Voyages from Mexico to Caribbean islands might take only a week or two, and so required no chain of susceptible hosts on shipboard. And susceptible hosts were easier for a pathogen to find in the Americas than anywhere in Atlantic Europe or West Africa, so the odds of a batch of active virus making it intact from Mexico to Cuba were orders of magnitude higher than of one making it from Seville to Cuba. Thus, once smallpox and measles were on the loose on the mainland, by the mid-1530s, they could easily leap to the islands, igniting epidemics as long as enough non-immunes remained.

Assessment of the role of epidemic diseases in the population catastrophe in the Caribbean is complicated by the Black Legend. It originated with Spaniards themselves. Several churchmen found Spanish conduct in the West Indies reprehensible and sought royal intervention on behalf of Amerindians. Foremost among them was Bartolome Las Casas, who arrived in the West

Indies in 1502 as a teenager. He became a landowner and slave owner and took part in massacres of the indigenous inhabitants of Cuba. He came to repent his actions, became a Dominican friar, and took up the cause of the native peoples of the Caribbean. His descriptions of the loss of life left no doubt who was to blame:

> There are two main ways in which those who have traveled to this part of the world pretending to be Christians have uprooted these pitiful peoples and wiped them from the face of the earth. First, they have waged war on them: unjust, bloody, cruel and tyrannical war. Second, they have murdered anyone and everyone who has shown the slightest sign of resistance, or even wishing to escape the torment to which they have subjected him. This latter policy has . . . led to the annihilation of all adult males, whom they habitually subject to the harshest and most iniquitous and brutal slavery that man has ever devised.[76]

Las Casas was not alone in condemning Spanish cruelty. Gonzalo Fernández de Oviedo, the aristocrat charged with overseeing gold smelting operations on Hispaniola in 1514, wrote that Spanish colonists worked Indians to death, uprooted them from their communities through labor drafts, and starved them. Las Casas claimed that Oviedo's book, first published in 1526, contained as many lies as pages, but both men agreed that Spanish wickedness and greed lay behind the population catastrophe on Hispaniola. Subsequent authors eager to vilify Spaniards or Catholics found it congenial to quote Las Casas and Oviedo at length.

Today vilifying Spaniards is no longer high on anyone's agenda, but the Black Legend still has its appeal. It suits those who prefer to see historical events as proceeding from human intentions, rather than as unintended consequences of actions undertaken for other reasons or, more unsettling still, the mindless quests of microorganisms to survive and reproduce. The Black Legend viewpoint keeps humans comfortably sovereign over human history. Moreover, it is amply documented in a handful of eyewitness texts, whereas belief in mass destruction driven by epidemics in the West requires faith in the lethal power of diseases on scales (thankfully) beyond modern experience.[77] The Black Legend fits the sensible argument that colonialism was evil.[78] For all these reasons, the Black Legend interpretation has remained compelling. But for all its charms, and despite the documented cruelty of Spanish conquistadors, the Black Legend is fundamentally misleading as the foremost explanation for the Columbian catastrophe in the Caribbean. Spaniards were indeed guilty of mass murder, forced migration, and forced labor, but even that would not suffice to reduce population by upwards of 95 percent within three generations.[79]

Historical comparison may help assess the relative roles of disease and violence. Consider the repeated conquests of Egypt undertaken by Persian Achaemenids, Alexander's Greeks and Macedonians, Romans, Byzantines, Arabs, Fatimids, Ottomans, and British: all were violent, but none produced massive depopulation of Egypt. Or consider the Spanish and Portuguese conquests and attendant war crimes in sixteenth-century Morocco, performed by the same generation as the conquistadors in the Americas: they did not lead to dramatic—or even discernible—depopulation of the affected districts of Morocco. Conquests and occupations, while often enormously violent, did not normally lead to demographic catastrophes on the scale of what befell the indigenous populations of the Caribbean. In short, Spanish cruelty in the Americas and the Caribbean was probably no different: widespread but not a major cause of population catastrophe in the Caribbean. Its role was mainly indirect, helping to ignite a syndemic. On balance, faith in the great killing power of infectious disease in the Caribbean, and much of the Americas, is well justified.[80]

A closer look at Hispaniola may help too. Columbus's second expedition departed Spain in September 1493 with 17 ships and roughly 1,500 men. It stopped in the Canaries to take on supplies and arrived in the Caribbean in late November. In addition to all manner of plants and animals with which to found a colony, it brought some sort of infection. Columbus recorded that most of his men were sick upon arrival, and he himself was laid up between mid-December 1493 and mid-March 1494. A physician on this expedition, Pedro Alvarez Chanca, wrote that one-third of the Spaniards fell ill within four or five days of disembarking on Hispaniola.[81] Las Casas noted ill health among Spaniards and Amerindians alike. He detailed the suffering of Columbus's men in 1493–94 based on testimony from his father and uncles who had been present. Oviedo, writing well after the fact but with access to relevant accounts from eyewitnesses, confirmed that in 1494 "all through the land the Indians lay dead everywhere. The stench was very great and pestiferous. The ailments that fell upon the Christians were many besides hunger. . . . The Indians who escaped went hastily inland. From this and the great humidity of this land stemmed grave and incurable diseases for those who stayed alive."[82] Some scholars have diagnosed malaria or yellow fever, neither of which is plausible.[83] Typhus is plausible; an even likelier candidate is influenza. Among the supplies Columbus purchased in the Canaries in October 1493 were eight pigs, a species that often hosts influenza—to which Spaniard and Amerindian alike were vulnerable.[84] The evidence is strong that one or more highly infectious diseases ravaged both Spaniards and Amerindians on Hispaniola beginning shortly after Columbus and his men landed in 1493.

That was only the beginning. Las Casas reported that one-third of the previous Taíno population of Hispaniola was dead by 1496, due to massacres, starvation, and sickness.[85] The Spaniards suffered too, perhaps from the same diseases, perhaps from others. Most Spaniards who disembarked on Hispaniola in 1493 had died by 1502 when Las Casas arrived. When Columbus's third expedition arrived in 1498, having stopped at Trinidad and the Venezuelan coast before Hispaniola, many of its crews were sickly. His fourth expedition (1502–3), which stopped in the Cape Verde Islands before crossing the Atlantic, might have brought malaria, although more likely that scourge came to the Americas some years later.[86] In 1502 a new governor, Nicolás de Ovando, sailed to Hispaniola with a complement of 2,500 men. Soon after arrival, 1,000 were dead and more were sick.[87] There are no useful clues as to what infections these Spanish armadas brought with them to the Caribbean, aside from Columbus's pigs in 1493, but they surely brought several, and they communicated some of them to Amerindians.

Not only did large numbers of Amerindians on Hispaniola die fast, a few dispatched from that island to Spain did so as well. In January 1494, Columbus sent Antonio de Torres back to Spain with 12 ships and some 550 Amerindians intended as a gift to King Ferdinand. Before they made it to Spain, however, 200 were dead and half the remainder were sick. These unfortunates were not worked to death in mines or hunted down with dogs. They died on shipboard after weeks of contact with Spaniards who were trying to keep them alive.[88]

In 1518, smallpox made it across the Atlantic. Two Spanish churchmen, writing in January of 1519, guessed that on Hispaniola smallpox had already killed one-third of the remaining population and recorded that it had begun to ravage Puerto Rico. They noted that Spaniards, in contrast, were but little affected.[89] Las Casas suggested this wave of smallpox carried off one-third to one-half of remaining Amerindians.[90] Oviedo wrote that smallpox left Hispaniola, Puerto Rico, Jamaica, and Cuba "desolated of Indians."[91] Hernando Gorjón, who came to Hispaniola in 1502, wrote around 1520 that Spaniards had given smallpox (*viruelas*), measles (*sarampión*), and something he called *romadizo*—which in modern Spanish means a cold or runny nose—to the Amerindians. Measles probably first made it to the Americas only in 1531, but whatever the specific diagnosis, Gorjón recognized that on Hispaniola large numbers of people had been killed by diseases acquired by contact with Spaniards.[92] The catastrophe on Hispaniola was by 1518, and almost certainly by 1493, a syndemic involving a cluster of simultaneous infections and social conditions that conspired to deepen their impact.

Beyond Hispaniola, smallpox after 1518 ricocheted around the Caribbean and adjacent mainlands for several years. On the big islands, by 1518 populations had already declined so much that smallpox was killing a large share of a small remnant population. This was the context in which Oviedo claimed 2 million had died in Panama by 1530 (which should be interpreted to mean "a lot"). Pedro Cieza de León, who crossed the Panamanian isthmus in 1548, wrote that the indigenous populations died in droves from "the poor treatment they have received from Spaniards and the diseases they have contracted."[93] On other mainland coasts, smallpox was in some cases probably the first of the crowd diseases to arrive. Heavy mortality began in Guatemala and Yucatan in 1519, and Nicaragua in 1520. Smallpox accompanied Hernán Cortés to Mexico and ignited an outbreak helping him and his (also sickly) allies overthrow the Aztec state in 1519–21. Smallpox reached the Andes, via Panama, by 1526—before any Spaniards set foot there.[94] In several well-documented cases, smallpox alone within months killed 30 percent or more of populations to whom it was a new infection.

Measles contributed to the ongoing syndemic starting probably in 1531. It might have come from Spain, or perhaps West Africa, for by this time slave trading from Africa to the Caribbean had begun. A new epidemic hit Mexico and Guatemala in 1531 and soon affected Central America as far south as Panama. There a Spaniard wrote in 1531:

> From a ship that has arrived from Nicaragua the pestilence has struck this land, and it has been so great that although it has not yet ended, two parts of all the people that are in this land have died, native Indians as well as slaves, and among them some Christians. I attest to your Majesty that it is the most frightening thing that I have ever seen, because even the strongest does not last more than a day and a half, and some two or three hours, and now it reigns as at the beginning, and has become concentrated in Panama. The clerics are organizing processions, and praying, but not even these pleas to our Lord have lifted his ire, to the point that I do not think there will remain alive a single person in the all the land.[95]

Part of the impact of measles was probably diabolically indirect. Recent immunological research reports that the virus has the capacity to wipe clean one's immune system memory, rendering a body defenseless against other infections. "Immune amnesia" in modern populations lasts two to three years after a case of measles and, until effective vaccination regimes, led to surges in mortality from other infections, especially among children. If measles had the same insidious impact upon immune systems in 1531, it opened the door for infections to which survivors had acquired what, without measles, would have been lifetime immunity.[96] By the early 1530s, several pathogens were likely working together to devastate the Amerindian populations in and around the Caribbean, assisted by the capacity of measles to neutralize immune systems.

Another round of epidemics hit Mexico and Central America hard in the mid-1540s, perhaps a form of typhoid, a waterborne infection. Additional massive epidemics ravaged Mexico, and elsewhere on the mainland, in 1558–63 and 1576–80. Typhus, measles, mumps, influenza, plague, pneumonia, pertussis, scarlet fever, malaria, and smallpox were probably all involved.[97] The full effect of a century of epidemics upon the population of the Americas was a decline of somewhere between 60 percent and 95 percent, with considerable differences from place to place. The higher figure is probably closer to the mark.

One important, if rarely used, method for judging the plausibility of infectious disease as the strongest explanation for the Caribbean catastrophe is analogies from more recent and better documented cases elsewhere. Jesuits in Canada in the seventeenth century wrote detailed accounts of the fate of their allies, the Wendat people (also known as Huron) who lived north of Lake Ontario. After 1634, unspecified epidemics scythed down the Wendat. Smallpox in 1639–40 killed half of those who remained. The French did not enslave or murder the Wendat: violence played no role in their decline until in 1649–50 the neighboring Iroquois took advantage of Wendat demographic weakness, attacking and almost destroying them as a people. The Wendat suffered a disease syndemic for 15 years, compounded after 1649 by violence.[98]

In the late eighteenth and the early nineteenth centuries, Amerindians on the North American prairies suffered at least as severely from smallpox. Its first recorded ravages on the northern plains came in 1781, when it took a grievous toll among the Mandan people along the upper Missouri River. Then the virus left the Mandan alone for 56 years, returning only in 1837. The old people, who had survived smallpox in 1781–82, remained healthy. Almost everyone else died within a year.[99]

Perhaps the best analogues for the Caribbean are Pacific archipelagoes in Polynesia and Micronesia. Hundreds of Pacific islands acquired their first human population starting about 3,000 years ago and ending with the colonization of New Zealand about 750 years ago. Polynesians subsequently remained almost totally isolated from the rest of humankind for many centuries. First contact led to population catastrophes on every island. Observers, usually missionaries, regularly reported in the early nineteenth century that single epidemics, often of measles, influenza, or smallpox, killed a quarter or a third of an island's population. The scale of population loss in Polynesia was on the order of 60–95 percent over the four or five generations after contact. For the best documented cases, population loss of 2–8 percent per year were normal. Colonial violence, labor drafts, and forced migration played a modest role in these population catastrophes. The vast majority of the loss of life derived from disease mortality and reduced fertility, the latter abetted by newly introduced venereal infections.

Hawaii provides a good example, with better documentation than most. While the size of its population in 1778, when outsiders first arrived, is uncertain (recent estimates range from 200,000 to more than 500,000 for the archipelago), the evidence for a post-contact catastrophe is strong. By 1820, native Hawaiians numbered only about 140,000 and by 1850 a mere 85,000. Epidemics in 1848–49 alone scythed down 10 percent of Hawaiians, and smallpox in 1851 killed another 6,000 (or 7 percent) in 1851.[100]

As late as a century ago, Polynesian populations still suffered terribly from infectious disease. In the spring of 1911, measles killed about 19 percent of the people on the island of Rotuma.[101] On Samoa, 22 percent of the population succumbed to the 1918 flu in a few weeks. The influenza pandemic killed the inhabitants of French Polynesia at 31 times the rate it killed people in France (15.5 percent vs. 0.5 percent). Medical care had little impact on flu victims in 1918; a tender grandparent was just as effective as the best doctor, whether in Papeete or Paris. The difference lay partly in population density and partly in prior exposure to a wide variety of respiratory pathogens and the preparedness of the immune systems.[102]

In Micronesia, similar disasters befell populations soon after exposure to crowd diseases. Among the Chamorro, the indigenous people of the largest archipelago of the Marianas (Guam, Tinian, Saipan), there is no doubt about a disease catastrophe. Spanish ships first visited Guam in 1521 and more regularly after 1565, but since the island was so far from any populated lands, crowd diseases faced extreme obstacles in reaching it. Chamorro population declined after 1565, but slowly. After Spanish settlement began in 1668, however, a handful of Jesuits inadvertently imported pestilence to Guam. The Chamorro population of 24,000–30,000 sank to 8,000 by 1700, mainly as a result of smallpox, influenza, tuberculosis, and other killers—although hundreds died by violence.[103] This amounts to an average annual decline, 1668–1700, of 4–5 percent. On the Micronesian island of Kosrae in the nineteenth century, a people numbering about 3,000 dwindled to 300 in three generations. No warfare was involved, only killing diseases.[104] As recently as 1964, the western Caroline Islands in Micronesia lost 29 percent of their population to a single influenza epidemic.[105]

Island populations on the European fringe also suffered catastrophic mortality in epidemics. Iceland was first settled in the 870s. Its population remained so small that the crowd diseases could not become endemic but instead appeared from time to time carried by ships' crews. In one well-documented case, smallpox, reintroduced to Iceland in 1707 after a 35-year absence, killed 26–30 percent of the island's people, and about 40 percent of all those able to host the virus (most people over age 35 were immune). Unfamiliar infections—particularly the breathborne trio of smallpox, measles, and influenza—could bring catastrophic losses to any previously isolated human populations, whether European, Polynesian, or Amerindian, in any part of the world.[106]

Recent instances of first-contact epidemics from Amazonia confirm the power of acute infectious diseases. Data gathered on 117 epidemics among indigenous peoples in Amazonia, from 1874 to 2008, show that the average toll of a single measles, influenza, or malaria epidemic was 20–25 percent.[107] In general, first contact for Amazonian populations, from the sixteenth century to the twenty-first, resulted in concurrent epidemics—syndemics—and a loss of population of 80 percent on average, with violence normally playing a negligible role.[108]

These analogues, from Canada to Guam to Iceland to Amazonia, all of which are better documented than the Caribbean catastrophe, indicate that a single epidemic of an unfamiliar disease could easily wipe out a quarter or a third of a population. And those in the Pacific and Amazonia show that repeated epidemics could reduce a population by 80 percent or even 95 percent over the span of three or four generations. But in the Caribbean, population declines in the decades after 1492 were even worse.

The demographic impact of disease in the Columbian encounter proved disastrous everywhere in the Americas, but not evenly so. The indigenous population decline on the island Caribbean in the three generations after Columbus was almost certainly more than 99 percent. In proportional terms, this easily exceeded the misfortune of Mexico, Central America, and the Andes. Indeed, in those mainland zones, today's population is substantially of Amerindian descent, unlike the Caribbean population. The Caribbean catastrophe exceeded even the documented rates of decline for Polynesian and Micronesian island populations.

Why did the Caribbean get the worst of it? Many factors influenced severity of the Caribbean's Columbian syndemic. One circumstance that surely mattered is simply the geographical position of the Caribbean. Thanks to its location, imported pathogens were more frequently carried to the Caribbean than to anywhere else in the Americas. The patterns of prevailing winds in the Atlantic in effect funneled westward shipping into the Caribbean. Whether they set sail from West Africa or Western Europe, ships and their microbes normally made land first on the islands of the Caribbean. So Caribbean ports, and thus their hinterlands, repeatedly received cargoes of viruses and bacteria. This geographic position distinguished the Caribbean from nearly everywhere else in the Americas for the first century or so after 1492. It is impossible to document the frequency with which pathogens were introduced to various parts of the Americas or the quantities involved. But it seems a strong likelihood that the

Caribbean stood in the least desirable location from this point of view, directly downwind from the sources of new infections. Coastal Brazil, the chief destination for slave ships sailing from Angola and Kongo, probably occupied the second most hazardous position in this respect.

Another possibility is that Caribbean peoples were on the receiving end of more violence and exploitation than others. This is conceivable but seems unlikely with respect to the indigenous peoples elsewhere in the Spanish Empire, such as Mexico and the Andes. They felt the full effect of compulsory labor in mines, forced migration, and separation of families—on top of outright violence—and yet their populations survived in much greater proportion than did those in the Caribbean.

Could the Caribbean have suffered more from food shortage than the American mainland? There are many accounts of Spaniards appropriating food from Caribbean peoples. Newly arrived livestock, especially cattle and goats, chewed and trampled their way through Amerindian gardens. Several accounts also note that due to epidemics no one was available to plant or harvest crops. It is hard to know whether these circumstances were more common in the Caribbean than elsewhere. But by and large, root crops, such as the manioc favored in the Caribbean, could withstand the attentions of pigs, goats, and cattle better than could maize, the staple of most Amerindian farming communities on the mainland. And the accessibility of fish and fruit on the islands also suggests that, even when Spaniards seized or demanded food, indigenous people on the islands had more reliable reserves than on the mainland. So it seems unlikely that malnutrition can go far to explain the excessive mortality in the Caribbean above and beyond that experienced almost everywhere else in the Americas.

Yet another possibility is that Caribbean peoples' fertility collapsed more thoroughly than that of other populations battered by inexplicable misfortune. One Spanish churchman, Fray Pedro de Córdoba, who arrived on Hispaniola in 1510, lamented the collapse of morale and fertility among the native peoples:

> The women, worn out with work, avoid conception and childbearing; lest, being pregnant or with young children, they have twice the work to do. The situation is so bad that many pregnant women seek and induce abortion, others have killed their children with their own hands so that they shall not have to endure the same hardships. . . . I have never read or heard of any nation, not even among the heathen, who have done such harm to their enemies as Christians have done to these unfortunate people who have helped and befriended them in their own land, for . . . they have caused these poor people to lose all desire to procreate. They neither breed nor multiply nor can breed or multiply, nor have they any posterity, which is a very parlous state.[109]

When disease carried off so many spouses and other potential partners, and forced labor kept mates apart, reproduction surely slowed. As Fray Pedro noted, even couples still together might be unwilling to reproduce due to demoralization. Moreover, those children born faced extreme hazard. The epidemics that assaulted Caribbean peoples had age-specific effects that made them more deadly and more demoralizing than the same infections experienced as endemic childhood diseases. Smallpox, measles, and the rest attacked and disabled adults in the Americas, unlike most of China, India, or Europe where they were mainly childhood diseases. Sick (or dead) parents could not nurse their toddlers, and many children surely died as a result, above and beyond those killed directly by infections. That the diseases attacked parents as well as children helps to account for their vehemence in the Americas, and the likely acute loss of morale.[110]

Even in the age of COVID-19 it is hard to imagine the discouragement people must have felt when faced with the relentless lethality of smallpox, measles, influenza, and other infections running amok, their medicines useless, their leaders and religions apparently helpless.[111] It is easy to suppose the will to live evaporated for some people in such circumstances. Could it have evaporated any more for Caribbean peoples than the Wendat or Chamorros or Aztecs? It is possible. Perhaps the fact that in Mexico and Peru, for example, life had featured oppressive states and forced labor before the coming of the Spanish somehow inoculated those populations against despair. Perhaps the fact that more pre-Hispanic traditions and structures survived in Mexico and Peru than in the Caribbean made conquest and depopulation easier to bear. But it is impossible to know.

Two further possible explanations exist for why Caribbean peoples suffered more grievously than average in the Americas: lowland, mosquito-borne diseases and genetic homogeneity. The first and simpler of the two is the presence of additional diseases that were absent or minimally important elsewhere: malaria and yellow fever. In the Caribbean, the densest populations lived at low elevations near the coasts, unlike the Andes or Mesoamerica. Thus the great majority of people in the Caribbean lived in places that were both warm (and thus welcoming to a maximum range of infections) and frequently reinfected by newly arriving ships' crews.

The infections that require warmth are mainly those carried by mosquito vectors such as malaria, yellow fever, and dengue. Yellow fever probably played only a tiny role in the Amerindian catastrophe. It is mainly an urban disease, its vector mosquito did not exist in the Americas before 1492, it was hard for the virus to cross the Atlantic, and the textual evidence for any yellow fever epidemics is doubtful before 1647, by which time the indigenous Caribbean population catastrophe was complete.[112] Dengue could have arrived in the

Caribbean in the sixteenth century, but there is no clear evidence for it before about 1780 at the earliest.[113] In any case, in its most virulent form it typically kills only 10 percent of those infected and its more common forms are less dangerous. Even if combined with other infections, it could have played only a small role in the catastrophe. Probably neither yellow fever nor dengue can account for significant Amerindian mortality.

But malaria was another matter. All forms of malaria are caused by plasmodia and transmitted by one or more of species of mosquitoes of the genus Anopheles. Both the plasmodia and the mosquitoes prosper only in warm weather, so malaria infested areas that were warm at least seasonally. Unlike infection with smallpox or measles, a bout of malaria does not confer immunity. One can contract cases of malaria again and again and build up resistance slowly over the years. Some populations, notably in West and Central Africa, developed heritable resistance due to intensive malarial pressure sustained over many generations. It is especially dangerous to small children, the elderly, and the infirm.[114]

Malaria could cross the Atlantic easily because many Spaniards and just about every West African who set foot on a ship carried malarial parasites. Spaniards, especially those from the lowland southwest around Seville and Cadiz, were often malaria survivors carrying vivax malaria (a milder strain lethal to about 1 percent of those who contract it) in their blood.[115] West Africans almost all carried more deadly falciparum parasites. All malaria needed to become established in the Americas was suitable mosquitoes and sufficient human population. The Americas already contained several efficient vectors for malaria, such as Anopheles darlingi and Anopheles albimanus.[116] Human population in 1492 was large enough and dense enough on several islands to host malaria—although less so with each passing year.

It is impossible to specify when malaria first took hold in the Americas, though its leading historian suggests the 1520s or 1530s.[117] By the 1510s, nearly a thousand enslaved Africans crossed the ocean to Spanish America each year, and over the next few decades the number increased until a lull in the 1550s.[118] Every slave ship brought more malaria. In regions with abundant human and Anopheles mosquito populations, conditions were set for outbreaks of malaria. Caribbean lowlands had sufficient suitable species of Anophelines to ensure that malaria could persist and eventually become endemic. Until it did become endemic, malaria epidemics killed adults and children alike among those born and raised in the Caribbean. Once it became ever-present, truly endemic—a gradual process—it became less dangerous to adults, only because they had withstood many bouts of malaria and developed considerable resistance. Once endemic, it mainly killed children.[119] In sum, malaria likely played a significant role in the post-Columbian catastrophe, negligible until about 1510, growing until roughly 1540, and then falling again: by that time Caribbean populations were small enough that sustainable malarial infection would have been rare.[120]

One last possibility is that Caribbean populations suffered more grievously from waves of epidemics because they were somehow more susceptible than other populations in the Americas. All populations with no prior exposure and no acquired immunity to the crowd diseases (or heritable resistance to malaria) suffered heavily when they encountered these diseases. Their immune systems had never met these pathogens before and could not instantly "recognize" them and build the right antibodies quickly. Caribbean indigenous people in this respect were no different from the remotest tribes in Amazonia who in recent decades have suffered heavily from unfamiliar infections, Pacific islanders in the nineteenth century, Icelanders under age 35 in 1707, or anyone else when first encountering smallpox, measles, and all the rest.

It is important to emphasize that this differential vulnerability arises from acquired immunity and was not a matter of "race," of biological or genetic inferiority or superiority, of better or worse immune systems.[121] It was, rather, a matter of the calibration of immune systems to specific pathogens. Human (and other vertebrate) immune systems, in effect, "learn" to recognize some pathogens and thereafter mobilize immune response quickly so as to prevent infection upon repeat exposure. One bout, if survived, provides immunity (for greater or lesser lengths of time) to most acute viral infections. This was just as true of Taíno as of Iranians, Igbo, Icelanders, and Iroquois. But, in 1492, most East Asians, South Asians, Southwest Asians, Europeans, and many Africans had encountered most of the crowd diseases in childhood, whereas no Taíno did. Toddlers around the world in 1492, once weaned from their mothers' milk with its protective antibodies, stood approximately the same chances of infection and death when first infected with one or several of the crowd diseases. But not adults. Those whose immune systems had "learned" to recognize specific pathogens, by surviving infection, stood far better chances of survival than did those whose immune systems had never before met any of the crowd diseases. All this is summed up in the phrase "acquired immunity."[122]

But in one respect Caribbean peoples may have been particularly susceptible: their immune systems were very similar to one another's. Indigenous Caribbean people's genetic diversity was narrow by world standards because of "founder effects" and "genetic bottlenecks." Like all Amerindians, they descended from small founding populations who passed through Beringia thousands of years ago. In the ensuing 15 or 30 millennia, genetic differentiation provided much less diversity than among most other human populations around the world who either descended from a larger founding group or had more time to create diversity (or both). By any measure, Amerindian genetic diversity was small compared to that of their northeast Asian forebears. A typical African village contains more genetic diversity (on most measures) than the indigenous population of the Americas as a whole.[123]

A second bottleneck narrowed Caribbean genetic diversity further. As we have seen, small founding populations migrated into the Caribbean from South America and Yucatan. Thus the ancestors of the indigenous population of the Caribbean passed through a double bottleneck, one in Beringia and one in the passage from the Americas' continental mainland to the islands. These small founding populations' descendants had little time to diversify through genetic mutation. It stands to reason that their genetic diversity, because of the second bottleneck, should have been narrower than that of the Amerindian population as a whole. And it should have been narrower than that of the bigger populations of Mexico and the Andes, where far more reproduction took place, more mutations occurred, and (probably) more diversity resulted.

It is difficult to test these propositions because Caribbean island populations today carry less than 3 percent of indigenous DNA.[124] The Columbian catastrophe, in effect, destroyed most of the evidence concerning genetic diversity among pre-Columbian Caribbean populations. However, skeletons offer some information. A sample of 27 Taíno skeletons from La Caleta (Dominican Republic) shows extremely low genetic diversity by the standards of Amerindians generally. Another sample of 47 from western Cuba, from an indigenous population sometimes known as the Ciboney, shows the same, as does a smaller sample from Guadeloupe. Indeed, Taíno genetic diversity, to judge from skeletal remains, was among the lowest of any population yet studied anywhere.[125] The sample size is small, so the evidence and conclusions based upon it require caution. But the evidence suggests indigenous Caribbean populations' narrow genetic diversity resulted in immune systems that individually were just as good as anyone else's but collectively were not.[126]

The reason Caribbean people's immune systems in 1492 could have been equal to anyone's individually but less effective collectively is twofold. First, any given pathogen that by chance posed a particular challenge to anyone's immune system posed the same challenge to many other people nearby. Second, people's immune systems create selective pressures upon pathogens that strongly influence which ones survive and reproduce, and which ones don't. In big epidemics, people receive pathogens from many sources, and pathogens diverge into many different strains. Immune systems kill off some strains more quickly than others, but some strains more slowly than others—raising the odds of their spread. Immune systems select for precisely the strains of pathogens that are most difficult for them to cope with, and a population with homogeneous immune systems does so much more efficiently than a population with heterogeneous immune systems.[127] This selection process is broadly similar to that by which the modern proliferation of antibiotics has selected for resistant strains. Strains that a given antibiotic can kill spread very inefficiently when and where that antibiotic is in wide use; but resistant strains survive and spread uninhibitedly.

The degree to which homogeneity in immune systems selects for one or another resistant strain of pathogen depends in part on the speed with which pathogens reproduce and mutate. Measles (and other RNA-based viruses) create strains resistant to immune systems faster and more often than most. The relevance of the genetic homogeneity argument varies not only among human populations, but also among pathogens.[128]

This differential vulnerability, once again, is not a matter of inferiority or superiority of populations. Native peoples of the Americas had (and have) immune systems that can calibrate themselves for smallpox, measles, and influenza just as efficiently as anyone else's.[129] However, in 1492 they were not calibrated for any of these diseases. Moreover, however efficient their individual immune systems, collectively their immune systems were likely less efficient at coping with novel infections than those of more genetically diverse populations. This genetic argument was probably of only modest relevance for the Americas as a whole, and least so for the big populations of Mexico and the Andes, where more reproduction, mutation, and diversification took place. But for the Caribbean population, subject to a double bottleneck and with less time to diversify, this factor probably mattered more—because of narrower genetic diversity.[130]

It is impossible to sort out definitively which among these many possible factors played the largest role in explaining why the Columbian syndemic was deadlier in the Caribbean than elsewhere. And it would be rash to suppose that the hierarchy of importance among these factors was everywhere the same, from the coasts of Cuba to the mountains of Montserrat. But on balance it appears that location, in two senses, explains much of it. Living predominantly in warm and mosquito-infested lowlands, populations on Caribbean islands and in the adjacent mainland were at greater risk for malaria than most of those elsewhere in the Americas. Location downwind from Europe and West Africa, and more frequent reinfection with any number of pathogens brought by newly arriving ships' crews, was likely at least as important. Exploitation and violence were probably no more severe or consequential among Caribbean populations than among several others in the Americas. The argument based on narrow genetic diversity and homogeneity of immune systems is plausible but probably more trivial than significant in the balance. In short, if, as the evidence strongly suggests, the Caribbean's Columbian syndemic was on the whole worse than that elsewhere in the Americas, it was probably geography more than violence, genetics, or anything else that explains it.

The Second Syndemic: The Disease Regime of the Plantation Complex, 1650–1850

The Columbian syndemic eventually played itself out, and by about 1580 changing environmental and demographic conditions put a new and milder disease regime in place. Epidemics still popped up in the Caribbean, but much more rarely and more locally than in the first century after 1492. The main reason for that respite was that the population of the Caribbean by the late sixteenth century was tiny and scattered, and consisted chiefly of people born and raised in either Western Europe or West Africa, whose immune systems had in childhood faced most of the acute infections now either recurrent of ever-present in the Caribbean.[131] So between about 1580 and 1647, the Caribbean region was much healthier than before, even if port cities, such as Cartagena and Havana, like port cities everywhere, teemed with pathogens. That proved a lull before another storm.

In 1647 yellow fever made its deadly debut in the Caribbean, signaling the advent of a new disease regime and a second syndemic. The yellow fever epidemic lasted five years, killing 15 percent of Barbados's population and about 30–35 percent of Havana's, to take the best-documented cases, and faded out in 1652.[132] But the new syndemic continued for two centuries. Several diseases formed a cluster of infection, all of them made either possible or more prevalent by the social oppression characteristic of the Caribbean in the age of slavery. The architects of the new socioeconomic order accidentally built a paradise for pathogens, and a hell on earth for humankind. The plantation regime helped to shape the disease regime, while the disease regime helped to shape the plantation regime.

The disease regime of the West Indies from the mid-seventeenth century to the mid-nineteenth was in effect like that of a gigantic city or army of the era. The plantation complex,[133] so to speak, sucked in large numbers of young people, mostly males; diseases, abetted by deprivation and violence, killed many of them quickly. Its birth rate stood well below its death rate, so the survival of the plantation complex required constant influxes of people to take the places of the dead.[134] In the case of cities around the world, these influxes were of voluntary migrants. In the case of armies, they were both volunteers and conscripts. In the case of the plantation complex in the Caribbean, they were mainly enslaved Africans. In all cases, despite the undeniable violence of cities, armies, and plantations, the chief reason for elevated death rates was disease.

In 1620, Caribbean population both on the islands and adjacent coasts was a small fraction of what it had been in 1492. Cuba had about 7,000 people, and Jamaica perhaps 1,500. Depopulation, combined with the new ongoing seaborne connections to Europe and Africa, led to rapid ecological changes. Fewer people meant less cultivation, less frequent use of fire, and a resurgence of spontaneous vegetation and wildlife, including many newly introduced species from Eurasia or Africa. Important examples included big domestic mammals such as cattle, goats, pigs, and horses; crops such as bananas, citrus, rice, coffee, and sugar; and one species of mosquito—*Aedes aegypti*. The Caribbean increasingly supported motley assemblages of plants and animals in an unstable mix—a globalizing creole ecology.

From the 1620s, enterprising Europeans sought to transform patches of several small islands into tobacco plantations. For three decades they encouraged poor Britons and Frenchmen to come toil on plantations on islands such as St. Kitts or Martinique. Tens of thousands did so, spurred by political turmoil and economic disruption in their home countries—some of it the outgrowth of adverse climate change.[135] They typically came as bondsmen or indentured servants, who owed years of labor in exchange for the price of their passage across the Atlantic.

In the 1640s, sugar entered the picture. Beginning on Barbados, planters invested heavily in sugar plantations that promised, and occasionally delivered, fabulous returns. The Caribbean had most of what made sugar profitable: plenty of sunshine, adequate rainfall in most years, suitable soils, and fuel in the form of biomass with which to boil and crystallize cane juice. But, because of the Columbian syndemic, it lacked cheap labor. Destitute European indentured servants flooded in: Barbados, the only Caribbean island without Anopheles mosquitoes and thus without malaria, saw its population rise nearly 30-fold between 1629 and 1642, reaching 40,000. But by the late 1640s, when yellow fever had fastened its grip on Barbados, the bonded servants died too fast for plantations to remain viable.[136]

The domain of sugar spread from Barbados to other small islands of the eastern Caribbean. But after a few decades the small islands gradually lost two of the requirements for profitable sugar: fertile soils and cheap fuel. Sugar was hard on soil nutrients, and sugar boiling made great demands on combustible biomass. So by the late seventeenth century, planters increasingly moved their operations westward, to bigger islands with more fuel and as yet undepleted soils: Jamaica, Hispaniola, Puerto Rico, and Cuba. The sugar business blossomed especially on Jamaica; in the part of Hispaniola that became French in 1697 and was called Saint-Domingue; and, after 1750, on Cuba.

The ecological changes brought by the sugar boom after 1640 made the Caribbean a more deadly and sickly place. Like the yellow fever virus, its primary vector, *Aedes aegypti* mosquitoes, arrived in the Caribbean from West Africa, presumably via the holds of slave ships.[137] All ships had to carry barrels of water, but slave ships needed much more stored water for their human cargoes. As a result, they provided more *Aedes aegypti* incubators than any others, ensuring vigorous vector populations in every Caribbean port.

Like slave ships, sugar plantations provided ideal habitat for the *Aedes aegypti* mosquito. They offered countless containers in which to lay eggs, such as clay pots used during the initial stages of sugar refining but for most of each year lying around collecting water. They furnished nutrition, in the form of human blood for protein and endless supplies of cane juice for calories. Plantations hosted few birds, dragonflies, or frogs—or any other mosquito predator. The more suited to *Aedes aegypti* the plantations became, the more easily they hosted yellow fever outbreaks, and the faster unseasoned European-born indentured servants died.[138]

The Caribbean sugar plantation complex consisted of more than plantations. To get sugar to distant markets required maritime transportation infrastructure featuring hundreds of small ports and a handful of sizable ones, from which ships sailed to Europe. Each port included systems for water storage—cisterns, rain barrels, little aqueducts—providing habitat suited to *Aedes aegypti* eggs. These port cities, like the plantations, also provided endless blood meals for mosquitoes. Havana, Santiago de Cuba, Cartagena, Veracruz, San Juan, Port Royal, Bridgetown, Cap François, and Willemstad were almost as good as sugar plantations for the yellow fever mosquito—and in the dry season probably better.

The network of Caribbean port cities functioned as a super-city for mosquitoes and pathogens, and ships served as super-vectors carrying both from one group of human bodies to the next. Ship traffic shuttled among the harbors, ensuring that no port lacked for mosquitoes or pathogens for long. Even out-of-the-way ports would receive frequent resupply of both *Aedes aegypti* and yellow fever virus thanks to the prevalence of smuggling in the region. Sugar plantations, ships, and ports combined to provide an ecosystem supremely suited to the transmission of yellow fever.

Plantations suited anopheline mosquitoes almost as well as they did *Aedes aegypti*. The main malaria vector in the Caribbean, *Anopheles albimanus*, is a short-lived mosquito, so its population density is especially sensitive to breeding conditions. The ecological changes imposed by the plantation economy provided additional breeding grounds in the form of irrigation ditches, canals, and puddles.[139] Clearing of woodlands, the first task when carving out a plantation, also favored *An. albimanus*. They like to lay eggs in the open sun amid swampy lowland terrain that deforestation, erosion, and siltation often created or expanded.[140]

In addition, the built environment on sugar plantations favored anophelines and malaria. Sugar boiling houses often maintained small artificial ponds nearby to quench accidental fires. After the 1660s, plantations often had their own distilleries and after 1750 usually contained purpose-built ponds of 20,000 to 30,000 gallons to supply their stills. Ponds surely extended the peak mosquito season further into the dry months and thus prolonged the seasonal risk of mosquito-borne disease for the people who worked in or lived near plantation distilleries.[141]

For these ecological and economic changes to foment epidemics, mosquitoes had to find enough people to bite. Here again the plantation complex inspired the necessary changes. In 1600, the total population of the island Caribbean stood below 100,000. By 1640, after the arrival of tens of thousands of indentured servants from the British Isles, it surpassed 200,000. By 1750, the total reached about 1 million, a consequence of the arrival of masses of enslaved Africans. In round numbers, Cuba had 150,000 people; Saint-Domingue 180,000; and Jamaica 140,000. Even small islands such as those of the Danish West Indies witnessed population surges: a nine-fold increase to 45,000 between 1720 and 1835.[142] About 70 percent of the people across the island Caribbean in 1750 were enslaved. By 1850, the total for the island Caribbean was about 2.2 million or 11 times the figure as of 1640.[143]

Caribbean populations gradually became large and dense enough to sustain frequent epidemics. Although Cuba in 1750 had a population density only about 1 percent of that of Barbados, Havana alone contained enough people, maybe 35,000,[144] to keep some pathogens in circulation. Despite low overall population densities, Jamaica and Saint-Domingue also featured urban landscapes crowded enough for the easy transmission of infectious disease. For infections such as yellow fever or smallpox that conferred immunity upon survivors, the outbreak of epidemics also required that populations contain sufficient proportions of non-immunes. That required the arrival of babies or immigrants.[145]

The bodies that came to the Caribbean to serve the plantation complex normally arrived teeming with pathogens and suffering from poor nutrition. Roughly 4.5 million enslaved Africans disembarked in Caribbean ports between 1600 and 1850, of whom 65–70 percent were male. They had first endured voyages on foot or in canoes, often in chains, from their homes to African coastal ports. They had been imprisoned there in barracks or pens (called barracoons in the Atlantic slave trade), held cheek by jowl with people from far-flung regions of Atlantic Africa. Crowded barracoons put the newly enslaved at risk of many infections unfamiliar to them. Somewhere between 10 and 40 percent of enslaved Africans died between enslavement and embarkation on a slave ship, and many of the survivors were in poor health, although normally not showing it, when their ship weighed anchor.

Slave health typically deteriorated after embarkation. Transatlantic slave voyages lasted for an average of 70–90 days, and the shortest took 50–55 days. Food often spoiled on shipboard in the equatorial heat. On voyages departing

West African coasts long after the yam harvest, mortality in the Middle Passage was half again as great as on voyages that departed months earlier when yams were fresh and plentiful. On long voyages, drinking water ran short. Dehydration may have been the single most deadly killer in the transatlantic slave trade.[146] If it wasn't, then dysentery claimed that doubtful honor: by one estimate, it killed about 40 percent of those Africans who died in the Middle Passage.[147] Although they hoped to preserve their human cargoes for sale,[148] slavers confined each transported African for months in about as much space as a passenger has today on an economy flight. Whether driven by law or self-interest, slavers typically employed doctors on board for the Middle Passage, but they did as much harm as good. Voyages on which the doctor died suffered nearly identical average slave and crew mortality as voyages on which the doctor survived.[149] Slave mortality on the Middle Passage in the early decades of the transatlantic trade averaged about 25 percent, falling to about 10 percent in the late eighteenth century, and 5 percent in the early nineteenth century.[150]

The survivors were often in perilous condition upon arrival in the Caribbean. About 3 percent of them died in the days or weeks before they could be sold; somewhat more died if they arrived in summer.[151] Once sold, three out of four of them went to work on sugar plantations, among the unhealthiest of environments on Earth.[152]

Europeans, a minority of arrivals to Caribbean shores after 1660, on average enjoyed better health than enslaved Africans until disembarkation. That may not have been true of slave-trade crewmen: their Middle Passage mortality rates were broadly similar to those of slaves.[153] But those who crossed directly from Europe without a detour to the coasts of Africa enjoyed survival rates far higher than anyone's on the Middle Passage. Their condition upon arrival in Cuba or Jamaica was far better. Their prospects plummeted, however, the moment they came within range of Caribbean mosquitoes.

The first year in the Caribbean was the most dangerous for new arrivals, whether African or European. Perhaps as many as one-third of newly arrived enslaved Africans died within 12 months.[154] European newcomers, after 1650 at least, ran even greater risks upon disembarking in Caribbean ports: one estimate is that 45 percent died before the "seasoning" period (the first 6 to 12 months in the region) ended.[155] In seventeenth-century Cartagena, a Jesuit noted that newcomers felt "languid and weakened," as if "injured by a serious disease."[156] One French author recommended that Europeans refrain from indulgences, including "intellectual work," for 18–24 months after setting foot in the Caribbean lest an overtaxed constitution bring on illness.[157] Everyone knew that new arrivals ran a terrible risk. In early nineteenth-century Jamaica, according to Renny's *An History of Jamaica*, black women taunted white newcomers with the verse:

New-come buckra,
He get sick,
He tak fever,
He be die;
He be die;
New-come buckra.[158]

While violence and accidents accounted for some proportion of the catastrophic mortality among new arrivals, the lion's share resulted from the Caribbean disease environment. The gauntlet of lethal infections included almost all the crowd diseases, notably the viruses smallpox, measles, mumps, rubella, and influenza, and the bacterial infections pneumonia, scarlet fever, pertussis, typhus, and plague.[159] It also included yellow fever and malaria. Any of these diseases might kill victims within days. In addition, a handful of potentially lethal diseases killed more slowly or brought years of suffering and disability: yaws, leprosy, filiariasis (guinea worm), and tetanus prominent among them. This disease regime formed gradually over the centuries between 1493 and 1700. It deteriorated after 1647, thanks to the installation of the sugar complex, the arrival of yellow fever, the slow buildup of population density, and the quickening of traffic bringing reinfection from Africa and Europe and the latest strains of influenza. By 1730, it had attained nearly its full ferocity, worsened slightly by the addition of dengue probably late in the eighteenth century.

Seventeenth- and eighteenth-century authors on health and disease in the Caribbean tended to organize their discussions into diseases of whites and diseases of blacks, exaggerating their difference.[160] A few also commented on differences in health between males and females.[161] They also emphasized a very real distinction in health between new arrivals and longtime residents of the region.[162] An alternative, followed here, is to recognize the importance of where people lived and worked, and identify the distinct disease environments of plantations, cities, and armies.[163]

The plantations of the Caribbean, especially the sugar plantations, were among the most hazardous disease environments anywhere in the two centuries between 1650 and 1850.[164] The fundamental reasons for that were geographical, historical, and social—and synergistic. First, the islands were warm year-round and usually well supplied with rainfall, ensuring a high diversity of pathogens once the Caribbean became linked to the rest of the world. This circumstance was no different from other parts of the world that were similarly warm, wet, and well connected by shipping to global circuits. It ensured continual reinfection with whatever pathogens lurked in London, Bordeaux, Seville, Ouidah, or Benguela. New strains of influenza, rubella, or plague were likelier to make it to the Caribbean than to other parts of the Americas. In the interval between about

1580 and 1647 when the Caribbean had been much healthier than either before or after, it was less well connected by shipping. It also had too few people to allow efficient circulation of infections until the plantation economy took hold.

Beyond matters of economic geography, the plantations of the Caribbean featured at least three forms of social oppression that contributed to the second syndemic. The most important of these was malnutrition among the enslaved.[165] Texts and skeletal remains confirm that enslaved populations were severely underfed, frequently on the edge of starvation, and routinely lacking in nutrients essential to human health.[166] In the best of times, slave diets throughout the region tended to be poor in protein, fats, vitamin B, vitamin A, iron, calcium, and other minerals.[167] Planters usually tried to economize on slave provisions, whether that meant food purchased or time granted to slaves to grow, gather, hunt, or fish for their own food.[168] Where enslaved workers relied on their own labor and provisioning grounds, the autumn was often a hungry season. In the early nineteenth century in the Danish West Indies, for example, where the enslaved obtained about 30 percent of their food themselves through provisioning grounds, autumn witnessed the highest mortality especially among children, due above all to seasonal malnutrition and malaria.[169] Across the region, those producing their own food relied heavily on manioc, sweet potatoes, yams, bananas, and other starchy foods. Children especially suffered from kwashiorkor—a deficiency of protein and calories. Babies suffering from thiamine shortage typically developed beriberi, often fatally. Everyone suffered food shortages when insect plagues, hurricanes, or drought ravaged crops, but slaves were the first to starve. For those who relied on food purchased by masters, nutrition was no less precarious. Price hikes, spoilage in shipping, and above all interruption of commerce in time of war routinely led to deprivation. Malnutrition frequently weakened the immune response of enslaved West Indians—as had often been true of Amerindians in the wake of Columbus.

A second form of oppression that led to higher disease burdens on plantations was the use of the whip. Overseers used the lash liberally as an integral part of the terror regime that underpinned plantations' social hierarchy. Skin sliced open by the whip invited infection. Yaws and tetanus, which afflicted enslaved bodies far more than free ones, were among the diseases that whipping made more common.[170]

A third form of oppression reflected in the burden of disease on plantations was sexual. Males in positions of authority routinely raped and assaulted enslaved women. By his count, Thomas Thistlewood, a plantation overseer on Jamaica, had sex with 138 different enslaved women over four decades.[171] Marriage was rare on plantations, and so were monogamy and chastity.[172] This situation ensured the prevalence of venereal diseases, including venereal syphilis, among both enslaved and free, black and white. Venereal diseases killed adults slowly if at all, but 25–50 percent of infants born with syphilis acquired in utero from their mothers died very young.[173] Evidence from skeletal bone lesions from a Barbados cemetery suggests that about 10 percent of the adult enslaved population on that island suffered from one or another form of syphilis. Women infected with syphilis often could not conceive, and if they could, they were likelier to miscarry, and if they carried to term, the result in 25–50 percent of cases was stillbirth. Syphilis was a major reason why enslaved populations had low birth rates.[174]

Sugar plantations were the deadliest among all the plantations. They were at lower elevations than indigo or coffee plantations, and for that reason, warmer and more hospitable to mosquito disease vectors. Moreover, sugar plantations were likelier environments for cross-species infection (there are about 300 infections humans can get from animals) because they had many mules, horses, and oxen used for hauling felled tree trunks and cartloads of manure or harvested cane. A large proportion of the livestock lived and worked next to humans, exacerbating sanitation problems.[175] In addition, work in sugar mills and boiling houses posed more serious risk of severe injury than any routine labor on coffee, cotton, indigo, or tobacco plantations.

On sugar plantations, enslaved populations on average grew less tall and died more quickly than those working on other types of plantations. Enslaved children on sugar plantations on average were shorter than their parents, indicating more pervasive malnutrition than in other settings.[176] In Jamaica in the early 1830s, slave populations on sugar plantations had a crude birth rate of 23/1,000 and a crude death rate of 35/1,000, amounting to an annual decline of 1.2 percent. Other Jamaican plantations at that time averaged a 0.2 percent increase annually, mainly due to lower death rates.[177] In the Danish West Indies, elevated infant and child mortality on sugar plantations lasted into the 1880s, decades after the end of slavery (1848), whereas on other plantations abolition brought fairly rapid improvements in health. An especially arduous work regime, combined with the higher risks of yellow fever, probably accounted for the distinctive peril to health posed by sugar plantations.[178]

The specific infections behind the plantations' contribution to the second syndemic included mosquito-borne diseases, especially malaria, yellow fever, and dengue; crowd diseases, especially smallpox and measles; most forms of dysentery; plus yaws, tuberculosis, tetanus, hookworm, and other worms and parasites. Malaria was mainly a rural disease, prevalent where conditions favored the vector mosquitoes *Anopheles albimanus* or *Anopheles darlingi*; where human population was dense; and where a sufficient proportion of those humans were not resistant to malaria infection. In practice, these requirements confined malaria mainly to well populated rural areas, mostly plantations, where it took a heavy toll upon children in particular, but also on any adults born and raised in

Figure 2.2 "View of a Sugar Plantation, French West Indies, 1762." The sugar plantation was the unhealthiest of all Caribbean disease environments. This image of a mid-eighteenth century French Caribbean sugar plantation gives a sense of the landscape transformation required to produce sugar. The key includes cane fields (5); manioc plots (13); slave quarters (2); water-powered mill for grinding cane (6); and sugar boiling house (7). From Denis Diderot, *Encyclopédie, ou, Dictionnaire Raisonné des Sciences, des Arts et des Metiers ... Recueil de Planches, sur les Sciences ...* (Paris, 1762), vol. 1, plate I. From Special Collections Department, University of Virginia Library.

cooler climates where few if any anopheline mosquitoes or malarial plasmodia lurked.

Yellow fever also bedeviled sugar plantations, especially among adults without prior experience of the virus. Among newly arrived Europeans, yellow fever inspired more dread than any other disease—and with good reason. It generally left children unscathed, but killed roughly 15–50 percent of adults who encountered it for the first time, especially young adults in the prime of life. People born and raised between Senegal and Angola, or with a few months' experience in those lands, were likely to have contracted yellow fever and to be immune for life. The same was true after 1647 for those who had lived for many years in the Caribbean. While many observers in the Caribbean after 1650 thought that black people were immune to yellow fever and whites were not, it was, almost certainly, people's prior exposure and acquired immunity that rendered them invulnerable to yellow fever.[179]

The crowd diseases, especially smallpox, visited plantations regularly. One British author, writing of smallpox on Barbados in the 1730s and 1740s, claimed, "we are seldom free from it in some part of the island or other."[180] Saint-Domingue hosted a smallpox outbreak every five or six years between 1750 and 1790, most seriously in 1782–84.[181] Among large and dense populations, smallpox typically was a childhood diseases that immunized survivors. But it was possible for a given plantation to avoid infection for a decade or two, in which case when the virus visited it killed many young adults. And smallpox could rage in the wake of measles, if the latter infection caused immune-system amnesia.

Except for those who had recently hosted measles, people born and raised in thickly populated parts of Europe or Africa were likely to be immune to most of the crowd diseases by the time they arrived in the Caribbean. Moreover, anyone passing through any of the major seaports that sent ships to the Caribbean would likely encounter the crowd diseases and either die or acquire immunity to them. People born and raised on plantations in the Caribbean itself, regardless of ancestry, were probably likelier than newcomers to remain susceptible into adulthood—one of the few respects in which the African-born and European-born enjoyed better odds than did the Caribbean-born once in the West Indies.

Dysenteries of every sort plagued plantations too. Poor sanitation, the proximity to livestock, and the routine handling of manure and animal byproducts ensured frequent infection, especially among small children. In the Danish West Indies in the 1840s, dysenteries ranked second to fevers as a recorded cause of death among the enslaved population.[182] They also ranked near the top on Jamaican plantations, from 1760 to 1830.[183]

Tuberculosis and several forms of pneumonia seem to have affected the enslaved far more severely than free people on Caribbean plantations. The likeliest explanation is crowding in slave quarters combined with malnutrition. In Africa, both diseases were much less prevalent than they became among Africans on Caribbean plantations. In one slave cemetery on Guadeloupe, slightly more than 10 percent of skeletons showed signs of tuberculosis.[184] One sample from the British West Indies implies that tuberculosis accounted for 12 percent of deaths among plantation slaves, although other samples suggest 4–6 percent might be closer to the average.[185]

Tetanus, a bacterial infection that lurks in soil and feces, especially where livestock are common, seriously afflicted plantation populations too. It commonly enters human bodies through a cut or wound in the skin. People such as cane workers who went barefoot and were subject to frequent abrasions, cuts, and other wounds—sometimes inflicted by an overseer's whip—were more likely to develop tetanus than others. Neonatal tetanus, often the result of contamination of a snipped umbilical cord, was a major killer of newborns born to enslaved mothers on Caribbean plantations. It killed 90 percent who contracted it. Somewhere between 25 percent and 50 percent of all babies born of West Indian enslaved mothers died in the first two weeks of life from tetanus. Even after the abolition of slavery, neonatal tetanus still killed a large share of infants on plantations. Babies born of European women suffered far less from neonatal tetanus, presumably due to better sanitary conditions in the planters' houses.[186]

After the simple fact of the presence and regular reintroduction of so many pathogens, the main reason behind the Caribbean's second syndemic was the dismal living and working conditions of plantation slavery, especially on sugar plantations. These conditions were bad throughout, at their deadliest in the mid- to late eighteenth century, and slightly better by the nineteenth.[187]

Cities also contributed mightily to the second syndemic. Urban populations in the Caribbean remained below one-tenth of the total until well after 1850. Smaller islands might have a substantial urban proportion if one counts settlements of 1,000 or 2,000 people as urban. Among the large islands, Cuba was exceptional: perhaps a quarter of Cuba's population lived in and around Havana by 1780. But across the Caribbean throughout the eighteenth century, the urban proportion stood closer to 5–10 percent, a little higher than the global average of 3–5 percent. In the Caribbean, it climbed sharply only after 1870 or so—partly a result of improvements to city sanitation.[188]

Caribbean cities were almost all port cities, and travel among them by sea was swift and frequent. So in epidemiological terms, the dozens of small cities functioned almost as a single city of roughly 100,000 people in 1750 and twice that in 1850. Their interconnectedness also tightened over time. Havana's ship traffic, for example, more than doubled in the decades between 1715 and 1760.[189] To take an extreme case, the Danish West Indies as a whole received only 1 convoy per week from Denmark, from 1752 to 1838, but the little island of St. Thomas alone welcomed 40–80 vessels weekly between the 1840s and 1860s.[190] Caribbean cities, like those on the shores of the Mediterranean or the South China Sea, were tightly linked to one another, and to the wider world, and efficiently conveyed pathogens from one host population to another.[191]

While Caribbean cities were networked so as—inadvertently—to maximize disease transmission, their populations were in one respect configured so as to have the opposite effect. From the sixteenth century on, their populations came from all over Atlantic Africa, tapping into the most genetically diverse human population anywhere (i.e., Africans), as well as from many places in Europe. On several islands, many people carried a small genetic inheritance from in- digenous populations of the Caribbean. Moreover, those populations quickly mixed and merged, producing creoles who were, genetically speaking, among the most global citizens on earth in the seventeenth and eighteenth centuries.[192] The extreme genetic heterogeneity of Caribbean urban populations meant that, collectively, their immune systems, because so different one to the next, were more effective in checking disease transmission than those of other populations elsewhere—other things being equal. However, Caribbean cities swirled with

Figure 2.3 Vue Generale de la Havana. Ca. 1840. Havana was the most active port in the Caribbean, a crucial node in the movement of pathogens from host to host among the islands and mainlands. Wikimedia Commons.

infection, and genetic heterogeneity could offer only modest protection to Caribbean city dwellers against the onslaught of pathogens.

In most cases, the prevalent diseases of Caribbean cities were the same as on the plantations but with different frequencies and patterns. Malaria was comparatively rare in cities, although urban dwellers who visited the countryside could easily acquire it. Yellow fever, however, was commonplace because *Aedes aegypti* thrive amid water storage infrastructure. By 1650, if not before, every port city harbored the necessary mosquito population for an outbreak of yellow fever. By 1750, if not before, every port city was sufficiently networked with others that if the yellow fever virus was not present it soon would be introduced. The annals of Cartagena, Portobello, Veracruz, Havana, Santiago de Cuba, Port Royal, Cap-Nord, Pointe-à-Pitre, Port-of-Spain, Bridgetown, New Orleans, Paramaribo, Cayenne, and dozens of other cities of the Greater Caribbean were rife with yellow fever epidemics from 1647 until about 1900. Cities were less dangerous to people who had grown up in the Caribbean, or West Africa, and acquired yellow fever immunity than to newcomers from elsewhere. An Englishman in Havana in 1820 noted, "The foreign vessels that arrive here suffer greatly. Whole crews are swept off within a few weeks of their arrival."[193] According to Humboldt, in the early nineteenth century denizens of Veracruz welcomed outbreaks of yellow fever because they knew they would remain unaffected through immunity conferred by prior exposure, while interlopers from the countryside who competed for trade and jobs would be decimated.[194]

Other infections that spread amid water infrastructure also beset Caribbean cities and were more prevalent there than on plantations. In the absence of piped water and in most cases reliant on streams, cisterns, or shallow wells, urban water supplies were easily contaminated by pathogens. Cartagena and Havana, for example, lacked reliable sources of clean water.[195] So did populations in the Danish West Indies, Surinam, and Saint-Domingue and no doubt elsewhere in the Caribbean.[196] In this respect they were not at all unusual before 1850: impure water was normal for most people around the world, urban or rural, especially those in big cities or living amid livestock. They lived and died with typhoid, polio, dysentery, twenty or more less famous waterborne infections, and, after 1832, cholera.

Cholera kills roughly half those whom it infects, often within a couple of days. The pathogen, a bacterium known as *Vibrio cholerae*, typically infects people who drink water contaminated by the diarrhea of someone already infected. Thus it spreads fastest in crowded communities with poor sanitation infrastructure—such as cities and ships anywhere before about 1870. Children and undernourished people are at higher risk of dying from it. Endemic to brackish waters around the Bay of Bengal, cholera escaped in the early nineteenth century in the first of six pandemic waves. Caribbean port cities met the pathogen's requirements nicely.[197]

It arrived in the Americas and the Caribbean, at least Cuba and Mexico, by 1832. It returned intermittently thanks to the maritime traffic between the Caribbean and the wider world. In 1833, cholera in Havana in the span of four months killed 9,300 (of a city population of 160,000).[198] By 1836, some 23,000 had succumbed in and around Havana and another 7,000 elsewhere in Cuba.[199] In coastal Mexico, cholera killed a quarter of Campeche's 20,000 people in a few weeks in 1833 and one-third of Veracruz's inhabitants. It hit other Mexican port cities such as Tampico.[200] A second wave of cholera washed over Caribbean ports in the 1850s. It killed some 50,000 on Cuba, 40,000 to 50,000 on Jamaica, nearly 25,000 on Barbados, and 30,000 on Puerto Rico. Cholera returned to Havana in 1867–68, carrying off another 6,000 to 8,000 but thereafter vanished from the Caribbean for the rest of the nineteenth century. Cholera's three visits cost about 200,000 lives on Cuba, Jamaica, and Puerto Rico combined, and more elsewhere in the Caribbean.[201] It found its victims chiefly in port cities.

With the twin scourges of yellow fever and cholera repeatedly stalking Caribbean cities, abetted by several other less fearsome diseases, they remained deadly environments well past 1850. Whereas conditions on plantations by 1850 had almost entirely stopped killing people faster than others were born, the disease environments of Caribbean cities continued to do so until the end of the nineteenth century.

Military duty at times presented disease risks even more dangerous than those of Caribbean cities or plantations. The plantation economy invested the Caribbean with a military value it had previously lacked. More islands, after the 1640s, seemed worth attacking and defending. Britain, France, and Spain carried the conflicts of the European continent to the Caribbean on an increasing scale. As the islands' populations became mainly enslaved people with doubtful loyalties to their masters' countries, warfare in the Caribbean of necessity became expeditionary warfare. The last major campaign on which a large share of troops hailed from the Caribbean was the English conquest of Jamaica in 1655, for which soldiers were recruited among the poor whites of Barbados and other islands. Thereafter, as the white proportion of island populations fell to 10–15 percent, local authorities and elites would no longer contemplate mobilizing Caribbean-based whites to go seize another island while leaving homes and plantations undefended. Instead, soldiers came from afar.

Expeditionary warfare entailed a high risk of heavy losses to disease. Soldiers and sailors recruited from outside the Caribbean generally lacked the requisite immunities to withstand the region's disease environments. Those from Europe and North America, in particular, normally had no prior exposure to either yellow fever or falciparum malaria. These two acute infections, in combination with the routine diseases of pre-modern military life anywhere—typhus and dysentery prominent among them—resulted in frequent catastrophic mortality, sometimes amounting to the annihilation of an expedition.

While typhus and dysentery affected combatants more or less equally, yellow fever and malaria in the Caribbean were partisan. They hardly affected those born and raised in endemic yellow fever and malaria zones, whether in the Caribbean or Africa, but they struck down legions of non-immunes serving in European armies and navies. For that reason, these mosquito-borne diseases helped to defend the geopolitical status quo in the Caribbean from 1690 to 1790, in particular preventing Spain from suffering more than it did from British assaults. After 1790, when Caribbean populations, beginning in Saint-Domingue/Haiti, rose in rebellion against European colonial masters, the political meaning of the military disease ecology of the Caribbean shifted, favoring revolutionaries and working against colonial rule.[202]

The dismal record for 21 expeditions or cruises from 1690 to 1865 for which archives preserve reasonably reliable quantitative data appears in Table 2.2. Several additional expeditions suffered from high disease mortality, as evidenced by words chosen by survivors to describe them, but the available documentation includes no numbers. As a Jamaican planter and politician put it, referring to British troops sent out to undo the Haitian Revolution, they "dropt like the leaves in autumn . . . without a contest with any other enemy than sickness."[203] Disease mortality on military expeditions often reached 50–70 percent.[204]

Table 2.2 **Disease Losses in Expeditionary Warfare in the Caribbean, 1690–1865**

Year	Campaign	Invader	Size of Invasion Force	Proportion of Force Lost to Disease	Notes
1690	St. Kitts	Britain	??	50%	
1693	Barbados	France	??	Almost half	
1695	Saint-Domingue	Britain	??	77% of those put ashore	
1697	Cartagena	France	5,600	40%	Including those lost to disease aboard fleeing ships
1702	Saint-Domingue coast cruise	Britain	4,000	35%	A naval cruise, not an invasion
1703	Guadeloupe	Britain	3,500	12–15%	Another 9% killed in combat
1726	Cartagena and environs	Britain	4,750	84%	Mostly sailors; a cruise, not an invasion
1741–42	Cartagena and Santiago de Cuba	Britain	29,000	71%	Another 3% lost in combat
1756	cruise	France	2,200	15%	
1758	Cruise off Saint-Domingue	France	1,200	17%	
1759	Guadeloupe	Britain	5,000	50%	
1762	Havana	Britain	15,000	65%	Another 3–4% killed in combat
1762	cruise	France	3,840	9%	

Date	Place	Power	Deaths	Percentage	Notes
1774–77	Surinam	Dutch	1,650	90%?	6–8% survived the expedition, but the ratio of combat-to-disease deaths is uncertain
1780	Nicaragua	Britain	1,800	77%	Minimal combat
1780	Gulf Coast forts	Spain	7,000	57%	
1793–98	Saint-Domingue	Britain	25,000	60–63%	
1795–96	St. Lucia	Britain	??	96%	Minimal combat
1802–04	Saint-Domingue/Haiti	France	60,000–65,000	55–75%	Figures are less precise here
1813–21	Venezuela	Spain	16,000–17,000	??	91–96% dead from all causes; maybe 75% from disease?
1861–65	Santo Domingo	Spain	51,000	40–60%	93% of all Spanish army deaths from disease

Source: McNeill, *Mosquito Empires*, 144–48, 166–67, 185–86, 189–91, 197, 247, 258–59, 265, 283, 295; Christian Buchet, *La lutte pour l'espace Caraïbe et la façade Atlantique de l'Amérique central et sud (1672–1763)* (Paris: Librairie de l'Inde, 1991), 2: 785–97. For the 1861–65 Dominican case, Micheal Clodfelter, *Warfare and Armed Conflicts: A Statistical Encyclopedia of Casualty and Other Figures, 1492–2015* (Jefferson, NC: McFarland, 2017), 306; partial data appear in Santiago Castro Ventura, *La Guerra Restauradora* (Santo Domingo: Manati, 2014), 284–85.

Note: Lower figures for French disease mortality in 1802 appear in the careful account by Philippe Girard, *The Slaves Who Defeated Napoleon: Toussaint L'Ouverture and the Haitian War of Independence, 1801–1804* (Tuscaloosa: University of Alabama Press, 2011), 179–80. He says that using conservative estimates, 43% died of yellow fever, 8% other diseases, 14% in combat, and 20% were in hospital or convalescent; overall in 1802, disease killed or incapacitated more than 70% of French forces.

The variability in disease mortality among expeditions was considerable. By and large, the healthiest results came from small, brief expeditions, outside the rainy season, that required putting few if any men ashore. The deadliest, on the other hand, exposed large numbers of men to conditions on land for many months (or years), including the rainy summer season. Naval cruises involved less risk than sieges. The reasons for these differences boiled down to the risk of yellow fever and malaria. The risk spiked when the proportion of non-immunes within reach of mosquitoes was highest—in other words, when a large expeditionary force put ashore and stayed through one or more rainy season, as in sieges and occupations of Cartagena in 1741, Havana in 1762, and Saint-Domingue 1793–1804.

The deadliest expeditions mounted by Britain also often coincided with mortality crises at home caused either by bad harvests or epidemics at home. The most severe mortality in England between 1670 and 1830 came in 1694–95, 1741–42, and 1762–63—all of them years in which British expeditions to the West Indies met disease disasters. If it is not coincidence, the connection likely consists of sickly and undernourished men eager to take the king's shilling, many of whom were recent measles survivors with compromised immune systems.[205] The disastrous French expedition to Cartagena of 1697–98 also came on the heels of repeated mortality crises in France that lowered population by about 9 percent between 1691 and 1695, with starvation, typhus, and dysentery rampant.[206] The desperate condition of France in the early and mid-1690s could also have driven many unhealthy men into the armed forces and to their deaths from infections acquired while assaulting Cartagena in 1697. Similar tandem misfortunes befell Scotland's effort to install a trading colony in today's Panama in 1698: the colonists left in the midst of the coldest decade in Scotland since about 1250 and the worst famine in Scotland's recorded history. About 80 percent of them died, mainly of disease, on shipboard or in Panama.[207]

As army doctor John Bell noted in 1791 concerning British forces in the Caribbean, "the number of those who have perished by disease has, in every instance, greatly exceeded the loss occasioned by the sword of the enemy."[208] The disease toll in a two-month siege at Havana in 1762 outstripped all losses to the British Army throughout North America for the duration of the Seven Years' War. In the War of the American Revolution (1775–83), in which Britain fought France and Spain as well as the fledgling United States, mosquito-borne infections killed more British soldiers on a brief expedition against a Spanish fort in Nicaragua in 1780 than did the Continental Army at the battles of Bunker Hill, Long Island, White Plains, Trenton, Princeton, Brandywine, Germantown, Monmouth, King's Mountain, Cowpens, and Guilford Courthouse put together.[209] The French and Spanish armies suffered similar fates. In spring of 1782, they assembled a force in the French Windward Islands of perhaps 30,000 men with the intention of taking Jamaica from Britain. A naval defeat scuttled their mission, but 20,000 of them took refuge in northern Saint-Domingue. In 90 days, fevers killed more soldiers marooned in Saint-Domingue than the British Army did in all of North America in all eight years of combat in the American Revolution. Men died so fast that graves at Cap Français cemetery had to be reopened to admit more corpses.[210]

It took decades for strategists to absorb the unfamiliar implications of the military disease ecology of the Caribbean. But by the 1740s some military planners in European capitals, Jamaica, Cuba, and elsewhere recognized the likelihood of heavy disease mortality on expeditions to the Caribbean and the necessity, as they saw it, of sending extra manpower to offset it. (That extra manpower itself would further raise the chances of epidemics.) They also understood the importance of conducting operations in the dry months, usually December through April, when yellow fever and malaria abated, although in practice often failed to do so. British war planners tried to recruit men from hotter climates, including North America, on the theory that they would stay healthier in the Caribbean than could lads from Lancashire or Lothian. Celebrated Scottish naval physician James Lind, known for his efforts against scurvy and a veteran of West Indies postings, estimated in the 1760s that 1 seasoned soldier or sailor was worth 10 unseasoned.[211]

The Spanish, more often than not in the defensive role, grasped by the 1740s, if not before, that their strategy for Caribbean defense could consist of the combination of fortification and epidemic disease, or, as they put it, "*el clima.*" If they built fortifications stout enough to stymie invaders for six or eight weeks, they had every reason to expect they would be rescued by yellow fever, malaria, and perhaps other infections as well. This strategy worked well and led to the enormous losses experienced by British amphibious assault forces. It failed at Havana in 1762 because yellow fever destroyed the British Army only after the stronghold had fallen. Spain's mosquito allies bit a few days too late to save the city.[212]

The carnage reached a crescendo between 1791 and 1821. Recurrent warfare in the Caribbean in those decades killed perhaps 250,000 European soldiers. Probably 80 percent of them died from disease. The dangers of expeditionary warfare by this time surprised no one, but the stakes—whether or not Haiti and Spanish America should be independent—seemed high enough to justify the campaigns, at least to decision makers in London, Paris, and Madrid. The larger scale of operations in these revolutionary wars offered mosquitoes, viruses, and plasmodia, a banquet in the form of huddled masses of non-immune soldiers larger than any seen before in the Caribbean.[213]

The military disease regime of the Caribbean took its toll among sleepy garrisons as well as among troops on campaign. Garrisons often resided in or near port cities to ease supply and allow quick deployment. That merged the dangers of urban and military disease ecology. Rotating army units into the Caribbean maximized disease risks by bringing fresh susceptibles within range of mosquitoes and pathogens. Spain addressed the problem after 1717 by creating permanent regiments for Caribbean garrisons, composed of men who were, or would become if they lived, well seasoned. While these regiments might lose 10–50 percent of their strength within a year when initially sent to Cartagena or Havana, soldiers who survived a seasoning year were a good bet to live another 10 or more.[214] These permanent garrisons had to be topped up periodically with fresh recruits, some of whom would also usually die quickly, but more than half of whom would survive to join the seasoned population. In the 1850s, Havana's garrison lost about 1,000 men per year to yellow fever, and Spanish military authorities figured the *vómito negro* would claim a quarter of all soldiers sent to Cuba.[215] Britain and France relied more heavily on naval power than on fortification and permanent garrisons, and usually rotated army units in and out of the Caribbean when war came, with predictably enormous losses among the fresh arrivals.

In any case, British and French garrisons died fast in the West Indies until the abolition of slavery. From 1764 to 1786, British garrison troops uninvolved in combat died at an annual rate of 14.5 percent for men in their first year, and 6.6 percent thereafter. British commanders on Jamaica in the 1780s reported

Figure 2.4 "Paramaribo, Surinam, 1808." The port of Paramaraibo, Surinam, was under British control in 1808 when naval surgeon John Waller visited. The bastion housed a small garrison, stationed where it could guard the entrance to the Surinam River—but also where soldiers stood at high risk to mosquito-borne disease. John A. Waller, *A Voyage in the West Indies* (London, 1820), facing p. 60.

15 percent annual mortality to disease among their garrisons.[216] Garrisons on Jamaica between 1817 and 1836 shrank by 14.3 percent annually, while in the Bahamas in the same years the annual decline was 20 percent annually. The Leewards and Windwards were healthier: 8.5 percent of soldiers died annually. Meanwhile, garrisons at home in Britain itself suffered 1.6 percent annual mortality—about one-ninth that of their comrades in the West Indies.[217] French peacetime garrisons on Guadeloupe and Martinique, from 1819 to 1836, averaged 11 percent annual mortality—a little healthier than Jamaica.[218] Thanks to the ever-present possibility of slave insurrection, garrisons could not enjoy postings at cooler upland elevations. Instead, they sweltered in the lowlands, near the ports and plantations, poised to crush uprisings and repel invasions. In this way, the political requirements of the plantation regime maximized the dangers of military disease ecology.

Four major changes gradually diminished the disease toll upon garrisons and armies operating in the West Indies. First, the slave trade wound down so fewer ships arrived from African coasts with cargoes including yellow fever and falciparum malaria, which improved everyone's health, not merely soldiers'. The Haitian Revolution sharply reduced slave imports to the Caribbean after 1791. The British abolished their slave trade in 1807, and other slaving nations gradually followed. Only Spanish and Cuban ships continued to bring captives to the Caribbean after the 1840s, and by 1870 the slave trade was over.

Second, big wars with large expeditionary forces became rare after 1823. Mosquitoes transmit diseases efficiently only when non-immunes are plentiful and in close quarters, and after the Spanish attempt to regain Venezuela ended in 1823, big European armies came to the Caribbean only twice, when Spain sought to prevent the independence of Santo Domingo in the 1860s and Cuba in the 1890s. After 1823, military forces in the region consisted mainly of small garrisons, less able to sustain large epidemics.

Third, in recognition of the high death rates at low elevations, commanders and governors, led by the viceroy of New Spain, finally chose to garrison some troops at higher and healthier altitudes. In the quarter century after 1780, officials in New Spain frequently expected assaults on Veracruz from either the French or British. They debated how to prepare for the eventuality, and most of the time settled on a strategy of posting small local—and disease-experienced—militia units and a "fixed battalion" of seasoned troops in Veracruz, while maintaining larger garrisons a few days' march away at much higher elevations where yellow fever posed only a minimal risk. On those occasions when they garrisoned Veracruz more heavily, their soldiers paid a heavy price in disease mortality. In 1799, for example, when Spanish military planners feared an imminent British assault on Veracruz, they stationed 4,000 recruits from highland Mexico on the coast. A quarter of them died from disease within a year.[219] The British in Jamaica about 1840 settled on a similar approach, decades after Dr. Lind recommended it in 1768. After the abolition of slavery in 1833, and fears of French invasions dwindled, British military planners and white Jamaicans felt more at liberty to consider the health and survival of soldiers. They put some units at higher elevations where malarial and yellow fever mosquitoes rarely ventured—1,135 meters (3,700 feet) at Newcastle barracks—which dramatically reduced their mortality rates (see the second map at the beginning of this volume).[220]

Fourth, was the recruitment of black men into European armies. On account of childhood exposure in either Africa or the Caribbean, these men on average suffered less as adults from yellow fever and malaria than did people born and raised elsewhere. Some people of African descent also had a heritable resistance to falciparum malaria. At the time, these facts were widely misinterpreted as evidence of innate racial disease resistance, leading to the—nonetheless accurate—conclusion that blacks would survive military duty in the West Indies at higher rates than whites. Militia units in Spanish America had included people of African ancestry (*pardos*) since the sixteenth century. The Spanish Army garrison in Cuba included enslaved Africans trained in artillery by 1763. The Spanish and British armies bought or rented enslaved men for heavy labor in the large-scale campaigns at Cartagena (1741) and Havana (1762), and allowed some to bear arms.[221] The French began to expand the "free colored" militia units in Saint-Domingue in 1780.[222] The British Army recruited Africans for newly created West Indian Regiments beginning in 1795, specifically because they expected them to stay healthier than white troops.[223] The relentless mortality among European troops in the Caribbean campaigns of the 1790s resulted in much larger recourse to African and Afro-Caribbean soldiers in British, French, and Spanish armies.

That created an unnatural experiment. Overall in the West Indies, African recruits in the early nineteenth century suffered death rates about one-third as high as those of British-born troops: on Jamaica, they died at one-quarter the rate of soldiers in general and in the Leewards and Windwards at one-half the overall rate.[224] They were several times likelier than British-born soldiers to die from respiratory ailments, especially tuberculosis, but their survival odds against malaria and yellow fever more than made up for it.[225] With these developments—the decline of the slave trade and of big wars in the region, and the deliberate policies of stationing garrisons at higher elevations and recruiting men of African birth or ancestry—armies in the Caribbean improved their health.

Parallel improvements took place in naval health. Whereas in 1730–48 the British Royal Navy annually lost to disease about 12–14 percent of those crews venturing to Caribbean waters, that rate fell to 4–6 percent by 1800. Anchoring well offshore kept sailors safer from mosquito-borne infections. Improvements in water purity, sanitation, and other realms helped boost sailors' health too.[226]

By 1850, the military disease regime of the West Indies had lost its special ferocity. Soldiers and sailors sickened and died at far lower rates than a century before. Garrison mortality remained worse in the West Indies than in France or Britain, but no longer six or eight times worse. Expeditions were fewer after 1823 and less catastrophic. The US Army attacked Veracruz in March 1847 with minimal losses to disease, partly because the commanders so feared yellow fever that they designed their campaign to avoid it.[227] Although the Spanish Army suffered acute disease mortality in its efforts to recolonize Santo Domingo (1861–65) and to prevent Cuban independence (1895–98),[228] overall, after 1850, the Caribbean was losing its distinctively dangerous military disease regime. By 1910, after effective measures to control mosquito-borne disease and the advent of water filtration, Caribbean postings no longer inspired dread among soldiers and sailors of any nation.

Implications of Caribbean Plantation, Urban, and Military Disease Ecologies

Taken together, the plantation, urban, and military disease ecologies of the Caribbean carried several important consequences. First, they more than anything else created the dismal demographic regime of the West Indies between 1650 and 1850, which expanded the scale and extended the career of the slave trade. In the unhealthiest situations—sugar plantations in their first half century of operation—slave populations experienced natural decrease of 3–5 percent per year, offset by purchase of yet more Africans.[229] Morgan's Table 1.2 in Chapter 1 of this book shows the prevalence of natural decrease among slave populations, 1715–90, in the Caribbean holdings of each colonial power. Spanish islands appear to show a natural increase in the slave populations, as did Danish islands before 1750, although, as he notes, this may well be a mirage based on underreporting of slave imports.[230] Elsewhere, natural decrease was the rule, especially on British-held islands. Cuba, Jamaica, and Saint-Domingue each imported between 800,000 and 1 million enslaved people in the century before effective abolition of the trade (1867, 1807, 1791 for each colony, respectively), yet all had between 290,000 and 470,000 when imports ceased. On Jamaica, at the time of the end of the slave trade in 1807, the island held only 385,000 people of African descent, slave or free.[231] In the British West Indies as a whole after 1807, during the next quarter century while slavery still endured, the slave population fell from 770,000 to 665,000 (14 percent in all and 0.5 percent per year). In Saint-Domingue in the 1780s, the decline was 2 percent per year. In the Danish West Indies in 1780–1804, it came to 1.1 percent per year.[232] In

Surinam in the late eighteenth century, the natural decrease was about 2 percent per year.[233] The only notable slave society in the Caribbean to register natural increase was malaria-free Barbados after about 1810. Elsewhere natural increase began shortly after abolition. In Cuba, death rates still exceeded birth rates among the enslaved population as late as 1879.[234] Part of the reason for this demographic record throughout the Caribbean plantation world was the sex ratio, which until the early nineteenth century always included more males, sometimes many more, than females, thereby constraining fertility rates. But death rates often mattered even more. Slave mortality stood two to four times higher than among populations in Europe at the same time; and death rates among whites in the Caribbean often rose to five times those prevailing in Europe. The demographic record of slavery in the Caribbean compared dismally with that of the US South, where the enslaved population quadrupled to 4 million in the half century after imports ceased in 1808. The Caribbean's second syndemic constituted one of the most acute and sustained demographic calamities in world history.[235]

A second consequence of the Caribbean disease regime was helping to make the modern Caribbean population mainly one of African ancestry. The acquired immunity to yellow fever among most adult West Africans and their frequent resistance to malaria, both acquired and in many cases inherited, allowed them somewhat longer life expectancies than other populations in the Caribbean after 1647. Greater resistance to fevers that killed so many Europeans contributed to the popular belief among planters and slavers that Africans, or blacks generally, were uniquely fit for hard work under the tropical sun or destined by providence for slavery. The cost-benefit calculations made by planters, based largely on perceptions of superior disease resistance among blacks, led them to prefer enslaved Africans to any other laboring population they could get. There were several reasons why more than 4 million enslaved Africans were dragged to the Caribbean, but planters' understanding of their own economic self-interest ranked high among them. Paying wages sufficient to attract free labor—from anywhere—was less economically rational after yellow fever took hold in the seventeenth century, partly because so few people wished to risk their lives in the Caribbean disease environment, and partly because on average enslaved Africans outlived those few who did.[236]

A third consequence of the Caribbean's disease ecology and its lethality was an unusually fluid market in both medical ideas and medical services.[237] Demand for both folk healers and accredited physicians ran high. Countless quacks and charlatans rushed to meet it. The uselessness of almost all medicines for so many ailments encouraged experimentation. Whites occasionally showed interested in the pharmacopeia of Africans in the West Indies, aware that even the best European-trained doctors could do little to help in many cases. Colonial states maintained hospitals from the seventeenth century and slave plantations employed doctors; by the late eighteenth they were legally obliged to do so on some islands and by 1816 on most islands. But these hospitals and doctors did little good before 1770.[238]

Eventually medical efforts began to bear modest fruit in civil society as in armies and navies. Quarantines, in use from the sixteenth century in the Caribbean, became tighter in the eighteenth. Cinchona bark, potent against malaria, came into wider use. Variolation (or inoculation) against smallpox, in use in Saint-Domingue by 1745 if not before, was replaced after 1805 by vaccination, which proved remarkably effective. The fact that masters legally owned enslaved bodies encouraged experimentation and innovation in medicine: inoculation spread faster in Caribbean slave colonies than it did among free subjects and citizens in European metropoles. Many planters, as well as colonial officials, sought to raise the birth rate and survival rate among the enslaved population, especially as slave prices rose (from about 1780) and as planters recognized (by the 1790s) that the end of the slave trade might be coming. After the trade officially ceased, efforts to stem the toll of disease redoubled—but still with modest effect.[239]

The last of the important implications of the Caribbean plantation, urban, and military disease ecologies was geopolitical. The partisan impact of yellow fever and malaria helped Spain to preserve its Caribbean holdings against foreign assaults and more broadly favored the status quo in international politics before 1790. After revolutions began, with Haiti in 1791 being the first, the implication of a partisan disease regime favored the revolutionaries and undermined the political status quo.

* * *

The recent disease history—most of the last 530 years—of the Caribbean is unusually bleak by global standards. A useful way to think of it is with the concept of sequential syndemics.

Caribbean disease history of the millennia before 1492 remains obscure. The combined power of archaeology, paleopathology, and paleogenomics is still far from adequate to reconstruct seven millennia years of disease history in detail. The picture available, imprecise and incomplete to be sure, is one in which acute infections played a minor role but diseases of malnutrition were, at least at times, widespread. On balance, Caribbean populations before 1492 were healthier than most others around the world.

That came to an end in 1492–93. The first syndemic—a self-reinforcing swirl of acute infections, recurrent malnutrition, and several forms of sustained social oppression—followed, reaching its fiercest form between 1519 and 1580 or so. It nearly eliminated the indigenous population of the West Indies and on some

of the adjacent mainland coasts. From about 1580 to 1647, the Caribbean became healthier for those few who remained. Its tiny population was now mainly
of European or African birth or descent. Its less lethal health regime was a result
of low population density and reduced ship traffic from European and African
centers of endemic infections.

It did not last because between 1630 and 1650 Europeans took the portentous step of installing the beginnings of a sugar plantation economy, igniting the
second syndemic in Caribbean history. It featured all of the infections prominent in the first syndemic, with the daunting additions of yellow fever and, after
1832, cholera. The acute social oppression of the slave system magnified the
syndemic, intensifying the natural decrease among all enslaved and most of the
free populations for 150 to 200 years. For that span, only strong currents of in-
migration, chiefly the slave trade from Africa, prevented Caribbean populations
from withering away entirely. The second syndemic attained its deadliest form
between 1730 and 1823, when sugar flourished, traffic from Europe and Africa
boomed, population density climbed, and linkages among Caribbean ports
strengthened enough to sustain constant tides of pathogens washing ashore—
and tens of thousands of hapless soldiers lacking sufficient immunities were
thrown into the mix like fuel on a fire.

After 1850, the second syndemic abated. The ongoing abolitions of slave
trading and slavery—beginning in 1791 and ending in 1886 in the Caribbean—
combined with several triumphs of medical science to improve health on plantations, in cities, and in armies and navies. The second syndemic flared up only now
and again in the remainder of the nineteenth century, for the last time during the
struggle for Cuban independence in 1895–98. As the Conclusion shows, since
1900 the region's health record has compared poorly to many others worldwide
but nonetheless amounts to a vast improvement over what came before for the
people of the Caribbean—who are, because of the two syndemics, now mainly
of African rather than Amerindian descent.

Natural Disasters in the Caribbean to 1850

STUART B. SCHWARTZ AND MATTHEW MULCAHY

European migrants who ventured to the Caribbean in the early modern era encountered a world of simultaneously great promise and peril, both a utopia and dystopia. Islands and surrounding mainland territories with climates of "eternal spring," lush tropical vegetation, and a seemingly endless promise of profit, and perhaps even redemption, created Edenic expectations among many colonists. But if the attractions of the region seemed promising, a paradise, its perils, particularly in the form of various natural disasters, made life there usually uncomfortable, risky, and at times deadly. These were climates, wrote one observer, in which "the tremendous irregularities of nature are dreadfully frequent." Joshua Peterkin, a St. Christopher sugar planter, expressed his frustration in practical terms: "Nature seems to have waged war with us;—the insect class—the vegetable world—and the elements: so that this gainful genus of plants [sugar cane] has to encounter with a great many enemies." New arrivals soon realized that a slim line separated disaster and success in the Caribbean, and the region's precarious physical environment called for individuals of a peculiar temperament, those willing to accept a high level of "risk and hazard . . . and . . . [who] put no medium between being great and being undone."[1]

No such stark distinctions existed for enslaved Africans and their creole descendants, the great majority of the region's population. Disasters were not a hellish counterpoint to an earthly paradise. Instead, they formed a deeper, Dantesque layer of an existing hell. As the historical geographer Bonham Richardson observed, enslaved people "might be said to have suffered all of the Caribbean environment's negative consequences and almost none of its benefits." Natural disasters cost many European colonists their fortunes and some their lives, but they exacted an exponentially higher toll among enslaved

Sea and Land. Philip D. Morgan, J. R. McNeill, Matthew Mulcahy, and Stuart B. Schwartz, Oxford University Press.
© Oxford University Press 2022. DOI: 10.1093/oso/9780197555446.003.0004

people during the early modern period. The physical destruction wrought by some disasters generated increased labor for enslaved Africans and Afro-Caribbeans who had to rebuild shattered plantations and towns, while damage to food supplies often resulted in severe shortages and increased mortality. It is difficult to disentangle the cause of death when inadequate food and/or shelter combined with grueling labor conditions to render individual bodies more prone to disease, but it is abundantly clear that, at various times and places, disasters of one sort of another—hurricanes, earthquakes, drought, flooding—combined with disease to kill hundreds and sometimes thousands of enslaved people. At individual moments and across time, disasters played a central role in making the Caribbean a "Reaper's Garden" for the enslaved.[2]

Disasters of one kind or another were not unknown to Europeans or Africans. Farmers in all parts of the "Old World" battled the elements of the natural world as they fought to extract a living from the earth. Residents of towns and cities feared fires, storms, and floods, which far too frequently wrought havoc in their lives. The rumbling of earthquakes sent shocks of fear through most, for whom the earth still seemed an immovable object, despite the advancements of Galileo and Copernicus. Too much or too little rain could threaten famine. Nevertheless, few of those who migrated to the Caribbean (voluntarily or involuntarily) were prepared for the frequency, scale, and magnitude of disasters they experienced on the islands. In some cases, colonists encountered entirely new phenomena, such as hurricanes, which routinely swept across the colonies with a violence far surpassing even the worst storms of Europe or West Africa. For good reason, hurricanes became a defining symbol of all that was different and dangerous about the Caribbean environment. In other cases, colonists suffered from disasters—earthquakes, floods, and droughts—that were not unfamiliar to them, but that seemed far more powerful and far more frequent in the Caribbean than in Europe. As one eighteenth-century commentator stated bluntly, "the Number of Risques" on the islands was "manifestly greater" than anything in Europe. "There is no Year or Season that does not bring some Calamity to us," wrote one Jamaican planter. Together, new and old hazards made life in the Caribbean precarious for all who lived there.[3]

The cumulative threat and impact of these hazards shaped everyday life in the region and, over time, gave rise to distinct social and cultural forms. Architecture, religious practices, *mentalities*, and economic and political concerns all reflected to varying degrees the reality of living in a space subjected to routine hurricanes, earthquakes, drought, and other disasters. In this sense natural hazards served as "agents of culture formation" as well as agents of physical destruction in the early modern Caribbean. Shared experience of repeated hazards and acceptance of such hazards as part of life fostered the emergence of cultures of disaster across the region, ones that crossed political boundaries and were characterized by broadly similar understandings of, and adaptations to, the threat from disasters. That said, significant differences also existed in response to disasters, differences between European colonies, between religious groups, between Europeans and Africans, and between island geographies and their respective vulnerability to different hazards. These factors influenced how various individuals and groups coped with catastrophe. As with other elements of Caribbean history, disasters highlight the tension between definitions of the region as a relatively unified social, cultural, and economic space and those that highlight the individuality of islands divided by different political and historical identities and trajectories.[4]

That disasters occupy a key place in the history of the Caribbean is no novel insight. Beginning in the nineteenth century, scientists sought to unravel the natural forces at work in events like hurricanes and earthquakes. Their modern counterparts have traced the frequency and characteristics of such events, in part to better understand, respond to, and protect against future events. Recent concern about climate change has spurred even greater investigative work on the region's historical climatology, specifically by identifying and cataloguing various disasters to determine their frequency. This scholarship provides an essential foundation for anyone investigating natural disasters in the region. And, of course, disasters are not absent from existing general histories of the region. Indeed, one would be hard pressed to find a history of an individual island or the region as a whole that failed to discuss hurricanes, earthquakes, drought, and the like. Nevertheless, relatively few of these histories provide much explicit analysis of the impact of such events on the development of colonial societies over time.[5]

More recently, historians have explored in some detail various disasters in the early modern Caribbean. Several studies focus on hurricanes, but earthquakes, drought, and other hazards are emerging as part of what might be termed "the new disaster history." This scholarship demonstrates that while natural hazards exist in the world, they become disasters only when the hazard affects human communities. As a result, the impact of any given disaster is shaped by the social, political, economic, and cultural conditions in which they strike, and by choices made before, during, and after the event itself. "Disasters," in short, are defined as much by human forces and actions as by natural processes. Moreover, while large-scale disasters can and did affect entire populations, especially on smaller islands, not all individuals or groups experienced a disaster the same way. Vulnerability and resilience are, and were, socially determined.[6]

In assessing the impact of disasters, this chapter highlights shifting conditions across the various islands and across time but pays particular attention to the development of the plantation complex—the combination of large-scale landholdings, a dominant export crop, and the use of enslaved labor—during the seventeenth and eighteenth centuries. During the first decades of colonization, European colonists experienced disasters in much the same way as Native

Americans had for centuries, but the rise of the plantation complex dramatically transformed the region's physical landscape and, with it, the impact of disasters. The physical destruction, social disruption, and human suffering that followed various disasters worsened as the plantation complex deepened. The focus on one or two staple crops for export at the expense of provision crops, for example, often rendered these societies, and especially enslaved peoples, vulnerable to famine when disaster struck. Likewise, while colonists across the region celebrated what they viewed as "improvements" to the region's landscape—house, towns, windmills, fences, and so on—such developments rendered colonial settlements more vulnerable to natural hazards.[7]

Scholars who see disasters as the product of various human forces nonetheless often distinguish between natural forces and human-induced events—that is, those caused directly by humans, either deliberately or accidently.[8] That distinction has been challenged recently by those who argue that human actions are directly affecting natural processes, so any separation of natural and human forces is meaningless.[9] This argument would have made sense to many residents of the early modern Caribbean, who at first did not distinguish between hazards of natural or human origins. Spanish residents of Hispaniola in 1580, referring to their "many calamities and travails," for example, mentioned in the same breath storms, famine, Caribs, the French, and worms that destroyed the food supplies.[10]

Nevertheless, this chapter differentiates between natural and human hazards with focus on the former. In good measure this is done for simplicity's sake, but also because, by the eighteenth century, many in the region differentiated among the various dangers that threatened their colonies. A writer like Bryan Edwards separated natural phenomena such as "hurricanes, inundations, earthquakes, volcanic eruptions" in his history of the West Indies from "conflagrations, mutinies and insurrections," because he believed humans had no control over the former while the latter "were wholly occasioned by [man's] negligence or his crimes."[11]

Although various hazards are analyzed separately, one kind of disaster often could produce another, what researchers sometime call "cascading disasters." Hurricanes, for example, often resulted in flooding, whose effects intensified after the storm itself had passed. Likewise, the widespread damage and destruction that accompanied major hurricanes and earthquakes often resulted in food shortages, contaminated water supplies, and damaged housing, which in turn created conditions that promoted dysentery or other diseases. The death toll from any one event often climbed higher as result. Conditions accompanying two of the most common natural hazards in the Caribbean, hurricanes and drought, sometimes resulted in insect infestations that threatened provision and export crops. In short, early modern residents often found themselves confronting multiple environmental hazards amid deteriorating living conditions. Just as diseases sometimes clustered in what McNeill and others identify as syndemics, so, too, different forms of disaster could cluster together or become linked with disease, causing even greater distress.[12]

The chapter offers a broad survey of the primary natural hazards that threatened colonists during the early modern period, providing some sense of the frequency of such events and examples of the damage and problems they caused for inhabitants. It then focuses on how people interpreted various disasters over time and how local and imperial officials responded to calamities. Disasters, of course, made no political distinctions, striking islands claimed by the British, French, Spanish, Dutch, and Danes. Examples are given from colonies belonging to all the European empires throughout, but some islands (and empires) get more attention than others.

Finally, a word of caution. Various natural hazards have played a fundamental role in shaping the development of societies in the Caribbean. At times, individual disaster events contributed to larger social, political, or economic transformations. More often than not, however, disasters were disruptive rather than transformative during the early modern period. Their cumulative threat helped define life in the region, but only rarely did a single disaster event result in fundamental change in individual islands.

Hurricanes

Of all the natural hazards that the peoples of the Caribbean encountered, none was more characteristic or symbolic of the region's dangers than the great storms of the north Atlantic that the Spaniards called *huracanes* and eventually other Europeans called by cognate terms (hurricane, *ouragan*, *orkan*) in their languages. The term first appeared in print in 1511 along with the Mediterranean term *torbellino* (or whirlwind), but a 1526 description of the damages to Puerto Rico from a "storm of water and wind, that here they call huracán" reveals that term was already in use on the islands. Whether the word was acquired from the Maya of Yucatan, the Taíno of the Greater Antilles, the Caribs of the Lesser Antilles, or from no indigenous people at all has still not been established with any certainty. Whatever its origins, the word and the storms came to symbolize for European newcomers both the novelty and the savagery of the New World.[13]

The world's most powerful storms, hurricanes struck fear in the hearts of residents of the early modern Caribbean. Sixteenth-century Spanish missionary Bartolomé de Las Casas called them the "worst storms of all the world's seas," and a later English observer noted that their violence "exceeds all Storms of Wind in the World." Learned humanists and old salt mariners warned of the hurricanes' power and dangers, and these storms, so violent and unrestrained, became in the hands of artists like the German engraver Theodore De Bry or in works like Shakespeare's *Tempest* a metaphor for the untamed wildness of the New World.[14] It is thus not surprising that the storms have attracted a great deal of attention from scholars, past and present. Serious historical and scientific study of the great storms began in the mid-nineteenth century, and hurricanes have remained the most studied hazards of the Caribbean region.[15]

Hurricanes are cyclonic storms that form from low pressure weather systems that develop over tropical ocean waters with temperatures over at least 81°F (27°C). Thus, the great majority of the hurricanes in the North Atlantic region are born in the months from June to November when sea surface temperatures (SST) are favorable to their formation. The air warmed by the sea surface rises, which creates atmospheric instability and promotes the formation of thunderstorms. As winds converge in an area of atmospheric instability and moisture rises by convection through the troposphere, the genesis of a tropical depression takes place. If this occurs at least 300 miles from the equator, the Coriolis force produced by the earth's rotation deflects the winds and facilitates cyclonic rotation. If the conditions of moisture, atmosphere, and upper level winds (wind shear) remain favorable, the depression can become a tropical storm, and if winds reach a minimum of 74 mph (Category 1 according to the Saffir-Simpson scale), a hurricane forms.[16]

Hurricanes can exceed 200 miles in circumference. They usually last 7 to 10 days and are often accompanied by torrential rains and by a sea surge that inundates coastal areas and port cities if the cyclonic winds come ashore. Modern measurements reveal that the most intense hurricanes (Category 5) have wind speeds of over 156 mph, a storm surge of over 18 feet, and pressures below 920 mbars, underlining the potential destructive power of the storms. While early modern survivors could not quantify these elements, their accounts always emphasized the destruction of buildings, the flooding of rivers, torrential rains, the devastation of crops, seed beds, and livestock, and a feeling of terror and desperation. Colonists compared the destruction caused by the wind, waves, and flooding—the fallen houses, damaged fortifications, great and ancient trees uprooted, vegetation blackened or stripped of its foliage—to war-torn battlefields or to the European countryside in winter.[17]

The north Atlantic (5–20°N latitude) annually produces only about 11 percent of the world's cyclonic storms, but most of the island Caribbean and the adjacent mainland of Mexico, the Gulf Coast, and southeast of the present United States lies within these latitudes. All peoples of the region—indigenous, African, and European—eventually came to fear and respect the violence of the storms and were forced to learn their characteristics by observation and experience.

Figure 3.1 "Overtaken in a Hurricanes in Jamaica, 1812." Catherine Street. Little is known about the painter or the painting, which is part of a collection of various scenes, mostly military, from England, France, Belgium, and some from Jamaica. The painting highlights the powerful winds and flooding that accompanied major storms in the region. Anne S. K. Brown Military Collection, Brown University Library.

Hurricanes had the power to profoundly impact the environment. Their wind, storm surges, and rains reshaped coastal landscapes, deforested large areas, and changed habitats, reproductive strategies, and food resources for various species. They caused a series of ecological changes on forests, fields, swamplands, coral reefs, and shorelines, some of them long term and not immediately perceptible. The native peoples of the region had learned to adjust their lives in many ways to the great storms. The Maya of Yucatan and Central America avoided placing cities and population concentrations on the coasts to reduce the risk from the storm surges associated with the hurricanes. The Taínos of the Greater Antilles in their mounded *conuco* agriculture depended on root crops like manioc, sweet potatoes, and ages (ajes) that were less susceptible to wind damage and more resistant to flooding. The Caribs of the Lesser Antilles organized their raiding cycle to avoid the hurricane season.[18]

In the Caribbean, where reading the weather signs was a matter of survival, Europeans came to respect indigenous knowledge about the seasonality, frequency, and patterns of hurricane visitations. European knowledge, whether

based on the Bible or classical sources like Aristotle's *Meterologica*, provided
little guidance for understanding hurricanes, climatic phenomena almost unknown in the Mediterranean world. Instead, they turned instead to indigenous
informants and often remained dependent on them, even as their populations
declined due to warfare and disease. Having defeated the Caribs on the small
island of St. Christopher, for example, colonists soon realized that they could
no longer predict the coming of the storms and began to send messengers to the
Caribs on Dominica to gather information.[19]

Eventually, a kind of local or "creole" knowledge developed throughout the
region. It drew on indigenous wisdom, traditional European ideas about weather
and astrology, limited reference to classical authorities, but mostly on maritime
and local experience. Time and hard-won experience taught colonists the signs
of approaching storms and the disastrous effects of their passage. They learned
to watch for signs in the sky, the swell of the sea, and the habits of native and
introduced fauna. The flight of frigate birds inland or the movement of cattle
from uplands to lowlands were taken as signs of an approaching storm. Some
colonists, following native informants, thought that circles around the moon at
certain times of the year indicated an approaching storm. Perhaps most importantly, colonists learned that the threat from hurricanes occurred only at certain
times of the year, wisdom that eventually became a regional proverb: "June too
soon, July stand by, August you must, September remember, October all over."[20]

As colonists, administrators, and mariners gradually acquired more knowledge and experience to the storms, they learned to build houses with a low profile, to adopt hipped rather than gabled roofs, to forgo high steeples on their
churches, and to build homes with looser construction that fared better than traditional European constructions. On occasion, early colonists altered or abandoned settlement sites to reduce potential damage. Planters learned not to buy
new enslaved people until the hurricane season had passed lest they die immediately in a storm and they encouraged slaves to cultivate crops on their own plots
that could survive the storms. The result was a distinctly colonial landscape.[21]

The Spanish were the first European power to learn about the storms and to
face the damage they wrought. An August 1545 hurricane that struck Hispaniola
completely flooded the town of Azua and most of the estates and sugar mills in
the vicinity. Thousands of pounds of sugar were lost, canes were torn up at the
roots, and many ships were grounded, sunk, or set adrift. Chronicler and royal
official Gonzalo Fernández de Oviedo, who lived through the storm and suffered
considerable personal losses, reported that it also battered the capital city of
Santo Domingo and damaged many stone houses and the fortifications as well
as the monasteries of the Franciscans and the Dominicans. Oviedo estimated
the damages as 200,000 gold pesos. That September, another hurricane struck
Santo Domingo, sinking 20 ships, some of them fully loaded with cargo.[22]

Subsequent European colonial settlements followed the Spanish/indig-
enous examples in confronting the storms, but soon added their own experience and traditions about the weather. The first French and English colonists at
St. Christopher in the Leeward Islands were battered by *hericanos* in 1624 and
1626, the latter leaving them totally without supplies. Early French observers
like Fathers Jean-Baptiste Du Tertre and Jean-Baptiste Labat were familiar with
the Spanish chroniclers' accounts of the hurricanes, but they also wrote about
their own repeated experience with the storms that struck Martinique and
Guadeloupe.[23]

The decades of the 1650s and 1660s were particularly difficult for the French
in the Lesser Antilles. Martinique and St. Christopher were battered by a fierce
storm in 1651 that caused heavy losses, including 28 ships. Guadeloupe was
struck twice in 1656 and again in 1657, the last storm driving aground any ship
that was unable to get to the open sea, felling great trees, destroying homes, and
killing most domestic animals. It was followed by an infestation of worms and
by a serious famine. A hurricane in 1664 carried so much rain that it ruined the
cassava and potatoes, causing extreme shortages and high prices. In August
1666 a major storm struck Guadeloupe, St. Christopher, and Martinique. At
Guadeloupe, the winds and waves destroyed houses and fortifications, and
the sea rose to a great height, washing away walls and heavy cannon. At St.
Christopher, the population sought refuge by lying flat in open fields.[24]

We now know that there are periods of greater and lesser hurricane activity
and that they are influenced by ENSO (El Niño–Southern Oscillation), the
two- to seven-year cycle of El Niño (warming)/La Niña (cooling) events in the
Pacific during which the eastward shift of warm water in the Equatorial Pacific
into areas of normally cooler water helps to shift thunderstorm activity farther
eastward than normal. The concurrent atmospheric anomalies produce unusually strong westerly winds aloft (vertical shear) and stronger than usual trade
winds at the surface that inhibit the formation of hurricanes in the Caribbean
Sea. The cycle results in a variety of world climatic anomalies. In the Caribbean,
the El Niño phase usually produces a decrease in rainfall, often causing droughts,
especially in the southern part of the region, and a reduction in the frequency
(but not necessarily the intensity) of cyclonic storms due to increased wind
shear. The opposite conditions, and an increase in hurricanes, occur during a La
Niña phase. Usually the phases last for a year or two, but they may be of minor,
moderate, or intense duration and occasionally, like the El Niños of 1718–24
and 1789–93 or the La Niña of 1622–32, may extend for much longer periods
with the resultant decrease or increase in hurricanes.[25]

Fragmentary evidence and studies of the historical record suggest that the
late fifteenth century was a period of reduced hurricane frequency, but the sixteenth century witnessed periods of increased hurricane activity around 1530,

1550, and 1570 associated with La Niña conditions. Those spikes in activity were followed by a long period of relative quiescence, from about 1590 to the 1640s, a period that produced some of the coldest decades of the so-called "Little Ice Age" (ca. 1300–1850 CE) when temperatures were about 1°C cooler and sea surface temperatures were thus less likely to generate cyclonic storms. A moderate upsurge in hurricanes occurred in the last two decades of the seventeenth century. Between 1700 and 1740, the region experienced 41 hurricanes with a notable increase around 1713–18, followed by a long period of less frequent hurricane formation until around 1766 when a new period of intense hurricane activity began, lasting until the end of the 1780s, a decade that produced another deadly series of storms. Another intensive period of storms followed from about 1806–16.[26]

A general regional chronology, however, is an insufficient tool for explaining the impact of the storms on individual island societies or their responses to them. The northern Windwards and the southern Leewards of Antigua, Montserrat, Nevis, and St. Kitts, as well as Martinique and Guadeloupe, were particularly vulnerable, lying within latitudes (12–16°N) where many of the major Atlantic storms moved westward into the Caribbean, including the infamous storms that form off the African coast around the latitude of the Cape Verde islands (16–17°N), and gather strength as they traverse the Atlantic. Guadeloupe was struck 4 times between 1699 and 1720, another 4 between 1738 and 1740, and then suffered 3 blows from 1765 to 1767. The Greater Antilles had their own vulnerabilities. Jamaica suffered strikes in 1712 and then again in 1722 and 1726. Puerto Rico experienced a rough decade in the 1730s with storms in 1730, 1738, and 1739. Cuba, a large island, almost a thousand miles in length, was struck frequently, with 57 storms of varying intensity hitting that island between 1494 and 1820. Cuba's worst storms were the October hurricanes that are generated in the southern sectors of the Caribbean and tend to move to the north and east.[27]

The relative impact of these periods of greater or lesser hurricane activity was to some extent a product of the changes in the population, built environment, and landscape. As these elements changed, so, too, did the effects of the storms. More importantly, the shift to large-scale plantation agriculture with the clearing of forests, the introduction of large numbers of livestock, and the concentration of population in port cities or along major water courses all increased vulnerabilities to wind and flood damage from the storms, as well as erosion and disease transmission.

As the English, French, and Dutch created settlements in the middle decades of the seventeenth century, occasional hurricanes facilitated a transformation from small farming to sugar plantation agriculture. With the prices of sugar high in European markets, colonists grew as much sugar as possible, and even small operators invested in sugar on some lands. When hurricanes struck, however, smaller farmers often did not have access to the capital or credit needed to rebuild or survive until the next harvest. Many were forced to sell their lands to better capitalized neighbors, which consolidated landholding in the hands of a small group of wealthy planters. Later, in the eighteenth century, damage from hurricanes forced indebted planters to mortgage their lands to metropolitan merchants. As a result of hurricanes and other "accident[s]," observed the eighteenth-century planter and historian Bryan Edwards, many British merchants became absentee owners "of estates in the West Indies which they have never seen."[28]

The irregularity and unpredictability of hurricanes contributed to a restless mobility among seventeenth-century colonists. English migrants who survived great storms often sought refuge in other colonies. Beginning in 1670, many moved to the new mainland colony of Carolina, which soon revealed its own vulnerability to hurricanes. Jamaica appeared as promising location until a series of strong storms hit between 1712 and 1752. Farther southward, Grenada, Tobago, and Trinidad had a deserved reputation as relatively protected from hurricanes. The Dutch colonies at Curacao, Aruba, and Bonaire were also far enough south to be relatively free from hurricanes, but the Dutch outposts at Saba, St. Maarten, and St. Eustatius shared the hazardous situation of their sister isles in the Leewards.[29]

Voluntary out-migration to escape the shadow of hurricanes was not a strategy available to all. Enslaved populations, which by the 1680s were increasing rapidly on the English and French islands as they shifted to sugar agriculture, did not have the ability to seek safety in the same way as freemen. The damage and destruction wrought by powerful storms took a heavy toll on enslaved populations, who were ill fed in the best of times, let alone in the wake of hurricanes. One St. Kitts planter wrote that two hurricanes in the later summer and fall of 1681 "destroyed our provisions, and hath occasioned a sickly and scarce time amongst us." A century later, Leeward Island officials warned they were in "sad distress for want of Negro provision" following a 1772 hurricane. Enslaved people on many of the islands relied on plantains as an essential part of their diet, but hurricanes proved especially destructive to the trees. The timely arrival of outside supplies from Europe or North America helped ease crises, but at times the intersection of natural disasters and political crises could initiate full-scale subsistence crises. Such was the case between 1776 and the 1790s when the British islands could not import food from the rebellious North American colonies, their usual suppliers, and then were hit by an awful decade with six successive hurricanes in the 1780s. One Jamaican planter recalled encountering enslaved individuals who were starving and "hunting about in the Savannas" for food following the 1781 hurricane.[30]

One other factor likely contributed to suffering in the slave quarters. Because of the horrific mortality rates on sugar plantations, colonists imported massive numbers of new Africans during the seventeenth and eighteenth centuries. These "salt water slaves" from West Africa had no experience with the storms and were often unprepared for the violence. Creoles provided some guidance, but advice was not always heeded, sometimes with tragic results. A 1784 hurricane, for example, killed one small child and severely injured two African women on a Jamaican plantation. The women, "not being used to Hurricanes, they would not take advise of the rest of the Negros . . . but remained in their Houses untill they fell in upon them."[31]

The official response following hurricanes concentrated on maintaining order in the slave quarters, providing adequate food and housing for the enslaved population, and restoring the productive capacity of sugar mills. Those practical considerations were accompanied by the fear that the chaos caused by the storms diminished or destroyed the symbols and signs of order. In some post-disaster situations whites complained that enslaved people had become recalcitrant, "defiant," or "arrogant." The markers of social order were weakened. "All artificial distinctions [were] leveled in the dust," wrote one observer, and the disappearance of clothing, houses, and other marks of rank and order undercut the social hierarchy of these slave societies, at least temporarily.[32]

The hurricanes' disruption of communications and trade, and the damage visited on plantations, fortifications, barracks, and government buildings, bred a fear that enslaved individuals would become disorderly and turn to looting, or rise in rebellion. On the French islands where control of the enslaved was mostly in the hands of the constabulary, largely made up of free people of color, officials did not commonly express post-hurricane fears of slave revolts, nor did those in the Spanish colonies, where the percentage of enslaved people remained low until the 1790s. Such fears were expressed with greater concern in the British colonies. There were, in fact, instances of what planters termed looting (in reality, scavenging for survival) after storms, but most of the time these fears of disorder or revolt were much exaggerated since enslaved people were too concerned with their own survival to plan a major revolt. Moreover, governments often called out troops or militia to impose order. In the case of Barbados after the hurricane of 1780, even Spanish prisoners being held captive in Bridgetown supported their captors' efforts to keep the enslaved population under control.[33]

To maintain order and quickly restore productivity, governors mobilized troops and militias, sought information from neighboring islands, and at times circumvented or ignored restrictions on commerce with other nations and their colonies; they contended that necessity forced such action in emergencies. Intercolonial cooperation became a common feature of Caribbean life, encouraged by hurricanes and other natural disasters and promoted at times by royal administrators.

Despite continual competition and imperial rivalries, such collaboration created a sense of common bonds and shared experience within the Caribbean region. Those sentiments were perhaps most strikingly demonstrated during periods of military hostilities, when storm-battered men and ships often were liberated by their captors who recognized a certain brotherhood in the face of calamity and nature's vagaries. This happened in 1746 when the governor at Havana refused to take as a prize a British ship that sought shelter from a storm, and again in 1780 when the Marquis de Bouillé, governor of Martinique, returned to Barbados the survivors of a storm-tossed British man-of-war because, as he said, "in a common catastrophe, all men should be brothers."[34]

Maritime commerce and warfare were central aspects of Caribbean life directly affected by the hurricanes. By 1555, Spain had organized its convoy system to avoid as much as possible the hurricane season by sending out a fleet from Seville in April that sailed to New Spain, and a second fleet a few months later that sailed for Panama to pick up Peruvian silver and then refit at Cartagena on the coast of New Granada. This latter fleet sailed in the Caribbean during hurricane season, but at latitudes that were far enough south and close enough to the Equator to be relatively safe. Moreover, this schedule kept the fleet out of the Caribbean ports like Portobello during the deadly summer months when insect-borne diseases were prevalent. The two fleets then met at Havana in the late spring of the following year and sailed, if possible, for Spain before July in order to avoid the hurricane season in the Caribbean and the winter storms on the coast of Andalucía. Delays and mistiming, however, often resulted in disasters like the loss of three silver-bearing galleons in 1622. Moreover, the schedule's regularity and predictability made the fleets and Spanish shipping in general an attractive target for corsairs and foreign rivals who could lay in wait off the Florida keys or the Bahamas.[35]

As commercial shipping increased with the development of plantation economies in the seventeenth and eighteenth centuries, other European planters and merchants sought to avoid the dangers of summer months. Shipping in and out of many islands decreased in the late summer, and insurance rates doubled or tripled. Planters often complained that the efforts and expenses of a whole year could be lost in a day, and while they pursued strategies like planting root crops for provisions or dividing cargoes into smaller lots in multiple vessels, they remained particularly vulnerable to the vagaries of nature.[36]

After commerce and trade, the principal concern of the competing European powers was imperial control and expansion. The hurricane season became an important factor in military operations, and the storms randomly became a fickle ally or a dreaded enemy. Many Spanish ships went down in the hurricanes, but in 1545 Puerto Rico was spared when a large fleet of Carib canoes with 2,000 warriors was caught in a hurricane. A French attempt in 1565 to destroy the Spanish settlement at St. Augustine failed when a hurricane destroyed much of the invading fleet, but a century later in 1666, a large English armada under Lord Willoughby was caught by a tremendous hurricane off of Guadeloupe with the loss of almost all the ships and about 2,000 men. The French considered it a "divine wind," one that island annually celebrated with a mass thereafter. The winds shifted for France in 1680 when it lost 25 ships in a hurricane during an attack against Santo Domingo.[37]

During the American Revolution when the Caribbean was awash with troops and ships, a number of storms wrought havoc on military operations. In mid-October 1780 the British benefited when a powerful storm caught a large Spanish fleet sailing from Cuba to attack British-held Pensacola, and the commander, Admiral Solano, faced with a battered fleet and loss of 2,000 men or half of his troops, abandoned the effort. Earlier that month, however, a different hurricane after passing over western Jamaica and eastern Cuba struck two British fleets operating against the rebels on the continental seaboard with disastrous results. No imperial strategy or military planning in the Caribbean could ignore or discount the role of the storms.[38]

Although it is difficult to disentangle the effects of different types of natural disasters because they were often temporally related, it has been argued that hurricanes tended to be more destructive of capital than of labor. More people died in epidemics, droughts, and major earthquakes than in most hurricanes, and while a few particularly deadly storms like the 1666 storm that struck Guadeloupe and Martinique, the "Great Hurricane" of 1780, the 1791 storm that struck Cuba, or the Barbados hurricane of 1831 that killed or injured thousands of people, the damage to buildings, infrastructure, and capital stock from the storms seemed more apparent. However, spikes in mortality levels after hurricanes due to famine or epidemic disease underline the difficulty in disentangling the types of natural disaster and make it difficult to simply characterize hurricanes as destructive of capital rather than of labor.[39]

Still, capital losses were sometimes spectacular, and they grew proportionally over time as plantations expanded. Of course, the impact of hurricanes varied according to the crops under cultivation. Tree crops like plantains did poorly in even minor storms, and in some instances, hurricanes dealt crushing blows to production of coffee, as in western Cuba in 1844. Tobacco, originally a small farmers' crop, suffered badly in the Leewards on various occasions. Most important was the impact on sugar, by far the region's leading export. Sugar, a perennial grass, could survive if the roots were not torn up by the wind, but the storms often wrought havoc on standing crops. Since sugar canes required processing, damage to the necessary mills, boiling houses, and curing sheds also disrupted production. A major storm could cripple an island. A hurricane in 1733 destroyed 30 of the 36 sugar mills on Montserrat and three-quarters of all the buildings on Antigua. Reports of damage consistently concentrated on such losses and the need for rebuilding in order to return the colony to production.[40]

The long-term economic impact of hurricanes on the region is difficult to estimate. Beyond immediate loss of crops and the processing infrastructure, the longer-term impact of a diminished labor force is less calculable. Following a storm there was usually an immediate contraction of economic production accompanied by an increase of imports of food and materials, which worsened the balance of trade. Government expenditures rose while tax revenues fell and the affected population clamored for a suspension of taxes or a moratorium on debt payments or foreclosures. Hurricanes often devastated a single year's sugar crop, and sometimes it took two or three years for exports to recover to pre-storm levels. English sugar imported from the Leeward Islands fell by 39 percent after a 1707 hurricane, remained low in 1709, and then returned to its former levels in 1710. A 1722 hurricane in Jamaica caused imports to London to fall by 49 percent, but production rebounded the following year. A similar situation prevailed in St. Vincent following the 1831 hurricane: sugar production fell by roughly 25 percent from the average of the preceding five years, rum production

Figure 3.2 "Memorable Huracan de 11 de Octubre de 1846." Following so soon after a destructive hurricane of 1844, this Category 5 storm destroyed over 100 ships in Havana harbor. The combined effect of the two storms on Cuban agriculture was an increasing concentration on sugar since many coffee planters did not have the resources to recover. From B. May, *Mapa Historico Pintoresco Moderno de la Isla de Cuba*, [Cuba?], 1853, Beinecke Library, Yale University.

by 44 percent, and overall exports dropped by 46 percent, but planters generally recovered within two years.[41]

These short-term losses were serious, but they could be offset to some extent by higher sugar prices caused by shortages. For this reason, administrative and planter correspondence after a hurricane was often filled with requests for information about the results of disasters on the crops of neighboring islands and foreign competitors. When the Antigua planter Walter Tullideph wrote following a destructive 1751 hurricane that battered all the Leewards, "if Jamaica should have suffered much in the storm, I think there was never a fairer Chance for a good Price for our Sugars all this year," he revealed a common post-hurricane preoccupation of many planters and merchants.[42]

A truly tragic example of the use of information about a hurricane's effects for personal profit involved the infamous *Zong* affair in 1781. The captain and mate of the slave ship *Zong*, running low on water, had thrown 122 enslaved Africans overboard in order to collect maritime insurance. The case was contested by the insurance company. The trial seemed to reveal that the shipowners and the captain had brought the ship to western Jamaica following a hurricane of 1780, but not to the main port at Montego Bay, which already had too many individuals for sale, nor to the harbor of Savanna-la-Mar that had been inundated by the hurricane, but to a minor port at Black River. There the remaining 208 Africans were sold at a good price in a single day, perhaps because the captain knew there was a high demand to replace those killed in the storm and many slave owners had been compensated for their losses in the storm and had cash on hand. Such commercial strategies in the face of climatic and economic circumstances were a regular aspect of doing business in the region.[43]

While limited data for the early modern period complicates efforts to determine the long-term economic impact of hurricanes, in general, it seems that the effects on small islands like Antigua and Nevis were much greater than on larger, more diversified islands like Cuba, Jamaica, and Hispaniola. Moreover, impact depended as well on the degree of sugar monoculture. One estimate has placed the hurricane-caused loss of sugar exports from 1700 to 1850 at over 739 metric tons (1.6 million lbs.), but this calculation does not take into consideration the possible increase in subsequent production that the storms' ecological impact may have promoted by the clearing of insect pests, reinvigoration of soils, and elimination of competing plant species.[44]

While hurricanes came to be accepted as a normal if dangerous environmental reality, there were periods when they weighed more heavily on life in the region. The last half of the eighteenth century witnessed a series of extended periods of drought followed by periods of heavy rain and frequent hurricanes. The mid-1760s were particularly bad. La Niña conditions in 1766 generated a devastating season of storms that year: 15 hurricanes made landfall, affecting all of the empires. The storms hit Puerto Rico three times and Cuba twice. Guadeloupe and Martinique were struck, the latter island suffering a thousand dead or injured and the loss of 80 ships. Louisiana, St. Kitts, Montserrat, Jamaica, St. Eustatius, and the Danish West Indies all suffered blows. Two years later, the Santa Teresa hurricane of 1768 struck western Cuba, killing some 40 people and destroying much shipping at Havana.[45]

Food shortages and in some cases high mortality from disease followed in the aftermath of these storms. Such shortages, in turn, caused all the imperial governments to temporarily violate their traditional policies of exclusive trade and to take a more active role in responding to these crises with trade concessions, tax relief, or direct assistance. After a few years, the colonial governments tended to return to former policies, but another bad hurricane season in 1772 with nine major storms forced governments to continue relief efforts.[46]

The worst was yet to come. The 1770s and 1780s proved to be one of the most active hurricane periods in history. In 1780 alone eight major storms struck the Caribbean and Gulf Coast. The "Great Hurricane," a Cape Verde storm that struck Barbados and then proceeded up the chain of the Lesser Antilles, killed between 20,000 and 30,000 people. The death toll was so high not only because of the violence and trajectory of the storm, but also because it struck during the American Revolution and the Caribbean was full of troops and ships that were caught in the wind and waves. Not a house or tree was left standing in Bridgetown, Barbados, and over 4,500 people died in what the governor called "universal destruction." At St. Lucia, 6,000 died, Guadeloupe reported similar losses, and at Martinique a sea surge of 25 feet ruined much of St. Pierre. A French fleet visiting the island at the time lost some 4,000 men when it tried to ride out the storm in open water. Just before and after the "Great Hurricane," two other storms caused extensive damage to Jamaica and Cuba.[47]

The 1780 hurricanes were the first of many during a tempestuous decade. Jamaica experienced five storms between 1780 and 1786. Still recovering from the 1780 disaster, Barbados was hit again in 1786. The Leewards were hit in 1785 and again in 1787, the latter storm also battering the Yucatan Peninsula and Honduras. Tiny Dominica was struck by three different storms in that year. An abrupt change took place from 1789 to 1794, as a major El Niño decreased hurricane activity for a period of time, but the storms continued to hit the region with frequency into the following century.[48] Perhaps the most significant in its impact and importance was the hurricane that struck a number of islands in the eastern Caribbean, including St. Lucia, Grenada, and especially Barbados, on August 10–11, 1831. The storm came at a delicate moment of social and political change: during and after a string of slave insurrections from Virginia to Demerara and at a moment when the abolitionist movement in England was on the verge of securing gradual emancipation. Barbados was devastated, the island denuded of vegetation, and the survivors threatened with starvation. The enslaved population of the island fought against the reinstitution of the plantation system and were forced violently back to work. The planters, their power challenged, could not stop the march toward emancipation in 1834, but they used the moment to insist on compensation and on a required apprenticeship of their former enslaved laborers until 1838.

The hurricane of 1831 also signaled a significant turning point in the history of science and meteorology, making it perhaps the last early modern hurricane. Colonel William Reid, a Royal Engineer sent to Barbados after the storm to assist with rebuilding, became fascinated with hurricanes and in 1838 published *An Attempt to Develop the Law of Storms*. He also began to correspond with an American self-taught meteorologist, William C. Redfield, who in 1831 had begun to publish on the structure and physics of the storms. Their exchanges were soon followed by the writing and debates of a number of other academics and amateurs in England, France, Cuba, and the United States who ushered in a new era in the international scientific study of hurricanes. By 1857, the year of Redfield's death, the Spanish government had created a chair of meteorology and a weather observatory on the island of Cuba. The following year, the Jesuits of Havana, in their efforts to reconcile science and providentialism, had erected their own observatory.[49]

Earthquakes, Volcanoes, and Tsunamis

Even as scientific advancements in the nineteenth century help unlock the workings of hurricanes, many observers, perhaps influenced by Aristotelian concepts about winds beneath the earth's surface, continued to believe that hurricanes were often accompanied by another frequent and dangerous natural phenomenon, earthquakes. Earthquakes shook the foundations of colonial society repeatedly during the early modern era, at times with devastating force. They had long inspired a particular terror among those who experienced them: the Roman poet Seneca asked following an earthquake in 62 CE, "What can seem safe enough to anyone if the world itself is shaken?" Migrants to the Caribbean quickly discovered they had frequent occasion to ponder that question.[50] Although a few single events have attracted historians' attention, much of the literature on earthquakes (and the related topics of volcanoes and tsunamis) is more scientific than historical. Recent years have witnessed the publication of several earthquake catalogues for various islands that build from impressive primary-source foundations, although they often contain little historical analysis. Moreover, there are several specific earthquake events that deserve greater attention, particularly the 1770 disaster in Saint-Domingue and the 1843 earthquake in Guadeloupe. In general, as one French scholar has noted, "over research is not yet a problem for the historical seismology of the West Indies," and, more specifically, for the social history of earthquakes in the region.[51]

The challenges associated with earthquakes differ from those of hurricanes in several ways. There was no earthquake season in the Caribbean. Tremors can strike at any time, suddenly and without warning. Colonists occasionally commented on weather conditions preceding earthquakes, suggesting, for example, that hot and dry weather often foreshadowed earthquakes, but these were broad generalizations. The duration of an earthquake was measured in minutes, not hours, but the damage done in those few minutes could be immense. Aftershocks, moreover, could continue long after the main event had passed. Finally, earthquakes were not a new phenomenon for colonists. Earthquakes occurred periodically in Spain and Portugal throughout the early modern period, and in at least one case, the great Lisbon earthquake of 1755, with devastating results. Even places like London suffered occasional shocks, as happened in 1580, 1692, and 1750. Earthquakes are even less common in most parts of West Africa, but not unknown. One major tremor occurred in what is now Ghana in 1615, damaging the Portuguese slave-trading castle Elmina.[52]

Unlike the generally minor events that caused little or no significant damage in Europe, earthquakes occurred in the Caribbean with great frequency and, at times, tremendous power. Modern seismographs located in Jamaica register some 200 earthquakes a year. Those in the Lesser Antilles report over 1,000 a year. Most of these tremors register only on instruments, but others are felt by humans, and some have resulted in catastrophic destruction. Both the routine rumbling of the earth and the destruction that followed major earthquakes further underscored for colonists the power of natural forces in the region and the vulnerability of their societies to those forces. As one visitor to Antigua in the 1780s wrote, "We live here on shaking ground."[53]

Earthquakes in the Caribbean, as in the rest of the world, result from the movement of tectonic plates. The islands of the Greater and Lesser Antilles are situated along the northern, eastern, and part of the southern edges of the Caribbean plate, which itself is sandwiched between the North American, South American, Cocos, and Nazca plates. There are also a number of smaller microplates, including the Gonàve microplate along the northern boundary of Caribbean plate (see the fourth map at the beginning of this volume). The movement among these various plates makes the Caribbean "one of the geologically complex regions on earth."[54]

Among the smaller islands of the Lesser Antilles, earthquakes generally arise from the collision between the North and South American and Caribbean plates as the former two slide beneath—are subducted—under the Caribbean plate. The stress that builds as one plate is forced under the other is released in the form of an earthquake. Subduction can also produce volcanic eruptions. As the plates are thrust down, rising temperatures melt the crust and produce magma, which then forces itself up through the earth and erupts on the sea floor. Over time, these submarine volcanoes rise above sea level, forming islands. This process created the arc of islands in Lesser Antilles.[55]

All of these islands were volcanic at some point, but the outer arc (the so-called limestone Caribbees) ceased to be active millions of years ago. Most of the islands of the inner arc from Saba to Grenada remain active and volcanoes have wrought tremendous devastation at times—the deadliest was the 1902 Mt. Pelée eruption in Martinique that killed over 30,000. The most recent major eruptions occurred in Montserrat in 1995 and St. Vincent in 2021. Dominica has nine active volcanic sites, ranking it among the most active locations in the world, while one currently active submarine volcano, Kick-'em Jenny, located north of Grenada, eventually will give rise to a new island (see the fifth map at the beginning of this volume).[56]

At least 11 notable eruptions occurred prior to 1840, but none resulted in any significant damage to colonial settlements. Colonists on Guadeloupe and Martinique likely heard occasional rumblings from Mts. Soufrière and Mt. Pelée, respectively, during the seventeenth century, and colonists on the former witnessed at least one dome-forming eruption in 1690, but it did not scare them away from settling on the islands' rich soils. Perhaps the most significant events were the 1797–98 eruption of La Soufrière on Guadeloupe and the 1812 La Soufrière eruption on St. Vincent. The 1797–98 eruption lasted for several days. Several inches of dust reportedly covered the streets of Basse-Terre, and the ash and debris damaged or destroyed several coffee plantations on the island. The 1812 eruption on St. Vincent in late April and early May shot forth "showers of stones, & earth & rocks." The spectacle captured the imagination of J. M. W. Turner, who depicted it in a painting first exhibited in 1815. The economic impact was relatively small and concentrated in the island's northern and leeward areas. Indeed, planters on the island's windward side saw production almost double in the wake of the eruption. Although several dozen individuals perished, the loss of life also was relatively small in part because minor earthquakes and smoke provided some warning of what was to come. The greatest loss appears to have occurred weeks after the eruption. Downed trees and buildings had dammed a river on the Wallibou plantation. When the dam broke, it washed through a small slave village, killing 33 individuals. In addition, strong winds carried dust from the 1812 eastward to Barbados, where it combined with drought and an infestation of insects to produce severe shortages of provisions.[57]

Barbados and Trinidad have somewhat different geologic histories. Barbados emerged from an accretion of sediments as the North American plate buckled under the Caribbean plate. Limestone then collected along the ridge at the plate boundary and was gradually thrust upward above sea level. Trinidad was at one point connected to the South American mainland, but eventually separated into a distinct island. Although not volcanic in origin, both islands experienced occasional earthquakes. Barbados residents, for example, occasionally felt the ground move beneath their feet, but one eighteenth-century commentator noted the shocks were "slight" and caused little damage.[58]

Subduction produces earthquakes in the Greater Antilles as well. The North American plate is subducted under the Caribbean plate along the Puerto Rico trench, the deepest part of the Atlantic Ocean, stretching from eastern Hispaniola to Guadeloupe. Farther to the west, along the Cayman Trough, the North American and Caribbean plates slide past one another horizontally. Three of the Greater Antilles islands—Jamaica, Hispaniola, and Puerto Rico—sit at the northern edge of the Caribbean plate, while Cuba sits on the southern edge of the North American plate. The boundary is subdivided further by microplates. Stresses created as the plates and microplates move horizontally are released along several strike-skip faults that run though these islands.[59]

One other threat associated with earthquakes are tsunamis, huge waves that can travel great distances and strike with devastating force. Most tsunamis result from earthquakes or, on occasion, landslides and volcanic eruptions. In some events, called teletsunamis, the source of the waves is thousands of miles away. This was the case following the great Lisbon earthquake of 1755 that produced tsunamis throughout the Caribbean, especially at Cuba, Martinique, and Antigua. More commonly, an offshore fault can produce tsunami waves on nearby islands. Traveling at speeds of over 400 miles per hour, tsunamis can cause great destruction with little advance warning. While the height of a tsunami wave in the open ocean might hardly be visible, in the shallows offshore the height of an oncoming wave rises rapidly and can reach over 30 feet and sometimes up to 100 feet. As a result, damage from a major tsunami often can be far greater than that associated with an earthquake.[60]

Reconstructing the early history of tsunamis is difficult, especially before the nineteenth century. Many earthquakes were unreported and descriptions of inundations did not distinguish between tidal surges caused by hurricanes and tsunami waves. Some of the earliest evidence of tsunami impact comes from the coast of Venezuela, which experienced a series of earthquakes in the sixteenth century. Local inhabitants informed the Spaniards that a destructive wave had caused much damage shortly before Columbus' visit to that coast in 1498. Spanish chroniclers later reported a series of quakes and damaging waves in 1530, 1539, 1541, and 1543 along that coast where wave heights over 100 feet were observed. This was an area where the Spaniards had developed an active pearl fishery that was much disrupted by these natural events by the end of the century.[61]

Tsunamis associated with earthquakes periodically struck other colonies in the region. During a 1690 earthquake, the sea at Nevis "for a time forsook the Shoar for about three quarters of a Mile together . . . till it return'd again: which violent Motion of the Water happen'd diverse times," suggesting a possible tsunami. Tsunami waves likely swept over the town of Port Royal during the 1692 earthquake, although there had been some debate about the cause of the town's flooding. That strike-slip faults such as the Enriquillo-Plantain Garden fault generally were not seen as producing tsunamis lent support to this idea. Recent research in the wake of the 2010 Haitian earthquake, however, suggests the strike-slip faults can cause underwater landslides that in turn can result in tsunamis, and recent scholarship has again suggested that the 1692 event resulted in a tsunami.[62]

As with hurricanes, the first European accounts of earthquakes in the Caribbean came from Spanish colonizers. While early colonists likely experienced tremors, the earliest recorded major earthquake struck northern Hispaniola along the Septentrional fault on December 2, 1562. The earthquake, which some scholars estimate as a magnitude 7.0, leveled the towns of Santiago de los Cabelleros and Concepcion de la Vega. Among the severely damaged structures were Concepcion's church and the Franciscan monastery, both masonry buildings. Concerned about future damage, colonists abandoned the towns. They rebuilt Santiago on a new site on what they hoped was more secure ground.[63]

The 1562 earthquake was only one of many to rock Spanish settlements on Hispaniola. Major earthquakes (often characterized as those with a magnitude greater than 6.5) rattled the southern coast of the island in 1615, 1665, 1673, 1684, and 1691. The 1673 tremor caused significant damage to the capital city of Santo Domingo, and the colony's economic troubles at linked to the collapse of the cacao industry a few years earlier hindered rebuilding efforts. Almost twenty years later, the governor reported that while the city's cathedral and government building had been restored, other structures around the central square remained in ruins.[64]

Spanish colonists on nearby Puerto Rico also suffered from earthquakes, including a major one in 1670 that caused significant damage in San Juan. Earthquakes periodically rattled colonists in Cuba, particularly the southeastern part of the island. One of the largest occurred in Santiago de Cuba in June 1766. The tremors struck in the middle of the night, when many residents were indoors and asleep. Colonists ran to escape collapsing buildings, but between 34 and 40 died in the disaster, and another 700 were injured. Buildings in the city and nearby towns, including fortifications and churches, suffered considerable damage, although reports suggested the surrounding plantation zone escaped relatively unscathed. Aftershocks continued to be felt for 66 days, leaving residents on edge.[65]

As other Europeans arrived elsewhere in the region, they soon encountered earthquakes as well. French colonists on St. Kitts, Martinique, and Guadeloupe experienced at least six earthquakes during the seventeenth century, although this is almost certainly an undercount. The first documented earthquake on Martinique occurred in 1657, and major earthquakes rattled the island again in 1727, 1736, and 1767. A major earthquake struck the English colony of Montserrat on Christmas Day, 1672, destroying numerous stone buildings and killing several colonists. The English and French on St. Kitts experienced an earthquake in 1664, while their counterparts on Barbados reported tremors in 1670 and 1690.[66]

The regular occurrence of earthquakes quickly became a defining feature of life in the Caribbean for colonists. Coming from the relatively quiet seismic zone of Western Europe, the number of felt earthquakes astonished newcomers. Hans Sloane reported in the 1680s that earthquakes occurred so often in Jamaica that colonists expect at least one every year. By the eighteenth century, newspaper accounts noted that Jamaica "is remarkable for earthquakes." French colonist Médéric Louis Élie Moreau de Saint-Méry wrote that the occurrence of routine earthquakes on Hispaniola was "well known."[67]

New migrants often panicked whenever the earth trembled, but over time seasoned colonists came to accept periodic earthquakes as part of life in the region. Even events that caused some damage passed with relatively little commentary from established creoles. John Luffman wrote that the frequent earthquakes on Antigua frightened him when he first arrived, but after a few months, "I begin to be used to them, and now they hardly alarm me." A French colonist living in Santo Domingo in 1751 reported that ""we did not pay much attention" to several minor tremors that occurred prior to the major earthquakes in October and November. After experiencing frequent tremors and a major earthquake on his travels on the Caribbean coast of South America and further south, Alexander von Humboldt wrote that he "never would have thought [earlier] that ... I would get as used to these often violent ground movements as in Europe we get used to thunder," but he became as accustomed to such tremors as "sailors do to rough waves."[68]

If frequent, relatively minor tremors resulted in a certain laisse-faire attitude at times among colonists, numerous major earthquakes served as powerful reminders of the danger and uncertainty that accompanied life in an earthquake zone. Major earthquakes struck periodically across the region during the seventeenth and eighteenth centuries, leveling towns and plantations, and claiming the lives of hundreds, and sometimes thousands, of colonists.

One of these occurred on April 6, 1690. The earthquake was felt throughout the Lesser Antilles as far south as Martinique and Barbados, but damage was greatest in the northern Leewards. Brick and stone structures on French St. Kitts collapsed, including the Jesuit college building and Governor de Poincy's chateau, reportedly one of the most impressive structures in the region. Twelve million pounds of sugar were damaged when stone pots holding the drying sugar crashed and broke. Nearby Nevis suffered perhaps the greatest damage. All brick and stone houses in the colony's major town, Charlestown, collapsed to the ground, although many wooden structures remained intact.[69]

Two years later, an even more serious earthquake swallowed up part of a town in Jamaica. The tremors began on June 7, just before noon. The first shocks were relatively minor, leading some long-term residents of the island to dismiss them, but the tremors intensified. At Port Royal, Jamaica's principal town and commercial trading center, brick and stone houses began to crack and fall, and then suddenly, the earth opened up and whole streets facing the harbor sank into the water. At the same time, several accounts reported that the sea flowed in over the town's fortifications, flooding the parts that remained above water.[70]

Much of the damage at Port Royal resulted from a process known as liquefaction. When an earthquake shakes loose, sandy, water-saturated ground, the tremors cause an upsurge in water pressure, which in turn causes the sand particles to separate. Relatively solid ground becomes quicksand, unable to support any large structures. The destruction at Port Royal was especially pronounced because much of the town was built on landfill. Some contemporaries emphasized that at least some part of the damage resulted from having "great heavy Brick Houses, whose Weight, on so sandy a Foundation, may be supposed to contribute much to their Downfall."[71]

The dramatic demise of Port Royal dominates discussion of the 1692 earthquake, but other parts of Jamaica suffered as well. In nearby Spanish Town, the earth rolled like sea waves, and all the buildings, except those built by the Spanish, suffered considerable damage. The earthquake left "scarce left a Planters House or Sugar-work standing all over the Island." At Yallahs, east of Port Royal, the tremors triggered a mountain slide that overwhelmed several settlements and killed 19. Accounts estimated that, overall, between 1,500 and 2,000 people perished in the disaster. In the following weeks perhaps as many as 2,000 more died from malnutrition and disease.[72]

In the wake of the disaster, officials laid plans for new town across the harbor on what they hoped was more stable ground, but Kingston's development stalled because its location near several mosquito-infested swamps rendered it "sickly." Many colonists decided to return to Port Royal, but a series of subsequent calamities, including a 1703 fire and a hurricane in 1712, pushed more and more colonists across the harbor to steadily expanding Kingston. By the time another

Figure 3.3 "A True and Perfect Relation of that Most Sad and Terrible Earthquake, at Port-Royal in Jamaica." Accounts of the 1692 earthquake that devastated the town of Port Royal in Jamaica circulated widely across the Atlantic world, as in this London broadside. The images of half-submerged people and buildings indicate liquefaction of the ground during the earthquake. Kozak Collection, NISEE-PEER, UC Berkeley.

hurricane washed over low-lying Port Royal in 1722, Kingston had secured its position as Jamaica's commercial hub.[73]

The 1692 earthquake thus helped alter Jamaica's economic geography, although Kingston's rise and Port Royal's demise as the island's major port took some time and involved multiple disasters, not just the earthquake. Other earthquakes, however, had a more direct impact on colonial economies. On November 7, 1727, a major earthquake rocked the French island of Martinique. Almost as soon as the tremors ceased, torrential winds and rains pounded the island. Numerous slave houses were swept away by flood waters, and reports indicated that a significant number of enslaved individuals drowned. Despite the devastation associated with the earthquakes and floods, sugar planters weathered the disaster well. The sugar cane in Martinique's fields escaped damage, and planters moved quickly to rebuild mills and boiling houses and to resume operations. The Church suspended observation of several saints' days so that planters could continue production. The result was a strong harvest in the spring of 1728.[74]

That was not the case on Martinique's cacao plantations. The earthquake and heavy rains that followed uprooted some 8 million cacao trees. Because the trees require nutrient-rich soil and years to grow, the earthquake signaled the end of cacao production on Martinique. Facing bleak economic prospects, many small planters looked for new opportunities on other islands, including nearby English or Spanish colonies. Martinique officials, worried about the loss of white colonists who not only grew cacao but also much of the island's food, responded by promoting coffee production and distributing coffee seeds to distressed cacao planters. Coffee, introduced to Martinique in 1721, grew well in the island's environment. By 1727, colonists and their enslaved laborers cultivated roughly 100,000 coffee bushes, almost all of which was consumed on the island. The Company of the Indies controlled the coffee market in France and prohibited the importation of coffee from Martinique to protect its producers in the Levant and East Indies. The Company protested the governor's actions, but facing the prospect of losing colonists, French officials proposed a compromise: Martinique could send its coffee to France, but the coffee had to be re-exported immediately to other European markets, thereby protecting the Company's home market. Even with this limitation, the number of coffee bushes on Martinique exploded from roughly 100,000 in 1727 to over 1,800,000 in 1731. By the middle of the eighteenth century, some 10 million coffee bushes grew on the island. Sugar remained Martinique's primary crop, but the 1727 earthquake marked an important transition in the island's secondary crop. Rising prices in the ensuing decades helped solidify coffee's presence on the island's plantation landscape.[75]

Various regions in the island of Hispaniola—divided after 1697 into French Saint-Domingue (now Haiti) in the west and Spanish Santo Domingo (now the Dominican Republic) in the east—suffered from significant earthquakes in 1701, 1713, and 1734. Then in the fall of 1751, a series of small tremors struck the island, followed by a far more powerful event on October 18. The earthquake, with an estimated magnitude of 7.4–7.5, resulted in some damage to towns on the French side, but Spanish settlements experienced the worst devastation. An account reported that that the village of Banique was "swallowed up," while in the capital of Santo Domingo, church and convent buildings were "overthrown." The city of Azua, which had been destroyed in a 1691 earthquake, again suffered extensive damage. Jittery residents decided the area was too vulnerable and moved the city from an area near what is now Puerto Viejo on the coast to its present location, to the northeast and farther inland.[76]

Then on November 21, another earthquake struck along the Enriquillo fault. This time the French part of the island suffered most. The tremors destroyed the town of Port-au-Prince, settled just two years earlier. Sugar mills, refining houses, and other plantation buildings in the neighboring Cul-du-Sac district suffered extensive damage. Twenty-five thousand pots of curing sugar were broken and "buried under the Ruins of the Houses." Residents of major towns slept in tents in open fields for several weeks, as violent aftershocks destroyed early efforts at rebuilding.[77]

An even worse disaster occurred in the evening of June 3, 1770, the day of Pentecost. The first tremors were "so violent that no man or animals could stand upright" and were felt in Jamaica as well as on Hispaniola. One account stated that the "earth boiled and that it had become fluid; for its movement imitated the motion of waves on the sea," suggesting liquefaction occurred. Sugar estates throughout the island suffered major damage to their mills and buildings, and one account listed the damage at Saint-Domingue at £4,000,000 sterling, not including the loss of lives. The earthquake (which scholars now estimate as a magnitude 7.5) completely demolished Port-au-Prince, and few structures remained standing. Several hundred people perished, some trapped under falling buildings. Fortunately, the evening the earthquake struck was hot and muggy, so many people were outside in the town's relatively wide streets and thus safe from falling buildings, or the number of immediate deaths likely would have been higher. Violent aftershocks continued for several days, and minor ones continued for weeks, leaving residents on edge.[78]

The death toll across the island climbed quickly in the weeks following the disaster. One account suggested there were 100 deaths a day for two weeks before the numbers diminished slowly, although by mid-July they were still at a "level which in all other times would have caused anxiety and fright." Many of these deaths likely resulted from shortages of food, disease, or a combination of both. It is also unclear whether accounts of the number of deaths during and after the disaster included enslaved people, although one planter in Leogane wrote that the "prodigious ravages" of disease meant "we bury daily between ten and twelve people." Another early nineteenth-century account suggested that enslaved individuals suffered tremendously during and after the earthquake. The author, Michel-Placide Justin, stated that as many as 15,000 enslaved people died from starvation in subsequent months. A lack of rain in the months before the earthquake exacerbated conditions after it. Crops in the field withered for want of water. Moreover, Justin claimed that few provisions arrived from France because ship captains avoided the island, fearing that the drought and earthquake limited their ability to load return cargoes of sugar.[79]

In addition, Justin argued that thousands more colonists died from disease caused by eating rotten meat. Spanish ranchers in neighboring Santo Domingo had been losing cattle to disease throughout the spring of 1770, but rather than simply disposing of the dead animals, they smoked and salted the meat and shipped it to Saint-Domingue, where earthquake damage created a huge demand for any and all food. Disease from the spoiled meat, which modern historians suggest may have been intestinal anthrax, killed an additional 15,000. All told, the earthquake and conditions that resulted from the devastation amid an on-going drought may have claimed the lives of some 30,000 colonists, free and enslaved. If so, it was perhaps the single deadliest disaster of the early modern Caribbean and the deadliest earthquake in the region prior to the 2010 Haiti disaster. Following five major eighteenth-century earthquakes, no significant earthquakes occurred on the Septentrional fault prior to 2010, leading some geologists to posit that the latest event may signal the beginning of a new cycle of seismic activity.[80]

Other major earthquakes continued to rattle the region on occasion during the early decades of the nineteenth century, including a major tremor in Martinique in 1839 that destroyed the capital Fort-au-France and another one along the Septentrional fault in May 1842 that claimed the lives of roughly 5,000 people in Cap Haitian (out of a population of 9,000) and caused widespread damage across Hispaniola. Houses were "utterly destroyed" in Cap-Haitian, with walls "laid flat on the ground . . . like leaves in a book." A fire broke out in the city the next day and was followed by intense storm, which added to the misery among residents living in tents, and likely to the death toll. The destruction and chaotic conditions that followed furthered existing opposition to Haiti's leader at the time, Jean-Pierre Boyer, and contributed to the overthrow of his govern-ment in early 1843.[81]

At roughly the same time, in early February 1843, the Lesser Antilles expe-rienced what many believe was the most powerful earthquake ever to strike the region. Centered in Guadeloupe, recent researchers estimate the earthquake magnitude as at least 8.5. Its effects were felt throughout the Lesser Antilles from St. Thomas to Grenada and Trinidad and as far away as Baltimore and New York City. In Guadeloupe, the earthquake demolished the town of Pointe-â-Pitre, particularly stone structures; what wooden buildings remained standing were burned in subsequent fires that broke out amongst the wreckage. An estimated 1,500–3,000 people died from either the collapse of buildings or from disease in the wake of the disaster. On nearby Antigua, one witness reported that the water in English Harbor "foamed and bubbled," while a "great stone" in a nearby wharf "was split diagonally in two parts, as if cut by a knife." English naval barracks and other structures collapsed, except "those built of wood and the hospital," which had an iron frame. Sugar mills, churches, and other structures in Dominica, Nevis, Montserrat, St. Christopher, Martinique, and several other islands like-wise suffered significant damage.[82]

The frequent minor tremors and the less frequent—but still all-too-common—major earthquakes required colonists to make adjustments to the new environmental realities they faced. Some of the adjustments involved

Figure 3.4 "Destruction de la ville de Pointe-à-Pitre par un tremblement de terre, le 8 février 1843." The 1843 earthquake was among the most powerful ever to strike in the region. It killed several thousand people and destroyed the town of Pointe-à-Pitre in Guadeloupe. Masonry building were especially vulnerable to the tremors, as illustrated in this print. Kozak Collection, NISEE-PEER, University of California, Berkeley.

practical matters, such as where to locate towns and cities and how to build houses and other structures. In the wake of major earthquakes colonists occasionally moved (or debated moving) cities and towns from sites that appeared especially vulnerable to tremors to less vulnerable locations. Sometimes this occurred immediately after the disaster, as happened with Santiago de los Caballeros. At other times, as was the case with Azua and Port Royal, the process spanned decades and sometimes involved more than one disaster. Although some towns, or at least economic functions, were relocated, most often colonists simply rebuilt towns and cities in the same spot, deciding it was too impractical or too expensive to relocate.[83]

Colonists took a variety of other steps to provide greater security against the dangers of earthquakes. New or rebuilt towns like Kingston often had wider streets and central squares to provide greater protection against falling buildings. In addition, colonists throughout the region, led by the Spanish, lowered the height of many buildings. The English and French were slower to adapt to earthquakes, but that changed over the course of the eighteenth century. One visitor to French Saint-Domingue reported that "the dread of earthquakes has, for a long time, occasioned the houses to be built of only one story." Likewise, after witnessing English buildings collapse during earthquakes and hurricanes while older, shorter Spanish buildings remained standing, colonists in Jamaica and elsewhere gradually altered their architectural practices.[84]

Finally, colonists altered the materials with which they constructed buildings, although residents of many islands then faced a variation of what the historian William McNeill termed the "conservation of catastrophe," in which efforts to adapt to one threat create new vulnerabilities to others. Thus, colonists gradually discovered that brick and stone buildings almost uniformly collapsed during major earthquakes, their rigid structure proving no match for the trembling earth. More flexible wooden structures, by contrast, fared better. Building in wood, however, rendered cities and towns more vulnerable to fire, a constant threat throughout the region. Many residents of Saint-Domingue learned the lessons of 1770 and built their houses with wood, but the fires that followed the major earthquake in May 1842, burned many of the buildings in Cap-Haitian that remained standing. The combination of the earthquake and fire killed several thousand and left the city looking like an "assemblage of ruined tombs" in the words of an observer. Wooden structures also were less likely to survive during major hurricanes.[85]

In addition to increased vulnerability to fire and storms, colonists viewed wooden structures as less impressive, less permanent than those made of brick and stone. These latter materials appealed to those colonists in all the islands anxious to use architecture to proclaim their mastery of land and laborers, the stability of their governments, and, in the case of churches, the depth of their devotion to God. As a result, regulations mandating wooden construction were not always followed, especially as years passed with no earthquakes. In other cases, colonists compromised and built wood-framed structures atop stone foundations. Overall, construction choices varied as individual colonists in different islands weighed the relative risks of various hazards.[86]

Drought and Flooding

Hurricanes and earthquakes often produced spectacular scenes of damage and destruction and, for that reason, usually top any accounting of Caribbean hazards. Equally devastating in their own way, however, were other forms of disaster, drought, and its opposite, flooding. Indeed, drought and resulting scarcity of food may have caused more deaths (cumulatively) and, in some islands, had a greater economic impact over time during the early modern period than any of the other calamities. Likewise, according to some, flooding has been the most common disaster to strike in the region across time. In short, as one scholar has noted, "Anyone who has spent significant time in the Caribbean is forced to consider water as a central factor in everyday life—both in its scarcity and in its abundance."[87]

Drought events differ from other disasters in several ways. First, they are not sudden events, but reveal themselves over time, making it difficult for contemporaries to determine when a drought began or ended. Drought conditions can linger for months, even years, and short-term relief in the form of rainfall may not signal the end of a drought. Second, there are multiple ways to define drought. Scientists often distinguish between four different kinds of drought: meteorological, hydrological, agricultural, and socioeconomic. Lack of rainfall is a key factor in all, but the definitions reveal the myriad forces at work. Because different plants have different moisture requirements, what constitutes a drought for one plant might not for another. In addition, while human activity shapes the impact of all "natural" disasters, human activity can actually cause a drought. Erosion from over-farming, deforestation, and/or excessive use of existing water sources all can contribute to a drought event. Socioeconomic drought thus occurs when the available water supply cannot meet the demand for water. Finally, although drought does not destroy infrastructure, its impact on humans and the economy can be immense.[88]

Precipitation in the Caribbean region follows a rough seasonal cycle. A dry season characterizes all of the islands from roughly December/January through May, followed by a wet season between June and November, although recent research has highlighted a midsummer dry period between peak rainy periods in May–June and September–October. Most precipitation in the region falls during the rainy season, in some cases, 70–80 percent of the total annual rainfall.[89] A number of climatic factors influences weather and rainfall in the Caribbean. One is the seasonal movement of the North Atlantic High (NAH). Stronger trade winds and drier weather emerge as the NAH moves south and decreases in size during the winter months. Conversely, weaker trade winds and wetter weather develop as the NAH shifts northward and expands in the summer. Droughts or excessive rains can emerge at any time during years when persistently strong (weak) trade winds persist, thereby inhibiting (promoting) the development of clouds, rain, and storms. Another is the El Niño/La Niña sequence in the Pacific, which generally results in higher frequency of droughts in the Caribbean during warmer El Niño events and greater rainfall (and more frequent hurricanes) during the cooler periods of La Niña, although recent research has suggested significant temporal and spatial variation across the region. Other factors also influence precipitation in the region, such as southward-moving cold fronts from North America that can produce significant rains on the northern coasts of the Greater Antilles during winter months.[90]

The end result is that precipitation fluctuates considerably in the region from year to year, and "average" rainfall figures over time can obscure wild swings from periods of drought to abundance. Moreover, significant variation in precipitation exists across the region and among the islands. In Jamaica and Hispaniola, for example, mountains influence rainfall patterns on various parts of the islands. The orographic effect (air masses forced upward by topography) means that locations to the windward and in higher elevations generally receive significantly more rain than those to the leeward side, which fall into what is called a rain shadow. Port Antonio on Jamaica's north coast receives 125 inches of rain a year. Twenty miles inland, but higher up, the Blue Mountains receive over 200 inches. Kingston, by contrast, on Jamaica's southern, leeward coast, receives less than 30 inches a year. On nearby Saint-Domingue, the north coast is relatively wet, with jungle-like mountain areas. By contrast, the nearby Artibonite Plain receives only 30 inches a rain a year, leading colonists to label the area "little Egypt." The existence of such microclimates meant that drought was often a localized experience, especially on some of the larger islands: some planters in Jamaica suffered losses from parched fields while others harvested fine crops, the result of what one called the "partial" rains.[91]

Drought has long played a key role in circum-Caribbean history. Perhaps most famously, an extended drought contributed to the massive decline of the Maya civilization in the lowlands of the Yucatan Peninsula and Mesoamerica in the period between 750 and 950 CE. Scientists suggest that periods of drought led to abandonment of native sites on islands such as Guadeloupe, which were re-established during periods of greater rainfall. Drought and the accompanying scarcity of provisions likewise pushed people off of Hispaniola to other nearby islands in search of food. Settlements in the Bahamas and Turks and Caicos during the period 1050–1250 CE likely developed from these drought-induced out-migrations.[92]

European colonists soon found themselves struggling against drought and, over the course of the seventeenth century, accounts of drought became more common as English and French colonists increasingly developed plantations on various islands. Colonists in Barbados complained of drought and associated shortages in the late 1640s, and some reports suggested that as much of one-fifth of the island's population perished from the combination of drought and disease between 1647 and 1650. The island suffered droughts again in 1668, 1670, 1700–1702, periodically during the 1730s, and then across the eighteenth century. Accounts of drought also appear from the Leeward Islands beginning in the 1680s. Indeed, the Leeward Islands experienced perhaps the most frequent and frequently severe droughts. One colonist wrote that "the surest and severest of all [calamities] is the dry Weather." The early decades of the eighteenth century were especially hard, a period of extended drought that ranks among the worst in the last 10,000 years.[93]

The French islands also suffered. Martinique experienced a serious drought in 1671 that left the sugar cane so damaged that the mills stopped production. Older residents claimed it was of a duration never seen before. In 1718, the French islands of Grenada, Guadeloupe, Marie Galante, and Martinique all suffered from drought. The area near Cap-François in Saint-Domingue experienced significant droughts in 1726, 1743, 1754, and 1757.[94] The impact of drought had some political consequences as well. Sustained dry conditions undermined French efforts to develop the island of St. Croix in the early eighteenth century and prompted the sale of the island to the Danes in 1733, who soon encountered the danger of drought. A Moravian missionary who arrived in the Danish West Indies in 1767 wrote that months without rain often scorched the sugar cane, turning the stalks red and souring the juice. Slave gardens withered and fires linked to the dry conditions became a major threat to plantation buildings, homes, and crops. When the rains finally came, they made the situation worse by flooding parts of the island, which promoted more illness and mortality.[95]

Drought created a number of issues for planters. Most obviously, the lack of rainfall withered crops and, by extension, planter profits. Planters across the region routinely complained of "burnt" fields that produced few crops. "Worse times were never known in the West Indies," wrote one colonist in 1759 in Antigua describing a drought that year that extended from "Barbados to all our Leeward Islands except Jamaica." Fields that were "totally scortch up for want of Rain" produced only 20 hogsheads of sugar, if there were lucky, rather than 100. And Jamaican planters were not always so lucky. One overseer in Jamaica reported in 1771 that he anticipated only 7 hogsheads of sugar from the 50 acres of new canes and 150 acres of ratoons on account of drought that had stretched from 1768 through 1771. Estates in St. Andrew parish had produced 1,700 hogsheads a few years before but struggled to ship 100 hogsheads that year. Drought reduced production on some Saint-Domingue plantations by almost 50 percent in the late 1770s. In addition to lost crops, lack of water also interrupted the operation of still houses and the processing of rum on many plantations.[96]

Only a few scholars have examined the economic impact of drought in any detail. Alexander Berland and David Barry Gaspar's work on Antigua at different points in the eighteenth century provide some of the best evidence of the economic losses. In the tumultuous 1730s, regular drought, insects, and a major hurricane considerably reduced sugar exports on the island. Following strong exports in 1728 and 1729, drought and the blast (see below) combined to reduce exports by 40 percent in 1731. Output remained low in 1732 and 1734 (a hurricane in 1733 contributed to a weak harvest the following year) and its nadir in 1737 at only 1,732 tons. The governor reported that some 90 percent of the island's crop was lost to drought. Likewise, Berland notes that during the extended drought that plagued Antigua in the late 1770s. sugar production on the island plummeted, reaching its nadir in 1780. Although output rebounded briefly in 1781, the result of "very favourable" weather early in the year, and again in 1782, drought conditions then re-emerged and production dropped. Many planters found themselves deeply in debt, which prompted the Assembly in 1779 to renew legislation to prevent bankrupted colonists from leaving the island before settling their debts.[97]

In addition to lost export crops and income, drought destroyed provision crops, which forced planters to rely even more on imported food, often at high prices. The price of corn skyrocketed in Barbados during a drought in 1690, and the price a barrel of beef tripled. Colonists also often had to import fresh water from other islands or find other sources of water. Poorer colonists in the Danish islands, for example, purified ground water by boiling it with white cinnamon, then skimming off the cloudy residue before drinking it.[98]

Animals, essential to plantation operations on most islands, also suffered from the dry weather. "The Loss of Horses, Mules, and Cattle, in Dry-weather Years especially, is very considerable," reported one Leeward Island planter. One account suggested during the severe drought on Saint-Domingue in 1779–80 that desperate animals turned to eating cactus, which provided some water even though the spines ripped their mouths. Antigua reportedly lost some 5,000 cattle in the first year of an extended period of drought between 1789 and 1791.[99]

Drought conditions also increased the chance of fires, as happened in Jamaica in 1754 when thousands of acres of woodlands burned. Between October 1768 and May 1770, Jamaica experienced "the longest and severest drought ever remembered in this island," according to the eighteenth-century planter and historian Edward Long. One overseer wrote of the "amazing devastation occasioned by the expanded drought" in March 1770.[100]

All colonists felt the impact of drought, but it created especially difficult conditions for enslaved laborers. They had to spend more time weeding to get the best results from the canes that survived, and that task became more difficult as the dry ground hardened. One planter in Jamaica noted that during dry weather, the ground had the "hardness of a brick." An observer in the Leeward Islands emphasized that picking grass for animal feed during period of drought was particularly difficult work, and "the most frequent cause" of enslaved laborers running away. In addition to field work, many enslaved people found themselves working to supply plantations with water. "It cost the daily labour of near twenty slaves to supply me and my family with water from ponds eight miles distant," reported the governor of the English Leeward Islands in April 1689. Fresh water acquisition, purification, and storage became a preoccupation for all classes of people, but, with the plantation's transformation of landscapes, the impact of water scarcity fell most heavily on the enslaved themselves.[101]

As drought conditions lingered, hunger became a bigger issue for enslaved people. Many islands relied heavily on food imported from Europe or North America, but enslaved people on all of the islands also produced some of their own food. Drought rendered those fields as barren as cane fields. Moreover, the loss of profits from diminished sugar yields combined with increased demand and higher prices for imported food meant that planters often were unable or unwilling to purchase enough food to make up for any shortfall. One English absentee owner was particularly blunt: Rachel Tudway wrote from London that "returns being so small and sugars so low hinders me" from sending out more food during a drought in Antigua in 1717–18. Responding to reports of shortages on her plantation during a drought in 1754, another Jamaican absentee planter responded she was "contended about it, knowing we must submit to God's will: whether it be drought, rains or hurricanes." Drought may have resulted in localized shortages, but such parsimony and inhumanity greatly exacerbated the suffering and privation experienced by enslaved people.[102]

Those conditions in turn exacted a horrific toll in human lives. Modern scholarship on famine notes that most people perish from diseases that attack weakened immune systems or that flourish amid the breakdown of "routine" social conditions rather than actual starvation. While such distinctions are difficult to make for the early modern Caribbean, it is clear that periods of drought and scarcity heightened mortality in the region. Already high mortality rates among the enslaved on Nevis reportedly doubled during periods of drought: observers suggested 1 in 7 enslaved people perished during drought years, compared to 1 of out every 15 during other periods. Some Leeward Island planters sought enslaved Africans from the Gold Coast because they perceived that the heat and "scarcity of Provisions" in that region rendered captives better able to survive similar conditions in the Caribbean. Enslaved Africans from Congo and Angola, by contrast, were less valued because planters thought "the Plenty of Provision in their own, more temperate, and more cool Countries, renders them lazy, and consequently, not so able to endure Work and Fatigue." Lack of clean water was also an issue. Fifteen enslaved laborers who hauled water for Governor Nathaniel Johnson in 1689 perished from the "bloody flux" (dysentery from drinking unclean water), as did Johnson's daughter and secretary.[103]

Droughts became particularly deadly at those times when supplies of outside food were disrupted, as often occurred during periods of warfare. European navies often sought to blockade enemy islands and create shortages during the War of Austrian Secession (1744–48) and again during the Seven Years' War (1756–63)[104] The worst situation developed during the American Revolution when an extended period of dry weather coincided with wartime disruptions to trade, a combination that proved catastrophic for enslaved laborers throughout large sections of the Caribbean. The Leeward Islands, which depended heavily on imported food from British North America, were especially hard hit when trade was cut off with the mainland colonies. Individual planters reported the death of hundreds, and sometimes thousands, of enslaved people on their plantations. Antigua was perhaps the most hard-hit of the British Leewards. Several planters reported that 10–15 percent of the enslaved people on their plantations perished for lack of food, "bad water," and diseases such as dysentery that resulted from both.[105]

Drought continued to stalk the region across the 1780s and 1790s. The severe dry weather in the later years was part of a larger global crisis linked to a series of El Niño events between 1789 and 1793. Antigua and Montserrat were especially hard hit, but colonists in other islands, including St. Vincent, also felt the effects of El Niño-induced drought. In Jamaica, drought withered cane fields and provision grounds in the summer of 1786, and enslaved people perished by the hundreds. One colonist wrote it was "not uncommon . . . in many places to find two or three of them lying dead upon the common roads." A committee of the Jamaican Assembly reported that the combined impact of "repeated Calamities" of hurricanes and droughts between 1780 and 1786, and "the unfortunate Measure of interdicting foreign Supplies" meant that as many as 15,000 enslaved people perished from "Famine, or of Diseases contracted by scanty and unwholesome diet." Another period of dry weather from August through December 1789 left many Jamaican planters bewildered. plantations resembled a "Brick yard," reported Simon Taylor. "I never saw any thing like it in my Life."[106]

"The curse of drought" struck Spanish and French colonies during the Revolutionary period as well. Vera Cruz, Yucatan, and other circum-Caribbean regions of New Spain as well as much of the interior areas of Mexico were particularly affected by drought and hunger in the mid-1780s and rising food prices thereafter. A drought on Saint-Domingue in 1775–76 reportedly claimed the lives of 30,000 enslaved people. "Extreme dryness" in 1786, 1788, and 1790 claimed the lives of enslaved individuals on plantations outside of Cap François in the island's northern province. In the region around Port-à-Priment, on the island's southern coast, no rain fell for a period of 18 months in 1779–80. Puerto Rico suffered a general drought in 1777, more localized droughts in the following decades, and then another deadly island-wide drought 1847 and 1849. Cuba suffered a series of droughts (alternating with hurricanes) in the period between the 1760s and 1790s. Drought began in the island's Oriente province in late 1769, but soon spread across the island the following year and lingered for two more years. Ranchers required to supply cattle to military garrisons sought exemptions because dry weather was killing their stocks. Similar conditions prevailed in different parts of the island in 1775, 1777, and the early 1790s.[107]

Many colonists were quick to blame the loss of life during these droughts on forces beyond their control. The lack of rain, of course, was a major factor, but late eighteenth-century planters on many islands also blamed imperial policies that limited trade as a major reason for the loss of life. British colonists routinely sought exemptions from the Navigation Acts that cut off trade with other European nations (and their colonies) and from the prohibitions on trading with North Americans during and after the Revolution. French planters in Martinique, Guadeloupe, and Saint-Domingue went even further, arguing that a conspiracy existed among French merchants to maintain exclusive trading rights. Merchants, planters claimed, had no concern for the well-being of planters or enslaved people because they profited from colonial distress by charging higher prices for essential supplies and for newly enslaved Africans who would replace those who died. The tens of thousands of enslaved who died at Saint-Domingue, one writer charged, did so because traders stayed away, fearing that drought conditions on the island meant they could get no cargoes of sugar for the trip home. For their part, merchants suggested that planters exaggerated the impact of droughts to support their case for free trade.[108]

Few on either side, however, considered the extent to which the plantation system itself was a key factor in the shift from drought to famine, at least until the late eighteenth and early nineteenth centuries when many planters took steps to expand provision grounds. Until then, the steady expansion of sugar production on the islands at the expense of provisions placed colonists and, more accurately, enslaved people, in positions of heightened vulnerability over time. Moreover, chronic malnutrition was a fact of life for enslaved people in the best of times, so, when the rains ceased, conditions deteriorated and mortality rates increased. Even then, some planters or their agents appeared unwilling to sacrifice space in the fields for provisions, hoping that outside provisions would arrive rather than take steps to grow their own. Thus dry weather was never the only, and sometimes not even the prime, cause of shortages and deaths. As one scholar of the French islands concluded, planters focused attention on environmental forces as the cause privation and suffering rather than as "the consequences of human choices" and of "political economic policies that deliberately regarded slave subsistence below the demands of export agriculture." Such conditions became politicized in the British Empire by the 1790s and early 1800s when debates over what constituted adequate provisioning for enslaved people and who or what forces were responsible for failure to meet such standards factored into abolitionists' critiques of slavery and plantation system more broadly.[109]

The severe shortages that accompanied droughts contributed to increased resistance among hungry enslaved laborers. Some colonists worried that enslaved people would flee plantations if they could not provide them with food. As early as the 1670s, French officials on the islands warned that if the enslaved lacked food, "then planters would lack slaves, because those slaves with strength would flee plantations or desert." An even greater concern was that enslaved people would turn to more violent measures. Reports of rebellions or planned rebellions during droughts emerged throughout the region, especially during the late seventeenth and eighteenth centuries as the plantation complex spread. Rumors circulated on Nevis in 1725 that hungry and desperate enslaved laborers were plotting to take over the island and jittery officials jailed 10 purported conspirators and executed 2. In 1733, the combination of drought, a hurricane, and an insect infestation created famine conditions and helped ignite a major slave rebellion on the Danish island of St. John that lasted for months. Similar factors may have spurred enslaved laborers in Antigua to plot to take over the island in 1736. The plot was uncovered, 88 enslaved people executed, and 47 more banished. At roughly the same time, food shortages contributed to an uprising in Guadeloupe, after which French officials forced planters to take steps to provide more food for the enslaved. Drought and the accompanying food shortages may have played some role in the alleged rebellion in Hanover Parish, Jamaica, in 1776. Famine "(the worst of all Evils) approaches fast," wrote on overseer on Antigua at the same time, "which may, & probably will bring on a rebellion of our slaves."[110]

It is difficult to determine the extent to which severe shortages alone or in some combination with other factors prompted rebellions, or even if reports of conspiracy to rebel had any basis in reality. If nothing else, however, white colonists linked drought, provision shortages, and rebellion (or rumored rebellions) among the enslaved. One planter in Jamaica articulated what was likely a common thought among many in the wake of the Hanover rebellion when he stated that, along with removing some soldiers from the island, one "chief cause" was a "scarcity of provisions. If the enslaved had "full bellies" and full employment, Nathaniel Phillips claimed, the enslaved would not have rebelled. Phillips's reasoning may be questionable, but in Jamaica and elsewhere across the region, others agreed that a link existed between drought, food shortages, and resistance by the enslaved. Antigua's governor believed that allowing the importation of provisions from French islands in 1778 "prevented Insurrections among the slaves."[111]

Here again, drought differed from other forms of disaster. White colonists feared the breakdown of order following hurricanes or earthquakes, but there is little evidence that enslaved people took advantage of the chaotic conditions to do anything more than secure (planters and officials would say loot) food and essential supplies. Most enslaved people were more concerned with their own survival than with striking against the plantocracy. Moreover, the relative suddenness of hurricanes and earthquakes left little time to prepare any coordinated resistance. Large-scale resistance by enslaved peoples often involved careful planning, not spur-of-the moment action. By contrast, ongoing drought events not only generated steadily increasing suffering, but also provided ample time for planning such actions. In short, far more than other kinds of disasters, drought and the privation that accompanied it appear to have generated active resistance among enslaved people. It is perhaps no coincidence that hot dry weather and drought marked the years 1786 and 1788 in Saint-Domingue or that conditions grew even worse in 1790, the year before the great slave uprising in 1791.[112]

Colonists and colonial officials took a number of steps to deal with drought. In the short term, trade restrictions sometimes were eased, either officially or unofficially. Colonial officials regularly sent ships to other islands in search of food and water during periods of drought. In other situations, individual governors opened island ports to ships of any nation to bring in food. In the longer term, colonists sought to preserve existing water supplies, increase rainfall, and ensure a more regular supply of water to their fields. By the eighteenth century, colonists on various islands gradually recognized that large-scale forest clearing for agriculture contributed to dry conditions, and they began to take steps to preserve trees and forests. In 1721 and again in 1724, the Antigua Assembly passed laws that prohibited cutting timber within 30 feet of public ponds to limit the evaporation of water. Beginning in the second half of the eighteenth century, local and imperial officials began to preserve whole sections of forests on some of the islands. The first such effort came in 1764, when British officials laid plans for the preservation of a certain number of acres on the newly acquired Ceded Islands of Grenada, Tobago, Dominica, and St. Vincent. These areas would remain forested "in order to preserve the seasons [i.e., rainfall] so essential to the fertility of the islands." Barbados enacted a similar measure the following year "to prevent that drought which in these climates is the usual consequence of a total removal of the woods." Spanish laws had long sought to protect water resources and had limited tree clearing on riverbanks, but they were often ignored before the nineteenth century. In 1824, the hard-nosed Conde de Torrepando, Governor of Puerto Rico, noted that clear-cutting to expand agriculture had so diminished the available water that formerly fertile and flourishing lands had become sterile. An astute British visitor to the island with long West India experience warned in 1834 that with the lack of water, "this beautiful and fertile island will at once be deprived of its enchanting verdure, its fertility, and its riches." The success of such conservation plans on individual islands varied, but the ordinances represented a real attempt to ease the threat of drought.[113]

In addition, colonists on islands with significant rivers sought ways to tap those rivers to irrigate their cane fields and to protect themselves from the ravages of drought. The most significant and extensive irrigation systems emerged in Saint-Domingue during the middle of the eighteenth century as planters and officials sought to irrigate fields in the Artibonite plain, the Cul de Sac plain, and the Les Cayes plain. Engineers from France arrived on the island and, over the next few decades, deploying huge numbers of enslaved labors, they laid out an elaborate series of irrigation canals to water these regions. Saint-Domingue's success spurred some planters in nearby Jamaica to develop their own irrigation projects in an effort to keep pace.[114]

Planters and officials in Saint-Domingue embraced irrigation efforts not only to combat drought but also to help control extreme rain and flooding. Indeed, irrigation efforts in the Artibonite plain were less successful than elsewhere because the river flooded so frequently and powerfully. Flooding has received little focused attention from historians of the Caribbean compared to other disasters, but at times, floods caused tremendous damage to plantations throughout the region. In some cases, flooding was linked to the storm surges that accompanied hurricanes and tropical storms, but at other times, flooding resulted from excessive rains and overflowing rivers. While violent rains and flooding were not unknown dangers to European colonists, the intensity of rainfall and flooding in the Caribbean astonished newcomers. One visitor to Spanish Santo Domingo wrote, "one must have seen these rains fall to form an idea of the prodigious volume of water they pour down. . . . Drops of water, each of which seems to contain fifty of those Europe, form, by their union, a shower, the noise of which indicates its weight. In an instant, gutters are overflowed, and the streets impassable; a minute after and the streets become rivers; in a few hours the smallest brooks are changed into torrents, and rivers into floods." Edward Long of Jamaica concurred: "rain precipitates in this island with a violence rarely seen in England." As Long and others noted, the violence of the rains rendered traveling and transporting plantation goods risky endeavors as swollen rivers and overflowed roads became "extremely dangerous."[115]

The danger of flooding was most pronounced on mountainous islands and places with large rivers. "Violent" rains at Montserrat in 1737 swept away part of the islands' major fortification, eroded hundreds of acres of cane fields, and claimed the lives of 67 enslaved individuals. Heavy rains sometimes washed away crops, as happened on Nevis in the 1728 when "Great rains" in August and September destroyed the island's potato crops and left enslaved people "pinc'd in their bell[ies]" for several months. Jamaica experienced frequent floods following periods of heavy rain. Simon Taylor wrote that rainy weather in the spring of 1788 resulted in "the severest & heaviest flood" during the previous 23 years, and the water levels were "infinitely higher than in any of the Hurricanes." Heavy rains in April 1792 destroyed many cane fields in St. Christopher, and "many lives were lost" when flood waters "carried into the Sea" several houses in Basse-Terre.[116]

Flatter, dryer islands such as Barbados and Antigua were less susceptible (Antigua's limestone foundation also helped by absorbing water), but they, too, at times experienced significant and dangerous floods. By the 1660s, accounts from Barbados suggested colonists often experienced severe "land floods" during the rainy season (August to December) in which water rushed through "Severall gullies" and frequently killed humans and animals. Four days of "incessant rain" in Barbados in November 1669 "deluged" many houses, undermined the foundations on stone buildings, which then collapsed, and washed away hundreds of corpses and coffins from the Christ Church Parish graveyard, "a dismal spectacle" in the words of one observer.[117]

As with drought, flooding was not simply the result of too much rain, but was linked at times to human activity, namely deforestation driven by the expanding plantation complex. The elimination of forests on many islands meant that soils did not hold as much water, which in turn promoted greater runoff, erosion, and flash flooding. Significant deforestation on land west of Havana during the second half of the eighteenth century, for example, transformed the rainfall of a relatively minor storm in June 1791 into a major disaster that reportedly killed 3,000 people. An especially rainy spring in Jamaica in 1765 produced overflowing rivers that carried away bridges and dams, washed away roads and fields, killed numerous animals, and damaged cane fields. Enslaved people on several plantations scurried onto the tops of houses to avoid being swept away. "It is inconceivable what devastations it has made," wrote one observer. Finally, soil erosion linked to heavy rains played some role in the end of the island's coffee boom in the early nineteenth century. At least 78 coffee estates were abandoned in the decade between 1805 and 1815, the result of "devastating soil erosion" linked to storms, rains, and deforestation.[118]

Many of the French islands also suffered from floods. Repeated flooding in the early years of colonization in Guadeloupe reconfigured town planning. One early settlement on the Riviere St. Louis was "twice carried away by the overflowing of the river in a hurricane, which bore down all before it, leaving nothing but the bare rock, on which it was impossible to build again without great expense." After the second flood, colonists abandoned the post and began constructing a new town, what became the capital, Basse-Terre. Saint-Domingue experienced frequent floods during the eighteenth century, many with devastating consequences, the result of the island's numerous rivers, high rugged mountains, significant rainfall, and the steady expansion of plantation agriculture across large areas in highlands and lowlands. Two hundred people died in 1722 when the Grande Riviere overflowed its banks. The entire town of Limbe in the northern province was washed away in 1744 when the Limbe River flooded. Damage was often immense: it reportedly required some 2,000 enslaved laborers to repair damage from a flood on the Artibonite River in 1761.[119]

Flooding sometimes followed in the wake of hurricanes. Even as the winds subsided, rains sometimes continued for days, creating new threats for colonists. The early June 1791 storm that hit western Cuba, for example, was likely no more than a Category 1 event, but the subsequent four days of rain produced catastrophic flooding that claimed the lives of some 3,000 residents and over 11,000 head of cattle. Excessive deforestation added to crisis as floodwaters poured down through gullies and ravines for days after the storm.[120]

Drought and flooding thus had significant social and economic consequences that shaped the lives and fortunes of many colonists throughout the Caribbean. Colonists—and later historians—often pointed to hurricanes as the greatest natural threat to colonial societies. Their fury seemed to symbolize all that was new and dangerous about life in the region. Unfolding slowly over time and without affecting infrastructure, drought, too, exacted a heavy human toll, especially among the region's enslaved population. It also created conditions that promoted infestations of various pests, which posed yet another environmental challenge to colonists throughout the region.[121]

Pests

The St. Christopher planter Joshua Peterkin listed the "insect class" alongside "the elements" in his survey of the major challenges confronting early modern Caribbean planters, although scholars have paid relatively little attention to such lamentations beyond the diseases insects carried.[122] Early modern people were fascinated by insects, as exemplified by their efforts to catalogue the new world of insects in the Caribbean, but for planters and farmers, insects proved far more menacing than fascinating. Insects often had a significant impact on agricultural production, the cornerstone of empire in the region. They routinely destroyed crops and fields and threatened the economic livelihood of individuals and communities. As Gilbert White proclaimed in his *Natural History and Antiquities of Selborne* (1789), "The most insignificant insects . . . are of much more consequence, and have much more influence in the oeconomy of Nature"—and, he might have added, the economic affairs of humans—"than the incurious are aware of." This was especially the case in the early modern Caribbean.[123]

Tropical insects created a number of minor annoyances for colonists. Chiggers, small mites that burrowed into their feet and caused a stinging sensation and terrible itching, were a major irritant. Ants, mosquitoes, and cockroaches constantly hovered around colonists' feet and heads, requiring special measures to keep them at bay. Colonists placed table and cupboard legs in bowls of water to keep ants from climbing up and slept under mosquito nets to fend off bites. Residents often felt they were under constant siege from battalions of insects.[124]

At times, however, insects and other pests created havoc on a scale that rendered them disastrous. Indeed, the challenge of insect infestations increased as colonists expanded their agricultural projects in the region, creating what one scholar has termed the "insect paradox": as much as colonists sought to control or eliminate insects, their economic activities created conditions that allowed insect population to flourish. Like drought, pests did not threaten plantation infrastructure, but the loss of sugar, cacao, and other export crops often had major consequences for planter profits. At times, insects (and/or plant diseases linked to insects) transformed the plantation landscape of the region, as planters abandoned one crop in favor of another, either temporarily or permanently. Moreover, insects often attacked and destroyed provision crops and livestock, significantly heightening privation and hardship, especially for enslaved people. As one Barbados planter wrote in the 1790s, planting provisions was like "throwing the Seed away," because the crops were so quickly destroyed by "exterminating insects" and dry weather.[125]

One of the first insect challenges came within a generation of Columbus's arrival in the region. The first settlement on Hispaniola was relocated after a hurricane in 1502 in part because of the bothersome infestation of ants. A few years later, Bartolomé de Las Casas reported a plague of stinging ants spread across large portions of Hispaniola and Puerto Rico. In addition to the pain they inflicted, the ants destroyed recently planted cassia trees as well as orange and pomegranate trees. Numerous tree groves in the city of Santo Domingo were lost, including those belonging to the Franciscan and Dominican missions. The loss of cassia trees was especially distressing, as colonists had hoped they would provide a new source of revenue after the collapse of the island's mining sector. Colonists tried a variety of methods of dealing with the ants, including drowning them, burning them, and poisoning them with mercury chloride, but to no avail. Colonists then turned to the protection of St. Saturnine, organizing a grand procession and public prayers beseeching the saint's intervention. According to Las Casas, the rituals proved effective: "from that day on, one saw by plain sight that the plague was diminishing." What ants remained, Las Casas suggested, testified to colonists' continued sins.[126]

The ants in question were *Solenopis geminata*, the tropical fire ant native to the Caribbean, although according to naturalist E. O. Wilson, they were not responsible for the devastating the trees. Instead, tropical fire ants have a symbiotic relationship with a host of other homopterous insects that do eat plants, including aphids, coccids, tree-hoppers, and mealy bugs. The ants provided protection in return for the insects' sugar-rich excrement. Colonists identified the ants as the culprit because the ants were biting them, but they missed the other insects involved. The infestation developed after new homopterans arrived on the island, likely alongside plantains, which were imported from the Canary Islands in 1516.[127]

Ants (likely fire ants) plagued other early Spanish settlements in the region as well. The town of Santi Spiritus in Cuba moved across the Yayabo River to escape an outbreak of ants in 1522. Colonists selected a new patron saint, St.

Ann, to seek relief and protection. An infestation in the 1530s contributed to the decision by Spanish colonists to abandon the towns of Sevilla Nueva and Mellila on the northern coast of Jamaica in 1534. One early eighteenth-century account reported that the "any are said to have killed the *Spanish* Children by eating their Eyes when they were left in their Cradles." Though likely apocryphal, the story's lingering hold on the imagination of Spanish and English residents in Cuba and Jamaica provides some testimony of the sheer volume of ants colonists encountered.[128]

In addition to various ants, infestations of caterpillars and/or locusts (sometimes termed grasshoppers) also periodically created major problems for colonists. An "abundance" of caterpillars plagued Barbados in the mid-seventeenth century and caused "very great harm" to potato crops. The governor of Barbados complained in 1663 that that "produce of the island has been eaten up by strange and unusual caterpillars and worms this year," and that only the timely arrival of provision ships from New England averted a crisis. Caterpillars and locusts struck at provision fields in the 1670s. Some historians have suggested that shortages of food, as much as a shortage of land, facilitated the outmigration of colonists from Barbados during the second half of seventeenth century and that insect infestations played some role in that process. The challenge continued into the eighteenth century. Griffith Hughes reported that swarms of the insects "destroyed almost every green tender Plant" in Barbados in 1734–35. The loss of potatoes in particular hurt poorer farmers who relied on the crop for food and resulted in an island-wide charity collection to ease their suffering.[129]

These pests appeared at other times and in other places as well. An infestation of caterpillars undermined early efforts to develop cotton plantations on Dutch Curacao in the mid-1680s. Colonists in Guadeloupe experienced an infestation in 1657, which created serious food shortages. A plague of insects, likely caterpillars, descended on Danish St. John in the summer of 1733. The insects attacked provision crops, threatening the island with famine and helping spur a rebellion by increasingly hungry and desperate enslaved individuals in November 1733. In the early 1770s, caterpillars damaged grasslands in Jamaica used for animal feed, leaving "Cattle rather low."[130]

Sugar fields seemed to have escaped any serious infestations for much of the seventeenth century and into the eighteenth century, although Hans Sloane and Dalby Thomas both suggested worms periodically damaged canes on some of the British islands. Insects became a much greater, and more frequent, problem during the eighteenth century as sugar production expanded across the region. The decision by many planters to concentrate exclusively on sugar production rendered their plantations—and their profits—more vulnerable to infestations.[131]

Among the most serious insect infestations occurred in the 1760s and 1770s when ants ravaged plantations in Martinique, Grenada, Tobago, and Barbados in numbers that left observers astonished. One observer wrote, "I have seen the roads coloured by them for miles together; and so crowded were they in many places, that the print of the horses feet would appear for a moment or two, till they were filled up by the surrounding multitudes. This is no exaggeration." Another claimed that some heaps of ants were 11 inches deep.[132] Planters quickly felt the effects, as the infestation rendered "some of the finest and most productive plantations . . . entirely ruined." In Grenada the ants destroyed a 12-mile stretch of plantation lands between St. George and St. John parishes. On nearby Martinique, ants rendered the windward side of the island "almost a desert." Plantations that had produced 300 or 400 hogsheads of sugar, according to one account, "now make none." The economic losses in sugar cane fields were significant enough that Martinique officials conceded a four-year moratorium on taxes to the afflicted areas. In addition, officials in Martinique and Grenada offered large monetary rewards to any individual who could figure out a means of destroying the ants. French planters from Martinique traveled to Barbados to discuss measures used to combat the ants, another example of how disasters sometimes broke through imperial boundaries.[133]

Ants and associated insects remained a major issue in several islands throughout the 1770s. Many desperate planters switched from sugar to cotton, indigo, or coffee in an effort to salvage some profits from their fields. Others abandoned their plantations altogether. Many French planters in Martinique and Grenada took advantage of generous incentives from the Spanish Crown and migrated to underdeveloped Trinidad. Roughly 1,532 white colonists and some 33,322 enslaved people arrived in Trinidad from Martinique, Grenada, and Dominica amidst the ant infestation of the 1770s. These migrants and their enslaved laborers played a key role in establishing the sugar plantation complex in Trinidad. Wary Spanish officials, however, soon urged "most vigilant precaution that the Pestilence of Ants be not brought into the Island," by requiring the inspection of clothing and personal effects belonging to migrants from other islands.[134]

While colonists blamed the damage on ants, the ants alone were not responsible for the devastation in the fields. The ants in question were likely *Phedidole megacephala*, an African species imported to the Caribbean at some point in the seventeenth century, that are not plant eaters but rather consume the sugary and amino acid–rich excrement from a variety of homopterous insects (cane flies, aphids, mealybugs, etc.). The ants, in turn, provide protection against flies, beetles, and other predators.[135]

This symbiotic relationship between ants and other insects was also likely responsible for earlier insect infestations of sugar fields that eighteenth-century colonists labeled "the blast," a term used to describe any sudden destruction of

crops. The idea harkened back to older medieval ideas of an ill wind or unfavorable constellation of stars as the cause of crop misfortune. In reference to sugar
cultivation, colonists often discussed the black blast, yellow blast, and the borer
but were not consistent in how they employed those terms, making it difficult to
determine what was happening in various infestations. Moreover, some sources
conflated the insects and a fungus that grew on the canes rather than recognizing
the relationship between the two. Nevertheless, it seems clear that what colonists
described as attacks of the "blast," and specifically the "black blast," refers to the
same symbiotic process.[136]

The black blast was most likely what scientists now call the cane fly
(*saccharosydne sacchariova*), although other suspects have been suggested. The
insects suck out cane juice and excrete honeydew. If not consumed by ants, or if
the quantity was too great, the honeydew promoted the growth of a black fungus
on the cane leaves, rendering them, in the words of one planter, "as dark as soot,
and a Sort of Soot comes off them when you touch them." Another planter wrote
that within a few days, infected canes "become almost absolutely black." In addition to damage from the insects, the black fungus blocked photosynthesis,
which reduced further the amount of sucrose in the cane juice.[137]

The first well-documented "blast" infestation occurred in the Leeward Islands
in the early 1730s, although at least one account referred to it as "the Barbados
Blast," suggesting the insects had plagued that island earlier. Antigua appears
to have been the first of the Leewards to suffer. Governor Mathew informed
London officials in 1734 that one "reason for small produce from this Island
is a blast that destroys the canes in a most extraordinary manner, and which
has encreas'd within five years last past surprizingly." From Antigua it spread to
nearby islands. Some commentators linked the emergence of the blast to the aftermath of a 1733 hurricane in the Leeward Islands, but if Mathew is correct, the
infestation existed prior to the storm, although the hurricane may have spread
the insects around the archipelago.[138]

Accounts described the blast as "Swarms of little Insects, at first invisible to the
naked Eye." Significantly, they also noted that "Multitudes of Ants are . . . seen on
blasted Canes," and at least a few contemporary observers suggested that "there
seems to be some sort of Alliance between them [the insects] and the Ant." St.
Kitts poet and planter James Grainger even discussed the link in verse, writing of
the blast, "With bugs confederate, in destructive league/the ants' republic joins;
a villain crew." To be sure, no one at the time fully discerned the specifics of the
relationship between ants and insects, although Griffith Hughes in the 1740s
and Samuel Martin in the 1780s came close. Both thought the ants consumed
the honeydew that oozed out after the insects—"the blast"—had pierced the
cane leaves, a theory echoed by Moreau de Saint-Méry on Saint-Domingue.[139]

A distinct but related threat was the sugar cane borer (*diatraea saccharalis*), which some commentators labeled the yellow blast, although, confusingly, others viewed the borer and yellow blast as separate insects. The caterpillars burrowed in cane stalks and fed off the plant's juice, depriving the cane of nutrients and turning the leaves a brownish-yellow. Even when the borer did not destroy the cane, contemporaries suggested that the plants produced only poor-quality sugar. The borer larva eventually turned into a yellowish moth. Reference to the pest first appeared in the 1770s. In a long list of pests that troubled his Barbados plantation, William Senhouse gave "pre-eminence to the Borer (a plague utterly unknown in Barbadoes until this period) . . . [and] horribly destructive of the hopes and industry of the Planter." From Barbados and the Windwards, the borer spread across the Lesser Antilles.[140]

Infestations of both the blast and the borer did not strike uniformly but were "particularly destructive to some parts of an Island, & not at all to others." Indeed, even on individual plantations sometimes some fields were "blasted" while others remained free from the insects. For those infested, however, the economic impact was often enormous. On William Stapleton's Nevis plantation, for example, sugar exports plunged from 163 hogsheads in 1733 to zero in 1734 when the blast hit (although lingering drought may have also played some role in this decline). Likewise, production from plantations in Nevis and St. Christopher plummeted when the borer invaded in the 1790s. Walter Nisbet reported that instead of 400 or 500 hogsheads of sugar, his St. Christopher plantation shipped only 120 hogsheads. Other estates experienced drops in production of roughly 50 percent. Nisbet planted some of his fields in cotton rather sugar and wrote that he planned to shift even more to cotton, but instead gambled that the borer would disappear. It did not, and by 1791, Nisbet wrote his past four crops were short on average of 200 hogsheads a year, a loss he calculated as roughly "twenty thousand Guineas."[141]

Nisbet and other planters took what action they could to combat both the blast and borer. Nathaniel Phillips wrote that in Martinique and Grenada, planters had devised a poison by crushing worm grass (*Spigelia anthelmia*) in a mortar and adding various other substances including "pomme rose" and molasses. Phillips reported that although it took 22 days for the poison to work, several estates had been cleared of the ants by this method. Other planters sent enslaved laborers into the fields to pick off insects from infected leaves or to wipe the blades with a wet cloth. Samuel Martin recommended dipping the cloth in a mixture formed from one barrel of water, country peppers, "Stinking-weed roots," some aloe, and a quart of lime juice. Picking or wiping off the insects was difficult work, however, and one Jamaican planter stated that swirling masses of insects often temporarily blinded slaves.[142]

Some planters turned to the more drastic step of cutting infected leaves, digging up whole fields, or burning the fields and crops to rid themselves of the insects. Burning cane fields, however, meant no income, so many planters hesitated to take this step. Simon Taylor complained that a neighbor's failure to clear the blast from their fields allowed the insects to spread to his estate. Samuel Martin advocated empowering magistrates to inspect plantation fields for the blast and, if any insects were found, to order planters to take immediate steps to eradicate them, or if they failed to do so, to burn the fields.[143]

Most of these methods failed to eradicate the pests. So, too, the lucrative rewards offered by officials in Grenada and Martinique prompted suggestions on defeating the armies of ants from far and wide, but to little effect. Ultimately, in the case of Barbados, Martinique, and Grenada, it took the power of hurricanes to rid the islands of the blast. A hurricane in 1766 briefly killed off the ant population in Martinique, although the insects returned by the early 1770s. A few years later, the "great hurricane" of 1780, finally washed away the insects and the ants. As one early nineteenth-century historian remarked, "the same Divine Power which brought the plague upon the inhabitants, provided for their deliverance from it." Although the hurricane was a huge disaster, at least a few colonists wondered if, by destroying the insects, the storm was as beneficial as harmful. One French commentator went so far as to observe that, without hurricanes to diminish insect populations, the Antilles would be uninhabitable.[144]

The economic damage caused by the blast and other insects, along with lingering concerns about drought, contributed to interest among planters in new species of canes that could better withstand these hazards. By the 1780s, planters throughout the region had adopted new varieties of cane introduced from the Pacific, specifically Bourbon and Otaheite. Both had thicker stems, which planters thought helped protect against insect damage, and both grew more quickly, which helped lessen the threat from drought. In addition, they yielded more juice than older varieties of canes. Planters in the British and French islands quickly adopted the new plants, as did those in Cuba and Puerto Rico during the early nineteenth century.[145]

A different kind of "blast" struck cacao trees throughout the Caribbean at various times in the seventeenth and eighteenth centuries and may have been spread by insects. Columbus first encountered cacao off the coast of Honduras during his fourth voyage to the region in 1502, but it took some time for Europeans to develop a taste for *chocolatl* (the Nahuatl name for chocolate). By the beginning of the seventeenth century, regular shipments of cacao beans had begun to arrive in Europe, and chocolate quickly became a luxury drink. As demand grew, Spanish colonists began to plant cacao tress in Hispaniola, Cuba, and Jamaica during the 1630s and 1640s, and on Trinidad by the 1670s (if not earlier). The English inherited established cacao "walks" or plantations when they conquered

Jamaica from the Spanish in 1655 and quickly expanded production so that by 1670, some 60 properties produced between 200,000 and 300,000 pounds of cacao each year. The French planted trees in Martinique and Guadeloupe by the 1660s and later at St.-Domingue. Production expanded dramatically in the early eighteenth century, with exports from Martinique alone more than doubling between 1710 and 1722. The Dutch established cacao walks in Surinam by the early eighteenth century.[146]

Cacao, however, turned out to be a star-crossed crop. At various times throughout the seventeenth and eighteenth centuries, drought, earthquakes, and most of all a blast—or some combination thereof—decimated cacao walks throughout the region. The first to suffer were colonists in the Greater Antilles. Great hopes for building a plantation economy around cacao came to a halt in 1670–71 when a blast struck cacao trees on Jamaica, Cuba, and Santo Domingo. In Santo Domingo, the blast stalled the emerging plantation sector on the island and pushed many colonists back to subsistence farming and cattle ranching. One measure of the economic impact is the level of tithing to the archdiocese of the town of Santo Domingo, which fell from over 13,000 pesos in 1666 to 4,000 pesos in 1669 following the appearance of the blast. In Jamaica, the demise of cacao helped spur the development of sugar plantations on the island, as many early planters who had sought to develop cacao walks turned to sugar following the blast.[147]

A similar blight struck Trinidad cacao walks in the mid-1720s. Cacao production began in the late seventeenth century as an alternative to tobacco, and it quickly became the island's primary cash crop. The blast, however, struck it quickly and thoroughly, devastating trees across the island. As production plummeted, so, too, did the island's population as colonists sought economic opportunities elsewhere and Trinidad lapsed into poverty.[148] The blast may also have been a factor in the collapse of cacao on Martinique at roughly the same time. The earthquake that year that destroyed millions of cacao tree was the primary factor in dooming the industry on Martinique, but the blast that followed completed the ruin. Reports circulated in early 1728 that the cacao trees that survived the earthquake were "consumed by a kind of worm and by interior decay." Instead of cacao, colonists turned to coffee as a secondary crop.[149]

The blast mystified contemporaries. Governor Lynch of Jamaica wrote, "Neither we nor our Neighbors of [Hi]Spaniola or Cuba know what to attribute this last Blast of the Cacao to, some fancy tis age, others think tis worms, some believe it to be a want of Shade or an ill quality of the Winds. But most judge it's some Constellation, or ill Disposition of the Climate." Indeed, some Jamaican colonists claimed a comet a few years earlier had foreshadowed the decline of the trees. Likewise, one eighteenth-century account suggested that enslaved laborers had foretold the failure of the crop, suggesting the English failed to employ the necessary religious ceremonies that had been used by the Spanish. Lynch reported that in Cuba, when any trees showed signs of life, colonists "bring a Priest and exorcise it ... [and] apply some part of its fruit to some particular Saints devotion," but he concluded, "I understand their Piety has succeeded as little as our Husbandry." Lynch believed a lack of water was the prime culprit.[150]

Modern scholars remain equally puzzled. Most suggest the blast was some kind of fungus, which various insects may have played a role in spreading. One candidate is Ceratocystis wilt, a fungus spread via cuts in the stems, sometimes caused by insects but also by the sharp instruments like machetes. Historians looking at the Trinidad case argue that climatic conditions, specifically somewhat cooler temperatures in the 1720s, undermined the *criollo* trees, although they conclude, it may be "impossible to conclusively resolve the true factors that contributed to the demise of the cacao industry" in Trinidad and elsewhere. Regardless, the blast undermined cacao production and remade the agricultural landscape of various islands during the seventeenth and eighteenth centuries.[151]

Other insects (and associated diseases or fungi) from time to time threatened crops in the region, including West Indian cotton worms and coffee borers, both of which occasionally caused extensive damage to their respectively named hosts. In short, insects of one kind or another at times ravaged plantations fields as thoroughly as a hurricane's winds, and the impact of those losses were felt by both planters and enslaved laborers.[152]

Caribbean Cultures of Disaster

As early colonists to the Caribbean encountered disasters both new and old, they drew upon long-established traditions and practices to make sense of such events. Over time, however, the high frequency of natural hazards and the increased familiarity with the particulars of the Caribbean environment led them to new ideas regarding the causes of different disasters and new ways to respond to such events. In addition to building styles and methods, interpretations, rituals, and political policies emerged from, or were reshaped by, the encounter with various disasters. Responses varied by empire and religion (Catholic, Protestant, Jewish, and traditional African and Afro-Caribbean), but a creole understanding of disasters also developed along similar lines across the region during the seventeenth and eighteenth centuries, contributing to something of a shared disaster culture. As European and Africans discovered over time, disasters were a routine, if unwelcome, feature of life in the Caribbean.[153]

The most dominant explanation for disasters during the early modern period was divine providence. European colonists, Catholic and Protestant, lived in a providential world in which natural events were infused with meaning.

Hurricanes, earthquakes, floods, and the like were "special providences" sent by God as punishments or as warnings of greater punishments to come if humans did not make amends. Victims of disaster needed to look no further than their own sinful actions to understand the cause of their misery. Colonists in Santo Domingo were reminded in the wake of a 1680 hurricane that the storm's winds were "executive ministers of divine justice" that reflected God's "just disgust" with their sins. One survivor of the 1770 tremor in Saint-Domingue did not hesitate to assert that earthquakes "were one of the most horrible events through which divine rage can terrify the human being." God often showed mercy amidst the destruction, as even the most terrible disaster could have been worse, but disasters, whether as a judgment or warning, signaled divine displeasure.[154]

Colonists, both Catholic and Protestant, also recognized that the Devil and his minions might be at work in any seeming "disruption" of the natural world. The ability of Indians to predict hurricanes in particular led to charges that they were in league with the Devil, that "old astrologer" who knew how to manipulate weather, according to the Spanish writer Oviedo. English and French colonists on St. Christopher likewise perceived diabolical arts at work in the Carib ability to forecast the onset of hurricanes, although that did not stop them from seeking information from natives about the storms.[155]

Providentialism formed the dominant interpretive lens through which colonists viewed disasters, but as was the case in Europe, other explanations circulated as well. Some colonists prognosticated on disasters by linking them to the movement of moon, stars, and planets. Both Catholic and Protestant authorities denounced astrology, but the practice had many adherents in colonies throughout the region. Numerous colonists in Port Royal, Jamaica, fled the town after an astrologer predicted an earthquake in 1686. Comets were viewed as portentous events, as in the case of the 1670 blasting of cacao trees in Jamaica. Catholic officials likewise condemned astrology and many associated "folk beliefs," such as the idea that particular saints' days could indicate future weather, but these beliefs had broad popular support.[156]

Of greater importance than astrology were efforts to discern and describe the natural forces at work in various calamities. Early modern natural philosophers, who would now be called "scientists," placed increasing emphasis on the natural mechanisms at work in various disasters. God remained the primary cause of all disasters, but such events occurred through "secondary causes," that is, through natural forces and processes that were observable and understandable to humans. Classical texts remained important to many European philosophers, but they also sought to accumulate new information based upon experience and observation. The Caribbean was often at the vanguard of early modern scientific inquiry, and a Baconian emphasis appeared especially pronounced among those writing about the Caribbean because so much about the region's natural disasters (and natural world more generally) was new and different from anything known in Europe. Information about hurricanes and other such events, one Oxford scholar wrote in 1671, was "not to be had in Colleges or Books, but must be fetch'd fro[m] both Indies." Exploring these natural forces did not diminish the power of God. Rather, they highlighted the wonder of God's "general providence" and his wisdom in establishing the complex natural forces that caused the earth to shake, winds to howl, or rains either to cease or pour down too powerfully. Religion and natural philosophy—special and general providences—thus did not challenge one another; they offered different, but complementary, ways of understanding the power and glory of God as manifested through various calamities.[157]

Because major disasters were acts of divine providence, the proper response was prayer and supplication, although ritual practices varied between Catholic and Protestant colonies. Both employed traditional ceremonies they had carried with them from the Old World, including prayers, processions, and fasts, but as colonists became more attuned to the vagaries of the region's climate, they made use of such rituals in different ways.

Catholic colonists in the region employed a hierarchy of ritual responses to disaster. The most basic response involved special prayers and liturgies. In Cuba and Puerto Rico, church leaders added the prayer *ad repelendas tempestates* during the hurricane months to seek divine protection against the storms. French colonists on St. Lucia sang *Miserere mei Deus* (by the Italian composer Allegri) throughout the hurricane months and offered another prayer, the *Te Deum*, at the end of the season.[158] In addition, colonists turned to talismans, shrines, effigies, and/or saints for protection and aid in recovering from disasters. Saint Barbara, for example, was generally considered a protector against thunder, lightning, and hurricanes. Colonists in Santiago de Cuba in 1766 prayed to a local Marian effigy, the Virgin of Dolores, hoping that "with her protection this community may be redeemed from the dreaded ruins brought about by the earthquake." Catholic towns and colonies often had more than one patron saint or special shrine, not all of which were local. When drought struck Santiago de Cuba in the early 1780s, for example, local officials declared St. Anthony of Padua to be the patron saint of the town's fields and gardens. Colonists in parts of Spanish America carried images of San Nicholás de Tolentino to help fight off locust infestations during the seventeenth and eighteenth centuries.[159]

At other times, Catholic colonists employed more elaborate rituals, often formal processions. Such processions had a long history in Europe as a means of coping with disasters, including earthquakes, storms, and especially drought. Indeed, so common was a procession in response to drought that historians use records of them to reconstruct climatic history for various regions in Catholic Europe.[160]

Colonists imported the practice to the Caribbean. Only scattered references to the format of these processions on the islands exist, but they appear to have followed European practices and procedures and reflected social hierarchy. Church officials, followed by local government officials and prominent colonists, led them. Others (including enslaved people) marched behind. Religious leaders carried relics, effigies, or the Eucharist at the front of the procession with hopes of bringing divine favor. Some processions may have remained inside the church, with prayers being offered in the presence of relics, but most likely wound their way through the stricken town or proceeded to a significant site linked to the disaster. The procession marking the one-year anniversary of the 1770 earthquake in Saint-Domingue, for example, ended at Bel Air in Port-au-Prince, where a cross had been erected a few days after the disaster.[161]

Church-sanctioned prayers and processions served colonists both as a means of humbling themselves before God during or after disasters and pleading for mercy and avoidance of future calamities, but colonists also did not hesitate to invoke other, unsanctioned practices to ward off calamity. The firing of canons or the ringing of church bells to disperse storms was common. On some islands, palms blessed on Palm Sunday were placed at entry points of houses as a means of countering storms. Other colonists burned the palms when a hurricane threatened, believing the smoke would disperse storm clouds, a practice that lingered into the early twentieth century in parts of Cuba and Puerto Rico.[162]

Colonists in the English, Dutch, and Danish islands also turned to God in the face of calamity, but they had little time for what they viewed as the superstitious processions, relics, and effigies employed by their counterparts on Catholic islands. Protestant ritual instead centered on fast days, during which colonists ceased work, refrained from food and drink, and attended church services marked by lengthy sermons interpreting disasters and outlining the reforms needed to appease a just and angry God. Although Catholics also engaged in fast days, such rituals occupied a more central place in Protestant responses to disaster. Colonists in the Jamaica called for a day of fasting in the wake of the Port Royal earthquake in 1692 and again following the 1722 hurricane. Prolonged drought in Leeward Islands resulted in numerous fast days, including ones in 1711, 1725, 1726, and 1741. Drought combined with the blast occasioned a fast in Antigua in 1736. Although the evidence is fragmentary, it appears that drought occasioned specific fasts and thanksgivings (as opposed to annual fasts noted below) more frequently than any other form of disaster.[163]

Jewish colonists on various islands took part in these officially declared fasts within their congregations, but they also created their own rituals and prayers. Following a period of drought in the early 1710s on Curacao, for example, a local rabbi drafted a special prayer for rain. It was later added to and published in the 1770s. As part of the ritual, a *shofar* was blown frequently. The Jewish community of Barbados introduced in 1835 a general fast and prayer to com-memorate the 1831 hurricane. Likewise, on Danish St. Thomas, the hymn "O Hurricane" was added to the liturgy after a storm destroyed the synagogue and damaged the cemetery of the Jewish community.[164]

Fast days generally were called during or immediately after the disaster, but they also became part of the colonists' ritual calendar. In some cases, this occurred through "anniversary fasts" marking the date of particularly terrible calamities. Colonists in Jamaica, for example, fasted each year on June 7 (the date of the Port Royal earthquake) and August 22 (the date of both the 1712 and 1722 hurricane). In other cases, colonists adapted ritual forms to the new envi-ronmental realities. The well-defined hurricane season, for example, led to the creation of standardized ritual days. For example, Danish islands held an annual fast at the beginning of hurricane season (July 25) and an annual thanksgiving (October 25) to mark a year with no storms. The practice continues informally to this day in St. Croix, St. John, and St. Thomas, where the fourth Monday in July remains Hurricane Supplication Day. British colonists on St. Christopher designated alternate Fridays in the months of July, August, and September as fast days, while those in Nevis set aside the last Friday of those months for prayer.[165]

Processions and fast days—and the providential *mentality* they represented—remained in use during the seventeenth and eighteenth centuries throughout the region and continued into the nineteenth century. Christian congregations on various islands, as well as the Jewish community on Barbados, for example, called for a day of humiliation following the powerful 1843 earthquake that caused extensive damage on several islands. Nevertheless, island residents ap-pear to have invoked such ceremonies infrequently. Indeed, the absence of such rituals after many events in this disaster-stricken region is striking. While colonists experienced numerous disasters, relatively few were followed by fasts or processions. Existing evidence, mostly from the British colonies, suggests that many storms, earthquakes, and floods occasioned little moral reflection and often no ritual response.[166]

One major reason for this was the sheer frequency of events. Put simply, calamities occurred so often that many ceased to be wondrous. The case of earthquakes is illustrative. Europeans generally viewed earthquakes as provi-dential events, especially during the seventeenth century, in part because they were so rare. "The Hand of God is not to be overlooked in such things . . . es-pecially such rare and unusual Instances as Earthquakes," wrote one English pamphleteer in 1693." This was not the case in the Caribbean. Earthquakes were common and even expected events. As one observer in the Danish island wrote, "Earthquakes are so common in all the West Indian islands that at least some occur every year." Many residents in Jamaica ignored the initial rumbling of the earth in June 1692 because it was such a routine occurrence. The same was true when minor tremors initially shook Hispaniola in May 1751 prior to the major earthquake in October. The initial tremors were "not minded by any Body, as there is no Island in the West-Indies where such Shocks are not some-times felt." Because most tremors caused little damage, they did not provoke the immediate panic and appeals to providence that often appeared in the wake of similar events in Europe or in other parts of the Americas. Major earthquakes and other disasters in the Caribbean remained distinctly providential events, but such events stand out in part because most other earthquakes, even rela-tively significant ones, did not occasion fasts or processions. Instead, colonists increasingly accepted earthquakes as part of the God's general ordering of the natural world in the region.[167]

Similar attitudes characterized other storms, drought, and floods. Negative evidence is problematic, but the absence of rituals in the British colonies is nonetheless suggestive of the extent to which the encounter with the realities of the Caribbean environment altered colonists' ideas about providence and the natural world. While Caribbean residents continued to view major disasters as acts of God, the sheer number of "minor" events rendered many alarming but not wondrous occurrences.[168]

Such shifting attitudes and interpretations also reflected, in part, an increas-ingly scientific approach to the natural world. Beginning in the second half of the seventeenth century and continuing across the eighteenth century, scientifically minded colonists (and their financial and intellectual supporters in London, Paris, Madrid, and elsewhere) increasingly gathered data and information about the natural world of the Caribbean generally, including natural disasters. Institutions such as the Royal Society in London and the Royal Academy of Sciences in Paris sent out barometers, thermometers, and questionnaires to resident correspondents, who returned detailed descriptions and instrument readings from their respective colonies. Over time, increasing numbers of let-ters and reports on hurricanes, earthquakes, and unusual insects, as well as bar-ometric and temperature readings, accounts of rainfall, and other data, made their way into the *Philosophical Transactions*, the acts of the Académie Royale des Sciences, and other metropolitan publications. Local publications in the Caribbean began to report on weather conditions because of their utility for commerce and agriculture. By the 1790s the *Papel periódico de La Habana* in-cluded them weekly. An interesting exception to this was the principal French learned society in the Caribbean in the 1780s, the *Cercle des Philadelphes*, which met at Cap François in Saint-Domingue. It decided not to bother recording in-strumental measurements because they served no purpose in the case of events like hurricanes. "[One never sees causes], one only sees outcomes," it noted, and such measurements provided "no power to control, no ability to prevent or to remedy anything." In general, however, increased knowledge about conditions before and after disasters gradually influenced colonists' (or at least elite colonists') understanding of the natural causes of such events.[169]

Increased experience with disasters contributed to other intellectual shifts during the eighteenth century. As eighteenth-century colonists increasingly emphasized the natural forces at work in many disasters, particularly hurricanes and earthquakes, they also increasingly suggested that these calamities must play some larger role in what one called "the admirable order with which the universe is governed." This Enlightenment era optimism found many adherents among Caribbean naturalists and observers. Edward Long, for example, wrote that hurricanes were "always accompanied with great rains, and a cool state of the air; however destructive therefore they may be in some respects, they fertilize the earth, purge the atmosphere from malignant vapours, and bring with them a healthful season." Likewise, Long believed that earthquakes "answer some wise, and perhaps salutary purpose in the oeconomy of nature" and suggested that the discharge of underground "effluvia" might produce rains. Moreau de Saint-Méry concluded that without "such extraordinary movements of nature . . . perhaps the Antilles would have been uninhabitable." The widely read French journalist Abbé Raynal was unsure whether the storms that tore up the soil made it more fertile or if their winds carried substances that promoted vegetation, but he was convinced that destruction was essential for regeneration, and so the hurricanes were "the source of partial evil and of general good." Even individual colonists who suffered severe losses from various hazards often saw some silver lining. A colonist in Antigua confessed his first experience with a hurricane was "dreadful," but he also observed "the Damage is not equal to the Benefit brought with it" in the form of plentiful rains for the island's parched cane fields... Likewise, the Jamaican planter Nathaniel Phillips remarked that "sometimes good arises from evil, for the destructive Hurricanes [of the mid-1780s] have led me on to make very great improvements" on his plantation, including strengthening buildings and installing a water mill.[170]

It is noteworthy that such comments concern large-scale and spectacular events such as hurricanes and earthquakes. The more quotidian calamities of drought and insect infestations do not appear to have generated the same philosophical musings, perhaps because their impact unfolded more slowly and appeared confined to fields rather than the colonies' physical and economic infrastructure. For whatever reason, fewer colonists seemed ready to celebrate the blast in shaping the general well-being of life in the Caribbean, although one early nineteenth-century observer thought that in small numbers insects could act as a "stimulus, wisely sent to rouse the inattentive planter to cleaner and more careful modes of husbandry." Moreover, whatever "benefits" accompanied many large-scale disasters were not shared widely. The early nineteenth-century historian Richard Schomburgk perceptively understood that only those with enough credit or capital usually had the resources to eventually reap the long-term benefits of events like hurricanes. Whatever the "general and future good from partial and present evil," for most people major disasters remained "sharp and afflictive remed[ies]."[171]

How the majority of the population in those colonies interpreted and responded to disasters is less clear. Enslaved peoples living in such region filled with natural hazards must have developed a rich and vibrant set of customs, beliefs, and rituals linked to various disasters, but the evidence of such activities appears in archival materials only sporadically. White colonists made few references to slave rituals and beliefs, mainly because many such ceremonies took place away from whites. When planters and others did observe such practices, their comments were often negative, dismissive, and frustratingly brief. What is clear is that enslaved Africans experienced the worst of the ravages wrought by hurricanes, drought, and other hazards.

Like Europeans, West Africans had little or no experience with hurricanes and earthquakes, and most West African groups viewed such events as divinely ordained. As with European colonists, such attitudes likely persisted among enslaved people in the Caribbean, although adapted to New World conditions. Charles Leslie wrote that enslaved people in Jamaica worshiped "two Gods, a good and a bad One," and that the evil God sends "Storms, Earthquakes, and all kinds of Mischief." Yoruba-speaking enslaved people in Cuba prayed to the guardian spirit Chango during storms and, out of deference to him, refrained from smoking. They also sought help from the *orisha* (deity) called Oyá, who controlled wind, lightning, and storms and who was syncretized as the Virgin of Candelaria, a protector against natural disasters. Enslaved people in the Danish islands recognized one god who created the universe, but worshiped a variety of gods, or spirits, who attended to the affairs of this world, including disasters.[172]

Because of high mortality rates and constant importation of new slaves from West Africa, diverse African rituals and beliefs remained powerful on most of the islands. One enslaved woman in Barbados named Ashy contrasted that relative power of the Fanti god to the Christian one during an ongoing drought in the late 1790s. "When we want rain in my country," she informed one planter who transcribed her words, "we all take de Black Caps and put on our head" and then made an offering with prayers of one "Blackee sheep and Negur Man." Then the "Big Blackee man *de same dat you call God,*" took the man and sheep and rains followed. One of the more detailed accounts of slave rituals following a drought comes from the Danish islands. Moravian missionary C. G. A. Oldendorp reported that during a period of extreme dryness in the 1730s, slaves from different ethnic groups invoked a variety of rituals. The Wawus (possibly Ewe speakers from the Bight of Benin) tied leaves around their heads and bodies and marched in a "sorrowful procession" to the "schambu hut" in which dwelled the "tiger" god, pleading with him to send rain. The Loango (from Kongo) sacrificed a cow in a ritual that concluded with penitents running home to escape that rain they expected to follow. "Karamnti" (likely Coromantee) women formed a procession that offered various fruits to a priest (called Udum), asking for rain. Echoing Ashy's testimony, Oldendorp reported that regarding animal sacrifices, enslaved people in the Danish islands "on joyous occasions . . . offer white animals and on calamitous occasions, black ones."[173]

Many of these offerings took place in the houses of sacred figures or in "sacred groves" on the island or involved persons seen as possessing special powers. Inquisition cases of "*mohanes*," ritual practitioners of African origin, for example, revealed individuals like Antonio Congo who in 1690 claimed he had the power to dissipate a hurricane and otherwise control nature. Enslaved individuals in many of the British islands may have looked to *obeah* men to help protect themselves or their crops from damage during storms or droughts. After the Jamaican maroon Plato, a powerful brigand and practitioner of *obeah*, was sentenced to death in 1780, he threatened the court and jailer that a great storm would be his revenge. Shortly thereafter a hurricane destroyed Savanna-la-Mar. This story may be apocryphal, but it reflects the possibility of alternative cosmologies. While evidence remains scattered and limited, it seems clear that the enslaved integrated natural hazards into their own understandings, hopes, and expectations.[174]

Although African beliefs and practices remained pervasive in slave quarters, by the latter decades of the eighteenth century some enslaved people became converts to Christianity, or at least began to incorporate elements of Christian belief into their cosmologies, and disasters sometimes played a role in that process. Anglican missionary James Ramsay, for example, claimed that many slaves became interested in baptism in the wake of the 1772 hurricane, while Methodist missionaries reported an increase in conversation among the enslaved population in Antigua. Likewise, accounts of the 1770 earthquake in Saint-Domingue reported that blacks and whites crowded into the colony's churches to hear preaching. Mary Prince's narrative suggests that some slaves embraced elements of a Christian providential view of disasters, although they saw distinct meanings in some events. Prince recounted a flood that struck Grand Turk shortly after whites had destroyed a simple structure that enslaved laborers had erected for prayers. "I do think that this [flood] was for their wickedness, for the Buckra men [whites] there were very wicked," she wrote.[175]

Whites, however, often dismissed such responses to disasters by suggesting that enslaved people did not fully understand or embrace Christian beliefs. One observer described the enslaved and free blacks in Saint-Domingue as "gullible . . . superstitious and roguish" for embracing the prophecy of a former Jesuit following the 1770 earthquake who preached that the island "was going to be destroyed, but that only the whites would perish." Moravian missionaries in the Danish West Indies during the 1730s reported that faith in a Christian god among some enslaved people remained strong during a violent hurricane in July 1733, although their spiritual condition "deteriorate[d]" as food became scarce and rebellion roiled St. John. What whites regarded as "deterioration," however, may simply reflect the limited willingness of some enslaved people to embrace Christianity in its entirety, choosing instead to incorporate elements of Christian beliefs within their own cosmologies. Regardless, it is clear that enslaved Africans drew upon a variety of beliefs in making sense of disasters, and that, as with European colonists, providential or supernatural explanations figured prominently in their responses across much of the early modern period.[176]

Just as interpretations of disasters evolved across time, so, too, did political responses by colonists and by local and imperial officials. As with religious rituals, some differences existed based on national character and political circumstances. The Spanish Crown from the inception of colonization had assumed responsibility for the success and survival of New World settlements. When calamity struck the colonies, the Crown often granted tax exemptions, a moratorium on debt collection, and at times even direct aid. Such assistance came in response to appeals generated by local town councils (*cabildos*) that emphasized their hardships, pointed out their colony's place in Spain's larger strategic interests, and underlined that Spain's justification for possession of the New World was based on its missionary responsibility to spread the "true faith." Spain's response combined strategic considerations with a sense of Christian paternalism. Aid, however, usually favored communities or important groups rather than victims as a whole.[177]

That approach was eventually adopted by other European states as well. The English and French early settlements, while undertaken under royal licenses, had been carried out by noble proprietors or by private companies, and thus natural calamities were not viewed as a direct royal responsibility for the most part. That was also true of the Dutch and later Danish settlements in the Caribbean. Instead of government aid, private charity, much of it religiously based, provided the most immediate aid to victims. Much of this assistance was also local, as churches in disaster-stricken areas raised food or money for victims. At times, however, news of disaster in the Caribbean touched those living in far-off colonies. In some cases, religious groups came to the aid of the brethren, as was the case when English Quakers sent funds to their Jamaican counterparts following the Port Royal earthquake or Jewish colonists on Curacao sent aid to rebuild a synagogue on St. Eustatius following the 1772 hurricane. In other cases, economic relationships between colonies or an increasing sense of nationalism helped spur donations. This was particularly true in the eighteenth century, when victims of disaster received relief funds or other aid from neighboring islands and from London, Bristol, New York, and Philadelphia. Similar developments spurred occasional donations in France, such as occurred after the 1780 hurricane when banks in Paris and Nantes set up subscription campaigns to coordinate donations to victims in the French islands.[178]

Private and religious assistance remained the primary forms of disaster relief in the eighteenth century, but governments—local and imperial—occasionally played an important role, especially in the English and French colonies. These efforts reflected both heightened royal power in the colonies by the latter part of the seventeenth century and, in the following decades, increased awareness among royal officials of the economic value of the colonies to their empires. As a result, beginning in the mid-eighteenth century, the Crown—and in England, Parliament—became more responsive to colonial appeals for help, in part because the symbolism of paternalism and state response had important political dimensions. Such relief remained sporadic, but was noteworthy nonetheless, with the most notable occurrence coming in 1780 when Parliament sent £120,000 to victims of hurricanes in Jamaica and Barbados. Parliament furnished smaller amounts of direct aid to colonists after the 1812 eruption on St. Vincent and to St. Vincent and Barbados following the 1831 hurricane. At other times, the king granted money from his royal bounty or provided provisions and supplies to distressed colonists, while Parliament occasionally subsidized the purchase of food, as happened during a drought in Antigua in 1779. The British government also occasionally granted tax relief to victims of disaster, as occurred following the 1772 hurricane in the Leeward Islands. Colonists in Montserrat and St. Vincent, likewise, sought tax relief during the great drought of 1791–92.[179]

The French throne also came to the aid of its colonial subjects. Royal officers in France and in the colonies often urged tax exemptions for victims, which were often granted. Cacao growers on Martinique received an exemption from a capitation tax following the 1727 earthquake and blast that destroyed cacao trees. Residents of Guadeloupe and Marie Galante likewise received tax relief in the wake of a hurricane in September 1740, as did planters on Martinique suffering from the ravages of ants in the 1760s and 1770s.[180] To some extent, the state was forced to act in these circumstances since French merchants assumed that disasters created precarious economic situations that made voyages unprofitable and repayment of debts unlikely. Statements by officials in France and on the islands also demonstrated that the justification of an *etat protecteur* (protective or welfare state) was taking shape over the course of the eighteenth century, although such efforts remained sporadic. As was the case in Britain, the largest direct government aid to the French colonies followed the 1780 hurricane. Louis XVI and his council voted 1 million crowns (*écus*) to victims of the disaster as a "gift from the nation." Such efforts continued sporadically across the nineteenth century. One particularly noteworthy example was a grand charity bazaar organized by Queen Marie-Amélie of France in the Palais-Royal that reportedly raised over 100,000 francs for victims of the 1843 earthquake in Guadeloupe, part of a much larger imperial relief effort.[181]

In the Dutch island colonies, by contrast, it appears that little or no state aid was available to victims of disaster. Despite having one the most advanced systems of charitable institutions in Europe, the Dutch government provided no assistance to victims on the colonies. That the Dutch West India Company retained control of the colonies during the seventeenth and most of the eighteenth centuries likely delayed the process of state intervention after calamities. Even after the WIC went bankrupt and the States General assumed control of the colonies in 1791, the government maintained a policy that each colony should be self-supporting. Thus, colonists in St. Martin had to fend for themselves after a devasting hurricane in 1819 leveled most of the island and resulted in damage in excess of 1.4 million florins (in a colony whose annual revenues totaled only ƒ31,162). Disaster victims in the Dutch colonies instead relied on private aid and assistance. Not until 1913 was a permanent fund created for disaster relief in the Netherlands Antilles.[182]

The history of broad disaster relief efforts deserves more focused attention than it has received, since relatively little is known about when and why aid was granted and who received it. In general, however, it appears that relief tended to aid planter elites in their effort to control labor and laborers, a trend that continued after the ending of slavery on many of the islands. In addition, local governments in the Caribbean region routinely took steps to ease suffering and aid rebuilding by loosening trade restrictions and requesting support from neighboring islands of any and all nations. Indeed, requests to open trade with foreign ports in post-disaster situations became ubiquitous in the British and Spanish islands during the eighteenth century, where local interests wished to ignore or circumvent mercantilist policies that restricted trade. Spanish trade with North American ports like Charleston and Philadelphia grew considerably after disasters, especially after the 1780s. Colonial requests were often supported and enacted by royal administrators, despite their charge to enforce trade laws, and on occasion when they were not, pressure mounted in the colonies to force government action. Such was the case when the Spanish governor of Cuba, Luis de Las Casas, was recalled in 1796 in part because his reluctance to lift trade restrictions and alleviate taxes following a series of hurricanes in the 1790s rendered him deeply unpopular among many Cubans.[183]

Even France, the mercantilist model for exclusivist policies, was forced to seek supplies on the open market after several mid-eighteenth-century calamities, although governors were usually careful to justify these "temporary" measures. Conditions became worse in the 1760s after the loss of Canada left French colonists even more dependent on shipments from the home country, or on goods smuggled in from British North America or from neighboring foreign islands. After a major hurricane in August 1788, the governor of Martinique, while awaiting relief from France, allowed in foreign supplies to ensure the survival of the slaves, "whose hunger would lead to the loss of the colony," but promised to avoid trade that would harm French commerce.[184]

Such modifications of mercantilist policy did not go unnoticed in the halls of power across the Atlantic, and more than one governor had to defend himself against charges that he bowed to pressure from local planters rather than fulfilling their duty to enforce imperial laws. Overall, mercantilist policies of exclusive trade within the colonial holdings of various empires were continually undercut by the subsistence crises created by drought, hurricanes, and other disasters and by the subsequent pressure from local elites anxious to secure outside supplies rather than sacrifice space in their sugar fields for provisions. In practice that also meant an embrace of contraband trade to provide essential supplies. The regular loosening of trade restrictions or turning a blind eye to interlopers in the late eighteenth century, both as a wartime necessity and a swelling demand for foodstuffs given the expansion of slavery, only heightened calls from colonists for free and open trade with foreign merchants.[185]

The post-disaster subsistence crises that drove these actions generally did not impact the planter class, although planters at times felt the pinch of shortages. Instead, shortages compounded suffering among poorer colonists and the enslaved. Poorer whites often struggled to recover from various disasters.[186] Shortages of food and water in the wake of hurricanes, earthquakes, and drought often resulted in outmigration from various islands as poorer colonists sought "better furnished" places, meaning colonies with seemingly better resources, fewer trade restrictions, or fewer environmental hazards. In some cases, colonists had little choice; in addition to the immediate crisis of food, water, and shelter, losses to crops and/or infrastructure required access to capital or credit to rebuild, and poorer colonists had less access to both. Indeed, at various times and places, disasters further consolidated lands in the hands of wealthy planters who had access to credit and bought out their poorer neighbors, as happened in Barbados following the 1675 hurricane. The outmigration of poor white colonists, however, generated regular concern among local and at times imperial officials who feared already pronounced black–white ratios would worsen.[187]

Conditions were even worse for enslaved Africans and Afro-Caribbeans. Hunger routinely stalked the slave quarters in the wake of disasters. Whether from hurricanes, earthquakes, drought, or insect infestation, the destruction of existing supplies, the loss of crops in provision grounds, and the disruption to trade in and out of the islands combined to generate tremendous privation and misery among the enslaved. The frequency of such circumstances increased across the seventeenth and much of the eighteenth century as the plantation complex intensified, island planters became more committed to sugar monoculture, and the enslaved populations expanded dramatically. The need for outside assistance and relief, in turn, became more pronounced, as did critiques of metropolitan mercantilist policies that planters feared threatened their physical and economic security. This was especially true during the revolutionary decades at the end of the eighteenth century. Pamphlets and newspaper accounts, in Europe and the colonies, issued charges and countercharges as each side sought to blame the actions of the other for the death of slaves. Disasters were not singularly responsible for growing calls for ending mercantilist policies and opening trade in the region, nor for calls for abolishing slavery, but they did play a central role in vigorous debates that ensued in European and colonial capitals at the end of the eighteenth and into the early nineteenth century.[188]

Finally, the threat from disasters of one kind or another marked the mental worlds of all who lived in the region and confronted its myriad dangers. Large-scale hazards such as earthquakes, hurricanes, and flooding not only threatened the economic foundation of the colonies but also undermined the physical and social foundations of their worlds. As the planter Joshua Peterkin saw it, disasters rendered the Caribbean something of a battleground between human efforts to dominate the natural world and natural forces that resisted such subjugation and, indeed, routinely destroyed the markers by which Europeans measured their domination: their houses, fences, fields, and mills. As a result, a sense of precariousness and fragility defined life in the region and gave rise to a mentality that emphasized living in the moment, of seeking immediate returns as a hedge against the potential catastrophic losses. The danger posed by disasters helped create a culture in which, as one visitor observed of Jamaicans, colonists grew "careless of Futurity." Likewise, hazards came to occupy a prominent place in colonists' daily thoughts and, sometimes, in their dreams. Thomas Thistlewood recalled a neighbor who could not sleep for weeks in the aftermath of the 1780 hurricane that pummeled western Jamaica. "He is afraid to fall asleep, as such dreadful hurricanes and confusion present themselves to him, as far exceed the real one," Thistlewood wrote. "Just so with myself and several others, the nerves so affected." Robert Graham, a reluctant absentee who returned to Scotland in the 1770s, missed much about his life in Jamaica, including the climate, but he also admitted to one correspondent that he slept well at night in part because he "fear[ed] neither hurricanes or blasts" in his fields.[189]

The anxiety wrought by disasters revealed itself in the region's more formal literary culture. The entire second book (of four) of James Grainger's poem

The Sugar-Cane (1764) outlined the various threats with which planters had to contend, including hurricanes, earthquakes, volcanoes, rats, drought, and the blast. "Say, will my Shenstone lend a patient ear / And weep at woes unknown to Britain's Isle?" he wrote. Hurricanes figure prominently as well in John Singleton's blank verse poem "A General Description of the West-Indian Islands" (1767). Cuban poet Jose Maria Heredia's "The Hurricane" (1825) emphasized the sublime power of the storms and their ability to disrupt progress. Indeed, the novelty and frequency of hurricanes meant that the storms served as particularly vivid symbols of the region's distinct environment and, by extension, culture, a role it would continue to play across the nineteenth century and beyond. As Barbadian historian and poet Kamau Brathwaite would note in his call for a truly Caribbean language that escaped the legacy of colonialism, "the hurricane does not roar in pentameter."[190]

* * *

Surveying the history of the British colonies in the Caribbean at the end of the eighteenth century, Bryan Edwards remarked that owning plantations and other property in the region constituted a "species of lottery. As such, it gives birth to a spirit of adventure and enterprise, and awakens extravagant hopes and expectations; too frequently terminating in perplexity and disappointment."[191] Myriad factors contributed to that perplexity and disappointment, including the almost constant warfare that raged among the European nations that laid claim to various islands. Natural disasters, however, played an equally important role in making life in the Caribbean a lottery.

Throughout the early modern period, disasters—hurricanes, earthquakes, droughts, flood, and various pests—wrought havoc upon plantations and towns, in sugar fields and provision grounds, in coffee estates and cacao groves. The damage and destruction had significant consequences for the settlement and development of colonies. In the initial years, disasters threatened the very existence of the colonies. Over time, as colonists adjusted to the dangers, disasters influenced the emergence of a distinct creole landscape and architecture. Moreover, disasters transformed the layout of the colonies, as towns were destroyed and rebuilt, or abandoned and new towns laid out in different parts of an island.

Disasters also shaped the economic geography of the region. Sugar emerged as the single most important export crop in the Caribbean during the early modern period, and while various disasters often caused enormous losses in production, and thus profits, colonists remained committed to the crop. So great were the profits from sugar that most planters absorbed the losses, rebuilt their plantations, and pushed forward. Colonists, at times, temporarily shifted to other crops when insects or drought attacked, but most returned to sugar when conditions improved. They did, however, continue to innovate, seeking out new species of sugar cane in the late eighteenth century they hoped would prove better able to withstand a variety of natural forces in the region. Smaller, poorer planters who lacked access to capital, by contrast, sometimes found themselves unable to rebuild in the wake of a disaster and sold out to larger planters. Even some "wealthy" planters at times found themselves so heavily indebted that a major hurricane or drought pushed them into insolvency and their plantations ended up in the hands of fellow colonists or metropolitan creditors. Ownership may have changed, but sugar cane remained in the fields.[192]

While disasters did not dislodge sugar as the region's primary export, they did at various times alter secondary crops grown on many of the islands, as happened with cacao production in Jamaica and Cuba in the 1670s and in Trinidad and Martinique in the 1720s. Likewise, hurricanes and erosion helped undermine the emerging coffee industry in Jamaica in the later part of the eighteenth and early nineteenth centuries. A series of hurricanes in Cuba in the 1840s had an even greater impact, destroying coffee crops and facilitating the shift to sugar cultivation. Many slaves found themselves transferred from the relatively less intense work of coffee production into the far harsher regime of sugar.[193]

Damage to sugar, cacao, coffee, and other export crops hurt planter profits, but losses in the provision fields and plantain groves, combined with higher prices for imported food, frequently created severe shortages of provisions for enslaved laborers and often led to heightened misery and mortality. The worst disasters claimed the lives of thousands of enslaved people who perished during the event itself or from the subsequent devastation, disruption, and displacement. Natural disasters were not the primary cause of the horrific mortality rates among enslaved people that necessitated the massive and ongoing importation of Africans to the region during the early modern period, but at various times and in various places, they contributed significantly to this vicious cycle.

In the wake of the 1785 hurricane, Robert Graham wrote to his brother-in-law Simon Taylor in Jamaica that the hurricanes and other disasters that struck so frequently in the Caribbean were "visitations which neither the wisdom, or learning of man can prevent or guard against and which from the nature of our situation in this world, we must submit to." In one sense, of course, Graham was correct. Hurricanes, earthquakes, heavy rains, and periodic droughts resulted from natural forces well beyond colonists' control. Living in the Caribbean meant living with the damage, disruption, and death that accompanied what Graham called "strokes of bad fortune." But in another sense Graham was mistaken, as he failed to recognize the extent to which the impact of those visitations was shaped by human actions. Colonists could do nothing to prevent hurricanes or other calamities, but human actions (or inaction) did shape the impact of these events and often heightened the suffering that accompanied them. Colonists were often quick to blame disasters on forces beyond their control, but they themselves played a central role in shaping the landscapes and the ecological conditions that, in turn, created the challenges that emerged during and after calamities. If, as one French traveler to the region concluded, "want and covetousness" explained why so many European colonists endured in a region plagued by calamity, such factors also did much to shape the devastating impact of those disasters in the early modern Caribbean and beyond.[194]

Conclusion: Caribbean Environmental History since 1850

PHILIP D. MORGAN, J. R. MCNEILL, MATTHEW MULCAHY, AND
STUART B. SCHWARTZ

Although the environmental history of the Greater Caribbean began with the initial human settlement of the islands more than 7,000 years ago, all but the latest 530 years of Caribbean history are poorly known. Nonetheless, the pre-Columbian history is in many respects essential to the understanding of the dramas that followed. During the better documented early modern centuries, ca. 1492–1850, the Caribbean underwent drastic reconfigurations. Sustained contact with the wider world, in particular the Atlantic world, bringing epidemics, conquests, colonial settlements, plantations, race-based slavery and eventually its abolition, recast the region's populations, its role within an increasingly global economy, its image in the minds of people everywhere—and its environment. Those social, political, economic, cultural, and ecological changes were thorough and quick, even by the standards of the American hemisphere, much of which was also recast in the same centuries. Environmental changes in the Caribbean of course continued after 1850. This conclusion provides a sketch of the continuing evolution of Caribbean landscapes and seascapes, the regimes of disease and health, and that of natural disasters.

When Humboldt, the so-called second discoverer of America, died in 1859, some key new forces transforming the Caribbean environment were already evident. He was aware, for example, of the burgeoning power of the United States, although he forecast that economic progress would center in the torrid zone or equinoctial region, the very heart of the Americas, which he considered to have superior natural resources. Thus Venezuela's coastline had "enormous advantages over that of the United States," he claimed, "thanks to the beauty of its ports, the tranquility of the sea, and its superb timber forests." Venezuela

Sea and Land. Philip D. Morgan, J. R. McNeill, Matthew Mulcahy, and Stuart B. Schwartz, Oxford University Press.
© Oxford University Press 2022. DOI: 10.1093/oso/9780197555446.003.0005

had "immense ship-building resources on its coastline"; and its "superb ships" were long-lasting because of the "properties of tropical wood." Nowhere else were the "anchorages so close, nor ports so conducive to the establishment of military settlements," he added. Storms and hurricanes from the Antilles "never reach the *Costa firme* [Venezuela's mainland coast]," he averred. The environmental assets of Venezuela, he therefore predicted, were greater than those of the United States. Humboldt's prophecy has, of course, not proven accurate. He both underestimated the United States' expansive power and exaggerated Venezuela's strengths. Geographical assets are possibilities, not determinations.[1]

Nevertheless, Humboldt was correct in seeing that the colonial system was fracturing even as the Caribbean region came under the influence of the rising new power to the north. Haiti proclaimed its independence from France in 1804; the rimland colonies of Venezuela, Colombia, and Panama threw off Spain's imperial yoke in 1819; and the Dominican Republic emerged from Haitian occupation in 1844. A sharp critic of colonial exploitation, Humboldt was in favor of states controlling their own destinies. While he would have applauded the development of independent nations in the Caribbean region—today numbering some 13 among the islands, and another 10 or so on the neighboring rimland— he did not anticipate that the United States, by both informal and formal means, would replace European nations as the hegemonic imperial power in the region. Through trade, investments, and capital flows, as well as invasions, occupations, and acquisitions, the United States came to dominate the region. As early as the mid-nineteenth century, it was the single largest market for Cuba's and Puerto Rico's exports (primarily sugar), absorbing almost a half of their output; in 1851 the US consul at Havana declared Cuba a de facto economic dependency of the United States. As a result, the Caribbean area has given rise to some of the longest-lasting examples of colonialism in world history. Even as late as 1945, only Cuba, Haiti, and the Dominican Republic were sovereign states. Today, Anguilla, the three Cayman Islands, and Montserrat are among the last colonies in the world; Martinique and Guadeloupe are overseas *départements* of France; and Puerto Rico is an internally self-governing territory of the United States, or, as some would say, the oldest colony in the world.[2]

An impassioned opponent of slavery, Humboldt was gratified that the institution was on its way to extinction in his lifetime. By the time he died in 1859, slavery had been abolished in a number of Caribbean territories and was under threat in others. Haiti led the way in 1804, following the world's only successful slave revolution; 30 years later, the combination of abolitionists and the enslaved dismantled the institution in the British colonies; in 1847 the Swedes prohibited slavery in their small island of St. Barthelémy, followed by the French and Danish colonies in 1848 and Venezuela in 1854. Four years after Humboldt's death, the Dutch abolished slavery in their domains, leaving only two Caribbean colonies, both Spanish, to complete the process of abolition, which Puerto Rico did in 1873 and Cuba in 1886, the last in the Americas except for Brazil two years later. The persistence of slavery well into the nineteenth century has been termed, a "second slavery," a reinvigorated institution, because of its scale, technological sophistication, onerous work demands, and harsh regimentation.[3]

Even after slavery's demise, the sugar plantation remained the dominant economic institution in the region—and generally more concentrated in its ownership and larger than ever before—through the 1970s. By 1870 Cuba's more than 1,000 mills produced 725,000 tons of sugar, accounting for about 40 percent of world exports. In the 1870s, for the first time in its history, the Caribbean region as a whole exported over 1 million tons of sugar. Sugar production continued on its sharp upward trajectory. In 1925 Cuba's fewer than 200 mills produced 5 million tons of sugar, rising to about 7 million in 1970, more than twice as much as the rest of the Caribbean combined. This dramatic expansion owed much to a huge enlargement of scale, fueled by massive steam-powered mills, serving whole districts, and the construction of a network of narrow-gauge railroads. The acreage of the average plantation grew enormously; the trend toward latifundia, or large landed estates, accelerated. By the last decade of the nineteenth century, for instance, the largest sugar factory in the world, located in Cuba, processed as much sugar as the whole island of Jamaica. In 1945 the world's largest plantation, La Romana in the Dominican Republic, stretched over 60,000 acres and produced 125,000 tons of sugar. But widespread land degradation and the rise of other competitors displaced Cuba as the world's largest exporter in the 1990s; today it is twenty-first in the world rankings. In 1960 Caribbean sugar accounted for about a fifth of world production; today, its contribution is minuscule. In the Caribbean region, Colombia now produces more sugar than Cuba, and Brazil out-produces the island more than twentyfold.[4]

Alongside the late nineteenth-century expansion of the sugar plantation, peasant small holdings and other economic alternatives mushroomed. Down to the Second World War, agriculture remained the foundation of almost all Caribbean economies, and the peasant population grew rapidly, peaking in the early twentieth century. One mainstay of peasant farmers was the banana tree. Introduced into the Caribbean ca. 1512, the tree was widespread in the plots of the enslaved. Humboldt extolled its potential. An acre planted with bananas, he explained, "produces nearly twenty times as much food as the same space sown with cereals." A large population, he claimed, "can be fed from a small plot of land covered with banana, cassava, yams and maize." Once rapid and reliable steamships became available from the 1860s onward, peasants could export their surplus fruit. It was not long before North American entrepreneurs saw the potential in this trade in bananas, leading some multinational corporations such as United Fruit Company to take advantage of the new opportunities that steamships presented. Peasant smallholdings began to be consolidated into larger, more economically profitable units. Large plantations devoted to the crop arose.[5]

As in the days of slavery, a range of crops and other economic activities existed outside of sugar estates. Small-farm peasant proprietors in Cuba produced a fine-quality tobacco, accounting for 40 percent of the island's exports in 1900. The golden age of cacao production in Trinidad lasted from 1870 to 1920. Another hillside crop, coffee, was a favorite of peasant farmers in the Blue Mountains of Jamaica. A number of Caribbean territories remained major producers of dyewood, most notably logwood, until the 1930s when synthetic dyes undermined the industry. Ginger, pimento, nutmeg, and arrowroot were other small-cultivator products that for some places and at specific times supported peasants economically. Maritime industries continued to deplete stocks and resources, whether turtling in the Caymans, whaling in the Windward Islands, or sponge fishing in the Bahamas. Various extractive industries—most notably oil production—contributed to Caribbean output while presenting environmental challenges.[6]

The late nineteenth and early twentieth centuries were marked by a continuing and increasingly intensive search for agricultural exports, expanded scientific networks, new technologies such as railroads and steamships that accelerated the pace of change, and far-reaching ecological globalization. The proliferation of agricultural experiment stations, botanical gardens, and nurseries provided the institutional infrastructure for the diffusion of plants and scientific knowledge. The spread of monoculture created genetically homogeneous plant communities that were susceptible to disease, to which the imperial and transnational scientific networks then responded. New varieties of sugar cane and new cane hybrids proliferated; the widespread introduction of fast-growing trees, such as the eucalyptus, sought to combat deforestation; a hardy breed of cattle, the Zebu from South Asia, proved a superior draft animal and better adapted to dry savanna environments than the Criollo strain; the mongoose introduced into the Caribbean in the late nineteenth century from India soon helped, in the words of one authority, "to endanger or exterminate more species of mammals, birds and reptiles within a limited area than any other animal deliberately introduced by man anywhere in the world." By the early twentieth century, new breeds of plants and animals, imported from Africa, Asia, and the Pacific—in what has been labeled a Neo-Columbian Exchange—dominated the Greater Caribbean agricultural landscape.[7]

Humboldt was well aware that the Caribbean population was growing fast. He was one of the first to meticulously chart the increase. He knew that the rapidly growing population was putting increasing pressure on resources. By time of his death, the Caribbean island population was approaching 4 million people, a more than threefold increase from a century earlier. Between 1860 and 1945 the region's population more than tripled, growing from 4 million to 15 million. It almost tripled again from 1945 to 2020; today the Caribbean population stands at about 44 million. The fastest growing territory has been the Dominican Republic. Cuba probably has the most people of any sovereign state, but the island of Hispaniola, with its two independent states, has almost twice as many people as Cuba. This dramatic increase in population from the late nineteenth century owes less to immigration than to increases in fertility; reduced mortality, especially among infants; and improved health conditions. By the early twentieth century, the Caribbean no longer imported but rather exported people— primarily to the United States, but also to Canada, the United Kingdom, France, and the Netherlands. By the late twentieth century, about half the native-born population of Puerto Rico lived outside the island. Within the region, there was considerable movement—to build the Panama Canal, to construct railroads in Costa Rica, and to cut canes in Cuba and the Dominican Republic. Perhaps a million people of Haitian descent live in the Dominican Republic today. Even with these internal and external migrations, population densities have increased markedly—producing some of the highest concentrations in the world and increasingly pushing people toward towns and cities, or off the islands altogether.[8]

From the late nineteenth century on, rural populations began to grow so quickly that the agricultural sector could not support them, and the movement to towns intensified. Initially, urban places had reputations as death traps; occupational opportunities were limited; and the allure of a smallholding in the countryside was strong. Yet, by the beginning of the twentieth century, 15 percent of Cuba's population lived in Havana and almost a third of Cubans were urban dwellers, making it the most urbanized Caribbean country. Over the course of the twentieth century, the degree of urbanization has soared throughout the region, putting it well above the global average. The share of urban populations in the Caribbean rose from 37 percent in 1960 to 58 percent in 1990 to about 70 percent today. Generally, there is one dominant city in each country—Santo Domingo in the Dominican Republic, Port-au-Prince in Haiti, Havana in Cuba, San Juan in Puerto Rico, and so on. In 2019, among the Caribbean islands, the Dominican Republic had the most urban dwellers at 8.8 million, or 82 percent of its population, followed closely by Cuba at 8.7 million, or 77 percent of its population, and then Haiti at 6.3 million, or 56 percent of its population. Rapid, unplanned, and uncontrolled urban growth has resulted in poor housing in inner cities, squatter settlements on the fringes, widespread overcrowding, and extensive suburban development.[9]

A rapidly rising population and urban sprawl placed increasing pressure on terrestrial resources. Deforestation occurred earliest, fastest, and most extensively on the small islands of the region. Wherever it happened, massive

nutrient loss and soil erosion followed. Still, even by the late nineteenth century, some territories—mostly larger islands and rimlands—retained fairly extensive forests. By 1870, for example, three-quarters of Puerto Rican forests had
not been felled. Much of Guyana is still pristine tropical rainforest, even today.
Nevertheless, by the late nineteenth century, most Caribbean island rainforests
had little timber left for building and furniture making. Islands generally became net importers of tropical hardwoods. Cuba was stripped of its vast forests
in a little over a century—the island was 80 percent forested in the early nineteenth century, but only about 15 percent remained by the early twentieth century—due to the freedom private property owners had to fell their woodlands
and the highly industrialized and mechanized form of sugar production that
consumed vast amounts of lumber and firewood. Nevertheless, vegetative re-
colonization and reforestation also occurred in some Caribbean territories.
Perhaps the most dramatic example is Puerto Rico, where forest covered just
10 percent of the island in the 1940s, but recovered 40 percent a half-century
or so later. This rapid growth was largely a function of the scale of agricultural
abandonment and secondary woodland replacement, which produced a more
homogenized forest than ever before. The most dramatic ecological catastrophe
occurred in twentieth-century Haiti. Since Haitians produced and consumed
charcoal as their primary source of domestic energy, the toll they have exacted
on their woodlands has been immense. In the 1920s forest covered about 60 percent of the country; today, the percentage is contested but at best 30 percent.
Accompanying this extensive land clearance has been major soil loss, gullying,
landslides, and silting of streams. The steep decline in the productivity of the
land has been dramatic and drastic.[10]

A debate has ensued about why the ecological histories of the Dominican
Republic and Haiti, two countries sharing the same island, have unfolded so
differently. Part of the answer involves environmental differences. The island of
Hispaniola's rains come mainly from the east, so the Dominican (eastern) part
of the island receives more rain and thus supports higher rates of plant growth.
Hispaniola's highest mountains (over 10,000 feet high) are on the Dominican
side, and the rivers from those high mountains mainly flow eastward into the
republic. The Dominican side also has broad valleys, plains, plateaus, and richer
soils. In particular, the Cibao Valley in the north is one of the richest agricultural areas in the world. In contrast, the Haitian side is drier because the barrier of high mountains blocks rains from the east. Compared to the Dominican
Republic, mountainous Haiti has a much smaller area of flat land good for intensive agriculture. There is more limestone terrain, and the soils are thinner
and less fertile and have a lower capacity for recovery. Yet these environmental
differences are not necessarily determinative. If so, why was Haiti a much richer
place than the Dominican Republic in colonial days? Over the course of the

nineteenth century, the lack of international recognition, role of foreign intervention, population growth rate and density, peasant predominance, and
constrained space characterized Haiti. Haiti's poverty forced its people to remain dependent on forest-derived charcoal for fuel, thereby accelerating the destruction of its forests. Differential government action also played a role, with 74
natural reserves in the Dominican Republic, "relatively the most comprehensive
and largest in the Americas," compared to just 4 tiny parks in Haiti.[11]

Another comparative puzzle is why Jamaica has trailed Barbados on the
path to sustained growth. Simply comparing size, the advantage seems to favor
Jamaica, which is more than 25 times larger than Barbados in area, 10 times
larger in population, and possessed of more natural resources, such as bauxite,
the ore that yields aluminum. More important, however, according to sociologist Orlando Patterson, is that "Jamaica is an extremely mountainous island
with deep, densely forested inland valleys that are difficult to reach, whereas
Barbados is a flat, coral island." As a result, the entire island of Barbados was
suitable for sugar cane production, whereas the crop was confined only to the
fertile coastal regions of Jamaica. On Barbados during the era of slavery, security
was stringent. On Jamaica, by contrast, slaves produced their own food, largely
in the backlands, that they then sold in local markets, giving them a measure
of autonomy. Mountainous interiors also offered opportunities for refuge and
resistance. In addition, Jamaica lies in major hurricane paths and frequently
experiences devastating destruction. Furthermore, it is located near a major
earthquake fault. Barbados's location to the south and farthest east of any of the
Lesser Antilles means that its hurricane risk is less than half that of Jamaica's;
it experiences fewer and less powerful earthquakes; and the whole island is
cooler than most parts of Jamaica. Barbados had a more stable elite, and a much
greater presence of white women and poor whites than in Jamaica. In addition,
Barbados, uniquely among populated Caribbean islands, never hosted malaria,
which until the mid-twentieth century hamstrung health in Jamaica.[12]

Perhaps the most perplexing conundrum is weighing the extent of environmental degradation in the Caribbean region as a whole against the promise
of environmental renewal. Small islands are especially vulnerable to natural
misfortunes. They enjoy a high degree of endemic plant and animal life, so species extinction rates can be extraordinarily high. The continuing destruction of
habitat as a result of increasing populations, agricultural development, urbanization, and rising sea levels poses problems for a wide range of fauna. Fruit-eating
bats, for example, have suffered from extensive forest felling. Many coral reefs
are being destroyed by effluent from cities and tourist complexes, and because
of climate change. Technological changes, such as the growing use of pesticides,
have had negative consequences. Bauxite mining, significant in Jamaica, the
Dominican Republic, Suriname, and Guyana, is particularly damaging, leaving

behind toxic red mud lakes and polluting groundwater aquifers. The introduction of alien animal species is no longer on the scale of the early arrival of domesticated livestock, but has had enduring aftereffects. For example, the mongoose, a notably voracious predator, was transplanted in the late nineteenth century to eradicate cane-field snakes, but went on to kill rice rats, nesting birds, and the Cuban solenodon. Extinctions have continued to mount in modern times: the Cuban red macaw in 1864; the Martinique muskrat in 1902; the monk seal in 1952. The problems of unsustainability are at least well known, enabling responses such as a growing range of protection laws, conservation areas, and national parks. Abandoned city lots have been converted to gardens in Cuba. The use of natural and artificial fertilizers—guano and rock phosphates—are helping to restore soil quality. In 2009, the Association of Caribbean States optimistically proclaimed the "Greater Caribbean" the world's first sustainable tourism zone.[13]

Fueled by the notion that the tropical climate is healthy, tourism is now the major industry in much of the Caribbean region. It employs, directly and indirectly, about 15 percent of the regional workforce and generates about the same proportion of the gross national product. Beginning in the 1920s but booming by the 1960s, regular international airplane flights made vacations to the Caribbean more affordable and increased the number of visitors. As early as 1921 a Barbadian government brochure bragged that the island was "the healthiest spot on the globe." Tourism has encouraged investment in infrastructure and lessened a reliance on agricultural exports; but for its critics, it exchanges one form of unhealthy dependence for another. Even though more visitors arrive by air than sea, the international cruise ship has replaced the sugar plantation as the region's iconic institution. However, cruise ship passengers spend more of their money on the ship itself than in the ports they visit; the companies hire foreign crews; and most of their supplies come from outside the region. In general, international corporations, not local entrepreneurs, earn most of the profit from tourism; two-thirds of the region's hotel rooms are foreign owned. Mass tourism also comes at an environmental price, as historian Duncan Macgregor notes, with "eroded beaches, polluted waters, inappropriate garbage and sewage disposal, destroyed mangroves, and blighted coral reefs." All-inclusive resorts are difficult to sustain, and for some years the Caribbean tourism industry has been losing market share. Ecotourism is one way of providing environmental protection. Farm-to-table operations can supply tourists' demand for high-quality food, thereby providing a stimulus to domestic agriculture. The future of tourism in the Caribbean is hard to predict, but the pandemic of 2020 has exposed the dangers of a reliance on such an industry.[14]

One small example of ecotourism's encounter with a local activity of long standing occurred in 2017 when horrified whale watchers off the island of St.

Vincent witnessed the killing of two orcas by local fishermen. Whaling has a long history in the Caribbean. When Yankee whaling declined in Caribbean waters in the late nineteenth century, locally based whaling operations found a niche. During the peak period of Caribbean whaling between 1870 and 1925, the tiny island of Bequia, one of the Grenadines, hosted at least five whaling stations, one of which employed nearly a hundred men. Today, Caribbean whalers venture to sea in small boats almost daily from a single small village on the leeward (western) coast of St. Vincent in search of spinner dolphins (and other dolphin species), pilot whales, and occasional orcas, which they harpoon and tow back to shore to use as food and local exchange. Whale and dolphin meat is much cheaper on the island than any other source of animal protein. Capturing on average about 350 cetaceans annually for the past half-century, Vincentian whalers seem to be involved in a sustainable enterprise, as long as tourists—the primary source of revenue in the region—do not object too vociferously. In fact, the greatest environmental challenge artisanal whaling faces in the Caribbean is probably the high level of mercury found in whales and dolphins, due to industrial pollutants. However, since St. Vincent and the Grenadines control a marine area 90 times larger than its terrestrial extent, its nutritional future is likely to be tied inextricably to the sea, if not necessarily to whales.[15]

The Caribbean, with its enormous range of social and economic systems contained in just 0.15 percent of the world's land surface, constitutes something of a laboratory of natural experiments. These experiments can be inward-looking, contrasting the ecological trajectories of Haiti and the Dominican Republic, or the divergent developmental paths of Jamaica and Barbados. The experiments can also look beyond the region, say, by contrasting the natural endowments of Venezuela and the United States, as Humboldt did. Binaries and dyads abound. The Caribbean region combines promise and peril, bewitching beauty and nightmarish horrors, efflorescence and degradation, exuberance and menace. Dyads drawn from three maritime technologies—canoe, caravel, and cruise ship—and three terrestrial institutions—conuco, plantation, and tourist resort—can serve as symbols of the main eras of Caribbean environmental history. The first period lasted at least 7,000 years as people paddled canoes from mainland to island, and from island to island, transporting plants, animals, and pottery, binding together archipelago and continental hinterlands. Their mound-building agriculture, the conucos, with their mixes of crops, sustained them. The caravel ushered in a period that lasted about 450 years. European imperialism, carried in the sailing ship, brought an even wider assortment of people, plants, animals, technologies, and pathogens to the region. No single empire dominated, so in one respect the Caribbean fragmented. At the same time, the key institution, the plantation, together with its signature product and distinctive mode of labor organization, provided some underlying unity. The last period, beginning about 60 years ago, symbolized by the cruise ship (the largest so big that ironically, it was unable to dock in most Caribbean ports), to which can be added the container vessel, tanker, and airliner, helped shape an increasingly globalized world. This world has been characterized by standardization and homogeneity, on the one hand, and hybridization and creolization, on the other. The Caribbean region has come to depend on mass tourism, so that the all-inclusive resort, for many, is the region's iconic institution. The close and changing relationship of land and sea, summarized by these symbolic dyads, has been at the heart of Caribbean development over successive ages.[16]

* * *

The dismal disease history of the Caribbean between 1493 and ca. 1850 has few parallels. The more cheerful story of the region's health history after 1850 has several. In the last 170 years, and especially in the last 50, Caribbean health and disease history has ceased to be an outlier and has instead joined the global trend. That trend since 1850 and especially since 1970, broadly speaking, is toward better health overall, and a reduction in the toll of infectious disease in particular. Today the island Caribbean's roughly 44 million people, 0.6 percent of humankind, are more numerous than ever before—and between 10 and 100 times more so than in 1492.

The simplest measure of changes in health is life expectancy at birth. In 1900, average life expectancy in the island Caribbean, and the world as a whole, was probably between 30 and 35 (it was 48 in North America). By 1950, the island Caribbean had extended life expectancy to 51—six years longer than the global average. By 2019, it had climbed to 77, and only in Haiti did life expectancy lag far behind the global average of 73. In some countries it stood well above, and even approached the world's longest-lived population, the Japanese (see Table C.1).

Some populations on the Caribbean littoral lagged a little behind the global average in 2019: Guyana at 70 and Suriname at 72. But Martinique's population outlived Canadians and Puerto Ricans outlasted the mainland US population. All in all, this is an extraordinary change in the health of the Caribbean and its position with respect to other world regions.

This improvement is the result of an unusually rapid epidemiological transition from an old regime in which infectious disease and child malnutrition exerted the strongest influences upon mortality to a new one in which "diseases of affluence" end the vast majority of lives. Almost every region in the world has made similar epidemiological transitions, or is doing so. The Caribbean is distinctive only in that its epidemiological old regime was so ferocious and its transition so fast. By 2005, heart disease, cancer, stroke, and diabetes caused half of all deaths in the Caribbean.[17] This is all the more remarkable because

Table C.1 **2019 Average Life Expectancies in the Island Caribbean, the World, and Japan (rounded to the nearest whole number)**

Haiti	64
Grenada	72
WORLD	73
Montserrat	74
Dominican Republic	74
Trinidad and Tobago	74
Jamaica	75
Dominica	75
St. Lucia	76
Curacao	79
British Virgin Islands	79
Barbados	79
Cuba	79
Puerto Rico	80
Anguilla	81
Guadeloupe	82
Martinique	83
Cayman Islands	84
(Japan)	84

Source: Max Roser, Esteban Ortiz-Ospina, and Hannah Ritchie (2019), "Life Expectancy." Published online at OurWorldInData.org. Retrieved from https://ourworldindata.org/life-expectancy.

the island Caribbean, in terms of income or wealth per capita, is not affluent by global standards. Among world regions, only Africa suffers more from malnutrition than the Caribbean.[18]

Part of the reason its epidemiological transition was fast was the information flowed freely among the islands and littoral. Successful disease control measures were quickly imitated both within and among the British, French, Dutch, Spanish, and, after 1898, American empires. This was not peculiar to the Caribbean, but characteristic of the colonial world at large after 1900, by which time research institutes, training programs, military medicine, and public health services were growing apace, and shuttling information around the world.[19]

The first important component of the Caribbean's great leap forward in health was mosquito control. In the 1880s and 1890s scientists in Italy, colonial Algeria, and India figured out that malaria was transmitted from human to human by mosquitoes. They quickly identified the vector species. At much the same time, Carlos Finlay and Walter Reed in Cuba unraveled the mysteries of yellow fever and its mosquito vector.

With that knowledge it became comparatively easy to control yellow fever because of the peculiar egg-laying habits of *Aedes aegypti*. Covering water containers, or adding a drop of oil to float on water surfaces, deprived yellow fever mosquitoes of satisfactory habitat for eggs and larvae. In Havana, occupied by the US Army after the Spanish-American War (1898), and the Canal Zone of Panama, acquired by the United States in 1903, systematic control of *Aedes aegypti* was proven possible and yellow fever incidence plummeted. Other cities and towns quickly took the same path. An extremely effective vaccine was developed in the 1930s, and ever since yellow fever has been of marginal significance in the Caribbean—a far cry from the situation between 1650 and 1850.

Anophelines, several of which can transmit malaria, proved harder to control. They lay eggs in puddles, ponds, swamps, and other natural features. Malaria remained an important rural disease in much of the Caribbean through the first third of the twentieth century. But between 1930 and 1950 its incidence declined quickly, and by 1980 it, too, had become rare in the region. The reasons included rural exodus and urbanization of the population, better housing, chemical assaults on mosquito populations featuring DDT, and antimalarial medications.[20] Successful reductions in yellow fever and malaria took place in several parts of the world between 1900 and 1960, but probably nowhere (with the possible exception of Brazil) did they matter as much as in the Caribbean—because few places outside of Africa had shouldered a similar burden from the two diseases. In Africa, reductions in yellow fever and especially malaria were much smaller before 1960.

Puerto Rico helped lead the way in the control of hookworm and bilharzia as well as malaria. In 1900, anemia caused by hookworm (*Necator americanus*) infestations killed roughly 12,000 Puerto Ricans annually. It affected about one-third of the island's population of a million, damaging fetuses, stunting growth, and causing mental debilities. After the United States acquired Puerto Rico in the Spanish-American War, US and Puerto Rican doctors researched the transmission cycle of hookworm, which normally enters human bodies through the skin of bare feet, and found that shoes, latrines, and public health education could sharply reduce the rate of infection. Bilharzia, for which snails serve as vectors, flourished early in the twentieth century in the irrigated cane fields along Puerto Rico's south coast. Snail control campaigns after 1953 quickly drove down bilharzia rates. US and Puerto Rican public health officials trumpeted their triumphs, partly in an effort to legitimate US rule over Puerto Rico, and partly to encourage other Caribbean islands to imitate Puerto Rico's successes.[21]

The other main components of the health transition in the Caribbean were also part and parcel of global changes in public health. They did not originate in the Caribbean, as yellow fever control did, and they did not change the Caribbean more than other places. The first of these, chronologically speaking, was the provision of clean drinking water. Between 1880 and 1950 most communities in the Caribbean sharply reduced the incidence of waterborne diseases such as typhoid, cholera, and dysentery, which had long taken a heavy toll especially among children. The second was the development of vaccines for common infectious diseases such as cholera, typhoid, and plague (ca. 1890–1930) and then tetanus, diphtheria, polio, and measles (ca. 1940–70). Vaccination regimes took hold only gradually and incompletely, but still made a large difference in the region's health. So did the arrival of antibacterial drugs after 1945, beginning with penicillin.

One important boost to better health throughout the region after 1960 was the Cuban Revolution led by Fidel Castro. The revolutionary government—no doubt aware of the US successes in public health propaganda on Puerto Rico—created public health programs that came to serve as one of the foundations of its shaky legitimacy. Castro, in a unique choice among communist governments in world history, claimed Cuba would become a "world medical power."[22] He wanted to show the merit of his revolution by overtaking the United States in various health metrics. His government built a healthcare system that was universal, community-based, free, and administered by the state. That meant it was also authoritarian, politicized, and at times dishonest in its compilation of data, as health authorities sometimes concealed disease outbreaks that they felt would embarrass or irritate the leadership.[23] Nonetheless, the Cuban Revolution's health service did register real reductions in disease, and its reputation, even if bolstered at times by statistical chicanery, put pressure on other Caribbean countries to improve their healthcare systems. The record and reputation of Cuban healthcare became a minor arena of Cold War competition, and redoubled the interest of the United States in the health of populations in Puerto Rico, and to some extent in Jamaica, the Dominican Republic, and anywhere else that might be contrasted with communist Cuba.

Contrasting life expectancy in Cuba to a handful of other Caribbean countries reveals a few relevant trends (see Table C.2). The official data for the post-1960 period is probably reasonably accurate despite Cuba's (and perhaps not only Cuba's) political temptations to falsification.[24]

Table C.2 **Life Expectancy at Birth in Cuba, the Caribbean, and the World, 1900–2019**

	Cuba	Aruba	Dominican Republic	Jamaica	Barbados	Puerto Rico	WORLD
1900	32	No data	No data	37.8	No data	No data	32
1930	42	No data	26	45.3	No data	No data	No data
1960	63.8	65.7	51.6	64.8	64.5	68.7	50.1
1990	74.6	73.5	66.6	73.2	74.7	74.2	64.2
2019	78.8	76.3	74.1	74.5	79.2	80.1	72.6

Source: Max Roser, Esteban Ortiz-Ospina, and Hannah Ritchie (2019), "Life Expectancy." Published online at OurWorldInData.org. Retrieved from https://ourworldindata.org/life-expectancy.

Cuba overtook Aruba and Jamaica in life expectancy between 1960 and 1990, and closed the gap on Puerto Rico. Its record closely parallels that of Barbados, which was slightly ahead of Cuba in 1960 and remained so in 1990 and in 2019; both added 15 years to life expectancy between 1960 and 2019. The Dominican Republic made even faster progress than Cuba between 1960 and 2019, adding more than 22 years to life expectancy, likely a reflection of comparatively easy measures—cleaner water, mosquito control, more vaccinations—that other Caribbean countries, including Cuba, had taken already. Many other countries around the world followed broadly similar trajectories, but few extended life quite so long as the Caribbean average.[25]

Of course this sunny picture of modern Caribbean health has some clouds. As everywhere, good health and good healthcare are unequally distributed in the Caribbean. That is true among societies: Haiti stands out for the comparatively poor health of its population. And it is true within societies: everywhere, even to some extent in Cuba, richer and better-connected citizens, which on some islands means whiter citizens, enjoy better health and better access to healthcare. Such inequities are widespread, and there is nothing specific to the Caribbean about them.

Since the nineteenth century, several rampaging pandemics have reached the Caribbean. The first of these, chronologically, was the 1918–19 influenza pandemic that killed about 50 million people worldwide, roughly 3 percent of the global population. In the Caribbean, while data is scarce, it is clear that its impact varied greatly from place to place. In the British Caribbean, it killed perhaps 30,000 in total, between 1 percent and 2 percent of the population. It affected the indigenous populations of British Honduras (Belize) and British Guiana grievously, and in those colonies killed 3–5 percent of the total population. In British Honduras, according to the chief medical officer, "some of the Indian villages were wiped out."[26] In contrast, in Jamaica the pandemic killed about 1 percent of the population, and in Barbados and Trinidad and Tobago, much less than that. In the Caribbean as whole, pandemic influenza probably killed about 100,000 in 1918–19, roughly 1 percent of the population.[27]

The second of these global pandemics was HIV/AIDS, a viral infection new to humans as of the early twentieth century. It remained confined to Africa until the 1970s, when it appeared (undiagnosed) in the Americas. In 1982, Haiti reported the first Caribbean case of HIV, after which it soon became conspicuous in the region. As a cause of death it peaked around 2000, when it killed about 1 in every 2,500 people annually in the Caribbean. For a while early in the twenty-first century it was the leading cause of death for the cohort aged 15 to 44. But HIV treatments have improved, in the Caribbean as elsewhere, and it has become more of a chronic illness than a death sentence. About 1 percent of the region's population is HIV-positive. Haiti's rate is above 2 percent, and the Bahamas and Trinidad are also well above the average. Cuba, according to official data, has the lowest infection rate. As everywhere in the world, infection is much more common among some subpopulations such as sex workers.[28]

Dengue has flourished in the Caribbean since the 1980s. It had already existed for at least a century, and probably three, in the Caribbean. It is easily mistaken for other fever-inducing diseases, and so just when it arrived, and how prevalent it may have been, is unknown. It is a mosquito-borne disease carried by *Aedes aegypti* and others of the *Aedes* genus. As such, its prevalence probably declined with the successful control of *Aedes aegypti* population beginning at the turn of the twentieth century. However, the advent of a yellow fever vaccine reduced the public health logic for *Aedes* control in the Caribbean and throughout the Americas, and unease about the ecological effects of heavy insecticide use led to relaxation of anti-*Aedes* measures. By 1970 that relaxation allowed resurgent mosquito populations and, in time, a dengue pandemic that gathered pace in the 1980s and only intensified in the twenty-first century, spanning the warm latitudes of the globe. It is centered in Southeast and South Asia, but conspicuous in the Caribbean as well. Globally, in 2010, perhaps 100 million people suffered from dengue and 300 million more hosted the virus without symptoms.[29] In the Caribbean, epidemics occurred in Cuba in 1981, and almost everywhere in 2002 (worst in the Dominican Republic and Trinidad and Tobago). Since 2004, major outbreaks have come at irregular intervals, usually about one every 3–5 years, a pattern shared with the rest of the warm latitudes in the Americas. In a bad year, dengue kills a few thousand in the Caribbean. The general trend remains one of growing incidence, with roughly five times as many cases today as in the 1980s. Mosquito control programs have proven difficult to maintain year in and year out. A vaccine was licensed in 2015 but as yet is available only in limited supply.[30]

Another cloud in the sunny picture of modern Caribbean health was the cholera outbreak in Haiti—the first in more than a century in the Caribbean. It arrived late in 2010 with UN relief efforts in the wake of the catastrophic earthquake and since then has infected over 800,000 Haitians and killed nearly 10,000.[31] It never escaped Haiti. Clean water and sanitation are far less reliable in Haiti than anywhere else in the Caribbean. But since 2018, Haiti has reported no new cholera cases, thanks mainly to an oral vaccine.[32] So this cloud has passed.

More recently, the COVID-19 pandemic took hold in the Caribbean in early 2020, as almost everywhere else in the world. As of the summer of 2021, its impact had registered more strongly upon the economy of the region than on its health, as tourism receipts fell off sharply. In 2020, the region's economy shrank by 7 percent.[33] Nonetheless, COVID-19 brought challenges to public health on several islands. Frequent connection to COVID-19 hotspots such as Spain, South Florida, Mexico, Colombia, and—for Martinique and Guadeloupe—France guaranteed frequent importation of the novel coronavirus. Reliance on the United States and United Kingdom for assistance proved impractical, as both floundered in their response to the pandemic. The Trump administration barred the export of various medical supplies that Caribbean countries, except Cuba, had for decades received from the United States in moments of crisis. (China and Taiwan stepped into the breach.) Cuba, as it has often done, sent emergency teams of doctors and nurses to other islands. Every Caribbean country enacted combinations of travel bans, quarantines, lockdowns, and physical distancing.

As of September 2021, the results of these efforts were mixed. According to data on excess deaths compiled by *The Economist*, pandemic mortality around the perimeter of the Caribbean rivaled that of the hardest hit countries in the world.[34] In Mexico, excess deaths over the 17 months since COVID-19 first arrived amounted to 410 per 100,000; in Colombia, 300; the United States, 240; Panama, 180; and Venezuela, 170. Among countries more conventionally reckoned as Caribbean, Belize stood in a class by itself with excess deaths of 280 per 100,000. Cumulative excess deaths in the Bahamas reached 180 per 100,000, and in Cuba, Haiti, the Dominican Republic, St. Lucia, and Trinidad and Tobago they stood between 120 and 130. Cuba's controversial health system achieved outcomes very similar to those elsewhere in the big islands. Jamaica was doing slightly better, at 93 per 100,000. A dozen or more of the smaller countries showed minimal excess death rates during the first year and a half of the pandemic, and a few, including Barbados and the Dutch islands taken as a whole, even showed negative excess deaths, meaning that fewer people than normal died over these 17 months, testament to the effectiveness of health measures in combating not only COVID-19 but other infections as well. These data are provisional.

In facing COVID-19, Caribbean populations have had two advantages that they put to good use. First, island nations find it easier than others to control the movement of people, including those carrying a virus, in and out of their countries. Second, in the spring and summer of 2020, almost everyone in the

Caribbean was aware of the ongoing disasters in nearby Florida, Mexico, and Colombia, lands where those in authority and many in the population at large were slow to admit the danger and consequently allowed explosions of infection. West Indians were under no illusion that their hospitals and health services had the resources of those in Florida, and understood that should COVID-19 run amok on their island they would be, to a large degree, on their own—as, with respect to other plagues, their ancestors had so often been.

* * *

As with epidemics, various natural disasters continued to batter the Caribbean across the rest of the nineteenth and twentieth centuries, and into the twenty-first. Indeed, some of the most dramatic and traumatic events in the region's history occurred after the long early modern period had given way to the modern and then postmodern worlds. These included, among others: the 1844–46 hurricanes in Cuba that destroyed the island's coffee industry; the eruption of Mt. Pelée on Martinique in 1902 that claimed the lives of some 30,000 people (as well as a second eruption between 1929 and 1932 that claimed fewer lives but caused significant economic disruptions); the 1907 earthquake that leveled much of Kingston, Jamaica; the series of hurricanes that struck in years between 1926–35, an unusually frequent recurrence of storms and with significant effects on politics and economics; the eruption of Soufrière Hills in Montserrat beginning in 1995, which forced the evacuation of almost two-thirds of the island's population; the devastating 2010 earthquake in Haiti; the twin Category 5 hurricanes Irma and Maria, which battered numerous islands (some twice) in the span of two weeks in the fall of 2017, resulting in enormous physical destruction and thousands of deaths; and most recently, the eruption of La Soufrière on St. Vincent, which forced the evacuation of 20,000 people, a crisis situation exacerbated by the ongoing coronavirus pandemic.[35]

As was the case across earlier centuries, disasters both shaped and revealed underlying social, political, economic, and cultural forces at work on individual islands and across the region as whole. At various points in time, disasters provided opportunities for individuals and governments to demonstrate their merits—or have their weaknesses revealed. Raphael Trujillo used the devastating San Zenón hurricane in 1930 to consolidate power in the Dominican Republic. While effectively responding to the challenges wrought by the storm, his directives morphed into a repressive regime that ruled the island for the next 31 years. When Hurricane Flora struck the Greater Antilles in 1963, brutal dictator François "Papa Doc" Duvalier prohibited any news of the impending storm and provided little effective relief after it struck, which proved disastrous for Haitians and an embarrassment for his government (and his US backers). On Cuba, by contrast, Fidel Castro's energetic relief and recovery efforts following

Flora helped consolidate his relatively new socialist regime in that country. In fact, not unlike public health, Castro's success in 1963, and later policies developed based on that experience, made Cuba a model for disaster preparation and mitigation in the region and beyond.[36]

Experience of disasters likewise continued to shape both shared and distinct cultural responses in the Caribbean. Disasters remained signal markers in the history of islands and in the lives of individuals. Fidel Castro lived through major hurricanes in the 1930s, which he believed "must have marked me" and distinguished him from younger revolutionaries born in the 1940s who had little experience with storms before Flora. The Catholic Bishop of Montserrat quipped in 1980 that any residents named Gale likely were born in 1899, 1924, or 1928, the years when major storms battered the island. Hurricane Gilbert in 1988 inspired Jamaican musicians to compose at least 16 different songs commemorating the storm in genre ranging from reggae to calypso to dance hall and gospel (with varying degrees of commercial success). There is a rich history of music and hurricanes in the region across the twentieth century, although shared experience with storms also gives way to local culture: the musical response to hurricanes in Jamaica is not the same as in Cuba or Martinique.[37]

One reason for that, of course, is the history of these individual islands. The idea that "there is no such thing as a natural disaster" and that humans play a key role in shaping the impact of disasters has become commonplace in recent years, but an important, obvious, yet often unstated corollary is that disasters are products of historical forces and historical actors and actions. The conditions that exist when any given disaster strikes and the choices made by individuals in that moment are shaped by choices made (and not made) by people in the past, sometimes with knowledge of the repercussions or potential repercussions of their actions, but often without such knowledge. In Martinique the lessons of 1902, for better or worse, shaped the response to the eruption of 1929, just as Castro's experiences as a young man influenced his actions in 1963. Disasters thus reveal not only existing institutions, structures, and relationships, but also the history of those institutions and forces. They are both singular events that often occur quickly and parts of larger processes that unfold slowly over time. History and memory matter.[38]

This is especially the case in the Caribbean, vulnerable as it is and has been to various hazards and battered by competing imperial forces for centuries. To borrow historian Laurent Dubois's suggestive phrase, disasters in this sense are the "aftershocks of history." Anthropologist Laura Wagner notes that in the case of Haiti, the island's modern disasters have been foretold, "created and exacerbated by the centuries of political, ecological, and social histories than preceded them." Any adequate reckoning and response to disasters requires engaging with that history. This was true for the first Europeans and Africans who arrived in the Caribbean in the sixteenth and seventeenth centuries and confronted a Native American history of disasters, which they simultaneously learned from, appropriated, disparaged, and/or discarded, and it remains true in the region today.[39]

Perhaps nothing in recent memory reveals this collision between hazard and history more clearly than the earthquake that struck Haiti on January 12, 2010. The earthquake was a powerful one, registering 7.0 magnitude, but it was not simply the violent movement of the Plantain-Garden fault that resulted in the death of between 200,000–300,000 people (and perhaps more) and widespread destruction in Port-au-Prince and across many parts of the country. The disaster resulted from a combination of the earthquake's energy and the island's history. The second oldest independent nation in the Americas, Haiti's enslaved liberators found few friends among European colonial powers and the still-young (and slaveholding) United States that refused to extend diplomatic recognition even as they sought out commercial connections to the new nation. France's demand that Haiti pay reparations in exchange for diplomatic recognition in the 1820s created a legacy of debt and poverty from which the island has never escaped. The United States invaded in 1915 (one of many US incursions into the region in the nineteenth and twentieth centuries) and occupied the country for almost two decades. "The true causes of Haiti's poverty and instability are not mysterious," Dubois notes, "and they have nothing to do with any inherent shortcomings on the part of Haitians themselves." Instead, "Haiti's present is the product of its history." As the historian Matthew J. Smith observed, the damage along the Enriquillo Plantain-Garden fault in Kingston in 1907 and Port-au-Prince in 2010 came from "histories that . . . no seismograph can measure." The combination of these natural forces and external and internal conflicts across time have rendered the country exceedingly vulnerable to natural hazards, both major and minor, in the past and present.[40]

The tremendous death and damage in Port-au-Prince also reflected larger shifts that have occurred in many other islands over the past half-century. One is increased urbanization. As agriculture declined as a major economic activity in many Caribbean islands, residents increasingly migrated to urban areas in search of work. But island cities often lacked the infrastructure to house these ever-growing populations that packed in urban areas. The impact of poverty, a lack of planning, poor construction, overcrowding, inadequate sanitation facilities, and degradation of the local environment rendered (and continue to render) these urban areas increasingly vulnerable to a variety of disasters, including floods, landslides, earthquakes, and disease. In the case of Haiti, Port-au-Prince's metropolitan area's population in 1960 was roughly 247,000; it had grown to almost 1.1 million by 1990, and then nearly doubled to 2.1 million in 2010. Despite the huge loss of life in the earthquake and in the subsequent outbreak of cholera, today the metropolitan area's population exceeds 2.7 million. On other islands like Jamaica, flooding in and around urban areas has emerged as the most common form of disaster affecting local populations, in part the result of urban growth and development.[41]

Shifting economic structures have also altered the Caribbean geography of disaster. In some ways, the story of disasters in the modern Caribbean mirrors that of the early modern period: hurricanes batter the islands, destroying fields and crops; major earthquakes topple buildings and damage infrastructure; drought and flooding remain common, if less dramatic, hazards to farmers in the region. Even though the sugar industry suffered from new global competition and the rise of beet sugar during the nineteenth century, sugar cane continued to occupy a significant place in the Caribbean's economic and physical landscape across much of the twentieth century and continues to do so today on many islands. Nevertheless, agriculture generally, and sugar production specifically, has declined in recent decades (as measured in terms of contribution to GDP). Indeed, commercial production of the crop that dominated the region's economic history for centuries ended on some islands such as St. Kitts in the early twenty-first century. Even in Cuba, tourism now outpaces sugar as a generator of foreign exchange.[42]

Thus, while agriculture remains important in many islands, especially on the larger islands in terms of land use and labor force participation, a different calculus now measures the economic impact of disasters: tourism. When Hurricane Ivan roared across Grenada in 1988, the storm destroyed over 80 percent of nutmeg trees, and it took three years for the industry to recover. More importantly, the storm destroyed roughly 90 percent of Grenada's hotel rooms, which represented almost three times as great a loss in terms of the island's GDP. As tourism plays an ever larger role in the economy of many islands, the impact of disasters increasingly is measured by losses to hotels, beaches, golf courses, port facilities for cruise ships, and the like. In short, no longer do officials calculate losses simply in terms of declining exports of crops; instead, they fear the loss of inputs to local economies in the form of tourist dollars.[43]

Scholars often talk about "differential vulnerability" in assessing the impact of disasters, which is really shorthand for highlighting how historical developments and contemporary conditions shape the relative impact of disasters in particular locations. Differential vulnerability will likely become even more pronounced in the Caribbean as climate change intensifies. Rising sea levels linked to global warming threaten to overwhelm low-lying, coastal parts of many islands. One study of Caribbean Community (CARICOM) nations in 2010 concluded that a conservative 1-meter SLR (sea-level rise) across this century would displace over 110,000 people and damage of up to 1 percent of agricultural land across the region, but as much as 5 percent in places like Dominica, St. Kitts, and Nevis.

A 2-meter SLR would displace roughly 260,000 people and damage 3 percent of agricultural land, although some islands could lose between 8 percent and 12 percent of their agricultural land. Sea-level rises higher than that would have an even greater impact.[44] Likewise, rising sea-surface temperatures likely will result in more frequent powerful (Category 4 and 5) hurricanes in the region, if not more frequent storms overall, although some islands will be more vulnerable than others. As happened with the back-to-back hurricanes of Irma and Maria in 2017, these storms will likely carry increased amounts of rain.[45] Several studies suggest that the Caribbean region overall will likely experience a significant decline in rainfall and more intense drought events if global temperatures exceed preindustrial levels by 1.5°, although the data collection is ongoing and projections for precipitation vary across the region. Such shortfalls likely will result in a longer dry season, including an extended period of mid-summer drought. While many islands will receive less rainfall overall, what rains may come in more intense periods so, ironically, future periods of decreased rainfall could also witness increased flooding, erosion, and landslides, especially on mountainous islands. That is already happening, as recent studies have found "the intensity of daily rainfall and the heavy rainfall events has been significantly rising over the past 25 years."[46]

The impact of such dry periods likewise will be different than in the past. Drought continues to pose challenges to agriculture, as it did throughout the early modern period, but there are also new challenges. The 2009–10 drought in Grenada, for example, significantly reduced yields of nutmeg and provision crops like yams but also affected the island's tourist industry. Major hotels reported having to truck in water to supply guests and at times rationed water. During an intense drought in Cuba in 2004–5, some 2.6 million residents relied on water brought into communities on trucks. More problematic in the long term is how much water tourists and tourist resorts consume: studies focused on Barbados found that per capita water consumption by tourists was three times as much as that by local residents. In addition, rising seas and decreases in rainfall threaten aquifers with salinity and reduce fresh water availability. Island states like Barbados, Cuba, and the Dominican Republic, where demand on aqueous resources is already high, are particularly vulnerable. Some, like Trinidad, Jamaica, and Barbados, have already begun to ration and recycle water.[47]

Historical developments help explain modern vulnerability, but of course, so too does geography. The island nations of the Caribbean, especially the smaller islands, remain especially vulnerable for many reasons, not least of which is that large-scale disasters like hurricanes and earthquakes often threaten the entirety of their physical space. Ninety percent of houses in Grenada were damaged during Hurricane Ivan, for example. The entire island of Barbuda was evacuated before (or in a few cases, after) Hurricane Irma ripped across the island. "For the first time in 300 years there is not a single person living on the island of Barbuda," one official commented in the storm's wake. Moreover, even larger islands often lack the necessary equipment and/or financial resources to deal with major disasters that inflict damage greater than annual GDP, affect large segments of their population, and threaten transport hubs, which can limit relief and recovery efforts. A one meter-rise in sea levels would inundate or damage 21 airports in CARICOM nations (28 percent of the total) and roughly 80 percent of port facility lands, and increasing storms surges would exacerbate that danger. Political geography matters in assessing the past, present, and future of disasters in the region.[48]

The historical hazards of the Caribbean remain threats today, just as they did for the region's indigenous peoples and for the European colonists and enslaved Africans who arrived during the long early modern period. But if the hazards themselves are familiar, the context in which they strike and their impact on the region's human communities continue to evolve. While the specific effects of climate change in the next century remain uncertain, there is little doubt that Caribbean rimlands and islands, especially those that are now called "small island developing states" (SIDS), are increasingly vulnerable to rising seas and temperatures. In this critical period of the "Great Acceleration," of human influence on the environment, creative human responses to the challenge of climatic change ironically will be particularly important for the Caribbean region given its history and its geophysical realities. The Caribbean's natural hazards will not disappear, but its "natural disasters" hopefully can be mitigated.[49]

In sum, the environmental history of the Caribbean since 1850 has remained a function of the region's place within the global economy and of its geographical and deep historical legacies. The slave trade, slavery, the plantation system, the dominance of sugar, the intermittent imperial warfare, and the savage disease environment—all this gradually diminished or disappeared from the Caribbean. But in important ways many things remained the same, as the long legacies of the past still exert their grip across the region, even as they recede further in time. The Caribbean's environmental history is still shaped by the extinctions that occurred soon after the original human settlement some 7,000 years ago. It is still marked by the introduced animals, plants, and pathogens of the Columbian Exchange and of the Neo-Columbian Exchanges of the later eighteenth and nineteenth centuries. It still reflects land tenure arrangements put in place at the various moments of slavery's abolition. In a hundred ways, great and small, the distant past, like the region's physical geography and its evolving place in a larger global system, continues to mold the present—precisely what Alexander von Humboldt would have expected.

NOTES

Introduction

1. Alexander von Humboldt, *Selected Writings*, ed. Andrea Wulf (New York: Alfred A. Knopf, 2018), 51–52 (Tobago); 54 (Cumaná); Alexander von Humboldt, *Political Essay on the Island of Cuba: A Critical Edition*, ed. Vera M. Kutzinki and Ottmar Ette (Chicago: University of Chicago Press, 2011), 176 (Antillean Mediterranean).

2. Humboldt, *Political Essay*, vii (Ortiz); 23 (importance). There is a book on Humboldt in Mexico—Myron Echenberg, *Humboldt's Mexico; In the Footsteps of the Illustrious German Scientific Traveller* (Montreal and Kingston: McGill-Queen's University Press, 2017)—but to our knowledge, none that focuses on the Caribbean or circum-Caribbean part of his travelogue, which lasted almost two years in total.

3. Humboldt, *Brief aus Amerika 1799–1804*, ed. Ulrike Moheit (Berlin: Akademie Verlag, 1993), 42, as cited and translated in *Political Essay*, xiv (letter); *Selected Writings*, 146 (memory).

4. Humboldt, *Political Essay*, 26 (vigor); and Humboldt, *Selected Writings*, 54–56, 61–62 (Guaiqueri).

5. Humboldt, *Selected Writings*, 51 (Tobago)—and for more on the Gulf of Sadness, see 430, 128–29 (Cariaco), 145 (La Guaira), 307 (lancha), 309 (American ship), 313–14 (Catalonian sloop); 326 n. 9, 328 n. 25 (observations and experiments); Humboldt, *Political Essay*, 5 (seafarers), 23 (Mediterranean).

6. Humboldt, *Political Essay*, 171 (aroma); Andrea Wulf, *The Invention of Nature: Alexander von Humboldt's New World* (New York: Alfred A. Knopf, 2015), 52 (spiders); Humboldt, *Selected Writings*, 190, 337 n. 89 (boas); 314 (crocodile); 315–16 (suckerfish); 317 (fireflies).

7. Humboldt, *Political Essay*, 171 (mosquitoes); Humboldt, *Selected Writings*, 65 (termites); 319 (acacia and ants); 321 (mosquitoes); 172 (ants and Saint Saturnin). The last story echoes a tale, including mention of a lottery and Saint Saturnin, told almost 300 years earlier by Bartolomé de Las Casas.

8. Humboldt, *Political Essay*, 166–67.

9. Wulf, *The Invention of Nature*, 5, 57–59, 104–5; Humboldt, *Selected Writings*, 56, 81–82 (pearls); 165–66 (deforestation).

10. Humboldt, *Selected Writings*, 50–54 (fever and good fortune), 148 (La Guaira), 312 (Havana) [see also 320 (Cartagena)]; Humboldt, *Political Essay*, 28 (Havana), 34–35 (yellow fever).

11. Humboldt, *Selected Writings*, 58, 61, 64–74, 142–44, 157–58, 480.

12. Humboldt, *Political Essay*, 58–60 (hurricanes) [he relies on Alexandre Moreau de Jonnès, *Histoire Physique des Antilles Françaises* (1822), for some of this information]; Humboldt, *Selected Writings*, 78–79 (Araya hurricane); Aaron Sachs, *The Humboldt Current: Nineteenth-Century Exploration and the Roots of American Environmentalism* (New York: Viking,

2006), 1–2 (storm); Maren Meinhardt, *Alexander von Humboldt: How the Most Famous Scientist of the Romantic Age Found the Soul of Nature* (Katonah, NY: BlueBridge, 2019), 7–8 (storm); Wulf, *The Invention of Nature*, 94 (storm, which she calls a hurricane). On the frequency of storms in Cuba and their central place in Cuba's history, see Louis Perez, *Winds of Change: Hurricanes and the Transformation of Nineteenth-Century Cuba* (Chapel Hill: University of North Carolina, 2001), especially 28–36.

13. Humboldt, *Selected Writings*, 92–93, 107, 150; Humboldt, *Political Essay*, 28, 341 n. I.16.

14. Humboldt, *Political Essay*, 91, 117.

15. Humboldt, *Political Essay*, 144 (he probably had a field hand rather than a sugar mill worker in mind); Wulf, *The Invention of Nature*, 106.

16. Humboldt, *Political Essay*, 269–70; Humboldt, *Selected Writings*, 90.

17. B. W. Higman, *A Concise History of the Caribbean* (New York: Cambridge University Press, 2011), 7; V. S. Naipaul, *The Overcrowded Barracoon* (New York: Alfred A. Knopf, 1973), 254; V. S. Naipaul, *The Middle Passage: Impressions of Five Societies—British, French and Dutch—in the West Indies and South America* (Harmondsworth, UK: Penguin, 1969), 27, 29; Orlando Patterson, *The Sociology of Slavery: An Analysis of the Origins, Development and Structure of Negro Slave Society in Jamaica* (London: MacGibbon & Kee, 1967), 9; E. J. Hobsbawm, "Passionate Witness: Review of *Frantz Fanon: A Critical Study* by Irene L. Gendzier," *New York Review of Books*, February 22, 1973, 8.

18. Sidney W. Mintz, "The Caribbean Region," in Sidney W. Mintz, ed., *Slavery, Colonialism, and Racism* (New York: W. W. Norton, 1974), 45–72; Sidney W. Mintz, "The Caribbean as a Sociocultural Area," *Cahiers d'Histoire Mondiale*, 9 (1966), 916–41, and reprinted in Michael M. Horowitz, ed., *Peoples and Cultures of the Caribbean: An Anthropological Reader* (Garden City, NY: American Museum of Natural History, 1971), 17–46. For the first book written in the Americas in a European language, see Fray Ramón Pané, *An Account of the Antiquities of the Indians*, ed. José Juan Arrom, trans. Susan C. Griswold (Durham, NC: Duke University Press, 1999).

19. Sidney W. Mintz, *Caribbean Transformations* (Baltimore: Johns Hopkins University Press, 1974), 33; Ida Altman and David Wheat, eds., *The Spanish Caribbean and the Atlantic World in the Long Sixteenth Century* (Lincoln: University of Nebraska Press, 2019), xiii–xxv.

20. J. R. McNeill, *Mosquito Empires: Ecology and War in the Greater Caribbean, 1620–1914* (New York: Cambridge University Press, 2010), 23. A large literature exists on the term *creole* and the process of creolization. A selective list includes: J. Arrom, "Criollo definición y matices de un concepto," *Hispania*, 34, no. 2 (1951), 172–76; Dell Hymes, ed., *Pidginization and Creolization of Languages* (Cambridge: Cambridge University Press, 1971); Edward Brathwaite, *The Development of Creole Society in Jamaica, 1770–1820* (Oxford: Clarendon Press, 1971); Richard Price, "The Miracle of Creolization: A Retrospective," *New West Indian Guide*, 75 (2001), 35–64; Charles Stewart, ed., *Creolization: History, Ethnography, Theory* (Walnut Creek, CA: Left Coast Press, 2007); Richard Price, "The Concept of Creolization," in David Eltis and Stanley L. Engerman, eds., *The Cambridge World History of Slavery*, vol. 3, *AD 1420–AD 1804* (New York: Cambridge University Press, 2011), 513–37; and Linda M. Rupert, *Creolization and Contraband: Curaçao in the Early Modern Atlantic World* (Athens: University of Georgia Press, 2012).

21. For example, Fernando Ortiz, *El Huracán: Su mitología y sus símbolos* (Mexico City: Fondo de Cultura Económica, 1947); Manuel Moreno Fraginals, *El ingenio: Complejo económico social cubano del azúcar*, 3 vols. (Havana: Comisión Nacional Cubana de la UNESCO, 1978); Luis Salívia, *Historia de los temporales de Puerto Rico y Las Antillas* (San Juan, PR: Editorial Edil, 1972); and Lucien-Rene Abénon, *La Guadeloupe de 1671 à 1759: étude politique, économique et sociale* (Paris: L'Harmattan, 1987).

22. David Watts, *The West Indies: Patterns of Development, Culture and Environmental Change since 1492* (Cambridge: Cambridge University Press, 1987), 531; Shawn William Miller, *An Environmental History of Latin America* (New York: Cambridge University Press, 2007), 10, 50, 55, 59–61, 77, 84–87, 112–15, 119–25, 197–98, 221, 229–35.

23. Alfred W. Crosby, Jr., *The Columbian Exchange: Biological and Cultural Consequences of 1492* (Westport, CT: Greenwood Press, 1972), 45–47, 65–68, 74–81, 95–97. See also Alfred W. Crosby, Jr., *Ecological Imperialism: The Biological Expansion of Europe, 900–1900*

(New York: Cambridge University Press, 1986), 50, 108, 116–17, 139–40, 151, 173–77, 182, 187, 198–200; and Alfred W. Crosby, Jr., *Germs, Seeds, & Animals: Studies in Ecological History* (Armonk, NY: M. E. Sharpe, 1993), 4, 10, 17, 24–25, 50–54, 57–58, 82–87, 89, 197.

24. Carl Ortwin Sauer, *The Early Spanish Main* (Berkeley: University of California Press, 1966), 5, 69; Bonham C. Richardson, *The Caribbean in the Wider World, 1492–1992: A Regional Geography* (Cambridge: Cambridge University Press, 1992); Richard H. Grove, *Green Imperialism: Colonial Expansion, Tropical Island Edens, and the Origins of Environmentalism, 1600–1860* (Cambridge: Cambridge University Press, 1995), 6.

25. The Latin American and Caribbean Society of Environmental History (the Spanish acronym is SOLCHA) was created in 2004. It meets annually. The Association of Caribbean Historians now includes panels in environmental history on a regular basis in its annual meetings. For a work be a leading figure in a new generation of hispanophone environmental historians, see the work of Cuban scholar Reinaldo Funes Monzote, *From Rainforest to Cane Field in Cuba: An Environmental History since 1492*, trans. Alex Martin (Chapel Hill, NC: University of North Carolina Press, 2008 [orig. pub., 2004]).

26. Higman, *A Concise History*, 1, 6–7; Mark Kurlansky, *A Continent of Islands: Searching for the Caribbean Destiny* (Cambridge, MA: Perseus Publishing, 1992), x–xi; Joshua M. Torres and Reniel Rodríguez Ramos, "The Caribbean: A Continent Divided by Water," in Basil A. Reid, ed., *Archaeology and Geoinformatics: Case Studies from the Caribbean* (Tuscaloosa: University of Alabama Press, 2008), 13–29; Antonio Benítez-Rojo, *The Repeating Island: The Caribbean and the Postmodern Perspective*, trans. James Maraniss, 2nd ed. (Durham, NC: Duke University Press, 1996), 2, 4.

27. Jamaica Kincaid, *A Small Place* (New York: Farrar, Straus, and Giroux, 1988), 52; Reid, "Introduction" in Reid, ed., *Archaeology and Geoinformatics*, 3. See also David Lowenthal, "The Range and Variation of Caribbean Societies," in Vera Rubin, ed., *Social and Cultural Pluralism in the Caribbean: Annals of the New York Academy of Sciences*, 83 (1960), 786–95; and Stuart Schwartz, Franklin Knight, et al., "The Caribbean from the Perspective of the Social Sciences," in Ileana Rodríguez and Marc Zimmerman, eds., *Process of Unity in Caribbean Society: Ideologies and Literature* (Minneapolis, MN: Institute for the Study of Ideologies and Literature, 1983), 57–95.

28. Scott M. Fitzpatrick, "Synthesizing Island Archaeology," in Scott M. Fitzpatrick, ed., *Voyages of Discovery: The Archaeology of the Islands* (Westport, CT: Praeger, 2004), 3–18; Irving Rouse, *The Tainos: Rise & Decline of the People Who Greeted Columbus* (New Haven, CT: Yale University Press, 1992), 7.

29. Higman, *A Concise History*, xi. For the Caribbean basin or Rimland, see Robert C. West and John P. Augelli, *Middle America: Its Lands and Peoples* (Englewood Cliffs, NJ: Prentice Hall, 1966), esp. 11–16. For the Greater Caribbean, see Immanuel Wallerstein, *The Modern World System*, vol. 2, *Mercantilism and the Consolidation of the European World Economy, 1600–1750* (New York: Academic Press, 1974), 103; Peter Hulme, *Colonial Encounters: Europe and the Native Caribbean, 1492–1797* (London: Methuen, 1986), 4–5; David Gaspar and David Geggus, eds., *A Turbulent Time: The French Revolution and the Greater Caribbean* (Bloomington: University of Indiana Press, 1997), viii; Matthew Mulcahy, *Hurricanes and Society in the British Greater Caribbean, 1624–1783* (Baltimore: Johns Hopkins University Press, 2006), 2, 6–7, and passim; McNeill, *Mosquito Empires*, 2 and passim; D. Ross Robertson and Katie L. Cramer, "Defining and Dividing the Greater Caribbean: Insights from the Biogeography of Shorefishes," *PLOS ONE*, 9, no. 7 (July 23, 2014), 1–16; Stuart B. Schwartz, *Sea of Storms: A History of Hurricanes in the Greater Caribbean from Columbus to Katrina* (Princeton, NJ: Princeton University Press, 2015); Ernesto Bassi, *An Aqueous Territory: Sailor Geographies and New Granada's Transimperial Greater Caribbean World* (Durham, NC: Duke University Press, 2016). Sauer, *Early Spanish Main*, 4.

30. See chapters by McNeill and Morgan in this volume.

31. Christopher M. Church, *Paradise Destroyed: Catastrophe and Citizenship in the French Caribbean* (Lincoln: University of Nebraska Press, 2017), 24, 27–28, 51–55, 65–66, 147; Schwartz, *Sea of Storms*, esp. 129–91.

32. Frederic G. Cassidy, *Jamaica Talk: Three Hundred Years of the English Language in Jamaica* (London: Macmillan, 1961), 178–79.

Chapter 1

1. "Directions for Sea-Men, Bound for Far Voyages," *Philosophical Transactions*, 1 (1665–66), 140–43, and "Appendix to the Directions for Seamen, Bound for Far Voyages," ibid., 147–49; Robert Boyle, "Other Inquiries Concerning the Sea," ibid., 315–16; ""Directions for Observations and Experiments to Be Made by Masters of Ships, Pilots, and Other Fit Persons in Their Sea-Voyages," *Philosophical Transactions*, 2 (1666–67), 433–48 (thanks to Kathleen Murphy for these references); Theodore W. Pietsch, "Charles Plumier (1646–1704) and His Drawings of French and American Fishes," *Archives of Natural History*, 28, no. 1 (2001), 1–57. See also Christopher P. Iannini, *Fatal Revolutions: Natural History, West Indian Slavery, and the Routes of American Literature* (Chapel Hill: University of North Carolina Press, 2012), 82; James Delbourgo, "Divers Things: Collecting the World under Water," *History of Science*, 49, no. 2 (June 2011), 149–85.

2. Brian Fagan, *Fishing: How the Sea Fed Civilization* (New Haven, CT: Yale University Press, 2017), ix; Lawrence Waldron, *Handbook of Ceramic Animal Symbols in the Ancient Lesser Antilles* (Gainesville: University of Florida Press, 2016), xvii; Lee A. Newsom and Elizabeth S. Wing, *On Land and Sea: Native American Uses of Biological Resources in the West Indies* (Tuscaloosa: University of Alabama Press, 2004), 201; James B. Peterson, "Taino, Island Carib, and Prehistoric Amerindian Economies in the West Indies: Tropical Forest Adaptations to Island Environments," in Samuel M. Wilson, ed., *The Indigenous People of the Caribbean* (Gainesville: University of Florida Press, 1997), 118–30), esp. 128. The late sixteenth-century illustrated *Histoire Naturelle des Indes* devotes its first 62 illustrations to plants, followed by almost another 60 to marine animals or marine settings. Land animals, birds, and, even more so, insects get short shrift. See Verlyn Klinkenborg, ed., and Ruth S. Kraemer, trans., *The Drake Manuscript in the Pierpont Morgan Library: Histoire Naturelle des Indes* (London: André Deutsch, 1996).

3. Pernille Røge, *Economistes and the Reinvention of Empire: France in the Americas and Africa, c. 1750–1802* (Cambridge: Cambridge University Press, 2019), 29; Kay Dian Kris, *Slavery, Sugar, and the Culture of Refinement: Picturing the British West Indies, 1700–1840* (New Haven, CT: Yale University Press, 2008), 16–29; Iannini, *Fatal Revolutions*, 62–74; Jefferson Dillman, *Colonizing Paradise: Landscape and Empire in the British West Indies* (Tuscaloosa: University of Alabama Press, 2015), esp. 2–3, 38–66, 106–36.

4. David Watts, *The West Indies: Patterns of Development, Culture and Environmental Change since 1492* (Cambridge: Cambridge University Press, 1987), 40. See also Lizabeth Paravisini-Gebert, "Extinctions: Chronicles of Vanishing Fauna in the Colonial and Postcolonial Caribbean," in Greg Garrard, ed., *Oxford Handbook of Ecocriticism* (New York: Oxford University Press, 2014), 341–57; and for a later period, Christopher M. Church, *Paradise Destroyed: Catastrophe and Citizenship in the French Caribbean* (Lincoln: University of Nebraska Press, 2017), esp. 2–6, 50–56, 63–69, 109–68, 191–231.

5. Isabel C. Rivera-Collazo, "Gone with the Waves: Sea-Level Rise, Ancient Territories and the Socioenvironmental Context of Mid-Holocene Maritime Mobility in the Pan-Caribbean Region," in Corinne L. Hofman and Andrzej T. Antczak, eds., *Early Settlers of the Insular Caribbean: Dearchaizing the Archaic* (Leiden: Sidestone Press, 2019), 47–56, esp. 48.

6. The *Columbia Gazeteer of the World* (New York: Columbia University Press, 1998) estimates the Caribbean Sea at 2,512,300 square kilometers and the South China Sea at 2,590,000 square kilometers. The Mediterranean is third largest, at 2,499,350 square kilometers. Some other listings put the Mediterranean first and the Caribbean second. Seemingly, the International Hydrographic Organization has not pronounced definitively on the size of world seas. The average depth of the Caribbean Sea is 2,647 meters. By contrast, the total land area of the Caribbean islands is small: 235,689 square kilometers. The insular land expanse is roughly the size of the United Kingdom, and one island, Cuba, accounts for nearly half. Jack E. Davis, *The Gulf: The Making of an American Sea* (New York: W. W. Norton, 2017), 16–19. For good accounts of the Caribbean environment, see, in addition to Watts, *The West Indies*, B. W. Higman, *A Concise History of the Caribbean* (New York: Cambridge University Press, 2011), 1–8; and David Barker, "Geographies of Opportunity, Geographies of Constraint," in Stephan Palmié and Francisco A. Scarano, eds., *The Caribbean: A History of the Region and Its Peoples* (Chicago: University of Chicago Press, 2011), 25–38.

7. Stan Ulanski, *The Gulf Stream: Tiny Plankton, Giant Bluefin, and the Amazing Story of the Powerful River in the Atlantic* (Chapel Hill: University of North Carolina Press, 2008), 4, 7–10; Richard Drayton, "Maritime Networks and the Making of Knowledge," in David Cannadine, ed., *Empire, the Sea, and Global History: Britain's Maritime World, c.1760–c.1840* (Basingstoke, UK: Palgrave Macmillan, 2007), 72–82; Carlos A. Andrade and Eric D. Barton, "Eddy Development and Motion in the Caribbean Sea," *Journal of Geophysical Research*, 105 (2000), 26191–202; A. L. Gordon, "Circulation of the Caribbean Sea," *Journal of Geophysical Research*, 72 (1967), 6207–23; Georg Wüst, *Stratification and Circulation in the Antillean-Caribbean Basins* (New York: Columbia University Press, 1964); Greg Bankoff, "Aeolian Empires: The Influence of Winds and Currents on European Maritime Expansion in the Days of Sail," *Environment and History*, 23 (2017), 163–96; Davis, *The Gulf*, 17–18.

8. William E. Johns, Tamara L. Townsend, David M. Frantanoni, and W. Douglas Wilson, "On the Atlantic Inflow to the Caribbean Sea," *Deep Sea Research Part 1*, 49 (2002), 211–43; Joshua M. Torres and Reniel Rodríguez Ramos, "The Caribbean: A Continent Divided by Water," in Basil A. Reid, ed., *Archaeology and Geoinformatics: Case Studies from the Caribbean* (Tuscaloosa: University of Alabama Press, 2008), 13–29, esp. 22–25.

9. Ian K. Steele, *The English Atlantic, 1675-1740: An Exploration of Communication and Community* (New York: Oxford University Press, 1986), 6–9, 21–40; N. A. M. Rodger, "Atlantic Seafaring," in Nicholas Canny and Philip Morgan, eds., *Oxford Handbook of the Atlantic World, c. 1450–c. 1850* (Oxford: Oxford University Press, 2011), 71–86, esp. 81; Johns et al., "On the Atlantic Inflow"; Nicolás Wey Gómez, *The Tropics of Empire: Why Columbus Sailed South to the Indies* (Cambridge, MA: MIT Press, 2008); Bankoff, "Aeolian Empires."

10. "Documents Relating to the Ship Zong," REC/19, National Maritime Museum, Greenwich, London; James Walvin, *The Zong: A Massacre, The Law, and the End of Slavery* (New Haven, CT: Yale University Press, 2011), 87–101; Trevor Burnard, *Jamaica in the Age of Revolution* (Philadelphia: University of Pennsylvania Press, 2020), 174–93; for early Spanish voyages that encountered trouble sailing eastward, see Ida Altman, "Key to the Indies: Port Towns in the Spanish Caribbean, 1493-1550," *The Americas*, 74, no. 1 (2017), 5–26, esp. 12–13; L. Antonio Curet and M. Hauser, eds., *Islands at the Crossroads: Migration, Seafaring, and Interaction in the Caribbean* (Tuscaloosa: University of Alabama Press, 2011). One reason for thinking that Ceramic Age migrants bypassed islands is that carbon dating for settlements in Puerto Rico and the Leeward Islands are much older than the Windward Islands. Another is simulation of possible travel routes. The work of Richard T. Callaghan is particularly noteworthy. For a summary essay, see his "Archaeological Views of Caribbean Seafaring," in William F. Keegan, Corinne L. Hofman, and Reniel Rodríguez Ramos, eds., *The Oxford Handbook of Caribbean Archaeology* (New York: Oxford University Press, 2013), 283–95.

11. Richard T. Callaghan and Stephanie J. Schwabe, "Watercraft of the Islands," *Proceedings of the XVIIIth Congress of the International Association for Caribbean Archaeology* (Martinique, St. Georges, Grenada, 2001), 231–42; Callaghan, "The Question of the Aboriginal Use of Sails in the Caribbean Region," *Proceedings of the XXIInd Congress of the International Association for Caribbean Archaeology* (Kingston, Jamaica, 2011), 121–35; William F. Keegan and Lisabeth A. Carlson, *Talking Taíno: Essays on Caribbean Natural History from a Native Perspective* (Tuscaloosa: University of Alabama Press, 2008), 7, 13, 16, 25–26, 81–87, 97, 112; Scott M. Fitzpatrick, "Seafaring Capabilities in the Pre-Columbian Caribbean," *Journal of Maritime Archaeology*, 8, no. 1 (2013), 101–38; William F. Keegan, "Mobility and Disdain: Columbus and Cannibals in the Land of Cotton," *Ethnohistory*, 62 (2015), 1–15; Emma Ruth Slayton, *Seascape Corridors: Modeling Routes to Connect Communities across the Caribbean Sea* (Leiden: Sidestone Press, 2018), 38–47, 81–195; Isaac Shearn, "Canoe Societies in the Caribbean: Ethnography, Archaeology, and Ecology of Precolonial Canoe Manufacturing and Voyaging," *Journal of Anthropological Archaeology*, 57 (2020), 101–40.

12. Scott M. Fitzpatrick, M. Kappers, and C. M. Giovas, "The Southward Route Hypothesis: Examining Carriacou's Chronological Position in Antillian Prehistory," in Scott M. Fitzpatrick and Ann H. Ross, eds., *Island Shores, Distant Pasts: Archaeological and Biological Approaches to the Pre-Columbian Settlement of the Caribbean* (Gainesville: University

of Florida Press, 2010), 163–76; and Fitzpatrick, "The Southward Route Hypothesis," in Keegan, Hofman, and Ramos, eds., *The Oxford Handbook of Caribbean Archaeology*, 198–204.

13. Keegan et al., "Introduction," in Keegan, Hofman, and Ramos, eds., *The Oxford Handbook of Caribbean Archaeology*, 1–18, esp. 5–6 (counts five archipelagos); William F. Keegan and Corinne L. Hofman, eds., *The Caribbean before Columbus* (New York: Oxford University Press, 2017), 3–4 (counts six archipelagos).

14. Jonathan B. Losos, *Lizards in an Evolutionary Tree: Ecology and Adaptive Radiation of Anoles* (Berkeley: University of California Press, 2009), 62–68; Robert Ricklefs and Eldredge Bermingham, "The West Indies as a Laboratory of Biogeography and Evolution," *Philosophical Transactions of the Royal Society*, 363 (2008), 2393–2413. The Bahamas is part of the Caribbean, for most geographers, though obviously it lies outside the sea, in the Atlantic Ocean.

15. For the key basic works, see T. W. Donnolly, "Geologic History of the Caribbean and Central America," in Albert W. Bally and Allison R. Palmer, eds., *The Geology of North America: An Overview* (Boulder, CO: Geological Society of America, 1989), 299–321; Gabriel Dengo and J. E. Case, eds., *The Geology of North America*, vol. H, *The Caribbean Region* (Boulder, CO: Geological Society of America, 1990); and Stephen K. Donovan and Trevor A. Jackson, eds., *Caribbean Geology: An Introduction* (Kingston, Jamaica: University of the West Indies Press, 1994). See also Jan Lindsay, "Kick 'Em Jenny," in Rosemary G. Gillespie and David A. Clague, eds., *Encyclopedia of Islands* (Berkeley: University of California Press, 2009), 510–12. Other counts of the Bahamas are 25 islands and 3,000 cays: Keegan and Hofman, *Caribbean before Columbus*, 170.

16. Watts, *The West Indies*, 3–13; Richard E. A. Robertson, "Antilles, Geology," in Gillespie and Clague, eds., *Encyclopedia*, 29–35; and Peter E. Siegel, ed., *Island Historical Ecology: Socionatural Landscapes of the Eastern and Southern Caribbean* (New York: Berghahn Books, 2018), 10.

17. R. T. Callaghan, "On the Question of the Absence of Archaic Age Sites on Jamaica," *Journal of Island and Coastal Archaeology*, 3 (2008), 54–71; William F. Keegan, "Situating Jamaica," in Hofman and Antczak, eds., *Early Settlers*, 191–99.

18. William F. Keegan, Scott M. Fitzpatrick, Kathleen Sullivan Sealey, Michelle J. LeFebvre, and Peter T. Sinelli, "The Role of Small Islands in Marine Subsistence Strategies: Case Studies from the Caribbean," *Human Ecology*, 36, no. 5 (2008), 635–54; Nanny Carder, Elizabeth J. Reitz, and John G. Crock, "Fish Communities and Populations during the Post-Saladoid Period (AD 600/800–1500) Anguilla, Lesser Antilles," *Journal of Archaeological Science*, 34 (2007), 588–99.

19. Shawn William Miller, *An Environmental History of Latin America* (New York: Cambridge University Press, 2007), 2; J. R. McNeill, "The Ecological Atlantic," in Canny and Morgan, eds., *Oxford Handbook of the Atlantic World*, 289–304, esp. 291. For Amazonia, see Robert C. West and John P. Augelli, *Middle America: Its Lands and Peoples* (Englewood Cliffs, NJ: Prentice-Hall, 1966), esp. 11–12; Neil L. Whitehead, ed., *Wolves from the Sea: Readings in the Anthropology of the Native Caribbean* (Leiden: Brill, 1995). For the Greater Caribbean, see Immanuel Wallerstein, *The Modern World-System*, vol. 2, *Mercantilism and the Consolidation of the European World Economy, 1600–1750* (New York: Academic Press, 1974), 103; Peter Hulme, *Colonial Encounters: Europe and the Native Caribbean, 1492–1797* (London: Methuen, 1986), 4–5; David Barry Gaspar and David Patrick Geggus, eds., *A Turbulent Time: the French Revolution and the Greater Caribbean* (Bloomington: University of Indiana Press, 1997), viii; Matthew Mulcahy, *Hurricanes and Society in the British Greater Caribbean, 1624–1783* (Baltimore: Johns Hopkins University Press, 2006), 2, 6–7, and passim; and J. R. McNeill, *Mosquito Empires: Ecology and War in the Greater Caribbean, 1620–1914* (New York: Cambridge University Press, 2010), 2 and passim; D. Ross Robertson and Katie L. Cramer, "Defining and Dividing the Greater Caribbean: Insights from the Biogeography of Shorefishes," *PLOS ONE*, 9, no. 7 (July 23, 2014), 1–16.

20. Jessica Vance Roitman, "Dutch Colonization on the 'Wild Coast,'" in L. H. Roper, ed., *The Torrid Zone: Caribbean Colonization and Cultural Interaction in the Long Seventeenth Century* (Columbia: University of South Carolina Press, 2018), 61–75, esp. 62; Lesley-Gail

Atkinson, ed., *The Earliest Inhabitants: The Dynamics of the Jamaican Taíno* (Kingston, Jamaica: University of the West Indies Press, 2006), 1; James Knight, *The Natural, Moral, and Political History of Jamaica...*, ed. Jack P. Greene (Charlottesville: University of Virginia Press, 2021), 23; B. W. Higman, *Proslavery Priest: The Atlantic World of John Lindsay, 1729–1788* (Kingston, Jamaica: University of the West Indies Press, 2011), 157–67; Rev. John Lindsay in *Gentleman's Magazine*, 51 (1781), 558–60, 615–16; 53 (1783), 984, 1027; 55, no. 2 (1785), 594–98.

21. Church, *Paradise Destroyed*, 50–51.

22. Watts, *The West Indies*, 13–17; Jago Cooper, "The Climatic Context for Pre-Columbian Archaeology in the Caribbean," in Keegan, Hofman, and Ramos, eds., *The Oxford Handbook of Caribbean Archaeology*, 47–58; Michael Chenoweth, *The 18th Century Climate of Jamaica Derived from the Journals of Thomas Thistlewood, 1750–1786, Transactions of the American Philosophical Society*, vol. 93, pt. 2 (Philadelphia: American Philosophical Society, 2003), 52–55. This is a remarkably detailed study of a person who "has left the world's earliest continuous daily weather record kept by one person from anywhere outside of Europe and the United States. His rainfall record . . . is the world's oldest instrumental rainfall record of this length from the Tropics" (quote on 15–16).

23. Watts, *The West Indies*, 13–22; Chenoweth, *The 18th Century Climate of Jamaica*, 48, 55–62; Newsom and Wing, *On Land and Sea*, 14. See also C. Fitzhugh Talman, "Climatology of Haiti in the Eighteenth Century," *Monthly Weather Review* (February 1906), 64–73.

24. Christian Depraetere and Marc Morell, "Hydrology," in Gillespie and Clague, eds., *Encyclopedia*, 421–22; Mark W. Hauser, *Mapping Water in Dominica: Enslavement and Environment under Colonialism* (Seattle: University of Washington Press, 2021), esp. 28, 38, 47, 109, 110, 111, 179; Michel-Rolph Trouillot, *Peasants and Capital: Dominica in the World Economy* (Baltimore: Johns Hopkins University, 1988), esp. 27–50. Another example of variations within a single island concerns Hispaniola. For an account of the differences between eastern and western parts of the island—rainfall, soils, and extent of deforestation—see Jared Diamond, *Collapse: How Societies Choose to Fail or Succeed* (New York: Viking Penguin, 2005), 329–57, and "Intra-Island and Inter-Island Comparisons," in Diamond and James A. Robinson, eds., *Natural Experiments of History* (Cambridge, MA: Belknap Press, 2010), 120–41.

25. Watts, *The West Indies*, 23–24; Chenoweth, *The 18th Century Climate of Jamaica*, 55–62; A. Martis, G. J. van Oldenborgh, and G. Burgers, " Predicting Rainfall in the Dutch Caribbean—More than El Niño?" *International Journal of Climatology*, 22 (2002), 1219–34.

26. Björn Malmgren, Amos Winter, and Deliang Chen, "El Niño-Southern Oscillation and North Atlantic Oscillation Control of Climate in Puerto Rico," *Journal of Climate*, 11 (1998), 2713–17; A. Anthony Chen and Michael A. Taylor, "Investigating the Link between Early Season Caribbean Rainfall and the El Niño + 1 Year," *International Journal of Climatology*, 22 (2002), 87–106; Mark Jury, Bjorn Malmgren, and Amos Winter, "Subregional Precipitation Climate of the Caribbean and Relationship with ENSO and NAO," *Journal of Geophysical Research*, 112 (2007), https://doi.org/10.1029/2006JD007541; Douglas W. Gamble, Darren B. Parnell, and Scott Curtis, "Spatial Variability of the Caribbean Mid-summer Drought and Relation to North Atlantic High Circulation," *International Journal of Climatology*, 28 (2008), 343–50; Joëlle L. Gergis and Anthony M. Fowler, "A History of ENSO Events since A.D. 1525: Implications for Future Climate Change," *Climatic Change*, 92, nos. 3–4 (2009), 343–87; McNeill, *Mosquito Empires*, 59; Geoffrey Parker, *Global Crisis: War, Climate Change and Catastrophe in the Seventeenth Century* (New Haven, CT: Yale University Press, 2013), 14–17, 464.

27. G. A. Milne and M. C. Peros, "Data-Model Comparison of Holocene Sea-Level Change in the Circum-Caribbean Region," *Global and Planetary Change*, 107 (2013), 119–31; Jago Cooper, "The Climatic Context," 47–58; Jago Cooper and Richard Boothroyd, "Living Islands of the Caribbean: A View of Relative Sea Level Change from the Water's Edge," in Corinne L. Hofman and Anne van Duijvenbode, eds., *Communities in Contact: Essays in Archaeology, Ethnohistory & Ethnography of the Amerindian Circum-Caribbean* (Leiden: Sidestone Press, 2011), 393–405.

28. For some key works, see David A. Hodell et al., "Reconstruction of Caribbean Climate Change over the Past 10,500 Years," *Nature*, 352 (August 29, 1991), 790–93; Jason

Curtis and David Hodell, "An Isotopic and Trace Element Study of Ostracods from Lake Miragoane, Haiti: A 10,500 Year Record of Paleosalinity and Paleotemperature Changes in the Caribbean," in P. K. Swart et al., eds., *Climate Change in Continental Isotopic Records* (Washington, DC: American Geophysical Union, 1993), 135–52; Antonia Higuera-Gundy et al., "A 10,300 14 C Yr Record of Climate and Vegetation Change from Haiti," *Quaternary Research*, 52, no. 2 (1999), 159–70; Cay J. Beets et al., "Climate and Pre-Columbian Settlements at Anse à la Gourde, Guadeloupe, Northeastern Caribbean," *Geoarchaeology: An International Journal*, 21, no. 3 (2006), 271–80; E. Gischler et al., "A 1500-Year Holocene Caribbean Climate Archive from the Blue Hole, Lighthouse Reef, Belize," *Journal of Coastal Research*, 246 (2008), 1495–1505; B. Malaizé et al., "September Hurricanes and Climate in the Caribbean during the Past 3700 Years B.P." *The Holocene*, 216 (2011), 911–24; Chad S. Lane et al., "Beyond the Mayan Lowlands: Impacts of the Terminal Classic Drought in the Caribbean Antilles," *Quaternary Science Reviews*, 86 (2014), 89–98; B. R. Gregory et al., "Middle–Late Holocene Caribbean aridity Inferred from for Aminifera and Elemental Data in Sediment Cores from Two Cuban Lagoons," *Palaeogeography, Palaeoclimatology, Palaeoecology*, 426 (2015), 229–41.

29. Rivera-Collazo, "Gone with the Waves," 47–55; Siobhán B. Cooke et al., "The Extinction of *Xenothrix mcgregori*, Jamaica's Last Monkey," *Journal of Mammalogy*, 98, no. 4 (2017), 937–49; for a similar argument, see J. Angel Soto-Centeno and David W. Steadman, "Fossils Reject Climate Change as the Cause of Extinction of Caribbean Bats," *Nature: Scientific Reports*, 5, no. 7971 (2015), 1–7, DOI: 10.1038/srep07971; Christina Giovas, "Pre-Columbian Amerindian Lifeways at the Sabazan Site, Carriacou, West Indies," *The Journal of Island and Coastal Archaeology*, 13, no. 2 (2018),161–90; Nathalie Serrand and Dominique Bonnissent, "Interacting Pre-Columbian Amerindian Societies and Environments: Insights from Five Millennia of Archaeological Invertebrate Record on the Saint-Martin Island (French Lesser Antilles)," *Environmental Archaeology* (2018), 1–16, DOI:10.1080/14614103.2018.1450463; Alexander Jorge Berland and Georgina Endfield, "Drought and Disaster in a Revolutionary Age: Colonial Antigua during the American Independence War," *Environment and History*, 24, no. 2 (2018), 209–35. See also Peter E. Siegel et al., "Paleoenvironmental Evidence for First Human Colonization of the Eastern Caribbean," *Quaternary Science Reviews*, 129 (2015), 275–95; and Siegel, ed., *Island Historical Ecology*, 8, 10, 13, 36–37, 77–80, 155, 157, 198, 301–5, 318, 319, 362, 366.

30. Chenoweth, *The 18th Century Climate of Jamaica*, 52, 75. For some of the rich literature on this topic, see K. H. Kilbourne, T. M. Quinn, R. Webb, T. Guilderson, J. Nyberg, and A. Winter, "Paleoclimate Proxy Perspective on Caribbean Climate since the Year 1751: Evidence of Cooler Temperatures and Multidecadal Variability," *Paleoceanography*, 23 (2008), 1–14; Tsuyoshi Watanabe, Amos Winter, and Tadamichi Oba, "Seasonal Changes in Sea Surface Temperature and Salinity during the Little Ice Age in the Caribbean Sea Deduced from Mg/Ca and $^{18}O/^{16}O$ Ratios in Corals," *Marine Geology*, 173 (2001), 21–35; Amos Winter, Hiroshi Ishioroshi, Tsuyoshi Watanabe, Tadamichi Oba, and John Christy, "Caribbean Sea Surface Temperatures: Two-to-Three Degrees Cooler than Present during the Little Ice Age," *Geophysical Research Letters*, 27 (2000), 3365–68.

31. McNeill, "The Ecological Atlantic," 293; Michael Chenoweth and Dimitry Divine, "A Document-Based 318-Year Record of Tropical Cyclones in the Lesser Antilles, 1690–2007," *Geochemistry, Geophysics, Geosystems: G3*, 9, no. 8 (August 2008), 1–21; Chenoweth, "A Reassessment of Historical Atlantic Basin Tropical Cyclone Activity, 1700–1855," *Climatic Change*, 76 (2006), 169–240; R. Garcia-Herrera, L. Gimeno, P. Ribera, & E. Hernandez, "New Records of Atlantic Hurricanes from Spanish Documentary Sources," *Journal of Geophysical Research*, 110 (2005), 1–7; and Cary J. Mock, Michael Chenoweth, Isabel Altamarino, Matthew D. Rodgers, and Ricardo Garciá-Herrera, "The Great Louisiana Hurricane of August 1812," *Bulletin of the American Meteorological Society*, 91 (December 2010), 1653–63.

32. Thomas R. Knutson et al., "Tropical Cyclones and Climate Change," *Nature Geoscience*, (February 21, 2010), 1–7, https://doi.org/10.1038/ngeo779; Michael E. Mann, Jonathan D. Woodruff, Jeffrey P. Donnelly, and Zhihua Zhang, "Atlantic Hurricanes and Climate over the Past 1,500 Years," *Nature*, 460 (August 13, 2009), 88—883; J. B. Nyberg, A. Malmgren,

A. Winter, M. R. Jury, K. Halimdea Kilbourne, and T. M. Quinn, "Low Atlantic Hurricane Activity in the 1970s and 1980s Compared to the Past 270 Years," *Nature*, 447 (June 7, 2007), 698-702; J. P. Donnelly and J. D. Woodruff, "Intense Hurricane Activity over the Past 5,000 Years Controlled by El Niño and the West African Monsoon," *Nature*, 447 (May 24, 2007), 465-68; Jonathan A. Hanna, Michael P. Pateman, Lindsay Bloch, and William F. Keegan, "Human-Environment Interactions in a Bahamian Dune Landscape: A Geoarchaelogical Study of a New Lucayan Burial Site," *Geoarchaeology* (2021), 1-19, DOI: 10.1002/ gea.21866; J. P. Donnelly et al., "Intense Climate Forcing of Unprecedented Hurricane Activity in the Last 2000 Years," *Earth's Future*, 3 (2105), 49-65.

33. Mulcahy, *Hurricanes and Society*, 14, 16-18; Captain Brayne to the Proprietors, November 20, 1670, *South Carolina Historical Society Collections*, vol. V (Charleston: South Carolina Historical Society, 1897), 226-32; Stuart B. Schwartz, *Sea of Storms; A History of Hurricanes in the Greater Caribbean from Columbus to Katrina* (Princeton, NJ: Princeton University Press, 2015), esp. 33-69; S. D. Smith, "Storm Hazard and Slavery: The Impact of the 1831 Great Caribbean Hurricane on St. Vincent," *Environment and History*, 18 (2012), 98. For spatial and temporal variations regarding hurricanes, see Eleonora Rohland, "Hurricanes on the Gulf Coast: Environmental Knowledge and Science in Louisiana, the Caribbean, and the United States, 1722-1900," in Patrick Manning and Daniel Rood, eds., *Global Scientific Practice in an Age of Revolutions, 1750-1850* (Pittsburgh: University of Pittsburgh Press, 2016), 38-53.

34. Sherry Johnson, *Climate and Catastrophe in Cuba and the Atlantic World in the Age of Revolution* (Chapel Hill: University of North Carolina Press, 2011), 1, 4, 22, 53-54, 74, and passim; Schwartz, *Sea of Storms*, esp. 1-32. See also Gergis and Fowler, "A History of ENSO Events"; and César N. Caviedes, "Five Hundred Years of Hurricanes in the Caribbean: Their Relationship with Global Climatic Variations," *Geojournal*, 23 (1991), 301-10.

35. Natalie A. Zacek, *Settler Society in the English Leeward Islands, 1670-1776* (New York: Cambridge University Press, 2010), 22-23; Chenoweth, *The 18th Century Climate of Jamaica*, 47-49, 62, 76; Niklas Thode Jensen, *For the Health of the Enslaved: Slaves, Medicine and Power in the Danish West Indies, 1803-1848* (Copenhagen: Museum Tusculanum Press, 2012), 139; Alexander Berland, "Extreme Weather and Social Vulnerability in Colonial Antigua, Lesser Antilles, 1770-1890" (PhD diss., University of Nottingham, 2015).

36. Chenoweth, *The 18th Century Climate of Jamaica*, 4, 7, 49; Peter Boomgaard, "The Tropical Rain Forests of Suriname: Exploitation and Management 1600-1975," *New West Indies Guide* [hereafter, *NWIG*], 66, nos. 3-4 (1992), 207-35, esp. 217, 227-28; *A true and perfect Narrative of the late dreadful fire . . . at Bridge-Town in the Barbadoes, April 18, 1668* (London, n.d.); Robert Schomburgk, *The History of Barbados* (London: Frank Cass, 1971 [orig. pub. 1848]), 241, 243, 322; "For the Unfortunate Inhabitants of Bridgetown, Barbados," Barbados Council Minutes, April 20, 1767, CO 28/50/188; *A Further and More Particular Account of the late Dreadful Fire* (London, n.d. [1703]); Matthew Mulcahy, "'That Fatall Spott': The Rise and Fall—and Rise and Fall Again—of Port Royal, Jamaica," in Carole Shammas, ed., *Investing in the Early Modern Built Environment: Europeans, Asians, Settlers and Indigenous Societies* (Leiden: Brill, 2012), 191-218; Zacek, *Settler Society in the English Leeward Islands*, 23-24; Bonham C. Richardson, *Igniting the Caribbean's Past: Fire in British West Indian History* (Chapel Hill: University of North Carolina Press, 2004), 19-32; Joseph L. Scarpaci, "Forts and Ports," in Jordana Dym and Karl Offen, eds., *Mapping Latin America: A Cartographic Reader* (Chicago: University of Chicago Press, 2011), 98-102; Thistlewood Diaries, Apr. 12, 1754; Parker, *Global Crisis*, 61-62, 464, 523, 635-36. On fire engines and fire insurance, see the correspondence of Simon Taylor, for example, Taylor to Chaloner Arcedencke, July 5, 1789; June 2, 12, 17, Sept. 7, Dec. 5, 1790; May 23, 1793; Christer Petley, *White Fury: A Jamaican Slaveholder and the Age of Revolution* (Oxford: Oxford University Press, 2018), 80, 129; Knight, *The Natural, Moral, and Political History of Jamaica*, 401.

37. R. Macdonald, C. J. Hawkesworth, and E. Heath, "The Lesser Antilles Volcanic Chain: A Study in Arc Magnetism," *Earth-Science Reviews*, 49 (2000), 1-76; Jan M. Lindsay, Richard E. A. Robertson, John B. Shepherd, and Shahiba Ali, eds., *Volcanic Hazard Atlas of the Lesser*

Antilles (Trinidad and Tobago: Seismic Research Centre, 2005); Robertson, "Antilles, Geology," in Gillespie and Clague, eds., *Encyclopedia*, 29–35.

38. John F. Cherry, "Insights from the Outside: Some Wider Perspectives and Future Directions in Caribbean Island Historical Ecology," in Siegel, ed., *Island Historical Ecology*, 345–66, esp. 352–57; Guillaume Lalubie, "La perception des aléas naturels aux Petites Antilles par les Amérindiens Kalinago" (paper presented at the 24th Congress of the International Association of Caribbean Archaeologists, Martinique July 25–29, 2011), 389–407.

39. Simon D. Smith, "Volcanic Hazard in a Slave Society: The 1812 Eruption of Mount Soufrière in St. Vincent," *Journal of Historical Geography*, 30 (2010), 1–13.

40. Schwartz, *Sea of Storms*, 27–28, 349 n. 83. These counts are largely based on G. R. Robson, "An Earthquake Catalogue for the Eastern Caribbean 1530–1960," *Bulletin of the Seismological Society of America*, 54, no. 2 (April 1964), 785–832; Judith M. Tomblin and Geoffrey R. Robson, "A Catalogue of Felt Earthquakes for Jamaica, with References to Other Islands in the Greater Antilles, 1564–1971," Ministry of Mining and Natural Resources, Special Publication 2, August 1977, typescript; and William McCann, Lawrence Feldman, and Maribel McCann, "Catalog of Felt Earthquakes for Puerto Rico and Neighbouring Islands, 1493–1899 with Additional Information for some 20th Century Earthquakes" (typescript, 2009); D. M. Manaker et al., "Interseismic Plate Coupling and Strain Partitioning in the Northeastern Caribbean," *Geophysical Journal International*, 174 (2008), 889–903. An early nineteenth-century listing of French Caribbean earthquakes, reports 6 in the seventeenth, 65 in the eighteenth, and 43 in the first two decades of the nineteenth century: Alexandre Moreau de Jonnés, *Histoire physique des Antilles françaises; savoir: La Martinique et les îles de la Guadeloupe* (Paris: Imprimerie de Migneret, 1822), 106, 110–16.

41. Larry Gragg, "The Port Royal Earthquake," *History Today*, 50 (September 2000), 28–34; Matthew Mulcahy, "The Port Royal Earthquake and the World of Wonders in Seventeenth-Century Jamaica," *Early American Studies*, 6 (Fall 2008), 391–422, and Mulcahy, "'That Fatall Spott,'" 391–421; Roger H. Leech, "Impermanent Architecture in the English Colonies of the Eastern Caribbean: New Contexts for Innovation in the Early Modern Atlantic World," in Kenneth Breisch and Alison Hoagland, eds., *Building Environments: Perspectives in Vernacular Architecture*, 10 (Knoxville: University of Tennessee Press, 2006), 153–68; David Manning, "Reformation and the Wickedness of Port Royal, Jamaica," in Crawford Gribben and Scott Spurlock, eds., *Puritans and Catholics in the Trans-Atlantic World, 1600–1850* (New York: Palgrave Macmillan, 2016), 131–63; Louis D. Gerdelan, "The Royal Society, Port Royal, and the Great Trans-Atlantic Earthquake of 1692," *Studi Storici*, 60, no. 4 (October–December, 2019), 845–74.

42. For disease after the 1770 earthquake, see Michel-Placide Justin, *Histoire politique et statistique de l'Ile d'Hayti, Sainte-Domingue, écrite sur les documents officiels et des notes communiqués par Sir James Barskett . . .* (Paris: Brière, 1826), 117–22; and David M. Morens, "Epidemic Anthrax in the Eighteenth Century, the Americas," *Emerging Infectious Diseases*, 8, no. 10 (2002), 1160–62. In addition to the counts in n. 40, for Hispaniola, see Uri ten Brink, William Bakun, and Claudia Flores, "Historical Perspective on Seismic Hazard to Hispaniola and the Northeast Caribbean Region," *Journal of Geophysical Research*, 116 (December 2011), 1–15; and William H. Bakun, Claudia H. Flores, and Uri S. ten Brink, "Significant Earthquakes on the Enriquillo Fault System, Hispaniola, 1500–2010: Implications for Seismic Hazard," *Bulletin of the Seismological Society of America*, 102, no. 1 (February 2012), 18–30, doi: 10.1785/0120110077.

43. Karen Fay O'Loughlin and James F. Lander, *Caribbean Tsunamis: A 500-Year History from 1498–1998* (Dordrecht, Netherlands: Kluwer Academic Publishers, 2003), 37–42, 56, 58–59, 85–86, 93, 118–42; James F. Lander, "A Brief History of Tsunamis in the Caribbean Sea," *Science of Tsunami Hazards, the International Journal of the Tsunami Society*, 20, no. 2 (2002), 57–94.

44. Noble David Cook, *Born to Die: Disease and New World Conquest, 1492–1650* (Cambridge: Cambridge University Press, 1998), 15–59.

45. Philip D. Curtin, *The Rise and Fall of the Plantation Complex: Essays in Atlantic History* (New York: Cambridge University Press, 1990), 81; Paul E. Kopperman, "The British Army in North America and the West Indies, 1755/83: A Medical Perspective," in Geoffrey L.

Hudson, ed., *British Military and Naval Medicine, 1600–1830* (Amsterdam: Rodopi, 2007), 51–86; John R. McNeill, "The Ecological Basis of Warfare in the Caribbean, 1700–1804," in Maarten Ultee, ed., *Adapting to Conditions: War and Society in the Eighteenth Century* (Tuscaloosa: University of Alabama Press, 1986), 26–42; Wendy D. Churchill, "Efficient, Efficacious and Humane Responses to Non-European bodies in British Military Medicine, 1780–1815," *Journal of Imperial and Commonwealth History,* 40, no. 2 (2012), 137–58; Michael Joseph, "Military Officers, Tropical Medicine, and Racial Thought in the Formation of the West India Regiments, 1793–1802," *Journal of the History of Medicine,* 72, no. 2 (2017), 142–65; Tim Lockley, *Military Medicine and the Making of Race: Life and Death in the West India Regiments, 1795–1874* (Cambridge: Cambridge University Press, 2020), esp. 19–112. In the rest of his book, Lockley documents a transformation in the largely positive view of black soldiers' suitability for military service in the tropics; for the origins of this view, see Maria Alessandra Bollettino, "'Of Equal or of More Service': Black Soldiers and the British Empire in the Mid-eighteenth-century Caribbean," *Slavery and Abolition,* 38, no. 3 (2017), 510–33 and for early and continuing opposition from white West Indians, see David Lambert, "'[A] Mere Cloak for their Proud Contempt and Antipathy towards the African Race': Imagining Britain's West India Regiments in the Caribbean, 1795–1838," *Journal of Imperial and Commonwealth History,* 46, no. 4 (2018), 627–50.

46. McNeill, *Mosquito Empires,* 105; McNeill, "The Ecological Basis of Warfare," in Ultee, ed., *Adapting to Conditions,* 26–42; Erica Charters, "The Caring Fiscal-Military State during the Seven Years' War, 1756–1763," *The Historical Journal,* 52, no. 4 (2009), 921–41; and Erica Charters, *Disease, War and the Imperial State: The Welfare of the British Armed Forces during the Seven Year's War* (Chicago: University of Chicago Press, 2014).

47. McNeill, "The Ecological Atlantic," in Canny and Morgan, eds., *Oxford Handbook,* 302; McNeill, *Mosquito Empires,* 44–46. See also Kenneth Kiple, *The Caribbean Slave: A Biological History* (New York: Cambridge University Press, 1984), 15–17, 18–20, 164–65, 177–78; and Rana A. Hogarth, *Medicalizing Blackness: Making Racial Difference in the Atlantic World, 1780–1840* (Chapel Hill: University of North Carolina Press, 2017), 17–77.

48. McNeill, *Mosquito Empires,* 106–36; Julie Orr, *Scotland, Darien, and the Atlantic World, 1698–1700* (Edinburgh: Edinburgh University Press, 2018), 7, 28, 68; Emma Rothschild, "A Horrible Tragedy in the French Atlantic," *Past and Present,* 192 (2006), 67–108; Stanley L. Engerman and B. W. Higman, "The Demographic Structure of the Caribbean Slave Societies in the Eighteenth and Nineteenth Centuries," in Franklin W. Knight, ed., *General History of the Caribbean,* vol. III, *The Slave Societies of the Caribbean* (Paris: Unesco, 1997), 45–104, esp. 49, 52, 63.

49. Richard B. Sheridan, *Doctors and Slaves: A Medical and Demographic History of Slavery in the British West Indies, 1680–1834* (Cambridge: Cambridge University Press, 1985), 42; Charles Leslie, *A New History of Jamaica: From the Earliest Accounts, to the Taking of Porto Bello . . .* (London: J. Hodges, 1740), 49; Michael E. O'Neal, "The Historical Context of Medical Practice in the British Virgin Islands," *Caribbean Perspectives,* I (1991), 30–41; Douglas J. Hamilton, *Scotland, the Caribbean and the Atlantic World, 1750–1820* (Manchester, UK: Manchester University Press, 2005), 112–39; McNeill, *Mosquito Empires,* 77; Mark Harrison, *Medicine in an Age of Commerce and Empire: Britain and Its Tropical Colonies, 1660–1830* (Oxford: Oxford University Press, 2010); John Bell, *An Inquiry into the Causes which Produce, and the Means of Preventing Diseases among British Officers, Soldiers, and Others in the West Indies . . .* (London: J. Murray, 1791), 3–4; John Hunter, *Observations on the Diseases of the Army in Jamaica* (London: G. Nicol, 1788); Bloch, "Slavery and Inter-Imperial Leprosy Discourse in the Atlantic World," *Atlantic Studies,* 14, no. 2 (February 2017), 243–62; Katherine Paugh, "Yaws, Syphilis, Sexuality, and the Circulation of Medical Knowledge in the British Caribbean and the Atlantic World," *Bulletin of the History of Medicine,* 88, no. 2 (2014), 225–52; Katherine Paugh, *The Politics of Reproduction: Race, Medicine, and Fertility in the Age of Abolition* (Oxford: Oxford University Press, 2017), 12, 107–21; Thomas Dancer, *The Medical Assistant, or Jamaica Practice of Physic* (Kingston, Jamaica: Alexander Aikman, 1801), reviewed in *Medical Repository, First Hexade,* vol. V (1802), 432–36. For early hospitals, see Pablo F. Gómez, "Hospitals and Public Health in the Sixteenth-Century Spanish Caribbean," in Ida Altman and David Wheat, eds., *The Spanish Caribbean and the*

Atlantic World in the Long Sixteenth Century (Lincoln: University of Nebraska Press, 2019), 211–32.

50. Antoine Poissonnier-Desperrières, *Traité des fièvres de l'isle de St.-Domingue* (Paris: P. G. Cavelier, 1763), xvi and 6; Antoine Poissonnier-Desperrières, *Traite des Maladies des Gens de Mer* (Paris: De L'imprimeur royale, 1767); Bertie Mandelblatt, "'On the Excellence of the Vegetable Diet': Scurvy, Antoine Poissonnier-Desperrières's New Naval Diet and French Colonial Science in the Atlantic World," *Early American Studies*, 19, no. 2 (Spring 2021), 322–59; Harrison, *Medicine in an Age of Commerce*, 83, 108–9, 188; J. F. Eckard, "Correction of Chisholm's Misstatement Respecting the Prevalence of Malignant Fever at St. Thomas's," *Medical Repository*, (1804), 336–38; Catherine E. Kelly, *War and the Militarization of British Army Medicine, 1793–1830* (London: Routledge, 2011), 11–31; Adrien Lopez-Denis, "Disease and Society in Colonial Cuba, 1790–1840" (PhD diss., UCLA, 2007); Katherine Arner, "The Malady of Revolutions: Yellow Fever in the Atlantic World, 1793–1828." (PhD diss., Johns Hopkins University, 2014); David Geggus, "Yellow Fever in the 1790s: The British Army in Occupied St. Domingue," *Medical History*, 23, no. 1 (1979), 38–58; Colin Chisholm, *An Essay on the Malignant Pestilential Fever, Introduced into the West Indian Islands from Boullam, on the Coast of Guinea, . . .* (Philadelphia: Thomas Dobson, 1799); José G. Rigau-Pérez, "The Introduction of Smallpox Vaccine in 1803 and the Adoption of Immunization as a Government Function in Puerto Rico," *Hispanic American Historical Review*, 69, no. 3 (1989), 393–423, esp. 400; Jensen, *For the Health of the Enslaved*, 197–99, 209–15. Interestingly, the British navy's growing preference for Caribbean limes instead of Mediterranean lemons, which was partly based on cost, unwittingly undermined faith in an accepted remedy for scurvy, since the West Indian citrus contained a negligible amount of ascorbate: Jonathan Lamb, *Scurvy: The Disease of Discovery* (Princeton, NJ: Princeton University Press, 2016), 32, 36–38.

51. Richard Price, *First-Time: The Historical Vision of an Afro-American People* (Baltimore: Johns Hopkins University Press, 1983), 153–59; Sheridan, *Doctors and Slaves*, 37–40, 69, 82, 266, 335; Londa Schiebinger, "Scientific Exchange in the Eighteenth-Century Atlantic World," in Bernard Bailyn and Patricia L. Denault, eds., *Soundings in Atlantic History: Latent Structures and Intellectual Currents, 1500–1830* (Cambridge, MA: Harvard University Press, 2011), 294–328, esp. 301, 308; Edward Long, *History of Jamaica . . .*, 3 vols. (London: T. Lowndes, 1774), 2:134–37, 380–81; Diana Paton, *The Cultural Politics of Obeah: Religion, Colonialism and Modernity in the Caribbean World* (Cambridge: Cambridge University Press, 2015), 19, 27, 31–34, 53; Karol K. Weaver, *Medical Revolutionaries: The Enslaved Healers of Eighteenth-Century Saint Domingue* (Urbana: University of Illinois Press, 2006), 72–73; Juanita De Barros, "'Setting Things Right': Medicine and Magic in British Guiana, 1803–38," *Slavery and Abolition*, 25 (2004), 28–50; Juanita De Barros, Steven Palmer, and David Wright, eds., *Health and Medicine in the Circum-Caribbean, 1800–1968* (New York: Routledge, 2009); Kelly Wisecup, "Communicating Disease: Medical Knowledge and Literary Forms in Colonial British America" (PhD diss., University of Maryland–College Park, 2009), esp. 192–252; McNeill, *Mosquito Empires*, 81–86; Jensen, *For the Health of the Enslaved*, 134–37; George Pinckard, *Notes on the West Indies . . .*, 2 vols. (London: Longman, Hurst, Rees, and Orme, 1806), 1:388–89; Andrew Curran, *The Anatomy of Blackness: Science and Slavery in an Age of Enlightenment* (Baltimore: Johns Hopkins University Press, 2011). See also Kristen Bloch, *Holistic Medicine, Spiritual Healing and Dis-ease in the Early Caribbean* (forthcoming).

52. The most comprehensive study is Chelsea Berry, "Poisoned Relations: Medicine, Sorcery, and Poison Trials in the Greater Caribbean, 1680–1850" (PhD diss., Georgetown University, 2019). For a few selective prior studies, see John Savage, "'Black Magic' and White Terror: Slave Poisoning and Colonial Society in Early 19th Century Martinique," *Journal of Social History*, 40, no. 3 (Spring 2007), 635–62; Natalie Zemon Davis, "Judges, Masters, Diviners: Slaves' Experience of Criminal Justice in Colonial Suriname," *Law and History Review*, 29, no. 4 (November 2011), 925–84; Diana Paton and Maarit Forde, eds., *Obeah and Other Powers: The Politics of Caribbean Religion and Healing* (Durham, NC: Duke University Press, 2012); Diana Paton, "Witchcraft, Poison, Law, and Atlantic Slavery," *William and Mary Quarterly* [hereafter, *WMQ*], 3rd Ser., 69, no. 2 (April 2012), 235–64; Sasha Turner Bryson, "The Art of Power: Poison and Obeah Accusations and the Struggle

for Dominance and Survival in Jamaica's Slave Society," *Caribbean Studies*, 41, no. 2 (2013), 61–90; Caroline Oudin-Bastide, *L'effroi et la terreur: Esclavage, poison et sorcellerie aux Antilles* (Paris: La Découverte, Les Empêcheurs de tourner en rond, 2013); Trevor Burnard and John Garrigus, *The Plantation Machine: Atlantic Capitalism in French Saint-Domingue and British Jamaica* (Philadelphia: University of Pennsylvania Press, 2016), 101–36; John Garrigus, "'Like an epidemic one could only stop with the most violent remedies': African Poisons versus Livestock Disease in Saint Domingue, 1750–88," *William and Mary Quarterly*, 3rd Ser., 78, no. 4 (2021), 617–50; and John Garrigus, '*Macandal Is Saved!': Disease, Conspiracy, and the Coming of the Haitian Revolution* (forthcoming).

53. Ida Altman, "Vasco Porcallo de Figueroa: Ambition, Fear, and Politics in Early Cuba," in Altman and Wheat, eds., *The Spanish Caribbean*, 71–90, esp. 78–79; Hogarth, *Medicalizing Blackness*, 81–103, 109, 111; Londa Schiebinger, *Secret Cures of Slaves: People, Plants, and Medicine in the Eighteenth-Century Atlantic World* (Stanford, CA: Stanford University Press, 2017), 29; Pablo F. Gómez, *The Experiential Caribbean: Creating Knowledge and Healing in the Early Modern Atlantic* (Chapel Hill: University of North Carolina Press, 2017), 112; Sheridan, *Doctors and Slaves*, 216–19; Jerome S. Handler, "Diseases and Medical Disabilities of Enslaved Barbadians, from the Seventeenth Century to around 1838 Pt. 2," *West Indian Medical Journal*, 58 (2009), 33–49; Jerome S. Handler, "Slave Medicine and Obeah in Barbados, circa 1650–1834," *NWIG*, 74 (2000), 57–90; Kiple, *Caribbean Slave*, 96–103; Claire Gherini, "Experiment and Good Sense Must Direct You": Managing Health and Sickness in the British Plantation Enlightenment, 1756–1815 (PhD diss., Johns Hopkins University, 2016), 232–301. For the modern science, see John M. Hunter, "Geophagy in Africa and the United States: A Culture Nutrition Hypothesis," *Geographical Review*, 63, no. 2 (April 1973), 170–95; Peter W. Abrahams and Julia A. Parsons, "Geophagy in the Tropics: A Literature Review," *Geographical Journal*, 162 (March 1996), 63–72; Sera L. Young et al., "Why on Earth? Evaluating Hypotheses about the Physiological Functions of Human Geophagy," *Quarterly Review of Biology*, 86, no. 2 (June 2011), 97–120; Philip T. B. Starks and Brittany L. Slabach, "The Scoop on Eating Dirt," *Scientific American*, 306, no. 6 (June 2012), 30–33.

54. Ann Appleton Storrow to Penny Butlier, June 6, 1793, Ann Appleton Storrow Papers, Ms N-979, Massachusetts Historical Society; James Lind, *An Essay on Diseases Incidental to Europeans in Hot Climates with the Method of Preventing Their Fatal Consequences* (London: T. Becket and P. A. de Hondt, 1768); Edmund Halley, "An Historical Account of the Trade Winds, and Monsoons, Observable in the Seas between and near the Tropicks, with an Attempt to Assign the Physical Cause of the Said Winds," *Philosophical. Transactions*, 16 (1686), 153–68; Benjamin Vaughan to Thomas Jefferson, Jan. 26, 1787, *The Papers of Thomas Jefferson Digital Edition*, ed. Barbara B. Oberg and J. Jefferson Looney (Charlottesville: University of Virginia Press, Rotunda, 2008). The key secondary works are Harrison, *Medicine in an Age of Commerce*, 41, 44, 48–50, 72, passim; and David Arnold, ed., *Warm Climates and Western Medicine: The Emergence of Tropical Medicine, 1500–1900* (Amsterdam: Rodopi, 1996).

55. Anya Zilberstein, *A Temperate Empire: Making Climate Change in Early America* (New York: Oxford University Press, 2016), 118–47. For other migration schemes see, for example, B. W. Higman, "The Chinese in Trinidad, 1806–1838," *Caribbean Studies*, 12 (1972), 21–44; and Claudius Fergus, "'Dread of Insurrection': Abolitionism, Security, and Labor in Britain's West Indian Colonies, 1760–1823," *WMQ*, 3rd Ser., 66, no. 4 (October 2009), 757–80.

56. Harrison, *Medicine in an Age of Commerce*, 69, 74, 84–88; 106–8, 113, 126, 128–29; Sarah Knott, *Sensibility and the American Revolution* (Chapel Hill: University of North Carolina Press, 2009), esp. 69–107; Benjamin Moseley, *A Treatise on Tropical Diseases; on Military Operations; and on the Climate of the West Indies* (London: T. Cadell, 1789), 52, 84; Pratik Chakrabarti, "Empire and Alternatives: *Swietenia Febrifuga* and the Cinchona Substitutes, *Medical History*, 54 (2010), 75–94; McNeill, *Mosquito Empires*, 74. One sidelight is the popularity of waxwork models, showing the nervous system: see William Shaw Miller, "Abraham Chovet: An Early Teacher of Anatomy in Philadelphia," *Anatomical Record*, 5 (1911), 147–71, and extended in *Annals of Medical History* 8 (1926): 375–93. Chovet had lived in the Caribbean for 27 years before moving to North America.

57. Benjamin Breen, *The Age of Intoxication: Origins of the Global Drug Trade* (Philadelphia: University of Pennsylvania Press, 2019), 3, 8–11, 22–27, 38–39, 43–50, 97, 105–8, 112–21, 132–36, 144–51, 183–87; Zachary Dorner, *Merchants of Medicines: The Commerce and Coercion of Health in Britain's Long Eighteenth Century* (Chicago: University of Chicago Press, 2020), 9, 72–83, 86, 90–98, 103–5, 167.

58. Harrison, *Medicine in an Age of Commerce*, 179–88 (quote on 187), 213–14; Katherine Johnston, "Atlantic Bodies: Health, Race, and the Environment in the Greater British Caribbean" (PhD diss., Columbia University, 2016); Claire Gherini, "Experiment and Good Sense Must Direct You" (PhD diss., Johns Hopkins University, 2016).

59. J. Edward Hutson, ed., *On the Treatment and Management of the More Common West-India Diseases (1750–1802)* (Kingston, Jamaica: University of the West Indies Press, 2005), 11–12; Katherine Johnston, "The Constitution of Empire: Place and Bodily Health in the Eighteenth-Century Atlantic," *Atlantic Studies*, 10, no. 4 (2013), 443–66; and Katherine Johnston, "Atlantic Bodies," esp. 130–218; Gherini, "Experiment and Good Sense Must Direct You," esp. 30–31.

60. Karen Kuppperman, "Fear of Hot Climates in the Anglo-American Cultural Experience," *WMQ*, 3rd Ser., 41 (1984), 213–40; James Chisholme to Dr. Ewart, Feb. 16, 1795, MS 5464, ff. 174–75, Papers of William and James Chisholme, National Library of Scotland; J. Hector St. John de Crèvecoeur, *Letters from an American Farmer and Sketches of Eighteenth-Century America*, ed. Albert E Stone (New York: Penguin, 1981 [orig. pub. 1782]), 167; Peter McCandless, *Slavery, Disease, and Suffering in the Southern Lowcountry* (New York: Cambridge University Press, 2011), 19–22, 29–40, 154. For movements, see Edward Cranfield to Board of Trade, 1684, CO 1/52, f. 18; Samuel Martin correspondence, MS Add 41348, ff. 153, 157, 183, 206, British Library; Janet Schaw, *Journal of a Lady of Quality; Being a Narrative of a Journey from Scotland to the West Indies, North Carolina, and Portugal in the Years 1774 to 1776*, eds. Evangeline Walker Andrews and Charles McLean Andrews (New Haven, CT: Yale University Press, 1921), 105. For natural benefits of the tropics, see Thomas Dancer, *A Short Dissertation on the Jamaica Bath Waters . . .* (Kingston, Jamaica: D. Douglass and Alex. Aikman, 1784), and his *The Medical Assistant*. See also Mark Carey, "Inventing Caribbean Climates: How Science, Medicine, and Tourism Changed Tropical Weather from Deadly to Healthy," *Osiris*, 26, no. 1 (2011), 129–41.

61. Diaries of George Washington (11 March 1748–13 December 1799), Volume 1 (11 March 1748–13 November 1765), *The Papers of George Washington Digital Edition*, ed. Theodore J. Crackel (Charlottesville: University of Virginia Press, Rotunda, 2008). On Hillary, see Christopher C. Booth, "William Hillary, Pupil of Boerhaave," *Medical History*, 7 (1963), 297–315; and Harrison, *Medicine in an Age of Commerce*, 54–56. For a later trip by his nephew to Barbados, sponsored by George Washington, see George Augustine Washington to GW, Aug. 11, 14, 1784; diary entry, May 13, 1785; GW to David Parry, May 25, 1785; Papers of GW Digital, Rotunda. See also Sheila Rothman, *Living in the Shadow of Death: Tuberculosis and the Social Experience of Illness in American History* (Baltimore: Johns Hopkins University Press, 1995), 13, 19–22, 32–35, 50, 53–56, 58–60, 68–71, 73, 124, 221.

62. Mark Catesby, *The Natural History of Carolina, Florida, and the Bahama Islands . . .*, 2 vols. (London: W. Innys and R. Manby, 1729–47), II:xxxix; Kenneth F. Kiple and Kriemhild Coneè Ornelas, "Race, War and Tropical Medicine in the Eighteenth-Century Caribbean," in Arnold, ed., *Warm Climates and Western Medicine*, 65–79; William Hillary, *Observations on the Changes of the Air, and the Concomitant Epidemical Diseases in the Island of Barbadoes . . .* (London: C. Hitch and L. Hawes, 1759); *The Journal of Nicholas Cresswell, 1774–1777* (New York: The Dial Press, 1924), 37; Long, *History of Jamaica*, II:508; McNeill, *Mosquito Empires*, 28–29.

63. Harrison, *Medicine in an Age of Commerce*, 1, 3, 153, and passim; William Wright, "Practical Observations on the Treatment of Acute Diseases; Particularly Those of the West Indies," *Medical Facts and Observations*, 7 (1797), 1–25, esp. 23–24; Thomas Dancer, *A brief history of the late expedition against Fort San Juan, so far as it relates to the diseases of the troops: together with some observations on climate, infection and contagion; and several of the endemial complaints of the West-Indies* (Kingston, Jamaica: D. Douglass and W. Aikman, 1781).

64. Gómez, *The Experiential Caribbean*, 1–2, 3, 36, 78, 79, 105, 145, passim; "Pablo F. Gómez, Caribbean Stones and the Creation of Early-Modern Worlds," *History and Technology*, 34, no. 1 (2018), 11–20; Schiebinger, *Secret Cures of Slaves*, esp. 45–64.

65. Philip D. Burden, *The Mapping of North America: Vol 1. A List of Printed Maps 1511–1670* (Rickmansworth, UK: Raleigh Publications, 1996), xv, xvii–xviii, xix–xx, 3, 13–14; Kenneth Nebenzahl, *Atlas of Columbus and the Great Discoveries* (Chicago: Rand McNally, 1990), 26, 30; David Buisseret, "The Cartography of the Caribbean, 1500–1650," in Pieter C. Emmer and German Carrera Damas, eds., *General History of the Caribbean*, vol. II, *New Societies: The Caribbean in the Long Sixteenth Century* (London: Unesco, 1999), 308–18; Buisseret, "Spanish Colonial Cartography, 1450–1700," in David Woodward, ed., *The History of Cartography* (Chicago: University of Chicago Press, 2007), vol. 3, pt. 1, 1095–171; María M. Portuondo, *Secret Science: Spanish Cosmography and the New World* (Chicago: University of Chicago Press, 2009), 68–79, plates 1–3, 8.

66. Buisseret, "The Cartography of the Caribbean," 308–18; James E. McClellan III and François Regourd, *The Colonial Machine: French Science and Overseas Expansion in the Old Regime* (Turnhout, Belgium: Brepols, 2011), 428; Neil L. Whitehead, "Indigenous Cartography in Lowland South America and the Caribbean," in David Woodward and G. Malcolm Lewis, eds., *The History of Cartography*, vol. 2, bk. 3, *Cartography in the Traditional African, American, Arctic, Australian, and Pacific Societies* (Chicago: University of Chicago Press, 1987), 301–26; Karl H. Offen, "Creating Mosquitia: Mapping Amerindian Spatial Practices in Eastern Central America, 1629–1779," *Journal of Historical Geography*, 33, no. 2 (2007), 254–82.

67. McClellan and Regourd, *The Colonial Machine*, 60–61. For Dutch maps, see Wim Renkema, *Karten van de Nederlandse Antillen: Curaçao, Aruba, Bonair, Saba, Sint Eustatius en Sin Maarten tot 1900* (Leiden: Brill Hes & De Graaf, 2012); and C. Koeman et al., *Links with the Past: The History of Cartography of Suriname 1500–1971* (Amsterdam: Theatrum Orbis Terrarum, 1973).

68. B. W. Higman, *Jamaica Surveyed: Plantation Maps and Plans of the Eighteenth and Nineteenth Centuries* (Kingston, Jamaica: Institute of Jamaica, 1988); David Buisseret, ed., *Rural Images: The Estate Plan in the Old and New Worlds* (Chicago: University of Chicago Press, 1988); Kees Zandvliet, *Mapping for Money: Maps, Plans and Topographic Paintings and Their Role in Dutch Overseas Expansion during the 16th and 17th Centuries* (Amsterdam: Batavian Lion International, 1998), 207–8; Daniel Hopkins, "An Extraordinary Eighteenth-Century Map of the Danish Sugar-Plantation Island St. Croix," *Imago Mundi*, 41 (1989), 44–58; Daniel Hopkins, Philip Morgan, and Justin Roberts, "The Application of GIS to the Reconstruction of the Slave-Plantation Economy of St. Croix, Danish West Indies," *Historical Geography*, 39 (2011), 85–104; Marco G. Meniketti, *Sugar Cane Capitalism and Environmental Transformation: An Archaeology of Colonial Nevis, West Indies* (Tuscaloosa: University of Alabama Press, 2015), 98–99; S. Max Edelson, *The New Map of Empire: How Britain Imagined America before Independence* (Cambridge, MA: Harvard University Press, 2017).

69. Le plan d'arpentage de la Grande-Terre, drawn by François Marie Amaudric de Sainte-Maure, 1732, Dépôt des fortifications des colonies, Guadeloupe, 69, 70 et 89 A, Centre des archives d'Outre-mer, Aix-en-Provence; Plan du port du Petit Cul de Sac de l'isle Guadeloupe et de ses environs, DFCG 133, CAOM; and Carte générale de l'isle de Guadeloupe, 1768–69, Département des Cartes et Plans, Service hydrographique de la Marine, 155, div. 2, 14, BN, Paris. For some discussion, see Anne Pérotin-Dumon, *La Ville aux Îles, La Ville dans L'Île: Basse-Terre et Pointe-à-Pitre, Guadeloupe, 1650–1820* (Paris: Karthala, 2000), 347–51, 763–64, and various plates following p. 415; Monique Pelletier, "La Martinique et la Guadeloupe au lendemain du traité de Paris (10 février 1763). L'oeuvre des ingénieurs géographes," *Chroniques d'histoire maritimes*, 9 (1984), 22–30); Danielle Bégot, Monique Pelletier, and Catherine Bousquet-Bressolier, eds., *La Martinique de Moreau du Temple, 1770: la carte des ingénieurs géographes* (Paris: Éditions du Comité des travaux historiques et scientifiques, 1998); and McClellan and Regourd, *The Colonial Machine*, 216. See also François Regourd, "L'Expédition hydrographique de Chastenet de Puységur à Saint-Domingue (1784–1785)," in Silvia Marzagalli and Hubert Bonin, eds., *Négoce, ports et océans XVIè–XXè siècles mélanges offerts à Paul Butel* (Pessac, France: Presses universitaires de

Bordeaux, 2000), 247–62; Jean-Louis Glenisson, "La défense et la mise en valeur de Saint-Domingue au lendemain du traité de Paris (1763): le rôle de la cartographie," *Le Monde des cartes*, 180 (2004), 17–35; and Emilie d'Orgeix, "French Military Engineers in the American Colonies (1635–1776)," in Bruce Lenman, ed., *Military Engineers and the Development of the Early Modern World* (Dundee, UK: Dundee University Press, 2013), 245–58.

70. Cameron B. Strang, *Frontiers of Science: Imperialism and Natural Knowledge in the Gulf South Borderlands, 1500–1850* (Chapel Hill: University of North Carolina Press, 2018), 46–50; Paul W. Mapp, *The Elusive West and the Contest for Empire, 1713–1763* (Chapel Hill: University of North Carolina Press, 2011); Edelson, *The New Map of Empire*, 21–101, 197–247, 289–351; Jesse Cromwell, *The Smugglers' World: Illicit Trade and Atlantic Communities in Eighteenth-Century Venezuela* (Chapel Hill: University of North Carolina Press, 2018); Adrian Finucane, *The Temptations of Trade: Britain, Spain, and the Struggle for Empire* (Philadelphia: University of Pennsylvania Press, 2016); Jorge Cañizares-Esguerra, ed., *Entangled Empires: The Anglo-Iberian Atlantic, 1500–1830* (Philadelphia: University of Pennsylvania Press, 2018), esp. 124–58, 197–235.

71. Charles A. Woods and Florence E. Sergile, "Antilles, Biology," in Gillespie and Clague, eds., *Encyclopedia of Islands*, 20–29; Brendan S. Holland, "Land Snails," in Gillespie and Clague, eds., *Encyclopedia of Islands*, 537–42; Christopher K. Starr, "Trinidad and Tobago," in Gillespie and Clague, eds., *Encyclopedia of Islands*, 926–29; Ricklefs and Bermingham, "The West Indies as a Laboratory"; Michael Leonard Smith et al., "Caribbean Islands," in Russell. A. Mittermeier et al., eds., *Hotspots Revisited: Earth's Biologically Richest and Most Endangered Terrestrial Ecoregions* (Mexico City: Agrupacion Sierra Madre, 2004), 112–18; Charles A. Woods and Florence E. Sergile, eds., *Biogeography of the West Indies: Patterns and Perspectives*, 2nd ed. (Boca Raton, FL: CRC Press, 2001). On insects, see J. K. Liebherr, ed., *Zoogeography of Caribbean Insects* (New York: NCROL, 1988), and Julio A. Genaro and Ana E. Tejuca, "Patterns of Endemism and Biogeography of Cuban Insects," in Woods and Sergile, eds., *Biogeography of the West Indies*, 77–81. On plants, see Eugenio Santiago-Valentin and Richard G. Olmstead, "Historical Biogeography of Caribbean Plants: Introduction to Current Knowledge and Possibilities from a Phylogenetic Perspective," *Taxon*, 53, no. 2 (2004), 299–319; Pedro Acevedo-Rodríguez and Mark T. Strong, "Floristic Richness and Affinities in the West Indies," *Botanical Review*, 74 (2008), 5–36, and other articles in this special issue; also Pedro Acevedo-Rodríguez and Mark T. Strong, "Catalogue of Seed Plants of the West Indies," National Museum of Natural History, Smithsonian Institution (2007), http://botany.si.edu/antilles/WestIndies/catalog.htm.

72. Watts, *The West Indies*, 25–34; Newsom and Wing, *On Land and Sea*, 3–6, 15–16, 141 Alan Graham, *A Natural History of the New World: The Ecology and Evolution of Plants in the Americas* (Chicago: University of Chicago Press, 2011), 4, 20, 60–63; Megan Raby, *American Tropics: The Caribbean Roots of Biodiversity Science (Flows, Migrations, and Exchanges)* (Chapel Hill: University of North Carolina Press, 2017), 6–7, 26–28, 39; D. T. MacDougal, "Mimosa: A Typical Sensitive Plant," in Joseph Charles Arthur and D. T. MacDougal, eds., *Living Plants and Their Properties: A Collection of Essays* (New York: Baker and Taylor, 1898), 47–62, esp. 49.

73. Newsom and Wing, *On Land and Sea*, 4–5, 20–23, 63–67, 95–100, 104, 109–10, 120–28, 129–35, 143–62; 182–86; Carl Ortwin Sauer, *The Early Spanish Main* (Berkeley: University of California Press, 1966), 56–58; Francisco Watlington, "The Physical Environment: Biogeographical Teleconnections in Caribbean Prehistory," in Jalil Sued-Badillo, ed., *General History of the Caribbean*, vol. 1, *Autochthonous Societies* (London: UNESCO, 2003), 30–92, esp. 71–85; Patricia Miloslavich et al., "Marine Biodiversity in the Caribbean: Regional Estimates and Distribution Patterns." *PloS One*, 5, no. 8 (2010), e11916.

74. Klinkenborg, ed., *Drake Manuscript*, ff. 2–33.

75. Davis, *The Gulf*, 52; Alexander O. Exquemelin, *The Buccaneers of America*, trans. Alexis Brown (Mineola, NY: Dover Publications, 1969 [orig. pub. 1678]), 42; *Journal of Cresswell*, 38; Holger Weiss, Laura Hallston, and Stefan Norrgård, "Cotton and Salt: Swedish Colonial Aspirations and the Transformation of Saint Barthélemy in the Eighteenth Century,"

Environment and History, 26, no. 2 (May 2020), 261–87, esp. 271; Newsom and Wing, *On Land and Sea*, 67; Klinkenborg, ed., *Drake Manuscript*, f. 27.

76. Long, *History of Jamaica*, III:838–42; W. Adolph and E. Hecker, "On the Active Principles of the Spurge Family, X: Skin Irritants Cocarcinogens, and Cryptic Cocarcinogens from the Latex of the Manchineel Tree," *Journal of Natural Products*, 47 (1984), 482–96; J. F. Pitts et al., "Manchineel Keratoconjunctivitis," *British Journal of Ophthalmology*, 77 (1993), 284–88; Nicola H. Strickland, "My Most Unfortunate Experience: Eating a Manchineel 'Beach Apple,'" *British Medical Journal*, 321 (August 12, 2000), 428; Henry Lowe et al., *Poisonous Plants of Jamaica* (Kingston, Jamaica: Pelican, 2002), 65–66; Denis Boucaud-Maitre et al., "Severity of Manchineel Fruit (*Hippomane mancinella*) Poisoning: A Retrospective Case Series of 97 Patients from French Poison Control Centers," *Toxicon*, 161, no. 1 (April 2019), 28–32.

77. Watts, *The West Indies*, 29–31, 34–37; Allison Bain et al., "Landscape Transformation during Ceramic Age and Colonial Occupations of Barbuda, West Indies," *Environmental Archaeology*, 23, no. 1 (2018), 36–46; Daniel R. Muhs et al., "Geochemical Evidence for African Dust Inputs to Soils of Western Atlantic Islands: Barbados, the Bahamas, and Florida," *Journal of Geophysical Research*, 112 (2007), 1–26. For a largely nation-state approach, see Nazeer Ahmad, *Soils of the Caribbean* (Kingston, Jamaica: Ian Randle, 2011).

78. Davis, *The Gulf*, 26; Watts, *The West Indies*, 37; D. Graham Burnett, *Masters of All They Surveyed: Exploration, Geography, and a British El Dorado* (Chicago: University of Chicago Press, 2000), 180; Stéphen Rostain, "Agricultural Earthworks on the French Guiana Coast," in Helaine Silverman and William Isbell, eds., *Handbook of South American Archaeology* (New York: Springer, 2008), 217–34; Rostain, "Agricultural Earthworks (the Guianas)," in Basil A. Reid and R. Grant Gilmore III, eds., *Encyclopedia of Caribbean Archaeology* (Gainesville: University of Florida Press, 2014), 33–36.

79. Watts, *The West Indies*, 53–61; Joost Morsink, "Catalytic Environments," *Environmental Archaeology*, 24, no. 2 (2019), 149–60, esp. 155; Morsink, "The Power of Salt: A Holistic Approach to Salt in the Prehistoric Circum-Caribbean Region" (PhD diss., University of Florida, 2012), 255–61.

80. Watts, *The West Indies*, 119, 121, 166–67, 194, 221–23, 237, 384, 396–97; Diane Wallman, "Histories and Trajectories of Socio-Ecological Landscapes in the Lesser Antilles: Implications of Colonial Period Zooarchaeological Research," *Environmental Archaeology*, 23, no. 1 (2018), 13–22; E. Christian Wells et al., "Plantation Soilscapes: Initial and Cumulative Impacts of Colonial Agriculture in Antigua, West Indies," *Environmental Archaeology*, 23, no. 1 (2018), 23–35; E. Christian Wells et al., "Agroindustrial Soilscapes in the Caribbean: A Geochemical Perspective from Betty's Hope, Antigua," *Environmental Archaeology*, 22, no. 4 (2017), 381–93; Lauren R. Gallant et al., "A Bat Guano Deposit in Jamaica Recorded Agricultural Changes and Metal Exposure over the Last >4300 Years," *Palaeogeography, Palaeoclimatology, Palaeoecology*, 538 (2020), https://doi.org/10.1016/j.palaeo.2019.109470.

81. Miloslavich et al., "Marine Biodiversity"; Paul Rose and Anne Laking, *Oceans: Exploring the Hidden Depths of the Underwater World* (Berkeley: University of California Press, 2008), 14, 54, 74; Richard Ellis, *The Empty Ocean: Plundering the World's Marine Life* (Washington, DC: Island Press, 2003), 103; Patricia E. Rosel et al., "A New Species of Baleen Whale (Balaenoptera) from the Gulf of Mexico, with a Review of Its Geographic Distribution," *Marine Mammal Science*, 37 (2021), 577–610, https://doi-org.proxy1.library.jhu.edu/10.1111/mms.12776; Lynn W. Lefebvre et al. "Status and Biogeography of the West Indian Manatee" in Woods and Sergile, eds., *Biogeography of the West Indies*, 425–74; Watlington, "The Physical Environment," 48–62; Waldron, *Handbook of Ceramic Animal Symbols*, 82–86; Anghiera, *De orbe novo*, I:373–74, as cited in Marcy Norton, "The Chicken or the *Iegue*: Human-Animal Relationships and the Columbian Exchange," *American Historical Review*, 120, no. 1 (February 2015), 28–60, esp. 44.

82. Christopher Columbus, *The Log of Christopher Columbus*, trans. Robert H. Fuson (Camden, ME: International Marine Publishing Company, 1987), 84; Gonzalo Fernández de Oviedo, *The Natural History of the West Indies* (1526), as cited in W. Jeffrey Bolster, *The Mortal Sea: Fishing the Atlantic in the Age of Sail* (Cambridge, MA: Harvard University Press, 2012),

13; Catesby, *Natural History*, II:xlii; Higman, *Proslavery Priest*, 147; Newsom and Wing, *On Land and Sea*, 187.

83. Newsom and Wing, *On Land and Sea*, 58–74, 172–88, 192–93; John G. Crock, Nanny Carder, and Wetherbee Dorshow, "'Marineness', the Underwater Seascape and Variability in Maritime Adaptations in the Late Ceramic Age Northern Lesser Antilles," *Environmental Archaeology*, 24, no. 2 (2019), 199–210; G. Villamizar, and F. Cervigón, "Variability and Sustainability of the Southern Subarea of the Caribbean Sea Large Marine Ecosystem," *Environmental Development*, 22 (2017), 30–41.

84. Patricia E. Bradley and Robert L. Norton, eds., *An Inventory of Breeding Seabirds of the Caribbean* (Gainesville: University Press of Florida, 2009), 5, 270; Waldron, *Handbook of Ceramic Animal Symbols*, 136–71. See also Herbert A. Raffaele, and Tracy Pederson, *A Guide to the Birds of the West Indies* (Princeton, NJ: Princeton University Press, 1998).

85. Ma. Magdalena Antczak, Andrzej T. Antczak, and Miguel Lentino, "Avian Remains from Late Pre-colonial Amerindian Sites on Islands of the Venezuelan Caribbean," *Environmental Archaeology*, 24, no. 2 (2019), 161–81; Keegan and Hofman, *The Caribbean before Columbus*, 73, 92, 109, 172, 182, 186, 191, 194, 198, 205, 227–28; Jaime R. Pagán-Jiménez, Reniel Rodríguez Ramos, and Corinne L. Hofman, "On the Way to the Islands: The Role of Domestic Plants in the Initial Peopling of the Antilles," in Hofman and Antczak, eds., *Early Settlers of the Insular Caribbean*, 89–106, esp. 103.

86. Watts, *The West Indies*, 37–40; David Lack, "The Numbers and Species of Humming Birds in the West Indies," *Evolution*, 27 (1973), 326–37; Paul Slud, "Geographic and Climatic Relationships of Avifaunas with Special Reference to Comparative Distribution in the Tropics," *Smithsonian Contributions to Zoology*, no. 212 (Washington, DC: Smithsonian Institution Press, 1976), 1–149; Christopher Benfy, "'A Searing Bolt of Turquoise,'" *New York Review of Books*, 68, no. 13 (August 19, 2021), 24–26; Iris Montero Sobrevilla, "The Slow Science of Swift Nature: Hummingbirds and Humans in New Spain," in Manning and Rood, eds., *Global Scientific Practice*, 127–46; Waldron, *Handbook of Ceramic Animal Symbols*, 113–125; Raffaele et al., *A Guide to the Birds of the West Indies*, 112–17, 320–29. Physician and naturalist Dr. Anthony Robinson (d. 1768), made 163 drawings of Jamaican birds.

87. Catesby, *Natural History*, I:10; J. Christopher Crocker, "My Brother the Parrot," in Gary Urton, ed., *Animal Myths and Metaphors in South America* (Salt Lake City: University of Utah Press, 1985), 13–47; N. F. R. Snyder, J. W. Wiley, and C. B. Kebler, *The Parrots of Luquillo: Natural History and Conservation of the Puerto Rican Parrot* (Los Angeles: Western Foundation of Vertebrate Zoology, 1987); M. I. Williams and D. W. Steadman, "The Historic and Prehistoric Distribution of Parrots (Psittacidae) in the West Indies," in Woods and Sergile, eds., *Biogeography of the West Indies*, 175–89; Thomas Boehrer, *Parrot Culture: Our 2,500-Year-Long Fascination with the World's Most Talkative Bird* (Philadelphia: University of Pennsylvania Press, 2004), 20, 50–55, 114, 152–53; Samuel T. Turvey, "A New Historical Record of Macaws on Jamaica," *Archives of Natural History*, 37, no. 2 (2010), 348–51; Matt Cameron, *Parrots: The Animal Answer Guide* (Baltimore: Johns Hopkins University Press, 2012), 4, 44, 87–88, 104, 173–76; Marcy Norton, "Going to the Birds: Animals as Things and Beings in Early Modernity," in Paula Findlen, ed., *Early Modern Things: Objects and Their Histories, 1500–1800* (New York: Routledge, 2013), 53–83; Mary Jane Berman et al., "The Bahama Archipelago," in Keegan et al., eds., *Oxford Handbook of Caribbean Archaeology*, 265; Waldron, *Handbook of Ceramic Animal Symbols*, 161–171.

88. Michael R. Gannon et al., *Bats of Puerto Rico: An Island Focus and a Caribbean Perspective* (Kingston, Jamaica: University of the West Indies, 2005); Armando Rodríguez-Durán and Thomas H. Kunz, "Biogeography of West Indian Bats; An Ecological Perspective," and Gary S. Morgan, "Patterns of Extinction in West Indian Bats," in Woods and Sergile, eds., *Biogeography of West Indies*, 355–68, and 369–407; Nathan S. Upham, "Past and Present of Insular Caribbean Mammals: Understanding Holocene Extinctions to Inform Modern Biodiversity Conservation," *Journal of Mammalogy*, 98, no. 4 (2017), 913–17; Burton K. Lim et al. "Phylogeography of Dominican Republic Bats and Implications for Systematic Relationships in the Neotropics," *Journal of Mammalogy*, 98, no. 4 (2017), 986–93; Ricardo Moratelli et al., "Caribbean Myotis (Chiroptera, Vespertilionidae), with description of a new species from Trinidad and Tobago," *Journal of Mammalogy*, 98, no. 4 (2017), 994–1008;

Waldron, *Handbook of Ceramic Animal Symbols*, 98–111; Manuel A. Garcia Arévalo, "The Bat and the Owl: Nocturnal Images of Death," in Fatima Bercht, Estrellita Brodsky, John Alan Farmer, and Dicey Taylor, eds., *Taíno: Pre-Columbian Art and Culture from the Caribbean* (New York: The Monacelli Press, 1997), 112–23.

89. Watts, *The West Indies*, 37–38; Arie Boomert, *The Indigenous Peoples of Trinidad and Tobago: From the First Settlers until Today* (Leiden: Sidestone Press, 2016), 6

90. Charles A. Woods et al., "Insular Patterns and Radiations of West Indian Rodents," in Woods and Sergile, eds., *Biogeography of the West Indies*, 335–54; Watlington, "The Physical Environment," esp. 44 (quote); Elizabeth S. Wing, "Pets and Camp Followers in the West Indies," in Elizabeth Reitz et al., eds., *Case Studies in Environmental Archaeology*, 2nd ed. (New York: Springer, 2008), 405–26; Michelle LeFebvre and Susan deFrance, "Guinea Pigs in the Pre-Columbian West Indies," *Journal of Island and Coastal Archaeology*, 9, no. 1 (2014), 16–44; Birgitta K. Kimura et al., "Origins of Pre-Columbian Guinea Pigs from Caribbean Archaeological Sites," *Journal of Archaeological Science Reports*, 5 (2016), 442–52; Waldron, *Handbook of Ceramic Animal Symbols*, 93–96; Christina M. Giovas, "The Beasts at Large—Perennial Questions and New Paradigms for Caribbean Translocation Research. Parts I & II: Mammalian Introductions in Cultural Context," *Environmental Archaeology*, 24, no. 2 (2019), 182–98; and 24, no. 3 (2019), 294–305; Michelle J. LeFebvre et al., "Bahamian Hutia (*Geocapromys ingrahami*) in the Lucayan Realm: Pre-Columbian Exploitation and Translocation," *Environmental Archaeology*, 24, no. 2 (2019), 115–31.

91. Newsom and Wing, *On Land and Sea*, 6, 80, 87, 93, 95, 107, 135, 137, 164, 180, 200, 202, 204, 210–11; Marion Schwartz, *A History of Dogs in the Early Americas* (New Haven, CT: Yale University Press, 1997), 76–78, 97–98, 164; Peter W. Stahl, "Early Dogs and Endemic South American Canids of the Spanish Main," *Journal of Anthropological Research*, 69, no. 4 (2013), 515–33; E. Plomp, "The Evolving Relationship Between Humans and Dogs in the Circum-Caribbean," *Archaeological Review from Cambridge*, 28, no. 2 (2013), 96–112; Sandrine Grouard, Sophia Perdikaris, and Karyne Debue, "Dog Burials Associated with Human Burials in the West Indies during the Early Pre-Columbian Ceramic Age (500 BC–600 AD)," *Anthropozoologica*, 48, no. 2 (2013), 447–65; Jason E. Laffoon et al., "The Movement and Exchange of Dogs in the Prehistoric Caribbean: An Isotopic Investigation," *International Journal of Osteoarchaeology*, 25 (2015), 454–65; Jeffrey P. Blick et al., "Dogs of the Bahamas and Caribbean: Evidence from Columbus's Diario, Historical Documents, and Archaeology," in R. Erdman and R. Morrison, eds., *Proceedings of the Fifteenth Symposium on the Natural History of the Bahamas* (San Salvador, Bahamas: Gerace Research Centre, 2016), 109–23; Waldron, *Handbook of Ceramic Animal Symbols*, 76–82; Jason E. Laffoon et al. "A Multi-isotope Investigation of Human and Dog Mobility and Diet in the Pre-colonial Antilles," *Environmental Archaeology*, 24, no. 2 (2019), 132–48; Fray Ramón Pané, *An Account of the Antiquities of the Indians*, ed. José Juan Arrom, trans. Susan C. Griswold (Durham, NC: Duke University Press, 1999), 28–29.

92. Albert Schwartz and Robert W. Henderson, *Amphibians and Reptiles of the West Indies: Descriptions, Distributions, and Natural History* (Gainesville: University Press of Florida, 1991); Waldron, *Handbook of Ceramic Animal Symbols*, 172–80; Corentin Bochaton et al., "Fossil Dipsadid Snakes from the Guadeloupe Islands (French West-Indies) and Their Interactions with Past Human Populations," *Geodiversitas*, 41, no. 2 (2019), 501–23; Church, *Paradise Destroyed*, 50–51; Gary S. Morgan et al., "The Cuban Crocodile (*Crocodylus rhombifer*) from Late Quaternary Underwater Cave Deposits in the Dominican Republic," *American Museum Novitates*, 3916 (December 2018), 1–56; Lawrence Waldron, "The Caimans of Carriacou," *Proceedings of XXV Congress of the International Association for Caribbean Archaeology* (Puerto Rico, 2013), 614–32.

93. Rafe M. Brown, "Frogs," in Gillespie and Clague, eds., *Encyclopedia of Islands*, 347–51; Hans Sloane, *A Voyage to the Islands Madeira, Barbados, Nieves, St Christophers, and Jamaica . . .*, 2 vols. (London: R. Bentley and M. Magnes, 1707–1725), I:lxv; M. P. Heinicke, W. E. Duellman, and S. B. Hedges, "Major Caribbean and Central American Frog Faunas Originated by Ancient Oceanic Dispersal," *Proceedings of the National Academy of Sciences USA*, 104 (2007), 10092–97; Hauser, *Mapping Water in Dominica*, 23, 136, 164, 180;

Schwartz and Henderson, *Amphibians and Reptiles of the West Indies*; Waldron, *Handbook of Ceramic Animal Symbols*, 183–93, 204–209.

94. Losos, *Lizards in an Evolutionary Tree*, x, xvii–xviii, 10, 12, 20, 21, 29, and passim; Matthew R. Helmus et al., "Island Biogeography of the Anthropocene," *Nature* 513 (September 25, 2014), 543–46; Emma Sherratt et al., "Amber Fossils Demonstrate Deep-Time Stability of Caribbean Lizard Communities," *Proceedings of the National Academy of Sciences of the United States of America*, 112 (2015), 9961–66; James T. Stroud and Jonathan B. Losos, "Ecological Opportunity and Adaptive Radiation," *Annual Review of Ecology, Evolution and Systematics*, 47 (2016), 507–32; Ambika Kamath and Jonathan B. Losos, "Does Ecological Specialization Transcend Scale? Habitat Partitioning among Individuals and Species of *Anolis* Lizards," *Evolution*, 71 (2017), 541–49; Waldron, *Handbook of Ceramic Animal Symbols*, 180–83.

95. Losos, *Lizards in an Evolutionary Tree*, 66, 69–70, 386, 409; Woods and Sergile, "Antilles, Biology," in Gillespie and Clague, eds., *Encyclopedia of Islands*, 27.

96. Archie Carr, *The Windward Road: Adventures of a Naturalist on Remote Caribbean Shores* (Gainesville: University Press of Florida, 2003 [orig. pub. 1956]), xxxi, passim; Carr, *"So Excellent a Fishe": A Natural History of Sea Turtles* (Gainesville: University Press of Florida, 2011 [orig. pub. 1967]), 13–15, passim; James J. Parsons, *The Green Turtle and Man* (Tallahassee: Florida State University Press, 1962), 2–3, 7, 10–16, 23–30, 35–37, 85–86, 94–95; Watts, *The West Indies*, 40, 61–62; Watlington, "The Physical Environment," 59; Newsom and Wing, *On Land and Sea*, 61, 63, 71,188, 213; Waldron, *Handbook of Ceramic Animal Symbols*, 195–209; Sharika D. Crawford, *The Last Turtlemen of the Caribbean: Waterscapes of Labor, Conservation, and Boundary Making* (Chapel Hill: University of North Carolina Press, 2020), 17–25.

97. Lawrence Waldron, *Pre-Columbian Art of the Caribbean* (Gainesville: University Press of Florida, 2019), 215–16; James Delbourgo, *Collecting the World: Hans Sloane and the Origins of the British Museum.* (Cambridge, MA: Harvard University Press, 2017), 117–25; Klinkenborg, ed., *Drake Manuscript*, f. 72; Keegan and Carlson, *Talking Taíno*, 16; Keith McE. Kevan, "Mid-eighteenth-century Entomology and Helminthology in the West Indies: Dr. James Grainger," *Journal of the Society for the Bibliography of Natural History*, 8, no. 3 (1977), 193–222. For the European context concerning insects, see three key works: Thomas Moffet's *Insectorum . . .* (1634), Robert Hooke's *Micrographia* (1665), and Bernard Mandeville's *Fable of the Bees* (1714). For an excellent appraisal of insects as pests, see Matthew Mulcahy and Stuart Schwartz, "Nature's Batallions: Insects as Agricultural Pests in the Early Modern Caribbean," *William and Mary Quarterly*, 3rd Ser., 75, no. 3 (2018), 1–32, and chapter in this volume.

98. Delbourgo, *Collecting the World*, 118; Klinkenborg, ed., *Drake Manuscript*, f. 78; Amy Butler Greenfield, *A Perfect Red: Empire, Espionage, and the Quest for the Color of Desire* (New York: HarperCollins, 2005), 115–16, 122, 165–67, 169, 173–74, 184–85; Peter C. Mancall, *Nature and Culture in the Early Modern Atlantic* (Philadelphia: University of Pennsylvania Press, 2018), 71–83, 111–32; Du Simitière Papers Relating to Natural History, 963.F 22e, as cited in Ianinni, *Fatal Revolutions*, 148; Newsom and Wing, *On Land and Sea*, 113. The best early illustrator of Caribbean insects was Maria Sibylla Merian, who will be discussed later. See also Higman, *Proslavery Priest*, 146–47, and plates 10, 11, 15, 146.

99. Geoffrey H. Wallace, "The History and Geography of Beeswax Extraction in the Northern Maya Lowlands, 1540–1700" (PhD diss., McGill University, 2020), 305 (quote). See also Ana María Falchetti, "La ofrenda y la semilla: Notas sobre el simbolismo del oro entre los Uwa," *Boletín Museo del Oro*, 43 (1997), 2–37, as cited in Allison Margaret Bigelow, *Mining Language: Racial Thinking, Indigenous Knowledge, and Colonial Metallurgy in the Early Modern Iberian World* (Chapel Hill: University of North Carolina Press, 2020), 27–28; and Rani T. Alexander and Héctor Hernández Álvarez, "Agropastoralism and Household Ecology in Yucatán after the Spanish Invasion," *Environmental Archaeology*, 23, no. 1 (2018), 69–79, DOI: 10.1080/14614103.2017.1342396. Thanks to Geoff Wallace for his assistance.

100. Angelica Marquez-Osuna, a Harvard University graduate student, kindly supplied this information, for which I am most grateful. See also Donald D. Brand, "The Honey Bee in New Spain and Mexico," *Journal of Cultural Geography*, 9, no. 1 (1988), 71–82; Julio A. Genaro, "A History of Systematic Studies of the Bees of Cuba," *Zootaxa*, 1195 (2006), 39–60; James E.

McClellan III, *Colonialism and Science: Saint Domingue in the Old Regime* (Baltimore: Johns Hopkins University Press, 1992), 33; and Eva Crane, *The World History of Beekeeping and Honey Hunting* (New York: Routledge, 1999), 362.

101. Robert H. MacArthur and Edward O. Wilson, *The Theory of Island Biogeography* (Princeton, NJ: Princeton University Press, 1967); Newsom and Wing, *On Land and Sea*, 17–18; Jonathan B. Losos and Robert E. Ricklefs, eds., *The Theory of Island Biogeography Revisited* (Princeton, NJ: Princeton University Press, 2010), esp. xi–xiv, 1–12, 52–87, 116–42, 388–438.

102. David Quammen, *The Song of the Dodo: Island Biogeography in an Age of Extinction* (New York: Scribner, 1997), esp. 17–20, 38, 136–37, 158, 174–75, 193, 252, 164, 378–79, 387–88, 414, 421; Shai Meiri and Pasquale Raia, "Dwarfism," and Pasquale Raia, "Gigantism," in Gillespie and Clague, eds., *Encyclopedia of Islands*, 235–23 and 372–76.

103. Woods and Sergile, "Antilles, Biology," in Gillespie and Clague, eds., *Encyclopedia of Islands*, 20–29; Lawrence R. Heaney and Steven M. Goodman, "Mammal Radiations," in Gillespie and Clague, eds., *Encyclopedia of Islands*, 589–91; Jose A. Ottenwalder, "Systematics and Biogeography of the West Indian Genus Solenodon," in Woods and Sergile, eds., *Biogeography of the West Indies*, 253–329; Morgan, "Patterns of Extinction in West Indian Bats," ibid., 369; Williams and Steadman, "The Historic and Prehistoric Distribution of Parrots," ibid., 175–89; Brian K. McNab, "Functional Adaptation to Island Life in the West Indies," ibid., 55–62; Ricklefs and Bermingham, "The West indies as a Laboratory," *Philosophical Transactions of the Royal Society*, 363 (2008), 2393–413; Klinkenborg, ed., *Drake Manuscript*, ff. 52–53, p. 260; Michael J. Jarvis, *In the Eye of All Trade: Bermuda, Bermudians, and the Maritime Atlantic World, 1680–1783* (Chapel Hill: University of North Carolina Press, 2010), 234.

104. R. E. Ricklefs and E. Bermingham, "History and the Species–Area Relationship in Lesser Antillean Birds," *American Naturalist*, 163 (2004), 227–39; Jacqueline Y. Miller and Lee D. Miller, "The Biogeography of the West Indian Butterflies (Lepidoptera): An Application of a Vicariance/Dispersalist Model," in Woods and Sergile, eds., *Biogeography of the West Indies*, 127–55, esp. 133; Losos, *Lizards in an Evolutionary Tree*, 241–42; Thomas Schoener, "The MacArthur-Wilson Equilibrium Model: A Chronicle of What It Said and How It Was Tested," in Losos and Ricklefs, eds., *The Theory of Island Biogeography Revisited*, 52–87, esp. 60–65; Robert E. Ricklefs, "Dynamics of Colonization and Extinction on Islands: Insights from Lesser Antillean Birds," ibid., 388–414; G. C. Mayer and R. M. Chipley, "Turnover in the Avifauna of Guana Island, British Virgin Islands," *Journal of Animal Ecology*, 61 (1992), 561–66.

105. Waldron, *Handbook of Ceramic Animal Symbols*, 60; David Spencer-Smith et al., "Biogeographical Affinities of the Butterflies of a 'Forgotten' Island: Mona (Puerto Rico)," *Bulletin of the Allyn Museum*, 121 (1988), 1–35; and David Spencer Smith et al., *The Butterflies of the West Indies and South Florida* (Oxford: Oxford University Press, 1994); Alice V. M. Samson and Jago Cooper, "History on Mona Island: Long-Term Human and Landscape Dynamics of an 'Uninhabited' Island, *New West Indian Guide*, 89, no. 1–2 (2015,) 30–50; Jago Cooper et al., "The Mona Chronicle: The Archaeology of Early Religious Encounter in the New World," *Antiquity*, 90, no. 352 (2016), 1054–71; A. Samson et al., "Artists before Columbus: A multi-method Characterization of the Materials and Practices of Caribbean Cave Art," *Journal of Archaeological Science*, 88 (2017), 24–36. https://doi.org/10.1016/j.jas.2017.09.012. See also A. Samson et al., "European Visitors in Native Spaces: Using Palaeography to Investigate Religious Dynamics in the New World," *Latin American Antiquity*, 27, no. 4 (2016), 443–61; Keegan et al., "The Role of Small Islands in Marine Subsistence Strategies," 635–54; and Keegan and Hofman, *Caribbean before Columbus*, 173–74.

106. William F. Keegan, "Island Shores and 'Long Pauses,'" in Fitzpatrick and Ross, eds., *Island Shores, Distant Pasts*, 11–20; Wing, "Pets and Camp Followers," 418, 420; Waldron, *Handbook of Ceramic Animal Symbols*, 96.

107. Andrzej T. Antczak and Corinne L. Hofman, "Dearchaizing the Caribbean Archaic," in Hofman and Antczak, eds., *Early Settlers of the Insular Caribbean*, 29–42; Rivera-Collazo, "Gone with the Waves," in ibid., 48.

108. Keegan et al., eds., *Oxford Handbook of Caribbean Archaeology*, 4, 127–130, 141–143, 198, 284, 286, 380, 394, 438, 442; Boomert, *Indigenous Peoples of Trinidad and Tobago*, 1–24.

109. For differing views on the migrations and their origins, see Keegan and Hofman, *Caribbean before Columbus*, 23–27; Keegan et al., eds., *Oxford Handbook of Caribbean Archaeology*, 62–63, 126–40, 155–70, 283–95, 391–406; Ivan Roksandic, ed., *Cuban Archaeology in the Caribbean* (Gainesville: University Press of Florida, 2016), esp. 7–32, 229–32.

110. Hofman and Antczak, eds., *Early Settlers*, esp. 30, 40, and works in preceding note.

111. Keegan and Hofman, *Caribbean before Columbus*, 23–50; Keegan et al., eds., *Oxford Handbook of Caribbean Archaeology*, esp. 126–40.

112. Christina M. Giovas and Scott M. Fitzpatrick, "Prehistoric Migration in the Caribbean: Past Perspectives, New Models, and the Ideal Free Distribution of West Indian Colonization," *World Archaeology*, 46, no. 4 (2014), 569–89; Keegan et al., eds., *Oxford Handbook of Caribbean Archaeology*, 131–132.

113. Keegan and Hofman, *Caribbean before Columbus*, 48–50; Giovas and Fitzpatrick, "Prehistoric Migration in the Caribbean," 569–89; Keegan, "Situating Jamaica," in Hofman and Antczak, eds., *Early Settlers*, 191–99; Callaghan, "On the Question of the Absence of Archaic Age Sites," 54–71; S. Scheffers et al., "Tsunamis, Hurricanes, the Demise of Coral Reefs and Shifts in Prehistoric Human Populations in the Caribbean," *Quarternary International*, 195 (2009), 69–87; and Jay B. Haviser, "Archaeological Evidence and the Potential Effects of Paleotsunami Events during the Archaic Age in the Southern Caribbean," in Hofman and Antczak, eds., *Early Settlers*, 57–63.

114. Keegan and Hofman, *Caribbean before Columbus*, 51–82; Keegan et al., eds., *Oxford Handbook of Caribbean Archaeology*, 62–63, 111–25, 184–97, 221–31; Keegan, "Island Shores and 'Long Pauses,'" in Fitzpatrick and Ross, eds., *Island Shores, Distant Pasts*, 11–20.

115. Irving Rouse, *The Tainos: Rise & Decline of the People Who Greeted Columbus* (New Haven, CT: Yale University Press, 1992); Keegan, "The 'Classic' Taino," in Keegan et al., eds., *Oxford Handbook of Caribbean Archaeology*, 70–83; Higman, *A Concise History*, 39.

116. Keegan and Hofman, *Caribbean before Columbus*, 13–14, 102–4, 112, 115–16, 138–39, 169, 246, 259; Ann H. Ross and Douglas H. Ubelaker, "A Morphometric Approach to Taino Biological Distance in the Caribbean," in Fitzpatrick and Ross, eds., *Island Shores, Distant Pasts*, 108–26; Alfredo Coppa et al., "New Evidence of Two Different Migratory Waves in the Circum-Caribbean Area during the Pre-Columbian period from the Analysis of Dental Morphological Traits," in Corinne L. Hofman et al., eds., *Crossing the Borders: New Methods and Techniques in the Study of Archaeological Materials from the Caribbean* (Tuscaloosa: University of Alabama Press, 2008), 195–213.

117. Ann H. Ross, William F. Keegan, Michael P. Pateman, and Colleen B. Young, "Faces Divulge the Origins of Caribbean Prehistoric Inhabitants," *Scientific Reports*, 10, no. 1 (2020), 1–9.

118. Kathrin Nägele et al., "Genomic Insights in Early Peopling of the Caribbean," *Science* (June 4, 2020), 1–9, 10.1126/science.aba8697; Daniel M. Fernandes et al., "A Genetic History of the Pre-contact Caribbean," *Nature*, https://www.biorxiv.org/content/10.1101/2020.06.01.126730v1. See also M. G. Vilar et al., "Genetic Diversity in Puerto Rico and Its Implications for the Peopling of the Island and the West Indies," *American Journal of Physical Anthropology*, 155 (2014), 352–68; F. Mendisco et al., "Where Are the Caribs? Ancient DNA from Ceramic Period Human Remains in the Lesser Antilles," *Philosophical Transactions of Royal Society. London B: Biological Sciences*, 370 (2015), https://doi.org/10.1098/rstb.2013.0388; H. Schroeder et al., "Origins and Genetic Legacies of the Caribbean Taino," *Proceedings of the National Academy of Sciences U.S.A.*, 115 (2018), 2341–46; M. A. Nieves-Colón et al., "Ancient DNA Reconstructs the Genetic Legacies of Pre-contact Puerto Rico Communities," *Molecular Biology and Evolution*, 37 (2020), 611–26.

119. Louis Allaire, "On the Historicity of Carib Migrations in the Lesser Antilles," *American Antiquity*, 45 (1981), 238–45; Allaire, "The Lesser Antilles before Columbus," and "The Caribs of the Lesser Antilles," in Wilson, ed., *The Indigenous People of the Caribbean*, 20–28 and 177–85; Allaire, "Ethnohistory of the Caribs," in Keegan et al., eds., *Oxford Handbook of Caribbean Archaeology*, 97–108; Keegan and Hofman, *Caribbean before Columbus*, 14–15, 229, 241–43. For the ceramics and movements of these peoples, see Cristiana Barreto, Helena Pinto Lima, Stéphen Rostain, and Corinne Hofman, eds., *Koriabo, from the Caribbean Sea to*

the Amazon River (Belém: Museu Paraense Emílio Goeldi, Leiden University, 2020), esp. 13–30, 33–53; and Corinne L. Hofman et al., "Island Networks: Transformations of Inter-community Social Relationships in the Lesser Antilles at the Advent of European Colonialism," *Journal of Island and Coastal Archaeology* (2020), DOI: 10.1080/15564894.2020.1748770.

120. Keegan and Hofman, *Caribbean before Columbus*, 202; Hofman and Antczak, eds., *Early Settlers*, 65–76, 123–30, 245–62; David W. Steadman et al., "Asynchronous Extinction of Late Quaternary Sloths on Continents and Islands," *Proceedings of the National Academy of Sciences*, 102 (2005), 11763–68; David W. Steadman and Anne Stokes, "Changing Exploitation of Terrestrial Vertebrates during the Past 3000 Years on Tobago, West Indies," *Human Ecology*, 30, no. 3 (September 2002), 339–67.

121. Keegan and Hofman, *Caribbean before Columbus*, 23–49, 152–55, 169; Jaime Pagán-Jiménez, "Human-Plant Dynamics in the Precolonial Antilles: A Synthetic Update," in Keegan et al., eds., *Oxford Handbook of Caribbean Archaeology*, 391–406.

122. Keegan and Hofman, *Caribbean before Columbus*, 58, 64, 224; Keegan et al., "The Role of Small Islands," 635–54; Giovas and Fitzpatrick, "Prehistoric Migration in the Caribbean," 569–89; Tom Brughmans et al., "Exploring Transformations in Caribbean Indigenous Social Networks through Visibility Studies: The Case of late Pre-colonial Landscapes in East-Guadeloupe (French West Indies)," *Journal of Archaeological Method and Theory*, 25 (2018), 475–519.

123. Keegan and Hofman, *Caribbean before Columbus*, 73; Sauer, *Early Spanish Main*, 53–54. For a good account of manioc or cassava, see B. W. Higman, *Jamaican Food: History, Biology, Culture* (Kingston, Jamaica: University of the West Indies Press, 2007), 33–34, 61–69.

124. Sloane, *Voyage to . . . Jamaica*, I:xxv; M. Arroyo-Kalin, "The Amazonian Formative: Crop Domestication and Anthropogenic Soils," *Diversity*, 2, no. 4 (2010), 473–504; K. M. Olsen, and B. A. Schaal, "Evidence on the Origin of Cassava: Phylogeography of *Manihot esculenta*," *Proceedings of the National Academy of Sciences of the United States of America*, 96, no. 10 (1999), 5586–91.

125.. Higman, *Concise History*, 27–28; Keegan and Hofman, *Caribbean before Columbus*, 135. Bill Keegan thinks the reason that manioc is considered so important is because it was vital to the Spanish. Cassava bread replaced hardtack on the continuing voyages of discovery and was essential to the enterprise of the Indies. Other native crops were not as important to the Spanish (communication, September 16, 2019).

126. Keegan and Hofman, *Caribbean before Columbus*, 105, 107, 210, 250; Corinne L. Hofman and Menno L. P. Hoogland, "Beautiful Tropical Islands in the Caribbean Sea: Human Responses to Floods and Droughts and the Indigenous Archaeological Heritage of the Caribbean," in Willem J. H. Willems and Henk P. J. van Schaik, eds., *Water and Heritage: Material, Conceptual and Spiritual Connections* (Leiden: Sidestone Press, 2015), 99–119; Basil A. Reid, ed., *The Archaeology of Caribbean and Circum-Caribbean Farmers (6000 BC–AD 1500)* (New York: Routledge, 2018); LeFebvre and deFrance, "Guinea Pigs," 16–44; Morsink, "Catalytic Environments," 149–60.

127. Jaime R. Pagán-Jiménez et al., "Early Dispersals of Maize and Other Food Plants into the Southern Caribbean and Northeastern South America," *Quaternary Science Reviews*, 123 (2015), 231–46; Alfredo E. Figueredo, "Manioc Dethroned and Maize Triumphant: Interpretations on the Ethnohistory and Archaeology of the Bahamas (with Sundry Notes on Relations of Production," *Journal of Caribbean Archaeology*, 15 (2015), 120–34; Mary Jane Berman and Deborah M. Pearsall, "At the Crossroads: Starch Grain and Phytolith Analyses in Lucayan Prehistory," *Latin American Antiquity*, 19, no. 2 (2008), 181–203; L. Antonio Curet, *Caribbean Paleodemography: Population, Culture History, and Sociopolitical Processes in Ancient Puerto Rico* (Tuscaloosa: University of Alabama Press, 2005), 164, 170–71; Peter E. Siegel, ed., *Ancient Borinquen: Archaeology and Ethnohistory of Native Puerto Rico* (Tuscaloosa: University of Alabama Press 2005), 70, 126, 180, 189.

128. Bain et al., "Landscape Transformation," 36–46; Boomert, *Indigenous Peoples of Trinidad*, 48; William F. Keegan, Roger W. Portell, and John Slapcinsky, "Changes in Invertebrate Taxa at Two Pre-Columbian Sites in Southwestern Jamaica, AD 800–1500," *Journal of Archaeological Science*, 30 (2003), 1607–17, esp. 1615; Reinaldo Funes Monzote, *From Rainforest to Cane Field in Cuba: An Environmental History since 1492*, trans. Alex Martin

(Chapel Hill: University of North Carolina Press, 2008), 7–15. For the percentage of forest remaining in the West Indies, see figure 1 at http://botany.si.edu/antilles/WestIndies. For the difficulties in distinguishing between fires ignited naturally as opposed to human action, see Isabel Rivera-Collazo, "*Por el camino verde:* Long-Term Tropical Socioecosystem Dynamics and the Anthropocene as Seen from Puerto Rico," *The Holocene,* 25 (2015), 1604–11; Maria A. Caffrey and Sally P. Horn, "Long-Term Fire Trends in Hispaniola and Puerto Rico from Sedimentary Charcoal: A Comparison of Three Records," *The Professional Geographer,* 67, no. 2 (2015), 229–41; and Lisa M. Kennedy, Sally P. Horn, and Kenneth H. Orvis, "A 4000-year Record of Fire and Forest History from Valle de Bao, Cordillero Central, Dominican Republic," *Palaeogeography, Palaeoclimatology, Palaeoecology,* 231 (2006), 279–90.

129. Siobhán B. Cooke et al., "Anthropogenic Extinction Dominates Holocene Declines of West Indian Mammals," *Annual Review of Ecology, Evolution, and Systematics,* 48 (2017), 301–27; David W. Steadman et al., "Late Holocene Historical Ecology: The Timing of Vertebrate Extirpation on Crooked Island, Commonwealth of the Bahamas," *Journal of Island and Coastal Archaeology,* 12, no. 4 (2017), 572–84; Upham, "Past and Present of Insular Caribbean Mammals," 913–17; Samuel T. Turvey et al., "The Last Survivors: Current Status and Conservation of the Non-volant Land Mammals of the Insular Caribbean," in Upham, "Past and Present Insular Caribbean Mammals," 918–36; Cooke et al., "The Extinction of *Xenothrix mcgregori,*" 937–49; David W. Steadman et al., "Vertebrate Community on an Ice-Age Caribbean Island," *Proceedings of the National Academy of Science, USA,* 112, no. 44 (2015), E5963–71; James Hansford et al., "Taxonomy-Testing and the 'Goldilocks Hypothesis': Morphometric Analysis of Species Diversity in Living and Extinct Hispaniolan Hutias," *Systematics and Biodiversity,* 10, no. 4 (2012), 491–507; David W. Steadman et al., "The Paleoecology and Extinction of Endemic Tortoises in the Bahamian Archipelago," *The Holocene,* 30, no. 3 (2020), 420–27.

130. Newsom and Wing, *On Land and Sea,* 4, 120–21, 200–201; Elizabeth S. Wing, "Native American Use of Animals in the Caribbean," in Woods and Sergile, eds., *Biogeography of the West Indies,* 418–518; Wing, "Pets and Camp Followers," 405–26; Elizabeth S. Wing, "Zooarchaeology of West Indian Land Mammals," in R. Borroto-Páez, C. A. Woods, and F. E. Sergile, eds., *Terrestrial Mammals of the West Indies: Contributions* (Gainesville: University of Florida Press, 2012), 341–56; Giovas, "Beasts at Large"; Michelle J. LeFebvre and Susan D. deFrance, "Pre-Columbian Animal Management and Manipulation: A Caribbean Island Perspective," in Reid, ed., *The Archaeology of Caribbean and Circum-Caribbean Farmers,* 149–70; Kimura et al., "Origins of Pre-Columbian Guinea Pigs," 442–52; LeFebvre and deFrance, "Guinea Pigs," 16–44; LeFebvre et al., "Bahamian Hutia," 115–31.

131. Gonzalo Fernández de Oviedo, *Historia general y natural de las Indias,* ed. Juan Pérez de Tudela Bueso, 2nd ed., 5 vols. (Madrid: Ediciones Atlas, 1992), 1:221–22, as cited in Norton, "The Chicken or the *Iegue,*" 28–60; Norton, "Going to the Birds," in Findlen, ed., *Early Modern Things,* 53–83. For close attachments between humans and peccaries, see R. A. Donkin, *The Peccary—With Observations on the Introduction of Pigs to the New World, Transactions of the American Philosophical Society,* 75, Pt. 5 (Philadelphia: American Philosophical Society, 1985), esp. 97–98.

132. C. Bochaton et al., "From a Thriving Past to an Uncertain Future: Zooarchaeological Evidence of two Millennia of Human Impact on a Large Emblematic Lizard (Iguana delicatissima) on the Guadeloupe Islands (French West Indies)," *Quaternary Science Reviews,* 150 (2016), 172–83; Keegan and Hofman, *Caribbean before Columbus,* 33, 37, 65, 70, 73, 84–85, 172; William F. Keegan et al., "A Crab-Shell Dichotomy Encore: Visualizing Saladoid Shell Tools," *Journal of Caribbean Archaeology,* 18, (2018), 1–33.

133. Keegan and Hofman, *Caribbean before Columbus,* 33, 34, 48; Nanny Carder and John G. Crock, "A Pre-Columbian Fisheries Baseline from the Caribbean," *Journal of Archaeological Science,* 39 (2012), 3115–24; Carder et al., "Fish Communities and Populations," 588–99; Ma. Magdalena Antczak and Andrzej T. Antczak, "Between Food and Symbol: The Role of Marine Molluscs in the Late Pre-Hispanic North-Central Venezuela," in Andrzej Antczak and Roberto Cipriani, eds., *Early Human Impact on Megamolluscs,* (Oxford: British Archaeological Reports, 2008), 231–45; Andrzej Antczak and Maria Magdalena Mackowiak

de Antczak, "Pre-Hispanic Fishery of the Queen Conch, Strombus gigas, on the Islands off the Coast of Venezuela," in Patricia Miloslavich and Eduardo Klein, eds., *Caribbean Marine Biodiversity: The Known and Unknown,* (Lancaster, PA: DEStech Publications, 2005), 213–43; Keegan et al., "Changes in Invertebrate Taxa," 1607–17.

134. Keegan and Hofman, *Caribbean before Columbus,* 172, 224; Todd J. Braje et al., "Archaeology, Historical Ecology and Anthropogenic Island Ecosystems," *Environmental Conservation,* 44, no. 3 (2017), 286–97; Marah J. Hardt, "Lessons from the Past: The Collapse of Jamaican Coral Reefs," *Fish and Fisheries,* 10 no. 2 (2008), 143–58; Scott M. Fitzpatrick, William F. Keegan, and Katherine Sullivan Sealey, "Human Impacts on Marine Environments in the West Indies during the Middle to Late Holocene," in T. C. Rick and J. M. Erlandson, eds., *Human Impacts on Ancient Marine Ecosystems: A Global Perspective* (Berkeley: University of California Press, 147–64; David W. Steadman and Sharyn Jones, "Long-Term Trends in Prehistoric Fishing and Hunting on Tobago, West Indies," *Latin American Antiquity,* 17 (2006), 316–34; Newsom and Wing, *On Land and Sea,* 102–4, 111–12, 134, 138–40, 165–66, 177–79, 187–88, 197; L. A. Carlson, W. F. Keegan, and S. M. Fitzpatrick, "Resource Depletion in the Prehistoric Northern West Indies," in Scott M. Fitzpatrick, ed., *Voyages of Discovery: The Archaeology of Islands* (London: Praeger, 2004), 85–107; S. R. Wing and E. S. Wing, "Prehistoric Fisheries in the Caribbean," *Coral Reefs,* 20 (2001), 1–8. A vigorous debate about the extent of prehistoric overfishing is in Julio A. Baisre, "Setting a Baseline for Caribbean Fisheries," *Journal of Island and Coastal Archaeology,* 5, no. 1 (January 2010), 120–47; and for the respondents, see ibid., 148–69; and for Baisre's rebuttal, ibid., 170–72. See also Rick J. Schulting et al., "Six Centuries of Adaptation to a Challenging Island Environment: AMS 14C Dating and Stable Isotopic Analysis of Pre-Columbian Human Remains from the Bahamian Archipelago Reveal Dietary Trends," *Quaternary Science Reviews,* 254 (2021), 106780.

135. Carder et al. "Fish Communities and Populations," 588–99; Giovas, "Pre-Columbian Amerindian Lifeways, 161–90; William F. Keegan et al., "Child Labor in Saladoid St. Thomas, U.S.V.I. (300–500 CE)," *Journal of Anthropological Archaeology,* 53 (2019), 222–28; A. S. Poteate et al., "Intensified Mollusk Exploitation on Nevis (West Indies) Reveals Six Centuries of Sustainable Exploitation," *Archaeological and Anthropological Sciences,* 7 (2015), 361–74; Newsom and Wing, *On Land and Sea,* 187–88, 193. A study of Guadeloupe has found similar evidence, but there the reef system was not all that rich: S. Grouard, "Faunal Remains Associated with Late Saladoid and Post-Saladoid Occupations at Anse a la Gourde, Guadeloupe, West Indies: Preliminary Results," *Archaeo Fauna,* 10 (2001), 71–98. Perhaps the relatively late development of the island (not settled till about AD 30–210) and its large relative area (1702 square kilometers, compared to Anguilla's 188) explains the lack of pressure there on marine resources.

136. Keegan and Hofman, *Caribbean before Columbus,* 128–36, 171–73, 176, 204, 228 176; Fitzpatrick, Keegan, and Sealey, "Human Impacts on Marine Environments," in Rick and Erlandson, eds., *Human Impacts on Ancient Marine Ecosystems,* 147–64.

137. Keegan and Carlson, *Talking Taíno,* 37–38; Morsink, "The Power of Salt," 266; Boomert, *Indigenous Peoples of Trinidad and Tobago,* 18; Crock, Carder, and Dorshow, "'Marineness,'" 199–210; Christine M. Giovas, "Though She Be but Little: Resource Resilience, Amerindian Foraging, and Long-Term Adaptive Strategies in the Grenadines, West Indies," *Journal of Island and Coastal Archaeology,* 11 (2016), 238–63. For interesting parallels between Spain's southwestern coast and the Caribbean with regard to fishing, see the forthcoming work of Molly A. Warsh.

138. Waldron, *Handbook of Ceramic Animal Symbols,* 210–11; Waldron, *Pre-Columbian Art of the Caribbean,* 54, 171, 195–98, 279, 311, 314, 323; Klinkenborg, ed., *Drake Manuscript,* f. 38; Keegan and Carlson, *Talking Taíno,* 21–30, 36, 124, 139, 140; Keegan et al., eds., *Oxford Handbook of Caribbean Archaeology,* 457; Sarah Barber, "Indigeneity and Authority in the Lesser Antilles: The Warners Revisited," in L. H. Roper, ed., *The Torrid Zone: Caribbean Colonization and Cultural Interaction in the Long Seventeenth Century* (Columbia: University of South Carolina Press, 2018), 46–57, esp. 48; Ulises M. González–Herrera, "Food Preparation and Dietary Preferences among the Arawak Aboriginal Communities of Cuba," in Roksandic, ed., *Cuban Archaeology,* 168–84, esp. 174. For a scientific perspective, see Andrea

M. Bernard et al., "Genetic Connectivity of a Coral Reef Ecosystem Predator: The Population Genetic Structure and Evolutionary History of the Caribbean Reef Shark (Carcharhinus perezi)," *Journal of Biogeography*, 44 (2017), 2488–500.

139. Menno L. P. Hoogland and Corinne L. Hofman, "Archaeological Investigations at Spanish Water, Curaçao," *Proceedings of the Twenty-Third Congress of the International Association for Caribbean Archaeology* (Antigua, 2011), 631–40; Crock et al., "Marineness," 199–210; Keegan and Hofman, *Caribbean before Columbus*, 133–34; Keegan and Carlson, *Talking Taíno*, 137; William F. Keegan, "The Ecology of Lucayan Arawak Fishing Practices," *American Antiquity*, 51, no. 4 (October 1986), 816–25; David Abulafia, *The Discovery of Mankind: Atlantic Encounters in the Age of Columbus* (New Haven, CT: Yale University Press, 2008), 3, 5, 122; Annelou Van Gijn and Corinne L. Hofman, "Were They Used as Tools? An Exploratory Functional Study of Abraded Potsherds from Two Pre-colonial Sites on the Island of Guadeloupe, Northern Lesser Antilles," *Caribbean Journal of Science*, 44, no. 1 (2008), 21–35; Richard Price, "Caribbean Fishing and Fishermen: A Historical Sketch," *American Anthropologist*, 68, no. 6 (December 1966), 1363–83.

140. Allaire, "Ethnohistory of the Caribs," in Keegan et al., eds., *Oxford Handbook of Caribbean Archaeology*, 100–101; Keegan and Hofman, *Caribbean before Columbus*, 75, 99, 107, 177, 183, 185–87, 202, 251; Joost Morsink, "Exchange as a Social Contract: A Perspective from the Microscale," in Keegan et al., eds., *Oxford Handbook of Caribbean Archaeology*, 320; Morsink, "The Power of Salt," 34, 228, 236–46.

141. Keegan and Hofman, *Caribbean before Columbus*, 65, 74; Susan D. Defrance, "Zooarchaeology in the Caribbean: Current Research and Future Prospects," in Keegan et al., eds., *Oxford Handbook of Caribbean Archaeology*, 378–90; Edwin F. Crespo-Torres et al., "The Study of Pre-Columbian Human Remains in the Caribbean Archipelago: From Descriptive Osteology to a Bioarchaeological Approach," in ibid., 436–51; Hayley Mickleburgh, "Reading the Dental Record: A Dental Anthropological Approach to Foodways, Health and Disease, and Crafting in the Pre-Columbian Caribbean" (PhD diss., University of Leiden, 2013); Jason Laffoon and Bart de Vos, "Diverse Origins, Similar Diets: An Integrated Isotopic Perspective from Anse à la Gourde, Guadeloupe," in Hofman and van Diijvenbdoe, eds., *Communities in Contact*, 187–204; Watts, *The West Indies*, 62; Yadira Chinique de Armas and William Pestle, "Assessing the Association between Subsistence Strategies and the Timing of Weaning among Indigenous Archaeological Populations of the Caribbean," *International Journal of Osteoarchaeology*, 28 (2018), 492–509; Boomert, *Indigenous Peoples of Trinidad and Tobago*, 71, 84; Davis, *The Gulf*, 35; Edwin F. Crespo-Torres, "Ancient Bones Tell Stories: Osteobiography of Human Remains from Tibes," in L. Antonio Curet and Lisa M. Stringer, eds., *Tibes: People, Power, and Ritual at the Center of the Cosmos* (Tuscaloosa, AL: University of Alabama Press, 2010), 191–208, esp. 203.

142. L. Antonio Curet, "The Archaeological Perspective: Comment on Julio Baisre's 'Setting a Baseline for Caribbean Fisheries,'" *Journal of Island and Coastal Archaeology*, 5 (2010), 152–55; Dave Davis and Kevin Oldfield, "Archaeological Reconnaissance of Anegada, British Virgin Islands," *Journal of Caribbean Archaeology*, 4 (2003), 1–11; Fitzpatrick et al., "Human Impacts on Marine Environments," 147–64, esp. 148; Loren McClenachan and Andrew B Cooper, "Extinction Rate, Historical Population Structure and Ecological Role of the Caribbean Monk Seal," *Proceedings of the Royal Society, Biological Sciences*, 275 (2008), 1351–58; Jeremy B. C. Jackson, "What Was Natural in the Coastal Oceans?" *Proceedings of the National Academy of Sciences*, 98, no. 10 (May 8, 2001), 5411–18; J. B. C. Jackson, "Reefs since Columbus," *Coral Reefs*, 16, suppl. (1997), S23–S32.

143. Berman et al., "Bahama Archipelago," 264–80; W. C. Schaffer et al., "Lucayan-Taino Burials from Preacher's Cave, Eleuthera, Bahamas," *International Journal of Osteoarchaeology*, 22, no. 1 (2012), 45–69; Keegan and Carlson, *Talking Taíno*, 7, 57–58.

144. Sauer, *Early Spanish Main*, 32, 35, 77, 87–91, 93, 99, 159–60, 191, 194, 213, 249–50, 254, 283; Luis N. Rivera-Pagán, "Freedom and Servitude: Indigenous Slavery and the Spanish Conquest of the Caribbean," in Sued-Badillo, ed., *General History of the Caribbean*, 1: 316–62; Murdo MacLeod, *Spanish Central America: A Socio-economic History, 1520–1720* (Berkeley: University of California Press, 1973), 52; William L. Sherman, *Forced Native Labor in Sixteenth-Century Central America* (Lincoln: University of Nebraska Press, 1979),

3, 20, 28–29, 33–34, 39–67, 82; David R. Radell, "The Indian Slave Trade and Population of Nicaragua during the Sixteenth Century," in William M. Denevan, ed., *The Native Population of the Americas in 1492*, 2nd ed. (Madison University of Wisconsin Press, 1992), 67–76; Erin Woodruff Stone, "Chasing 'Caribs': Defining Zones of Legal Indigenous Enslavement in the Circum-Caribbean, 1493–1542," in Jeff Fynn-Paul and Damian Alan Pargas, eds., *Slaving Zones: Cultural Identities, Ideologies, and Institutions is the Evolution of Global Slavery* (Boston: Brill, 2018), 118–47; Stephan Lenik, "Carib as a Colonial Category: Comparing Ethnohistorical and Archaeological Evidence from Dominica, West Indies," *Ethnohistory*, 59, no. 1 (2012), 79–107. For a general overview, see Andrés Reséndez, *The Other Slavery: The Uncovered Story of Indian Enslavement in America* (Boston: Houghton Mifflin Harcourt, 2016).

145. Genaro Rodríguez Morel, "The Sugar Economy of Española in the Sixteenth Century," in Stuart B. Schwartz, ed., *Tropical Babylons: Sugar and the Making of the Atlantic World, 1450–1680* (Chapel Hill: University of North Carolina Press, 2004), 87–88, 103 (quote); Dicey Taylor, Marco Biscione, and Peter G. Roe, "Epilogue: The Beaded Zemi in the Pigorini Museum," in Bercht et al., eds., *Taíno*, 158–69; Joanna Ostapkowicz, Fiona Brock, Alex C. Wiedenhoeft, Rick Schulting, and Donatella Saviola, "Integrating the Old World into the New: An 'Idol from the West Indies,'" *Antiquity*, 91, no. 359 (2017), 1314–29. See also Joanna Ostapkowicz and Lee Newsom, "'Gods Adorned with Embroiderer's Needle': The Materials, Making, and Meaning of a Taíno Cotton Reliquary," *Latin American Antiquity*, 23, no. 3 (2012), 300–326; Ostapkowicz, "'Made . . . with Admirable Artistry': The Context, Manufacture and History of a Taíno Belt," *Antiquaries Journal*, 93 (2013), 287–317; Ostapkowicz et al., "To Produce 'A Pleasing Effect': Taíno Shell and Stone Cibas and Spanish Cuentas in the Early Colonial Caribbean," *Beads*, 30 (2018), 3–15; and Ostapkowicz, "New Wealth from an Old World: Glass, Jet and Mirrors in the 16th Century Indigenous Caribbean," in Dirk Brandherm et al., eds., *Gifts, Goods and Money: Comparing Currency and Circulation Systems in Past Societies* (Oxford, UK: Archaeopress, 2018), 153–93.

146. Nicholas J. Saunders, "Shimmering Worlds: Brilliance, Power, and Gold in Pre-Columbian Panama," in Nicholas J. Saunders, John W. Hoopes, and Thomas Gilcrease, eds., *To Capture the Sun: Gold of Ancient Panama* (Tulsa: University of Oklahoma Press, 2011), 79–113; Bigelow, *Mining Language*, 23–101, esp. 23, 33–34.

147. Linda Newson, "The Depopulation of Nicaragua in the Sixteenth Century," *Journal of Latin American Studies*, 14 (1982), 253–86; C. S. Alexander, "Margarita Island, Exporter of People," *Journal of Inter-American Studies*, 3 (October 1961), 548–57; William F. Keegan, *The People Who Discovered Columbus: The Prehistory of the Bahamas* (Gainesville: University of Florida Press, 1992), 218–22; Tessa Murphy, "Kalinago Colonizers: Indigenous People and the Settlement of the Lesser Antilles," in Roper, ed., *The Torrid Zone*, 17–30.

148. David Wheat, "Afro-Portuguese Maritime World and Foundations of Spanish Caribbean Society, 1570–1640" (PhD diss., Vanderbilt University, 2009), 48–49; Jerome S. Handler, "The Amerindian Slave Population of Barbados in the Seventeenth and Eighteenth Centuries," *Caribbean Studies*, 8 (1968), 38–64; Jerome S. Handler, "Amerindians and Their Contributions to Barbadian Life in the Seventeenth Century," *Journal of Barbados Museum and Historical Society*, 35, no. 3 (1977), 189–210; Carolyn Arena, "Indian Slaves from Guiana in Seventeenth-Century Barbados," *Ethnohistory*, 64, no. 1 (January 2017), 65–90; Carolyn Arena, "Aphra Behn's *Oroonoko*, Indian Slavery and the Anglo-Dutch Wars," in Roper, ed., *The Torrid Zone*, 31–45; Carolyn Arena, *Yarico's Caribbean: Indigenous Trade, Diplomacy, and Enslavement in the 17th Century* (Chapel Hill: University of North Carolina Press, forthcoming); Richard Ligon, "A Topographicall Description . . . of the Yland of Barbados . . .," 1657, British Library; Alan Gallay, *The Indian Slave Trade: The Rise of the English Empire in the American South, 1670–1717* (New Haven, CT: Yale University Press, 2003); Brett Rushforth, *Bonds of Alliance: Indigenous and Atlantic Slaveries in New France* (Chapel Hill: University of North Carolina Press, 2013), 165–73, 299–367.

149. Elena Schneider and Paul Conrad have generously helped me with this topic. See Christon I. Archer, "The Deportation of Barbarian Indians from the Internal Provinces of New Spain, 1789–1810," *The Americas*, 29 (January 1973), 376–85; Evelyn Powell Jennings, "State Enslavement in Colonial Havana, 1763–1790," in Verene A. Shepherd, ed.,

Slavery without Sugar: Diversity in Caribbean Economy and Society Since the 17th Century (Gainesville: University Press of Florida, 2002), 152–82, esp. 160, 162; Jason M. Yaremko, "Colonial Wars and Indigenous Geopolitics: Aboriginal Agency, the Cuba-Florida-Mexico Nexus, and the Other Diaspora," *Canadian Journal of Latin American & Caribbean Studies*, 35, 70 (2010), 165–96; Elena A. Schneider, *The Occupation of Havana: War, Trade, and Slavery in the Atlantic World* (Chapel Hill: University of North Carolina Press, 2018), 77–78, 82, 147, 151, 190, 208, 250, 261; Paul Conrad, "Indians, Convicts, and Slaves: An Apache Diaspora to Cuba at the turn of the Nineteenth-Century," in Bonnie Martin and James F. Brooks, eds., *Linking the Histories of Slavery: North America and Its Borderlands* (Santa Fe: School for Advanced Research Press, 2015), 67–95; Sigfrido Vázques Cienfuegos and Antonio Santamaria Garcia, "Indio foráneos en Cuba a principios del siglo XIX: historia de un suceso en el contexto de la movilidad poblacional y la geoestrategia del imperio español," *Colonial Latin American Historical Review*, 2nd Ser., 1, no. 1 (Winter 2013), 1–34; Gabino La Rosa Corzo, *Runaway Slave Settlements in Cuba: Resistance and Repression*, trans. Mary Todd (Chapel Hill, University of North Carolina Press, 2003 [orig. pub. 1988]), 40, 88–90.

150. For general context and other forms of slavery, see, for example, William G. Clarence-Smith and David Eltis, "White Servitude" in David Eltis and Stanley L. Engerman, eds., *The Cambridge World History of Slavery*, vol. 3, *AD 1420–AD 1804* (New York: Cambridge University Press, 2011), 132–59; and David Wheat, "Mediterranean Slavery, New World Transformations: Galley Slaves in the Spanish Caribbean, 1578–1635," *Slavery & Abolition*, 31, no. 3 (2010), 327–44.

151. Watts, *The West Indies*, 104–5, 107–8, 115–26, 134, 198–99, 547 n. 13, esp. 115 and 125; Exquemelin, *The Buccaneers of America*, 50 [he also claimed that hunters killed a hundred pigs for every ten or so they dressed]: Philip P. Boucher, *France and the American Tropics to 1700: Tropics of Discontent?* (Baltimore: Johns Hopkins University Press, 2008), 123]; Alfred W. Crosby, Jr., *The Columbian Exchange: Biological and Cultural Consequences of 1492* (Westport, CT: Greenwood, 1972), 74–121; Virginia DeJohn Anderson, *Creatures of Empire: How Domestic Animals Transformed Early America* (New York: Oxford University Press, 2004), 121; Lauren Derby, "Bringing the Animals Back In: Writing Quadrupeds into the Environmental History of Latin America and the Caribbean," *History Compass*, 9, no. 8 (2011), 602–21; Jean-Pierre Tardieu, "Cimarrón-Maroon-Marron: An Epistemological Note," *Outre-Mers: Revue d'Histoire*, 94, nos. 350–51 (2006), 237–47. The central concept seems to be *cima*, or "peak," perhaps a reference to feral cattle escaping to mountainous interiors (thanks to Molly Warsh).

152. Robert Cunninghame Graham et al., *Horses of the Conquest: A Study of the Steeds of the Spanish Conquest* (Norman: University of Oklahoma Press, 1949); John Grier Varner and Jeannette Johnson Varner, *Dogs of the Conquest* (Norman: University of Oklahoma Press, 1983); Norton, "The Chicken or the *Iegue*," esp. 29, 32, 45; Anderson, *Creatures of Empire*, 97; Elizabeth J. Reitz, "The Spanish Colonial Experience and Domestic Animals," *Historical Archaeology*, 26, no. 1 (1992), 84–91. For the diversity of the earliest settlers and their lack of dietary adaptation, see T. Douglas Price et al., "Home Is the Sailor: Investigating the Origins of the Inhabitants of La Isabela, the First European Settlement in the New World," *Current Anthropology*, 61, no. 5 (October 2020), 583–602.

153. Selina Brace et al., "Evolutionary History of the Nesophontidae, the Last Unplaced Recent Mammal Family," *Molecular Biology and Evolution*, 33 (2016), 3095–103, esp. 3095; Richard S. Dunn, *Sugar and Slaves: The Rise of the Planter Class in the English West Indies, 1624–1713* (Chapel Hill: University of North Carolina Press, 1972), 191, 275; William Beckford, *Descriptive Account of the Island of Jamaica...*, 2 vols. (London: T and J. Egerton, 1790), 1:56; Knight, *The Natural, Moral, and Political History of Jamaica*, 549; Kevan, "Mid-Eighteenth-Century Entomology," esp. 199; Bonham C. Richardson, *Economy and Environment in the Caribbean: Barbados and the Windwards in the late 1800s* (Gainesville: University Press of Florida, 1997), 156; J. R. Ward, *British West Indian Slavery, 1750–1834: The Process of Amelioration* (Oxford, UK: Clarendon Press, 1988), 97; Nigel Turvey, *The Cane Toads: A Tale of Sugar, Politics, and Flawed Science* (Sydney, Australia: Sydney University Press, 2013), 27–29. See also Robert Graham to Angus MacBean, June 6, 1785, Graham of Gartmore Papers, NLS, Acc. 11335/181; Rev. William Smith, *A Natural History of Nevis, and the Rest*

of the English Leeward Islands in America (Cambridge: J. Bentham, 1745), 209; Watts, *The West Indies*, 120, 153, 163–64, 215, 429, 515; J. L. Carstens, *A General Description of All the Danish, American or West Indian Islands*, ed. and trans. Arnold Highfield (St. Croix: Virgin Islands Humanities Council, 1997), 120; and Joshua Peterkin, *A Treatise on Planting* . . . (St. Christophers, Basseterre, St. Kitts and Nevis: E. L. Low, 1790), 44. My thanks to Matt Mulcahy for some of these references.

154. Norton, "The Chicken or the *Iegue*," 28–60; Norton, "Going to the Birds," 53–83; Crosby, *The Columbian Exchange*, 97; Louise. E. Robbins, *Elephant Slaves and Pampered Parrots: Exotic Animals in Eighteenth-Century Paris* (Baltimore: Johns Hopkins University Press, 2002), 23–31, 117, 125–30. For a good overview of the various introductions of terrestrial vertebrate species into the Caribbean since the beginning of human occupation, see Melissa E. Kemp et al., "7000 Years Of Turnover: Historical Contingency and Human Niche Construction Shape the Caribbean's Anthropocene Biota," *Proceedings of the Royal Society B*, 287 (2020), http://dx.doi.org/10.1098/rspb.2020.0447.

155. Karl Jacoby, "Slaves by Nature? Domestic Animals and Human Slaves," *Slavery & Abolition*, 15 (1994), 89–99; Philip D. Morgan, "Slaves and Livestock in Eighteenth-Century Jamaica: Vineyard Pen, 1750–175," *WMQ*, 3rd Ser., 52 (1995), 47–76; Anya Zilberstein, "Bastard Breadfruit and Other Cheap Provisions: Early Food Science for the Welfare of the Lower Orders," *Early Science and Medicine*, 21, no. 5 (2016), 492–508, esp. 507; David Lambert, "Runaways and Strays: Rethinking (Non)Human Agency in Caribbean Slave Societies," in Sharon Wilcox and Stephanie Rutherford, eds., *Historical Animal Geographies* (Abingdon, UK: Routledge 2018), 185–98.

156. David Lambert, "Master-Horse-Slave: Mobility, Race and Power in the British West Indies, c. 1780–1838," *Slavery & Abolition*, 36 (2015), 618–41; Ligon, "A Topographicall Description," 1657, British Library; Reinaldo Funes Monzote, "Animal Labor and Protection in Cuba: Changes in Relationships with Animals in the Nineteenth Century," trans. A. Hidalgo, in Martha Few and Zeb Tortorici, eds., *Centering Animals in Latin American History* (Durham, NC: Duke University Press, 2013), 209–43; Philippe Girard, *Toussaint Louverture: A Revolutionary Life* (New York: Basic Books, 2016), 33, 58–60; Sudhir Hazareesingh, *Black Spartacus: The Epic Life of Toussaint Louverture* (New York: Farrar, Straus, and Giroux, 2020), 2, 14, 22, 213, 282; David A. Bell, *Men on Horseback: The Power of Charisma in the Age of Revolution* (New York: Farrar, Straus, and Giroux, 2020), 14–15, 139; Sara E. Johnson, "'You Should Give Them Blacks to Eat': Waging Inter-American Wars of Torture and Terror," *American Quarterly*, 61, no. 1 (March 2009), 65–92; Christopher M. Blakley, *If We Were Dogs: Human-Animal Relationships and the Making of British Atlantic Slavery* (Baton Rouge: Louisiana State University Press, forthcoming).

157. Funes Monzote, *From Rainforest to Cane Field in Cuba*, 17–19; David Wheat, *Atlantic Africa and the Spanish Caribbean, 1570–1640* (Chapel Hill, NC: University of North Carolina Press, 2016), 11–12, 68, 182, 185–87, 190–99, 209–11; Andrew Sluyter, *Black Ranching Frontiers: African Cattle Herders of the Atlantic World, 1500–1900* (New Haven, CT: Yale University Press, 2012), 19–60; Terry G. Jordan, *North American Cattle-Ranching Frontiers: Origins, Diffusion, and Differentiation* (Albuquerque: University of New Mexico Press, 1993).

158. Wheat, *Atlantic Africa and the Spanish Caribbean*, 11–12, 18, 26–27, 117–18, 150–54, 168, 181–95, 197–215.

159. Funes Monzote, *From Rainforest to Cane Field in Cuba*, 20–25, 39–43, 59–82; Alejandro de la Fuente, *Havana and the Atlantic in the Sixteenth Century* (Chapel Hill: University of North Carolina Press, 2008), 21, 32–33, 119, 127–33; John R. McNeill, *Atlantic Empires of France and Spain: Louisbourg and Havana, 1700–1763* (Chapel Hill: University of North Carolina Press, 1985), 174.

160. Jarvis, *In the Eye of All Trade*, 80, 89–90, 277; Jennifer L. Anderson, *Mahogany: The Costs of Early American Luxury* (Cambridge, MA: Harvard University Press, 2012), 92–94.

161. Ibid., 24–25, 231–32; Antonio Barrera, "Local Herbs, Global Medicines: Commerce, Knowledge, and Commodities in Spanish America," in Pamela H. Smith and Paula Findlen, eds., *Merchants and Marvels: Commerce, Science, and Art in Early Modern Europe* (New York: Routledge, 2002), 163–81; McNeill, *Mosquito Empires*, 30–31; McNeill,

"Ecological Atlantic," in Canny and Morgan, eds., *Oxford Handbook of the Atlantic World*, 300; J. Harry Bennett, "William Whaley, Planter of Seventeenth-Century Jamaica," *Agricultural History*, 40, no. 2 (1966), 113–23.

162. John Taylor, *Jamaica in 1687: The Taylor Manuscript at the National Library of Jamaica*, ed. David Buissseret (Kingston, Jamaica: University of the West Indies Press, 2008), 295; *The laws of Jamaica passed by the assembly, and confirmed by His majesty in council, Feb. 23. 1683: to which is added, A short account of the island and government thereof, with an exact map of the island* (London: H. Hills, 1683, 105–14; James Robertson, "Making Jamaica English: Priorities and Processes," in Roper, ed., *The Torrid Zone*, 104–17, esp. 115.

163. Anderson, *Mahogany*, 3, 4–5, 7, 8, 14, and passim.

164. Anderson, *Mahogany*, 214, 216–21, 231; Chandra Mukerji, *Territorial Ambitions and the Gardens of Versailles* (Cambridge: Cambridge University Press, 1997), 73–82; Boucher, *France and the American Tropics*, 124.

165. Boomgaard, "The Tropical Rain Forests of Suriname," 207–35.

166. Watts, *The West Indies*, 154–55, 168, 184–85, 193, 195, 202–3, 219 (quote), 221–23, 231, 238, 301, 325, 393–95, 398–99, 434–35, 438; Bradley and Norton, eds., *An Inventory of Breeding Seabirds*, 184; J. H. Galloway, *The Sugar Cane Industry: An Historical Geography from Its Origins to 1914* (Cambridge: Cambridge University Press, 1989), 113; Carl Bridenbaugh and Roberta Bridenbaugh, *No Peace beyond the Line: The English in the Caribbean, 1624–1690* (New York: Oxford University Press, 1972), 185; McNeill, *Mosquito Empires*, 28. Other islands did not move quite as rapidly as Barbados to denude their forests, but a similar process occurred. Thus heavily wooded Montserrat, which turned to sugar cultivation in the 1650s, had lost a third of its forest a generation later. By the 1770s, the island was almost completely bare of trees. By the early eighteenth century, French Martinique was importing fuel for its sugar mills. See Lydia M. Pulsipher, *Seventeenth-Century Montserrat: An Environmental Impact Statement* (Norwich, UK: GEO Books, 1986), 41; Clarissa T. Kimber, *Martinique Revisited: The Changing Plant Geographies of a West Indian Island* (College Station: Texas A&M University Press, 1988), 176, 181, 209, 212–13; and also more generally Richard H. Grove, *Green Imperialism: Colonial Expansion, Tropical Island Edens and the Origins of Environmentalism, 1600–1860* (New York: Cambridge University Press, 1995), 5, 63–71, 269–84, 292–97.

167. Funes Monzote, *From Rainforest to Cane Field in Cuba*, 3, 15–126, 131–34, 270; McNeill, *Mosquito Empires*, 27–32; Clifford L. Staten, *The History of Cuba* (New York: St. Martin's Press, 2005), 20; Dale Tomich, "World Slavery and Caribbean Capitalism: The Cuban Sugar Industry, 1760–1869," *Theory and Society*, 20, no. 3 (June 1991), 297–319.

168. Sidney W. Mintz, *Sweetness and Power: The Place of Sugar in Modern History* (New York: Penguin, 1985), esp. 21–73; Galloway, *Sugar Cane Industry*; B. W. Higman, "The Sugar Revolution," *Economic History Review*, 2nd Ser., 53 (May 2000), 213–38; B. W. Higman, "The Making of the Sugar Revolution," in Alvin O. Thompson, ed., *In the Shadow of the Plantation: Caribbean History and Legacy—in Honour of Professor Emeritus Woodville K. Marshall* (Kingston, Jamaica: Ian Randle, 2002), 40–71; Schwartz, ed., *Tropical Babylons*, 3–21, 85–157, 289–330; Justin Roberts, *Slavery and the Enlightenment in the British Atlantic, 1750–1807* (New York: Cambridge University Press, 2013), esp. 16–79; Caitlin Rosenthal, *Accounting for Slavery: Masters and Management* (Cambridge, MA: Harvard University Press, 2018), esp. 9–63, 69–70.

169. Anderson, *Mahogany*, 75; Higman, *Jamaica Surveyed*, 5, 78–79, 80–84, 291; Buisseret, ed., *Rural Images*, 91–167.

170. Watts, *West Indies*, 383–84, 391–92, 397–447, 533, 538; Roberts, *Slavery and the Enlightenment*, 13, 144–53; Stuart McCook, *States of Nature: Science, Agriculture, and Environment in the Spanish Caribbean, 1760–1940* (Austin: University of Texas Press, 2002), 79–81.

171. Chris Evans, "The Plantation Hoe: The Rise and Fall of an Atlantic Commodity," *WMQ*, 3rd Ser., 69, no. 1 (2012), 71–100. J. R. Ward, "The Amelioration of British West Indian Slavery, 1750–1834: Technical Change and the Plough," *NWIG*, 63, nos. 1/2 (1989), 41–58.

172. Randy M. Browne, *Surviving Slavery in the British Caribbean* (Philadelphia: University of Pennsylvania Press, 2017), 5 and passim; Roberts, *Slavery and the Enlightenment*, 1–7, 241.

173. Verene A. Shepherd, ed., *Slavery without Sugar: Diversity in Caribbean Economy and Society since the 17th Century* (Gainesville: University Press of Florida), 1-18; Philip Morgan, "Caribbean Slavery," in Philip Misevich and Kristin Mann, eds., *The Rise and Demise of Slavery and the Slave Trade in the Atlantic World* (Rochester, NY: University of Rochester Press, 2016), 64-99, esp. 72-79.

174. Schwartz, ed., *Tropical Babylons*, 85-157; Wheat, *Atlantic Africa and the Spanish Caribbean*, 11-12, 181-215.

175. David Geggus, "Saint-Domingue on the Eve of the Haitian Revolution," in David Patrick Geggus and Noman Fiering, eds., *The World of the Haitian Revolution* (Bloomington: University of Indiana Press, 2009) 3-20.

176. David Geggus, "Indigo and Slavery in Saint Domingue," in Shepherd, ed., *Slavery without Sugar*, 19-35.

177. Jack P. Greene, *Settler Jamaica in the 1750s: A Social Portrait* (Charlottesville: University of Virginia Press, 2016), 29; B. W. Higman, *Slave Population and Economy in Jamaica, 1807-1834* (Cambridge: Cambridge University Press, 1976), 9, 12-14, 21-24, passim; S. D. Smith, "Coffee and the "Poorer Sort of People' in Jamaica during the Period of African Enslavement," in Shepherd, ed., *Slavery without Sugar*, 102-28; David P. Geggus, "Sugar and Coffee Cultivation in Saint Domingue and the Shaping of the Slave Labor Force," and Michael-Rolph Trouillot, "Coffee Planters and Coffee Slaves in the Antilles: The Impact of a Secondary Crop," in Ira Berlin and Philip D. Morgan, eds., *Cultivation and Culture: Labor and the Shaping of Slave Life in the Americas* (Charlottesville: University of Virginia Press, 1993), 73-98 and 124-37. For more on the demographic impact of sugar, see McNeill's essay in this volume.

178. Roberts, *Slavery and the Enlightenment*, 80-130; Nicholas Crawford, "'In the Wreck of a Master's Fortune': Slave Provisioning and Planter Debt in the British Caribbean," *Slavery & Abolition*, 37, no. 2 (June 2016), 353-74; Nicholas Crawford, "Feeding Slavery: Scarcity, Subsistence, and the Political Economy of the British Caribbean, c. 1783-1825" (PhD diss., Harvard University, 2016); Bertie Mandelblatt, "Feeding the French Atlantic: Colonial Food Provisioning Networks in the Franco-Caribbean during the Ancien Régime" (PhD diss., University of London, 2008); Bertie Mandelblatt, "A Transatlantic Commodity: Irish Salt Beef in the French Atlantic World," *History Workshop Journal*, 63 (2007), 18-47; Bertie Mandelblatt, "How Feeding Slaves Shaped the French Atlantic: Mercantilism and the Crisis of Food Provisioning in the Franco-Caribbean during the Seventeenth-Century," in Sophus Reinert and Pernille Røge, eds., *The Political Economy of Empire in the Early Modern World* (London: Palgrave Macmillan, 2013), 192-220; Bertie Mandelblatt, "'A Land Where Hunger Is in Gold and Famine Is in Opulence': Plantation Slavery, Island Ecology, and the Fear of Famine in the French Caribbean," in Lauric Henneton and L.H. Roper, eds., *Fear and the Shaping of Early American Societies* (Leiden: Brill, 2016), 243-64; Jennifer L. Anderson, "Barbuda and the Provisioning of the Codrington Estates on Antigua," in Georgia L. Fox, ed., *An Archaeology and History of a Caribbean Sugar Plantation on Antigua* (Gainesville: University of Florida Press, 2020), 55-67; Verene A. Shepherd, *Livestock, Sugar and Slavery: Contested Terrain in Colonial Jamaica* (Kingston, Jamaica: Ian Randle, 2009); Sluyter, *Black Ranching Frontiers*, 98-139. See also David Watts, "Cycles of Famine in Islands of Plenty: The Case of the Colonial West Indies in the Pre-emancipation Period," in Bruce Currey and Graeme Hugo, eds., *Famine as a Geographical Phenomenon* (Dordrecht, Netherlands: D. Reidel, 1984), 49-70.

179. S. G. Stephens, "Cotton Growing in the West Indies During the 18th and 19th Centuries," *Tropical Agriculture*, 21, no. 2 (1944), 23-29; Roberts, *Slavery and the Enlightenment*, 97-101; George F. Tyson, "On the Periphery of the Peripheries: The Cotton Plantations of St. Croix, Danish West Indies, 1735-1815," in Tyson, ed., *Bondmen and Freedmen in the Danish West Indies: Scholarly Perspectives* (St. Thomas: Virgin Islands Humanities Council, 1996), 83-107; Michael Craton and Gail Saunders, *Islanders in the Stream: A History of the Bahamian People*, vol 1, *From Aboriginal Times to the End of Slavery* (Athens: University of Georgia Press, 1992), 192, 196-97, 213; David Beck Ryden, "'One of the Finest and Most Fruitful Spots in America': An Analysis of Eighteenth-Century Carriacou," *Journal of Interdisciplinary History*, 43, no. 4 (Spring 2013), 539-70; Sven Beckert, *Empire of Cotton: A Global History* (New York: Alfred A. Knopf, 2014), 8-9, 31, 88-97, 100-102, 113, 204, 267, 390; Weiss, Hallston, and Norrgård, "Cotton and Salt," 261-87. For a 1766 drawing of a Jamaican cotton

bush, accompanied by the layout of a cotton field, as well as a 1767 drawing of a cotton gin, showing three black workers, see Higman, *Proslavery Priest*, 144, and plate 4. I have also benefitted from Alexey Krichtal, "Liverpool, Slavery, and Atlantic Cotton Frontier, 1763–1833" (PhD diss., Johns Hopkins University, forthcoming).

180. Justin Roberts, "Working between the Lines: Labor and Agriculture on Two Barbadian Sugar Plantations, 1796–1797," *WMQ*, 63, no. 3 (July 2006), 551–86; Justin Roberts, "Uncertain Business: A Case Study of Barbadian Plantation Management, 1770–1793," *Slavery & Abolition*, 32, no. 3 (September 2011), 247–68; Justin Roberts, *Slavery and the Enlightenment*, 101–3, 289; Ward, *British West Indian Slavery*, 18–23, 65, 76, 108–18; Higman, *Jamaica Surveyed*, 261–76, 291.

181. There is a huge literature on the Haitian Revolution and second slavery. For a few highlights, see Daniel B. Rood, *The Reinvention of Atlantic Slavery: Technology, Labor, Race, and Capitalism in the Greater Caribbean* (New York: Oxford University Press, 2017), esp. 1–120; Julia Gaffield, *Haitian Connections in the Atlantic World: Recognition after Revolution* (Chapel Hill: University of North Carolina Press, 2015); Ada Ferrer, *Freedom's Mirror: Cuba and Haiti in the Age of Revolution* (New York: Cambridge University Press, 2014); José Guadalupe Ortega, "Machines, Modernity, and Sugar: The Greater Caribbean in a Global Context, 1812–50," *Journal of Global History*, 9, no. 1 (2014), 1–25; Leida Fernández-Prieto, "Islands of Knowledge, Science and Agriculture in the History of Latin America and the Caribbean," *Isis*, 104, no. 4 (December 2013), 788–97; Leida Fernández-Prieto, "Mapping the Global and Local Archipelago of Scientific Tropical Sugar: Agriculture, Knowledge, and Practice, 1790–1880," in Manning and Rood, eds., *Global Scientific Practice*, 181–98; Geggus and Fiering, eds., *The World of the Haitian Revolution*; Anthony Kaye, "The Second Slavery: Modernity in the Nineteenth-Century South and the Atlantic World," *Journal of Southern History*, 75 (August 2009), 627–50; Dale Tomich and Michael Zeuske, "Introduction, The Second Slavery: Mass Slavery, World-Economy and Comparative Microhistories," *Review of the Fernand Braudel Center*, 31, no. 2 (2008), 91–100; David Patrick Geggus, ed., *The Impact of the Haitian Revolution in the Atlantic World* (Columbia: University of South Carolina Press, 2001). For the French Caribbean in this era, see the impressive work of Joseph la Hausse de Lalouvière, "Enslavement and Empire in the French Caribbean, 1793–1848" (PhD diss., Harvard University, 2019).

182. Jarvis, *In the Eye of All Trade*, 185–256; Crawford, *The Last Turtlemen of the Caribbean*, 6–7, 25–38, 90; Anderson, *Mahogany*, 156–83; O. Nigel Bolland, "Timber Extraction and the Shaping of Enslaved People's Culture in Belize," in Shepherd, ed., *Slavery without Sugar*, 36–62.

183. The net migration of Africans into the Spanish Caribbean has probably been undercounted. I expect that the 3 percent rate of natural increase of slaves in the Spanish Caribbean in the first half of the eighteenth century is too high. But even if it is half or even a third as high, it would still be striking. For the latest estimates of the slave trade into the Spanish Caribbean, see Alex Borucki, David Eltis, and David Wheat, eds., *From the Galleons to the Highlands: Slave Trade Routes in the Spanish Americas* (Albuquerque: University of New Mexico Press, 2020), esp. 201–22.

184. Riva Berleant-Schiller and Lydia Pulsipher, "Subsistence Cultivation in the Caribbean," *NWIG*, 60, nos. 1–2 (1986), 1–40; Woodville K. Marshall, "Provision Ground and Plantation Labor in Four Windward Islands: Competition for Resources during Slavery," in Berlin and Morgan, eds., *Cultivation and Culture*, 203–20; Dale Tomich, "*Une Petite Guinée*: Provision Ground and Plantation in Martinique, 1830–1848," in Berlin and Morgan, eds., *Cultivation and Culture*, 221–42; Judith Carney, "African Traditional Plant Knowledge in the Circum-Caribbean Region," *Journal of Ethnobiology*, 23, no. 2 (2003), 167–85; Judith A. Carney and Richard Nicholas Rosomoff, *In the Shadow of Slavery: Africa's Botanical Legacy in the Atlantic World* (Berkeley: University of California Press, 2009), 1–2, 7, 88–94, 100–138, 155–74; Tinde R. van Andel et al., "Local Plant Names Reveal that Enslaved Africans Recognized Substantial Parts of the New World Flora," *Proceedings of the National Academy of Sciences* [*PNAS*] (December 2014), https://doi.org/10.1073/pnas.1418836111; Judith Carney, "'The Mangrove Preserves Life': Habitat of African Survival in the Atlantic World," *Geographical Review*, 107, no. 3 (2017), 433–51; Judith A. Carney, "Subsistence in the

Plantationocene: Dooryard Gardens, Agrobiodiversity, and the Subaltern Economies of Slavery," *Journal of Peasant Studies*, 48, no. 5 (2021), 1075–99.

185. Altman, "Key to the Indies," 5–26; J. M. H. Clark, "Environment and the Politics of Relocation in the Caribbean Port of Veracuz, 1519–1599," in Altman and Wheat, eds., *The Spanish Caribbean*, 189–210; Richard L. Kagan, *Urban Images of the Hispanic World, 1493–1793* (New Haven, CT: Yale University Press, 2000), 28; Richard L. Kagan, "A World without Walls: City and Town in Colonial Spanish America," in James D. Tracy, ed., *City Walls: The Urban Enceinte in Global Perspective* (Cambridge: Cambridge University Press, 2000), 117–52; Ana Maria Silva, "Roots in Stone and Slavery: Permanence, Mobility, and Empire in 17th-C. Cartagena de Indias" (PhD diss., University of Michigan, 2018); Jane Landers, "The African Landscape of Seventeenth-Century Cartagena de Indias and Its Hinterlands," in Jorge Cañizares-Esguerra, Matt D. Childs, and James Sidbury, eds., *The Black Urban Atlantic in the Age of the Slave Trade* (Philadelphia: University of Pennsylvania Press, 2013), 147–62; Pérotin-Dumon, *La Ville aux Îles, la ville dans L'Île*, esp. 47–164; David Geggus, "Urban Development in Eighteenth-Century Saint-Domingue," *Bulletin du Centre of d'Histoire des Espaces Atlantiques*, 5 (1990), 197–228. For a rare inland town, see James Robertson, *Gone Is the Ancient Glory: Spanish Town, Jamaica, 1554–2000* (Kingston, Jamaica: Ian Randle, 2005).

186. Allan J. Keuthe, "Havana in the Eighteenth Century," in Franklin W. Knight and Peggy K. Liss, eds., *Atlantic Port Cities: Economy, Culture, and Society in the Atlantic World, 1650–1850* (Knoxville: University of Tennessee Press, 1991), 13–39; Higman, *A Concise History*, 82–84; de la Fuente, *Havana and the Atlantic*, 9, passim; Guadalupe García, *Beyond the Walled City: Colonial Exclusion in Havana* (Berkeley: University of California Press, 2016), 8, 24; Schneider, *The Occupation of Havana*, 26–28, passim; Aaron Graham, "Towns, Government, Legislation and the 'Police' in Jamaica and the British Atlantic, 1770–1805," *Urban History*, 47, no. 1 (2020), 41–62; Nadine Hunt, "Expanding the Frontiers of Western Jamaica through Minor Atlantic Ports in the Eighteenth Century," *Canadian Journal of History*, 45, no. 3 (Winter 2010), 485–502.

187. Geggus, "Urban Development in Eighteenth-Century Saint-Domingue"; David Geggus, "The Major Port Towns of Saint Domingue in the Later Eighteenth Century," in Knight and Liss, eds., *Atlantic Port Cities*, 87–116; David Geggus, "The Slaves and Free People of Color of Cap Français," in Jorge Cañizares-Esguerra, Matt D. Childs, and James Sidbury, eds., *The Black Urban Atlantic in the Age of the Slave Trade* (Philadelphia: University of Pennsylvania Press, 2013), 101–21; B. W. Higman, "Jamaican Port Towns in the Early Nineteenth Century," in Knight and Liss, eds., *Atlantic Port Cities*, 117–48; David Eltis and David Richardson, *Atlas of the Transatlantic Slave Trade* (New Haven, CT: Yale University Press, 2010), 234; Trevor Burnard, "'The Grand Mart of the Island': The Economic Function of Kingston, Jamaica in the Mid-eighteenth Century," in Kathleen E. A. Monteith and Glen Richards, eds., *Jamaica in Slavery and Freedom: History, Heritage and Culture* (Kingston, Jamaica: University of West Indies Press, 2002), 225–41; Gauvin Alexander Bailey, *Architecture and Urbanism in the French Atlantic Empire: State, Church, and Society, 1604–1830* (Montreal and Kingston, Jamaica: McGill-Queen's University Press, 2018), esp. 173–322.

188. Linda M. Rupert, *Creolization and Contraband: Curaçao in the Early Modern Atlantic World* (Athens: University of Georgia Press, 2012), esp. 103–62; Jarvis, *In the Eye of All Trade*, esp. 161–67; Ruud Stelten, *From Golden Rock to Historic Gem: A Historical Archaeological Analysis of the Maritime Cultural Landscape of St. Eustatius, Dutch Caribbean* (Leiden: Sidestone Press, 2019), 14–17, 50, 167–73; Wim Klooster and Gert Oostindie, *Realm between Empires; The Second Dutch Atlantic, 1680–1815* (Ithaca: Cornell University Press, 2018), esp. 163–92; Neville A. T. Hall, *Slave Society in the Danish West Indies: St Thomas, St. John, and St. Croix* (Mona, Jamaica: University of West Indies Press, 1992), esp. 87–109; Erik Göbel, "The Danish West Indies, 1660s–1750s: Formative Years," in Roper, ed., *The Torrid Zone*, 118–31; Schaw, *Journal of a Lady of Quality*, 137.

189. Ernesto Bassi, *An Aqueous Territory: Sailor Geographies and New Granada's Transimperial Greater Caribbean World* (Durham, NC: Duke University Press, 2017), 9, and passim. Other books that explore zones or microregions are Jarvis, *In the Eye of All Trade*, esp. 185–256, 318–74; Kit Candlin, *The Last Caribbean Frontier, 1795–1815* (New York: Palgrave Macmillan,

2012); Rupert, *Creolization and Contraband*; Cécile Vidal, *Caribbean New Orleans: Empire, Race, and the Making of a Slave Society* (Chapel Hill: University of North Carolina Press, 2019); Heather Freund, "A Negotiated Possession: Law, Race, and Subjecthood in the Ceded Islands, 1763–1797" (PhD diss., University of Illinois, Urbana-Champaign, 2019); Jeppe Mulich, *In a Sea of Empires: Networks and Crossings in the Revolutionary Caribbean* (Cambridge: Cambridge University Press, 2020); James Dator, "'To See a World in a Grain of Sand': Liberty and Slavery in the Leeward Caribbean, 1689–1739" (forthcoming); Tessa Murphy, *The Creole Archipelago: Race and Borders in the Colonial Caribbean* (Philadelphia: University of Pennsylvania Press, 2021).).

190. Aviva Ben-Ur, *Jewish Autonomy in a Slave Society: Suriname in the Atlantic World, 1651–1825* (Philadelphia: University of Pennsylvania Press, 2020), esp. 30–77; Natalie Zemon Davis, "Regaining Jerusalem: Eschatology and Slavery in Jewish Colonization in Seventeenth-Century Suriname," *Cambridge Journal of Postcolonial Literary Inquiry*, 3, no. 1 (January 2016), 11–38. For general context, see Richard L. Kagan and Philip D. Morgan, eds., *Atlantic Diasporas: Jews, Conversos, and Crypto-Jews in the Age of Mercantilism, 1500–1800* (Baltimore: Johns Hopkins University Press, 2009); and Jane S. Gerber, ed., *The Jews in the Caribbean* (Oxford, UK: The Littman Library of Jewish Civilization, 2014).

191. De La Fuente, *Havana*, 1, 71–78, 152; Schneider, *The Occupation of Havana*, esp. 6, 67–71; McNeill, *Mosquito Empires*, 138–44, 155–56, 173–74; Zachary M. Beier, "Everyday Entanglements: Labor and Diversity at the Cabrits Garrison, Dominica," in Christopher DeCorse and Beier, eds., *British Forts and Their Communities: Archaeological and Historical Perspectives* (Gainesville: University Press of Florida, 2018), 151–77; Gerald F. Schroedl, and Todd M. Ahlman, "The Maintenance of Cultural and Personal Identities of Enslaved Africans and British soldiers at the Brimstone Hill Fortress, St. Kitts, West Indies," *Historical Archaeology*, 36, no. 4 (2002), 38–49; Todd M. Ahlman, Gerald F. Schroedl, and Ashley H. McKeown, "The Afro-Caribbean Ware from the Brimstone Hill Fortress, St. Kitts, West Indies: A Study in Ceramic Production," *Historical Archaeology*, 43, no. 4 (2009), 22–41; Gerald F. Schroedl, "Enslaved Africans and the British Military at the Brimstone Hill Fortress, St. Kitts, West Indies," in *British Forts and Their Communities*, 178–205; Gerald F. Schroedl and Todd M. Ahlman, "Archaeological Evidence for Enslaved African Laborers from Two Locations at the Brimstone Hill Fortress, St Kitts, West Indies," in Roger Leech and Pamela Leech, eds., *The Colonial Landscape of the British Caribbean* (Woodbridge, UK: Boydell Press, 2021), 89–130; Tessa C. S. Machling, *The Fortifications of Nevis, West Indies, from the 17th Century to the Present Day: Protected Interests?* BAR International Series 2349 (Oxford, UK: Archaeopress, 2012), 70, 125; David Buisseret, *Historic Architecture of the Caribbean* (London: Heineman, 1980), 46–71; Laurent Dubois, *Haiti: The Aftershocks of History* (New York: Picador, 2012), 53–54. See also Eric Klingelhofer, ed., *First Forts: Essays on the Archaeology of Proto-colonial Fortifications* (Boston: Brill, 2010), esp. Kathleen A. Deagan, "Strategies of Adjustment: Spanish Defense of the Circum-Caribbean Colonies, 1493–1600," 17–39; Roger Leech, "'Within Musquett Shott of Black Rock'—Johnson's Fort and The Early Defenses of Nevis, West Indies," 129–40; and Jay B. Haviser, "The 'Old Netherlands Style' and Seventeenth-Century Dutch Fortification of the Caribbean," 167–87.

192. Louis P. Nelson, *Architecture and Empire in Jamaica* (New Haven, CT: Yale University Press, 2016), esp. 2, 4, 6, 36–64, 68, 80–81, 95, 187–217; Louis P. Nelson, "'Come Hell or High Water': Architectural Responses to Natural Disaster in the Early British Caribbean," in Leech and Leech, eds., *The Colonial Landscape*, 39–55; Jay D. Edwards, "The Evolution of Vernacular Architecture in the Western Caribbean," in Jeffery K. Wilkerson, ed., *Cultural Traditions and Caribbean Identity; The Question of Patrimony* (Gainesville: University Press of Florida, 1980), 291–339; Jay D. Edwards, "The First Comparative Studies of Caribbean Architecture," *NWIG*, 3&4 (1983), 173–200; Jay D. Edwards, "The Complex Origins of the American Domestic Piazza-Verandah-Gallery," *Material Culture*, 21, no. 2 (1989), 3–58; Jay D. Edwards, "The Origins of Creole Architecture," *Winterthur Portfolio*, 29 (Summer–Autumn 1994), 156–89; Jay D. Edwards, "Creole Architecture: A Comparative Analysis of Upper and Lower Louisiana and Saint Domingue," *International Journal of Historical Archaeology*, 10, no. 3 (September 2006), 241–71; Carol F. Jopling, *Puerto Rican Houses in*

Sociohistorical Perspective (Knoxville: University of Tennessee Press, 1988); Pilar Chias and Tomas Abad, *The Fortified Heritage: Cadiz and the Caribbean, A Transatlantic Relationship* (Madrid: Universidad de Alcalá, 2011); Bailey, *Architecture and Urbanism,* esp. 439–80.

193. Walter Raleigh, *The Discovery of the Empire of Guiana ... in 1595,* ed. Sir Robert Schomburgk (London: Hakluyt Society, 1848), 3; Christopher Columbus, *The Four Voyages,* ed. J.M. Cohen (London: Penguin, 1969), 64–65.

194. Molly A. Warsh, *American Baroque: Pearls and the Nature of Empire, 1492–1700* (Chapel Hill: University of North Carolina Press, 2018), esp. 31–127, 135–49; Warsh, "Enslaved Pearl Divers in the Sixteenth Century Caribbean," *Slavery and Abolition,* 31, no. 3 (September 2010), 345–62, esp. 346. See also Michael Perri, " 'Ruined and Lost': Spanish Destruction of the Pearl Coast in the Early Sixteenth Century," *Environment and History,* 15 (2009), 129–61; and A. Romero, "Death and Taxes: The Case of the Depletion of Pearl Oyster Beds in Sixteenth-Century Venezuela," *Conservation Biology,* 17 (2003), 1013–23.

195. Allan Greer, *Property and Dispossession: Natives, Empires and Land in Early Modern North America* (New York: Cambridge University Press, 2018), esp. 241–70, although there is no mention of the Caribbean; Gabriel de Avilez Rocha, *Common Currents of Empire: Political Ecologies of Colonialism and Slavery in the Early Atlantic* (Chapel Hill: University of North Carolina Press, forthcoming). See also Rocha's various articles and essays: "The Pinzones and the Coup of the *Acedares*: Fishing and Colonization in Fifteenth-Century Atlantic Africa and the Caribbean," *Colonial Latin American Review,* 28, no. 4 (2019), 427–29; "The Azorean Connection: Trajectories of Slaving, Piracy, and Trade in the Early Atlantic" in Altman and Wheat, eds., *The Spanish Caribbean,* 257–78; "Maroons in the *Montes*: Toward a Political Ecology of Marronage in the Sixteenth-Century Caribbean," in Cassander L. Smith, Nicholas R. Jones, and, Miles P. Grier eds., *Early Modern Black Diaspora Studies* (New York: Palgrave Macmillan, 2018), 15–35; "Plunder and Profit in the Name of Protection: Royal Iberian Armadas in the Early Atlantic" in Lauren Benton, Adam Clulow, and Bain Attwood, eds., *Protection and Empire: A Global History* (New York: Cambridge University Press, 2018), 72–90; "Politics of the Hinterland: Taxing Fowl in and beyond the Ports of Terceira Island, 1550–1600," *Early American Studies,* 15, no. 4 (2017), 740–68.

196. Loren McClenachan, Marah Hardt, Jeremy Jackson, and Richard Cooke, "Mounting Evidence for Historical Overfishing and Long-Term Degradation of Caribbean Marine Ecosystems: Comment on Julio Baisre's 'Setting a Baseline for Caribbean Fisheries,' " *Journal of Island and Coastal Archaeology,* 5, no. 1 (January 2010), 165–69; Hardt, "Lessons from the Past," *Fish and Fisheries,* 10, no. 2 (2009), 143–58; Peter J. Adam, "Monachus Tropicalis," *Mammalian Species,* 747 (2004), 1–9; A. Romero, R. Baker, J. E. Cresswell, A. Singh, A. McKie, and M. Manna, "Environmental History of Marine Mammal Exploitation in Trinidad and Tobago, WI and its Ecological Impact," *Environment and History,* 8 (2002), 255–74; McClenachan and Cooper, "Extinction Rate," 1351–1358; Jackson, "Reefs since Columbus," S23–S32; Sloane, *A Voyage to the Islands,* I:lvi; Delbourgo, *Collecting the World,* 79, 126–27, 191, 266, 307.

197. Bolster, *The Mortal Sea,* is by far the most sophisticated attempt to grapple with these issues.

198. Loren McClenachan, Jeremy B. C. Jackson, and Marah J. H. Newman, "Conservation Implications of Historic Sea Turtle Nesting Beach Loss," *Frontiers in Ecology and the Environment,* 4 (2006), 290–96; K. A. Bjorndal, and J. B. C. Jackson, "Role of Sea Turtles in Marine Ecosystems: Reconstructing the Past," in Peter L. Lutz, J. A. Musick, and J. Wyneken, eds., *Biology of Sea Turtles* (Boca Raton, FL: CRC Press, 2003), ch. 10; Jackson, "Reefs since Columbus," S23–S32; Crawford, *The Last Turtlemen of the Caribbean,* 1–38.

199. Jarvis, *In the Eye of All Trade,* 234–35; Mary Draper, "Timbering and Turtling: The Maritime Hinterlands of Early Modern British Caribbean Cities," *Early American Studies An Interdisciplinary Journal,* 15, no. 4 (2017), 769–800.

200. Loren McClenachan and Andrew B. Cooper, "Extinction Rate, Historical Population Structure and Ecological Role of the Caribbean Monk Seal," *Proceedings of the Royal Society, Biological Sciences,* 275 (June 2008), 1351–58; Peter J. Adam, "Monachus Tropicalis," *Mammalian Species,* no. 747 (2004), 1–9. Julio A. Baisres, "Setting a Baseline for Caribbean Fisheries," *Journal of Island & Coastal Archaeology,* 5, no. 1 (January 2010), 120–47, argues that the monk seal was a rare species in the Caribbean, citing some contemporary

commentators, noting that some respectable naturalists failed to mention them, and emphasizing their absence from archaeological sites. He makes some telling points, but I am still impressed by the number of breeding colonies in the region (which may well have been more than 13), even if a pre-Columbian population of 230,000–340,000 may be exaggerated.

201. Bolster, *The Mortal Sea*, 58; Jarvis, *In the Eye of All Trade*, 80, 502 n. 31; Marah J. Hardt, "Lessons from the Past: The Collapse of Jamaican Coral Reefs," *Fish and Fisheries*, 10 (2008), 1–16, esp. 5; Taylor, *Jamaica in 1687*, 295.

202. Grove, *Green Imperialism*, 6, 8, and passim; Funes Monzote, *From Rainforest to Cane Field in Cuba*, 22–23. Some parts of Northern Europe may well have been in advance of the Caribbean regarding forestry conservation. For circum-Caribbean exchanges, see Strang, *Frontiers of Science*, 13, 35, 64, 67–68, 80–81, 87, 98, 153–54, 172–73, 178, 189, 193, 197–98, 230, 241–42, 284, 313.

203. Harold J. Cook, *Matters of Exchange: Commerce, Medicine, and Science in the Dutch Golden Age* (New Haven, CT: Yale University Press, 2007), 111–12, 117–20, 130, 141, 210–25, 320, 327–29; McClellan and Regourd, *The Colonial Machine*, 337–44; Richard Drayton, *Nature's Government: Science, Imperial Britain, and the "Improvement" of the World* (New Haven, CT: Yale University Press, 2000), 64–65 (quotes), 72, 80, 108, 113, 132, 137, 156–57; Grove, *Green Imperialism*, 53, 74, 264, 269; McCook, *States of Nature*, 17; Susan Danforth, "Cultivating Empire: Sir Joseph Banks and the (Failed) Botanical Garden at Nassau," *Journal of the Bahamas Historical Society*, 23 (2001), 21–28.

204. McCook, *States of Nature*, 14; Grove, *Green Imperialism*, 268, 275; David Lambert, *White Creole Culture, Politics and Identity during the Age of Abolition* (Cambridge: Cambridge University Press, 2005), 6, 41, 50–51, 57–59; McClellan, *Colonialism and Science*, 183–272; Drayton, *Nature's Government*, 113; *Minutes of the Society for the Improvement of Plantership in the Island of Barbados* (Liverpool, UK: Thomas Kaye, 1811), as cited in Roberts, *Slavery and the Enlightenment*, 33–34; Jensen, *For the Health of the Enslaved*, 96–97.

205. Henry Barham, *Hortus Americanus: containing an account of the . . . vegetable productions of South-America and the West-India Islands, and particularly the Island of Jamaica* (Kingston, Jamaica: Alexander Aikman, 1794 [published posthumously, likely written in 1711]), 1, 2, 91, 143, 157, 187, 185; Patrick Browne, *Civil and Natural History of Jamaica* (London: T. Osborne and J. Shipton, 1756) and see his "Catalogue of the Plants of the English Sugar Colonies," Department of Botany, British Museum; Raymond Phineas Stearns, *Science in the British Colonies of America* (Urbana: University of Illinois Press, 1970), 376; Frans A. Stafleu, *Linnaeus and the Linnaeans: The Spreading of Their Ideas in Systematic Botany, 1735–1789* (Utrecht, Netherlands: Oosthoek, 1971), 202–3; Nicholas Joseph Jacquin, *Enumeratio Systematica Plantarum Quas in Insulis Caribaeis . . .* (Leiden: Lugduni Batavorum, apud Theodorum Haak, 1760), and *Selectarum Stirpium Americanarum Historia . . .* (Vienna: Joseph Kurtböck for Kraus, 1763); William Urban Buée to Joseph Banks, Nov. 22, 1796, Add. MS 8098, f. 438, and May 24, 1798, Add. MS 8099, ff. 149–50, British Library; William Urban Buée, "Some Account of the Cultivation of the Clove Tree, in the Island of Dominica," in Bryan Edwards, *History, Civil and Commercial, of the British Colonies in the West Indies*, 3 vols. (London: John Stockdale, 1801), 3:371–82; Richard A. Howard and Elizabeth S. Howard, eds., *Alexander Anderson's The St. Vincent Botanic Garden* (London: The Linnean Society, 1983), 40; Alexander Anderson to Joseph Banks, May 3, 1789, Dawson Turner Copies, Banks Correspondence, Vol. 6, ff. 159–60, Natural History Museum, London; Alexander Anderson to George Yonge, Jun. 5, 1790, WO 40/4, National Archives, Kew, England. My thanks to Kathleen Murphy for many of these references here and in the following notes.

206. Howard and Howard, eds., *Anderson's St. Vincent Botanic Garden*, 6, 20; Londa Schiebinger, *Plants and Empire: Colonial Bioprospecting in the Atlantic World* (Cambridge, MA: Harvard University Press, 2004), 35–44; Anderson to George Yonge, Apr. 7, 1793, WO 40/4; Matthew Wallen to Joseph Banks, Sep. 23, 1784, Add. MS 33977, f. 267, British Library; Hinton East to Joseph Banks, Jul. 19, 1784, Banks Letters, Vol. 1, f. 168, Archives of the Royal Botanic Gardens, Kew; Drayton, *Nature's Government*, 106–24. Joseph-Nicolas Thiery de Menonville smuggled cochineal from Oaxaca, New Spain to Saint-Domingue in 1777,

but the garden declined and its valuable insect inhabitants eventually disappeared after his death. McClellan, *Colonialism and Science*, 152–55; Greenfield, *A Perfect Red*, 169–83.

207. James Petiver to George Jesson, Jul. 20, 1716, Sloane 3340, f. 252, British Library, as cited in Kathleen S. Murphy, "Collecting Slave Traders: James Petiver, Natural History, and the British Slave Trade," *WMQ*, 3rd ser., 70, no. 4 (October 2013), 637–70; Kathleen S. Murphy, "Translating the Vernacular: Indigenous and African Knowledge in the Eighteenth-Century British Atlantic," *Atlantic Studies*, 8, no. 1 (March 2011), 29–48; Susan Scott Parrish, *American Curiosity: Cultures of Natural History in the Colonial British Atlantic World* (Chapel Hill: University of North Carolina Press, 2006), esp. 215–306; Schiebinger, *Plants and Empire*; Catesby, *Natural History*, II, Appendix 10; C. M. Harris, ed., *Papers of William Thornton*, vol. 1, *1781–1802* (Charlottesville: University Press of Virginia, 1995), 197, 207; William Thornton, "Some Account of Lettsom's Island—and some of its Productions, in a Letter to John Coakley Lettsom, M.D., F.R.S. &C," 1795–1800, William Thornton Papers, Library of Congress, kindly supplied by C. M. Harris; Long, *History of Jamaica*, II:72: Henry de Pointhieu to Banks, Jan. 23, 1778, as cited in Drayton, *Nature's Government*, 93; Alexander Anderson to Mr. Forsyth, June 6, 1786, *The Cottage Gardener*, 8 (May 6, 1852); Jill H. Casid, *Sowing Empire: Landscape and Colonization* (Minneapolis: University of Minnesota Press, 2005), 197–212. See also James Delbourgo, *A Most Amazing Scene of Wonders: Electricity and Enlightenment in Early America* (Cambridge, MA: Harvard University Press, 2006), 185–87; Schiebinger, "Scientific Exchange," in Bailyn and Denault, eds., *Soundings in Atlantic History*, 294–328; Miles Ogborn, "Talking Plants: Botany and Speech in Eighteenth-Century Jamaica," *History of Science*, 51 (2013), 251–82: Miles Ogborn, *The Freedom of Speech: Talk and Slavery in the Anglo-Caribbean World* (Chicago: University of Chicago Press, 2019), esp. 109–42.

208. Gonzalo Fernández de Oviedo, *De la natural historia de las Indias* (Toledo: Ramon Petras, 1526); Antonello Gerbi, *Nature in the New World: From Christopher Columbus to Gonzalo Fernández de Oviedo*, trans. Jeremy Moyle (Pittsburgh: University of Pittsburgh Press, 1985), esp. 255–305; Kathleen Ann Myers, *Fernández de Oviedo's Chronicle of America: A New History for a New World*, trans. Nina M. Scott (Austin: University of Texas Press, 2007); Charles Plumier, *Description des Plantes de l'Amerique avec leurs Figures* (Paris: Jean Anisson, 1693); McClellan, *Colonialism and Science*, 112–16; Pietsch, "Charles Plumier (1646–1704)," 1–57; Delbourgo, *Collecting the World*, esp. 37–172; Maria Sibylla Merian, *Metamorphosis insectorum Surinamensium* (Amsterdam: Gerard Valck, 1705); Natalie Zemon Davis, *Women on the Margins: Three Seventeenth-Century Lives* (Cambridge, MA: Harvard University Press, 1995), 140–202; Kim Todd, *Chrysalis: Maria Sibylla Merian and the Secrets of Metamorphosis* (New York: Mariner Books, 2007); Ella Reitsma, with Sandrine Ulenberg, *Maria Sibylla Merian and Daughters: Women of Art and Science* (Los Angeles: J. Paul Getty Museum, 2008); Kay Etheridge and Florence F. J. M. Pieters, "Maria Sibylla Merian (1647–1717): Pioneering Naturalist, Artist, and Inspiration for Catesby," in E. Charles Nelson and David Elliot, eds., *The Curious Mister Catesby: A "Truly Ingenious" Naturalist Explores New Worlds* (Athens: University of Georgia Press, 2015), 39–56; Kay Etheridge, "The History and Influence of Maria Sibylla Merian's Bird-Eating Tarantula: Circulating Images and the Production of Natural Knowledge," in Manning and Rood, eds., *Global Scientific Practice*, 54–70; Therese O'Malley and Amy R. W. Meyers, *The Art of Natural History: Illustrated Treatises and Botanical Paintings, 1400–1850* (Washington, DC: National Gallery of Art, 2010); Higman, *Proslavery Priest*, esp. 141–67; Frank Cundall, "Dr. Anthony Robinson of Jamaica," *Journal of Botany*, 60 (1922), 49–52; McClellan and Regourd, *The Colonial Machine*, 37; Douglas Hall, *Planters, Farmers and Gardeners in Eighteenth Century Jamaica*, Elsa Goveia Memorial Lecture (Kingston, Jamaica: University of West Indies Press, 1987), and "Botanical and Horticultural Enterprise in Eighteenth-Century Jamaica," in Roderick A. McDonald, ed., *West Indies Accounts: Essays on the History of the British Caribbean and the Atlantic Economy in Honour of Richard Sheridan* (Kingston, Jamaica: University of West Indies Press), 101–25. There are eighteenth-century manuscript collections of drawings of William Houstoun (d. 1733), Dr. Anthony Robinson (d. 1768), Department of Botany, British Museum; Rev. John Lindsay, Bristol Museum; Dr. John Lindsay, Edinburgh University and Royal Society; and Olaf Swartz, Royal Swedish Academy of Sciences. See also

William T. Stearn, "Grisebach's "Flora of the British West Indian Islands: A Biographical and Bibliographical Introduction," *Journal of the Arnold Arboretum*, 46, no. 3 (July 1965), 243–85. Prior to 1800, Ray Desmond's *Dictionary of British and Irish Botanists and Horticulturalists* (London: Taylor and Francis, 1977) lists 47 active in the West Indies (compared to 58 for the much bigger and populous North American mainland).

209. Stearns, *Science in the British Colonies*, 217, 356, 361–62; Theodore Feldman, "The Barometer," in Robert Bud and Deborah Jean Warner, eds., *Instruments of Science: an Historical Encyclopedia* (New York: National Museum of American History, 1998), 53–54; J. W. Olmsted, "The Scientific Expedition of Jean Richer to Cayenne (1672–1673)," *Isis*, 34 (1942), 117–28; M. Chenoweth, J. M. Vaquero, R. García-Herrera, and D. Wheeler, "A Pioneer in Tropical Meteorology: William Sharpe's Barbados Weather Journal, April–August 1680," *Bulletin of the American Meteorological Society*, 88 (2007), 1957–64; Nicholas Dew, "Vers la ligne: Circulating Measurements Around the French Atlantic," in James Delbourgo and Nicholas Dew, eds., *Science and Empire in the Atlantic World* (New York: Routledge, 2008), 53–72; Nicholas Dew, "Scientific Travel in the Atlantic World: The French expedition to Gorée and the Antilles, 1681–1683," *British Journal for the History of Science*, 43, no. 1 (March 2010), 1–17; F. Regourd, "Sciences et Colonisation sous l'ancien régime: le cas de la Guyane et des Antilles françaises, XVIIe–XVIIIe siècles" (doctoral thesis, Université de Bordeaux-III, 2000), esp. 233–358; McClellan and Regourd, *The Colonial Machine*, 73 and passim; Craig P. Waff and Stephen Skinner, "Thomas Stevenson of Barbados and Comet Halley's 1759 Return," in Richard Goddard, comp., *George Washington's Visit to Barbados 1751* (St. Michael, Barbados: Cole Printery, 1997); Johnson, *Climate and Catastrophe in Cuba*, 14; McCook, *States of Nature*, 15.

210. James Petiver, *Hortus Peruvianus medicinalis, or, The South-Sea Herbal* (London, 1715) and the text he translated and abridged was Louis Feuillée, *Journal des Observations physiques, mathematiques et botaniques, faites par l'ordre du Roy sur les Côtes Orientales de l'Amerique Meridionale, & dans les Indes Occidentales, depuis l'année 1707 jusques en 1712* (Paris: Pierre Giffart, 1714); Murphy, "Collecting Slave Traders"; Robert Millar to Hans Sloane, November 25, 1735, Sloane, 4054, f. 146, British Library; McClellan, *Colonialism and Science*, 159–60; Henry de Pointhieu to Banks, Jan. 23, 1778, as cited in Drayton, *Nature's Government*, 93; Harris, ed., *Papers of William Thornton*, 34–35. Richard Drayton, "A l'ecole des Francais: les sciences et le deuxieme empire britannique (1783–1830)," *Revue Francaise d'Histoire D'Outre Mer*, 86, nos. 322–23 (1999), 91–118.

211. McNeill, *Mosquito Empires*, 23; Casid, *Sowing Empire*, 1–44; J. Kumamoyo et al., "Mystery of the Forbidden Fruit: Historical Epilogue on the Origin of the Grapefruit, *Citrus paradise* (Rutaceae)," *Economic Botany*, 41 (1987), 97–107; Riva Berleant-Schiller, "Hidden Places and Creole Forms: Naming the Barbudan Landscape," *Professionaal Geographer*, 43, no. 1 (1991), 92–101; B. W. Higman and B. J. Hudson, *Jamaican Place Names* (Mona, Jamaica: University of the West Indies Press, 2009), esp. 4, 35, 118, 130, 159, 252–55. For a bizarre hybrid, a "feral cow . . . sired by a bull and a female deer," which "none of the Indians dares come near"; see Klinkenborg, ed., *Drake Manuscript*, f. 67.

212. Watts, *The West Indies*, 220–21; John H. Parry, "Plantation and Provision Ground: An Historical Sketch of the Introduction of Food Crops into Jamaica," *Revista de Historia de America*, 39 (1955), 1–20; John H. Parry, "Salt Fish and Ackee: An Historical Sketch of the Introduction of Food Crops into Jamaica," *Caribbean Quarterly*, 8, no. 4 (1962), 30–36; Berleant-Schiller and Pulsipher, "Subsistence Cultivation," 1–40; William C. Sturtevant, "History and Ethnography of Some West Indian Starches," in Peter J. Ucko and G. W. Dimbleby, eds., *The Domestication and Exploitation of Plants and Animals* (Chicago: Aldine, 1969), 177–99; John Rashford, "Arawak, Spanish, and African Contributions to Jamaica's Settlement Vegetation," *Jamaica Journal*, 24, no. 3 (1993), 17–23; John Rashford, "Jamaica's Settlement Vegetation, Agroecology, and the Origin of Agriculture," *Caribbean Geography*, 5 (1994), 32–50; Dulcie Powell, "The Botanic Garden, Liguanea (with a Revision of Hortus Eastensis)," *Bulletin of the Institute of Jamaica*, Science Ser., no. 15, part 1 (Kingston, Jamaica, 1972), 6–12; Grove, *Green Imperialism*, 268; Richard Sheridan, "Captain Bligh, the Breadfruit and the Botanic Gardens of Jamaica," *Journal of Caribbean History*, 23, no. 1

(1989), 28–50; and Zilberstein, "Bastard Breadfruit," *Early Science and Medicine*, 21, no. 5 (2016), 492–508.

213. Woodrow W. Denham, *West Indian Green Monkeys: Problems in Historical Biogeography*, Contributions to Primatology, vol. 24 (Basel: Karger, 1987), esp. 14–15, 26–28.

214. José de Acosta, *The Natural & Morall History of the Indies*, trans. Edward Grimeston (London, 1604), iv, xxv, 278 [see also José de Acosta, *Natural and Moral History of the Indies*, ed. Jane E. Mangan, with introduction and commentary by Walter D. Mignolo, trans. Frances Lopéz-Morillas (Durham, NC: Duke University Press, 2002), xviii, 215, 464, 473–74, 503–5]; William Dampier, *A Voyage to New Holland* (London: James and John Knapton, 1698), iv, 68; Jack P. Greene, "Changing Identity in the British Caribbean: Barbados as a Case Study," in Nicholas Canny and Anthony Pagden, eds., *Colonial Identity in the Atlantic World, 1500–1800* (Princeton, NJ: Princeton University Press, 1987), 213–66, esp. 235, 265. Some say the term first appears in Spanish in the mid-sixteenth century and refers to black slaves born in the Indies. It is an oppositional term, distinguishing, in some cases, locals from immigrants, whites from blacks (in Martinique and Louisiana, it refers primarily or solely to whites; in Haiti, to blacks). For good discussions of the term, see Edward Brathwaite, *The Development of Creole Society in Jamaica, 1770–1820* (Oxford, UK: Clarendon Press, 1971), xii–xvi and passim; D. A. Brading, *The First America: The Spanish Monarch, Creole Patriots, and the Liberal State, 1492–1867* (Cambridge: Cambridge University Press, 1991); O. Nigel Bolland, "Creolization and Creole Societies: A Cultural Nationalist View of Caribbean History," in Alistair Hennessy, ed., *Intellectuals in the Twentieth-Century Caribbean*, 2 vols. (London: Macmillan, 1992), I:50–79; Stuart B. Schwartz, "Spaniards, *Pardos*, and the Missing Mestizos: Identities and Racial Categories in the Early Hispanic Caribbean," *NWIG*, 71, nos. 1/2 (1997), 5–19; Richard D. E. Burton, *Afro-Creole: Power, Opposition, and Play in the Caribbean* (Ithaca, NY: Cornell University Press, 1997); Jorge Cañizares-Esguerra, "New World, New Stars: Patriotic Astrology and the Invention of Indian and Creole Bodies in Colonial Spanish America, 1600–1650," *American Historical Review*, 104 (1999), 33–68, and his *How to Write the History of the New World: Histories, Epistemologies, and Identities in the Eighteenth-Century Atlantic World* (Stanford, CA: Stanford University Press, 2001); David Buisseret and Steven G. Reinhardt, eds., *Creolization in the Americas* (Arlington: University of Texas Press, 2000); Richard Price, "The Miracle of Creolization: A Retrospective," *NWIG*, 75 (2001), 35–64; Verene A Shepherd and G. L. Richards, eds., *Questioning Creole: Creolisation Discourses in Caribbean Culture* (Kingston, Jamaica: Ian Randle, 2002); Michel-Rolph Trouillot, "Culture on the Edges: Caribbean Creolization in Historical Context," in Brian Keith Axel, ed., *From the Margins: Historical Anthropology and Its Futures* (Durham, NC: Duke University Press, 2002), 189–210; Lambert, *White Creole Culture*, 6, 17, 37–39, 173, 211; J. H. Elliott, *Empires of the Atlantic World: Britain and Spain in America, 1492–1830* (New Haven, CT: Yale University Press, 2006), 234–45; Sean X. Goudie, *Creole America: The West Indies and the Formation of Literature and Culture in the New Republic* (Philadelphia: University of Pennsylvania Press, 2006); Charles Stewart, ed., *Creolization: History, Ethnography, Theory* (Walnut Creek, CA: Left Coast Press, 2007); Ralph Bauer and José Antonio Mazzotti, eds., *Creole Subjects in the Colonial Americas: Empires, Texts, Identities* (Chapel Hill: University of North Carolina Press, 2009); Richard Price, "The Concept of Creolization," in Eltis and Engerman, eds., *The Cambridge World History of Slavery*, 3:513–37 (quote on 513); Rupert, *Creolization and Contraband*, esp. 11–12, 212–43.

215. Browne, *Civil and Natural History of Jamaica*, ii, iii, 422; Sidney W. Mintz and Sally Price, eds., *Caribbean Contours* (Baltimore: Johns Hopkins University Press, 1985), 6; the first known reference to a ship named the *Creole*, a French privateer, occurred during the Seven Years' War: Admiralty Office, *PaG*, May 13, 1762; the one eighteenth-century transatlantic slave ship with creole as part of its name was the Deux *Créoles*, which arrived in St. Domingue in 1772: Trans-Atlantic Slave Trade Database, http://www.slavevoyages.org, i.d. 30952. Between 1780 and 1799, a selection of North American newspapers contain 55 references to 5 ships—the *Amiable Creole, La Belle Creole, Favourite Creole, Jean Creole*, or simply *La Creole*—that tended to move back and forth between the French West Indies and

North America. Between 1780 and 1799, the newspaper references are: 1 in Rhode Island, 7 in Virginia, 9 in Massachusetts, 11 in South Carolina, and 28 in Pennsylvania.

216. *Boston Gazette,* Apr. 29, 1765; *Boston Evening Post,* Jan. 6, 1766; *Boston Newsletter and New England Chronicle,* Feb. 27, 1766; Extract of a letter from New-London, *Boston Post-Boy,* Mar. 24, 1766 and *Newport Mercury,* Mar 31, 1766; *Boston Gazette,* May 19, 1766; Long, *History of Jamaica,* II:260–86; "A Character of the Creoles," *City Gazette* (Charleston), Feb. 2, 1788; reprinted in Philadelphia's *American Museum* (November and December 1789), 359–60, 466–67, and cited in Ashli White, *Encountering Revolution: Haiti and the Making of the Early Republic* (Baltimore: Johns Hopkins University Press, 2010), 38–39, 127, but also see 36, 54–55; Knight, *The Natural, Moral, and Political History of Jamaica,* 483. John Elliott acutely notes that in 1764, the Boston lawyer James Otis observes that, while English officials "who borrow the term [creole] of the Spaniards," apply it to "all Americans of European extract," the "northern colonists apply it only to the islanders and others of such extract under the torrid Zone": "The Rights of the British Colonies Asserted and Proved," in Bernard Bailyn, ed., *Pamphlets of the American Revolution, 1750–1776,* vol. 1, *1750–1765* (Cambridge, MA: Harvard University Press, 1965), 440, cited in *Empires of the Atlantic World,* 234–35. Positive accounts of creoles certainly existed. One Scottish traveler thought West Indian white women were "more than commonly sensible, even those who have never been off the Island are amazingly intelligent and able to converse with you on any subject. They make excellent wives, fond attentive mothers." Her concluding pronouncement was that "I never admired my own sex more than in these amiable *creoles.*" Schaw, *Journal of a Lady of Quality,* 113–14.

217. Price, "Concept of Creolization," 514; Sidney W. Mintz, *Caribbean Transformations* (Chicago: Aldine, 1974), 33.

218. Kären Wigen, "Introduction" to "Forum: Oceans of History," *American Historical Review,* 111, no. 3 (2006), 717–80, esp. 717; Peter N. Miller, ed., *The Sea: Historiography and Thalassography* (Ann Arbor: University of Michigan Press, 2013); John Mack, *The Sea: A Cultural History* (London: Reaktion Books, 2011); and Jerry H. Bentley, Renate Bridenthal, and Kären Wigen, eds., *Seascapes: Maritime Histories, Littoral Cultures, and Transoceanic Exchanges* (Honolulu: University of Hawai'i Press, 2007). See also Ernesto Bassi, "Small Islands in a Geopolitically Unstable Caribbean World," in *Oxford Research Encyclopedia, Latin American History* (March 2019), DOI: 10.1093/acrefore/9780199366439.013.375.

219. Robin Blackburn, *The Making of New World Slavery: From the Baroque to the Modern, 1492–1800* (London: Verso, 1997), 403; Higman, "The Sugar Revolution," 213–36, esp. 213; Abbé [Guillaume-Thomas François] Raynal, *A Philosophical and Political History of the Settlements and Trade of the Europeans in the East and West Indies,* 6 vols., trans. J. O. Justamond (New York: Negro Universities Press, 1965 [orig. pub. 1770]), V: 107.

Chapter 2

1. Thanks for helping with all or parts of this chapter to Trevor Burnard, Cam Elliott, Monica Green, Kyle Harper, Emily Mendenhall, Andrew Meshnick, Phil Morgan, Matt Mulcahy, Tim Newfield, Philip Rotz, Eleanora Rohland, Stuart Schwartz, and Molly Warsh.

2. Smallpox comes in two main varieties, *Variola major* and *Variola minor.* The former is far deadlier, and in this chapter is what is meant by smallpox. *V. minor* rarely kills and yet immunizes survivors against *V. major.* Specialists in the analysis of ancient DNA currently are debating the antiquity of smallpox, but at the moment it seems secure to say that what is called smallpox in this chapter (and enters the story only in 1518) was indeed extremely close genetically to the variants in circulation in the twentieth century. Relevant recent papers include Ana T. Duggan et al., "17th Century Variola Virus Reveals the Recent History of Smallpox," *Current Biology,* 26 (2016), 1–6; Ashleigh F. Porter et al., "Comment: Characterization of Two Historic Smallpox Specimens from a Czech Museum," *Viruses,* 9 (2017), doi:10.3390/v9100276; Barbara Mühlemann et al., "Diverse Variola Virus (Smallpox) Strains Were Widespread in Northern Europe in the Viking Age," *Science,* 369 (July 24, 2020), DOI: 10.1126/science.aaw8977.

3. For quarantines, see Pablo Gómez, *The Experiential Caribbean: Creating Knowledge and Healing in the Early Modern Atlantic* (Chapel Hill: University of North Carolina Press, 2017),

Chapter 2. For scholarship on the history of medicine in the Caribbean before 1850, see, inter alia, Karol Weaver, *Medical Revolutionaries: The Enslaved Healers of Eighteenth-Century Saint Domingue* (Urbana: University of Illinois Press, 2006); Richard Sheridan, *Doctors and Slaves: A Medical and Demographic History of the British West Indies, 1680–1834* (Cambridge: Cambridge University Press, 1985); K. F. Kiple and K. C. Ornelas, "After the Encounter: Disease and Demography in the Lesser Antilles," in Robert Paquette and Stanley Engerman, eds., *The Lesser Antilles in the Age of European Expansion* (Gainesville: University of Florida Press, 1996), 51–67; Mark Harrison, "'The Tender Frame of Man': Disease, Climate, and Racial Difference in India and the West Indies, 1760–1860," *Bulletin of the History of Medicine*, 70 (1996), 68–93; Mark Harrison, *Medicine in an Age of Commerce and Empire: Britain and Its Tropical Colonies, 1660–1830* (Oxford: Oxford University Press, 2010); Francisco Guerra, *Epidemología americana y filipina* (Madrid: Ministerio de Sanidad y Consumo, 1999); Esteban Mira Caballos, "La medicina indígena en la Española y su commercialización (1492–1550)," *Asclepio: Revista de Historia de la Medicina y de la Ciencia*, 49 (1997), 185–98; Linda Newson, "Medical Practice in Early Colonial Spanish America: A Prospectus," *Bulletin of Latin American Research*, 25 (2006), 367–39; Jean-Claude Eymeri, *Histoire de la medicine aux Antilles et en Guyane* (Paris: L'Harmattan, 1992); Geneviève Leti, *Santé et société esclavagiste à la Martinique (1802–1848)* (Paris: L'Harmattan, 1998); Pierre Pluchon, *Histoire des médecins et pharmaciens de marine et des colonies* (Toulouse: [privately published], 1985); Niklas Thode Jensen, *For the Health of the Enslaved: Slaves, Medicine, and Power in the Danish West Indies, 1803–1848* (Copenhagen: Museum Tusculanum Press, 2012); Rana A. Hogarth, *Medicalizing Blackness: Making Racial Difference in the Atlantic World, 1780–1840* (Chapel Hill: University of North Carolina Press, 2017), 17–80; Suman Seth, *Difference and Disease: Medicine, Race, and the Eighteenth-Century British Empire* (Cambridge: Cambridge University Press, 2018); Pablo Gómez, *The Experiential Caribbean: Creating Knowledge and Healing in the Early Modern Atlantic* (Chapel Hill: University of North Carolina Press, 2017); and the early chapters of Juanita De Barros, Steven Palmer and David Wright, eds., *Health and Medicine in the Circum-Caribbean, 1800–1968* (London: Routledge, 2009). For the broader Atlantic, Londa Schiebinger, *Secret Cures of Slaves: People, Plants and Medicine in the Eighteenth-Century Atlantic World* (Stanford, CA: Stanford University Press, 2017); Manuel Barcia, *The Yellow Demon of Fever: Fighting Disease in the Nineteenth-Century Transatlantic Slave Trade* (New Haven, CT: Yale University Press, 2020), 166–93; and Kalle Kananoja, *Healing Knowledge in Atlantic Africa: Medical Encounters, 1500–1850* (Cambridge: Cambridge University Press, 2021).

4. Emily Mendenhall, "Syndemics: A New Path for Global Health Research," *The Lancet*, 389 (March 4, 2017), 889–91. Or, in the words of the originator of the concept, "The syndemics model of health focuses on the biosocial complex, which consists of interacting, co-present, or sequential diseases and the social and environmental factors that promote and enhance the negative effects of disease interaction." Merrill Singer et al., "Syndemics and the Biosocial Conception of Health," *The Lancet*, 389 (March 4, 2017), 941–50.

5. Samuel Fahlberg, *Utdrag, af Samlingar til natural-historien öfver ön St. Barthelemi i Vest-Indien* (Stockholm: Kungl. Vetenskapsakademien, 1786). Fahlberg was a polymath with a strong interest in disease conditions. For a useful overview of the medical tradition in which these authors wrote, see Thomas Rütten, "Early Modern Medicine," in Mark Jackson, ed., *The Oxford Handbook of the History of Medicine* (Oxford: Oxford University Press, 2011), 60–81.

6. Key papers in this debate include Gisela Grupe, "Zur Ätiologie der Cribra orbitalia: Auswirkungen auf das Aminosäureprofil im Knochenkollagen und den Eisengehalt des Knochenminerales," *Zeitschrift für Morphologie und Anthropologie*, Bd. 81, H. 1 (1995), 125–37; Nicole E. Smith-Guzman, "The Skeletal Manifestation of Malaria: An Epidemiological Approach Using Documented Skeletal Collections," *American Journal of Physical Anthropology*, 158 (2015), 624–35; R. L. Gowland and A. G. Western, "Morbidity in the Marshes: Using Spatial Epidemiology to Investigate Skeletal Evidence for Malaria in Anglo-Saxon England (AD 410–1050)," *American Journal of Physical Anthropology*, 147 (2012), 301–11. See also Lucie Biehler-Gomez and Cristina Cattaneo, "Infectious Diseases: Non-Specific and Specific Infections," in Lucie Biehler-Gomez and Cristina Cattaneo, eds., *Interpreting Bone Lesions and Pathology for Forensic Practice* (London: Academic Press, 2021), 39–59.

7. It cannot, of course, establish that a given infection was *not* present. An accessible guide to the findings from and the limits of paleopathology using bioarchaeological data for what is now the United States is Debra L. Martin and Anna J. Osterholtz, *Bodies and Lives in Ancient America: Health before Columbus* (London and New York: Routledge, 2016). More technical, and more focused on problems of data interpretation, is Stephanie Marciniak and H. N. Poinar, "Ancient Pathogens through Human History: A Paleogenomic Perspective," in Charlotte Lindqvist and Om P. Rajora, eds., *Paleogenomics: Genome-Scale Analysis of Ancient DNA* (Dordrecht: Springer, 2019), 115–38.

8. For a review of the perils and promise of paleogenomics generally, see Pontus Skoglund and Iain Mathieson, "Ancient Genomics of Modern Humans: The First Decade," *Annual Review of Genomics and Human Genetics* 19, no. 1 (2018), 381–404.

9. See Joseph Mackrill, *The History of Yellow Fever* (Baltimore: Hayes, 1796), for the earliest statement of African origin. Phylogenetic analysis indicates the probability of American origins of the yellow fever virus is less than 0.001; that the virus in its current forms is a minimum of 1,500 years old; and that the transmission to the Americas took place roughly 300–400 years ago, but with a wide margin of error attached to that estimate. Juliet Bryant, Edward C. Holmes, and Alan D. T. Barrett, "Out of Africa: A Molecular Perspective on the Introduction of Yellow Fever Virus into the Americas," *PLOS Pathogens*, May 18, 2007, https://doi.org/10.1371/journal.ppat.0030075. The dates inferred from molecular analyses must be treated with caution as RNA-based viruses like yellow fever are unstable. See also T. P. Monath and Pedro F. C. Vasconcelos, "Yellow Fever," *Journal of Clinical Virology*, 64 (2015), 160–73; David W. C. Beasley, Alexander J. McAuley, and Dennis A. Bente, "Yellow Fever Virus: Genetic and Phenotypic Diversity and Implications for Detection, Prevention and Therapy," *Antiviral Research*, 115 (2015), 48–70; on the vector as opposed to the virus, see J. R. Powell and W. J. Tabachnick, "History of Domestication and Spread of Aedes aegypti," *Memorias Instituto Oswaldo Cruz*, 108, suppl. (2013), 11–17; Jeffrey R. Powell, Andrea Gloria-Soria, and Panayiota Kotsakiozi, "Recent History of Aedes aegypti: Vector Genomics and Epidemiology Records," *BioScience*, 68, no. 11 (2018), 854–60; Jacob E. Crawford et al., "Population Genomics Reveals that an Anthropophilic Population of Aedes aegypti Mosquitoes in West Africa Recently Gave Rise to American and Asian Populations of This Major Disease Vector," *BMC Biology*, 15, no. 1/16 (2017), 1–16.

10. Important statements on this topic include Charles E. Rosenberg, "Framing Disease: The Creation and Negotiation of Explanatory Schemes," *The Milbank Quarterly*, 67, suppl. 1 (1989), 1–15; Jon Arrizabalaga, "Problematizing Retrospective Diagnosis in the History of Disease," *Asclepio*, 52 (2002), 51–70; Piers D. Mitchell, "Retrospective Diagnosis and the Use of Historical Texts for Investigating Disease in the Past," *International Journal of Paleopathology*, 1 (2011), 81–88.

11. Influenza is an exception because it comes in so many strains and is constantly brewing up new ones. So surviving a bout of influenza may provide resistance or immunity to that particular strain but not to all the others.

12. Epidemiologists refer to "basic reproduction numbers" for infectious diseases, commonly denoted as R_o. Measles has the highest R_o, 12–18, which means each case of measles is likely to lead to 12–18 additional cases among a non-immune population. Smallpox and rubella's R_o is 5–7, mumps 4–7, and the 1918 influenza 2–3.

13. Upwards of 60 percent of the nearly 1,500 identified human pathogens derive from animal pathogens and are originally zoonotic diseases. Bats and rodents—highly social creatures—are most commonly the source of zoonoses, although usually indirectly through an intermediate host such as a herd animal.

14. Kirsten Bos et al., "Pre-Columbian Mycobacterial Genomes Reveal Seals as a Source of New World Human Tuberculosis," *Nature*, 517 (2014), 494–97.

15. C. F. Ardelean, L. Becerra-Valdivia, M. W. Pedersen, et al., "Evidence of Human Occupation in Mexico around the Last Glacial Maximum," *Nature* (July 22, 2020), https://doi.org/10.1038/s41586-020-2509-0.

16. A helpful review is N. D. Wolfe, C. P. Dunavan, and J. Diamond, "Origins of Major Human Infectious Diseases," in Institute of Medicine (US), *Improving Food Safety through a One Health Approach: Workshop Summary* (Washington: National Academies Press, 2012), A16.

Available at http://www.ncbi.nlm.nih.gov/books/NBK114494/. A more accessible discussion of some of the same issues appears in Linda Newson, *Conquest and Pestilence in the Early Spanish Philippines* (Honolulu: University of Hawaii Press, 2009), 10–12. A. Drake and M. Oxenham, "Disease, Climate, and the Peopling of the Americas," *Historical Biology*, 25 (2013), 565–97, review the role of the Beringia bottleneck in shaping the disease burden of the Americas (and are doubtful that cold temperatures mattered much). Also helpful is the overview by Herbert S. Klein, "The First Americans: The Current Debate," *Journal of Interdisciplinary History*, 46, no. 4 (2016), 543–61; and that by Jennifer Raff, "Journey into the Americas," *Scientific American*, 324, no. 5 (May 2021), 26–33. On the size of the original migrant population—perhaps about 250—see Nelson Fagundes et al., "How Strong Was the Bottleneck Associated to the Peopling of the Americas? New Insights from Multilocus Sequence Data," *Genetics and Molecular Biology*, 41 (2018), 206–14.

17. The zooarchaeological evidence concerns introduced animals, all of which in pre-Columbian times hailed from South America. Peter W. Stahl, "Adventive Vertebrates and Historical Ecology in the Pre-Columbian Neotropics," *Diversity*, 1 (2009), 151–65, doi:10.3390/d1020151. Several studies of the genome of extant Caribbean populations are helpfully summarized in A. Moreno-Estrada et al., "Reconstructing the Population Genetic History of the Caribbean," *PLoS Genetics*, 9 (2013), doi:10.1371/journal.pgen.1003925; but due to poor DNA preservation only a tiny handful studies of ancient DNA in the Caribbean have been published: Hannes Schroeder et al., "Origins and Genetic Legacies of the Caribbean Taino," *Proceedings of the National Academy of Sciences*, 115 (2018), 2341–46, https://doi.org/10.1073/pnas.1716839115; F. Mendisco et al., "Where Are the Caribs? Ancient DNA from Ceramic Period Human Remains in the Lesser Antilles," *Philosophical Transactions of the Royal Society B*, 370 (2015), http://dx.doi.org/10.1098/rstb.2013.0388; C. Lalueza-Fox et al., "MtDNA from Extinct Tainos and the Peopling of the Caribbean," *Annals of Human Genetics*, 65 (2001), 137–51, doi:10.1046/j.1469-1809.2001.6520137.x; C. Lalueza-Fox et al., "Mitochondrial DNA from Pre-Columbian Ciboneys from Cuba and the Prehistoric Colonization of the Caribbean," *American Journal of Physical Anthropology*, 121 (2003), 97–108, doi:10.1002/ajpa.10236.

18. K. B. Tankersly, N. P. Dunning, L. A. Owen, J. Sparks, "Geochronology and Paleoenvironmental Framework for the Oldest Archaeological Site (7800–7900 cal BP) in the West Indies, Banwari Trace, Trinidad," *Latin American Antiquity*, 29 (2018), 681–95. A more cautious dating of 8400–7200 BP appears in Matthew F. Napolitano, Robert J. DiNapoli, Jessica H. Stone, Maureece J. Levin, Nicholas P. Jew, Brian G. Lane, John T. O'Connor, and Scott M. Fitzpatrick, "Reevaluating Human Colonization of the Caribbean Using Chronometric Hygiene and Bayesian Modeling," *Science Advances*, 5 (2019), DOI: 10.1126/sciadv.aar7806.

19. See Napolitano et al. (2019), which revisits 2,484 radiocarbon dates on more than 50 islands. In addition, see the recent compendium Corinne L. Hofman and Andrzej T. Antczak, eds., *Early Settlers of the Insular Caribbean: Dearchaizing the Archaic* (Leiden: Sidestone Press, 2019). For genomic analysis based on 93 human remains from 16 archaeological sites, see Kathrin Nägele et al., "Genomic Insight into the Early Peopling of the Caribbean, *Science* (June 24, 2020), 10.1126/science.aba8697. They find little admixture among indigenous populations.

20. I rely on Napolitano et al. (2019) here, but see also Jonathan A. Hanna, "Camáhogne's Chronology: The Radiocarbon Settlement Sequence on Grenada, West Indies," *Journal of Anthropological Archaeology*, 55 (2019), doi.org/10.1016/j.jaa.2019.101075. For details on Puerto Rico, see Isabel Rivera-Collazo, "*Por el camino verde*: Long-Term Tropical Socioecosystem Dynamics and the Anthropocene as Seen from Puerto Rico," *The Holocene*, 25 (2015), 1604–11. A recent summary of early settlement on Cuba appears in Luis Martínez-Fernández, *Key to the New World: A History of Early Colonial Cuba* (Gainesville: University of Florida Press, 2018), 23–25.

21. Pre-Columbian subsistence in the Caribbean is summarized in Lee A. Newson and Elizabeth S. Wing, *On Land and Sea: Native American Uses of Biological Resources in the West Indies* (Tuscaloosa: University of Alabama Press, 2004).

22. William F. Keegan and Corinne L. Hofman, *The Caribbean before Columbus* (Oxford: Oxford University Press, 2017), 30. Where this process has been most closely studied, on Abaco Island in the Bahamas, it seems the arrival of humans resulted in the greatest pulse of extinctions in the island's history. See David W. Steadman, Nancy A. Albury, Brian Kakuk, Jim I. Mead, J. Angel Soto-Centeno, Hayley M. Singleton, and Janet Franklin, "Vertebrate Community on an Ice-Age Caribbean Island," *PNAS*, 112 (2015), E5963–71. See also S. B. Cooke et al., "Anthropogenic Extinction Dominates Holocene Declines of West Indian Mammals," *Annual Review of Ecology and Evolution*, 48 (2017), 301–27.

23. Similar mass extinctions occurred after the first humans arrived in Australia, the Americas, and Madagascar. See Ross MacPhee, ed., *Extinctions in Near Time: Causes, Contexts, and Consequences* (Berlin: Springer, 2013); S. Kathleen Lyons, Joshua H. Miller, Danielle Fraser, Felisa A. Smith, Alison Boyer, Emily Lindsey, and Alexis M. Mychajliw, "The Changing Role of Mammal Life Histories in Late Quaternary Extinction Vulnerability on Continents and Islands," *Biology Letters*, 12 (2016), https://doi.org/10.1098/rsbl.2016.0342. For the Pacific story, see J. R. McNeill, "Of Rats and Men: A Synoptic Environmental History of the Island Pacific," *Journal of World History*, 5 (1994), 299–349.

24. Nägele et al. (2020).

25. Useful archaeological studies include Hofman and Antczak, eds., *Early Settlers of the Caribbean*; William Keegan and Corinne Hofman, *The Caribbean before Columbus* (Oxford: Oxford University Press, 2017); Samuel Wilson, *The Archaeology of the Caribbean* (Cambridge: Cambridge University Press, 2007); Lee Newson and Elizabeth Wing, *On Land and Sea: Native American Uses of Biological Resources in the West Indies* (Tuscaloosa: University of Alabama Press, 2004); M. Veloz Maggioli, *La isla de Santo Domingo antes de Colón* (Santo Domingo: Banco Central, 2003); P. Allsworth-Jones, *Pre-Columbian Jamaica* (Tuscaloosa: University of Alabama Press, 2008); Jalil Sued-Balillo, ed., *General History of the Caribbean*, vol. I, *Autochthonous Societies* (Paris: UNESCO, 2003); William Keegan, Corinne Hofman, and Reniel Rodríguez Ramos, eds., *The Oxford Handbook of Caribbean Archaeology* (New York: Oxford University Press, 2013).

26. A thorough review of what information can be derived from teeth is Hayley Mickleburgh, "Reading the Dental Record: A Dental Anthropological Approach to Foodways, Health and Disease, and Crafting in the pre-Columbian Caribbean" (PhD thesis, University of Leiden, 2013, especially pp. 57–59, 286–92, and 322–24). See also H. L. Mickleburgh, "Dental Wear and Pathology in the Precolonial Caribbean: Evidence for Dietary Change in the Ceramic Age," *International Journal of Osteoarchaeology*, 26 (2014), 290–302. Debra Martin and Anna Osterholtz, *Bodies and Lives in Ancient America: Health before Columbus* (New York: Routledge, 2016), summarizes much of the literature on pre-Columbian health in what is now the United States. See also Clark Spencer Larsen, "In the Wake of Columbus: Native Population Biology in the Postcontact Americas," *Yearbook of Physical Anthropology*, 37 (1994), 109–54, which is devoted to North America despite its title.

Bruce Rothschild, F. L. Calderon, A. Copra, and C. Rothschild, "First European Exposure to Syphilis: The Dominican Republic at the Time of Columbian Contact," *Clinical Infectious Diseases*, 31 (2000), 936–41. Paleogenomic work on treponemal infection is rare and recent and so far sheds no light on the Caribbean. V. J. Schuenemann, A. Kumar Lankapalli, R. Barquera, E. A. Nelson, D. Iraíz Hernández, V. Acuña Alonzo, et al., "Historic Treponema Pallidum Genomes from Colonial Mexico Retrieved from Archaeological Remains," *PLoS Neglected Tropical Diseases*, 12 (2018), e0006447, https://doi.org/10.1371/journal.pntd.0006447.

27. Bruce Rothschild et al., "First European Exposure to Syphilis." Paleogenomic work on treponemal infection is rare and recent and so far sheds no light on the Caribbean. V. J. Schuenemann et al., "Historic Treponema Pallidum Genomes."

28. Edwin F. Crespo Torres, "La enfermedad en los indios de Boriquén," *Revista del Instituto de Cultura Puertorriqueña*, 8 (2008), 3–15.

29. There is no doubt treponemal infections existed in the Americas. There is debate as to whether these included venereal syphilis; and as to whether syphilis existed in Eurasia and Africa before 1492 or not. As regards North America, see Mary Lucas Powell and Della Collins Cook, eds., *The Myth of Syphilis* (Gainesville: University of Florida Press, 2005). See also Kristin Harper et al., "The Origin and Antiquity of Syphilis Revisited: An Appraisal

of Old-World Pre-Columbian Evidence of Treponemal Infection," *American Journal of Physical Anthropology*, 146 (2011), 99–133; Molly Zuckerman and Kristin Harper, "Paleoepidemiological and Biocultural Approaches to Ancient Disease: The Origin and Antiquity of Syphilis," in Molly Zuckerman and Debra Martin, eds., *New Directions in Biocultural Anthropology* (Hoboken, NJ: WileyBlackwell, 2016), 317–35. The most recent evidence for European syphilis in the late fifteenth century is discussed in Karen Giffin et al., "A Treponemal Genome from an Historic Plague Victim Supports a Recent Emergence of Yaws and Its Presence in 15th-Century Europe," *Nature: Scientific Reports* (2020), https://doi.org/10.1038/s41598-020-66012-x.

30. A compact overview of TB history is Monica Green, "The Globalisations of Disease," in Nicole Boivin, Rémy and Michael Petraglia, eds., *Human Dispersal and Species Movement: From Prehistory to Present* (Cambridge: Cambridge University Press, 2017), 499–502.

31. Charlotte Roberts and Jane Buikstra, "The History of Tuberculosis from the Earliest Times to the Development of Drugs," in Peter Davies, Peter Barnes, and Stephen Gordon, eds., *Clinical Tuberculosis* (London: Hodder Arnold, 2008), 12–13; Mickleburgh, "Reading the Dental Record," 57–59; Ann Ramenofsky, Alicia Wilbur, and Anne Stone, "Native American Disease History: Past, Present, and Future Directions," *World Archaeology*, 35 (2003), 249–51.

32. George H. Perry, "Parasites and Human Evolution," *Evolutionary Anthropology*, 23, no. 6 (2014), 218–28.

33. Roberto Valcárel Rojas and Ángela Peña Obregón, "Las sociedades indígenas en Cuba," in José Abreu Cardet, ed., *Historia de Cuba* (Santo Domingo: Archivo General de la Nación, 2013), 26–30.

34. Crespo Torres, "La enfermedad en los indios de Boriquén."

35. Mickleburgh, "Reading the Dental Record," 323–24. On drought, for example, see Chad Lane, Sally Horn, and Matthew Kerr, "Beyond the Mayan Lowlands: Impacts of the Terminal Classic Drought in the Caribbean Antilles," *Quaternary Science Reviews*, 86 (2014), 89–98, which shows severe impacts on Hispaniola ca. AD 750–1100.

36. Guinea pigs can serve as reservoirs for infections that humans can also host, such as salmonella, ringworm, and scabies, but nothing that is highly lethal. On pre-Columbian guinea pigs: Michelle LeFebvre and Susan deFrance, "Guinea Pigs in the Pre-Columbian West Indies," *Journal of Island and Coastal Archaeology*, 9, no. 1 (2014), 16–44; E. Lord et al., "Complete Mitogenomes of Ancient Caribbean Guinea Pigs (Cavia porcellus)," *Journal of Archaeological Science*, 17 (2018), 678–88.

37. It is conceivable that Caribbean immune systems were not only calibrated by experience, but also genetically adapted to be efficient against the range of pathogens in circulation before 1492. An argument along these lines has been made for the indigenous population of the British Columbia coast based on comparison of aDNA to DNA in living populations. Apparently the pre-contact population showed different adaptations, as one might expect because their disease environment was much different from what it became after contact. See John Lindo, Emilia Huerta-Sánchez, Shigeki Nakagome, et al., "A Time Transect of Exomes from a Native American Population before and after European Contact," *Nature Communications* (November 15, 2016), DOI: 10.1038/ncomms13175.

38. Useful reviews of this issue appear in Suzanne Austin Alchon, *A Pest in the Land: New World Epidemics in a Global Perspective* (Albuquerque: University of New Mexico Press, 2003), 150–71; and Linda Newson, "The Demographic Impact of Colonization," in Victor Bulmer-Thomas, John Coatsworth, and Roberto Contés Conde, eds., *The Cambridge Economic History of Latin America* (Cambridge: Cambridge University Press, 2006), 143–84. Important overviews of depopulation in the Americas include N. D. Cook, *Born to Die: Disease and New World Conquest* (New York: Cambridge University Press, 1998); Massimo Livi-Bacci, *Conquest: The Destruction of the American Indios* (Cambridge, UK: Polity, 2008), and N. D. Cook and George Lovell, eds., *The Secret Judgments of God: Native Peoples and Old World Disease in Spanish Colonial America* (Norman: University of Oklahoma Press, 1992); and for North America, see Ann Ramenofsky, *Vectors of Death: The Archaeology of European Contact* (Albuquerque: University of New Mexico Press, 1987); Larsen, "In the Wake of Columbus."

39. Alchon, *A Pest in the Land*, 153.

40. David Henige, *Numbers from Nowhere: The American Indian Contact Population Debate* (Norman: University of Oklahoma Press, 1998). Henige tries to debunk high counters and offers no estimate of his own on the grounds that no responsible one is feasible.

41. A statistically sophisticated effort to split the distance among prior estimates comes in at 45–78 million. Alexander Koch et al., "Earth Systems Impacts of the European Arrival and Great Dying in the Americas after 1492," *Quaternary Science Reviews*, 207(2019), 13–36, here 15. As regards new techniques in archaeology, in the Maya lowlands and Amazonia (as well as Cambodia) the use of LiDAR within the past few years has revealed far denser settlements and caused scholars to boost their estimates of population, in some cases several-fold. Jonas Gregorio de Souza et al., "Pre-Columbian Earth-Builders Settled along the Entire Southern Rim of the Amazon," *Nature Communications*, 9 (2018), doi:10.1038/s41467-018-03510-7; W. E. Carter et al., "Estimating Ancient Populations by Aerial Survey," *American Scientist*, 107 (2019), 30–37, doi:10.1511/2019.107.1.30.

42. Among the latest of the low counters is Esteban Mira Caballos, who offers 300,000 for the population of the islands in 1492. He gives a total of 100,000 for Hispaniola and 80,000 for Cuba. See his *El indio antillano: repartimiento, encomienda y esclavitud* (1492–1542) (Seville: Muñoz Moya, 1997), 33–47.

43. Barry Higman, *A Concise History of the Caribbean* (New York: Cambridge University Press, 2011), 50. This range omits the implications for the Caribbean as a whole of the 8 million estimate for Hispaniola alone offered by Sherburne Cook and Woodrow Borah, *Studies in Population History* (Berkeley: University of California Press, 1971), I:408. Their figure of 8 million, based on methods they developed in the study of Mexico, remains an outlier in the debates over Hispaniola's population in 1492. It also omits the tentative conclusion in favor of much lower estimates derived from genetic data of living populations in D. M. Fernandes, K. A. Sirak, H. Ringbauer, et al., "A Genetic History of the Pre-contact Caribbean," *Nature*, 590 (2021), 103–10, https://doi.org/10.1038/s41586-020-03053-2. Some of the low estimates appear in Appendix 1 of Livi-Bacci, *Conquest*. See Alchon, *Pest in the Land*, 167, for a compilation of estimates.

44. Karen Anderson-Córdova, who recently studied the question in detail, prefers 250,000 to 500,000; Massimo Livi-Bacci settled on 200,000 to 300,000; N. D. Cook, who has looked at the textual evidence as closely as anyone, chose 500,000 to 750,000; Karen F. Anderson-Córdova, *Surviving Spanish Conquest: Indian Fight, Flight, and Cultural Transformation in Hispaniola and Puerto Rico* (Tuscaloosa: University of Alabama Press, 2017), 86. Livi-Bacci, *Conquest*, Appendix 6, for a range of estimates, and p. 105 for his own. Cook, *Born to Die*, 21–23.

45. Kathleen Deagan and José María Cruxent, "From Contact to Criollos: The Archaeology of Spanish Conquest in Hispaniola," in Warwick Bray, ed., *The Meeting of Two Worlds: Europe and the Americas, 1492–1650. Proceedings of the British Academy*, 81 (1993), 67–104. On p7.1 they offer a "few million" for the 1492 population of Hispaniola. Archaeologists Valcárel Rojas and Peña Obregón, "Las sociedades indígenas en Cuba," 50, prefer 200,000 for Cuba alone in 1492.

46. E.g., Mira Caballos, *El indio antillano*, passim.

47. D. M. Fernandes et al., "A Genetic History of the Pre-contact Caribbean." Working from genomic data from less than 200 skeletons on several islands, this group hypothesizes a population for Hispaniola in the tens of thousands, but for some unspecified number of generations prior to 1492.

48. Alonso de Castro, cited in Roberto Marte, ed., *Santo Domingo en los manuscritos de Juan Bautista Muñoz* (Santo Domingo: Fundación García Arévalo, 1981), 397.

49. Gonzalo Fernández de Oviedo, *Historia general y natural de las Indias* (Madrid: Atlas, 1992), 1: 66. Oviedo wrote the first volume in the early 1530s. The bulk of the work remained unpublished until the nineteenth century. Eleanora Rohland of Bielefeld University has found correspondence from the *cabildo* of Hispaniola in 1535 complaining about the absence of indigenous labor that prevented collection of gold: Archivo General de Indias, Gobierno, Audiencia de Santo Domingo, Cartas y expedientes Cabildo Secular de la Española (1530–1690), 28 Diciembre 1535: "y ya a mas de seys anos que en esta ysla no se coge oro ninguno con yndios de encomienda que no los ay."

50. Juan López de Velasco, *Geografía y descripción universal de las Indias* (Madrid: Atlas, 1971), 248: 99. A 1606 report by the Spanish governor Antonio Osorio found a single Amerindian in the several settlement on Hispaniola he surveyed, which with various necessarily heroic assumptions David Wheat extrapolates to a total of 365 for the entire island. David Wheat, *Atlantic Africa and the Spanish Caribbean, 1657–1640* (Chapel Hill: University of North Carolina Press, 2016), 280–81.

51. These figures come from Livi-Bacci, *Conquest,* 108. Other figures for Cuba appear in Martínez-Fernández, *Key to the New World,* 33–34.

52. Oliver Dunn, James E. Kelly, Jr. and William F. Keegan, "Beachhead in the Bahamas: Destruction of the Taíno," *Archaeology* 45 (1992), 50–56, 55.

53. A more cautious approach is evident in Newson, "Demographic Impact," 152: she says the population was "virtually extinct within a few generations."

54. For the argument made in cultural, not biological terms, see Tony Castanha, *The Myth of Indigenous Caribbean Extinction: Continuity and Reclamation in Borikén (Puerto Rico)* (London: Palgrave, 2011); Karen F. Anderson-Córdova, *Surviving Spanish Conquest: Indian Fight, Flight, and Cultural Transformation in Hispaniola and Puerto Rico* (Tuscaloosa: University of Alabama Press, 2017); Corinne Hofman, Roberto Valcárcel Rojas, and Jorge Ulloa Hung, "Colonization, Transformations, and Indigenous Cultural Persistence in the Caribbean," in Christine Beaule and John Douglass, eds., *The Global Spanish Empire: Five Hundred Years of Place Making and Pluralism* (Tucson: University of Arizona Press, 2020), 55–82.

55. Hannes Schroeder et al., "Origins and Genetic Legacies of the Caribbean Taino," *Proceedings of the National Academy of Sciences,* published ahead of print, February 20, 2018, https://doi.org/10.1073/pnas.1716839115. That proportion is not necessarily entirely Taíno. On Cuba: Martínez-Fernández, *Key to the New World,* 35.

56. J. B. Torres et al., "Genetic Diversity in the Lesser Antilles and Its Implications for the Settlement of the Caribbean Basin," *PLoS One* (2015), DOI: 10.1371/journal.pone.0139192. The data here come from St. Vincent and Trinidad. See also Theodore Schurr, Jada Benn Torres, Miguel Vilar, Jill Gaieski, and Carlalynne Melendez, "An Emerging History of Indigenous Caribbean and Circum-Caribbean Populations: Insights from Archaeological, Ethnographic, Genetic, and Historical Studies" In Molly Zuckerman and Debra Martin, eds., *New Directions in Biocultural Anthropology* (Hoboken: WileyBlackwell, 2016), 385–402.

57. Antonio García de León, *Tierra adentro, mar en fuera: El Puerto de Veracruz y su litoral a sotovento, 1519–1821* (Mexico City: Fondo de Cultura Económica, 2011), 132–33; Terry Rugeley, *The River People in Flood Time: The Civil Wars in Tabasco, Spoiler of Empires* (Stanford, CA: Stanford University Press, 2014), 31; Nancy Farriss, *Maya Society under Colonial Rule: The Collective Enterprise of Survival* (Princeton, NJ: Princeton University Press, 1984), 59; More recent work, compatible with Farriss, offers a population of perhaps 800,000 as of 1528, tumbling to 140,000 by 1580: Julie A. Hoggarth, Matthew Restall, James W. Wood, and Douglas J. Kennett, "Drought and Its Demographic Effects in the Maya Lowlands," *Current Anthropology,* 58, no. 1 (2017), 91, table 1; Martha Few, *For All of Humanity: Mesoamerican and Colonial Medicine in Enlightenment Guatemala* (Tuscon: University of Arizona Press, 2015), 30; Linda Newson, "Demographic Catastrophe in Sixteenth-Century Honduras," in D. J. Robinson, ed., *Studies in Spanish American Population History* (Boulder, CO: Westview Press, 1981), 234–35; Linda Newson, "The Depopulation of Nicaragua in the Sixteenth Century," *Journal of Latin American Studies,* 14 (1982), 253–86; Cook, *Born to Die,* 84; Oviedo, *Historia natural,* I:105; Pedro Cieza de León, *La crónica del Perú* (Madrid: Historia 16, 1984), 75.

58. The Cuban historian Juan Pérez de la Riva in 1972 offered a rare attempt at quantifying the reasons behind population decline in the sixteenth century (for Cuba alone) and came up with the following proportions: suicide, 35 percent; epidemics, 20 percent; violence, 12 percent; and starvation, 12 percent. Juan Pérez de la Riva, "Desaparición de la población indígena cubana," *Universidad de la Habana,* 196–97 (1972), 61–84, cited in Martínez-Fernández, *Key to the New World,* 77. These proportions seem unlikely to me. George Raudzens, ed., *Technology, Disease and Colonial Conquests, Sixteenth to Eighteenth Centuries*

(Leiden: Brill, 2001), however, offers essays skeptical of both violence and epidemics as proper explanation for European conquests in the Americas.

59. Lately, the liveliest debates along these lines concern North America. Catherine Cameron, Paul Kelton, and Alan Swedlund, eds., *Beyond Germs: Native Depopulation in North America* (Tuscon: University of Arizona Press, 2015) includes strong arguments against exaggeration of the power of diseases. They write (p. 4): "We may never know the full extent of Native depopulation, given the notoriously slim and problematic evidence that is available for indigenous communities during the colonial period, but what is certain is that a generation of scholars has significantly overemphasized disease as the cause of depopulation, downplaying the active role of Europeans in inciting wars, destroying livelihoods, and erasing identities. This scholarly misreading has given support to a variety of popular writers who have misled and are currently misleading the public." Two important works on southeastern North America in this vein are: Paul Kelton, *Epidemics and Enslavement: Biological Catastrophe in the Native Southeast, 1492–1715* (Lincoln: University of Nebraska Press, 2007); and Robin Beck, *Chiefdoms, Collapse, and Coalescence in the Early American South* (Cambridge: Cambridge University Press, 2013), especially pp. 6, 152. Andrés Reséndez, *The Other Slavery: The Uncovered Story of Indian Enslavement in America* (Boston: Houghton Mifflin Harcourt, 2016), also judges that historians have overemphasized disease in the population declines in the Caribbean, Mexico, and the US Southwest. Reséndez is best read alongside Fernando Santos-Granero, *Vital Enemies: Slavery, Predation, and the Amerindian Political Economy of Life* (Austin: University of Texas Press, 2009), which shows how commonplace pre-Columbian slavery was. A recent overview, again more attuned to North America than elsewhere, and one that insists on the centrality of infectious disease, is Seth Archer, "Colonialism and Other Afflictions: Rethinking Native American Health History," *History Compass*, 14 (2016), 511–21. See also Tai S. Edwards and Paul Kelton, "Germs, Genocides and America's Indigenous Peoples," *Journal of American History*, 107 (2020), 52–76, which, although focused on whether or not the term genocide is appropriate, reviews much of the literature on the relative roles of epidemics, violence, and displacement in the North American context. Many of the views here would apply more strongly to North America than to the Caribbean.

60. A general discussion is Jean-Frédéric Schaub, "Violence in the Atlantic: Sixteenth and Seventeenth Centuries," in Nicholas Canny and Philip Morgan, eds., *The Oxford Handbook of the Atlantic World, 1450–1850* (Oxford: Oxford University Press, 2011), 113–29.

61. Henige and Livi-Bacci fall into this category. I do not.

62. For slavery in the pearl fisheries, see Molly A. Warsh, "Enslaved Pearl Divers in the Sixteenth Century Caribbean," *Slavery and Abolition*, 31 (2010), 345–62.

63. Erin Woodruff Stone, *Captives of Conquest: Slavery in the Early Modern Spanish Caribbean* (Philadelphia: University of Pennsylvania Press, 2021), 7, extrapolating from the very limited documentation, suggests 250,000 to 500,000 for the circum-Caribbean including the mainland coasts and hinterlands of Florida, Mexico, Central and South America.

64. In 1514 on Hispaniola, records of labor drafts of Taíno indicate that 43 percent had no children. Miguel D. Mena, *Iglesia, espacio, y poder: Santo Domingo (1498–1521), experiencia fundacional del nuevo mundo* (Santo Domingo: Archivo General de la Nación, 2007), 285, cited in Stone, *Captives of Conquest*, 52. It is not clear the age distribution represented in these records or how Spanish clerks knew who had children and who did not. The baby teeth thus far found from pre-Columbian populations in the Caribbean suggest that the average age at which infants were weaned was low, one to two years on average (about half the global average). If that is accurate, it would allow higher than average fertility but not guarantee it. Mickleburgh, "Reading the Dental Record," 314–15.

65. Livi-Bacci, *Conquest*, makes this case throughout. David S. Reher, "Reflections on the Fate of the Indigenous Populations of America," *Population and Development Review*, 37 (2011), 172–77 emphasizes fertility decline for the hemisphere as a whole. Robert McCaa and colleagues have argued that Nahua speakers in Central Mexico had very high fertility and mortality rates before 1519, and that high fertility was necessary to maintain population. Any reduction in fertility necessarily brought population decline. Robert McCaa, "Marriageways in Mexico and Spain, 1500–1900," *Continuity and Change*, 9 (1994), 11–43;

Lourdes Marquez Morfin, Robert McCaa, Rebecca Storey, Andrés del Angel, "Health and Nutrition in Prehispanic Mesoamerica," in Richard H. Steckel and Jerome C. Rose, eds., *The Backbone of History: Health and Nutrition in the Western Hemisphere* (New York: Cambridge University Press, 2002), 307–38; R. McCaa, "Child Marriage and Complex Families among the Nahuas of Ancient Mexico," *Latin American Population History Bulletin*, 26 (1994), 2–11.

66. Peter Katona and Judit Katone-Apte, "The Interaction between Nutrition and Infection," *Clinical Infectious Diseases*, 46 (2008), 1582–88.

67. See Chapter 3 in this volume, by Schwartz and Mulcahy, on drought. On the intersections among drought, hunger, and epidemics in sixteenth-century central Mexico, see Bradley Skopyk, *Colonial Cataclysms: Climate, Landscape, and Memory in Mexico's Little Ice Age* (Tuscon: University of Arizona Press, 2020), 31–88.

68. Newson, "Demographic Impact," 153–54, says that between 1492 and 1600 some 250,000 to 300,000 Spaniards came to the Americas. Of the roughly 50,000 whose destination is recorded, about 10–11 percent stayed in the West Indies. After 1540, rather few chose to stay in the Caribbean. Moreover, many of those Spaniards recognized that their welfare depended on the survival of Amerindians as laborers. As a Franciscan friar in Guatemala wrote to the Spanish king in 1575: "each day the Indians become fewer in number, while Spaniards increase, and this is a matter of some urgency. If the Indians perish within two generations then the sons and grandsons of those who conquered in Your Majesty's name will suffer great hardships." Quoted and translated in W. George Lovell, "Disease and Depopulation in Early Colonial Guatemala," in Noble David Cook and W. George Lovell, eds., *Secret Judgments of God: Old World Disease in Colonial Spanish America* (Norman: University of Oklahoma Press, 1991), 57. Original: *los naturales son cada día menos, los españoles cada día más y asi ay grandísimas necesidades y si los indios no duran más de dos vidas padescerian los hijos y nietos de los conquistadores que han ganado a Vuestra Majestad toda esta tierra mucha necesidad.*

69. George Raudzens, "Outfighting or Outpopulating: Main Reasons for Early Colonial Conquests," in Raudzens, ed., *Technology, Disease and Colonial Conquests*, 39–43, reviews the evidence concerning violence in Hispaniola before 1514, and concludes it played little role.

70. Studies exist for California, the coast of Georgia, Ecuador, and the US Southwest, and only in the latter case did the frequency of cranial trauma rise with European contact. The value of this evidence as an index of trends in violence is reduced by the fact that Europeans brought new weaponry that created different kinds of wounds. The studies all appear in Richard Steckel, ed., *The Backbone of History: Health and Nutrition in the Western Hemisphere* (New York: Cambridge University Press, 2002), and are summarized in Joerg Baten and Richard Steckel, "The History of Violence in Europe: Evidence from Cranial and Postcranial Bone Trauma," in Richard Steckel, Clark Spencer Larsen, Charlotte A. Roberts, and Joerg Baten, eds., *The Backbone of Europe: Health, Diet, Work, and Violence over Two Millennia* (Cambridge: Cambridge University Press, 2019), 301–2

71. It would be revealing to compare the pace and scale of population loss in those parts of the Caribbean where slaving was rife, such as the Bahamas or the Lesser Antilles, with those where it was not, such as Jamaica.

72. Watts, "The Caribbean Environment and Early Settlement," in by P. C. Emmer, ed., *General History of the Caribbean. Volume II. New Societies: The Caribbean in the Long Sixteenth Century* (London: UNESCO, 1999), 38. Watts based his judgment on the account of Hugh Thomas, *The Conquest of Mexico* (London: Hutchinson, 1993), 609–14. Livi-Bacci, *Conquest*, 114, and Henige, *Numbers from Nowhere*, passim, share Watts's skepticism about the role of disease before 1518.

73. Pathogens swirled through Seville and other ports of embarkation in the early sixteenth century. See Alexandra Parma Cook and Noble David Cook, *The Plague Files: Crisis Management in Sixteenth-Century Seville* (Baton Rouge: Louisiana State University Press, 2009); and Kristy Wilson Bowers, *Plague and Public Health in Early Modern Seville* (Rochester, NY: University of Rochester Press, 2013).

74. There was one other route for smallpox. In ideal (dry and cool) conditions, the virus can stay viable for months in clothing that has rubbed against infective pustules. If that virus can then escape the clothing and slip into a cut or abrasion on a susceptible person's skin, it can survive and replicate in the welcoming environment of a non-immune body. But this route,

too, required a lot of viral luck. Against this there is the exception that proves the rule, the account of the 280-ton slave ship *Britannia* in the late eighteenth century. Its captain bought 450 slaves in New Calabar, one of which was a young girl suffering from smallpox. Before the ship made it to the West Indies, 230 slaves had died from the disease according to the testimony of William James. See Great Britain, House of Commons, *Report of the Lords of the Committee of Council Appointed for Consideration of All Matters Relating to Trade and Foreign Plantations* (London, 1789), Part II, 7–8.

75. Data on voyage duration, ship sizes, and so forth is compiled in Pierre Chaunu and Huguette Chaunu, *Séville et l'Atlantique* (Paris: SEVPEN, 1955–60), vols. 2 and 6. Roughly 20,000 bodies sailed from Spain to the West Indies, 1492–1518. The crossing took on average 48 days.

76. Bartolomé de las Casas, *A Short Account of the Destruction of the Indies* (London: Penguin, 1992), 12–13.

77. Eighteen months into the COVID-19 pandemic in the worst-hit country, Peru, the SARS-CoV-2 virus had killed about 0.6 percent of the population.

78. See, e.g., the Latvian-Chilean physician Alejandro Lipschutz, "La despoblación de las Indias después de la Conquista," *América indígena*, 26 (1966), quoted in Francisco Guerra, "El efecto demográfico de la epidemias tras el descrubrimiento de América," *Revista de Indias*, 46 (1986), 43: "the dominant cause behind the depopulation of the Americas was the violent imposition of decadent European feudalism of the fifteenth and sixteenth centuries, in the form of the *encomienda* upon the peoples of the Americas." On colonialism's evils, I incline toward the analysis and judgment of David Abernethy, *Dynamics of Global Dominance: European Overseas Empire, 1415–1980* (New Haven, CT: Yale University Press, 2000), 387–407.

79. Spaniards, in fact, often killed Amerindians accidentally through what they understood as acts of kindness. In the interest of spreading their faith, maximizing baptisms, and saving souls, religious orders embarked on programs of gathering Amerindian populations together, called *reducciones*. Priests and officials in most cases sincerely wished to save souls, and sometimes to rescue people from ruthless exploitation. But the policy was carried out at times with mixed motives, as on Hispaniola in 1517. Hieronymite priests gathered some 3,500 people into one settlement at Juan de Ampiés, where they were put to work mining gold—an assignment at odds with the ascetic and scholarly traditions of the Hieronymite order. In 1519 an epidemic, identified as smallpox, carried off three-quarters of them. From Paraguay to Peru to Florida to California, missions had a similar impact, clustering people together and maximizing their disease exposure. See Esteban Mira Caballos, *La Española, epicentro del Caribe en el siglo XVI* (Santo Domingo: Academia Dominica de la Historia, 2010), 350–67. Diseases spread at mission villages among Florida's Timicua (Amerindian) reduced population by up to 90 percent, 1600–80, according to John Worth, *The Timucuan Chiefdoms of Spanish Florida*, vol II, *Resistance and Destruction* (Gainesville: University of Florida Press, 1998), 10. Collecting Indians into California missions helped to account for the toll of smallpox in 1838–40, which killed up to 60 percent of California's Amerindians, or some 200,000 to 300,000 people, according to Benjamin Madley, "The Third Vector: Pacific Pathogens, Colonial Disease Ecologies, and Native America Epidemics North of Mexico," in Edward Melillo and Ryan Jones, eds., *Migrant Ecologies* (Honolulu: University of Hawaii Press, forthcoming). Madley cites volume 4, pp. 65–66 of the manuscript of the Spanish governor of California, Juan Alvarado, *Historia de California* (5 vols.) in the University of California's Bancroft Library, MSS C-D 4. See also the pioneering work S. F. Cook, *The Epidemic of 1830–1833 in California and Oregon* (Berkeley: University of California Press, 1955); and David Igler, "Diseased Goods: Global Exchanges in the Eastern Pacific Basin, 1770–1850," *The American Historical Review*, 109, no. 3 (June 2014), 693–719.

80. Much, but probably not all, of the Americas. The arguments of Kelton, *Epidemics and Enslavement*, and Beck, *Chiefdoms, Collapse, and Coalescence,* for the southeastern United States, viz., that epidemics played a smaller role in population decline than violent slave raiding undertaken by Amerindians to supply labor to English settlers, make sense. Settlements were scattered over nearly 1 million square miles, and separated by almost uninhabited buffer zones, so the connectivity of the Amerindian communities was too low to sustain widespread

epidemics. The Caribbean, where almost everyone lived near the sea and canoe traffic linked all the islands, was very different in this respect, and more conducive to disease transmission.

81. Pedro Alvarez Chanca, "The Letter of Dr Pedro Alvarez Chanca Dated 1494 Relating to the Second Voyage of Columbus," *Smithsonian Miscellaneous Collections*, 48 (1907), 453. A detailed archaeological account of the first settlement is Kathleen Deagan and José María Cruxent, *Columbus's Outpost among the Taínos: Spain and America at la Isabela, 1493–1498* (New Haven, CT: Yale University Press, 2002).

82. Oviedo, *Historia natural*, quoted in Francisco Guerra, "The Earliest American Epidemic: The Influenza of 1493," *Social Science History*, 12 (1988), 313.

83. E.g., Samuel Eliot Morison, *Admiral of the Ocean Sea* (Boston: Little, Brown, 1942). As discussed later, both malaria and yellow fever were introduced somewhat later to the Americas from Africa.

84. Details for this hypothesis are in Guerra, "The Earliest American Epidemic"; Francisco Guerra, "La epidemia americana de influenza en 1493," *Revista de Indias*, 45 (1985), 325–47; and Agustín Muñoz-Sanz, "La gripe de Cristóbal Colón: Hipótesis sobre una catástrofe ecológica," *Enfermedades Infecciosas y Microbiología Clínica*, 24 (2006), 326–34. Ducks, wild or domestic, might also have been present and assisted with the transmission of influenza. It appears that a 1494 hurricane in Hispaniola might have damaged crops, food supplies, and nutrition—and therefore reduced disease resistance.

85. Las Casas, *Historia de Indias*, 1: 419–20, cited in Cook, *Born to Die*, 37. In his most famous work, the *Brevísima relación de la destrucción de las Indias* (1542), Las Casas wrote that Amerindians were delicate and died easily from any disease. In his *Historia de las Indias*, he wrote that God sent pestilence to liberate *Indios* from suffering and to punish the Spaniards for their wickedness. Thus he could square observations of high disease mortality with his argument that Spanish conduct in the West Indies was so cruel as to warrant royal intervention.

86. James Webb, *Humanity's Burden: A Global History of Malaria* (New York: Cambridge University Press, 2009), 66–91.

87. Keegan, "Destruction of the Taino," citing Las Casas.

88. Cook, *Born to Die*, 31–32.

89. Cook, *Born to Die*, 61; Livi-Bacci, *Conquest*, 45.

90. Las Casas, *Historia de las Indias*, 3: 270.

91. Oviedo, *Historia natural*, I:105.

92. *Colección de documentos inéditos relativos al descrubimiento, conquista y colonización de las posesiones españolas en América y Oceania*, ed. J. F. Pacheco et al. (Madrid: Manuel B. de Quirós, 1864), I:429. See also Emilio Rodríguez Demorizi, *Los dominicos y las encomiendas de indios de la isla Española* (Santo Domingo: Editora del Caribe, 1971), 13–14.

93. Cieza de León, *Crónica del Perú*, 75.

94. Cook, *Born to Die*, 60–77; Newson, "The Depopulation of Nicaragua."

95. Raúl Porras Barrenechea, ed., *Cartas del Perú* (Lima: Sociedad de Bibliofilos Peruanos, 1959), 22, quoted in Cook, *Born to Die*, 91.

96. On measles and immune amnesia: Michael Mina et al., "Long-Term Measles-Induced Immunomodulation Increases Overall Childhood Infectious Disease Mortality," *Science*, 348 (May 8, 2015), 694–99; Michael Mina, "Measles, Immune Suppression and Vaccination: Direct and Indirect Nonspecific Vaccine Benefits," *Journal of Infection*, 74 (2017), S10– S17; Michael Mina et al., "Measles Virus Infection Diminishes Preexisting Antibodies that Offer Protection from Other Pathogens," *Science*, 366 (2019), 599–606.

97. In New Spain, 1545–50, an epidemic called *cocoliztli* ("pestilence" in the Nahua language) slashed population totals dramatically. Its identity remains mysterious, but the latest genetic evidence suggests a strain of *salmonella enterica*—a cause of typhoid and related infections—was involved, at least in the case of one cemetery in Oaxaca. See A. J. Vagene et al., "Salmonella enterica Genomes Recovered from Victims of a Major 16th-Century Epidemic in Mexico," *bioRxiv* (2017), 106740, http://dx.doi.org/10.1101/106740. See also Ewen Callaway, "Salmonella Suspected in Aztec Decline," *Nature*, 542 (February 23, 2017), 404. Typhus, measles, and smallpox have all been suggested previously as the infections called *cocoliztli*.

98. Kathryn Labelle, *Dispersed but Not Destroyed: A History of the Seventeenth-century Wendat People* (Vancouver: University of British Columbia Press, 2014), 14–16. The most detailed

demographic work on the Wendat is Gary Warrick, *A Population History of the Huron-Petun, A.D. 500–1650* (New York: Cambridge University Press, 2008), especially pp. 192–243. See also Neal Salisbury, "Native People and European Settlers in Eastern North America," in *The Cambridge History of the Native Peoples of the Americas*, vol. I, *North America* (New York: Cambridge University Press, 1996), 408. Salisbury also says that epidemics reduced the coastal populations between Newfoundland and Nantucket by 90 percent in 1616–19 (pp. 402–3).

99. Elizabeth Fenn, *Encounters at the Heart of the World: A History of the Mandan People* (New York: Hill & Wang, 2014), 325, says 90 percent of the Mandan died from the 1837 smallpox as well as 50 percent of their neighbors, the Hidatsa. Some of their neighbors had been vaccinated, but not the Mandan. The earlier smallpox epidemic of 1781–82 in the Dakotas killed about 68 percent of the Mandan, Hidatsa, and Arikaras according to Elizabeth Fenn, *Pox Americana: The Great Smallpox Epidemic of 1775–1782* (New York: Hill & Wang, 2002), 270–71. See also James Dashchuk, *Clearing the Plains: Disease, Politics of Starvation, and the Loss of Aboriginal Life* (Regina, Saskatchewan, Canada: University of Regina Press, 2013), 36–57, on the epidemics among First Nations on the Canadian prairies, 1781–1822. Smallpox in 1781–82 devastated plains people, and a combined measles and whooping cough syndemic in 1818–20 killed 40–65 percent of them.

100. Estimates from Seth Archer, *Sharks upon the Land: Colonialism, Indigenous Health, and Culture in Hawai'i, 1778–1855* (New York: Cambridge University Press, 2018), 217, 225, 231, 241–43.

101. G. Dennis Shanks et al., "Extreme Mortality after First Introduction of Measles Virus to the Polynesian Island of Rotuma, 1911," *American Journal of Epidemiology*, 173 (2011), 1211–22.

102. G. Dennis Shanks et al., "Epidemiological Isolation Causing Variable Mortality in Island Populations during the 1918–1920 Influenza Pandemic," *Influenza and Other Respiratory Viruses*, 6 (2019), 417–23. J. L. Rallu, "Pre- and Post-Contact Population in Island Polynesia," in P. V. Kirch and J. L. Rallu, eds., *The Growth and Collapse of Pacific Island Societies* (Honolulu: University of Hawaii Press, 2007), 15–34. It could also be the case that the age structure of populations affected overall mortality in the 1918 influenza pandemic, because it disproportionately killed young adults. France was low on young men in 1918 as a result of World War I, which had no parallel impact on French Polynesia. For details on the Marquesas in particular, see Jean-Louis Rallu, *Les populations océaniennes aux XIXe et XXe siècles* (Paris: Institut National d'Etudes Démographiques, 1990). On Samoa, see Sandra Tomkins, "The Influenza Epidemic of 1918–19 in Western Samoa," *Journal of Pacific History*, 27 (1992), 181–97.

103. Richard J. Shell, "The Marianas Population Decline: 17th Century Estimates," *Journal of Pacific History*, 34 (1999), 291–305. It is likely the 1668 population had already fallen from levels of 1565, but there is no firm evidence one way or another. See also Richard Shell, "The Ladrones Population," *Journal of Pacific History*, 36 (2001), 225–36; Cynthia Wiecko, *Guam: At the Crossroads of Spanish Militarization, Ecological Change, and Identity in World History* (PhD thesis, Washington State University, 2011), 194–95. After 1700, Spaniards inflicted considerable violence and dispossession upon Guam's indigenous people.

104. F. X. Hezel, "From Conversion to Conquest: The Early Spanish Mission in the Marianas," *Journal of Pacific History*, 17 (1982), 135, n. 64.

105. Ann Ramenofsky, *Vectors of Death*, 161. The key study is: P. Brown, D. C. Gajdusek, and J. A. Morris, "Epidemic A2 Influenza in Isolated Pacific Island Populations without Pre-epidemic Antibody to Influenza Virus Types A and B, and the Discovery of Other Still Unexposed Populations," *American Journal of Epidemiology*, 83 (1966), 176–88.

106. J. Steffensen, "Smallpox in Iceland," *Nordisk medicinhistorisk årsbok* (1977), 41–56. While not an island, the Cape Colony in South Africa was another place that smallpox could reach only infrequently. An outbreak in 1713 killed 20 percent of the European settler population and 21 percent of the enslaved African population according to tax rolls. Robert Ross, "Smallpox and the Cape of Good Hope in the Eighteenth Century," in C. Fyvie and D. McMasters, eds., *African Historical Demography* (Edinburgh: Centre for African Studies, University of Edinburgh, 1977), I:416–28.

107. More precisely, the median loss per epidemic of measles was 18 percent and the mean 24 percent. For influenza the median was 20 percent and the mean 28 percent. For malaria, 19 percent and 27 percent. Robert S. Walker, Lisa Sattenspiel, and Kim R. Hill, "Mortality from Contract-Related Epidemics among Indigenous Populations in Greater Amazonia," *Scientific Reports*, 5 (September 10, 2015), 14032, DOI: 10.1038/srep14032.

108. Marcus J. Hamilton, , Robert S. Walker, and Dylan C. Kesler, "Crash and Rebound of Indigenous Populations in Lowland South America," *Scientific Reports*, 4 (2014), [https://www.nature.com/articles/srep04541?message-global%3Dremove%26WT.ec_id%3DSREP-631-20140408]

109. Quoted in Nicolás Sánchez-Albornoz, *The Population of Latin America: A History* (Berkeley: University of California Press, 1974), 56.

110. This point is emphasized in James C. Riley, "Smallpox and American Indians Revisited," *Journal of the History of Medicine and Allied Sciences*, 65 (2010), 445–77.

111. I say "apparently" because leaders probably did find ways to mitigate the impact of repeated epidemics, even if not in the form of medical interventions.

112. Guerra, "El efecto," 52–53, argues for yellow fever arriving in the Caribbean as early as the late 1490s—unlikely in my view.

113. Enrique Beldarraín Chaple and Maira Celeiro Chaple, "Sinopsis histórica del clima y las enfermedades en Cuba," in Luz María Espinosa Cortés and Enrique Beldarraín Chaple, eds., *Cuba y México: Desastres, alimentación y salud: siglos XVIII y XIX* (Mexico City: Plaza y Valdés, 2005), 32, maintains that a dengue epidemic affected the whole island of Cuba in 1782. S. V. Mayer, R. B. Tesh and N. Vasilakis, "The Emergence of Arthropod-Borne Viral Diseases: A Global Perspective on Dengue, Chikungunya and Zika Fevers," *Acta Tropica*, 166 (2017), 155–63 suggest a pan-tropical dengue outbreak ca. 1779–88. Karen Bourdier, *Vie quotidienne et conditions sanitaires sur les grandes habitations sucrières du nord de Saint-Domingue à la veille de l'insurrection d'août 1791* (PhD thesis, Université de Pau et des Pays de l'Adour, 2005), 183–48, suggests dengue visited Saint-Domingue in the late eighteenth century. Dengue's first appearance in the Danish West Indies came in 1827 according to Jensen, *For the Health of the Enslaved*, 84–85.

114. World Health Organization, "Severe Falciparum Malaria," *Transactions of the Royal Society of Tropical Medicine and Hygiene*, 94, suppl. (2000), 1–90.

115. Roughly half of those heading to the Americas in the sixteenth century came from southern Spain.

116. See the Malaria Atlas Project of Oxford University for Anopheline vectoral capacity: https://map.ox.ac.uk/bionomics/. Mosquitoes that are long-lived and prefer human blood for their meals are the most efficient vectors.

117. James L. A. Webb, *Humanity's Burden: A Global History of Malaria* (New York: Cambridge University Press, 2009), 71.

118. Slave trade numbers from the Transatlantic Slave Trade Database at: http://www.slavevoyages.org/assessment/estimates

119. Malaria resistance is a devilishly complex subject imperfectly understood by experts. See Denise Doolan, Carlota Dobaño, and J. Kevin Baird, "Acquired Immunity to Malaria," *Clinical Microbiology Reviews*, 22 (2009), 13–36.

120. This account of malaria's arrival in the Americas draws on Webb, *Humanity's Burden*, 66–91. See, however, the argument in Linda Newson, *The Cost of Conquest: Indian Decline in Honduras under Spanish Rule* (Boulder, CO: Westview Press, 1986), 261–62, who argues that malaria's impact, like yellow fever's, could have come only after the catastrophe had unfolded.

121. The argument is sometimes made that some populations' immune systems were selected for general efficiency by virtue of their ancestors' long experience with infectious disease. While this appeals to the principles of evolutionary biology, my best guess—by no means expert—is that this sort of genetic adaptation took too long, and disease environments were too unstable, to have much bearing. With falciparum malaria, however, long experience could bring genetic adaptations that conferred protection.

122. Sometimes "adaptive immunity" or "adaptive resistance." I belabor this point because some authors (if I read them correctly) insist that there can be no difference in the preparedness

of immune systems among different populations of the world, seem to deny the possibility of acquired immunity, and suggest dark motives among those who disagree. See, e.g., David S. Jones, "Virgin Soils Revisited," *William & Mary Quarterly*, 60 (2003), 703–42; David S. Jones, *Rationalizing Epidemics: Meanings and Uses of American Indian Mortality Since 1600* (Cambridge, MA: Harvard University Press, 2004); Jones, "Death, Uncertainty and Rhetoric," in Cameron et al., eds., *Beyond Germs*, 16–49.

123. Dennis O'Rourke and Jennifer Raff, "The Human Genetic History of the Americas: The Final Frontier," *Current Biology*, 20 (February 23, 2010), R202–R207, DOI 10.1016/j.cub.2009.11.051. See also Sijia Wang et al., "Genetic Variation and Population Structure in Native Americans," *PLOS Genetics* (November 23, 2007), http://dx.doi.org/10.1371/journal.pgen.0030185. Wang et al. review the genetic diversity among populations in the Americas and find the longer the migration from Beringia, the lower the genetic diversity, emphasizing the role of serial founder effects. A useful recent summary is Deborah A. Bolnick et al., "Native American Genomics and Population Histories," *Annual Review of Anthropology*, 45 (2016), 319–40. See also Nelson Fagundes et al., "How Strong Was the Bottleneck Associated to the Peopling of the Americas? New Insights from Multilocus Sequence Data," *Genetics and Molecular Biology*, 41 (2018), 206–14.

124. J. Benn-Torres et al., "Admixture and Population Stratification in African Caribbean Populations," *Annals of Human Genetics*, 72 (2008), 90–98. For an effort to uncover the genetic history of the Caribbean more generally, using DNA from living populations, see A. Moreno-Estrada et al., "Reconstructing the Population Genetic History of the Caribbean," *PLoS Genetics*, 9 (2013), e1003925, doi:10.1371/journal.pgen.1003925.

125. C. Lalueza-Fox et al., "MtDNA from Extinct Tainos and the Peopling of the Caribbean," *Annals of Human Genetics*, 65 (2001), 137–51; C. Lalueza-Fox et al., "Mitochondrial DNA from Pre-Columbian Ciboneys From Cuba and the Prehistoric Colonization of the Caribbean," *American Journal of Physical Anthropology*, 121 (2003), 97–108; F. Mendisco et al., "Where Are the Caribs: Ancient DNA from Ceramic Period Human Remains in the Lesser Antilles," *Philosophical Transactions of the Royal Society B*, 370, no. 1160 (January 19, 2015), DOI: 10.1098/rstb.2013.0388.

126. Francis Black, "An Explanation of High Death Rates among New World Peoples When in Contact with Old World Diseases," *Perspectives in Biology and Medicine*, 37 (1994), 296–97, explains this in terms of Amerindians as a whole (not Caribbean peoples specifically), arguing that their genetic homogeneity appears evident in the range of histocompatibility antigens that can be produced by their immune systems. See also Francis Black, "Disease Susceptibility among New World Peoples," in Francisco Salzano and A. Magdalena Hurtado, eds., *Lost Paradises and the Ethics of Research and Publication* (Oxford: Oxford University Press, 2004), 146–63, especially pp. 153–58. The same was likely true of Iceland's population in 1707 and indeed earlier, because Iceland has, and presumably 400 years ago also had, narrower genetic diversity than the rest of Europe. See A. Helgason, G. Nicholson, K. Stefánsson, and P. Donnelly, "A Reassessment of Genetic Diversity in Icelanders: Strong Evidence from Multiple Loci for Relative Homogeneity Caused by Genetic Drift," *Annals of Human Genetics*, 67 (2003), 281–97, doi:10.1046/j.1469-1809.2003.00046.x. This paper speaks to the genetic homogeneity of Icelanders; the inferences about the disease vulnerability of Icelanders in 1707 is my own and should be treated with caution.

127. The probability that a specific pathogen will encounter antibodies that don't do it much harm is highly sensitive to the number of different alleles present in a population. A mathematical treatment of this issue appears in Black, "An Explanation of High Death Rates," 299–300. He says that on average the variety of relevant alleles is 15 times greater in populations of Africa and Eurasia than in indigenous Americans.

128. On this basis Riley, "Smallpox and American Indians Revisited," 468, says this argument may not matter for smallpox, a more stable virus, as opposed to measles. He refers to various cultural factors that might have made smallpox as lethal as it was among North American Amerindians, such as the indoor environment of the longhouse among peoples of the northeast.

129. Work examining immune response in Brazil has shown that indigenous people's immune systems are as adept as any other individual Brazilian's immune system. Black, "Disease

Susceptibility among New World Peoples," 153; and Black, "An Explanation of High Death Rates," 295. An accessible discussion of the relevant features of human immune systems appears in Andrew Noymer, "Population Decline in Post-Conquest America: The Role of Disease," *Population and Development Review*, 37 (2011), 178–83.

130. This line of argument might apply, but with lesser force, to the remoter populations of the Pacific, to Icelanders, and other populations whose ancestors migrated recently into what were isolated regions. On the Marianas, see M. Vilar et al., "The Origins and Genetic Distinctiveness of the Chamorros of the Marianas Islands: An mtDNA Perspective," *American Journal of Human Biology*, 25(2013), 116–22, which shows narrow genetic variation among Chamorros generally today, due both to a small founder population and to the disappearance of the majority of the population in the centuries after contact.

131. Wheat, *Atlantic Africa*, 280, estimates that 69 percent of the population of the Spanish Caribbean, ca. 1605–15, was African-born or of African descent and 23 percent were Spaniards.

132. J. R. McNeill, *Mosquito Empires: Ecology and War in the Greater Caribbean, 1620–1914* (New York: Cambridge University Press, 2010), 64, and the sources cited there. Interestingly, in the same years, the European port most closely connected to the Spanish Caribbean, Seville, suffered from a bubonic plague outbreak. Could plague have made it to the Caribbean or yellow fever to Seville, perhaps creating double epidemics in one or both?

133. A phrase from Philip Curtin, *The Rise and Fall of the Plantation Complex* (New York: Cambridge University Press, 1998).

134. This was not true of the southern colonies of British North America, where by 1710–30 natural increase prevailed among enslaved populations. In the West Indies natural decrease lasted until 1805–50, depending on the island.

135. Geoffrey Parker, *Global Crisis: War, Climate Change and Catastrophe in the Seventeenth Century* (New Haven, CT: Yale University Press, 2013).

136. David Watts, *The West Indies: Patterns of Development, Culture and Environmental Change since 1492* (Cambridge: Cambridge University Press, 1987), 127–228 offers a geographically sensitive account of the installation of the plantation regime.

137. On the coevolution of *Ae. aegypti* and human societies, see J. E. Brown, B. R. Evans, W. Zheng, V. Obas, L. Barrera-Martinez, A. Egizi, H. Zhao, A. Caccone, and J. R. Powell, "Human Impacts Have Shaped Historical and Recent Evolution in *Aedes aegypti*, the Dengue and Yellow Fever Mosquito," *Evolution*, 68 (2014), 514–25, doi:10.1111/evo.12281.

138. The connections between sugar plantations and *Aedes aegypti* habitat is detailed in McNeill, *Mosquito Empires*, 47–52, which expands upon James Goodyear, "The Sugar Connection: A New Perspective on the History of Yellow Fever," *Bulletin of the History of Medicine*, 52 (1978), 5–21. Philip Rotz finds a connection between sugar plantations in Natal and dengue epidemics for which *Aedes aegypti* serves as vector: Rotz, "Sweetness and Fever? Sugar Production, Aedes agypti, and Dengue Fever in Natal, South Africa, 1926–1927," *South African History Journal*, 68 (2016), 286–303.

139. On the expansion of irrigation to serve sugar plantations in Saint-Domingue, see Trevor Burnard and John Garrigus, *The Plantation Machine: Atlantic Capitalism in French Saint-Domingue and British Jamaica* (Philadelphia: University of Pennsylvania Press, 2016), 35. Surinam's sugar plantations featured abundant canals as the Dutch transplanted their refined water-management skills to their plantations. Alex van Stipriaan, *Surinaams contrast, Roofbouw en Overleven in een Caraïbische Plantagekolonie, 1750–1863* (Leiden: KITLV, 1993), 81–98; Gert Oostindie and Alex van Stipriaan, "Slavery and Slave Cultures in a Hydraulic Society," in Stephan Palmié, ed., *Slave Cultures and the Cultures of Slavery* (Knoxville: University of Tennessee Press, 1995), 80–82.

140. See Bourdier, *Vie quotidienne et conditions sanitaires sur les grandes habitations sucrières*, 110–17, on the quick and thorough deforestation of northern Saint-Domingue in the eighteenth century.

141. Jordan Smith, *The Invention of Rum* (PhD dissertation, Georgetown University 2018), 115–16. Plantations normally included cisterns to collect water both for boiling houses and for the homes of estate owners or managers. Marco Meniketti, *Sugar Cane Capitalism and Environmental Transformation: An Archaelogy of Colonial Nevis, West Indies* (Tuscaloosa: University of Alabama Press, 2015), has some data on cisterns.

142. Erik Gøbel, *The Danish Slave Trade and Its Abolition* (Leiden: Brill, 2016), 58.
143. Higman, *Concise History of the Caribbean*, 130–31, 158–61; www.populastat.info; McNeill, *Mosquito Empires*, 25–26. Similar figures appear in Stanley Engerman and Barry Higman, "The Demographic Structure of Caribbean Slave Societies in the Eighteenth and Nineteenth Centuries," in Franklin Knight, ed., *General History of the Caribbean* (London: UNESCO Publishing, 2003), 3: 48–52.
144. This estimate is from J. R. McNeill, *Atlantic Empires and France and Spain* (Chapel Hill: University of North Carolina Press, 1985), 38, based on raw data compiled in the *visita* of Bishop Morell y Santa Cruz in: Archivo General de Indias, Audiencia de Santo Domingo, legajos 534 and 2227.
145. Strictly speaking, it could also be elevated by a disproportionate death rate among immunes, but this was exceedingly unlikely.
146. Kenneth Kiple and Brian T. Higgins, "Mortality Caused by Dehydration during the Middle Passage," *Social Science History*, 13 (1989), 421–37.
147. Richard Steckel and Richard Jensen, "New Evidence on the Causes of Slave and Crew Mortality in the Atlantic Slave Trade," *Journal of Economic History*, 46 (1986), 57–77. In the Dutch slave trade, dysentery topped the list among causes of death. Johannes Postma, *The Dutch in the Atlantic Slave Trade, 1600–1815* (Cambridge: Cambridge University Press, 1990), 244. Among the many studies of the Middle Passage, the latest to consider health at length is Sowande' M. Mustakeem, *Slavery at Sea: Terror, Sex, and Sickness in the Middle Passage* (Urbana: University of Illinois Press, 2016).
148. The French Compagnie des Indes paid bonuses to captains who minimized slave mortality. Robert Harms, *The Diligent: A Voyage through the Worlds of the Slave Trade* (New York: Basic Books, 2002), 318.
149. Erik Gøbel, "Dansk slavehandel på trekantruten," *Danske Magazin*, 52 (2012), 522–23. Tardo-Dino, himself a physician, without evidence credited doctors on board slave ships with reducing mortality: Frantz Tardo-Dino, *Le Collier de servitude: la condition sanitaire des esclaves aux Antilles françaises du XVIIe au XIVe siècle* (Paris: Editions Caribéennes, 1985), 57. For African healers on shipboard during the waning years of the Angola-Brazil slave trade, see pp. 215–17 in Mariza de Carvalho Soares, "African Barbeiros in Brazilian Slave Ports," in Jorge Canizares-Esgurra, Matt Childs, and James Sidbury, eds., *The Black Urban Atlantic in the Age of the Slave Trade* (Philadelphia: University of Pennsylvania Press, 2016), 207–32. For efforts to combat disease on slave ships in the early nineteenth century, see Barcia, *The Yellow Demon of Fever*, 166–93.
150. Details of mortality on slave voyages to the Caribbean appear in David Eltis and David Richardson, *Atlas of the Transatlantic Slave Trade* (New Haven, CT: Yale University Press, 2010), 169–81. Mortality declines resulted from better diet, shorter average sailing times, and, after 1805, the increasing practice of inoculation against smallpox. For the health of slaves upon arrival in sixteenth- and seventeenth-century Havana, see Alejandro de la Fuente García, "Índice de morbilidad e incidencia de enfermedades entre los esclavos en La Habana, 1580–1699," *Asclepios*, 43 (1991), 7–22. He finds (pp. 17–18) that disembarking slaves in Havana suffered from malnutrition and dysentery above all other conditions.
151. Alexander von Humboldt remarked on the seasonality of mortality among newly arrived slaves in Havana in the early nineteenth century: *Political Essay on the Island of Cuba* (Chicago: University of Chicago Press, 2011 [orig. pub. 1826]), 92.
152. Three out of four: Stephen Behrendt, "Ecology and Seasonality in the Slave Trade," in Bernard Bailyn and Patricia Denault, eds., *Soundings in Atlantic History: Latent Structures and Intellectual Currents* (Cambridge, MA: Harvard University Press, 2009), 54.
153. Stephen Behrendt, "Crew Mortality in the Transatlantic Slave Trade in the Eighteenth Century," *Slavery and Abolition*, 18 (1997), 49–71, calculates 16–17 percent mortality for British and French voyages. For a review of diseases affecting the slave trade to Cuba and slave health once ashore, see M. Salvador-Vázquez and C. Menéndez de León, "Higiene y enfermedad del esclavo en Cuba durante la primera mitad del siglo XIX," *Anuario de Estudios Americanos*, 43 (1986), 419–45. Gøbel, *Danish Slave Trade*, 44, cites data showing that for 49 voyages conducted by Danish slavers, 1777–89, the crew mortality was 33–34 percent and that for slaves 16 percent.

154. Pablo Gómez, *The Experiential Caribbean: Creating Knowledge and Healing in the Early Modern Atlantic* (Chapel Hill: University of North Carolina Press, 2017), 45. The same proportion obtained in the Danish West Indies: Gøbel, *Danish Slave Trade*, 46, and Neville Hall, *Slave Society in the Danish West Indies* (Kingston, Jamaica: University of the West Indies Press, 1992), 85. Half of all newly arrived slaves to the West Indies died within three years according to Richard Follett, "The Demography of Slavery," in Gad Heumann and Trevor Burnard, eds., *The Routledge History of Slavery* (London: Routledge, 2012), 120. Among state slaves in Havana in 1764, 19 percent died within six months: Evelyn P. Jennings, *Constructing the Spanish Empire in Havana: State Slavery in Defense and Development, 1762–1835* (Baton Rouge: Louisiana State University, 2020), 106. In the years before the abolition of the British slave trade (1807), the toll in Jamaica had declined to about one-quarter dead in the first year: David Collins, *Practical Rules of the Management and Medical Treatment of Negro Slaves in the Sugar Colonies* (London: J. Barfield, 1811), 51. For Saint-Domingue, Bourdier, *Vie quotidienne et conditions sanitaires sur les grandes habitations sucrières*, 40–41, 45–47, and Frantz Tardo-Dino, *Le Collier de servitude: la condition sanitaire des esclaves aux Antilles françaises du XVIIe au XIVe siècle* (Paris: Editions Caribéennes, 1985).

155. Gómez, *Experiential Atlantic*, 45. Gómez notes this is a very rough estimate and applies it to the sixteenth century in "Hospitals and Health in the Sixteenth-century Spanish Caribbean," in Ida Altman and David Wheat, eds., *The Spanish Caribbean and the Atlantic World in the Long Sixteenth* Century (Lincoln: University of Nebraska Press, 2019), 211–32, here 214.

156. José Fernández, *Apostólica y penitente vida de el V.P. Pedro Claver de la Compañia de Iesús: sacada principalmente de informaciones juridicas hechas ante el Ordinario de la ciudad de Cartagena de Indias: a su religiosisima Provincia de el Nuevo Reyno de Granada* (Zaragoza, Spain: Diego Dormer, 1666), 102.

157. Antoine de Bertin, *Des moyens de conserver la santé des blancs et des nègres, aux Antilles ou climats chauds et humides de l'Amérique* (Paris: Chez Méquignon, 1786), 38–39, cited in Bourdier, *Vie quotidienne et conditions sanitaires sur les grandes habitations sucrières*, 44 (I do not find the quotation in the online version of Bertin available to me).

158. Robert Renny, *An History of Jamaica* (London: Cawthorn, 1807), 241.

159. Plague transmission normally involves rodents capable of hosting the bacillus. Whether they existed in the Caribbean in the sixteenth century is unclear. However, once again the ecological changes of the plantation complex may have exacerbated the disease regime: both port cities and plantations themselves offered superb rat habitat, and therefore improved the prospects for the plague bacillus *Yersinia pestis*. On the other hand, after 1660 the frequency of plague epidemics in Europe diminished, and with it the likelihood of plague introductions to the Americas.

160. Three among many: Jean Dazille, *Observations sur les maladies des nègres* (Paris: Didot, 1776); Francisco Barrera y Domingo, *Reflexiones historico, fisico naturales, medico quirurgicas: prácticos y especulativos entretenimientos acerca de la vida, usos, costumbres, alimentos, bestidos, color y enfermedades a que propenden los negros de Africa, venidos a las Americas* (Havana: Ediciones C.R. 1953 [orig. pub. 1798]), 66–505; Nicolas-Louis Bourgeois, *Voyage intéressants dans différentes colonies françaises* (Paris: Bastien, 1788), 471, claimed that blacks and whites rarely suffered from the same diseases. Some modern scholars also use this distinction. See Bourdier, *Vie quotidienne et conditions sanitaires sur les grandes habitations sucrières*, 195–204, for example, where, following her sources closely, she discusses "diseases specific to slaves." See also E. Beldarraín Chaple, "Sanidad y esclavitud: medidas para contrarrestar las enfermedades de los esclavos en Cuba," *Afro-Hispanic Review*, 34 (2015), 9–29.

161. Richard Dunn, *Tale of Two Plantations: Slave Life and Labor in Jamaica and* Virginia (Cambridge, MA: Harvard University Press, 2014), 434, provides cause of death data for a Jamaican plantation, 1762–1834, that does show notable differences between male and female, but the sample size is small. Jensen, *For the Health of the Enslaved*, 125 and 283, using a sample from the Danish West Indies in the 1840s that is nearly 100 times as large, says that aside from the risks of childbirth, health hazards for male and female were similar. On maternal health and childbirth, Bourdier, *Vie quotidienne et conditions sanitaires sur les grandes habitations sucrières*, 353–58.

162. Among the enslaved, the discrepancy in health was so great that by the 1780s in the British West Indies, the price of an African-born slave was half that of one born in the Caribbean. Schiebinger, *Secret Cures*, 144. Other factors besides health might contribute to the price differential, but Schiebinger and her source attribute it, plausibly in my view, to differences in immunities and therefore life expectancies.

163. One could also arrange a discussion island by island, or by type of island. But in general the differences in disease regimes among islands were small, except in the case of Barbados, which had no malaria. Jensen, *For the Health of the Enslaved*, 112, notes that fevers were reported more frequently on St. Croix than in the British West Indies and gastrointestinal disease less often. A more ecologically logical approach to understanding the Caribbean disease environment would be to organize it by elevation, but the data are inconvenient for that purpose. In any case, most people lived at low elevations. James Delle, *The Colonial Caribbean: Landscapes of Power in the Plantation System* (New York: Cambridge University Press, 2014), 35–61, shows that between 1676 and 1814, 80–90 percent of Jamaican plantations lay below 250 m elevation (and 45–60 percent of them stood within 5 km of the coast).

164. A crucial text on Caribbean plantation health history, although superseded in some particulars, is Kenneth Kiple, *The Caribbean Slave: A Biological History* (Cambridge: Cambridge University Press, 1984). See also Jerome Handler, "Diseases and Medical Disabilities of Enslaved Barbadians from the Seventeenth Century to around 1838 (Part I)," *Journal of Caribbean History*, 40 (2006), 1–38, and Part II, *Journal of Caribbean History*, 40 (2006), 177–214; Richard Sheridan, *Doctors and Slaves: A Medical and Demographic History of the British West Indies, 1680–1834* (Cambridge: Cambridge University Press, 1985; Karen Bourdier, *Vie quotidienne et conditions sanitaires sur les grandes habitations sucrières*; Leti, *Santé et société esclavagiste*; Gabriel Debien, *Les esclaves aux Antilles françaises* (Basse-Terre: Société d'Histoire de la Guadeloupe, 1974), 297–336.

165. To judge by adult heights, nutrition in Atlantic Africa, specifically protein intake in childhood, was even worse than that on Caribbean slave plantations at least in the early nineteenth century. Data from Cuba, Guyana, and Trinidad show African-born slaves were on average 2 or 3 cm shorter than the Caribbean-born. Barry W. Higman, "Growth in Afro-Caribbean Slave Populations," *American Journal of Physical Anthropology*, 50 (1979), 376; Kiple, *The Caribbean Slave*, 23; Ramiro Alberto Flores Guzmán, "The Feeding of Slave Population in the United States, the Caribbean, and Brazil: Some Remarks in the State of the Art," *América Latina en la Historia Económica. Revista de Investigación*, 20 (2013), 16–22.

166. J. Handler and R. S. Corruccini, "Plantation Slave Life in Barbados: A Physical Anthropological Analysis," *Journal of Interdisciplinary History*, 14 (1983), 78, 81; Kristin A. Shuler, "Life and Death on a Barbadian Sugar Plantation," *International Journal of Osteoarchaeology*, 21 (2011), 66–81; Jensen, *For the Health of the Enslaved*, 165–94; Gabriel Debien, *Les esclaves aux Antilles françaises* (Basse-Terre: Société d'Histoire de la Guadeloupe, 1974), 171–218; Bourdier, *Vie quotidienne et conditions sanitaires sur les grandes habitations sucrières du nord de Saint-Domingue*, 75–83, 232–76; Jensen, *For the Health of the Enslaved*, passim.

167. For the Cuban case, see Ismael Sarmiento Ramírez, "Del funche al ajiaco: La dieta que los amos imponen a los esclavos africanos en Cuba y la asimilación que estos hacen a la cucina criolla," *Anales del Museo de América*, 16 (2009), 127–54; M. Salvador-Vázquez and C. Menéndez de León, "Higiene y enfermedad del esclavo en Cuba durante la primera mitad del siglo XIX," *Anuario de Estudios Americanos*, 43 (1986), 428–31.

168. On the economics of slave nutrition, Bourdier, *Vie quotidienne et conditions sanitaires sur les grandes habitations sucrières*, 268–76; Vertus Saint-Louis, *Système colonial et problèmes d'alimentation: Saint-Domingue au XVIIIe siècle* (Montreal: Editions du CIDIHCA, 1999).

169. Jensen, *For the Health of the Enslaved*, 187. Yams were the staff of life on plantations relying on provisioning grounds in the Danish West Indies in the early nineteenth century.

170. Schiebinger, *Secret Cures*, 53; Lucille M. Mair, *A Historical Study of Women in Jamaica, 1655–1834* (Kingston, Jamaica: University of the West Indies Press, 2006), 223–25.

171. See Trevor Burnard, *Mastery, Tyranny and Desire: Thomas Thistlewood and His Slaves in the Anglo-Jamaican World* (Chapel Hill: University of North Carolina Press, 2004).

172. On the sexual customs on Saint-Domingue sugar plantations and their impact on venereal disease, Bourdier, *Vie quotidienne et conditions sanitaires sur les grandes habitations sucrières*, 330–37. In the Dutch West Indies, slaves of African birth were likelier to maintain longer marriages and relationships than those of Caribbean birth according to Huub Everaert, *Een zoektocht naar de aard van man-vrouw relaties onder Surinaamse slaven: de suikerplantages Fairfield, Breukelerwaard, Cannewapibo en La Jalousie in de periode voorafgaande aan de emancipatie* (PhD thesis, University of Amsterdam, 1999).

173. The standard treatment for syphilis, mercury, might have killed more adults faster than syphilis itself.

174. See Handler, "Diseases and Medical Disabilities," 14; Burnard and Garrigus, *The Plantation Machine*, 69; Burnard, *Mastery, Tyranny, and Desire*; Trevor Burnard and Richard Follett, "Caribbean Slavery, British Anti-slavery, and the Cultural Politics of Venereal Disease," *The Historical Journal*, 55 (2012), 427–51 for changing understandings of venereal infections in the eighteenth century; Katherine Paugh, "Yaws, Syphilis, Sexuality, and the Circulation of Medical Knowledge in the British Caribbean and the Atlantic World," *Bulletin of the History of Medicine*, 88 (2014), 225–52, reviews understandings of yaws and syphilis, sometimes considered the same disease; on the Danish West Indies, Jensen, *For the Health of the Enslaved*, 99–101, says that slaves tried to conceal venereal infections from whites and used obeah healers. On Saint-Domingue, see Bourdier, "Les conditions sanitaires sur les habitations sucrières de Saint-Domingue à la fin du siècle," *Dix-huitième siècle*, 43 (2011), 360–61.

175. Bourdier, *Vie quotidienne et conditions sanitaires sur les grandes habitations sucrières*, 278–309, on the presence of livestock in Saint-Domingue, which in the 1780s had 40,000 horses, 50,000 mules, and 250,000 cattle, sheep, and goats.

176. B. W. Higman, *Slave Populations of the West Indies* (Baltimore: Johns Hopkins University Press, 1984), 281–92. On slave heights, nutrition, and sugar, see also J. R. Ward, "The Amelioration of British West Indian Slavery: Anthropometric Evidence," *Economic History Review*, 71 (2018), 1199–226. G. C. Friedman, "The Heights of Slaves in Trinidad," *Social Science History*, 6 (1982), 482–515. David Eltis, "Nutritional Trends in Africa and the Americas: Heights of Africans, 1819–1839," *Journal of Interdisciplinary History*, 12 (1982), 453–75.

177. Follett, "Demography of Slavery," 123. Birth rates were also slightly higher on non-sugar plantations. The difference in crude death rates between sugar plantations and other plantations on Jamaica in 1830 was greater than the difference between London and the rest of England at any time after 1780: the demographic penalty of sugar plantations probably outlasted that of cities. John Landers, *Death and the Metropolis: Studies in the Demographic History of London, 1670–1830* (Cambridge: Cambridge University Press, 1993), 175, shows that the discrepancy between London's and England's crude death rate declined from about 17/1000 in the 1730s to 9/1000 in the 1780s and a mere 3/1000 in the 1820s. England's crude death rate, 1700–1800, almost always stood between 24/1000 and 28/1000. E. A. Wrigley, "British Population during the Long Eighteenth Century, 1680–1840," in Roderick Floud and Paul Johnson, eds., *The Cambridge Economic History of Modern Britain*, vol. I, *Industrialisation, 1700–1860* (Cambridge: Cambridge University Press, 2004), 64.

178. On the health of sugar plantation populations, see Jensen, *For the Health of the Enslaved*, 45–51; Leti, *Santé et société esclavagiste*, 28, 258–60; Higman, *Slave Populations*, 324–29; Stipriaan, *Surinaams contrast*, 316–18, which shows that population loss among slaves on Surinam's sugar plantations, 1752–1850, ranged 50–100 percent higher than on coffee plantations; for Jamaica in the eighteenth century, see Vincent Brown, *The Reaper's Garden: Death and Power in the World of Atlantic Slavery* (Cambridge, MA: Harvard University Press, 2008), 51–54; for Louisiana data, see Urmi Engineer Willoughby, *Yellow Fever, Race, and Ecology in Nineteenth-Century New Orleans* (Baton Rouge: Louisiana State University Press, 2017); Michael Tadman, "The Demographic Cost of Sugar: Debates on Slave Societies and Natural Increase in the Americas," *American Historical Review*, 105 (2000), 1534–75. Tadman maintains that the work regime of sugar is sufficient to explain the dismal demography of sugar plantations everywhere in the Americas.

179. There is a long debate in both the medical and historical literatures about the possibility of heritable immunity to yellow fever. Views from the eighteenth and nineteenth century are analyzed in Rita A. Hogarth, *Medicalizing Blackness: Making Racial Difference in the Atlantic World, 1780–1840* (Chapel Hill: University of North Carolina Press, 2017), 17–80. A strong argument against the idea of heritable immunity to yellow fever appears in Mariola Espinosa, "The Question of Racial Immunity to Yellow Fever in History and Historiography," *Social Science History*, 38 (2014), 437–53. Expert medical opinion remains open to the idea, however: see Thomas P. Monath and Pedro F. C. Vasconcelos, "Yellow Fever," *Journal of Clinical Virology*, 64 (2015), 160–73; Lauren E. Blake, Mariano A. Garcia-Blanco, "Human Genetic Variation and Yellow Fever Mortality during 19th Century U.S. Epidemics," *mBio*, 5, no. 3 (2014), e01253–14, DOI: 10.1128/mBio.01253-14.

180. Griffith Hughes, *The Natural History of Barbados* (London: printed for the author, 1750), 39. Hughes noted that since inoculation had come into practice, the death toll of smallpox in Barbados had fallen.

181. Bourdier, *Vie quotidienne et conditions sanitaires sur les grandes habitations sucrières*, 186–87. North America hosted a giant smallpox epidemic in roughly the same years: Fenn, *Pox Americana*. This is probably best understood as a single epidemic, ca. 1775–84, spanning the islands and mainland.

182. Jensen, *For the Health of the Enslaved*, 283. For dysentery in Saint-Domingue, Bourdier, *Vie quotidienne et conditions sanitaires sur les grandes habitations sucrières*, 191–94.

183. Dunn, *Tale of Two Plantations*, 434.

184. S. Lösch et al., "Evidence for Tuberculosis in 18th/19th Century Slaves in Anse Sainte-Marguerite (Guadeloupe—French Western Indies," *Tuberculosis*, 95 suppl. 1 (2015), 65–68. The actual rate of TB infection would have been higher than 10 percent, because normally only a small share of TB sufferers show a skeletal response. Usually lesions occur primarily on people who host the disease for many years.

185. Higman, *Slave Populations*, 341. Dunn, *Tale of Two Plantations*, 434, using a small sample size from Jamaica, 1762–1838, suggests that TB killed 4–7 percent of slaves. Data assembled by Jensen, *For the Health of the Enslaved*, 283, from the Danish West Indies in the 1840s attribute about 5 percent of slave deaths to "consumption and lungs." For tuberculosis in Saint-Domingue, Bourdier, *Vie quotidienne et conditions sanitaires sur les grandes habitations sucrières*, 207–8.

186. The toll upon babies taken by tetanus was sometimes blamed on "black midwives who like their fair sisters in Europe are always illiterate, generally careless, and often intoxicated." Robert Renny, *An History of Jamaica* (London: Cawthorn, 1807), 207. For more sober assessments, see Sasha Turner, *Contested Bodies: Pregnancy, Childrearing, and Slavery in Jamaica* (Philadelphia: University of Pennsylvania Press, 2017), 152–53; Bourdier, "Les conditions sanitaires, 361–62; Bourdier, *Vie quotidienne et conditions sanitaires sur les grandes habitations sucrières*, 199–201, 349–50; Handler, "Diseases and Medical Disabilities," 17–18; Schiebinger, *Secret Cures*, 142; Jensen, *For the Health of the Enslaved*, 88; Brown, *The Reaper's Garden*, 54–55. Among the authors of the time who comment on tetanus, see Jean-Baptiste Thibault de Chanvalon, *Voyage à la Martinique* (Paris: Bauche, 1763), 89; and Andrew Halliday, *The West Indies: The Natural and Physical History of the Windward and Leeward Colonies* (London: Parker, 1837), 19.

187. Ward, "The Amelioration of British West Indian Slavery," for an argument about improvement 1788–1838. By 1786, in Cap François (northern Saint-Domingue) plantations with more than 20 slaves were legally obliged to maintain an infirmary for slaves, although whether that improved their health or not is hard to say. Bourdier, "Les conditions sanitaires sur les habitations sucrières de Saint-Domingue." Planters could often regard the appalling mortality with detachment. The Gothic horror novelist and absentee estate owner Matthew Lewis visited his sugar plantations twice in 1816–18 and remarked, "Say what you will to the Negroes, and treat them as well as one can, obstinate devils, they will die." *Journal of a West Indian Proprietor* (London: J. Murray, 1834), 388. Lewis died of yellow fever en route home from Jamaica.

188. Stanley Engerman and Barry Higman, "The Demographic Structure of Caribbean Slave Societies in the Eighteenth and Nineteenth Centuries," in Franklin Knight, ed., *General*

History of the Caribbean (London: UNESCO Publishing), 3: 69–71, discusses the proportion of slaves living in cities.

189. Data in McNeill, *Atlantic Empires of France and Spain*, 191ff.

190. http://www.virgin-islands-history.dk/eng/vi_hist.asp. This page is maintained by Denmark's Statens Arkiver (consulted August 3, 2018). St. Thomas served as a mail distribution center and so handled more than its share of shipping.

191. One indication of urban disease is the meticulously collected data in Jennings, *Constructing the Spanish Empire in Havana*, 104–5. In 1765–68, at any given time 6 percent to 19 percent of state slaves working on fortifications in Havana were sick, and 13 percent to 35 percent of prisoners similarly employed.

192. A. Moreno-Estrada et al., "Reconstructing the Population Genetic History of the Caribbean," *PLoS Genetics*, 9 (2013), doi:10.1371/journal.pgen.1003925; Francesco Montinaro et al., "Unravelling the Hidden Ancestry of American Admixed Populations," *Nature Communications*, 6 (2015), https://www.nature.com/articles/ncomms7596.

193. Robert Jameson, *Letters from the Havana, during the Year 1820* (London: J. Miller, 1821), 59.

194. Myron Echenberg, *Humboldt's Mexico* (Montreal and Kingston, Jamaica: McGill-Queen's University Press, 2017), 170. During the American Civil War, natives of New Orleans looked forward to a yellow fever epidemic that would rid them of Union occupation. It did not come, thanks to a naval blockade. Kathryn Olivarius explores the ways that yellow fever influenced social hierarchy in nineteenth-century New Orleans in "Immunity, Capital, and Power in Antebellum New Orleans," *The American Historical Review*, 124 (2019), 425–55, and in a forthcoming book, *Necropolis*.

195. Gómez, *Experiential Atlantic*, 47.

196. Jensen, *For the Health of the Enslaved*, 140–44; Stipriaan, *Surinaams contrast*, 356–57; Bourdier, *Vie quotidienne et conditions sanitaires sur les grandes habitations sucrières*, 247–48.

197. A handy summary is Christopher Hamlin, *Cholera: The Biography* (Oxford: Oxford University Press, 2009).

198. G. Delgado García, "El cólera morbo asiático en Cuba: Apuntes históricos y bibliográficos," *Cuadernos de Historia de Salud Pública*, 78 (1993), 21–27. The original source is likely to be Ramón de la Sagra, *Tablas necrologicas del colera-morbus en la ciudad de la Habana* (Havana, 1833).

199. Kiple, *The Caribbean Slave*, 146. His chief source for Cuban data is Jorge LeRoy y Cassa, *Estudios sobre la mortalidad de la Habana durante el siglo XIX* (Havana, 1913). M. Salvador-Vázquez and C. Menéndez de León, "Higiene y enfermedad del esclavo en Cuba durante la primera mitad del siglo XIX," *Anuario de Estudios Americanos*, 43 (1986), 436, say the 1833–36 cholera killed 25–50 percent of Cuba's slave population, which is likely an exaggeration. Enrique Beldarrain Chaple, *Las epidemias y su enfrentamiento en Cuba 1800–1860* (PhD thesis, University of Havana 2012), 52–88, considers cholera in Cuba with much local detail.

200. On Mexico's experience, C. A. Hutchinson, "The Asiatic Cholera Epidemic in 1833 in Mexico," *Bulletin of the History of Medicine*, 32 (1958), 1–23. In Campeche in 1833, according to Dr. Henry Perrine, "the mortality was nominally but 20 percent. In a village only five miles distant, along the coast, where there was no medical assistance, at least forty percent of the original number perished. Finally the living began to envy the dead. Happy the dead, was the general remark, they had some aid during life, something like internment after death—but we must perish alone and be consumed by dogs and buzzards in our dwellings." Quoted in C. G. Shattuck, *The Peninsula of Yucatan: Medical, Biological, Meterological and Sociological Studies* (Washington DC: Carnegie Institution, 1933), 340–41.

201. Kenneth Kiple, "Cholera and Race in the Caribbean," *Journal of Latin American Studies*, 17 (1985), 157–77. Margaret Jones, *Public Health in Jamaica, 1850–1940* (Mona: University of the West Indies Press, 2013), 68, gives 20,000 to 30,000 for 1851 alone on Jamaica; Luis Figueroa, *Sugar, Slavery and Freedom in Nineteenth-Century Puerto Rico* (Chapel Hill: UNC Press 2005), 74, says Puerto Rico lost 12 percent of its slave population to cholera in the epidemic. On the impact of cholera in the 1850s in Yucatan, see Heather McCrea, *Diseased Relations: Epidemics, Public Health, and State-Building in Yucatán, Mexico, 1847–1924* (Albuquerque: University of New Mexico Press, 2010), 59–132; on p. 62 McRea mention a cholera outbreak on Guadeloupe in 1865 than killed 12,000.

202. Details of this argument appear in McNeill, *Mosquito Empires*.
203. Bryan Edwards, *The History, Civil and Commercial of the British Colonies in the West Indies* (London: Stockdale, 1801), 3: 174, cited in Tim Lockley, *Military Medicine and the Making of Race: Lie and Death in the West India Regiments, 1795–1874* (Cambridge: Cambridge University Press, 2020), 37.
204. Marjoleine Kars makes clear, even without quantification, the heavy toll taken by disease upon Dutch troops sent to quell a 1763 slave uprising along the Berbice River in what is now Guyana: *Blood on the River: A Chronicle of Mutiny and Freedom on the Wild Coast* (New York: Free Press, 2020).
205. Landers, *Death and the Metropolis*, 266–83, for mortality peaks in England. John Post, "Climatic Variability and the European Mortality Wave of the Early 1740s," *Journal of Interdisciplinary History*, 15 (1984), 1–30 reports a 20–25 percent mortality increase in the British Isles, 1740–42 (p. 13), attributed mainly to typhoid, bacillary dysentery, and typhus. It is not plausible that sickly men returning from the West Indies expeditions had anything more than a tiny statistical impact on Britain's elevated mortality rates, although if they landed in southeastern England with malarial parasites in their bloodstreams they might have added somewhat to the spiking rates of death by "fevers" in England and London, as Dobson suggests. The Thames estuary and the marshy coastal environs of southeastern England had anopheline mosquitoes and vivax malaria into the 1920s, although its prevalence declined from the mid-eighteenth century. Mary Dobson, *Contours of Death and Disease in Early Modern England* (Cambridge: Cambridge University Press, 1997), 343–50. Landers's breakdown of the data by month and cause of death suggests that fever deaths spiked between April of 1741 and April of 1742 and in May of 1762, too early in both cases, especially the latter, for the return to England of victims of Caribbean malaria. For the hardships of 1741–42 in Ireland, see David Dickson, *Arctic Ireland: The Extraordinary Story of the Great Frost and Forgotten Famine of 1740–41* (Belfast: White Row Press, 1997).
206. Marcel Lachiver, *Les années de misère: La famine au temps du Grand Roi, 1680–1720* (Paris: Fayard, 1991), 155–233, for the bad weather, famines, and searing epidemics of the 1690s, especially 1693–94 and 1697. The French expedition against Cartagena left Brest in January of 1697 in the middle of a very cold winter with high grain prices.
207. McNeill, *Mosquito Empires*, 106–23; Rosanne D'Arrigo et al., "Complexity in Crisis: The Volcanic Cold Pulse of the 1690s and the Consequences of Scotland's Failure to Cope," *Journal of Volcanology and Geothermal Research*, 389 (2020), 1–11.
208. John Bell, *An Inquiry into the Causes Which Produce and the Means of Preventing Diseases among British Officers, Soldiers, and Others in the West Indies* (London: J. Murray, 1791), 1.
209. McNeill, *Mosquito Empires*, 185, 191.
210. Burnard and Garrigus, *Plantation Machine*, 213–14, citing Justin Girod-Chantran, *Voyage d'un Suisse dans différentes colonies d'Amérique pendant la dernière guerre* (Neuchâtel, Switzerland: de l'Imprimerie de la Société typographique, 1785), 403.
211. Lind, *An Essay on Diseases Incidental to Europeans in Hot Climates* (London, 1768), 188. Cited in Erica Charters, *Disease, War and the Imperial State: The Welfare of the British Armed Forces during the Seven Years' War* (Chicago: University of Chicago Press, 2014), 70.
212. For details on the learning among European war planners, McNeill, *Mosquito Empires*, 137–91.
213. A minority of soldiers carried wide enough portfolios of immunities to weather the risks of Caribbean military disease ecology safely. Most of these were born and raised either in the Caribbean or in Atlantic Africa. Some served in specially raised British regiments, discussed later. The largest such contingents fought in the campaigns of the Haitian Revolution. No quantitative evidence survives concerning their health. See McNeill, *Mosquito Empires*, 236–67; and David Geggus, "Yellow Fever in the 1790s," *Medical History*, 23 (1979), 38–58; David Geggus, *Slavery, War and Revolution: The British Occupation of Saint Domingue, 1793–1798* (Oxford: Oxford University Press, 1982); Michael Duffy, *Soldiers, Sugar, and Seapower: The British Expeditions to the West Indies and the War against Revolutionary France* (Oxford: Oxford University Press, 1987); Julio Albi, *Banderas olvidadas: El ejército realista en América* (Madrid: Ediciones de Cultura Hispánica, 1990).

214. A governor in Cartagena in 1661 advised the king of Spain that he should expect a quarter of the city's garrison to be sick at any time: Gómez, *Experiential Atlantic*, 42. Whereas in 1587, before yellow fever arrived, a Cartagena official had extolled the healthfulness of the city: Miguel Hidalgo to Juan Martínez, 4 junio 1587, in Enrique Otte, ed., *Cartas privadas de emigrantes a Indias, 1540–1616* (Mexico City: Fondo de Cultura Económica, 1996), 302.

215. Kiple, *Caribbean Slave*, 173.

216. Burnard and Garrigus, *Plantation Machine*, 212. In 1779–83, fevers killed 3,500 British soldiers stationed at Jamaica, or about 700 annually; in 1793–1815, the figure was 8,000, or about 350 annually. McNeill, *Mosquito Empires*, 202, 265. John Bell, *An Inquiry into the Causes Which Produce and the Means of Preventing Diseases among British Officers, Soldiers, and Others in the West Indies* (London: J. Murray, 1791), 117, reported the disease killed 49 percent of the 23rd Regiment within three years of its arrival in the Caribbean in 1765.

217. Edward Balfour, "Statistical Data for Forming Troops and Maintaining Them in Health in Different Climates and Localities," *Journal of the Statistical Society of London*, 8 (1845), 194–95. Balfour drew much of his data from Alexander Tulloch's "Statistical Report on Sickness, Invaliding, and Mortality among Troops in the West Indies," published in Great Britain, *Parliamentary Papers*, 1837–38, XL (138). Garrisons in British India suffered 5–6 percent annual mortality, 1817–36.

218. Philip Curtin, *Death by Migration: Europe's Encounter with the Tropical World in the Nineteenth Century* (Cambridge: Cambridge University Press, 1989), 8.

219. Christon Archer, "The Key to the Kingdom: The Defense of Veracruz, 1780–1810," *The Americas*, 27 (1971), 426–49; Myron Echenberg, *Humboldt's Mexico*, 187.

220. Lind, *Diseases Incidental to Europeans*, 117–28; Curtin, *Death by Migration*, 27–28. It is not clear from Curtin's pages just when the British Army began to move its troops to higher ground in Jamaica, but Newcastle barracks opened in 1840. Average annual mortality in the Jamaica Command fell to 6.6 percent in 1837–46 and 2.1 percent in 1859–68.

221. Jennings, *Constructing the Spanish Empire in Havana*, 126–35; Elena Schneider, *The Occupation of Havana: War, Trade, and Slavery in the Atlantic World* (Chapel Hill: University of North Carolina Press, 2018), 119–20, 127–28; Maria Alessandra Bollettino, "'Of Equal or More Service': Black Solders and the British Empire in the Mid-eighteenth Century Caribbean," *Slavery and Abolition*, 38 (2017), 518–23; Tim Lockley, *Military Medicine and the Making of Race: Life and Death in the West India Regiments, 1795–1874* (Cambridge: Cambridge University Press, 2020), 22–25.

222. Burnard and Garrigus, *Plantation Machine*, 212–13.

223. Roger Buckley, *Slaves in Red Coats: The West India Regiments, 1795–1815* (New Haven, CT: Yale University Press, 1979); Lockley, *Military Medicine*; see also several chapters in Christopher L. Brown and Philip D. Morgan, *Arming Slaves: From Classical Times to the Modern Age* (New Haven, CT: Yale University Press, 2006).

224. Balfour, "Statistical Data for Forming Troops," 195–96.

225. Stephen Kunitz, "Diseases and Mortality in the Americas since 1700," in Kenneth Kiple, ed., *The Cambridge World History of Human Disease* (New York: Cambridge University Press, 1993), 329.

226. Duncan Crewe, *Yellow Jack and the Worm* (Liverpool: Liverpool University Press, 1993), 96; Coriann Convertito, *The Health of British Seamen in the West Indies, 1773–1806* (PhD thesis, University of Exeter, 2011), 138–40; Charters, *Disease, War, and the Imperial State*, 53–85.

227. Ulysses S. Grant, *Personal Memoirs* (New York: Barnes & Noble Books, 2003),62: "It was very important to get the army away from Vera Cruz as soon as possible in order to avoid the yellow fever, or vomito, which usually visits that city early in the year, and is very fatal to persons not acclimated." Grant was a lieutenant in this campaign. The strategy was mapped out by Gen. Winfield Scott, who was well acquainted with the French army's fate in the Haitian Revolution.

228. For Spanish Army health in Cuba, see John L. Tone, *War and Genocide in Cuba, 1895–1898* (Chapel Hill: University of North Carolina Press, 2008). For Santo Domingo, see Santiago Castro Ventura, *La Guerra Restauradora* (Santo Domingo: Manatí, 2014), 284–85.

229. David Eltis, F. Lewis, and D. Richardson, "Slave Prices, the African Slave Trade, and Productivity in the Caribbean, 1674–1804," *Economic History Review*, 58 (2004), 673–700.

Stipriaan, *Surinaams contrast*, 316, reports 3–5 percent annual natural decrease among slave populations in Surinam, 1750–80, and falling to 1–2 percent annually in 1780–1850; Philip Morgan, "Slavery in the British Caribbean," in David Eltis and Stanley Engerman, eds., *The Cambridge World History of Slavery*, vol. 3, *AD 1420–AD 1804* (Cambridge: Cambridge University Press, 2011), 383, reports 5 percent annual natural decrease among slaves in the British West Indies at the end of the seventeenth century, falling to 1 percent by the early nineteenth. A detailed study of a large sample is A. Meredith John, *The Plantation Slaves of Trinidad, 1783–1816* (Cambridge: Cambridge University Press, 1988). One environment even more deadly for enslaved laborers than sugar plantations was the royal shipyard in Havana. Levi Marrero, *Cuba: Economía y sociedad* (Madrid: Editorial Playor, 1978), 8: 17, calculates a 6.8 percent annual mortality.

230. Indeed I think it is a mirage. If many more slaves were imported than recorded, growth in the slave population would then appear to be due to natural increase rather than imports. On the undercounting of slave imports to eighteenth-century Cuba, Elena Schneider, "Routes into Eighteenth-Century Cuban Slavery," in Alex Borucki, David Eltis and David Wheat, eds., *From the Galleons to the Highlands: Slave Trade Routes in the Spanish Americas* (Albuquerque: University of New Mexico Press, 2019), 256, says the majority of slaves imported to Cuba were smuggled. McNeill, *Atlantic Empires*, 166–70, estimates slave imports to Cuba alone, 1700–1760, at 75,000 taking into account contraband. This is more than twice the quantity of slaves legally imported into Cuba based on archival documents as reported in David Eltis and Jorge Felipe-Gonzalez, "The Rise and Fall of the Cuban Slave Trade: New Data, New Paradigms," in Alex Borucki, David Eltis and David Wheat, eds., *From the Galleons to the Highlands: Slave Trade Routes in the Spanish Americas* (Albuquerque: University of New Mexico Press, 2019), 205. If anywhere close to accurate, and supplemented by the numbers for Puerto Rico and Santo Domingo, this would surely convert the natural increase in Morgan's table to natural decrease. See also the (mainly nineteenth-century) data on Cuban slave demography in Manuel Moreno Fraginals, "Africa in Cuba: A Quantitative Analysis of the African Population of the Island of Cuba," *Annals of the New York Academy of Sciences*, 292 (1977), 187–201;

231. Dunn, *Tale of Two Plantations*, 23–24. See also Higman, *Slave Populations*, 312.

232. Follett, "Demography of Slavery"; Bourdier, *Vie quotidienne et conditions sanitaires*, 360; Jensen, *For the Health of the Enslaved*, 43, 47. In the 1780s, the rate of natural decrease in the Danish West Indies was 1.6 percent annually according to a German-language report by a Danish state commission on the slave trade printed in Gøbel, *Danish Slave Trade*, 213; A Danish West Indies census of 1805–6 showed a natural decrease of 1.0 percent (Gøbel, *Danish Slave Trade*, 173).

233. Pieter Emmer, "Slavery and Slave Trade of Minor Atlantic Power," in David Eltis and Stanley Engerman, eds., *The Cambridge World History of Slavery*, vol. 3, *AD 1420–AD 1804* (Cambridge: Cambridge University Press, 2011), 465; Stipriaan, *Surinaams contrast*, 310–46.

234. Reinier Borrego Moreno, "'Lo importante aqui es no morirse': Azúcar, esclavitud y mortalided en Cuba (1841–1886)," in Josef Opatrny, ed., *Proyectos politicos y culturales en las realidades caribeñas de los siglos XVIII y XIX* (Prague: Ibero-Americana Pragiensia, Supplementum 43, 2016), 147–56.

235. For comparison, the Soviet Gulag during the Stalin years, 1929–53, had a mortality rate of 2–6 percent in ordinary years, but 15 percent during the famine year of 1933 and 22–25 percent in the war years of 1942–43—according to official records. Only in Stalin's last years, 1949–53, when the Gulag population shrank below 50,000, did mortality fall below 2 percent annually. Golfo Alexopoulos, *Illness and Inhumanity in Stalin's Gulag* (New Haven, CT: Yale University Press, 2017), argues that all these figures were kept artificially low by releasing millions on the verge of death. Anne Applebaum, *Gulag: A History* (New York: Anchor Books, 2003), 582–84, prints the official NKVD (secret police) figures from the Russian archives. The numbers are incomplete, and controversial, but it seems plausible to say that the Gulag population, absent new prisoners, would have wasted away even faster than the Caribbean slave population because of comparable mortality and even lower birth rates.

236. This issue is considered in works such as Kiple, *The Caribbean Slave*, and Curtin, *Plantation Complex*.

237. Yellow fever was especially baffling and inspired a broad spectrum of wrong explanations, e.g., that yellow fever's prevalence resulted from sailors drinking rum at an early age (National Archives of the United Kingdom, ADM 1/326 Admiral Cochrane to Admiralty, 25 July 1805). I owe this citation to Cameron Elliott.

238. Schiebinger, *Secret Cures*, 9, 24, 46, 131–32, et passim; Pablo Gomez, "The Circulation of Bodily Knowledge in the Seventeenth-Century Black Spanish Caribbean," *Social Science Medicine*, 26 (2013), 383–402; Esteban Mira Caballos, *La española, epicentro del Caribe en el siglo xix* (Santo Domingo: Academia dominica de la historia, 2010), 509–24; Enrique Beldarraín Chaple, *Apuntes sobre la medicina en Cuba: Historia y publicaciones* (Havana: ECIMED, 2005); Pratik Chakrabarti, *Materials and Medicine: Trade, Conquest and Therapeutics in the Eighteenth Century* (Manchester: Manchester University Press, 2010), chapter 2; Ryan Amir Kashanipour, "A World of Cures: Magic and Medicine in Colonial Yucatán" (PhD diss., University of Arizona, 2012); Cesar A. Mena and Armando F. Cobelo, *Historia de la medicina en Cuba*, vol. 1 (Miami, FL: Ed. Universal, 1992); Emilio Quevedo Vélez, *Historia de la medicina en Colombia* (Bogotá: Tecnoquímicas, 2007); Tulio Aristizábal Giraldo, *Iglesias, conventos y hospitales en Cartagena colonial* (Bogotá: El Ancora Editores, 1998); José López Sánchez, *Cuba: medicina y civilización, siglos XVII y XVIII* (Havana: Editorial Científico y Técnica, 1997); Stipriaan, *Surinaams contrast*, 362–68.

239. On quarantines: Gavin Milroy, "Operation and Results of Quarantine in British Ports since the Beginning of the Present Century," *Association Medical Journal*, 1, no. 29 (July 22, 1853), 638–39; Gómez, *Experiential Atlantic*, 44. On cinchona: Bourdier, *Vie quotidienne et conditions sanitaires*, 184; Matthew J. Crawford, *The Andean Wonder Drug: Cinchona Bark and Imperial Science in the Spanish Atlantic, 1630–1800* (Pittsburgh: University of Pittsburgh Press, 2016). On variolation and vaccination: Edward Long, *The History of Jamaica* (London: Lowndes, 1774), 2: 507; Sheridan, *Doctors and Slaves*, 250; Jones, *Public Health in Jamaica*, 66–68; Bourdier, *Vie quotidienne et conditions sanitaires*, 432–36; Jensen, *For the Health of the Enslaved*, 194–219; Enrique Beldarraín Chaple, "Notas sobre las guerras per la independencia nacional y su repercussiones en el estado de salud de la población cubana," in Luz María Espinosa Cortés and Enrique Beldarraín Chaple, eds., *Cuba y México: Desastres, alimentación y salud: siglos XVIII y XIX* (Mexico City: Plaza y Valdés, 2005), 83; E. Beldarraín Chaple, "Sanidad y esclavitud: medidas para contrarrestar las enfermedades de los esclavos en Cuba," *Afro-Hispanic Review*, 34 (2015), 14–16; Martha Few, *For All of Humanity: Mesoamerican and Colonial Medicine in Enlightenment Guatemala* (Tuscon: University of Arizona Press, 2015), 55–61; José Rigau-Pérez, "The Introduction of Smallpox Vaccine in 1803 and the Adoption of Immunization as a Government Function in Puerto Rico," *Hispanic American Historical Review*, 69 (1989), 393–423. On pro-natalism among planters: Karen Bourdier, "La mère et l'enfant dans les sucreries du nord de Saint-Domingue: entre profit économique et sauvegarde du capital humain," in Jacques de Cauna and Cécile Révauger, eds., *La société des plantations esclavagiste* (Paris: Les Indes savantes 2014), 46–48; Bourdier, *Vie quotidienne et conditions sanitaires*, 339–44, 420–28; Follett, "Demography of Slavery," 120; on African medical traditions and their uptake in the Caribbean, Bourdier, *Vie quotidienne et conditions sanitaires*, 392–407; Jensen, *For the Health of the Enslaved*, 68–75; Schiebinger, *Secret Cures*, passim, and two contemporary sources with a positive view of African healers, Nicolas Bourgeois, *Voyages intéressans dans différentes colonies françaises, espagnoles, anglaises &c* (London: J. Bastien, 1788); George Pinckard, *Notes on the West Indies* (London: Longman, Hurst, Rees and Orme, 1806), 3 vols.

Chapter 3

1. Bryan Edwards, *The History, Civil and Commercial, of the British Colonies in the West Indies* (Dublin: Luke White, 1793), 1:50; Joshua Peterkin, *A Treatise on Planting*, 2nd ed. (Basseterre, St. Christopher, 1790), 41–42; William and Edmund Burke, *An Account of the European Settlements in America*, 6th ed. (London: J. Dodsley, 1777), 2:106. More generally, see Richard Grove, *Green Imperialism: Colonial Expansion, Tropical Island Edens and the*

Origins of Environmentalism, 1600–1860 (Cambridge: Cambridge University Press, 1995), 16–71; Jefferson Dillman, *Colonizing Paradise. Landscape and Empire in the British West Indies* (Tuscaloosa: University of Alabama Press, 2015); Miguel Rodríguez-Ferrer, *Naturaleza y civilización de la grandiose isla de Cuba* (Madrid: J. Noguera, 1876).

2. Bonham Richardson, *Economy and Environment in the Caribbean: Barbados and the Windwards in the Late 1800s* (Gainesville: University Press of Florida, 1997), 3; Vincent Brown, *The Reaper's Garden: Death and Power in the World of Atlantic Slavery* (Cambridge, MA: Harvard University Press, 2010).

3. Robert Robertson, *A Detection of the State and Situation of the Present Sugar Planters, of Barbadoes and the Leeward Islands* (London: J. Wiltord, 1732), 26; Simon Taylor, quoted in Alexander X. Byrd, *Captives and Voyagers: Black Migrants across the Eighteenth-Century British World* (Baton Rouge: Louisiana State University Press, 2008), 103.

4. For disasters as "agents," see Greg Bankoff, *Cultures of Disaster: Society and Natural Hazards in the Philippines* (New York: Routledge, 2003), 3. See also James Robertson, "Island Time: Disasters in the Comprehension of Montserrat's Past," *Caribbean Quarterly*, 63, no. 4 (2017), 529–50. On unity and differences in the region, albeit with an emphasis on unity, see Franklin Knight, *The Caribbean: The Genesis of a Fragmented Nationalism*, 2nd ed. (New York: Oxford University Press, 1990).

5. One example of the excellent work by Michael Chenoweth, who has created the most accurate catalogue of hurricanes that struck during the past 500 years based on exhaustive research in newspapers, ship logs, and other sources. See Michael Chenoweth, "A Reassessment of Historical Atlantic Basin Tropical Cyclone Activity, 1700–1855," *Climatic Change*, 76, no. 1 (2006), 169–240. An even more comprehensive overview for the past 530 years by Chenoweth, which he shared with us in draft, will re-write and greatly expand the record of Atlantic hurricanes.

6. On the central role of disasters in the region's colonial history, see, for example, Richard Dunn, *Sugar and Slaves: The Rise of the Planter Class in the English West Indies, 1624–1713* (Chapel Hill: University of North Carolina Press, 1972). A classic statement on the social construction of disasters is Kenneth Hewitt, *Interpretations of Calamity: From the Viewpoint of Human Ecology* (Boston: Allen and Unwin, 1983). See also Susanna Smith and Anthony Oliver-Smith, eds., *Culture and Catastrophe: The Anthropology of Disaster* (Santa Fe: School for Advanced Research Press, 2002); Tania López-Marrero and Ben Wisner, "Not in the Same Boat: Disasters and Differential Vulnerability in the Insular Caribbean," *Caribbean Studies*, 40 (December 2012), 131.

7. David Watts, "Cycles of Famine in Islands of Plenty: The Case of the Colonial West Indies in the Pre-Emancipation Era," in Bruce Currey and Graeme Hugo, eds., *Famine as a Geographical Phenomenon* (Dordrecht, Netherlands: D. Reidel, 1984), 49–70.

8. A good summary of this argument, and of trends in the history of disasters generally is Monica Juneja and Franz Mauelshagen, "Disasters and Pre-industrial Societies: Historiographic Trends and Comparative Perspectives," *The Medieval History Journal*, 10 (2007), 1–31. Wars can often have unforeseen and ironic consequences, but humans do deliberately begin the process that results in death and destruction. Likewise, while infestations of insects or other pests and/or crop disease are often directly linked to human actions (as McNeill notes in his chapter, infestations often would not exist in a specific location but for human actions, unlike hurricanes, which exist regardless of human actions), early modern colonizers were usually not aware that they played a role in such events and thus perceived them as natural hazards. For some discussion of these issues in the context of Caribbean history, see Christopher M. Church, *Paradise Destroyed: Catastrophe and Citizenship in the French Caribbean* (Lincoln: University of Nebraska Press, 2017), 3–6.

9. Andrea Jamku, Gerrit Schenk, and Franz Mauelshagen, eds., *Historical Disasters in Context: Science, Religion, and Politics* (New York: Routledge, 2012), 1–14; Theodore Steinberg, "What Is a Natural Disaster," *Literature and Medicine*, 15 (Spring 1996), 33–47; Bas van Bavel et al., *Disasters and History: The Vulnerability and Resilience of Past Societies* (Cambridge: Cambridge University Press, 2020), 159–87.

10. Archivo General de Indias (Seville [hereafter AGI]), Patronato, leg. 179, ramo 1, n. 4, fls. 14–30 (17 Oct. 1580).

11. Bryan Edwards, *The History, Civil and Commercial, of the British West Indies*, 5th ed. (London: G. and W. B. Whittaker, 1819), 5:67–68; Robert Schomburgk, *The History of Barbados* (London: Brown, Green and Longmans, 1848), 37. Following Edward's definition, we pay relatively little attention to fires. Fires were a constant threat to colonists. Major fires at times engulfed port towns in all the colonies, their many wooden buildings providing ample fuel to transform even small sparks into major conflagrations. Fires also routinely burned plantation fields and buildings. Some of these fires resulted from natural forces such as lightning strikes, but as the foremost historian of the topic concludes, "with rare exceptions, fires in the region were and are attributed to human agency." In some cases, conflagrations came when humans lost control of fire set for a specific purpose (such as cooking or boiling sugar); in other cases, fire served as a weapon of resistance. While we have not considered fires in detail, we have at times noted when fires became linked to other disasters, such as drought. See Bonham Richardson, *Igniting the Caribbean's Past: Fire in British West Indian History* (Chapel Hill: University of North Carolina Press, 2004), 20.

12. Susan Cutter, "The Changing Nature of Hazard and Disaster Risk in the Anthropocene," *Annals of the American Association of Geographers*, 111, no. 3 (2021), 819–27. For a discussion of infestations following hurricanes and drought, see Matthew Mulcahy and Stuart Schwartz, "Nature's Battalions: Insects of Agricultural Pests in the Early Modern Caribbean," *William and Mary Quarterly*, 75 (July 2018), 433–64.

13. Salvador Arana Soto, *Historia de nuestras calamidades* (San Juan, PR, Printed by Tipografía Miguza1968), 37. Douglas Taylor, "Spanish Hurricane and Its Congeners," *International Journal of American Linguistics*, 22 (1956), 275–76. John Taylor, *Newes and Strange Newes from St. Christophers of a tempestuous Spirit which is called by the Indians a Hurry-Cano or whirlwind* (London, 1638). The association with savagery or the devil is discussed in Peter Hulme, *Colonial Encounters: Europe and the Native Caribbean, 1492–1797* (New York: Methuen, 1986), 94–101.

14. Bartolomé de Las Casas, *Historia de las Indias* (1561), chapter 69; "Captain Langford's Observations of his own Experience upon Hurricanes and their Prognostiks," *Philosophical Transactions of the Royal Society*, 20 (1698), 413.

15. Andrés Poëy y Aguirre, "A Chronological Table, Comprising 400 Cyclonic Hurricanes which have Occurred in the West Indies in the North Atlantic within 362 years, from 1493 to 1855," *Journal of the Royal Geographical Society*, 25 (1855), 291–28. Establishing an accurate listing continues. See Michael Chenoweth and Dmitry Divine, "A Document-Based 318-Year Record of Tropical Cyclones in the Lesser Antilles, 1690–2007," *Genochemsitry, Geophysics, Geosystems*, 9 (August 2008), doi.org/10.1029/2008GC002066; Ricardo Garćia-Herrara et al., "Identification of Caribbean Basin Hurricanes from Spanish Documentary Sources," *Climate Change*, 83 (2007), 55–85. There are also numerous chronologies regions like E. Garnier, J. Desarthe, and D. Moncoulon, "The Historic Reality of the Cyclonic Variability in the French Antilles, 1635–2007," *Climate of the Past Discussions*, 11, 1519–50 (2019), and others for individual islands. For a particularly good example, see Luis A. Salivia, *Historia de los temporales de Puerto Rico y Las Antillas 1492–1970*, 2nd ed. (San Juan, PR: Editorial Edil, 1972). On hurricanes prior to 1492, see Jonathan Nott, "Paleotempestology: The Study of Prehistoric Tropical Cyclones—a Review and Implications for Hazard Assessment," *Environment International*, 30, no. 3 (2004), 433–47. Since 2000, there has been a surge of social and political studies of the impact of hurricanes. See, for example, Sherry Johnson, *Climate and Catastrophe in Cuba and the Atlantic World in the Age of Revolution* (Chapel Hill: University of North Carolina Press, 2011); Louis Pérez, *Winds of Change: Hurricanes and the Transformation of Nineteenth Century Cuba* (Chapel Hill: University of North Carolina Press, 2001); Matthew Mulcahy, *Hurricanes and Society in the British Greater Caribbean, 1624–1783* (Baltimore: John Hopkins University Press, 2006); and Stuart Schwartz, *Sea of Storms: A History of Hurricanes in the Greater Caribbean from Columbus to Katrina* (Princeton, NJ: Princeton University Press, 2015).

16. Good overviews of hurricanes include Kerry Emanuel, *A Divine Wind: The History and Science of Hurricanes* (New York: Oxford University Press, 2005); Roger Pielke, *The Hurricane* (London: Routledge, 1999); and James Elsner and A Birol Kara, *Hurricanes of the North Atlantic: Climate and Society* (New York: Oxford University Press, 1999).

17. An excellent discussion of how to use modern classifications for older storms is Michael Chenoweth, "Objective Classification of Historical Tropical Cyclone Intensity," *Journal of Geophysical Research*, 112 (2007), doi:10.1029/2006JD007211.

18. James W. Wiley and Joseph W. Wunderle, Jr., "The Effects of Hurricanes on Birds with Special Reference to Caribbean Islands," *Bird Conservation International*, 3 (1993), 319–49; Emery R. Boose, Mayra I. Serrano, and David R. Foster, "Landscape and Regional Impacts of Hurricanes in Puerto Rico," *Ecological Monographs*, 74, no. 2 (2004), 335–52. Carl Ortwin Sauer, *The Early Spanish Main* (Berkeley: University of California Press, 1966), 51–54, presents an excellent summary of *conuco* agriculture.

19. "Captain Langford's Observations," 407.

20. Schwartz, *Sea of Storms*, 24–25; Mulcahy, *Hurricanes and Society*, 21.

21. Alexander X. Byrd, *Captives and Voyagers*, 66; Pablo Vila, "La destrucción de Nueva Cádiz: Terremoto o Huracán?" *Boletín de la Academia Nacional de la Historia*, 31, no. 123 (September 1948), 213–19; J. L. Carstens, *A General Description of all the Danish, American or West Indian Islands*, trans. and ed. Arnold Highfield (St. Croix: Virgin Islands Humanities Council, 1997), 49.

22. José Carlos Millás, *Hurricanes of the Caribbean and Adjacent Regions, 1492–1800* (Miami FL: Academy of the Arts and Sciences of the Americas, 1968), 67–69, provides a long translation of Oviedo's remarks.

23. Schwartz, *Sea of Storms*, 43–58.

24. Millás, *Hurricanes*, 129–33; Félix-Hilaire Fortuné, *Cyclones at autres cataclysms aux Antilles* (Fort-de-France, Martinique: Masure, 1986), 47–52.

25. Joelle Gergis and Anthony M. Fowler, "A History of ENSO Events since A.D. 1525: Implications for Future Climate Change," *Climatic Change*, 92, nos. 3–4 (2009), 343–87; César N. Caviedes, "Five Hundred Years of Hurricanes in the Caribbean: Their Relationship with Global Climatic Variabilities," *Geojournal*, 23, no. 4 (1991), 301–10; Roger A. Pielke, Jr., and Christopher Landsea, "La Niña, El Niño, and Atlantic Hurricane Damages in the United States," *Bulletin of the American Meteorological Society*, 80 (1999), 2027–33. A good visual discussion of this is found on the NOAA website: https://www.climate.gov/news-features/blogs/enso/impacts-el-ni%C3%B1o-and-la-ni%C3%B1a-hurricane-season.

26. Alison J. Reading and Rory P. D. Walsh, "Tropical Cyclone Activity within the Caribbean Basin since 1500," in David Barker and Duncan F. M. McGregor, eds., *Environment and Development in the Caribbean* (Kingston, Jamaica: University of the West Indies Press, 1995), 111–23. Other studies have offered a somewhat different periodization of frequency or have suggested within the period 1650–1765 there were some years of increased activity in the late seventeenth and early eighteenth centuries.

27. Pérez, *Winds of Change*, 28–33.

28. Edwards, *History, Civil and Commercial* (1793), 2:34; Mulcahy, *Hurricanes and Society*, 86–89.

29. See Mulcahy, *Hurricanes and Society*, 18–19; on Grenada, see John Davy, *The West Indies before and since Emancipation* (London: W. & F. G. Cash, 1854), 213; Schwartz, *Sea of Storms*, 42–53. The Swedes perceived their colony of St. Barthélemy (acquired from the French in 1784), as relatively free from hurricanes, although it experienced six significant storms between 1786 and 1819. See Holger Weiss, Laura Hollsten, and Steffen Norrgård, "Cotton and Salt: Swedish Colonial Aspirations and the Transformation of St. Barthélemy in the Eighteenth Century," *Environment and History*, 26 (May 2020), 261–87.

30. John Cordy Jeaffreson, ed., *A Young Squire of the Seventeenth Century: From the Papers of Christopher Jeaffreson* (London: Hurst and Blackett, 1878), 1:279; D. Walsh to James Scott, September 18, 1772, in Vere Langford Oliver., ed., *Caribbeana: Being Miscellaneous Papers Relating to the History, Genealogy, Topography, and Antiquities of the British West Indies* (London: Mitchell, Hughes, and Clarke, 1909–19), 2:322–23; Richard B. Sheridan, "The Crisis of Slave Subsistence in the British West Indies during and after the American Revolution," *William and Mary Quarterly*, 33, no. 4 (1976), 615–41. One estimate set the number of slave fatalities from the storm and famine in Jamaica alone at 15,000, which was 5.8 percent of the island's slave population of 256,000, but a contemporary placed the figure at 21,000 (8.0 percent). See pp. 632–33 and the sources cited therein. Simon Taylor quoted

in Trevor Burnard, *Jamaica in the Age of Revolution* (Philadelphia: University of Pennsylvania Press, 2020), 79.

31. Letter from Henry Rugeley, October 2, 1784, Rugeley Papers, Bedfordshire and Luton Archives, X311/127.

32. William Dickson, *The Mitigation of Slavery in Two Parts* (London: R. and A. Taylor, 1814), 362–63.

33. Mulcahy, *Hurricanes and Society*, 97–105; Schwartz, *Sea of Storms*, 102–4, 123–24; Johnson, *Climate and Catastrophe*, 122–54.

34. Schwartz, *Sea of Storms*, 122–24; Johnson, *Climate and Catastrophe*, 147–53; Michael Drexler, "Hurricanes and Revolutions," in Martin Brückner, ed., *Early American Cartographies*, (Chapel Hill: University of North Carolina Press, 2011), 458–59.

35. On the Spanish maritime system, the classic work is Pierre and Huguette Chaunu, *Seville et l'Atlantique, 1504–1650*, 13 vols. in 8 (Paris: Institut des Haute Études de L'Amérique Latine, 1955–60). On the Caribbean aspects of the fleet organization, see Alejandro de la Fuente, *Havana and the Atlantic in the Sixteenth Century* (Chapel Hill: University of North Carolina Press, 2008), 11–81.

36. See, for example, information on seasonal shipping patterns in Ian Steele, *The English Atlantic, 1675–1740: An Exploration of Communication and Community* (New York: Oxford University Press, 1986), 25–26; Mulcahy, *Hurricanes and Society*, 89–91.

37. AGI, Indiferente general, 419, libro v, f.133, cited in Álvaro Huerga, *Ataques de los caribes a Puerto Rico* (San Juan, PR: Academia Puertorriqueña de la Historia, 2006), 82–83; *Relación verdadera, en que se da quenta del horrible Huracàn que sobrevino a la Isla, y Puerto de Santo Domingo de los Españoles el dia quinze de Augusto de 1680* (Madrid: 1680?).

38. Schwartz, *Sea of Storms*, 97.

39. NOAA maintains a database of the deadliest hurricanes on record complied by Edward Rappaport and Jośe Fernández Partagás: "The Deadliest Atlantic Tropical Cyclones, 1492–Present," https://www.nhc.noaa.gov/pastdeadlyapp1.shtml?.

40. Mulcahy, *Hurricanes and Society*, 67–69, 72; Natalie Zacek, *Settler Society in the English Leeward Islands, 1660–1776* (Cambridge: Cambridge University Press, 2010), 20.

41. Export figures from Sheridan, *Sugar and Slavery: The Economic History of the British West Indies, 1623–1775* (Baltimore: Johns Hopkins University Press, 1973), 490, 497; S. D. Smith, "Storm Hazard and Slavery: The Impact of the 1831 Great Caribbean Hurricane on St. Vincent," *Environment and History*, 18 (2012), 97–123. For comparative purposes, see Tobias N. Rasmussen, "Macroeconomic Implications of Natural Disasters in the Caribbean," International Monetary Fund Working paper WP/04/224 (2004). For a broader discussion of the economic impact of hurricanes, see Mulcahy, "Weathering the Storms: Hurricanes and Risk in the British Greater Caribbean," *Business History Review*, 78 (Winter 2004), 635–53.

42. Cited in Richard Sheridan, *Sugar and Slavery*, 439.

43. Burnard, *Jamaica in the Age of Revolution*, 174–94.

44. Preeya Mohan and Eric Strobl, "The Economic Impact of Hurricanes in History: Evidence from Sugar Exports in the Caribbean from 1700 to 1960," *Weather, Climate, and Society*, 5 (January 2013), 5–13.

45. Schwartz, *Sea of Storms*, 87–88.

46. Johnson, *Climate and Catastrophe*, 92–95.

47. See Schwartz, *A Sea of Storms*, 93–104.

48. Caviedes, "Five Hundred Years of Hurricanes," 304–6; Schwartz, *Sea of Storms*, 104–13; Johnson, *Climate and Catastrophe*, 68–91.

49. Schwartz, *Sea of Storms*, 134–44.

50. Seneca quoted in Deborah Coen, "Introduction: Witness to Disaster: Comparative Histories of Earthquake Science and Response," *Science in Context*, 25 (March 2012), 1; on links between hurricanes and earthquakes, see Schomburgk, *History of Barbados*, 41.

51. Jean Vogt, "A Glimpse at Historical Seismology of the West Indies," *Annals of Geophysics*, 47 (April/June 2004), 465–76. Several recent catalogues provide good summary source material. See, for example, the catalogue of earthquakes for Hispaniola (but referencing other parts of the Antilles) that includes excerpts from various primary sources: Claudia

Flores, Uri ten Brink, and William Bakun, *Accounts of Damage from Historical Earthquakes in the Northeastern Caribbean to Aid in the Determination of Their Location and Intensity Magnitudes: U.S. Geological Survey, Open-File Report, 2011–1133* (Reston, VA: U.S. Geological Survey, 2012), 1–190, https://pubs.usgs.gov/of/2011/1133/pdf/ofr2011-1133_212012.pdf. For Puerto Rico, see William McCann, Lawrence Feldman, and Maribel McCann, "Catalog of Felt Earthquakes for Puerto Rico and Neighboring Islands, 1493–1899, with Additional Information for some 20th Century Earthquakes," *Revista Geofísica*, 62 (2010), 141–90. As with hurricanes, scientists are employing the natural archives to trace the occurrence of earthquakes beyond what written sources allow. A discussion of the methods is outlined at https://earthquake.usgs.gov/learn/topics/paleo-intro/.

52. On European background with earthquakes and their relative infrequency (with Lisbon being the notable exception), see Mark Molesky, *This Gulf of Fire: The Great Lisbon Earthquake, or Apocalypse in the Age of Science and Reason* (New York: Vintage, 2015), 111, 146; see also Jamie Bluestone, "Why the Earth Shakes: Pre-Modern Understandings and Modern Earthquake Science" (PhD diss., University of Minnesota, 2006), 124–25, 190–91. The 1580 earthquake, often called the "London earthquake," was felt across much of England, northern France, the Low Countries, and parts of Germany. See G. Neilson, R. M. W. Musson, and P. W. Burton, "The 'London Earthquake' of 1580," *Engineering Geology*, 20 (1984), 113–41; Paulina Ekua Amponsah, "Seismic Activity in Ghana: Past, Present, and Future," *Annals of Geophysics*, 47 (April/June 2004), 539–43. See also Augustín Udías, "Jesuit Studies of Earthquakes and Seismological Stations," in M. Kölbl-Ebert, ed., *Geology and Religion: A History of Harmony and Hostility*, Special Publications No. 310 (London: Geological Society of London, 2009), 137. For earthquakes in France, see Grégory Quenet, "Earthquakes in Early Modern France: From Old Regime to the Birth of a New Risk," in Jamku et al., *Historical Disasters in Context*, 94–114. See also Quenet, *Les Tremblements de terre aux dix-septième et dix-huitième siècles. La naissance d'un risque* (Seyssel: Champ Vallon, 2005).

53. John Luffman, *A Brief Account of the Island of Antigua* (London, 1789), 19 144 (quote); "Earthquakes in Jamaica," Earthquake Unit, University of the West Indies, Mona, https://www.mona.uwi.edu/earthquake/earthquakes-jamaica   Richard   Robertson, "Antilles, Geology," in Rosemary Gillespie and David Clague, eds., *Encyclopedia of Islands* (Berkeley: University of California Press, 2009), 32.

54. Alan Graham, *A Natural History of the New World* (Chicago: University of Chicago Press, 2011), 58–59. A good, general introduction to earthquake science is Susan Hough, *Earthshaking Science: What We Know (and Don't Know) about Earthquakes* (Princeton, NJ: Princeton University Press, 2002).

55. Graham, *Natural History of the New World*, 58; W. Travis Garmon, Casey Allen, and Kaelin Groom, "Geologic and Tectonic Background of the Lesser Antilles," in Casey Allen, ed., *Landscapes and Landforms of the Lesser Antilles* (Cham, Switzerland: Springer, 2017), 7–15; David Barker, "Geographies of Opportunity, Geographies of Constraint," in Stephan Palmié and Francisco Scarano, eds., *The Caribbean: A History of the Region and Its Peoples* (Chicago: University of Chicago Press, 2011), 25–31; see also Robert Potter, David Barker, Dennis Conway, and Thomas Klak, eds., *The Contemporary Caribbean* (New York: Pearson, 2004), 6–14.

56. The most thorough discussion of volcanoes in the region, including a list of active eruptions, is Jan Lindsey et al., eds., *Volcanic Hazard Atlas of the Lesser Antilles* (St. Augustine, Trinidad: University of the West Indies Press, 2005), especially p. xv, 10. See also Robertson, "Antilles, Geology," 32–34.

57. Lindsay et al., *Volcanic Hazard Atlas*, xiv–xv, 81–82, 248; Clarissa Kimber, *Martinique Revisited: The Changing Plant Geographies of a West Indian Island* (College Station: Texas A&M University Press, 1988), 129. *Pennsylvania Gazette*, December 13, 1797; S. D. Smith, "Volcanic Hazard in a Slave Society: The 1812 Eruption of Mt. Soufrière in St. Vincent," *Journal of Historical Geography*, 37 (2011), 55–67; Barry Higman, *Slave Populations of the British Caribbean, 1807–1834* (Baltimore: Johns Hopkins University Press, 1984), 214–15.

58. Barker, "Geographies of Opportunity, Geographies of Constraint," 25–31; Potter et al., *The Contemporary Caribbean*, 8–14; Griffith Hughes, *Natural History of Barbados* (London,

1750), 29. In 1728, the island's governor feared the powder magazine might have collapsed in an earthquake that struck a few years earlier, which might have exploded and destroyed Bridgetown. See Governor Worsley to the Duke of Newcastle, May 20, 1728, in *Calendar of State Papers, Colonial Series: America and the West Indies, 1574–1739* [hereafter *CSPC*], eds. W. Noel Sainsbury et al., 40 vols. (London: Her Majesty's Stationary Office, 1858–1994), 36:100.

59. Barker, "Geographies of Opportunity, Geographies of Constraint," 25–31; Potter et al., *The Contemporary Caribbean*, 8–14. The most notable are the Septentrional-Oriente Fault, which cuts across southern Cuba, northern Hispaniola, and north of Puerto Rico, and the Enriquillo-Plantain Garden Fault, which runs across southern Jamaica and southern Hispaniola. It was this fault that ruptured in the 2010 Haiti earthquake.

60. K. F. O'Laughlin and James Lander, *Caribbean Tsunamis: A 500-Year History from 1498–1998* (Dordrecht, Netherlands: Springer, 2003); Bruce Bolt, *Earthquakes* (New York: W.H. Freeman, 1978, revised 1993), 147–53. Tsunamis are occasionally spoken of as tidal waves, but this is incorrect because unlike ocean tides, tsunami waves are not associated with the gravitational pull of the sun and moon. On the 1755 tsunami reaching the Caribbean, see Molesky, *This Gulf of Fire*, 144; "Account of the Effects of the Late Earthquake in Several Parts," *Gentleman's Magazine*, 25 (1755), 589–90; "An Account of the Agitation of the Sea at Antigua, Nov. 1, 1755, By Capt. Affleck of the Advice Man of War," *Philosophical Transactions of the Royal Society*, 49 (1755–56), 668–70; in addition, see J. Rodger et al., "The Transoceanic 1755 Lisbon Tsunami in Martinique," *Pure Applied Geophysics*, 168 (2011), 1015–31.

61. O'Laughlin and Lander, *Caribbean Tsunamis*; On the pearl fishery, see Molly A. Warsh, "A Political Ecology in the Early Spanish Caribbean," *William and Mary Quarterly*, 71, no. 4 (October 2014), 516–48.

62. *An Account of the Late Dreadful Earth-Quake in the Island of Mevis* [sic], *St. Christophers, &c.* (London, 1690); on various scenarios for Port Royal, see Emanuela Guidoboni and John Ebel, *Earthquakes and Tsunamis in the Past: A Guide to Techniques in Historical Seismology* (Cambridge: Cambridge University Press, 2009), 516–17. For new perspectives on tsunami hazards following the 2010 earthquake, see M. J. Hornbach, et al., "High Tsunami Frequency as a Result of Combined Strike-Slip Faulting and Coastal Landslides," *Nature Geoscience*, 3 (2010), 783–88; C. B. Harbitz et al., "Tsunami Hazard in the Caribbean: Regional Exposure Derived from Credible Worst Case Scenarios," *Continental Shelf Research*, 38 (2012), 1–23. The latter contains an updated catalogue of Caribbean tsunamis.

63. Uri ten Brink, William Bakun, and Claudia Flores, "Historical Perspective on Seismic Hazard to Hispaniola and the Northeast Caribbean Region," *Journal of Geophysical Research*, 116 (December 2011), 1–15.

64. Uri ten Brink at al., "Historical Perspective on Seismic Hazard to Hispaniola." The amount of energy released by an earthquake is measured by the moment magnitude scale (the successor to the Richter scale). The intensity of an earthquake—the extent to which the earthquake is felt by humans and the level of damage that results—is captured by the modified Mercalli scale (scientists in Europe employ the roughly analogous European macroseismic scale). The Mercalli scale is particularly useful in examining early modern earthquakes because it allows for some standard measure of the impact of an earthquake. Reading historical documents with an eye to their descriptions of damage to houses, churches, trees, and the impact on the land itself allows scientists and historians to assess the magnitude of past disasters, but it requires some informed guesswork to assign a magnitude figure. On the 1673 earthquake, see Juan Jose Ponce Vázquez, "Atlantic Peripheries: Diplomacy, War, and Spanish-French Interactions in Hispaniola, 1660s–1690s," in D'Maris Coffman et al., eds., *The Atlantic World* (New York: Routledge, 2015), 305.

65. McCann et al., "Catalog of Felt Earthquakes," 141–90; M. O. Cotilla Rodríguez, "The Santiago de Cuba Earthquake of 11 June, 1766: Some New Insights," *Geofísica Internacional*, 42 (2003), 589–602.

66. Philip Boucher, *France and the American Tropics* (Baltimore: Johns Hopkins University Press, 2007), 19; Kimber, *Martinique Revisited*, 131, 207. "Answer to Inquiries Sent to Colonel Stapleton, Governor of the Leeward Islands," November 22, 1676, in *CSPC*, 9:500; Alexandre Moreau de Jonnés, *Histoire Physique de Antilles Francaises* (Paris, 1822), 110.

67. *Pennsylvania Gazette*, December 29, 1737; see also Hans Sloane, *Voyage to the Islands of Madera, Barbados, Nieves, S. Christophers, and Jamaica* (London, 1707–1725), 1:xliv; Médéric Louis Élie Moreau de Saint-Méry, *A Topographical and Political Description of the Spanish Part of Saint-Domingo, translated from the French by William Cobbett* (Philadelphia, 1798), 10.

68. Luffman, *A Brief Account of the Island of Antigua*, 123; M de Mairan, *Histoire de L'Académie Royale des Sciences, Année 1752*, quoted in Flores et al., "Accounts of Damage," 23; *Pennsylvania Gazette*, May 14, 1752. See also Rev. E. Heath, *A Full Account of the Late Dreadful Earthquake at Port Royal in Jamaica, Written in Two Letters from the Minister of that Place* (London, 1692); Alexander von Humboldt, *Selected Writings*, ed. Andrea Wulf (New York: Knopf, 2018), 144.

69. *An Account of the Late Dreadful Earth-Quake in the Island of Mevis*; John Oldmixon, *The British Empire in America* (London: John Nicolson, 1708), 2:215; Governor Codrington to Lords of Trade and Plantations, June 4, 1690, *CSPC*, 13:278–79; Lt. Governor Stede to Lords of Trade and Plantations, April 23, 1690, in *CSPC*, 13:250. Codrington's letter dates the earthquake as April 5, but this is an error. See also Boucher, *France and the American Tropics to 1700*, 226. Popular accounts sometimes assert that the smaller town of Jamestown was swallowed up by the sea during a 1680 earthquake, but this is myth. See Tessa Machling, *The Fortifications of Nevis, West Indies, from the Seventeenth Century to the Present Day* (Oxford: British Archaeological Reports, 2012), 106–7.

70. See, for example, *A True and Perfect Relation of that Most Sad and Terrible Earthquake, at Port Royal in Jamaica, which Happened on Tuesday the 7th of June, 1692* (London, 1692).

71. Accounts V and VIII in "A Letter from Hans Sloane, M.D., and S.R.S. with Several Accounts of the Earthquakes in Peru October the 20th 1687. And at Jamaica, February 19th, 1687/88 and June the 7th, 1692," *Philosophical Transactions of the Royal Society*, 18 (1694), 90–91. On liquefaction, see George R. Clark II, "The Quake that Swallowed a City," *Earth*, 4 (April 1995), 34–41. See also Matthew Mulcahy, "The Port-Royal Earthquake and the World of Wonders in Seventeenth-Century Jamaica," *Early American Studies*, 6 (Fall 2008), 391–421. An earthquake struck London in 1692 as well, and the two became linked in the minds of many contemporaries. See Louis Gerdelan, "The Royal Society, Port Royal, and the Great Trans-Atlantic Earthquake of 1692," *Studi Storici* (2019), 854–74.

72. "A Letter from Hans Sloane," 94–95; Henry Cadbury, "Quakers and the Earthquake at Port Royal, 1692," in *Jamaican Historical Review*, 8 (1971), 19–31.

73. This story is outlined in Matthew Mulcahy, "'That Fatall Spot': The Rise and Fall—and Rise and Fall Again—of Port Royal, Jamaica," in Carole Shammas, ed., *Investing in the Early Modern Built Environment: Europeans, Asians, Settlers, and Indigenous Societies* (Leiden: Brill, 2012), 191–218.

74. For a description of the 1727 earthquake, see Jean-Baptiste Labat, *Nouveau voyage aux isles de l'Amérique* (Paris: Ch. J. B. Delspoine, 1742), 351–53. See also Robert Harms, *The Diligent: A Voyage through the Worlds of the Slave Trade* (New York: Basic Books, 2002), 341–46.

75. Harms, *The Diligent*, 341–46; Kimber, *Martinique Revisited*, 202–3. Kimber notes that 6 million trees were destroyed in the earthquake and that a root fungus finished of many that survived. On the expansion of coffee exports from Martinique between the 1730s and 1750s, see S. D. Smith, "Sugar's Poor Relation: Coffee Planting in the British Indies, 1720–1833," *Slavery and Abolition*, 19 (December 1998), 71–72.

76. "An Authentick Account of the Earthquakes that happened last Year in the Island of St. Domingo, translated from the French," *Pennsylvania Gazette*, May 14, 1752; Flores et al., "Accounts of Damage," 19, 25–26; William H. Bakun et al., "Significant Earthquakes on the Enriquillo Fault System, Hispaniola, 1500–2010: Implications for Seismic Hazard," *Bulletin for the Seismological Society of America* 102, no. 1 (2012), 18–30.

77. "An Authentick Account of the Earthquakes"; Jean Vogt, "Deux séismes majeurs de Saint-Domingue au XVIIIéme siècle," *Généalogie et Histoire de la Caraibe*, 174 (October 2004), 4298–302.

78. *Relation du tremblement de terre arrive a L'Isle de St. Dominique Le 3 Juin 1770*, Boston Public Library, Haitian Collection; *Relation Tres-détaillée des malheurs arrives Isles de Saint-Domingue,*

par le Tremblement de Terre arrive le 3 Juin 1770 (Paris, 1770). Thanks to Malick Ghachem for this reference Translation by David Turnham. Jean Vogt, "Deux séismes majeurs de Saint-Domingue au XVIIIéme siècle," *Généalogie et Histoire de la Caraibe*, 178 (February 2005), 4424-32. Translation by Catherine Savell. See also *The Annual Register, or a View of the History, Politics, and Literature for the Year 1770* (London, 1770); *Pennsylvania Gazette*, July 5, 19, 26, 1770; Bakun et al., "Significant Earthquakes on the Enriquillo Fault System," 26; J. Scherer, "Great Earthquakes in the Island of Haiti," *Bulletin of the Seismological Society of America* (1912), 161-80; *Gentleman's Magazine* (August 1770), 348 (for monetary losses); Trevor Burnard and John Garrigus, *The Plantation Machine: Atlantic Capitalism in French Saint-Domingue and British Jamaica* (Philadelphia: University of Pennsylvania Press, 2016), 199.

79. *Relation Tres-détaillée des malheurs arrives Isles de Saint-Domingue*; Vogt, "Deux séismes majeurs de Saint-Domingue au XVIIIéme siècle," 4430; Michel-Placide Justin, *Histoire Politique et Statistique de L'Ile D'Hayti, Saint-Domingue* (Paris: Briére, 1826), 117-22; David Morens, "Epidemic Anthrax in the Eighteenth Century, the Americas," *Emerging Infectious Diseases*, 8 (October 2002), 1160-62.

80. Justin, *Histoire Politique et Statistique de L'Ile D'Hayti, Saint-Domingue*; Morens, "Epidemic Anthrax in the Eighteenth Century," 1160-62. See also John Garrigus, "'Like an epidmeic one could only stop with the most vioent remedies': African Posions versus Livestock Disease in Siant-Domingue, 1750-1788," *William and Mary Quarterly* 78 (October 2021): 617-52. On the absence of seismic activity after 1770, see Bakun et al., "Significant Earthquakes on the Enriquillo Fault System, Hispaniola," 18-30; Roger Bilham, "Lessons from the Haiti Earthquake," *Nature*, 463 (February 2010), 878-79.

81. Nathalie Feuillet, François Beauducel, and Paul Tapponnier, "Tectonic Context of Moderate to Large Historical Earthquakes in the Lesser Antilles and Mechanical Coupling with Volcanoes," *Journal of Geophyiscal Research*, 116 (2011), B10308; Uri ten Brink et al., "Historical Perspective of Seismic Hazard to Hispaniola and the Northeast Caribbean Region," 1-15; on the effects of the earthquake, see Matthew J. Smith, *Liberty, Fraternity, and Exile: Haiti and Jamaica after Emancipation* (Chapel Hill: University of North Carolina Press, 2014), 46-56, quote 48; Laurent Dubois, *Haiti: The Aftershocks of History* (New York: Picador, 2013), 121-23; Laurent Dubois et al., *The Haiti Reader: History, Culture, Politics* (Durham: Duke University Press, 2020), 83-89.

82. Susan Hough, "Missing Great Earthquakes," *Journal of Geophysical Research*, 118 (2013), 1098-108; Feuillet, Beauducel, and Tapponnier, "Tectonic Context of Moderate to Large Historical Earthquakes"; Joseph Ballio, "Louis-Eugène Lami's *Charity Bazaar for Victims of the Gaudeloupe Earthquake, 1843*," *Master Drawings*, 44 (Winter 2006), 498-510; José Grases Galofre, *Terremotos Destructores del Caribe 1502-1990: una contribución al Decenio Internacional para la Redución de los Desastres Naturales, Caracas, agosto de 1990* (Montevideo: UNESCO-Relacis, 1994). Excerpts of this source are posted on the website for the Seismic Research Centre at the University of the West Indies, https://uwiseismic. com/wp-content/uploads/2021/04/EqEC_1843_document_1.pdf. For recent materials that detail the 1843 event in French, see Claude Thiebaut, *Sur les Ruines de la Point-à-Pitre: Chronique du 8 février 1843—Hommage à l'Amiral Gourbeyre* (Paris: L'Harmattan, 2008); Jacqueline Picard, *La Pointe-à-Pitre n'existe plus!"—relations du tremblement de terre de 1843 en Guadeloupe* (Guadeloupe: Carat, 2003). Picard provides the most detailed discussion of the number of deaths, and is at the lower end.

83. Deciding to abandon a town site and rebuild elsewhere was a common response to earthquakes on both sides of the Atlantic. See Stephen Tobriner, "Safety and Reconstruction of Noto after the Sicilian Earthquake of 1693—the Eighteenth-Century Context," in Alessa Johns, ed., *Dreadful Visitations: Confronting Natural Catastrophe in the Age of Enlightenment* (New York: Routledge, 1999), 49-77, quote 57; Charles Walker, *Shaky Colonialism: The 1746 Earthquake-Tsunami in Lima, Peru, and Its Long Aftermath* (Durham: Duke University Press, 2008), 90-91.

84. Francis Alexander Stanislaus and Baron de Wimpffen, *A Voyage to Saint Domingo in the Years 1788, 1789, and 1790* (London: Cadell and Davies, 1797), 67, 101-2; Gauvin Bailey, *Architecture and Urbanism in the French Atlantic Empire: State, Church, and Society,*

1604–1830 (Montreal: McGill Queen's University Press, 2018), 14–15; Moreau de Saint-Méry, quoted in Scherer, "Great Earthquakes," 175; Edward Long, *The History of Jamaica* (London: T. Lowndes, 1774), 2:18–19.

85. William McNeill, *The Global Condition: Conquerors, Catastrophes, and Community* (Princeton, NJ: Princeton University Press, 1992), 148; Smith, *Liberty, Fraternity, and Exile*, 46–56. Smith notes that a fire a few months later (January 1843) also struck Port-au-Prince but was not related to the earthquake; 52–53. Vogt, "Deux séismes majeurs de Saint-Domingue au XVIIIéme siècle," 4427–28. See also Bailey, *Architecture and Urbanism*, 466. Similar building and design recommendations followed in the wake of other early modern earthquakes as well. See the discussion following the Lisbon earthquake in Molesky, *Great Gulf of Fire*, 309–17. In a contrary example, a fire in the city of Charlotte Amalie on Danish St. Thomas in 1832 destroyed much of the city. By royal order it was rebuilt with brick and stone that then caused high mortality in an earthquake in 1867. See Roy A. Watlington and Shirley H. Lincoln, *Disaster and Disruption in 1867: Hurricane, Earthquake, and Tsunami in the Danish West Indies* (St. Thomas: Eastern Caribbean Center, University of the Virgin Islands, 1997).

86. For a general discussion of building material debates, see Mulcahy, *Hurricanes and Society*, 117–44.

87. Ashok Mishra and Vijay Singh, "A Review of Drought Concepts," *Journal of Hydrology*, 391 (2010), 202–16; Douglas Gamble, "The Neglected Climatic Hazards of the Caribbean: Overview and Prospects for a Warmer Climate," *Geography Compass*, 8, no. 4 (2014), 221–34; See also Richardson, *Economy and Environment in the Caribbean*, 83. Potter et al., *The Contemporary Caribbean*, 175, terms flooding "the most frequently occurring and persistent hazard in the region." See also Tania López-Marrero and Ben Wisner, "Not in the Same Boat," 131. For a study that highlight the dangers posed by both, see Dave St. Aubyn Gosse, *Abolition and Plantation Management in Jamaica, 1807–1838* (Kingston, Jamaica: University of the West Indies Press, 2012), 123–52. For a more detailed discussion of Caribbean drought and its effects in the larger context of the Greater Caribbean, see Matthew Mulcahy, "'Miserably Scorched': Drought in the Plantation Colonies of the British Greater Caribbean," in Thomas Blake Earle and D. Andrew Johnson, eds., *Atlantic Environments and the American South* (Athens: University of Georgia Press, 2020), 65–89; Mark Hauser, *Mapping Water in Dominica: Enslavement and Environment under Colonialism* (Seattle: University of Washington Press, 2021), 49.

88. Mishra and Singh, "A Review of Drought Concepts." See also D. A. Wilhite and M. H. Glantz, "Understanding the Drought Phenomenon: The Role of Definitions," *Water International*, 10 (1985), 111–20; Hauser, *Mapping Water in Dominica*, 52. Drought also needs to be distinguished from aridity. The latter is a permanent feature of a particular place, while the former is an occasional occurrence linked to other forces. The two can often combine, as arid places may become subject to drought.

89. Alexander Berland, "Documentary Derived Chronologies of Rainfall Variability in Antigua, Lesser Antilles, 1770–1890," *Climate of the Past*, 9 (2013), 1331–43; Douglas Gamble and Scott Curtis, "Caribbean Precipitation: Review, Model, Prospect," *Progress in Physical Geography*, 32 (2008), 265–76; David Watts, *The West Indies: Patterns of Development, Culture, and Environmental Change Since 1492* (New York: Cambridge University Press, 1987), 17–25.

90. Berland, "Documentary Derived Chronologies of Rainfall Variability in Antigua," 1331–43. Michael Chenoweth, *The 18th Century Climate of Jamaica, Derived from the Journals of Thomas Thistlewood* (Philadelphia: American Philosophical Society, 2003), 2–4. César Caviedes, *El Nino in History: Storming Through the Ages* (Gainesville: University Press of Florida, 2001), 89–145. El Niño events can result in relatively heavy rainfall in parts of the Greater Antilles in May, June, and July, for example, but reduce later summer rainfall in the southern parts of the Lesser Antilles. Gamble, "The Neglected Climatic Hazards of the Caribbean," 221–34.

91. Watts, *The West Indies*, 17–25. For Jamaica, see Thomas Boswell, "The Caribbean: A Geographic Preface," in Richard Hillman and Thomas Agostino, *Understanding the Contemporary Caribbean*, 2nd ed. (Boulder, CO: Lynn Rienner, 2009), 24–25; for a contemporary observation of this regional variation, see "Observations Made by a Curious and Learned Person Sailing from England to the Caribe-Islands," *Philosophical Transactions of the Royal*

Society, 2 (December 1666), 499; on Saint-Domingue, see James McClellan, *Colonialism and Science: Saint-Domingue and the Old Regime* (Chicago: University of Chicago Press, 2010), 26–27; for Antigua, see Berland, "Documentary-Derived Chronologies of Rainfall Variability," 1332. On microclimates, see Katherine Johnston, "The Constitution of Empire: Place and Bodily Health in the Eighteenth-Century Atlantic," *Atlantic Studies*, 10 (2013), 443–66.

92. Gerald Haug, "Climate and the Collapse of Maya Civilization," *Science*, 299 (March 14, 2003), 1731–35; Gyles Iannone, ed., *The Great Maya Droughts in Cultural Context: Case Studies in Resilience and Vulnerability* (Boulder: University Press of Colorado, 2014). A good summary of the debate is in Charles Mann, *1491: New Revelations of the Americas before Columbus* (New York: Vintage, 2006), 274–79; C. J. Beets et al., "Climate and Pre-Columbian Settlement at Anse à La Gourde, Guadeloupe," *Geoarchaeology*, 21 (2006), 271–80; Chad Lane et al., "Beyond the Mayan Lowlands: Impacts of the Terminal Classic Drought in the Caribbean Antilles," *Quaternary Science Review*, 86 (2014), 89–98.

93. Watts, "Cycles of Famine," 62; Governor Sir Nathaniel Johnson to Lords of Trade and Plantations, June 2, 1688, *CSPC*, 12:553; "An Account of Governor Codrington's Proceedings as to the Settlement of St. Christopher," September 12, 1691, *CSPC*, 13:538; Robertson, *A Detection of the State and Situation of the Present Sugar Planters*, 49; Gregory Cushman review of Sherry Johnson, "Climate and Catastrophe in Cuba and the Atlantic World," *Hispanic American Historical Review*, 93, no. 1 (2013), 103–4.

94. McClellan, *Colonialism and Science*, 27–28; Archives Nationales d'Outre-Mer (Aix-en-Province, [hereafter ANOM]), C^{8A} 1 F. 120 (Gov. Gen. Baas-Castelmore, 12 June 1671); ANOM C^{8A} 24 F 197 (Gov. Gen. Marquis de Feuquières, 1 August 1718).

95. Watts, *The West Indies*, 247, 249; C. G. A. Oldendorp, *C.G.A. Oldendorp's History of the Mission of the Evangelical Brethren on the Caribbean Islands of St. Thomas, St. Croix, and St. John* (1777), ed. Johann Jakob Bossard, English trans. Arnold Highfield and Vladimir Barac (Ann Arbor, MI: Karoma Publishers, 1987), 53, 102, 460–61, 485, 520, 536–68.

96. Robert Stokell to Davenport and Wentworth, Feb. 26, 1759, Beinecke Lesser Antilles Collection, Hamilton College; Veront Satchell, *Hope Transformed: A Historical Sketch of the Hope Landscape, St. Andrew, Jamaica, 1669–1960* (Kingston, Jamaica: University of the West Indies Press, 2012), 120–21; Mulcahy, "Miserably Scorched," 72; Burnard and Garrigus, *Plantation Machine*, 224–25.

97. David Barry Gaspar, *Bondmen and Rebels: A Study of Master-Slave Relations in Antigua* (Baltimore: Johns Hopkins University Press, 1985), 223–24; Alexander Berland, "Extreme Weather and Social Vulnerability in Colonial Antigua, Lesser Antilles, 1770–1890" (PhD diss., University of Nottingham, 2015), 123–32.

98. Governor Kendall to Lords of Trade and Plantation, August 22, 1690, *CSPC*, 13:311; Governor Hart to the Council of Trade and Plantations, May 20, 1726, *CSPC*, 35:311; Keith Mason, "The Absentee Planter and the Key Slave: Privilege, Patriarchalism, and Exploitation in the Early Eighteenth-Century Caribbean," *William and Mary Quarterly*, 70 (January 2013), 92–93; Carstens, *A General Description of all the Danish, American or West Indian Islands*, 122–23; Watts, "Cycles of Famine," 62.

99. Robert Robertson, *A Detection*, 45; McClellan, *Colonialism and Science*, 27; Berland, "Extreme Weather and Social Vulnerability," 139.

100. Long, *History of Jamaica*, III:615; Satchell, *Hope Transformed*, 120–21; Chenoweth, *The 18th Century Climate of Jamaica*, 47–49; Oldendorp, *History of the Mission*, 102; Richardson, *Igniting the Caribbean's Past*, 91–92.

101. On drought and working conditions, see Justin Roberts, *Slavery and the Enlightenment in the British Atlantic, 1750–1807* (New York: Cambridge University Press, 2013), 95, 105; James Ramsay, *An Essay on the Treatment and Conversion of African Slaves in the British Colonies* (London: J. Phillips, 1784), 72; Governor Sir Nathaniel Johnson to the Lords of Trade and Plantations, April 20, 1689, *CSPC*, 13:24; see also *American Weekly Mercury*, August 22, 1734; McClellan, *Colonialism and Science*, 28; Mark William Hauser, "A Political Ecology of Water and Enslavement: Water Ways in Eighteenth-Century Caribbean Plantations," *Current Anthropology*, 58, no. 2 (2017), 227–56.

102. Rachel Tudway, quoted in J. R. Ward, *British West Indian Slavery, 1750–1835: The Process of Amelioration* (Oxford: Oxford University Press, 1988), 37; Rebecca Woolnough, quoted

Christine Walker, "To Be My Own Mistress: Women in Jamaica, Atlantic Slavery, and the Creation of Britain's American Empire, 1660–1770" (PhD diss., University of Michigan, 2014), 285; G. Debien, "La nourriture des esclaves sur les plantations des Antilles francaises aux XVIIe et XVIIIe siecles," *Caribbean Studies*, 4 (1964), 3–27; On food scarcity in the region generally, see Bertie Mandelblatt, "'A Land Where Hunger Is in Gold and Famine Is in Opulence': Plantation Slavery, Island Ecology, and the Fear of Famine in the French Caribbean," in Lauric Henneton and Louis Roper, eds., *Fear and the Shaping of Early American Societies* (Leiden: Brill, 2016), 243–64. Justin Roberts highlights planter efforts at increased self-sufficiency on Barbados and Jamaica. Roberts, *Slavery and the Enlightenment*, 101–5.

103. On famine and disease, see Joel Mokyr and Cormac Ó Gráda, "Famine Disease and Famine Mortality: Lessons from the Irish Experience, 1845–50," in Tim Dyson and Cormac Ó Gráda, eds., *Famine Demography: Perspectives in from the Past and Present* (Oxford: Oxford University Press, 2002), 19–43. Robertson, *A Detection of the State and Situation of the Present Sugar Planters*, 44; William Smith, *A Natural History of Nevis, and the Rest of the English Leeward Charibee Islands in America* (Cambridge, UK: J. Bentham, 1745), 225; Johnson to the Lords of Trade and Plantations, April 20, 1689, *CSPC*, 13:24. For a fuller discussion of the impact in British colonies, see Mulcahy, "Miserably Scorched," 74–75.

104. For Barbados, J. Harry Bennett, Jr., *Bondsmen and Bishops: Slavery and Apprenticeship on the Codrington Plantations of Barbados, 1710–1838* (Berkeley: University of California Press, 1958), 38; Burnard and Garrigus, *Plantation Machine*, 112–19; Tullideph to George Thomas, May 22, 1746, in Richard Sheridan, ed., "Letters from a Sugar Planter in Antigua, 1739–1758," *Agricultural History*, 31 (July 1957), 14; Robert Colhoun to William McDowall, May 30, 1757, and Wm Milliken to Capt. McDowall, June 2, 1757, National Archives of Scotland [hereafter NAS], GD 237/12/47. Thanks to Phil Morgan for sharing his transcriptions of the McDowall letters with us.

105. Sheridan, "The Crisis of Slave Subsistence in the British West Indies," 615–41; Alexander Berland and Georgina Endfield, "Drought and Disaster in a Revolutionary Age: Colonial Antigua during the American Independence War," *Environment and History*, 24 (May 2018), 209–35; Ward, *British West Indian Slavery*, 66; Andrew O'Shaughnessy, *An Empire Divided: The American Revolution and the British Caribbean* (Philadelphia: University of Pennsylvania Press, 2000), 162.

106. Richard Grove, "The Great El Niño of 1789–93 and Its Global Consequences: Reconstructing An Extreme Climate Event in World Environmental History," *Journal of Medieval History*, 10 (2007), 75–98; Johnson, *Climate and Catastrophe*, 193–201; William Taylor to Thomas Graham, August 8, 1786, Airth Mss 10924, f. 55–56, National Library of Scotland; Report of the Jamaica Assembly, cited in Edwards, *The History, Civil and Commercial* (1793), 2:397; Taylor quoted in Byrd, *Captives and Voyagers*, 89.

107. Enrique Florescano, *Precios de maíz y crisis agrícolas en México, 1708–1810* (Mexico City: El Colegio de México, 1969); Georgina H. Enfield, *Climate and Society in Colonial Mexico* (Hoboken, NJ: John Wiley and Sons, 2011); McClellan, *Colonialism and Science*, 27–28; Laurent Dubois, *Avengers of the New World: The Story of the Haitian Revolution* (Cambridge, MA: Harvard University Press, 2004), 93–4; see also *Pennsylvania Gazette*, July 5, 1786; Johnson, *Climate and Catastrophe*, 97–100, 204–6; Fernando Pico, *Puerto Rico y la sequía de 1847* (San Juan, PR: Ediciones Huracán, 2015), 28–29; Jean Baptiste Dubuc, *Lettres critiques et politiques sur les colonies et le commerce des villes maritimes de France* (Geneva, 1785), 124–26, 80–90.

108. Joseph Horan, "The Colonial Famine Plot: Slavery, Free Trade, and Empire in the French Atlantic, 1763–1791," *International Review of Social History*, 55 (2010), 103–21. One visitor to Saint-Domingue noted that planters often complained about drying up of fresh springs, but it was their "own imprudence" by cutting down trees that created this "sudden privation." See Stanislaus, *Voyage to Saint Domingo*, 192–93.

109. Mandelblatt, "Land Where Hunger Is in Gold," quote 256; see also Wm. Milliken to Capt. McDowall, June 2, 1757, NAS, GD 237/12/47; Nicholas Crawford, "Calamity's Empire: Slavery, Scarcity, and the Political Economy of Provisioning in the British Caribbean, c. 1775–1834" (PhD diss., Harvard University, 2016), 28; Katherine Johnston,

"Endangered Plantations: Environmental Change and Slavery in the British Caribbean, 1631–1807," *Early American Studies*, 18 (Summer 2020), 259–86.

110. For fear of running away, see Mandelblatt, "Land Where Hunger Is in Gold," quote p. 259; Robert Colhoun to William McDowall, 30 May 1757, NAS, GD 237/12/47; on Nevis revolt, see Mason, "The Absentee Planter and the Key Slave," 93; Jon Sensbach, *Rebecca's Revival: Creating Black Christianity in the Atlantic World* (Cambridge, MA: Harvard University Press, 2006), 22; Gaspar, *Bondmen and Rebels*, 29–34, 215–54; Lucien Abénon, *La Guadeloupe 1671 à 1759: Etude Politique, Economique, et Sociale* (Paris: L'Harmattan, 1987), 236–38; Richard B. Sheridan, "The Jamaican Slave Insurrection Scare of 1776 and the American Revolution," *Journal of Negro History*, 3 (1975), 290–308; Berland, "Extreme Weather and Social Vulnerability in Colonial Antigua," 132. Interestingly, accounts of slave conspiracies during these periods of dearth often included reports that rebels had hosted elaborate feasts. How slaves managed to acquire such abundance at a time when the islands suffered from dry weather and a want of provisions is unexplained, but such rumors furthered images of a world turned upside down in the eyes of panicked whites. See James Dator, "Search for a New Land: Imperial Power and Afro-Creole Resistance in the British Leeward Islands, 1624-1745" (PhD diss., University of Michigan, 2011), 312, 318, 339–43.

111. Nathaniel Phillips to John Purrier, March 25, 1777, Slebech Papers, Letters, Sept. 3, 1777, to Nov. 6, 1782, item 9050, image 23; British Archives Online: West Indies, Plantations, Slavery, and Trade, https://microform.digital/boa/collections/1/the-west-indies-slavery-plantations-and-trade-1759-1832/detailed-description, accessed July 9, 2020; Governor Burt, quoted in Berland and Endfield, "Drought and Disaster in a Revolutionary Age," 226.

112. On the need to read accounts of conspiracies with caution, see Jason Sharples, "Discovering Slave Conspiracies: New Fears of Rebellion and Old Paradigms of Plotting in Seventeenth-Century Barbados," *American Historical Review*, 120 (June 2015), 811–43. Waldemar Westergaard, *The Danish West Indies Under Company Rule, 1671-1754* (New York: Macmillan, 1917), 164, argues that food shortages were the "most persistent motive that led to general unrest." Dubois, *Avengers of the New World*, 93–94; *Pennsylvania Gazette*, July 5, 1786. On enslaved people's' struggles simply to survive during normal times, to say nothing of during subsistence crises, see Randy Brown, *Surviving Slavery in the British Caribbean* (Philadelphia: University of Pennsylvania Press, 2017).

113. Vere Lang Oliver, *The History of Antigua* (London, 1894), 1:xcv; Grove, *Green Imperialism*, 271; Miguel de la Torre, Circular of August 6, 1824; George Flinter, *An Account of the Present State of the Island of Puerto Rico* (London: Longman, Rees, et al., 1834). Both sources were cited in Jaime Bagué, "Enumeración de los bosques públicos (año de 1870) basado en el informe de Juan Francisco Ladón," typescript, Coleccion Portorriqueña, Biblioteca José Lázaro, University of Puerto Rico. These sources are discussed in Pico, *Puerto Rico y la sequía de 1847*, 102–5. Both sources are cited and discussed in Pico, *Puerto Rico y la sequía de 1847*, 102–5.

114. Watts, *The West Indies*, 299; McClellan, *Colonialism and Science*, 71–74; Burnard and Garrigus, *Plantation Machine*, 245–48; Satchell, *Hope Transformed*, 169–74.

115. McClellan, *Colonialism and Science*, 71–77; Moreau de Saint-Méry, *Spanish Part of Saint-Domingo*, 1:21; Long, *History of Jamaica*, 3:649–50 and 1:356.

116. On Montserrat, see Walter Tullideph to David Tullideph, Oct. 3, 1737, Tullideph Letterbook, NAS; on Nevis, see Joseph Herbert to Sir William Stapleton, Dec. 20, 1728, in Edwin Gay, ed., "Letter from a Sugar Plantation in Nevis, 1723–32," *Journal of Economic and Business History*, 1 (November 1928), 160; Taylor, quoted in Byrd, *Captives and Voyagers*, 89; Elsa Goveia, *Slave Society in the British Leeward Islands at the end of the Eighteenth Century* (New Haven, CT: Yale University Press, 1965), 114.

117. Frank Klingberg, *Codrington Chronicle: An Experiment in Anglican Altruism on a Barbados Plantation, 1710–1834* (Berkeley: University of California Press, 1949), 71; "A Briefe Description of the Island of Barbados," MS 736, f. 183, Trinity College Library, Dublin; Nicholas Blake to Joseph Williamson, Nov. 12, 1669, CSPC, 7:45. Blake initially reported 150 coffins were "carried into the sea," but in an addendum dated Nov. 15th, the minister told him "the coffins, corpses, and bones of nearer 1,500 than 150 persons were carried into the sea."

118. Sherry Johnson, *Climate and Catastrophe*, 16; Simon Taylor to Chaloner Arcedekne, April 23, 1765, and April 30, 1765, in Betty Wood, ed., *Travel, Trade, and Power in the Atlantic, 1765-1884* (Cambridge: Cambridge University Press, 2002), 12-15; B. W. Higman, "Jamaican Coffee Plantations, 1780-1860: A Cartographic Analysis," *Caribbean Geography*, 2 (1996), 73-91.

119. Thomas Jeffreys, *The Natural and Civil History of the French Dominions in North and South America* (London, 1760), 2:81; McClellan, *Colonialism and Science*, 26; Burnard and Garrigus, *Plantation Machine*, 246.

120. See Johnson, *Climate and Catastrophe*, 154-55, 163-68.

121. David Watts, "Long-Term Environmental Influences on Development in Islands of the Lesser Antilles," *Scottish Geographical Magazine* 109, no. 3 (1993), 133-41.

122. On insects and disease, see J. R. McNeill, *Mosquito Empires: Ecology and War in the Greater Caribbean, 1620-1914* (New York: Cambridge University Press, 2010) and Trevor Burnard, "'The Countrie Continues Sicklie': White Mortality in Jamaica, 1655-1780," *Social History of Medicine*, 12 (1999), 45-72. For a fuller discussion of insects in the region, see Mulcahy and Schwartz, "Nature's Battalions," 433-64.

123. Etienne Stockland, "'La Guerre aux Insects': Pest Control and Agricultural Reform in the French Enlightenment," *Annals of Science*, 70, no. 4 (2013), 435-60; Sheila Wille, "Governing Insects in Britain and the Empire, 1691-1816" (PhD diss., University of Chicago, 2014). White, quoted in Deirdre Coleman, "Entertaining Entomology: Insects and Insect Performers in the Eighteenth Century," *Eighteenth-Century Life*, 30 (Summer 2006), 110. See also James McWilliams, *American Pests: The Losing War on Insects from Colonial Times to DDT* (New York: Columbia University Press, 2008), 1-25; Janice Neri, *The Insect and the Image: Visualizing Nature in Early Modern Europe, 1500-1700* (Minneapolis: University of Minnesota Press, 2011); Lucinda Cole, *Imperfect Creatures: Vermin, Literature, and the Sciences of Life, 1600-1740* (Ann Arbor: University of Michigan Press, 2016); Eric Jorink, *Reading the Book of Nature in the Dutch Golden Age, 1575-1715* (Leiden: Brill, 2010); Peter Mancall, *Nature and Culture in the Early Modern Atlantic* (Philadelphia: University of Pennsylvania Press, 2018), especially 121-37; Mary Fissell, "Imagining Vermin in Early Modern England," *History Workshop Journal*, 47 (1999), 1-29; on the German-born botanical artist Maria Sibylla Merian (1647-1717) and her travels to Surinam in the early eighteenth century, see Neri, *Visualizing Nature*, 139-80; Sharon Valliant, "Maria Sibylla Merian: Recovering an Eighteenth-Century Legend," *Eighteenth-Century Studies*, 26 (1993), 467-79; and the chapter "Metamorphoses," in Natalie Zemon Davis, *Women on the Margins* (Cambridge, MA: Harvard University Press, 1995), 140-202. A fascinating study of insects in the Caribbean is D. Keith McE. Kevan, "Mid-Eighteenth Century Entomology and Helminthology in the West Indies: Dr. James Grainger," *Journal of the Society for the Bibliography of Natural History*, 8 (1977). 193-222. Studies (beyond Stockland) that explore insects as agricultural pests include: Philip Pauly, "Fighting the Hessian Fly: American and British Responses to Insect Invasion, 1776-1789," *Environmental History*, 7 (July 2002), 377-400; Diogo de Carvalho Cabral, "Into the Bowels of Tropical Earth: Leaf-Cutting Ants and the Colonial Making of Agrarian Brazil," *Journal of Historical Geography*, 50 (2015), 92-105. See also Diogo de Carvalho Cabral, "Meaningful Clearings: Human-Ant Negotiated Landscapes in Nineteenth-Century Brazil," *Environmental History*, 26 (2021), 1-24. Leaf-cutting ants were present in places like Cuba, but unlike Brazil, they do not appear to have had a major impact on plantation agriculture during this period. J. M. Cherrett, "Some Aspects of the Distribution of Pest Species of Leaf-Cutting Ants in the Caribbean," *Proceedings of the American Society of Horticultural Science* (Tropical Region) 12 (1968), 295-310.

124. Richard Ligon, *True and Exact History of the Island of Barbadoes* (London, 1657, reprint 1673), 63. See also AGI, Santo Domingo, leg. 77, ramo V, doc. 134 (undated).

125. For "insect paradox," see McWilliams, *American Pests*, 4-5; Wille, "Governing Insects," 172-97; Sampson Wood, quoted in Crawford, "Calamity's Empire," 67.

126. English translation of las Casas, "Plague of Ants," in Roberto González Echevarría, ed., *Oxford Book of Latin American Short Stories* (New York: Oxford University Press, 1997), 34-38, translation by Sandra Ferdman; see José Luiz Saenz, "Una carta anua de la residencia

de Santo Domingo (23 Octubre 1695)," *Archivum Historicum Societatis Iesu*, 62, no. 124 (1993), 281–312. See also René Antoine Ferchault de Réaumur, *The Natural History of Ants, from an Unpublished Manuscript* (1742), trans. William Wheeler (New York: Knopf, 1926), 235–36, fn. 37.

127. E. O. Wilson, "Early Ant Plagues in the New World," *Nature*, 433 (January 6, 2005), 32. A lengthier discussion of Wilson's research into this question is in E. O. Wilson, "Ant Plagues: A Centuries Old Mystery Solved," in Wilson, *Nature Revealed: Selected Writings, 1949–2006* (Baltimore: Johns Hopkins University Press, 2006), 344–50

128. E. O. Wilson, *The Creation: An Appeal to Save Life on Earth* (New York: W. W. Norton, 2006), 45; Long, *History of Jamaica*, 1:345; Edwards, *The History, Civil and Commercial* (1793), 1:129–31; Hans Sloane, *A Voyage to the Islands Madera, Barbados, Nieves, S. Christophers, and Jamaica . . .* (London, 1707), 1:lxviii.

129. Ligon, *True and Exact History*, 62; Lord Willoughby to the King, Nov. 4, 1663, *CSPC*, 5:167; Lord Willoughby to Sir Henry Bennet, Feb. 18, 1664, *CSPC*, 5:189; Lt. Governor Stede to Lords of Trade and Plantations, Oct. 19, 1687, *CSPC*, 12:454. For the impact of food shortages on outmigration, see Watts, "Cycles of Famine," 61. Note: all locusts are grasshoppers, but not all grasshoppers are locusts. Hughes, *Natural History of Barbados*, 84–85.

130. Wim Klooster, "Contraband Trade by Curacao's Jews with Countries of Idolatry, 1660–1800," *Studia Rosenthaliana*, 31 (1997), 58–73; for Guadeloupe, see Schomburgk, *History of Barbados*, 651; Westergaard, *The Danish West Indies*, 166–67; Simon Taylor to Arcedekne, July 24, 1771, in Wood, *Travel, Trade, and Power in the Atlantic*, 105.

131. On the absence of pests, see Watts, *The West Indies*, 239–40, 432. Dalby Thomas, *An Historical Account of the Rise and Growth of the West-India Collonies* (London, 1690), 20; Sloane, *A Voyage to the Islands*, 2:220. Caterpillars and other pests contributed to the decline of sugar in Madeira in an early period. See Jason Moore, "Madeira, Sugar, and the Conquest of Nature in the 'First' Sixteenth Century, Part II," *Review (Fernand Braudel Center)*, 33 (2010), 8–9.

132. "John Castles, Observations on the Sugar Ants: In a Letter from John Castles," *Philosophical Transactions of the Royal Society*, 80 (1790), 346–58.; Alfred Spencer, ed., *The Memoirs of William Hickey, 1775–1782* (London: Hurst & Blackett, 1925), 2:16–18.

133. Spencer, *The Memoirs of William Hickey*, 2:16–18; Castles, "Observations on the Sugar Ants," 346–58; see also Thomas Coke, *A History of the West Indies* (London, 1810), 2:313–14; *Anderson's Historical and Chronological Deduction of the Origin of Commerce* (Dublin, 1790), 5:304; Gov. Ennery to Sec. de la Marine, 12 March 1768, C8B 12 n. 196; Gov. Ennery to Sec. de la Marine, June 2, 1770, C8A 69 F347, Gov. Ennery to Sec. de la Marine, July 2, 1770, C8A 69 F348; Gov. Vallière to Sec. de la Marine, Sept. 16, 1771, C8A 70 F41, ANOM. See also M. Barboteau, "Essai sur La fourmi," *Journal de Physique*, 8 (1776–77), 383–95, 21–36, 88–96; Schomburgk, *History of Barbados*, 643. A good discussion of the situation in Martinique and how colonists responded to the threat is Pierre-Etienne Stockland, "Statecraft and Insect Oeconomies in the Global French Enlightenment (1670–1815)" (PhD diss., Columbia University, 2018), 298–301.

134. Nathaniel Phillips Diaries, Oct. 30, Nov. 2, and Nov. 6, 1775, Slebech Papers, Item 9402; Taylor to Arcedekne, January 25, 1773, in Wood, *Travel, Trade, and Power*, 114; "The Autobiographical Manuscript of William Senhouse," *JBMHS*, 2 (May 1935), 130; Schomburgk, *History of Barbados*, 642–43; Castles, "Observations on the Sugar Ants," 355; Walter Nisbet to Catherine Stapleton, May 23, 1788, Stapleton-Cotton Manuscripts, 18, University of Wales, Bangor; Pierre-Gustave Louis Borde, *The History of the Island of Trinidad Under the Spanish Government* (Paris: Maissoneuve Et Cie, 1883; reprint Port of Spain: Paria Publishers, 1982), 2:165–66. Thanks to Bridget Brereton for this reference. "Rules for the Population & Trade of the Windward Island Trinidad, abridged from the Spanish Ordinance Published at Madrid in 1783," CO 295/1/9. Thanks to Patrick Barker for this reference.

135. Wilson, "Early Ant Plagues," 349; Bert Hölldobler and Edward Wilson, *Journey to the Ants* (Cambridge, MA: Harvard university Press, 1994), 143–55, quotation 146. Fire ants also attend homopterans on sugar canes, but Wilson suggests the lack of commentary about stinging makes them unlikely candidates in this infestation. Thomas Coke in his 1810

history suggested that the ants may have arrived from Africa. See Coke, *History of the West Indies*, 2:314.

136. For the term *blast*, see the discussion in the *Oxford English Dictionary*. For an example of the some of the confusion surrounding the terms, consider Bryan Edwards, who viewed the yellow blast and borer as different pests, but his description of the yellow blast as "myriads of little insects," seems to indicate what others generally called the black blast. Edwards, *History, Civil and Commercial* (1793), 2:210-11.

137. Kevan, "Mid-Eighteenth Century Entomology," 202-3; Wilson, "Ant Plagues," 349; For planter comments, see Simon Taylor to Chaloner Arcedekne, January 25, 1773, in Wood, *Travel, Trade, and Power*, 114; William Beckford, *A Descriptive Account of the Island of Jamaica* (London: T. and J. Egerton, 1790), 1:53. See also Samuel Martin, *Essay on Plantership*, 7th ed. (London: Robert Mearns, 1785), 31-33; Schomburgk, *History of Barbados*, 646-47; R. G. Fennah, "Damage to Sugar Cane by Fulgoroidea and Related Insects," in J. R. Williams et al., eds., *Pests of Sugar Cane*, (Amsterdam, 1969), 367-89. See also H. A. Ballou, *Insect Pests of the Lesser Antilles* (Bridgetown, Barbados: Advocate Co., 1912), 60-62, 70-77.

138. "Extract of a Letter from St. Kitts," *American Weekly Mercury*, July 4-July 11, 1734; *American Weekly Mercury*, October 34-31, 1734; "A State of H.M. Leeward Carribee Islands in America," August 31, 1734, enclosed in Gov. Mathew to Mr. Popple, September 14, 1734, *CSPC*, 41:207-8; While Mathew suggested the blast existed in Antigua prior to 1734, a letter from Antigua stated that blast was "never was known in this Island before" that year. See the *Pennsylvania Gazette*, April 4, 1734. Likewise, the author of the 1734 report from St. Kitts (cited earlier) stated that insects were a new threat, as did planters from Nevis (see Charles Pym to William Stapleton, May 9, 1734, Stapleton Ms. 4/9/3; John Rylands Library), and that they only appeared following the hurricane. See also Dator, "Search for a New Land," 286-88.

139. Hughes, *Natural History of Barbados*, 245-46; "Extract of a Letter from St. Christopher's," *American Weekly Mercury*, July 4-July 11, 1734.James Grainger, *The Sugar-Cane: A Poem in Four Books* (London: R. and J. Dodsley, 1764), bk. II, 228-29; Martin, *Essay on Plantership*, 31-33. Martin noted that some people thought there was a connection between the blast insects and ants, but he implied the theory was that the ants ate the blast, which he dismissed. Médéric Louis Élie Moreau de Saint-Méry, *Description Topographique, Physique, Civile, Politique, et Histoire de la Partie Francaise de L'Isle Saint-Domingue* (Philadelphia, 1797), 2:573. John Castles in Grenada wrote that Henry Smeathman also advanced this theory, but Castles rejected it. "Observations on the Sugar Ants," 349. It is also possible that in a few cases, references to ants attacking sugarcane may refer to termite infestations. For some discussion of this, see Kevan, "Mid-Eighteenth Century Entomology," 202-3.

140. "The Autobiographical Manuscript of William Senhouse," 130; Beckford, for example, conflates the yellow blast and borer, as did Schomburgk, although Senhouse saw them as distinct threats. Beckford, *Descriptive Account of Jamaica*, 1:52-53; Schomburgk, *History of Barbados*, 642-45; on the borer and poor quality sugar, see Luffman, *A Brief Account of the Island of Antigua*, 122; Walter Nisbet to Catherine Stapleton, May 23, 1788, April 12, 1791, Stapleton-Cotton Manuscripts, STAP/D/18, Bangor University, Wales; Robert Thomson to William Shipley, July 21, 1794, Bodrhyddan Estate Papers, 58/107, NLW; Bryan Edwards, writing in 1790, claimed the borer had not reached Jamaica. Edwards, *History, Civil and Commercial* (1793), 2:211.

141. Some of the losses were also the result of a hurricane in 1733 than affected the 1734 crop. See Joseph Herbert to William Stapleton, July 28, 1733, Stapleton Mss. 4/5. On exports, see Keith Mason, "The World an Absentee Planters and His Slaves Made: Sir William Stapleton and His Nevis Sugar Estate, 1722-1740," *Bulletin of the John Rylands University Library*, 75 (1993), 103-31; Gaspar, *Bondmen and Rebels*, 224; Tullideph Letterbook, April 22, 1740, July 4, 1740, GD 205/53/8, NAS. Walter Nisbet to Catherine Stapleton, May 23, 1788, April 12, 1791, Stapleton-Cotton Manuscripts, 18. See also Nisbet to Stapleton, March 18, 1789, Stapleton Mss., 23 (vi); Nisbet to Stapleton, April 12, 1791. Nisbet was writing to update Catherine Stapleton on her plantations, but included information on his own estates in

the letters. For other estates, see Ward, *British West Indian Slavery*, 77; Selwyn Carrington, *The Sugar Industry and the Abolition of the Slave Trade, 1775–1810* (Gainesville: University Press of Florida, 2002), 221–26.

142. Nathaniel Phillips Diary, Nov. 6, 1775, Slebech Papers, Item 9402; Martin, *Essay on Plantership*, 31–33; Walter Tullideph to George Thomas, August 3, 1739, Tullideph Letterbook, GD 205/53/8, NAS. Tullideph recommended that Thomas hire 14 enslaved people, noting, "As the blast so often visits us believe you will have occasion for them." See also Beckford, *Descriptive Account*, 1:53; Peterkin, *A Treatise on Planting*, 11–13.

143. Tullideph to Thomas, April 22, 1740; on burning, see "Extract from a Letter from St. Christopher," *American Weekly Mercury*, July 4–July 11, 1734; Patrick Browne, *Civil and Natural History of Jamaica* (London: T. Osborne and J. Shipton, 1756), 435; Taylor to Arcedekne, Sept. 17, 1773, in Wood, *Travel, Trade, and Power*, 125; Martin, *Essay on Plantership*, 33.

144. Coke, *History of the West Indies*, 2:315–16; Moreau de St. Méry, *A Topographical and Political Description*, 1:29. The danger of ants to Martinique prompted vigorous debates among French scientists on the best means of dealing with the threat. See Stockland, "Statecraft and Insect Oeconomies," 301–2. John Castles speculated that because sugar cane leaves and stems provided the insects some protection from regular rains, it was only during a major storm when the canes were torn up and twisted that large numbers of ants and their nests were exposed directly to the wind and rain, and thus washed away. See Castles, "Observations on the Sugar Ants," 351–55.

145. See "Letter XI" in Clement Caines, *Letters on the Cultivation of the Otaheite Cane* (London: Messrs. Robinson, 1801), 59–73; Watts, *The West Indies*, 433–34. For doubts about quality, see Richard Pares, *A West-India Fortune* (London: Longmans, Green, and Co., 1950), 110–11.

146. Sophie D. Coe and Michael D. Coe, *The True History of Chocolate*, 3rd ed. (New York: Thames and Hudson, 2013), 21–26, 185; Dauril Alden, "The Significance of Cacao Production in the Amazon Region during the Late Colonial Period: An Essay in Comparative History," *Proceedings of the American Philosophical Society*, 120 (April 1976), 103–35; Lambert Motilal and Thayil Sreenivasan, "Revisiting 1727: Crop Failure Leads to the Birth of Trinitario Cacao," *Journal of Crop Improvement*, 26 (2012), 599–626. For Jamaica, see Richard Blome, *Description of the Island of Jamaica* (London, 1672), 9 and [Thomas Lynch?], "An Accurate Description of the Cacao-tree . . . given by an Intelligent Person now Residing in Jamaica," *Philosophical Transactions of the Royal Society*, 8 (1673), 6007–9.

147. Thomas Lynch to Earl of Sandwich, August 20, 1671, BL, Add. Mss., 11410, fol. 186; Thomas Lynch to Lord Arlington, December 17, 1671, BL, Add. Mss., 11410, f. 219–20; Ponce-Vázquez, "Atlantic Peripheries," 305; J. Harry Bennett, "Cary Helyar, Merchant and Planter in Seventeenth-Century Jamaica," *William and Mary Quarterly*, 21 (January 1964), 53–76.

148. Motilal and Sreenivasan, "Revisiting 1727"; Linda Newson, *Aboriginal and Spanish Colonial Trinidad: A Study in Cultural Contact* (London: Academic Press, 1976), 135, 157; Borde, *The History of the Island of Trinidad*, 90–93; Coe and Coe, *The True History of Chocolate*, 26, 195–97. Forestero and Trinitario eventually spread across the globe, supplanting criollo. Roughly 80 percent of today's chocolate is *Forestero*, another 10–15 percent *Trinitario*, and the small remainder is *Criollo*. Coe and Coe note that *Criollo* is still a well-regarded, high-end chocolate.

149. Governor Jan Noach de Fay [Curacao] to West India Company, January 30, 1728, Nationaal Archief, the Netherlands, Nieuwe West-Indische Compagnie 578, fol. 9. Thanks to Wim Klooster for this reference. See also Kimber, *Martinique Revisited*, 202–3, 214; Harms, *The Diligent*, 341–46.

150. Thomas Lynch to Sir Robert Moray, March 2, 1672, BL, Add. Mss. 11410, f. 242; Lynch to Captain Wilkinson, Dec. 25, 1672, f. 297–98. On the comet, see "A Journal Kept by Colonel [William] Beeston," in *Interesting Tracts Relating to the Island of Jamaica* (St. Jago de la Vega, 1800), 284–85; Pierre Charlevoix, *A Voyage to North-America . . .; also a Description and Natural History of the Islands in the West Indies* (Dublin: John Exshaw, 1766), 2:307.

151. Motilal and Sreenivasan, "Revisiting 1727," 619. See also G. A. R. Wood and R. A. Lass, *Cocoa*, 4th ed. (London: Longman, 1985), 3, 329–30; P. F. Entwistle, *Pests of Cocoa* (London: Longman, 1972), 3, 20, 630–37.

152. Both receive attention in Grainger's 1764 poem *The Sugar-Cane*, and in the entomological analysis of a poem presented by Kevan, "Mid-Eighteenth Century Entomology and Helminthology," 198–99.

153. Bankoff, *Cultures of Disaster*, 2–4.

154. *Relación verdadera, en que se da quenta del horrible Huracàn que sobrevino a la Isla, y Puerto de Santo*, 1; Terry Rey, *The Priest and the Prophetess: Abbé Ouvière, Romainee Rivière, and the Revolutionary Atlantic World* (New York: Oxford University Press, 2017), 114–15.

155. See, for example, John Taylor, *Newes and Strange Newes from St. Christophers*; Schwartz, *Sea of Storms*, 13–14, 23–24. For the central role of the Devil in both Spanish and English colonization projects, see Jorge Cañizares-Esguerra, *Puritan Conquistadors: Iberianizing the Atlantic, 1550–1700* (Stanford, CA: Stanford University Press, 2006), particularly 17, 123–25, 141; Dillman, *Colonizing Paradise*, 33–37, 54–59.

156. David Buisseret, ed., *Jamaica in 1687: The Taylor Manuscript in the National Library of Jamaica* (Kingston, Jamaica: University of the West Indies Press, 2009), 118–19; "An Journal kept by Col. William Beeston," Dec. 4, 1664, in *Interesting Tracts*, 284–85; Fernando Ortiz, *El huracán: Su mitología y sus símbolos* (Mexico City: Fondo de Cultura Ecoómica, 1947), 65–107.

157. R. Bohun, *A Discourse Concerning the Origine and Properties of Wind, with an Historical Account of Hurricanes and other Tempestuous Winds* (Oxford, 1671), 2–5; François Walter, "Pour une histoire culturelle des risques naturels," in François Walter, Bernardino Fantini, Pascal Delvaux, eds., *Les Cultures du Risque (xvi- xxi siècle)* (Geneva: Presses d'Histoire Suisse, 2009), 1–28.

158. Schwartz, *Sea of Storms*, 27, 37, 43.

159. Teodoro Vidal, *El control de la naturaleza: Mediante la palabra en la tradición puertorriqueña* (San Juan, PR: Alba, 2008); information on Santiago de Cuba is from Olga Portuondo Zúñiga, *¡Misericordia! Terremotos y otros calamidades en la mentalidad del santiaguero* (Santiago de Cuba: Editorial Oriente, 2014), 47–57, and from María Elena Díaz, *The Virgin, the King, and the Royal Slaves of El Cobre: Negotiating Freedom in Colonial Cuba, 1670–1780* (Stanford, Ca: Stanford University Press, 2000), 124–25' Martha Few, "Killing Locusts in Colonial Guatemala," in Martha Few and Zeb Tortorici, eds., *Centering Animals in Latin American History* (Durham, NC: Duke University Press, 2013), 73.

160. See, for example, Javier Martín-Vide and Mariano Barriendos Vallvé, "The Use of Rogation Ceremony Records in Climatic Reconstruction," *Climatic Change*, 30 (1995), 201–21. For historical context of these events, see Mariano Barriendos, "Climate and Culture in Spain: Religious Responses to Extreme Climatic Events in the Hispanic Kingdoms (16th–19th Centuries)," in Wolfgang Behringer et al., eds., *Cultural Consequences of the "Little Ice Age"* (Göttingen, Germany: Vandenhoeck & Ruprecht, 2005), 379–415.

161. Vogt, "Deux séismes majeurs de Saint-Domingue au XVIIIéme siècle: Le séisme du 3 juin 1770," 4429 (translation by Catherine Savell); Moreau de Saint-Méry, *Description Topographique*, 2:420. On European traditions, see Jussi Hanska, *Strategies of Sanity and Survival: Religious Responses to Natural Disasters in the Middle Ages* (Helsinki: Finnish Literature Society, 2002), 49–100. Examples of processions include one following the 1751 earthquake in Santo Domingo. See *An Authentick Account of the Earthquakes that Happened last Year in the Island of Santo Domingo*, reprinted in *Pennsylvania Gazette*, May 7, 1752. Colonists in Guatemala carried images of various saints to the cathedral in 1685 and left them there for eight days to help fight off a locust infestation. At times, priests blessed holy wafers with the image of San Nicolás de Tolentino, which farmers then buried in their fields to ward off locusts. See Few, "Killing Locusts in Colonial Guatemala," 73.

162. Schwartz, *Sea of Storms*, 22.

163. See Matthew Mulcahy, "Environmental Threats and Imperial Celebrations. Days of Fasting and Thanksgiving in the British Caribbean, 1670–1780" (paper presented at "National Worship in International Perspective" conference, Durham University, April 2010). Although enslaved people usually did not attend church services, it appears that many owners

did not require them to work on fast days. See Douglas Hall, *In Miserable Slavery: Thomas Thistlewood in Jamaica, 1750–86* (Kingston, Jamaica: University of the West Indies Press, 1989; reprint 1999), 57.

164. Isaac and Suzanne Emmanuel, *History of the Jews of the Netherlands Antilles* (Cincinnati, OH: American Jewish Archives, 1970), 1:65–66; Schwartz, *Sea of Storms*, 127. A manuscript of "A Form of Prayer for the General Fast," (Barbados, 1835) was offered for sale in Kestenbaum and Company, *Catalogue of Fine Judaica* (November 7, 2019). See www. Kestenbaum.net.

165. Charles Leslie, *A New and Exact Account of Jamaica* (Edinburgh: R. Fleming, 1740), 306–7; Oldendorp, *History of the Mission*, 45; "Monday Is Hurricane Supplication Day," *St. Thomas Source*, July 18, 2005, https://stthomassource.com/content/2005/07/18/monday-hurric ane-supplication-day/, accessed March 3, 2015; Mulcahy, *Hurricanes and Society*, 47–48; Schwartz, *Sea of Storms*, 126–27. There is some evidence that colonists in the Leewards also sought protection from earthquakes in these established fasts. See Zacek, *Settler Society in the English Leeward Islands*, 27–28.

166. For a broader context of such ritual in the British world, see the multivolume history (in progress) edited by Natalie Mears et al., including *National Prayers: Special Worship since the Reformation: Volume 1: Special Prayers, Fasts and Thanksgivings in the British Isles, 1533–1688* (Woodbridge, UK: The Boydell Press, 2013). On 1843 fast days, see *The Barbadian*, Saturday, March 4, 1843; *Form of Prayer to Be Observed by the Jewish Congregation as a Fast Day* (Unknown, 1843); see image of text at https://www.kestenbaum.net/auction/lot/ auction-55/055-015/, accessed July 13, 2020. The fast in Barbados was called to celebrate sparing the island the damage visited upon other islands.

167. John Shower, *Practical Reflections on the Late Earthquakes* (London, 1693), 120–21; Oldendorp, *History of the Mission*, 46; Mulcahy, "Port Royal Earthquake and the World of Wonders," 391–421; *Virginia Gazette*, June 5, 1752; Quenet, "Earthquakes in Early Modern France," 101; Moreau de Saint-Méry, *Description Topographique*, 2:417–22; Smith, *Natural History of Nevis*, 59–63. There is some evidence that increasing knowledge of events in places like the Caribbean began to alter European ideas about earthquakes by the middle of the eighteenth century, even if Europeans did not experience frequent tremors. See Kerrewin van Blanken, "Diligent Observers of Natural Things: Lay Observations and the Natural Philosophy of Earthquakes in the Royal Society of London 1665–1755" (MA thesis, Utrecht University, 2019), 24–25.

168. Curiously, while in the Andean region devastating earthquakes usually generated a literature of sermons and reports reflecting on sin as the cause of such calamities, in the Hispanic Caribbean, little similar response accompanied the events like hurricanes. The seasonality of the storms, their frequency, and their effect on the neighboring islands of other nations seem to have diminished a purely providential explanation of their origins. See Schwartz, *Sea of Storms*, 30–32.

169. McClellan, *Colonialism and Science*, 166–67. Some data, however, was collected by individuals in Saint-Domingue. See James E. McClellan III and François Regourd, *The Colonial Machine: French Science and Overseas Expansion in the Old Regime* (Turnhout, Belgium: Brepols Publishing, 2011), 272–80, 446–49. See also For a different approach to scientific observation's relation to the colonial project see Christopher P. Iannini, *Fatal Revolutions: Natural History, West Indian Slavery and the Routes of American Literature* (Chapel Hill: University of North Carolina Press, 2012). An older, but still useful study is Raymond Stearns, *Science in the British Colonies in America* (Urbana: University of Illinois Press, 1970).

170. Moreau de Saint-Méry, *Spanish Part of Saint-Domingo*, 1:29–30; Long, *History of Jamaica*, 3:622, 619; Abbé Raynal, *A Philosophical and Political History of the Settlements and Trade of the Europeans in the East and West Indies*, translated by J.O. Justamond (London: A. Strahan, 1788)), 5:24–28. See also Mulcahy, *Hurricanes and Society*, 57–58; Benjamin Mecom to Deborah Franklin, September 21, 1754, Benjamin Franklin Papers, America Philosophical Society, Philadelpia; Nathaniel Phillips to Thomas Hibbert, July 28, 1788, Phillips Correspondence, Item 9097, Slebech Papers, British Archives Online, Ref. 71811c20, https://microform.digital/boa/collections/1/volumes/43/correspondence#paginate

171. Lansdown Guilding, "Insects Infesting the Sugar-Cane," *Transactions of the Society, Instituted at London, for the Encouragement of Arts, Manufactures, and Commerce*, 46 (1827-28), 151; Schomburgk, *History of Barbados*, 45; Wille, "Governing Insects," 23.

172. See Stefan Norrgård, "Practicing Historical Climatology in West Africa: A Climatic Periodisation, 1750-1800," *Climatic Change*, 129 (2015), 131-43; Leslie, *New and Exact Account of Jamaica*, 323; Ortiz, *Huracán*, 501-3; Schwartz, *Sea of Storms*, 129; Oldendorp, *History of the Mission*, 191-92.

173. Jerome Handler, "Life Histories of Enslaved Africans in Barbados," *Slavery and Abolition*, 19 (1998), 87-100; especially footnotes 22 and 23; Oldendorp, *History of the Mission*, 191-92.

174. Pablo Gómez, *The Experiential Caribbean: Creating Knowledge and Healing in the Early Modern Atlantic* (Chapel Hill: University of North Carolina Press, 2017), 146-51. Gómez's assertion that Caribbean *mohanes* "invented a powerful phenomenological language and tools that enabled them to manipulate the natural world" (p. 194) is worthy of further debate. Kenneth Bilby and Jerome Handler, "Obeah: Healing and Protection in West Indian Slave Life," *Journal of Caribbean History*, 38 (2004), 153-83. On Plato and the integration of natural phenomena into the cosmologies of the enslaved, see Schwartz, *Sea of Storms*, 107, 136-37.

175. Ramsay, *Essay on the Treatment and Conversion of Slaves*, 176; Robert Glen, "An Early Methodist Revival in the West Indies: Insights from a Neglected Letter in 1774," *Wesley and Methodist Studies*, 9 (2017), 36-56; Vogt, "Deux Séismes majuers de Saint-Domingue au XVIIème siècle," 4298-4302; Mary Prince, *The History of Mary Prince*, ed. Sarah Salih (New York: Penguin, 2000), 23. See also Nicole Aljoe, *Creole Testimonies: Slave Narratives from the British West Indies* (New York: Palgrave Macmillan, 2012), 119-48.

176. Rey, *Priest and Prophetess*, 115; Oldendorp, *History of the Mission*, 288-89.

177. Francisco Moscoso, *El gran huracán: Las deudas y la resistencia en Puerto Rico, 1530* (San Juan, PR: Gaviota, 2013), provides a detailed analysis of the delicate and continuous balancing of the crown's need for revenue and the colonists' demands for a debt moratorium following a series of hurricanes from 1526 to 1530 in Puerto Rico.

178. A larger discussion of disaster relief is in Mulcahy, *Hurricanes and Society*, 141-64; for Curacao, see Emmanuel, *History of the Jews of Netherlands Antilles*, 167; Schwartz, *Sea of Storms*, 99.

179. The 1780 donation is discussed in Mulcahy, *Hurricanes and Society*, 165-88; Smith, "Volcanic Hazard in a Slave Society," 55-67; Berland, "Extreme Weather and Social Vulnerability," 134-35; Schomburgk, *History of Barbados*, 440-41; Oscar Webber, "An Intolerance of Idleness; British Disaster 'Relief' in the Caribbean, 1831-1907," *New West Indian Guide*, 93 (December 2019), 201-30; Grove, "The Great El Niño," 86.

180. Schwartz, *Sea of Storms*, 63-64; Harms, *The Diligent*, 344; on tax relief following infestations, see ANOM, C^{88} 12 n. 196 (12 March 1768); C^{8A} 69 FG347 (2 June 1770); ANOM, C^{8A} 69 F348 (2 July 1770); C^{8A} 70 F4 (16 September 1777).

181. Lucien-René Abenón, "Ouragans et cyclones à la Guadeloupe au xviiie siècle: Le problem alimentaire," in Alain Yacou, ed., *Les catastrophes naturelles aux Antilles : D'une Soufrière à une autre* (Paris: Karthala, 1999), 163-71; Élias Regnault, *Histoire des Antilles et des colonies Francaises, Espagnoles, Anglaises, Danois, et Suedoises* (Paris: Fermin Didot frères, 1849), 33, who reports that following a devastating hurricane in Martinique in 1766, instead of sending aid, French merchants suspended their transactions on the island. For details on specific relief in 1780, see Schwartz, *Sea of Storms*, 63-64, 99. The charity bazaar became the subject of a watercolor painting by Louis-Eugène Lami. See Ballio, "Louis-Eugène Lami's *Charity Bazaar for Victims of the Gaudeloupe Earthquake, 1843*," 498-510. An excellent discussion of French disaster relief efforts in the latter part of the nineteenth century is Church, *Paradise Destroyed*, 78-90, 134-38, 216-28.

182. On governing institutions in the Dutch Caribbean, see Wim Klooster and Gert Oostindie, *Realm between Empires: The Second Dutch Atlantic, 1680-1815* (Ithaca, NY: Cornell University Press, 2018), 57-69. On relief after 1819, see Han Jordaan and To Van der Lee, "The Hurricane of 1819: Destruction and Reconstruction of Buildings on St. Martin," in Henry Coomans et al., eds., *Building Up the Future from the Past: Studies in the Architecture*

and Historic Monuments in the Dutch Caribbean (Zutphen, Netherlands: De Walburg Pers, 1990), 99-108. See also Schwartz, *Sea of Storms*, 64-69, 98-100, 163.

183. Mulcahy, *Hurricanes and Society*, 141-88; Webber, "An Intolerance of Idleness," 201-30; Johnson, *Climate and Catastrophe*, 168-91.

184. Debien, "La nourriture des *esclaves* sur les plantations des *Antilles francaises*," 22; Vicomte de Damas (16 August 1788), ANOM, COL C8A 88 F 99; Schwartz, *Sea of Storms*, 113-15. For some discussion of the trade between Quebec, Ile Royale, and the Antilles prior to 1763, see J. R. McNeill, *Atlantic Empires of France and Spain: Louisbourg and Havana, 1700-1763* (Chapel Hill: University of North Carolina Press, 1985), 111-12, 185-90.

185. Johnson, *Climate and Catastrophe*, 122-54; Schwartz, *Sea of Storms*, 114-15; Mandelblatt, "Land Where Hunger Is in Gold," 261-64; Mulcahy, *Hurricanes and Society*, 103-16.

186. James Pritchard notes that planters in Guadeloupe faced serious shortages in the early 1720s after a series of hurricanes and torrential rains destroyed crops. *In Search of Empire: The French in the Americas, 1670-1730* (New York: Cambridge University Press, 2004), 77. Likewise, reports sometimes suggested whites were facing severe shortages in Jamaica in the 1780s. One account suggested, "Many, nay most of Estates have not an ounce of victuals to give their Negroes & upon several properties, the white people are in real want." See William Taylor to Thomas Graham, August 8, 1786, Airth Mss 10924, f. 55-56, National Library of Scotland.

187. William Byam to William Lord Willoughby, [1670 or 1671], *CSPC*, 7:205-6; Governor Sir Nathaniel Johnson to Lords of Trade and Plantations, June 2, 1688, *CSPC*, 12:553; Mulcahy, "Miserably Scorched," 69; Mulcahy, *Hurricanes and Society*, 83-89.

188. Vicomte de Damas (16 August 1788), ANOM, COL C8A 88 F 99; Mulcahy, *Hurricanes and Society*, 108-16; Horan, "Colonial Famine Plot"; Carl Lokke, *France and the Colonial Question: A Study of Contemporary French Opinion, 1763-1801* (New York: Columbia University Press, 1932), 60-116. For a broader perspective on the French case, see Bertie Mandelblatt, "How Feeding the Slaves Shaped the French Atlantic: Mercantilism and the Crisis of Food Provisioning in the Franco-Caribbean during the Seventeenth and Eighteenth Centuries," in Sophus Reinert and Pernille Røge, eds., *The Political Economy of the Early Modern World* (London: Palgrave Macmillan, 2013), 192-220. By the middle of the nineteenth century, concern about feeding freed people was replaced by a desire to control laborers and prevent "idleness." See Webber, "An Intolerance of Idleness," 201-30.

189. Leslie, *New and Exact Account*, 2; Thistlewood quoted in Trevor Burnard, *Mastery, Tyranny, and Desire: Thomas Thistlewood and His Slaves in the Anglo-Jamaica World* (Chapel Hill: University of North Carolina Press, 2004), 65; Robert Graham to Dougal Malcom, August 15, 1775, Letterbook 178, Graham of Gartmore and Ardoch Papers, AC 11335. See also Mulcahy, *Hurricanes and Society*, 26-32.

190. Grainger, *Sugar-Cane*, and John Singleton, *A General Description of the West-Indian Islands* (Barbados, 1767), both reprinted in Thomas Krise, ed., *Caribbeana: An Anthology of English Literature of the West Indies, 1657-1777* (Chicago: University of Chicago Press, 1999), 166-314. For discussion of Grainger's poem, see, as examples, Jim Egan, "The 'Long'd for Aera' of an 'Other Race': Climate, Identity, and James Grainger's *Sugar Cane*," *Early American Literature*, 38, no. 2 (2003), 189-212; Keith Sandiford, *The Cultural Politics of Sugar: Caribbean Slavery and Narratives of Colonialism* (Cambridge: Cambridge University Press, 2000), 67-87; on Heredia, see Raul Coronado, "The Poetics of Disenchantment: José Maria Heredia and the Tempests of Modernity," *J19: The Journal of Nineteenth-Century Americanists*, 1 (2013), 184-89; Kamau Brathwaite, *Roots* (Havana: Ediciones Casa de las Americas, 1986; reprint, Ann Arbor: University of Michigan Press, 1993), 265.

191. Edwards, *History*, 2:16.

192. Mulcahy, *Hurricanes and Society*, 87-89.

193. See Pérez, *Winds of Change*.

194. Graham to Simon Taylor, Dec. 10, 1785, Taylor Family Papers, 10/A/61, Institute of Commonwealth Studies, University College London; Richard Sheridan, *Doctors and Slaves: A Medical and Demographic History of Slavery in the West Indies* (Cambridge: Cambridge University Press, 2009); Jean Barbot, *A Description of the Coasts of North and South Guinea*, in Awnsham Churchill, ed., *Collection of Voyages and Travels* (London, 1746), 579.

Conclusion: Caribbean Environmental History since 1850

1. Alexander von Humboldt, in Vera M. Kutzinki and Ottmar Ette, eds., *Political Essay on the Island of Cuba: A Critical Edition* (Chicago: University of Chicago Press, 2011), 269–70.
2. B. W. Higman, *A Concise History of the Caribbean* (New York: Cambridge University Press, 2011), 7, 251, 266–75; Stephan Palmié and Francisco A. Scarano, eds., *The Caribbean: A History of the Region and Its Peoples* (Chicago: University of Chicago Press, 2011), 7, 375–76, 476–77.
3. David Brion Davis, *Inhuman Bondage: The Rise and Fall of Slavery in the New World* (New York: Oxford University Press, 2006), 157–74, 231–67; Gelien Matthews, *Caribbean Slave Revolts and the British Abolition Movement* (Baton Rouge: Louisiana State University Press, 2006); Higman, *Concise History of the Caribbean*, 146–58 (quote on 156); Daniel B. Rood, *The Reinvention of Atlantic Slavery: Technology, Labor, Race, and Capitalism in the Greater Caribbean* (New York: Oxford University Press, 2017), 2–7; Dale Tomich and Michael Zeuske, "Introduction: The Second Slavery: Mass Slavery, World-Economy and Comparative Microhistories," *Review of the Fernand Braudel Center*, 31, no. 2 (2008), 91–100.
4. Michael Zueske, "Alexander von Humboldt in Cuba, 1800/1801 and 1804: Traces of an Enigma," *Studies in Travel Writing*, 15, no. 4 (2011), 347–58; Higman, *Concise History of the Caribbean*, 222–26, 289–90; Alan Dye, *Cuban Sugar in the Age of Mass Production: Technology and the Economics of the Sugar Central, 1899–1929* (Stanford, CA: Stanford University Press, 1998); David Watts, *The West Indies: Patterns of Development, Culture and Environmental Change since 1492* (Cambridge: Cambridge University Press, 1987), 484–501; Duncan McGregor, "Contemporary Caribbean Ecologies: The Weight of History," in Palmié and Scarano, eds., *The Caribbean*, 41–42.
5. Alexander von Humboldt, *Selected Writings*, ed. Andrea Wulf (New York: Alfred A. Knopf, 2018), 90; Watts, *The West Indies*, 115–16, 504, 506–11; Higman, *Concise History of the Caribbean*, 226–27, 236–37, 290; Peter Clegg, *The Caribbean Banana Trade: From Colonialism to Globalization* (New York: Palgrave Macmillan, 2002); Steve Striffler and Mark Moburg, eds., *Banana Wars: Power, Production, and History in the Americas* (Durham, NC: Duke University Press, 2003); Jason M. Colby, *The Business of Empire: United Fruit, Race, and U.S. Expansion in Central America* (Ithaca, NC: Cornell University Press, 2011).
6. Watts, *The West Indies*, 501–5; Kathleen E. A. Monteith, *Plantation Coffee in Jamaica, 1790–1848* (Mona: University Press of the West Indies, 2019); Higman, *Concise History of the Caribbean*, 173, 229.
7. Stuart McCook, "The Neo-Columbian Exchange: The Second Conquest of the Greater Caribbean, 1720–1930," *Latin American Research Review*, 46 (2011), 11–31, and see his *States of Nature: Science, Agriculture, and Environment in the Spanish Caribbean, 1760–1940* (Austin, TX: University of Texas Press, 2002), esp. 1–10, 47–104, and "Greater Caribbean: Mexico, Central America, and the West Indies" in Hugh Richard Slotten, Ronald L. Numbers, and David N. Livingstone, eds., *Modern Science in National, Transnational, and Global Context* (Cambridge: Cambridge University Press, 2020), 8:782–98; J. H. Galloway, "Botany in the Service of Empire: The Barbados Cane-Breeding Program and the Revival of the Caribbean Sugar Industry, 1880s–1930s," *Annals of the Association of American Geographers*, 86 (2005), 682–706; Leida Fernández Prieto, "Islands of Knowledge: Science and Agriculture in the History of Latin America and the Caribbean," *Isis*, 104 (2013), 788–97, and her "Mapping the Global and Local Archipelago of Scientific Tropical Sugar: Agriculture, Knowledge, and Practice, 1790–1880," in Patrick Manning and Daniel Rood, eds., *Global Scientific Practice in an Age of Revolutions, 1750–1850* (Pittsburgh: University of Pittsburgh Press, 2016), 181–98; Megan Raby, *American Tropics: The Caribbean Roots of Biodiversity Science* (Chapel Hill: University of North Carolina Press, 2017); Frank Courchamp, Jean-Louis Chapuis, and Michel Pascal, "Mammal Invaders on Islands: Impact, Control and Control Impact," *Biological Reviews*, 78 (2003), 347–83, especially 353–54, 367.
8. Humboldt, *Political Essay on the Island of Cuba*, 29–37, 66–93, 209–20, 309–23; Higman, *Concise History of the Caribbean*, 158–64, 216–22, 275–84, 331; Watts, *The West Indies*, 456–65, 469–84, 519–21.

9. Watts, *The West Indies*, 460; Higman, *Concise History of the Caribbean*, 173–74, 218, 278–79; David Barker, "Geographies of Opportunity, Geographies of Constraint," in Palmié and Scarano, eds., *The Caribbean*, 36; Alejandro Portes, Carlos Dore-Cabral, and Patricia Landolt, eds., *The Urban Caribbean: Transition to the New Global Economy* (Baltimore: Johns Hopkins University Press, 1997); Rivke Jaffe, ed., *The Caribbean City* (Kingston, Jamaica: Ian Randle, 2008); C. Klaufus and R. Jaffe, "Latin American and Caribbean Urban Development," *European Review of Latin American and Caribbean Studies / Revista Europea de Estudios Latinoamericanos y del Caribe*, 100 (2015), 63–72; Robert. B. Potter, *The Urban Caribbean in an Era of Global Change* (London: Routledge, 2017 [orig. pub. 2000]); Olivier Dehoorne, Huhua Cao, and Dorina Ilies, "Étudier la ville caribéenne," *Études caribéennes*, 39–40 (Avril–Août 2018), 1–33. For the 2019 estimates, see https://data.worldbank.org/indicator/SP.URB.TOTL.IN.ZS?locations=ZJ-LC-AG&name_desc=false, which plots urban populations since 1960.

10. Watts, *The West Indies*, 514, 530, 536; Reinaldo Funes Monzote, *From Rainforest to Cane Field in Cuba: An Environmental History since 1492*, trans. Alex Martin (Chapel Hill: University of North Carolina Press, 2008), 1, 124, 127–31, 179–88, 219–51, 265–70; Jennifer L. Anderson, *Mahogany: The Costs of Luxury in Early America* (Cambridge, MA: Harvard University Press, 2012), 91, 101, 199–200, 210–11, 214, 259–60, 279, 286, 299, 312–13; Higman, *Concise History of the Caribbean*, 228–29, 311–12; Owen B. Evelyn and Roland Camirand, "Forest Cover and Deforestation in Jamaica: An Analysis of Forest Cover Estimates over Time," *International Forestry Review*, 5 (2003), 354–63; L. Alan Eyre, "The Tropical Rainforests of the Eastern Caribbean: Present Status and Conservation," *Caribbean Geography*, 9 (1998), 101–20.

11. Jared Diamond, *Collapse: How Societies Choose to Fail or Succeed* (New York: Penguin Books, 2005), 328–57 (quotation on 332); Blair Hedges, Warren B. Cohen, Joel Timyan, and Zhiqiang Yang, "Haiti's Biodiversity Threatened by Nearly Complete Loss of Primary Forest," *Proceedings of the National Academy of Science, USA*, 115 (2018), 11850–55; P. J. Wampler, A. Tarter, R. Bailis, K. Sander, and W. Sun, "Discussion of Forest Definitions and Tree Cover Estimates for Haiti," *Proceedings of the National Academy of Science, USA*, 116 (2019), 5202–3.

12. Orlando Patterson, *The Confounding Island: Jamaica and the Postcolonial Predicament* (Cambridge, MA: Harvard University Press, 2019), 21–119 (quotes on 39 and 106); William Hillary, *Observations on the Changes of the Air and the Concomitant Epidemical Disease in the Island of Barbadoes . . .* (Philadelphia: Kite, 1811 [orig. pub., 1766]), 21; E. A. Seagar, "Malaria in Barbados," *Tropical Agriculture*, 5, no. 3 (1928), 48–50; J. R. McNeill, *Mosquito Empires: Ecology and War in the Greater Caribbean, 1620–1914* (New York: Cambridge University Press, 2010), 28–29.

13. Watts, *The West Indies*, 525–29; Sergio Diaz-Briquets and Jorge Pérez-López, *Conquering Nature: The Environmental Legacy of Socialism in Cuba* (Pittsburgh: University of Pittsburgh Press, 2000); Higman, *Concise History of the Caribbean*, 273.

14. Robert Goddard, "Tourism, Drugs, Offshore Finance, and the Perils of Neoliberal Development," in Palmié and Scarano, eds., *The Caribbean*, 571–82; Mark Carey, "Inventing Caribbean Climates: How Science, Medicine, and Tourism Changed Tropical Weather from Deadly to Healthy," *Osiris*, 26, no. 1 (2011), 129–41; Polly Pattullo, *Last Resorts: The Cost of Tourism in the Caribbean* (New York: Monthly Review Press, 2005); Higman, *Concise History of the Caribbean*, 237–39, 280, 296, 299–301, 321.

15. Russell Fielding, *The Wake of the Whale: Hunter Societies in the Caribbean and North Atlantic* (Cambridge, MA: Harvard University Press, 2018), 5–8, 37, 42, 101–8, 153, 205–15, 228–31, 242, 253, 262, 271, 273; John E. Adams, "Historical Geography of Whaling in Bequia Island, West Indies," *Caribbean Quarterly*, 19, no. 4 (1971), 42–50.

16. David Lowenthal, "The Range and Variation of Caribbean Societies," in Vera Rubin, ed., *Social and Cultural Pluralism in the Caribbean: Annals of the New York Academy*, 83 (1960), 786–95; David Lowenthal, *West Indian Societies* (London: Oxford University Press, 1972); Higman, *Concise History of the Caribbean*, 301, 327–32, notes the three maritime technologies and their impact.

17. Francisco Sastre et al., "Improving the Health Status of Caribbean People: Recommendations from the Triangulating on Health Equity Summit," *Global Health Promotion*, 21 (2014), 19–28, https://doi.org/10.1177/1757975914523455. See also Dinesh Sinha, "Changing Patterns of Food, Nutrition and Health in the Caribbean," *Nutrition Research*, 15 (1995), 899–938.

18. About 17 percent of the region's population officially was malnourished in 2012: World Health Organization, World Food Programme, and International Fund for Agricultural Development, *The State of Food Insecurity in the World 2012. Economic Growth Is Necessary but Not Sufficient to Accelerate Reduction of Hunger and Malnutrition* (Rome: Food and Agricultural Organization of the United Nations, 2012).

19. For the American part of this story, see Alfred W. McCoy and Francisco Scarano, eds., *Colonial Crucible: Empire in the Making of the Modern American State* (Madison: University of Wisconsin Press, 2009), 273–326.

20. Richard Carter and Kamini Mendis, "Evolutionary and Historical Aspects of the Burden of Malaria," *Clinical Microbiology Reviews*, 15 (2002), 564–94; Matthew P. Johnson, "Swampy Sugar Lands: Irrigation Dams and the Rise and Fall of Malaria in Puerto Rico, 1898–1962," *Journal of Latin American Studies*, 51 (2019), 243–71.

21. Key figures in Puerto Rican hookworm control were Bailey Ashford and Isaac González Martínez. See Ana Rita Gonzalez and Elizabeth Fee, "Anemia in Puerto Rico as the Turn of the Twentieth Century," *American Journal of Public Health*, 105 (2015), 272–73; José G. Rigau-Pérez, "The Work of US Public Health Service Officers in Puerto Rico, 1898–1919," *Puerto Rican Health Sciences Journal*, 36 (2017), 130–39; Nicole Trujillo-Pagan, "Worms as a Hook for Colonising Puerto Rico," *Social History of Medicine*, 26 (2013), 611–32. For Bilharzia, see William R. Jobin, "Sugar and Snails: The Ecology of Bilharziasis Related to Agriculture in Puerto Rico," *The American Journal of Tropical Medicine and Hygiene*, 29 (1980), 86–94. For an example of contemporary admiration for Puerto Rico's disease control efforts, see Solón Núñez, "La sanidad en Jamaica y Puerto Rico," *Boletín de la Oficina Sanitaria Panamericana*, 13 (1934), 908–17, esp. pp. 913–14.

22. Julie Feinsilver, *Healing the Masses: Cuban Health Politics at Home and Abroad* (Berkeley: University of California Press, 1993), 1–2.

23. For a critique see Katherine Hirschfeld, *Health, Politics, and Revolution in Cuba since 1898* (New Brunswick, NJ, and London: Transaction Publishers, 2007), 203–26.

24. R. M. Gonzalez, "Infant Mortality in Cuba: Myth and Reality," *Cuban Studies* (2015), 19–39, presents plausible evidence that post-revolutionary Cuba has long falsified data on infant mortality. Assuming Gonzalez is right, corrected data would shorten overall life expectancy only by a year or so.

25. The record of the Cuban health service is controversial. For a laudatory judgment, Don Fitz, *Cuban Health Care: The Ongoing Revolution* (New York: Monthly Review Press, 2020). See also Richard S. Cooper, Joan F. Kennedy, Pedro Ordúñez-García, "Health in Cuba," *International Journal of Epidemiology*, 35 (2006), 817–24, as well as Feinsilver, *Healing the Masses*, and Hirschfeld, *Health, Politics, and Revolution*.

26. British Honduras, Medical Report for the Year 1919 (Belize City, 1922), 4cited by David Killingray, "The Influenza Pandemic of 1918–1919 in the British Caribbean," *Social History of Medicine*, 7 (1994), 72.

27. Killingray, "The Influenza Pandemic," 81.

28. J. P. Figueroa, "The HIV Epidemic in the Caribbean," *West Indian Medical Journal*, 57 (2008), 195–203.

29. Samir Bhatt et al., "The Global Distribution and Burden of Dengue," *Nature*, 496 (2013), 504–7, https://doi.org/10.1038/nature12060; World Health Organization, "Dengue and Severe Dengue," May 19, 2021, https://www.who.int/en/news-room/fact-sheets/detail/dengue-and-severe-dengue; Jaime Rafael Torres et al., "Epidemiological Characteristics of Dengue Disease in Latin America and in the Caribbean: A Systematic Review of the Literature," *Journal of Tropical Medicine* (2017), doi.org/10.1155/2017/8045435.

30. Olivia B. Dick et al., "The History of Dengue Outbreaks in the Americas," *American Journal of Tropical Medicine and Hygiene*, 87 (2012), 584–93.

31. Jocalyn Clark, "Cholera Cover Up in Haiti," *Lancet Infectious Diseases* 17, (2017), DOI:https://doi.org/10.1016/S1473-3099(16)30568-0.

32. Pan-American Health Organization, "Haiti Reaches One-Year Free of Cholera," https://www.paho.org/hq/index.php?option=com_content&view=article&id=15684:haiti-reaches-one-year-free-of-cholera&Itemid=1926&lang=en.

33. According to the World Bank, as reported in Congressional Research Service, "Latin America and the Caribbean: Impact of COVID-19," April 15, 2021, accessed June 1, 2021, https://fas.org/sgp/crs/row/IF11581.pdf.

34. "The Pandemic's True Death Toll," *The Economist*, accessed September 3, 2021, https://www.economist.com/graphic-detail/coronavirus-excess-deaths-estimates?utm_campaign=the-economist-today&utm_medium=newsletter&utm_source=salesforce-marketing-cloud&utm_term=2021-09-02&utm_content=article-link-2&etear=nl_today_2. The figures compiled here are arrived at by methods familiar to demographers and epidemiologists and everywhere are a better index than official numbers.

35. Christopher M. Church, "Rhythms of Catastrophe, Iterations of Inequity: Disaster Memory, Dislocation, and Disparity during Pelée's Eruption of 1929," *Environmental History*, 25 (2020), 335–60. The initial official death toll from Hurricane Maria was 64 but was later revised upward to almost 3,000. See "Nearly a Year after Hurricane Maria, Puerto Rico Revises Death Toll to 2,975," *New York Times*, August 28, 2018; "Caribbean Volcano Erupts, Spewing Ash and Smoke for Miles," *New York Times*, April 9, 2021.

36. See the discussion in Stuart Schwartz, *Sea of Storms: A History of Hurricanes in the Greater Caribbean from Columbus to Katrina* (Princeton, NJ: Princeton University Press, 2015), 244–50, 283–94. See also Mikael Wolfe, "'A Revolution Is a Force More Powerful than Nature': Extreme Weather and the Cuban Revolution, 1959–64," *Environmental History*, 25 (2020), 469–91.

37. Wolfe, "A Revolution Is a Force More Powerful than Nature," 476; James Robertson, "Island Time: Disasters in the Comprehension of Montserrat's Past," *Caribbean Quarterly*, 63 (2017), 529–50, quote 540–41. On Hurricane Gilbert, see Schwartz, *Sea of Storms*, 300–304; Pamela O'Gorman, "Gilbert Songs," *Jamaican Journal* (May–July 1989), 2–10; Joshua Jelly-Shapiro, "Listen to the Storm Songs of the Caribbean," *New York Times*, September 28, 2019, contains audio links to several sings from Cuba, Jamaica, Haiti, Trinidad, and Puerto Rico. On larger cultural responses in Cuba, see Louis Perez, *Winds of Changes: Hurricanes and the Transformation of Nineteenth-Century Cuba* (Chapel Hill: University of North Carolina Press, 2001), 139–55.

38. Church, "Rhythms of Catastrophe, Iterations of Inequity," 338; Ilan Kelman, "Why Do Bad Ideas Stick?" *Disaster and Social Crisis Research Network Electronic Newsletter*, no. 42 (September–November 2010), 9.

39. Laurent Dubois, *Haiti: The Aftershocks of History* (New York: Picador, 2012); Laura Wagner, "Chronicle of a Disaster Foretold," https://medium.com/dukeuniversity/chronicle-of-a-disaster-foretold-d560206e9a32.

40. Julia Gaffield, *Haitian Connections in the Atlantic World: Recognition after Revolution* (Chapel Hill: University of North Carolina Press, 2015); Dubois, *Haiti*, 4 and 369; Matthew J. Smith, "A Tale of Two Tragedies: Forgetting and Remembering Kingston (1907) and Port-au-Prince (2010)," *Karib-Nordic Journal for Caribbean Studies*, 4 (2019), 1–14.

41. David Barker, "Geographies of Opportunity, Geographies of Constraint," in Palmié and Scarano, ed. *The Caribbean*, 36–37; Tania López-Marrero and Ben Wiser, "Not in the Same Boat: Disasters and Differential Vulnerability in the Insular Caribbean," *Caribbean Studies*, 40 (December 2012), 129–68; Watson Denis, "Menaces hydrométéorologiques et risques geophysiques en Haiti," *Revue de la Société Haïtienne d'Histoire, de Géographie et de Géologie*, 241–44 (2011), 31–67. For urban populations in individuals countries, see https://data.worldbank.org/indicator/SP.URB.TOTL.IN.ZS?end=2019&locations=ZJ-HT&name_desc=false&start=1960&view=chart. UN population figures for Port-au-Prince came from https://www.macrotrends.net/cities/21133/port-au-prince/population.

42. Clinton Beckford and Donovan Campbell, *Domestic Food Production and Food Security in the Caribbean* (New York: Palgrave Macmillan, 2013), 3–13. On Cuba and St. Kitts, see David Barker, "Caribbean Agriculture in a Period of Global Change: Vulnerabilities and

Opportunities," *Caribbean Studies*, 40 (December 2012), 41–61, especially 45; Roger S. Pulwarty, Leonard Nurse, and Ulric O. Trotz, "Caribbean Islands in a Changing Climate," *Environment: Science and Policy for Sustainable Development*, 52 (November/December 2010), 16–27.

43. On Grenada, see Leonard Nurse and Rawleston Moore, "Adaptation to Global Climate Change: An Urgent Requirement for Small Island Developing States," *Review of European Community and International Environmental Law*, 14 (2005), 100–107; Pulwarty et al., "Caribbean Islands in a Changing Climate," 16–27.

44. On sea level rise and consequences, see M. C. Simpson et al., *Quantification and Magnitude of Losses and Damages Resulting from the Impacts of Climate Change: Modelling the Transformational Impacts and Costs of Sea Level Rise in the Caribbean* (United Nations Development Programme, Barbados, West Indies 2010), 10–12.

45. For a summary of current understanding of, and debates regarding the effects of global warning on hurricanes and tropical storms, see Thomas Knutson et al., "Climate Change is Probably Increasing the Intensity of Tropical Cyclones," *ScienceBrief* (March 2021), https://sciencebrief.org/uploads/reviews/ScienceBrief_Review_CYCLONES_Mar2 021.pdf, accessed May 2021; see also *Climate Science Special Report: Fourth National Climate Assessment, Volume I* (Washington DC, 2017), accessed at https://science2017.globalcha nge.gov/chapter/9/.

46. Douglas Gamble, "The Neglected Climatic Hazards of the Caribbean: Overview and Prospects in a Warmer Climate," *Geography Compass*, 8 (2014), 221–34; Kevon Rhiney, "Geographies of Caribbean Vulnerability in a Changing Climate: Issues and Trends," *Geography Compass*, 9, no. 3 (2015), 97–114; Michelle Mycoo, "Beyond 1.5°C: Vulnerabilities and Adaptation Strategies for Caribbean Small Island Developing States," *Regional Environmental Change*, 18 (2017), 2341–53; Pulwarty et al., "Caribbean Islands in a Changing Climate," 16–27; Jayaka Campbell et al., "Generating Projections for the Caribbean at 1.5, 2.0, an 2.5°C from a High-Resolution Ensemble," *Atmosphere*, 12 (2021), 328. On the decline in the region's precipitation since 1900, see Leonard Nurse and Graham Sem et al,"Small Island States," in *TAR Climate Change 2001: Impacts, Adaptions, and Vulnerability: third Assessment Report of the Intergovernmental Panel on Climate Change*. Edited by James J. McCarthy et al. (Cambridge: Cambridge University Press, 2001), 847. On the rise of daily rainfall and heavy rainfall events, see Tannecia S. Stephenson, et al., "Changes in Extreme Temperature and Precipitation in the Caribbean Region, 1961–2010," *International Journal of Climatology*, 34 (2014), 2957–71. See also Michael Taylor et al., "Climate Change and the Caribbean: Review and Response," *Caribbean Studies*, 40 (December 2012), 169–200. CARICOM is a group of 20 nations in the Caribbean basin but does not include all island nations. Guadeloupe, Martinique, Puerto Rico, and Cuba are among the islands that are not members.

47. Everson Peters, "The 2009/10 Caribbean Drought: A Case Study," *Disasters*, 39 (2015), 738–61; for Cuba, see Pulwarty et al., "Caribbean Islands in a Changing Climate," 16–27; "Drought Brings Hardship and Withered Crops to Eastern Cuba," *New York Times*, August 8, 2004; Nadam Charara, Adrian Cashman, Robert Bonnell, and Ronald Gehr, "Water Use Efficiency in the Hotel Sector in Barbados," *Journal of Sustainable Tourism*, 19 (2010), 231–45; Adrian Cashman, Leonard Nurse, and Charlery John, "Climate Change in the Caribbean: The Water Management Implications," *Journal of Environment and Development*, 19, no. 1 (2010), 42–67.

48. "Hurricane Ivan Devastates Grenada," *The Guardian*, September 9, 2004; "Hurricane Irma," *The Independent*, September 15, 2017; Rhiney, "Geographies of Caribbean Vulnerability," 100; Simpson et al., *Quantification and Magnitude of Losses*, 10–12.

49. Will Steffen, Paul T. Crutzen, and J. R. McNeill, "The Anthropocene: Are Humans Now Overwhelming the Great Forces of Nature," *Ambio*, 36 (December 2007), 614–21. J. R. McNeill and Peter Engelke, *The Great Acceleration: A Global Environmental History of the Anthropocene since 1945* (Cambridge, MA: Harvard University Press, 2016); Rhiney, "Geographies of Caribbean Vulnerability," 97–99.

BIBLIOGRAPHY

Archival Material

American Philosophical Society
    Franklin Papers Online
Archives Nationales d'Outre-mer (ANOM)
    Series C8A—General Correspondence of Martinique
Archivo General de Indias (AGI)
    Gobierno, Audiencia de Santo Domingo, Cartas y expedientes Cabildo Secular de la
        Española (1530–1690)
    Gobierno, Audiencia de Santo Domingo, legajos 534 and 2227
Bedfordshire and Luton Archives, X311/127
    Rugeley Papers
Beinecke Lesser Antilles Collection, Digital Collections, Hamilton College
Bibliothèque Nationale. Paris
    Carte générale de l'isle de Guadeloupe, 1768–69
Boston Public Library, Haitian Collection
    Relation du tremblement de terre arrive a L'Isle de St. Dominigue Le 3 Juin 1770,
British Library
    Add. Mss. 11410
    Add. MS 33977
    Add MS 41348
    Add. MS 8098–8099
    Ligon, Richard. "A Topographicall Description . . . of the Yland of Barbados . . .," 1657
    Sloane, 3340
    Sloane, 4054
British Museum, Department of Botany
    Browne, Patrick. "Catalogue of the Plants of the English Sugar Colonies"
Cambridge University Library
    Vanneck-Arcedeckne Papers
Centre des archives d'Outre-mer, Aix-en-Provence
    Le plan d'arpentage de la Grande-Terre, Guadeloupe
    Plan du port du Petit Cul de Sac de l'isle Guadeloupe
Institute of Commonwealth Studies, Senate House Library, University of London
    Letter of Simon Taylor, ICS 120/1/A
Library Company of Philadelphia
    Pierre Eugene Du Simitière Papers Relating to Natural History and the West Indies

Library of Congress
    William Thornton Papers
Lincolnshire Record Office
    Thomas Thistlewood Diaries
Massachusetts Historical Society
    Ann Appleton Storrow Papers
Nationaal Archief, the Netherlands
    Nieuwe West-Indische Compagnie 578, fol. 9
National Archives, Kew, England
    ADM 1/326
    CO 1/52
    CO 28/50/188
    CO 295/1
    WO 40/4
National Archives of Scotland
    McDowall Papers, National Archives of Scotland, GD 237/12
    Walter Tullideph Letterbook, National Archives of Scotland, GD 205/53
National Library of Scotland
    Papers of William and James Chisholme,
    Graham of Gartmore Papers
National Library of Wales
    Bodrhyddan Estate Papers
National Maritime Museum, Greenwich
    "Documents Relating to the Ship Zong"
Natural History Museum, London
    Banks Correspondence
Royal Botanic Gardens, Kew
    Banks Letters
Rylands Library, University of Manchester
    Stapleton Manuscripts
Trinity College Library, Dublin
    "A Briefe Description of the Island of Barbados." MS 736, f. 183
University of Wales, Bangor
    Stapleton-Cotton Manuscripts

                                    Newspapers

American Weekly Mercury
The Barbadian
Boston Evening Post
Boston Gazette
Boston Newsletter and New England Chronicle
Boston Post-Boy
Charleston City Gazette
The Guardian
Newport Mercury
The New York Times
The Pennsylvania Gazette
The Virginia Gazette

                        Published Material prior to ca. 1850

Acosta, José de. *The Natural & Morall History of the Indies.* Translated by Edward Grimeston.
    London, 1604.

Acosta, José de. *Natural and Moral History of the Indies.* Edited by Jane E. Mangan, with introduction and commentary by Walter D. Mignolo. Translated by Frances Lopéz-Morillas. Durham, NC: Duke University Press, 2002.

"Account of the Effects of the Late Earthquake in Several Parts." *Gentleman's Magazine* 25 (1755): 589–90.

"An Account of the Agitation of the Sea at Antigua, Nov. 1, 1755. By Capt. Affleck of the Advice Man of War." *Philosophical Transactions of the Royal Society* 49 (1755–56): 668–70.

An Account of the Late Dreadful Earth-Quake in the Island of Mevis [sic], *St. Christophers, &c.* London, 1690.

"An Accurate Description of the Cacao-tree, Tree, and the Way of It's Curing and Husbandry, & C; given by an Intelligent Person now Residing in Jamaica." *Philosophical Transactions of the Royal Society* 8 (1673): 6007–9.

"A Journal Kept by Colonel [William] Beeston." In *Interesting Tracts Relating to the Island of Jamaica.* St. Jago de la Vega, 1800.

"A Letter from Hans Sloane, M.D., and S.R.S. with Several Accounts of the Earthquakes in Peru October the 20th 1687. And at Jamaica, February 19th. 1687/88 and June the 7th, 1692." *Philosophical Transactions of the Royal Society* 18 (1694): 78–80.

Alexander Anderson to Mr. Forsyth, June 6, 1786. *The Cottage Gardener* 8 (May 6, 1852).

Alvarez Chanca, Pedro. "The Letter of Dr Pedro Alvarez Chanca Dated 1494 Relating to the Second Voyage of Columbus." *Smithsonian Miscellaneous Collections* 48 (1907 [orig. pub. 1494]): 428–57.

Anderson's Historical and Chronological Deduction of the Origin of Commerce. Dublin, 1790.

The Annual Register, or a View of the History, Politics, and Literature for the Year 1770. London, 1770.

Anonymous. *A Further and More Particular Account of the late Dreadful Fire.* London, n.d. [orig. pub. 1703].

Anonymous. *A true and perfect narrative of the late dreadful fire which happened at Bridge-Town in the Barbadoes, April 18, 1668 as the same was communicated in two letters from Mr. John Bushel, and Mr. Francis Bond, two eminent merchants there, to Mr. Edward Bushel, citizen and merchant of London: containing the beginning, progress, and event of that dreadful fire, with the estimation of the loss accrewing thereby, as it was delivered to His Majesty by several eminent merchants concerned in that loss.* London, n.d.

"Appendix to the Directions for Seamen, Bound for Far *Voyages*." *Philosophical Transactions* 1 (1665–66): 147–49.

A True and Perfect Relation of that Most Sad and Terrible Earthquake, at Port Royal in Jamaica, which Happened on Tuesday the 7th of June, 1692. London, 1692.

Bailyn, Bernard, ed. *Pamphlets of the American Revolution, 1750–1776,* vol. 1, *1750–1765.* Cambridge, MA: Harvard University Press, 1965.

Bakun, William H., et al. "Significant Earthquakes on the Enriquillo Fault System, Hispaniola, 1500–2010: Implications for Seismic Hazard," *Bulletin for the Seismological Society of America* 102, no. 1 (2012), 18–30.

Balfour, Edward. "Statistical Data for Forming Troops and Maintaining Them in Health in Different Climates and Localities." *Journal of the Statistical Society of London* 8 (1845): 193–209.

Barbot, Jean. *A Description of the Coasts of North and South Guinea.* In *Collection of Voyages and Travels.* Edited by Awnsham Churchill. London, 1746.

Barboteau, M. "Essai sur la fourmi." *Journal de Physique* 8 (1776–77): 383–95.

Barham, Henry. *Hortus americanus: containing an account of the trees, shrubs, and other vegetable productions, of South-America and the West-India Islands, and particularly of the island of Jamaica; interspersed with many curious and useful observations, respecting their uses in medicine, diet, and mechanics.* Kingston, Jamaica: Alexander Aikman, 1794 [published posthumously, likely written in 1711].

Barrera y Domingo, Francisco. *Reflexiones historico, fisico naturales, medico quirurgicas: prácticos y especulativos entretenimientos acerca de la vida, usos, costumbres, alimentos, bestidos, color y enfermedades a que propenden los negros de Africa, venidos a las Americas.* Havana: Ediciones C.R. 1953 [orig. pub. 1798].

Beckford, William. *A descriptive account of the island of Jamaica with remarks upon the cultivation of the sugar-cane; also observations and reflections upon what would probably be the consequences of an abolition of the slave-trade, and of the emancipation of the slaves.* 2 vols. London: T. and J. Egerton, 1790.

Bell, John. *An Inquiry into the Causes Which Produce and the Means of Preventing Diseases among British Officers, Soldiers, and Others in the West Indies.* London: J. Murray, 1791.

Bertin, Antoine de. *Des moyens de conserver la santé des blancs et des nègres, aux Antilles ou climats chauds et humides de l'Amérique.* Paris: Chez Méquignon, 1786.

Blome, Richard. *Description of the Island of Jamaica.* London, 1672.

Bohun, R. *A Discourse Concerning the Origine and Properties of Wind, with an Historical Account of Hurricanes and other Tempestuous Winds.* Oxford, 1671.

Bolt, Bruce. *Earthquakes* (New York: W.H. Freeman, 1978, revised 1993).

Bourgeois, Nicolas. *Voyages intéressans dans différentes colonies françaises, espagnoles, anglaises &c.* London: J. Bastien, 1788.

Boyle, Robert. "Other Inquiries Concerning the Sea." *Philosophical Transactions* 1 (1665–66): 315–16.

Brayne, Captain to the Proprietors, November 20, 1670. *South Carolina Historical Society Collections.* Vol. 5. Charleston, 1897: 226–32.

Browne, Patrick. *Civil and Natural History of Jamaica.* London: T. Osborne and J. Shipton, 1756.

Buée, William Urban. "Some Account of the Cultivation of the Clove Tree, in the Island of Dominica." In Bryan Edwards, *History, Civil and Commercial, of the British Colonies in the West Indies.* 3 vols. London: John Stockdale, 1801, 3: 371–82.

Burke, Edmund. *An Account of European Settlements in America.* 6th ed. London, 1777.

Caines, Clement. *Letters on the Cultivation of the Otaheite Cane.* London: Messrs. Robinson, 1801.

"Captain Langford's Observations of his own Experience upon Hurricanes and their Prognostiks." *Philosophical Transactions of the Royal Society* 20 (1698): 413.

Carstens, J. L. *A General Description of all the Danish, American or West Indian Islands.* Edited and translated by Arnold Highfield. St. Croix: Virgin Islands Humanities Council, 1997.

Catesby, Mark. *The Natural History of Carolina, Florida, and the Bahama Islands . . .* 2 vols. London: W. Innys and R. Manby, 1729–47.

Chanvalon, Jean-Baptiste Thibault de. *Voyage à la Martinique.* Paris: Bauche, 1763.

Charlevoix, Pierre. *A voyage to North-America: undertaken by command of the present King of France: containing the geographical description and natural history of Canada and Louisiana: with the customs, manners, trade and religion of the Inhabitants: a description of the lakes and rivers, with their navigation and manner of passing the Great Cataracts / by Father Charlevoix; also, a description and natural history of the islands in the West Indies belonging to the different powers of Europe.* 2 vols. Dublin, 1766.

Chisholm, Colin. *An essay on the malignant pestilential fever introduced into the West Indian Islands from Boullam, on the coast of Guinea, as it appeared in 1793 and 1794. By C. Chisholm, M.D. and surgeon to His Majesty's ordnance in Grenada.* Philadelphia: Thomas Dobson, 1799.

Cieza de León, Pedro. *La crónica del Perú.* Madrid: Historia 16, 1984 [orig. pub. 1553].

Coke, Thomas. *A History of the West Indies.* London, 1808.

Collins, David. *Practical Rules of the Management and Medical Treatment of Negro Slaves in the Sugar Colonies.* London: J. Barfield, 1811.

Columbus, Christopher. *The Four Voyages.* Edited by J. M. Cohen. London: Penguin, 1969.

Columbus, Christopher. *The Log of Christopher Columbus.* Translated by Robert H. Fuson. Camden, ME: International Marine Publishing Company, 1987.

Cresswell, Nicholas. *The Journal of Nicholas Cresswell, 1774–1777.* New York: The Dial Press, 1924.

Crèvecoeur, J. Hector St. John, de. *Letters from an American Farmer and Sketches of Eighteenth-Century America.* Edited by Albert E Stone. New York: Penguin, 1981 [orig. pub. 1782].

Dampier, William. *A Voyage to New Holland.* London: James and John Knapton, 1698.

Dancer, Thomas. *A brief history of the late expedition against Fort San Juan, so far as it relates to the diseases of the troops: together with some observations on climate, infection and contagion; and several of the endemial complaints of the West-Indies.* Kingston, Jamaica: D. Douglass and W. Aikman, 1781.

Dancer, Thomas. *A short dissertation on the Jamaica bath waters: to which is prefixed, an introduction concerning mineral waters in general: shewing the methods of examining them, and ascertaining their contents.* Kingston, Jamaica: D. Douglass and Alex. Aikman, 1784.

Dancer, Thomas. *The Medical Assistant, or Jamaica Practice of Physic.* Kingston, Jamaica: Alexander Aikman, 1801.

d'Anghiera [Anglerius], Pietro Martire. *Decadas del Nuevo Mundo.* Edited by E. O'Gorman. Mexico City: J. Porrua e Hijos, 1964 [orig. pub. 1530].

Dazille, Jean. *Observations sur les maladies des nègres.* Paris: Didot, 1776.

Dickson, William. *The Mitigation of Slavery in Two Parts.* London, 1814, reprint 1970.

"Directions for Observations and Experiments to Be Made by Masters of Ships, Pilots, and Other Fit Persons in Their Sea-Voyages." *Philosophical Transactions* 2 (1666–67): 433–48.

"Directions for Sea-Men, Bound for Far Voyages." *Philosophical Transactions* 1 (1665–66): 140–43.

Dubois, Laurent. *Haiti: The Aftershocks of History.* New York: Picador, 2013.

Dubuc, Jean Baptiste. *Lettres critiques et politiques sur les colonies et le commerce des villes maritimes de France.* Geneva, 1785.

Oliver Dunn, James E. Kelly, Jr. and William F. Keegan, "Beachhead in the Bahamas: Destruction of the Taíno," *Archaeology* 45 (1992), 50–56.

Eckard, J. F. "Correction of Chisholm's Misstatement respecting the Prevalence of Malignant Fever at St. Thomas's." *Medical Repository* Article III (Feb. to Apr., 1804): 336–38.

Edwards, Bryan. *The History, civil and commercial, of the British Colonies in the West Indies.* 3 vols. London: Stockdale, 1801.

Edwards, Bryan. *The History, civil and commercial, of the British West Indies.* 5th ed. 12 vols. London: G. and W. B. Whittaker, 1819.

Exquemelin, Alexander O. *The Buccaneers of America.* Translated by Alexis Brown. Mineola, NY: Dover Publications, 1969 [orig. pub. 1678].

Fahlberg, Samuel. *Utdrag, af Samlingar til natural-historien öfver ön St. Barthelemi i Vest-Indien.* Stockholm: Kungl. Vetenskapsakademien, 1786.

Feuillée, Louis. *Journal des Observations physiques, mathematiques et botaniques, faites par l'ordre du Roy sur les Côtes Orientales de l'Amerique Meridionale, & dans les Indes Occidentales, depuis l'année 1707 jusques en 1712.* Paris: Pierre Giffart, 1714.

Fernández, José. *Apostólica y penitente vida de el V.P. Pedro Claver de la Compañia de Iesús: sacada principalmente de informaciones juridicas hechas ante el Ordinario de la ciudad de Cartagena de Indias: a su religiosisima Provincia de el Nuevo Reyno de Granada.* Zaragoza, Spain: Diego Dormer, 1666.

Fernández de Oviedo y Valdés, Gonzalo. *Historia general y natural de las Indias.* Edited by Juan Pérez de Tudela Bueso. 2nd ed. 5 vols. Madrid, 1992 [orig. pub. 1526].

Flinter, George. *An Account of the Present State of the Island of Puerto Rico.* London: Longman, Rees, et al., 1834.

Form of Prayer to be Observed by the Jewish Congregation as a Fast Day. 1843.

Girod-Chantran, Justin. *Voyage d'un Suisse dans différentes colonies d'Amérique pendant la dernière guerre.* Neuchatel, Switzerland: de l'Imprimerie de la Société typographique, 1785.

Grant, Ulysses S. *Personal Memoirs.* New York: Barnes & Noble Books, 2003 [orig. pub. 1885].

Great Britain, House of Commons. *Report of the Lords of the Committee of Council Appointed for Consideration of All Matters Relating to Trade and Foreign Plantations.* London, 1789.

Guilding, Lansdown. "Insects Infesting the Sugar-Cane." *Transactions of the Society, Instituted at London, for the Encouragement of Arts* 46 (1827–28): 143–51.

Halley, Edmund. "An Historical Account of the Trade Winds, and Monsoons, observable in the Seas between and near the Tropicks, with an Attempt to assign the Physical Cause of the said Winds." *Philosophical. Transactions* 16 (1686): 153–68.

Halliday, Andrew. *The West Indies: The Natural and Physical History of the Windward and Leeward Colonies.* London: Parker, 1837.

Heath, Rev. E. *A Full Account of the Late Dreadful Earthquake at Port Royal in Jamaica, Written in Two Letters from the Minister of that Place.* London, 1692.

Hickey, William. *The Memoirs of William Hickey, 1775–1782.* Edited by Spencer. London: Hurst & Blackett, 1925.

Hillary, William. *Observations on the changes of the air and the concomitant epidemical diseases, in the island of Barbadoes: to which is added a treatise on the putrid bilious fever, commonly called the yellow fever and such other diseases as are indigenous or endemial, in the West India islands, or in the torrid zone.* London: C. Hitch and L. Hawes, 1759.

Howard, Richard A., and Elizabeth S. Howard, eds. *Alexander Anderson's The St. Vincent Botanic Garden.* London: The Linnean Society, 1983.

Hughes, Griffith. *The Natural History of Barbados.* London: printed for the author, 1750.

Hunter, John. *Observations on the Diseases of the Army in Jamaica.* London: G. Nicol, 1788.

Jacquin, Nicholas Joseph. *Enumeratio systematica plantarum: quas in insulis Caribaeis vicinaque Americes continente detexit novas, aut iam cognitas emendavit.* Leiden: Lugduni Batavorum, apud Theodorum Haak, 1760.

Jacquin, Nicholas Joseph. *Selectarum Stirpium Americanarum Historia.* Vienna: Joseph Kurtböck for Kraus, 1763.

Jameson, Robert. *Letters from the Havana, during the Year 1820.* London: J. Miller, 1821.

Jeaffreson, Christopher. *A Young Squire of the Seventeenth Century: From the Papers of Christopher Jeaffreson.* Edited by John Cordy Jeaffreson. London, 1878.

Jeffreys, Thomas. *The Natural and Civil History of the French Dominions in North and South America.* Vol. 2. London, 1760.

Jonnés, Alexandre Moreau de. *Histoire physique de Antilles françaises.* Paris, 1822.

Justin, Michel-Placide. *Histoire politique et statistique de l'Ile d'Hayti, Sainte-Domingue, écrite sur les documents officiels et des notes communiqués par Sir James Barskett.* Paris: Brière, 1826.

Klinkenborg, Verlyn, ed., and Ruth S. Kraemer, trans. *The Drake Manuscript in the Pierpont Morgan Library: Histoire Naturelle des Indes.* London: André Deutsch, 1996.

Knight, James. *The Natural, Moral, and Political History of Jamaica.* Edited by Jack P. Greene. Charlottesville: University of Virginia Press, 2021.

Labat, Jean-Baptiste. *Nouveau voyage aux isles de l'Amérique.* Paris: Ch. J. B. Delspoine, 1742.

The laws of Jamaica passed by the assembly, and confirmed by His majesty in council, Feb. 23. 1683: to which is added, A short account of the island and government thereof, with an exact map of the island. London: H. Hills, 1683.

Las Casas, Bartolome de. *Historia de las Indias.* 3 vols. Mexico City: Fondo de Cultura, 1951 [orig. pub. 1561].

Las Casas, Bartolome de. *A Short Account of the Destruction of the Indies.* London: Penguin, 1992 [orig. pub. 1552].

Leslie, Charles. *A New and Exact Account of Jamaica.* Edinburgh, 1740.

Leslie, Charles. *A new history of Jamaica: from the earliest accounts, to the taking of Porto Bello by Vice-Admiral Vernon.* London: J. Hodges, 1740.

Lewis, Matthew. *Journal of a West Indian Proprietor.* London: J. Murray, 1834.

Ligon, Richard. *True and Exact History of the Island of Barbadoes.* London, 1657, reprint 1673.

Lind, James. *An Essay on Diseases Incidental to Europeans in Hot Climates with the Method of Preventing their Fatal Consequences.* London: T. Becket and P. A. de Hondt, 1768.

Lindsay, Rev. John. "An Examination of the Hypothetical Doctrine of Water-spouts . . . "; "Letter on waterspouts"; and "Letter on Whirlwinds." in *Gentleman's Magazine* 51 (1781): 558–60, 615–16; 53 (1783): 984, 1027; 55, no. 2 (1785): 594–98.

Long, Edward. *The History of Jamaica, or, General Survey of the Antient and Modern State of that Island: with Reflections on its Situation, Settlements, Inhabitants, Climate, Products, Commerce, Laws, and Government.* 3 vols. London: Lowndes, 1774.

López de Velasco, Juan. *Geografía y descripción universal de las Indias.* Madrid: Atlas, 1971 [orig. pub. 1574].

Luffman, John. *A Brief Account of the Island of Antigua.* London, 1789.

Mackrill, Joseph. *The History of Yellow Fever.* Baltimore: Hayes, 1796.

Marrero, Levi. *Cuba: Economía y Sociedad,* Vol. 8 (Madrid: Editorial Playor, 1978).

Martin, Samuel. *Essay on Plantership.* 7th ed. London, 1785.

Merian, Maria Sibylla. *Metamorphosis insectorum Surinamensium.* Amsterdam: Gerard Valck, 1705.

Minutes of the Society for the Improvement of Plantership in the Island of Barbados. Liverpool, 1811.

Moreau de Jonnés, Alexandre. *Histoire physique des Antilles françaises; savoir: La Martinique et les îles de la Guadeloupe.* Paris: Imprimerie de Migneret, 1822.

Moreau de Saint-Méry, Mérédic-Louis-Élie. *Description topographique, physique, civile, politique, et histoire de la partie française de l'Isle Saint-Domingue.* Philadelphia, 1797.

Moreau de Saint-Méry, Mérédic-Louis-Élie. *A Topographical and Political Description of the Spanish Part of Saint-Domingo, translated from the French by William Cobbett.* Philadelphia, 1798.

Moseley, Benjamin. *A Treatise on Tropical Diseases; and on the Climate of the West Indies.* London: T. Cadell, 1789.

"Observations Made by a Curious and Learned Person Sailing from England to the Caribe-Islands." *Philosophical Transactions of the Royal Society* 2 (December 1666): 499.

"Observations on the Sugar Ants: In a Letter from John Castles." *Philosophical Transactions of the Royal Society* 80 (1790): 346–58.

Oldendorp, C. G. A. *History of the Mission of the Evangelical Brethren on the Caribbean Islands of St. Thomas, St. Croix, and St. John.* Edited by Johann Jakob Bossard. English translation by Arnold Highfield and Vladimir Barac. Ann Arbor, MI: Karoma Publishers, 1987 [orig. pub. 1777].

Oldmixon, John. *The British empire in America: containing the history of the discovery, settlement, progress and present state of all the British colonies on the continent and islands of America.* London, 1708.

Otte, Enrique, ed. *Cartas privadas de emigrantes a Indias, 1540–1616.* Mexico City: Fondo de Cultura Económica, 1996.

Pacheco, J. F., et al. *Colección de documentos inéditos relativos al descrubimiento, conquista y colonización de las posesiones españolas en América y Oceania.* 42 vols. Madrid: Manuel B. de Quirós, 1864–84.

Pané, Fray Ramón. *An Account of the Antiquities of the Indians.* Edited by José Juan Arrom. Translated by Susan C. Griswold. Durham, NC: Duke University Press, 1999.

Panum, Peter Ludwig. *Observations Made during the Epidemic of Measles on the Faeroe Islands in the year 1846.* New York: Public Health Association, 1940 [orig. pub. Copenhagen, 1847].

Peterkin, Joshua. *A treatise on planting, from the origin of semen to ebullition; with a correct mode of distillation and a melioration on the whole process progressively. Dedicated to the Planters of the Leeward Charribbee Islands.* St. Christophers, Basseterre: E. L. Low, 1790.

Petiver, James. *Hortus Peruvanius medicinalis, or The South-Sea Herbal.* London: n.p., 1715.

Pinckard, George. *Notes on the West Indies: written during the expedition under the command of the late General Sir Ralph Abercromby, including observations on the island of Barbadoes, and the settlements captured by the British troops, upon the coast of Guiana, likewise remarks relating to the creoles and slaves of the western colonies, and the Indians of South America, with occasional hints, regarding the seasoning, or yellow fever of hot climates.* 3 vols. London: Longman, Hurst, Rees, and Orme, 1806.

Plumier, Charles. *Description des Plantes de l'Amerique avec leurs Figures.* Paris: Jean Anisson, 1693.

Poissonnier-Desperrières, Antoine. *Traité des fièvres de l'isle de St.-Domingue.* Paris: P. G. Cavelier, 1763.

Poissonnier-Desperrières, Antoine. *Traite des Maladies des Gens de Mer.* Paris: De L'imprimeur royale, 1767.

Porras Barrenechea, Raúl, ed. *Cartas del Perú (1524–1543).* Lima: Sociedad de Bibliofilos Peruanos, 1959.

Prince, Mary. *The History of Mary Prince.* Edited by Sarah Salih. New York: Penguin, 2000 [orig. pub. 1831].

Raleigh, Walter. *The discovery of the large, rich, and beautiful empire of Guiana: with a relation of the great and golden city of Manoa (which the Spaniards call El Dorado), etc. performed in the year 1595*. Edited by Sir Robert Schomburgk. London: Hakluyt Society, 1848.

Ramsay, James. *Essay on the Treatment and Conversion of Slaves in the British Sugar Islands*. London, 1784.

Regnault, Élias. *Histoire des Antilles et des colonies francaises, espagnoles, anglaises, danoises et suédoises*. Paris: Fermin Didot, frères, 1849.

Relación verdadera en que se dá quenta del horrible huracan que sobrevino a la isla, y puerto de Santo Domingo de los Españoles el dia quinze de Agosto de 1680. Madrid: 1680?.

Relation Tres-détaillée des malheurs arrivés Isles de Saint-Domingue, par le Tremblement de Terre arrive le 3 Juin 1770. Paris, 1770.

Renny, Robert. *An History of Jamaica*. London: Cawthorn, 1807.

Review of Dancer, Thomas. *The Medical Assistant* in *Medical Repository*, first Hexade, vol. 5 (1802): 432–36.

Robertson, Robert. *A Detection of the State and Situation of the Present Sugar Planters, of Barbadoes and the Leeward Islands*. London, 1732.

Sagra, Ramón de la. *Tablas necrológicas del cólera-morbus en la ciudad de la Habana*. Havana: Impresa del Gobierno, Capitania general y Real Sociedad Patriótica por S.M., 1833.

Sainsbury, W. Noel, ed. *Calendar of State Papers, Colonial Series: America and the West Indies*. London, 1860.

Schaw, Janet. *Journal of a Lady of Quality; Being a Narrative of a Journey from Scotland to the West Indies, North Carolina, and Portugal in the Years 1774 to 1776*. Edited by Evangeline Walker Andrews and Charles McLean Andrews. New Haven, CT: Yale University Press, 1921.

Schomburgk, Robert H. *The history of Barbados; comprising a geographical and statistical description of the island; a sketch of the historical events since the settlement; and an account of its geology and natural productions*. London: Frank Cass, 1971 [orig. pub. 1848].

Senhouse, William. "The Autobiographical Manuscript of William Senhouse." *Journal of the Barbadian Museum and Historical Society* 2 (1935): 61–79, 115–34; and 3 (1935): 3–19, 87–99.

Shower, John. *Practical Reflections on the Late Earthquakes*. London, 1693.

Sloane, Hans. *A voyage to the islands Madera, Barbados, Nieves, S. Christophers and Jamaica: with the natural history of the herbs and trees, four-footed beasts, fishes, birds, insects, reptiles, &c. of the last of those islands; to which is prefix'd, an introduction, wherein is an account of the inhabitants, air, waters, diseases, trade, &c. of that place, with some relations concerning the neighbouring continent, and islands of America*. 2 vols. London: R Bentley and M. Magnes, 1707–25.

Smith, Rev. William. *A Natural History of Nevis, and the rest of the English Leeward Islands in America*. Cambridge: J. Bentham, 1745.

Stanislaus, Francis. *A Voyage to Saint Domingo in the Years 1788, 1789, and 1790*. London, 1817.

Taylor, John. *Jamaica in 1687: The Taylor Manuscript at the National Library of Jamaica*. Edited by David Buissseret. Kingston, Jamaica: University of the West Indies Press, 2008.

Taylor, John. *Newes and Strange Newes from St. Christopher of a tempestuous Spirit which is called by the Indians a Hurry-Cano or whirlwind*. London, 1638.

Thomas, Dalby. *An Historical Account of the Rise and Growth of the West-India Collonies*. London, 1690.

Thornton, William. *Papers of William Thornton*, vol. 1, *1781–1802*. Edited by C. M. Harris. Charlottesville: University Press of Virginia, 1995.

Tulloch, Alexander. *Statistical Report on Sickness, Invaliding, and Mortality among Troops in the West Indies*. Parliamentary Papers, vol. 40. London: Great Britain, War Office, 1837–38.

Vaughan, Benjamin, to Thomas Jefferson, Jan. 26, 1787. *The Papers of Thomas Jefferson Digital Edition*. Edited by Barbara B. Oberg and J. Jefferson Looney. Charlottesville: University of Virginia Press, Rotunda, 2008.

von Humboldt, Alexander. *Political Essay on the Island of Cuba: A Critical Edition*. Edited by Vera M. Kutzinki and Ottmar Ette. Chicago: University of Chicago Press, 2011 [orig. pub. 1826].

von Humboldt, Alexander. *Selected Writings*. Edited by Andrea Wulf. New York: Knopf, 2018.

Washington, George. *The Papers of George Washington Digital Edition* [diaries]. Edited by Theodore J. Crackel. Charlottesville: University of Virginia Press, Rotunda, 2008.

Wright, William. "Practical Observations on the Treatment of Acute Diseases; particularly those of the West Indies." *Medical Facts and Observations* 7 (1797): 1–25.

Published Material after ca. 1850

Abénon, Lucien. *La Guadeloupe 1671 à 1759: Etude politique, économique, et sociale*. Paris: L'Harmattan, 1987.

Abenón, Lucien-René. "Ouragans et cyclones à la Guadeloupe au xviiie siècle: Le problem alimentaire." In *Les catastrophes naturelles aux Antilles: D'une Soufrière à une autre*, edited by Alain Yacou. Paris: Karthala, 1999: 163–71.

Abernethy, David. *Dynamics of Global Dominance: European Overseas Empire, 1415–1980*. New Haven. CT: Yale University Press, 2000.

Abrahams, Peter W., and Julia A. Parsons. "Geophagy in the Tropics: A Literature Review." *Geographical Journal* 162 (March 1996): 63–72.

Abulafia, David. *The Discovery of Mankind: Atlantic Encounters in the Age of Columbus*. New Haven, CT: Yale University Press, 2008.

Acevedo-Rodríguez, Pedro, and Mark T. Strong. "Floristic Richness and Affinities in the West Indies." *Botanical Review* 74 (2008): 5–36.

Adam, Peter J. "Monachus Tropicalis." *Mammalian Species* 747 (2004): 1–9.

Adams, John E. "Historical Geography of Whaling in Bequia Island, West Indies." *Caribbean Quarterly* 19, no. 4 (1971): 42–50.

Adolph, W. and E Hecker. "On the active principles of the Spurge Family, X: Skin Irritants Cocarcinogens, and Cryptic Cocarcinogens from the Latex of the Manchineel Tree." *Journal of Natural Products* 47 (1984): 482–96.

Ahlman, Todd M., Gerald F. Schroedl, and Ashley H. McKeown. "The Afro-Caribbean Ware from the Brimstone Hill Fortress, St. Kitts, West Indies: A Study in Ceramic Production." *Historical Archaeology* 43, no. 4 (2009): 22–41.

Ahmad, Nazeer. *Soils of the Caribbean*. Kingston, Jamaica: Ian Randle, 2011.

Albi, Julio. *Banderas olvidadas: El ejército realista en América*. Madrid: Ediciones de Cultura Hispánica, 1990.

Alchon, Suzanne Austin. *A Pest in the Land: New World Epidemics in a Global Perspective*. Albuquerque: University of New Mexico Press, 2003.

Alden, Dauril. "The Significance of Cacao Production in the Amazon Region during the Late Colonial Period: An Essay in Comparative History." *Proceedings of the American Philosophical Society* 120 (April 1976): 103–35.

Alexander, C. S. "Margarita Island, Exporter of People." *Journal of Inter-American Studies* 3 (October 1961): 548–57.

Alexander, Rani T., and Héctor Hernández Álvarez. "Agropastoralism and Household Ecology in Yucatán after the Spanish Invasion." *Environmental Archaeology* 23, no. 1 (2018): 69–79. DOI: 10.1080/14614103.2017.1342396.

Alexopoulos, Golfo. *Illness and Inhumanity in Stalin's Gulag*. New Haven, CT: Yale University Press, 2017.

Aljoe, Nicole. *Creole Testimonies: Slave Narratives from the British West Indies*. New York: Palgrave Macmillan, 2012.

Allaire, Louis. "Ethnohistory of the Caribs." In Keegan et al., eds., *Oxford Handbook of Caribbean Archaeology*: 97–108.

Allaire, Louis. "On the Historicity of Carib Migrations in the Lesser Antilles." *American Antiquity* 45 (1981): 238–45.

Allaire, Louis. "The Lesser Antilles before Columbus" and "The Caribs of the Lesser Antilles." In Wilson, ed., *The Indigenous People of the Caribbean*: 20–28 and 177–85.

Allsworth-Jones, P. *Pre-Columbian Jamaica*. Tuscaloosa: University of Alabama Press, 2008.

Altman, Ida. "Key to the Indies: Port Towns in the Spanish Caribbean, 1493–1550." *The Americas* 74, no. 1 (2017): 5–26.

Altman, Ida. "Vasco Porcallo de Figueroa: Ambition, Fear, and Politics in Early Cuba." In Altman and Wheat, eds., *The Spanish Caribbean*: 71–90.

Altman, Ida, and David Wheat, eds. *The Spanish Caribbean and the Atlantic World in the Long Sixteenth Century*. Lincoln: University of Nebraska Press, 2019.

Amponsah, Paulina Ekua. "Seismic Activity in Ghana: Past, Present, and Future." *Annals of Geophysics* 47 (April/June 2004): 539–43.

Anderson, Jennifer L. "Barbuda and the Provisioning of the Codrington Estates on Antigua." In *An Archaeology and History of a Caribbean Sugar Plantation on Antigua*, edited by Georgia L. Fox. Gainesville: University of Florida Press, 2020: 55–67.

Anderson, Jennifer L. *Mahogany: The Costs of Early American Luxury*. Cambridge, MA: Harvard University Press, 2012.

Anderson, Virginia DeJohn. *Creatures of Empire: How Domestic Animals Transformed Early America*. New York: Oxford University Press, 2004.

Anderson-Córdova, Karen F. *Surviving Spanish Conquest: Indian Fight, Flight, and Cultural Transformation in Hispaniola and Puerto Rico*. Tuscaloosa: University of Alabama Press, 2017.

Andrade, Carlos A., and Eric D. Barton. "Eddy Development and Motion in the Caribbean Sea." *Journal of Geophysical Research* 105 (2000): 26191–202.

Antczak, Andrzej T., and Corinne L. Hofman. "Dearchaizing the Caribbean Archaic." In Hofman and Antczak, eds., *Early Settlers*: 29–42.

Antczak, Andrzej, and Maria Magdalena Mackowiak de Antczak. "Pre-Hispanic Fishery of the Queen Conch, Strombus gigas, on the Islands off the Coast of Venezuela." In *Caribbean Marine Biodiversity: The Known and Unknown*, edited by Patricia Miloslavich and Eduardo Klein. Lancaster, PA: DeStech Publications, 2005: 213–43.

Antczak, Ma. Magdalena, and Andrzej T. Antczak. "Between Food and Symbol: The Role of Marine Molluscs in the Late Pre-Hispanic North-Central Venezuela." In *Early Human Impact on Megamolluscs*, edited by Andrzej Antczak and Roberto Cipriani. Oxford: British Archaeological Reports, 2008: 231–45.

Antczak, Ma. Magdalena, Andrzej T. Antczak, and Miguel Lentino. "Avian Remains from Late Pre-colonial Amerindian Sites on Islands of the Venezuelan Caribbean." *Environmental Archaeology* 24, no. 2 (2019): 161–68.

Applebaum, Anne. *Gulag: A History*. New York: Anchor Books, 2003.

Archer, Christon I. "The Deportation of Barbarian Indians from the Internal Provinces of New Spain, 1789–1810." *The Americas* 29 (January 1973): 376–85.

Archer, Christon. "The Key to the Kingdom: The Defense of Veracruz, 1780–1810." *The Americas* 27 (1971): 426–49.

Archer, Seth. "Colonialism and Other Afflictions: Rethinking Native American Health History." *History Compass* 14 (2016): 511–21.

Archer, Seth. *Sharks upon the Land: Colonialism, Indigenous Health, and Culture in Hawai'i, 1778–1855*. New York: Cambridge University Press, 2018.

Arena, Carolyn. "Aphra Behn's *Oroonoko*, Indian Slavery and the Anglo-Dutch Wars." In Roper, ed., *The Torrid Zone*: 31–45.

Arena, Carolyn. "Indian Slaves from Guiana in Seventeenth-Century Barbados." *Ethnohistory* 64, no. 1 (January 2017): 65–90.

Arena, Carolyn. *Yarico's Caribbean: Indigenous Trade, Diplomacy, and Enslavement in the 17th Century*. Chapel Hill: University of North Carolina Press, forthcoming.

Arévalo, Manuel A. Garcia. "The Bat and the Owl: Nocturnal Images of Death." In Bercht et al., eds., *Taíno*: 112–23.

Ardelean, C. F., L. Becerra-Valdivia, M. W. Pedersen, et al. "Evidence of Human Occupation in Mexico around the Last Glacial Maximum." *Nature* (July 22, 2020). https://doi.org/10.1038/s41586-020-2509-0

Aristizábal Giraldo, Tulio. *Iglesias, conventos y hospitales en Cartagena colonial.* Bogotá: El Ancora Editores, 1998.

Arner, Katherine. "The Malady of Revolutions: Yellow Fever in the Atlantic World, 1793–1828." PhD diss., Johns Hopkins University, 2014.

Arnold, David, ed. *Warm Climates and Western Medicine: The Emergence of Tropical Medicine, 1500–1900.* Amsterdam: Rodopi, 1996.

Arrizabalaga, Jon. "Problematizing Retrospective Diagnosis in the History of Disease." *Asclepio* 52 (2002): 51–70.

Arrom, J. "Criollo definición y matices de un concepto." *Hispania,* 34, no. 2 (1951): 172–76.

Arroyo-Kalin, M. "The Amazonian Formative: Crop Domestication and Anthropogenic Soils." *Diversity* 2, no. 4 (2010): 473–504.

Atkinson, Lesley-Gail, ed. *The Earliest Inhabitants: The Dynamics of the Jamaican Taíno.* Kingston, Jamaica: University of the West Indies Press, 2006.

Bailey, Gauvin Alexander. *Architecture and Urbanism in the French Atlantic Empire: State, Church, and Society, 1604–1830.* Montreal and Kingston, Jamaica: McGill-Queen's University Press, 2018.

Bain, Allison, et al. "Landscape Transformation During Ceramic Age and Colonial Occupations of Barbuda, West Indies." *Environmental Archaeology* 23, no. 1 (2018): 36–46.

Baisre, Julio A. "Setting a Baseline for Caribbean Fisheries." *Journal of Island and Coastal Archaeology* 5, no. 1 (January 2010): 120–47; and respondents, ibid., 148–69; and Baisre's rebuttal, ibid., 170–72.

Bakun, William H., Claudia H. Flores, and Uri S. ten Brink, "Significant Earthquakes on the Enriquillo Fault System, Hispaniola, 1500–2010: Implications for Seismic Hazard." *Bulletin of the Seismological Society of America* 102, no. 1 (February 2012): 18–30. doi: 10.1785/0120110077.

Ballio, Joseph. "Louis-Eugène Lami's *Charity Bazaar for Victims of the Guadeloupe Earthquake,* 1843." *Master Drawings* 44 (Winter 2006): 498–510.

Ballou, H. A. *Insect Pests of the Lesser Antilles.* Bridgetown, Barbados: Advocate Co., 1912.

Bankoff, Greg. "Aeolian Empires: The Influence of Winds and Currents on European Maritime Expansion in the Days of Sail." *Environment and History* 23 (2017): 163–96.

Bankoff, Greg. *Cultures of Disaster: Society and Natural Hazards in the Philippines.* New York: Routledge, 2003.

Barber, Sarah. "Indigeneity and Authority in the Lesser Antilles: The Warners Revisited." In Roper, ed., *The Torrid Zone:* 46–57.

Barcia, Manuel. *The Yellow Demon of Fever: Fighting Disease in the Nineteenth-Century Transatlantic Slave Trade.* New Haven, CT: Yale University Press, 2020.

Barker, David. "Caribbean Agriculture in a Period of Global Change: Vulnerabilities and Opportunities." *Caribbean Studies* 40 (December 2012): 41–61.

Barker, David. "Geographies of Opportunity, Geographies of Constraint." In *The Caribbean: A History of the Region and Its Peoples,* edited by Stephan Palmié and Francisco Scarano. Chicago: University of Chicago Press, 2011: 25–38.

Barrera, Antonio. "Local Herbs, Global Medicines: Commerce, Knowledge, and Commodities in Spanish America." In *Merchants and Marvels: Commerce, Science, and Art in Early Modern Europe,* edited by Pamela H. Smith and Paula Findlen. New York: Routledge, 2002: 163–81.

Barreto, Cristiana, Helena Pinto Lima, Stéphen Rostain, and Corinne Hofman, eds. *Koriabo, from the Caribbean Sea to the Amazon River.* Belém, Brazil: Museu Paraense Emílio Goeldi, Leiden University, 2020.

Barriendos, Mariano. "Climate and Culture in Spain: Religious Responses to Extreme Climatic Events in the Hispanic Kingdoms (16th–19th Centuries)." In *Cultural Consequences of the Little Ice Age,* edited by Wolfgang Behringer et al. Göttingen, Germany: Vandenhoeck & Ruprecht, 2005: 379–415.

Barros, Juanita De, Steven Palmer, and David Wright, eds. *Health and Medicine in the Circum-Caribbean, 1800–1968.* London: Routledge, 2009.

Bassi, Ernesto. *An Aqueous Territory: Sailor Geographies and New Granada's Transimperial Greater Caribbean World.* Durham: Duke University Press, 2017.

Bassi, Ernesto. "Small Islands in a Geopolitically Unstable Caribbean World." In *Oxford Research Encyclopedia, Latin American History* (March 2019). DOI: https://doi.org/10.1093/acref ore/9780199366439.013.375.

Baten, Joerg, and Richard Steckel. "The History of Violence in Europe: Evidence from Cranial and Postcranial Bone Trauma." In *The Backbone of Europe: Health, Diet, Work, and Violence over Two Millennia,* edited by Richard Steckel, Clark Spencer Larsen, Charlotte A. Roberts, and Joerg Baten. Cambridge: Cambridge University Press, 2019: 300–324.

Bauer, Ralph, and José Antonio Mazzotti, eds. *Creole Subjects in the Colonial Americas: Empires, Texts, Identities.* Chapel Hill: University of North Carolina Press, 2009.

Bavel, Bas van, et al. *Disasters and History: The Vulnerability and Resilience of Past Societies.* Cambridge: Cambridge University Press, 2020.

Beasley, David W. C., Alexander J. McAuley, and Dennis A. Bente. "Yellow Fever Virus: Genetic and Phenotypic Diversity and Implications for Detection, Prevention and Therapy." *Antiviral Research* 115 (2015): 48–70.

Beck, Robin. *Chiefdoms, Collapse, and Coalescence in the Early American South.* Cambridge: Cambridge University Press, 2013.

Beckford, Clinton, and Donovan Campbell. *Domestic Food Production and Food Security in the Caribbean.* New York: Palgrave Macmillan 2013.

Beets, Cay J., et al. "Climate and Pre-Columbian Settlements at Anse à la Gourde, Guadeloupe, Northeastern Caribbean." *Geoarchaeology: An International Journal* 21, no. 3 (2006): 271–80.

Bégot, Danielle, Monique Pelletier, and Catherine Bousquet-Bressolier, eds. *La Martinique de Moreau du Temple, 1770: la carte des ingénieurs géographes.* Paris: Éditions du Comité des travaux historiques et scientifiques, 1998.

Behrendt, Stephen. "Crew Mortality in the Transatlantic Slave Trade in the Eighteenth Century." *Slavery and Abolition* 18 (1997): 49–71.

Behrendt, Stephen. "Ecology and Seasonality in the Slave Trade." In *Soundings in Atlantic History: Latent Structures and Intellectual Currents,* edited by Bernard Bailyn and Patricia Denault. Cambridge, MA: Harvard University Press, 2009: 44–85.

Beier, Zachary M. "Everyday Entanglements: Labor and Diversity at the Cabrits Garrison, Dominica." In DeCorse and Beier, eds., *British Forts and Their Communities:* 151–77.

Beldarraín Chaple, Enrique. *Apuntes sobre la medicina en Cuba. Historia y publicaciones.* Havana: ECIMED, 2005.

Beldarraín Chaple, Enrique. "Las epidemias y su enfrentamiento en Cuba 1800–1860." PhD diss., University of Havana, 2012.

Beldarraín Chaple, Enrique. "Notas sobre las guerras per la independencia nacional y su repercussiones en el estado de salud de la población cubana." In *Cuba y México: Desastres, alimentación y salud: siglos XVIII y XIX,* edited by Luz María Espinosa Cortés and Enrique Beldarraín Chaple. Mexico City: Plaza y Valdés, 2005: 51–83.

Beldarraín Chaple, Enrique. "Sanidad y esclavitud: medidas para contrarrestar las enfermedades de los esclavos en Cuba." *Afro-Hispanic Review* 34 (2015): 9–29.

Beldarraín Chaple, Enrique, and Maira Celeiro Chaple. "Sinopsis histórica del clima y las enfermedades en Cuba." In *Cuba y México: Desastres, alimentación y salud: siglos XVIII y XIXI,* edited by Luz María Espinosa Cortés and Enrique Beldarraín Chaple. Mexico City: Plaza y Valdés, 2005: 25–50.

Bell, David A. *Men on Horseback: The Power of Charisma in the Age of Revolution.* New York: Farrar, Straus, and Giroux, 2020.

Benfy, Christopher. "'A Searing Bolt of Turquoise.'" *New York Review of Books* 68, no. 13 (August 19, 2021): 24–26.

Benítez-Rojo, Antonio. *The Repeating Island: The Caribbean and the Postmodern Perspective.* Translated by James Maraniss. 2nd ed. Durham, NC: Duke University Press, 1996.

Benn-Torres, J., et al. "Admixture and Population Stratification in African Caribbean Populations." *Annals of Human Genetics* 72 (2008): 90–98.

Bennett, J. Harry. *Bondsmen and Bishops: Slavery and Apprenticeship on the Codrington Plantations of Barbados, 1710–1838*. Berkeley: University of California Press, 1958.

Bennett, J. Harry. "Cary Helyar, Merchant and Planter in Seventeenth-Century Jamaica." *William and Mary Quarterly* 21 (January 1964): 53–76.

Bennett, J. Harry. "William Whaley, Planter of Seventeenth-Century Jamaica." *Agricultural History* 40, no. 2 (1966): 113–23.

Bentley, Jerry, Renate Bridenthal, and Kären Wigen, eds. *Seascapes: Maritime Histories, Littoral Cultures, and Transoceanic Exchanges*. Honolulu: University of Hawai'i Press, 2007.

Ben-Ur, Aviva. *Jewish Autonomy in a Slave Society: Suriname in the Atlantic World, 1651–1825*. Philadelphia: University of Pennsylvania Press, 2020.

Bercht, Fatima, Estrellita Brodsky, John Alan Farmer, and Dicey Taylor, eds. *Taíno: Pre-Columbian Art and Culture from the Caribbean*. New York: Monacelli Press, 1997.

Berland, Alexander. "Documentary Derived Chronologies of Rainfall Variability in Antigua, Lesser Antilles, 1770–1890." *Climate of the Past* 9 (2013): 1331–43.

Berland, Alexander. "Extreme Weather and Social Vulnerability in Colonial Antigua, Lesser Antilles, 1770–1890." PhD diss., University of Nottingham, 2015.

Berland, Alexander, and Georgina Endfield. "Drought and Disaster in a Revolutionary Age: Colonial Antigua During the American Independence War." *Environment and History* 24, no. 2 (May 2018): 209–35.

Berleant-Schiller, Riva. "Hidden Places and Creole Forms: Naming the Barbudan Landscape." *Professional Geographer* 43, no. 1 (1991): 92–101.

Berleant-Schiller, Riva, and Lydia Pulsipher. "Subsistence Cultivation in the Caribbean." *New West Indies Guide* 60, nos. 1–2 (1986): 1–40.

Berlin, Ira, and Philip D. Morgan, eds. *Cultivation and Culture: Labor and the Shaping of Slave Life in the Americas*. Charlottesville: University of Virginia Press, 1993.

Berman, Mary Jane, and Deborah M. Pearsall. "At the Crossroads: Starch Grain and Phytolith Analyses in Lucayan Prehistory." *Latin American Antiquity* 19, no. 2 (2008): 181–203.

Berman, Mary Jane, et al. "The Bahama Archipelago." In Keegan et al., eds., *Oxford Handbook of Caribbean Archaeology*, 264–80.

Bernard, Andrea M., et al. "Genetic Connectivity of a Coral Reef Ecosystem Predator: The Population Genetic Structure and Evolutionary History of the Caribbean Reef Shark (Carcharhinus perezi)." *Journal of Biogeography* 44 (2017): 2488–2500.

Berry, Chelsea. "Poisoned Relations: Medicine, Sorcery, and Poison Trials in the Greater Caribbean, 1680–1850." PhD diss., Georgetown University, 2019.

Biehler-Gomez, Lucie, and Cristina Cattaneo. "Infectious Diseases: Non-Specific and Specific Infections." In *Interpreting Bone Lesions and Pathology for Forensic Practice*, edited by Lucie Biehler-Gomez and Cristina Cattaneo. London: Academic Press, 2021: 39–59.

Bigelow, Allison Margaret. *Mining Language: Racial Thinking, Indigenous Knowledge, and Colonial Metallurgy in the Early Modern Iberian World*. Chapel Hill: University of North Carolina Press, 2020.

Bilby, Kenneth, and Jerome Handler. "Obeah: Healing and Protection in West Indian Slave Life." *Journal of Caribbean History* 38 (2004): 153–83.

Bilham, Roger. "Lessons from the Haiti Earthquake." *Nature* 463 (February 2010): 878–79.

Bjorndal, K. A., and J. B. C. Jackson. "Role of Sea Turtles in Marine Ecosystems: Reconstructing the Past." In *Biology of Sea Turtles*, edited by Peter L. Lutz, J. A. Musick, and J. Wyneken. Boca Raton, FL: CRC Press, 2003: ch. 10.

Black, Francis. "Disease Susceptibility among New World Peoples." In *Lost Paradises and the Ethics of Research and Publication*, edited by Francisco Salzano and A. Magdalena Hurtado. Oxford: Oxford University Press, 2004: 146–63.

Black, Francis. "An Explanation of High Death Rates among New World Peoples When in Contact with Old World Diseases." *Perspectives in Biology and Medicine* 37 (1994): 292–307.

Blackburn, Robin. *The Making of New World Slavery: From the Baroque to the Modern, 1492–1800*. London: Verso, 1997.

Blake, Lauren E., and Mariano A. Garcia-Blanco. "Human Genetic Variation and Yellow Fever Mortality during 19th Century U.S. Epidemics." *mBio* 5, no. 3 (2014): e01253-14. DOI: 10.1128/mBio.01253-14.

Blakley, Christopher M. *If We Were Dogs: Human-Animal Relationships and the Making of British Atlantic Slavery*. Baton Rouge: Louisiana State University Press, forthcoming.

Blanken, Kerrewin van. "Diligent Observers of Natural Things: Lay Observations and the Natural Philosophy of Earthquakes in the Royal Society of London 1665–1755." MA thesis, Utrecht University, 2019.

Blick, Jeffrey P., et al. "Dogs of the Bahamas and Caribbean: Evidence from Columbus's Diario, Historical Documents, and Archaeology." In *Proceedings of the Fifteenth Symposium on the Natural History of The Bahamas*, edited by R. Erdman and R. Morrison. San Salvador, Bahamas, 2016: 109–23.

Bloch, Kristen. "Slavery and Inter-Imperial Leprosy Discourse in the Atlantic World." *Atlantic Studies* 14, no. 2 (February 2017): 243–62.

Bloch, Kristen. *Holistic Medicine, Spiritual Healing and Dis-ease in the Early Caribbean*. Forthcoming.

Bluestone, Jamie. "Why the Earth Shakes: Pre-Modern Understandings and Modern Earthquake Science." PhD diss., University of Minnesota, 2006.

Bochaton, C., et al. "From a Thriving Past to an Uncertain Future: Zooarchaeological Evidence of Two Millennia of Human Impact on a Large Emblematic Lizard (*Iguana delicatissima*) on the Guadeloupe Islands (French West Indies)." *Quaternary Science Reviews* 150 (2016): 172–83.

Bochaton, Corentin, et al. "Fossil Dipsadid Snakes from the Guadeloupe Islands (French West-Indies) and Their Interactions with Past Human Populations." *Geodiversitas* 41, no. 2 (2019): 501–23.

Boehrer, Thomas. *Parrot Culture: Our 2,500-Year-Long Fascination with the World's Most Talkative Bird*. Philadelphia: University of Pennsylvania Press, 2004.

Bolland, O. Nigel. "Creolization and Creole Societies: A Cultural Nationalist View of Caribbean History." In *Intellectuals in the Twentieth-Century Caribbean*, edited by Alistair Hennessy. 2 vols. London: Macmillan, 1992, I: 50–79.

Bolland, O. Nigel. "Timber Extraction and the Shaping of Enslaved People's Culture in Belize." In Shepherd, ed., *Slavery without Sugar*, 36–62.

Bollettino, Maria Alessandra. "'Of Equal or of More Service': Black Soldiers and the British Empire in the Mid-eighteenth-century Caribbean." *Slavery and Abolition* 38, no. 3 (2017): 510–33.

Bolnick, Deborah A., et al. "Native American Genomics and Population Histories." *Annual Review of Anthropology* 45 (2016): 319–40.

Bolster, W. Jeffrey. *The Mortal Sea: Fishing the Atlantic in the Age of Sail*. Cambridge, MA: Harvard University Press, 2012.

Boomert, Arie. *The Indigenous Peoples of Trinidad and Tobago: From the First Settlers until Today*. Leiden: Sidestone Press, 2016.

Boomgaard, Peter. "The Tropical Rain Forests of Suriname: Exploitation and Management 1600–1975." *New West Indies Guide* 66, nos. 3&4 (1992): 207–35.

Boose, Emery R., Mayra I. Serrano, and David R. Foster. "Landscape and Regional Impacts of Hurricanes in Puerto Rico." *Ecological Monographs* 74, no. 2 (2004): 335–52.

Booth, Christopher C. "William Hillary, Pupil of Boerhaave." *Medical History* 7 (1963): 297–315.

Borde, Pierre-Gustave Louis. *The History of the Island of Trinidad Under the Spanish Government*. 2 vols. Paris: Maissoneuve Et Cie, 1883; reprint, Port of Spain: Paria Publishers, 1982.

Borrego Moreno, Reinier. "'Lo importante aqui es no morirse': Azúcar, esclavitud y mortalided en Cuba (1841–1886)." In *Proyectos politicos y culturales en las realidades caribeñas de los siglos XVIII y XIX*, edited by Josef Opatrny. Prague: Ibero-Americana Pragiensia, Supplementum 43 (2016): 147–56.

Borucki, Alex, David Eltis, and David Wheat, eds. *From the Galleons to the Highlands: Slave Trade Routes in the Spanish Americas*. Albuquerque: University of New Mexico Press, 2020.

Bos, Kirsten, et al. "Pre-Columbian Mycobacterial Genomes Reveal Seals as a Source of New World Human Tuberculosis." *Nature* 517 (2014): 494–97.

Boswell, Thomas. "The Caribbean: A Geographic Preface." In *Understanding the Contemporary Caribbean*, edited by Richard Hillman and Thomas Agostino. 2nd ed. Boulder CO: Lynn Rienner, 2009: 19–40.

Boucaud-Maitre, Denis, et al. "Severity of Manchineel Fruit (*Hippomane mancinella*) Poisoning: A Retrospective Case Series of 97 Patients from French Poison Control Centers." *Toxicon* 161, no. 1 (April 2019): 28–32.

Boucher, Philip. *France and the American Tropics*. Baltimore: Johns Hopkins University Press, 2007.

Bourdier, Karen. "Les conditions sanitaires sur les habitations sucrières de Saint-Domingue à la fin du siècle." *Dix-huitième siècle* 43 (2011): 349–68.

Bourdier, Karen. "La mère et l'enfant dans les sucreries du nord de Saint-Domingue: entre profit économique et sauvegarde du capital humain." In *La société des plantations esclavagiste*, edited by Jacques de Cauna and Cécile Révauger. Paris: Les Indes savantes, 2014.

Bourdier, Karen. *Vie quotidienne et conditions sanitaires sur les grandes habitations sucrières du nord de Saint-Domingue à la veille de l'insurrection d'août 1791*. Lille: Atelier National de Reproduction des Thèses, 2008.

Bowers, Kristy Wilson. *Plague and Public Health in Early Modern Seville*. Rochester, NY: University of Rochester Press, 2013.

Brace, Selina, et al. "Evolutionary History of the Nesophontidae, the Last Unplaced Recent Mammal Family." *Molecular Biology and Evolution* 33 (2016): 3095–103.

Brading, D. A. *The First America: The Spanish Monarch, Creole Patriots, and the Liberal State, 1492–1867*. Cambridge: Cambridge University Press, 1991.

Bradley, Patricia E., and Robert L. Norton, eds. *An Inventory of Breeding Seabirds of the Caribbean*. Gainesville: University Press of Florida, 2009.

Braje, Todd J., et al. "Archaeology, Historical Ecology and Anthropogenic Island Ecosystems." *Environmental Conservation* 44, no. 3 (2017): 286–97.

Brand, Donald D. "The Honey Bee in New Spain and Mexico." *Journal of Cultural Geography* 9, no. 1 (1988): 71–82.

Brathwaite, Edward. *The Development of Creole Society in Jamaica, 1770–1820*. Oxford: Clarendon Press, 1971.

Brathwaite, Kamau. *Roots*. Havana: Ediciones Casa de las Americas, 1986; reprint, Ann Arbor: University of Michigan Press, 1993.

Breen, Benjamin. *The Age of Intoxication: Origins of the Global Drug Trade*. Philadelphia: University of Pennsylvania Press, 2019.

Bridenbaugh, Carl, and Roberta Bridenbaugh. *No Peace Beyond the Line: The English in the Caribbean, 1624–1690*. New York: Oxford University Press, 1972.

Brink, Uri ten, William Bakun, and Claudia Flores. "Historical Perspective on Seismic Hazard to Hispaniola and the Northeast Caribbean Region." *Journal of Geophysical Research* 116 (December 2011): 1–15.

British Honduras. *Medical Report for the Year 1919*. Belize City, 1922.

Brown, Christopher L. Brown, and Philip D. Morgan, eds. *Arming Slaves: From Classical Times to the Modern Age*. New Haven, CT: Yale University Press, 2006.

Brown, J. E., B. R. Evans, W. Zheng, V. Obas, L. Barrera-Martinez, A. Egizi, H. Zhao, A. Caccone, and J. R. Powell. "Human Impacts Have Shaped Historical and Recent Evolution in *Aedes aegypti*, the Dengue and Yellow Fever Mosquito." *Evolution* 68 (2014): 514–25. doi:10.1111/evo.12281.

Brown, P., D. C. Gajdusek, and J. A. Morris. "Epidemic A2 Influenza in Isolated Pacific Island Populations without Pre-epidemic Antibody to Influenza Virus Types A and B, and the Discovery of Other Still Unexposed Populations." *American Journal of Epidemiology* 83 (1966): 176–88.

Brown, Rafe M. "Frogs." In Gillespie and Clague, eds., *Encyclopedia of Islands*: 347–51.

Brown, Randy. *Surviving Slavery in the British Caribbean*. Philadelphia: University of Pennsylvania Press, 2017.

Brown, Vincent. *The Reaper's Garden: Death and Power in the World of Atlantic Slavery*. Cambridge, MA: Harvard University Press, 2010.

Brughmans, Tom, et al. "Exploring Transformations in Caribbean Indigenous Social Networks through Visibility Studies: The Case of Late Pre-colonial Landscapes in East-Guadeloupe (French West Indies)." *Journal of Archaeological Method and Theory* 25 (2018): 475–519.

Bryant, Juliet, Edward C. Holmes, and Alan D. T. Barrett. "Out of Africa: A Molecular Perspective on the Introduction of Yellow Fever Virus into the Americas." *PLOS Pathogens* (May 18, 2007). https://doi.org/10.1371/journal.ppat.0030075

Buchet, Christian. *La lutte pour l'espace Caraïbe et la façade Atlantique de l'Amérique central et sud (1672–1763)*. 2 vols. Paris: Librairie de l'Inde, 1991.

Buisseret, David. "The Cartography of the Caribbean, 1500–1650." In *General History of the Caribbean*, vol. II, *New Societies: The Caribbean in the Long Sixteenth Century*, edited by Pieter C. Emmer and German Carrera Damas. London: Unesco, 1999: 308–18.

Buisseret, David. *Historic Architecture of the Caribbean*. London: Heineman, 1980.

Buisseret, David, ed. *Rural Images: The Estate Plan in the Old and New Worlds*. Chicago: University of Chicago Press, 1988.

Buisseret, David. "Spanish Colonial Cartography, 1450–1700." In *The History of Cartography*, edited by David Woodward. Chicago: University of Chicago Press, 2007, vol. 3, pt. 1: 1095–171.

Buisseret, David, and Steven G. Reinhardt, eds. *Creolization in the Americas*. Arlington: University of Texas Press, 2000.

Buckley, Roger. *Slaves in Red Coats: The West India Regiments, 1795–1815*. New Haven, CT: Yale University Press, 1979.

Burden, Philip D. *The Mapping of North America*, vol. 1, *A List of Printed Maps 1511–1670*. Rickmansworth, UK: Raleigh Publications, 1996.

Burn, Michael, and Suzanne Palmer. "Atlantic Hurricane Activity during the Last Millennium." *Scientific Reports* (August 2015). DOI: 10.1038/srep12838.

Burnard, Trevor. "'The Countrie Continues Sicklie': White Mortality in Jamaica, 1655–1780." *Social History of Medicine* 12 (1999): 45–72.

Burnard, Trevor. "'The Grand Mart of the Island': The Economic Function of Kingston, Jamaica in the Mid-Eighteenth Century." In *Jamaica in Slavery and Freedom: History, Heritage and Culture*, edited by Kathleen E. A. Monteith and Glen Richards. Kingston, Jamaica: University of West Indies Press, 2002: 225–41.

Burnard, Trevor. *Jamaica in the Age of Revolution*. Philadelphia: University of Pennsylvania Press, 2020.

Burnard, Trevor. *Mastery, Tyranny, and Desire: Thomas Thistlewood and His Slaves in the Anglo-Jamaica World*. Chapel Hill: University of North Carolina Press, 2004.

Burnard, Trevor, and Richard Follett. "Caribbean Slavery, British Anti-slavery, and the Cultural Politics of Venereal Disease." *The Historical Journal* 55 (2012): 427–51.

Burnard, Trevor, and John Garrigus. *The Plantation Machine: Atlantic Capitalism in French Saint-Domingue and British Jamaica*. Philadelphia: University of Pennsylvania Press, 2016.

Burnett, D. Graham. *Masters of All They Surveyed: Exploration, Geography, and a British El Dorado*. Chicago: University of Chicago Press, 2000.

Burton, Richard D. E. *Afro-Creole: Power, Opposition, and Play in the Caribbean*. Ithaca, NY: Cornell University Press, 1997.

Bustamente, Miguel. *La fiebre amarilla en México y su origen en América: studio epidemiológico e histórico*. Mexico City: Secretaría de Salubridad y Asistencia, 1958.

Byrd, Alexander X. *Captives and Voyagers: Black Migrants across the Eighteenth-Century British World*. Baton Rouge: Louisiana State University Press, 2008.

Cabral, Diogo de Carvalho. "Into the Bowels of Tropical Earth: Leaf-Cutting Ants and the Colonial Making of Agrarian Brazil." *Journal of Historical Geography* 50 (2015): 92–105.

Cabral, Diogo de Carvalho. "Meaningful Clearings: Human-Ant Negotiated Landscapes in Nineteenth-Century Brazil." *Environmental History* 26 (2021): 1–24.

Cadbury, Henry. "Quakers and the Earthquake at Port Royal, 1692." *Jamaican Historical Review* 8 (1971): 19–31.

Caffrey, Maria A., and Sally P. Horn. "Long-Term Fire Trends in Hispaniola and Puerto Rico from Sedimentary Charcoal: A Comparison of Three Records." *The Professional Geographer* 67, no. 2 (2015): 229–41.

Callaghan, Richard T. "Archaeological Views of Caribbean Seafaring." In Keegan et al., eds., *The Oxford Handbook of Caribbean Archaeology*: 283–95.

Callaghan, Richard T. "On the Question of the Absence of Archaic Age Sites on Jamaica." *Journal of Island and Coastal Archaeology* 3 (2008): 54–71.

Callaghan, Richard T. "The Question of the Aboriginal Use of Sails in the Caribbean Region." *Proceedings of the XXIInd Congress of the International Association for Caribbean Archaeology.* Kingston, Jamaica, 2011: 121–35.

Callaghan, Richard T., and Stephanie J. Schwabe. "Watercraft of the Islands." *Proceedings of the XVIIIth Congress of the International Association for Caribbean Archaeology.* Martinique, St. Georges, Grenada, 2001: 231–42.

Callaway, Ewen. "Salmonella Suspected in Aztec Decline." *Nature* 542 (February 23, 2017): 404.

Cameron, Catherine, Paul Kelton, and Alan Swedlund, eds. *Beyond Germs: Native Depopulation in North America.* Tucson: University of Arizona Press, 2015.

Cameron, Matt. *Parrots: The Animal Answer Guide.* Baltimore: Johns Hopkins University Press, 2012.

Campbell, Jayaka, et al. "Generating Projections for the Caribbean at 1.5, 2.0, and 2.5°C from a High-Resolution Ensemble." *Atmosphere* 12 (2021): 328.

Candlin, Kit. *The Last Caribbean Frontier, 1795–1815.* New York: Palgrave Macmillan, 2012.

Cañizares-Esguerra, Jorge, ed. *Entangled Empires: The Anglo-Iberian Atlantic, 1500–1830.* Philadelphia: University of Pennsylvania Press, 2018.

Cañizares-Esguerra, Jorge. *How to Write the History of the New World: Histories, Epistemologies, and Identities in the Eighteenth-Century Atlantic World.* Stanford, CA: Stanford University Press, 2001.

Cañizares-Esguerra, Jorge. "New World, New Stars: Patriotic Astrology and the Invention of Indian and Creole Bodies in Colonial Spanish America, 1600–1650." *American Historical Review* 104 (1999): 33–68.

Cañizares-Esguerra, Jorge. *Puritan Conquistadors: Iberianizing the Atlantic, 1550–1700.* Palo Alto, CA: Stanford University Press, 2006.

Cañizares-Esguerra, Jorge, Matt D. Childs, and James Sidbury, eds. *The Black Urban Atlantic in the Age of the Slave Trade.* Philadelphia: University of Pennsylvania Press, 2013.

Canny, Nicholas, and Philip Morgan, eds. *Oxford Handbook of the Atlantic World, c.1450–c.1850.* Oxford: Oxford University Press, 2011.

Carder, Nanny, and John G. Crock. "A Pre-Columbian Fisheries Baseline from the Caribbean." *Journal of Archaeological Science* 39 (2012): 3115–24.

Carder, Nanny, Elizabeth J. Reitz, and John G. Crock. "Fish Communities and Populations during the Post-Saladoid Period (AD 600/800–1500) Anguilla, Lesser Antilles." *Journal of Archaeological Science* 34 (2007): 588–99.

Carey, Mark. "Inventing Caribbean Climates: How Science, Medicine, and Tourism Changed Tropical Weather from Deadly to Healthy." *Osiris* 26, no. 1 (2011): 129–41.

Carlson, L. A., W. F. Keegan, and S. M. Fitzpatrick. "Resource Depletion in the Prehistoric Northern West Indies." In *Voyages of Discovery: The Archaeology of Islands*, edited by Scott M. Fitzpatrick. London: Praeger, 2004: 85–107.

Carney, Judith. "African Traditional Plant Knowledge in the Circum-Caribbean Region." *Journal of Ethnobiology* 23, no. 2 (2003): 167–85.

Carney, Judith. "'The Mangrove Preserves Life': Habitat of African Survival in the Atlantic World." *Geographical Review* 107, no. 3 (2017): 433–51.

Carney, Judith A. "Subsistence in the Plantationocene: Dooryard Gardens, Agrobiodiversity, and the Subaltern Economies of Slavery." *Journal of Peasant Studies* 48, no. 5 (2021): 1075–99.

Carney, Judith A., and Richard Nicholas Rosomoff. *In the Shadow of Slavery: Africa's Botanical Legacy in the Atlantic World.* Berkeley: University of California Press, 2009.

Carr, Archie. *"So Excellent a Fishe": A Natural History of Sea Turtles*. Gainesville: University Press of Florida, 2011 [orig. pub. 1967].

Carr, Archie. *The Windward Road: Adventures pf a Naturalist on Remote Caribbean Shores.* Gainesville: University Press of Florida, 2003 [orig. pub. 1956].

Carrington, Selwyn. *The Sugar Industry and the Abolition of the Slave Trade, 1775–1810*. Gainesville: University Press of Florida, 2002.

Carter, Henry Rose. *Yellow Fever: An Epidemiological and Historical Study of Its Place of Origin.* Baltimore: Williams & Wilkins, 1931.

Carter, Richard, and Kamini Mendis. "Evolutionary and Historical Aspects of the Burden of Malaria." *Clinical Microbiology Reviews* 15 (2002): 564–94.

Carter, W. E., et al. "Estimating Ancient Populations by Aerial Survey." *American Scientist* 107 (2019): 30–37. doi:10.1511/2019.107.1.30.

Carvalho Soares, Mariza de. "African Barbeiros in Brazilian Slave Ports." In *The Black Urban Atlantic in the Age of the Slave Trade*, edited by Jorge Cañizares-Esguerra, Matt Childs, and James Sidbury. Philadelphia: University of Pennsylvania Press, 2016: 207–32.

Cashman, Adrian, Leonard Nurse, and Charley John. "Climate Change in the Caribbean: The Water Management Implications." *Journal of Environment and Development* 19, no. 1 (2010): 42–67.

Casid, Jill H. *Sowing Empire: Landscape and Colonization*. Minneapolis: University of Minnesota Press, 2005.

Cassidy, Frederic G. Cassidy. *Jamaica Talk: Three Hundred Years of the English Language in Jamaica.* London: Macmillan, 1961.

Castanha, Tony. *The Myth of Indigenous Caribbean Extinction: Continuity and Reclamation in Borikén (Puerto Rico)*. London: Palgrave, 2011.

Castro Ventura, Santiago. *La Guerra Restauradora*. Santo Domingo: Manatí, 2014.

Caviedes, César. *El Nino in History: Storming through the Ages*. Gainesville: University Press of Florida, 2001.

Caviedes, César N. "Five Hundred Years of Hurricanes in the Caribbean: Their Relationship with Global Climatic Variabilities." *Geojournal* 23, no. 4 (1991): 301–10.

Chakrabarti, Pratik. "Empire and Alternatives: *Swietenia Febrifuga* and the Cinchona Substitutes. *Medical History* 54 (2010): 75–94.

Chakrabarti, Pratik. *Materials and Medicine: Trade, Conquest and Therapeutics in the Eighteenth Century*. Manchester: Manchester University Press, 2010.

Charara, Nadam, Adrian Cashman, Robert Bonnell, and Ronald Gehr. "Water Use Efficiency in the Hotel Sector in Barbados." *Journal of Sustainable Tourism* 19 (2010): 231–45.

Charley John. "Climate Change in the Caribbean: The Water Management Implications." *Journal of Environment and Development* 19, no. 1 (2010): 42–67.

Charters, Erica. "The Caring Fiscal-Military State During the Seven Years' War, 1756–1763," *The Historical Journal* 52, no. 4 (2009): 921–41.

Charters, Erica. *Disease, War and the Imperial State: The Welfare of the British Armed Forces during the Seven Year's War*. Chicago: University of Chicago Press, 2014.

Chaunu, Pierre, and Huguette Chaunu. *Séville et l'Atlantique*. 12 vols. Paris: SEVPEN, 1955–60.

Chenoweth, Michael. *18th Century Climate of Jamaica, Derived from the Journals of Thomas Thistlewood*. Philadelphia: American Philosophical Society, 2003.

Chenoweth, Michael. "Objective Classification of Historical Tropical Cyclone Intensity." *Journal of Geophysical Research* 112 (March 16, 2007): 1–13. doi:10.1029/2006JD007211.

Chenoweth, Michael. "A Reassessment of Historical Atlantic Basin Tropical Cyclone Activity, 1700–1855." *Climate Change* 76 (May 2006): 169–240.

Chenoweth, Michael, and Dmitry Divine, "A Document-Based 318-Year Record of Tropical Cyclones in the Lesser Antilles, 1690–2007." *Genochemsitry, Geophysics, Geosystems* 9 (August 2008). doi.org/10.1029/2008GC002066.

Chenoweth, M., J. M. Vaquero, R. García-Herrera, and D. Wheeler. "A Pioneer in Tropical Meteorology: William Sharpe's Barbados Weather Journal, April–August 1680." *Bulletin of the American Meteorological Society* 88 (2007): 1957–64.

Cherrett, J. M. "Some Aspects of the Distribution of Pest Species of Leaf-Cutting Ants in the Caribbean." *Proceedings of the American Society of Horticultural Science* (Tropical Region) 12 (1968): 295–310.

Cherry, John F. "Insights from the Outside: Some Wider Perspectives and Future Directions in Caribbean Island Historical Ecology." In Siegel, ed., *Island Historical Ecology*: 345–66.

Chias, Pilar, and Tomas Abad. *The Fortified Heritage: Cadiz and the Caribbean, A Transatlantic Relationship*. Madrid: Universidad de Alcalá, 2011.

Chinique de Armas, Yadira, and William Pestle. "Assessing the Association between Subsistence Strategies and the Timing of Weaning among Indigenous Archaeological Populations of the Caribbean." *International Journal of Osteoarchaeology* 28 (2018): 492–509.

Church, Christopher M. *Paradise Destroyed: Catastrophe and Citizenship in the French Caribbean*. Lincoln: University of Nebraska Press, 2017.

Church, Christopher M. "Rhythms of Catastrophe, Iterations of Inequity: Disaster Memory, Dislocation, and Disparity during Pelée's Eruption of 1929." *Environmental History* 25 (2020): 335–60.

Churchill, Wendy D. "Efficient, Efficacious and Humane Responses to Non-European bodies in British Military Medicine, 1780–1815." *Journal of Imperial and Commonwealth History* 40, no. 2 (2012): 137–58.

Clarence-Smith, William G., and David Eltis. "White Servitude." In Eltis and Engerman, eds., *The Cambridge World History of Slavery*, 3: 132–59.

Clark, George R., II, "The Quake that Swallowed a City." *Earth* 4 (April 1995): 34–41.

Clark, J. M. H. "Environment and the Politics of Relocation in the Caribbean Port of Veracuz, 1519-1599." In Altman and Wheat, eds., *The Spanish Caribbean*: 189–210.

Clegg, Peter. *The Caribbean Banana Trade: From Colonialism to Globalization*. New York: Palgrave Macmillan, 2002.

Climate Science Special Report: Fourth National Climate Assessment, Volume I. Washington DC, 2017.

Clodfelter, Micheal. *Warfare and Armed Conflicts: A Statistical Encyclopedia of Casualty and Other Figures, 1492–2015*. Jefferson, NC: McFarland, 2017.

Coe, Sophie D., and Michael D. Coe. *The True History of Chocolate*. 3rd ed. New York: Thames and Hudson, 2013.

Coen, Deborah. "Introduction: Witness to Disaster: Comparative Histories of Earthquake Science and Response." *Science in Context* 25 (March 2012): 1–15.

Colby, Jason M. *The Business of Empire: United Fruit, Race, and U.S. Expansion in Central America*. Ithaca, NY: Cornell University Press, 2011.

Cole, Lucinda. *Imperfect Creatures: Vermin, Literature, and the Sciences of Life, 1600–1740*. Ann Arbor: University of Michigan Press, 2016.

Coleman, Deirdre. "Entertaining Entomology: Insects and Insect Performers in the Eighteenth Century." *Eighteenth-Century Life* 30 (Summer 2006): 107–34

Coleman, Jill S., and Steven A. LaVoie. "Paleotempestology: Reconstructing Atlantic Tropical Cyclone Tracks in the Pre-HURDAT Era." *Modern Climatology* (2012): 237–56.

Columbia Gazeteer of the World. New York: Columbia University Press, 1998.

Conrad, Paul. "Indians, Convicts, and Slaves: An Apache Diaspora to Cuba at the Turn of the Nineteenth-Century." In *Linking the Histories of Slavery: North America and Its Borderlands*, edited by Bonnie Martin and James F. Brooks. Santa Fe: School for Advanced Research Press, 2015: 67–95.

Convertito, Coriann. *The Health of British Seamen in the West Indies, 1773–1806*. PhD diss., University of Exeter, 2011.

Cook, Alexandra Parma, and Noble David Cook. *The Plague Files: Crisis Management in Sixteenth-Century Seville*. Baton Rouge: Louisiana State University Press, 2009.

Cook, Harold J. *Matters of Exchange: Commerce, Medicine, and Science in the Dutch Golden Age*. New Haven, CT: Yale University Press, 2007.

Cook, N. D. *Born to Die: Disease and New World Conquest*. New York: Cambridge University Press, 1998.

Cook, N. D., and George Lovell, eds. *The Secret Judgments of God: Native Peoples and Old World Disease in Spanish Colonial America*. Norman: University of Oklahoma Press, 1992.

Cook, S. F. *The Epidemic of 1830–1833 in California and Oregon*. Berkeley: University of California Press, 1955.

Cook, Sherburne F., and Woodrow W. Borah. *Studies in Population History*. 2 vols. Berkeley: University of California Press, 1971.

Cooke, Siobhán B., et al. "Anthropogenic Extinction Dominates Holocene Declines of West Indian Mammals." *Annual Review of Ecology, Evolution, and Systematics* 48 (2017): 301–27.

Cooke, Siobhán B., et al. The Extinction of *Xenothrix mcgregori*, Jamaica's Last Monkey." *Journal of Mammalogy* 98, no. 4 (2017): 937–49.

Cooper, Jago. "The Climatic Context for Pre-Columbian Archaeology in the Caribbean." in Keegan et al. eds., *The Oxford Handbook of Caribbean Archaeology*: 47–58.

Cooper, Jago, et al. "The Mona Chronicle: The Archaeology of Early Religious Encounter in the New World." *Antiquity* 90, no. 352 (2016): 1054–71.

Cooper, Jago, and Richard Boothroyd. "Living Islands of the Caribbean: A View of Relative Sea Level Change from the Water's Edge." In Hofman and Duijvenbode, eds., *Communities in Contact*: 393–405.

Cooper, Richard S., Joan F. Kennedy, and Pedro Orduñez-García. "Health in Cuba," *International Journal of Epidemiology* 35 (2006): 817–24.

Coppa, Alfredo, et al. "New Evidence of Two Different Migratory Waves in the Circum-Caribbean Area during the Pre-Columbian Period from the Analysis of Dental Morphological Traits." In *Crossing the Borders: New Methods and Techniques in the Study of Archaeological Materials from the Caribbean*, edited by Corinne L. Hofman et al. Tuscaloosa: University of Alabama Press, 2008: 195–213.

Coronado, Raul. "The Poetics of Disenchantment: José Maria Heredia and the Tempests of Modernity." *J19: The Journal of Nineteenth-Century Americanists* 1 (2013): 184–89.

Courchamp, Frank, Jean-Louis Chapuis, and Michel Pascal. "Mammal Invaders on Islands: Impact, Control and Control Impact." *Biological Reviews* 78 (2003): 347–83.

Crane, Eva. *The World History of Beekeeping and Honey Hunting*. New York: Routledge, 1999.

Craton, Michael, and Gail Saunders. *Islanders in the Stream: A History of the Bahamian People*, vol 1, *From Aboriginal Times to the End of Slavery*. Athens: University of Georgia Press, 1992.

Crawford, Jacob E., et al. "Population Genomics Reveals that an Anthropophilic Population of *Aedes aegypti* Mosquitoes in West Africa Recently Gave Rise to American and Asian Populations of This Major Disease Vector." *BMC Biology* 15, no. 1/16 (2017): 1–16.

Crawford, Matthew J. *The Andean Wonder Drug: Cinchona Bark and Imperial Science in the Spanish Atlantic, 1630–1800*. Pittsburgh: University of Pittsburgh Press, 2016.

Crawford, Nicholas. "Calamity's Empire: Slavery, Scarcity, and the Political Economy of Provisioning in the British Caribbean, c. 1775–1834." PhD diss., Harvard University, 2016.

Crawford, Nicholas. "'In the Wreck of a Master's Fortune': Slave Provisioning and Planter Debt in the British Caribbean." *Slavery & Abolition* 37, no. 2 (June 2016): 353–74.

Crawford, Sharika D. *The Last Turtlemen of the Caribbean: Waterscapes of Labor, Conservation, and Boundary Making*. Chapel Hill: University of North Carolina Press, 2020.

Crespo-Torres, Edwin F. "Ancient Bones Tell Stories: Osteobiography of Human Remains from Tibes." In *Tibes: People, Power, and Ritual at the Center of the Cosmos*, edited by L. Antonio Curet and Lisa M. Stringer. Tuscaloosa: University of Alabama Press, 2010: 191–208.

Crespo Torres, Edwin F. "La enfermedad en los indios de Boriquén." *Revista del Instituto de Cultura Puertorriqueña* 8 (2008): 3–15.

Crespo-Torres, Edwin F., et al. "The Study of Pre-Columbian Human Remains in the Caribbean Archipelago: From Descriptive Osteology to a Bioarchaeological Approach." In Keegan et al., eds., *Oxford Handbook of Caribbean Archaeology*: 436–51.

Crewe, Duncan. *Yellow Jack and the Worm*. Liverpool: Liverpool University Press, 1993.

Crock, John G., Nanny Carder, and Wetherbee Dorshow. "'Marineness', the Underwater Seascape and Variability in Maritime Adaptations in the Late Ceramic Age Northern Lesser Antilles." *Environmental Archaeology* 24, no. 2 (2019): 199–210.

Crocker, J. Christopher. "My Brother the Parrot." In *Animal Myths and Metaphors in South America*, edited by Gary Urton. Salt Lake City: University of Utah Press, 1985: 13–48.

Cromwell, Jesse. *The Smugglers' World: Illicit Trade and Atlantic Communities in Eighteenth-Century Venezuela*. Chapel Hill: University of North Carolina Press, 2018.

Crosby, Alfred W., Jr. *The Columbian Exchange: Biological and Cultural Consequences of 1492*. Westport, CT: Greenwood, 1972.

Crosby, Alfred W., Jr. *Ecological Imperialism: The Biological Expansion of Europe, 900–1900*. New York: Cambridge University Press, 1986.

Crosby, Alfred W., Jr. *Germs, Seeds, & Animals: Studies in Ecological History*. Armonk, NY: M. E. Sharpe, 1993.

Cundall, Frank. "Dr. Anthony Robinson of Jamaica." *Journal of Botany* 60 (1922): 49–52.

Curet, L. Antonio. "The Archaeological Perspective: Comment on Julio Baisre's 'Setting a Baseline for Caribbean Fisheries.'" *Journal of Island and Coastal Archaeology* 5 (2010): 152–55.

Curet, L. Antonio. *Caribbean Paleodemography: Population, Culture History, and Sociopolitical Processes in Ancient Puerto Rico*. Tuscaloosa: University of Alabama Press, 2005.

Curet, L. Antonio, and M. Hauser, eds. *Islands at the Crossroads: Migration, Seafaring, and Interaction in the Caribbean*. Tuscaloosa: University of Alabama Press, 2011.

Curran, Andrew. *The Anatomy of Blackness: Science and Slavery in an Age of Enlightenment*. Baltimore: Johns Hopkins University Press, 2011.

Curtin, Philip. *Death by Migration: Europe's Encounter with the Tropical World in the Nineteenth Century*. Cambridge: Cambridge University Press, 1989.

Curtin, Philip. *The Rise and Fall of the Plantation Complex*. New York: Cambridge University Press, 1998.

Curtis, Jason, and David Hodell. "An Isotopic and Trace Element Study of Ostracods from Lake Miragoane, Haiti: A 10,500 Year Record of Paleosalinity and Paleotemperature Changes in the Caribbean." In *Climate Change in Continental Isotopic Records*, edited by P. K. Swart et al. Washington, DC: American Geophysical Union, 1993: 135–52.

Cutter, Susan. "The Changing Nature of Hazard and Disaster Risk in the Anthropocene." *Annals of the American Association of Geographers* 111, no. 3 (2021): 819–27.

Danforth, Susan. "Cultivating Empire: Sir Joseph Banks and the (Failed) Botanical Garden at Nassau." *Journal of the Bahamas Historical Society* 23 (2001): 21–28.

D'Arrigo, Rosanne, et al. "Complexity in Crisis: The Volcanic Cold Pulse of the 1690s and the Consequences of Scotland's Failure to Cope." *Journal of Volcanology and Geothermal Research* 389 (2020): 1–11.

Dashchuk, James. *Clearing the Plains: Disease, Politics of Starvation, and the Loss of Aboriginal Life*. Regina, SK, Canada: University of Regina Press, 2013.

Dator, James. "Search for a New Land: Imperial Power and Afro-Creole Resistance in the British Leeward Islands, 1624–1745." PhD diss., University of Michigan, 2011.

Dator, James. "'To See a World in a Grain of Sand': Liberty and Slavery in the Leeward Caribbean, 1689–1739." Forthcoming.

Davis, Dave, and Kevin Oldfield, "Archaeological Reconnaissance of Anegada, British Virgin Islands." *Journal of Caribbean Archaeology* 4 (2003): 1–11.

Davis, David Brion. *Inhuman Bondage: The Rise and Fall of Slavery in the New World*. New York: Oxford University Press, 2006.

Davis, Jack E. *The Gulf: The Making of an American Sea*. New York: W. W. Norton, 2017.

Davis, Natalie Zemon. "Judges, Masters, Diviners: Slaves' Experience of Criminal Justice in Colonial Suriname." *Law and History Review* 29, no. 4 (November 2011): 925–84.

Davis, Natalie Zemon. "Regaining Jerusalem: Eschatology and Slavery in Jewish Colonization in Seventeenth-Century Suriname." *Cambridge Journal of Postcolonial Literary Inquiry* 3, no. 1 (January 2016): 11–38.

Davis, Natalie Zemon. *Women on the Margins: Three Seventeenth-Century Lives*. Cambridge, MA: Harvard University Press, 1995.

Davy, John. *The West Indies before and since Emancipation*. London: W. & F. G. Cash, 1854.

Deagan, Kathleen A. "Strategies of Adjustment: Spanish Defense of the Circum-Caribbean Colonies, 1493–1600." In Klingelhofer, ed., *First Forts*: 17–39.

Deagan, Kathleen, and José María Cruxent. *Columbus's Outpost among the Taínos: Spain and America at la Isabela, 1493–1498*. New Haven, CT: Yale University Press, 2002.

Deagan, Kathleen, and José María Cruxent. "From Contact to Criollos: The Archaeology of Spanish Conquest in Hispaniola." In *The Meeting of Two Worlds: Europe and the Americas, 1492–1650*, edited by Warwick Bray. Proceedings of the British Academy 81 (1993): 67–104.

De Barros, Juanita. "'Setting Things Right': Medicine and Magic in British Guiana, 1803–38." *Slavery and Abolition* 25 (2004): 28–50.

De Barros, Juanita, Steven Palmer, and David Wright, eds. *Health and Medicine in the Circum-Caribbean, 1800–1968*. New York: Routledge, 2009.

Debien, Gabriel. *Les esclaves aux Antilles françaises*. Basse-Terre: Société d'Histoire de la Guadeloupe, 1974.

Debien, Gabriel. "La nourriture des *esclaves* sur les plantations des *Antilles* francaises aux XVIIe et XVIIIe siecles." *Caribbean Studies* 4 (1964): 3–27.

DeCorse, Christopher, and Zachary M. Beier, eds. *British Forts and Their Communities: Archaeological and Historical Perspectives*. Gainesville: University Press of Florida, 2018.

Defrance. Susan D. "Zooarchaeology in the Caribbean: Current Research and Future Prospects." In Keegan et al., eds., *Oxford Handbook of Caribbean Archaeology*: 378–90.

Dehoorne, Olivier, Huhua Cao, and Dorina Ilies. "Étudier la ville caribéenne." *Études caribéennes* 39-40 (Avril–Août 2018): 1–33.

De la Fuente, Alejandro. *Havana and the Atlantic in the Sixteenth Century*. Chapel Hill: University of North Carolina Press, 2008.

Delbourgo, James. *Collecting the World: Hans Sloane and the Origins of the British Museum*. Cambridge, MA: Harvard University Press, 2017.

Delbourgo, James. "Divers Things: Collecting the World Under Water." *History of Science* 49, no. 2 (June 2011): 149–85.

Delbourgo, James. *A Most Amazing Scene of Wonders: Electricity and Enlightenment in Early America*. Cambridge, MA: Harvard University Press, 2006.

Delgado García, G. "El cólera morbo asiático en Cuba: Apuntes históricos y bibliográficos." *Cuadernos de Historia de Salud Pública* 78 (1993): 21–27.

Delle, James. *The Colonial Caribbean: Landscapes of Power in the Plantation System*. New York: Cambridge University Press, 2014.

Denevan, William, ed. *The Native Population of the Americas in 1492*. Madison: University of Wisconsin Press, 1992.

Dengo, Gabriel, and J. E. Case, eds. *The Geology of North America*, vol H, *The Caribbean Region*. Boulder, CO: Geological Society of America, 1990.

Denham, Woodrow W. *West Indian Green Monkeys: Problems in Historical Biogeography*, Contributions to Primatology, vol. 24. Basel: Karger, 1987.

Denis, Watson. "Menaces hydrométéorologiques et risques geophysiques en Haiti." *Revue de la Société Haïtienne d'Histoire, de Géograpghie et de Géologie* 241–44 (2011): 31–67.

Depraetere, Christian, and Marc Morell. "Hydrology." In Gillespie and Clague, eds., *Encyclopedia of Islands*: 421–22.

Derby, Lauren. "Bringing the Animals Back in: Writing Quadrupeds into the Environmental History of Latin America and the Caribbean." *History Compass* 9, no. 8 (2011): 602–21.

Desmond, Ray. *Dictionary of British and Irish Botanists and Horticulturalists*. London: Taylor and Francis, 1977.

Dew, Nicholas. "Scientific Travel in the Atlantic World: the French Expedition to Gorée and the Antilles, 1681–1683." *British Journal for the History of Science* 43, no. 1 (March 2010): 1–17.

Dew, Nicholas. "Vers la ligne: Circulating Measurements Around the French Atlantic." in James Delbourgo and Nicholas Dew, eds., *Science and Empire in the Atlantic World*. New York: Routledge, 2008: 53–72.

Diamond, Jared. *Collapse: How Societies Choose to Fail or Succeed*. New York: Viking Penguin, 2005.

Diamond, Jared. "Intra-Island and Inter-Island Comparisons." In *Natural Experiments of History*, edited by Diamond and James A. Robinson. Cambridge, MA: Belknap Press, 2010: 120–41.

Díaz, María Elena. *The Virgin, the King, and the Royal Slaves of El Cobre: Negotiating Freedom in Colonial Cuba, 1670–1780*. Stanford, CA: Stanford University Press, 2000.

Diaz-Briquets, Sergio, and Jorge Pérez-López. *Conquering Nature: The Environmental Legacy of Socialism in Cuba*. Pittsburgh: University of Pittsburgh Press, 2000.

Dickson, David. *Arctic Ireland: The Extraordinary Story of the Great Frost and Forgotten Famine of 1740–41*. Belfast: White Row Press, 1997.

Dillman, Jefferson. *Colonizing Paradise. Landscape and Empire in the British West Indies*. Tuscaloosa: University of Alabama Press, 2015.

Dobson, Mary. *Contours of Death and Disease in Early Modern England*. Cambridge: Cambridge University Press, 1997.

Donkin, R. A. *The Peccary—with Observations on the Introduction of Pigs to the New World*. Philadelphia: American Philosophical Society, 1985.

Donnelly, J. P., et al. "Intense Climate Forcing of Unprecedented Hurricane Activity in the Last 2000 Years." *Earth's Future* 3 (2105): 49–65.

Donnelly, Jeffrey P., and Jonathan D. Woodruff. "Intense Hurricane Activity over the Past 5,000 Years Controlled by El Niño and the West African Monsoon." *Nature* 447 (May 24, 2007): 465–68.

Donnolly, T. W. "Geologic History of the Caribbean and Central America." In *The Geology of North America: An Overview*, edited by Albert W. Bally and Allison R. Palmer. Boulder, CO: Geological Society of America, 1989: 299–321.

Donovan, Stephen K., and Trevor A. Jackson, eds. *Caribbean Geology: An Introduction*. Kingston, Jamaica: University of the West Indies Press, 1994.

Doolan, Denise, Carlota Dobaño, and J. Kevin Baird. "Acquired Immunity to Malaria." *Clinical Microbiology Reviews* 22 (2009): 13–36.

Dorner, Zachary. *Merchants of Medicines: The Commerce and Coercion of Health in Britain's Long Eighteenth Century*. Chicago: University of Chicago Press, 2020.

Drake, A., and M. Oxenham. "Disease, Climate, and the Peopling of the Americas." *Historical Biology* 25 (2013): 565–97.

Draper, Mary. "Timbering and Turtling: The Maritime Hinterlands of Early Modern British Caribbean Cities." *Early American Studies An Interdisciplinary Journal* 15, no. 4 (2017): 769–800.

Drayton, Richard. "A l'ecole des Francais: les sciences et le deuxieme empire britannique (1783–1830)." *Revue Francaise d'Histoire D'Outre Mer* 86, nos. 322–23 (1999): 91–118.

Drayton, Richard. "Maritime Networks and the Making of Knowledge." In *Empire, the Sea, and Global History: Britain's Maritime World, c. 1760–c.1840*, edited by David Cannadine. Basingstoke, UK: Palgrave Macmillan, 2007: 72–82.

Drayton, Richard. *Nature's Government: Science, Imperial Britain, and the "Improvement" of the World*. New Haven, CT: Yale University Press, 2000.

Drexler, Michael. "Hurricanes and Revolutions." In *Early American Cartographies*, edited by Martin Brückner. Chapel Hill: University of North Carolina Press, 2011: 442–66.

Dubois, Laurent. *Avengers of the New World: The Story of the Haitian Revolution*. Cambridge, MA: Harvard University Press, 2004.

Dubois, Laurent, et al. *The Haiti Reader: History, Culture, Politics*. Durham NC: Duke University Press, 2020.

Dubois, Laurent. *Haiti: The Aftershocks of History*. New York: Picador, 2012.

Duffy, Michael. *Soldiers, Sugar, and Seapower: The British Expeditions to the West Indies and the War against Revolutionary France*. Oxford: Oxford University Press, 1987.

Duggan, Ana T., et al. "17th Century Variola Virus Reveals the Recent History of Smallpox." *Current Biology* 26 (2016): 1–6.

Dunn, Richard. *Sugar and Slaves: The Rise of the Planter Class in the English West Indies, 1624–1713*. Chapel Hill: University of North Carolina Press, 1972.

Dunn, Richard. *Tale of Two Plantations: Slave Life and Labor in Jamaica and Virginia*. Cambridge, MA: Harvard University Press, 2014.

Dye, Alan. *Cuban Sugar in the Age of Mass Production: Technology and the Economics of the Sugar Central, 1899–1929*. Stanford, CA: Stanford University Press, 1998.

Echenberg, Myron. *Humboldt's Mexico*. Montreal and Kingston, Jamaica: McGill-Queen's University Press, 2017.

Echevarría, Roberto González, ed. *Oxford Book of Latin American Short Stories*. New York: Oxford University Press, 1997.

Edelson, S. Max. *The New Map of Empire: How Britain Imagined America before Independence*. Cambridge, MA: Harvard University Press, 2017.

Edwards, Jay D. "The Complex Origins of the American Domestic Piazza-Verandah-Gallery." *Material Culture* 21, no. 2 (1989): 3–58.

Edwards, Jay D. "Creole Architecture: A Comparative Analysis of Upper and Lower Louisiana and Saint Domingue." *International Journal of Historical Archaeology* 10, no. 3 (September 2006): 241–71.

Edwards, Jay D. "The Evolution of Vernacular Architecture in the Western Caribbean." In *Cultural Traditions and Caribbean Identity; The Question of Patrimony*, edited by Jeffery K. Wilkerson. Gainesville: University Press of Florida, 1980: 291–339.

Edwards, Jay D. "The First Comparative Studies of Caribbean Architecture." *New West Indies Guide* 57, nos. 3–4 (1983): 173–200.

Edwards, Jay D. "The Origins of Creole Architecture." *Winterthur Portfolio* 29 (Summer–Autumn 1994): 156–89.

Edwards, Tai S., and Paul Kelton. "Germs, Genocides and America's Indigenous Peoples." *Journal of American History* 107 (2020): 52–76.

Egan, Jim. "The 'Long'd for Aera' of an 'Other Race': Climate, Identity, and James Grainger's *Sugar Cane*." *Early American Literature* 38, no. 2 (2003): 189–212.

Elliott, J. H. *Empires of the Atlantic World: Britain and Spain in America, 1492–1830*. New Haven, CT: Yale University Press, 2006, 234–45.

Ellis, Richard. *The Empty Ocean: Plundering the World's Marine Life*. Washington, DC: Island Press, 2003.

Elsner, James, and A Birol Kara. *Hurricanes of the North Atlantic: Climate and Society*. New York: Oxford University Press, 1999.

Eltis, David. "Nutritional Trends in Africa and the Americas: Heights of Africans, 1819–1839." *Journal of Interdisciplinary History* 12 (1982): 453–75.

Eltis, David, and Stanley L. Engerman, eds. *The Cambridge World History of Slavery*, vol. 3, *AD 1420–AD 1804*. New York: Cambridge University Press, 2011.

Eltis, David, and Jorge Felipe-Gonzalez. "The Rise and Fall of the Cuban Slave Trade: New Data, New Paradigms." In *From the Galleons to the Highlands: Slave Trade Routes in the Spanish Americas*, edited by Alex Borucki, David Eltis, and David Wheat. Albuquerque: University of New Mexico Press, 2019: 201–22.

Eltis, David, F. Lewis, and D. Richardson. "Slave Prices, the African Slave Trade, and Productivity in the Caribbean, 1674–1804." *Economic History Review* 58 (2004): 673–700.

Eltis, David, and David Richardson. *Atlas of the Transatlantic Slave Trade*. New Haven, Ct: Yale University Press, 2010.

Emanuel, Kerry. *A Divine Wind: The History and Science of Hurricanes*. New York: Oxford University Press, 2005.

Emmanuel, Isaac, and Suzanne. *History of the Jews of the Netherlands Antilles*. Cincinnati, OH: American Jewish Archives, 1970.

Emmer, Pieter. "Slavery and Slave Trade of Minor Atlantic Power." In *The Cambridge World History of Slavery*, vol. 3, *AD 1420–AD 1804*, edited by David Eltis and Stanley Engerman. Cambridge: Cambridge University Press, 2011: 450–78.

Enfield, Georgina H. *Climate and Society in Colonial Mexico*. Hoboken, NJ: John Wiley and Sons, 2011.

Engelbrecht, Christine, et al. "Ceratocystis Wilt of Cacao—a Disease of Increasing Importance." *Phytopathology* 97 (2007): 1648–49.

Engerman, Stanley, and Barry W. Higman. "The Demographic Structure of Caribbean Slave Societies in the Eighteenth and Nineteenth Centuries." In *General History of the Caribbean*, edited by Franklin Knight. Paris/London: UNESCO Publishing, 3 (1997): 45–104.

Entwistle. P. F. *Pests of Cacao.* London: Longman, 1972.

Espinosa, Mariola. "The Question of Racial Immunity to Yellow Fever in History and Historiography." *Social Science History* 38 (2014): 437–53.

Etheridge, Kay. "The History and Influence of Maria Sibylla Merian's Bird-Eating Tarantula: Circulating Images and the Production of Natural Knowledge." In Manning and Rood, eds., *Global Scientific Practice*: 54–70.

Etheridge, Kay, and Florence F. J. M. Pieters. "Maria Sibylla Merian (1647–1717): Pioneering Naturalist, Artist, and Inspiration for Catesby." In *The Curious Mister Catesby: A "Truly Ingenious" Naturalist Explores New Worlds*, edited by E. Charles Nelson and David Elliot. Athens: University of Georgia Press, 2015: 39–56.

Evans, Chris. "The Plantation Hoe: The Rise and Fall of an Atlantic Commodity." *William and Mary Quarterly*, 3rd Ser., 69, no. 1 (2012): 71–100.

Evelyn, Owen B., and Roland Camirand. "Forest Cover and Deforestation in Jamaica: An Analysis of Forest Cover Estimates over Time." *International Forestry Review* 5 (2003): 354–63.

Everaert, Huub. *Een zoektocht naar de aard van man-vrouw relaties onder Surinaamse slaven: De suikerplantages Fairfield, Breukelerwaard, Cannewapido en La Jalousie in de periode voorafgaande aan de emancipatie.* PhD diss., University of Amsterdam, 1999.

Eymeri, Jean-Claude. *Histoire de la medicine aux Antilles et en Guyane.* Paris: L'Harmattan, 1992.

Eyre, L. Alan. "The Tropical Rainforests of the Eastern Caribbean: Present Status and Conservation." *Caribbean Geography* 9 (1998): 101–20.

Fagan, Brian. *Fishing: How the Sea Fed Civilization.* New Haven, CT: Yale University Press, 2017.

Fagundes, Nelson, et al. "How Strong Was the Bottleneck Associated to the Peopling of the Americas? New Insights from Multilocus Sequence Data." *Genetics and Molecular Biology* 41 (2018): 206–14.

Falchetti, Ana María. "La ofrenda y la semilla: Notas sobre el simbolismo del oro entre los Uwa." *Boletín Museo del Oro* 43 (1997): 2–37.

Farriss, Nancy. *Maya Society under Colonial Rule: The Collective Enterprise of Survival.* Princeton, NJ: Princeton University Press, 1984.

Feinsilver, Julie. *Healing the Masses: Cuban Health Politics at Home and Abroad.* Berkeley: University of California Press, 1993.

Feldman, Theodore. "The Barometer." In *Instruments of Science: An Historical Encyclopedia*, edited by Robert Bud and Deborah Jean Warner. New York: National Museum of American History, 1998: 53–54.

Fenn, Elizabeth. *Encounters at the Heart of the World: A History of the Mandan People.* New York: Hill & Wang, 2014.

Fenn, Elizabeth. *Pox Americana: The Great Smallpox Epidemic of 1775–1782.* New York: Hill & Wang, 2002.

Fennah, R. G. "Damage to Sugar Cane by Fulgoroidea and Related Insects." In *Pests of Sugar Cane*, edited by J. R. Williams et al. Amsterdam: Elsevier, 1969: 356–89.

Fergus, Claudius. "'Dread of Insurrection': Abolitionism, Security, and Labor in Britain's West Indian Colonies, 1760–1823." *William and Mary Quarterly*, 3rd Ser., 66, no. 4 (October 2009): 757–80.

Fernandes, D. M., K. A. Sirak, H. Ringbauer, et al. "A Genetic History of the Pre-contact Caribbean." *Nature* 590 (2021): 103–10. https://doi.org/10.1038/s41586-020-03053-2.

Fernández-Prieto, Leida. "Islands of Knowledge, Science and Agriculture in the History of Latin America and the Caribbean." *Isis* 104, no. 4 (December 2013): 788–97.

Fernández-Prieto, Leida. "Mapping the Global and Local Archipelago of Scientific Tropical Sugar: Agriculture, Knowledge, and Practice, 1790–1880." In Manning and Rood, eds., *Global Scientific Practice*: 181–98.

Ferrer, Ada. *Freedom's Mirror: Cuba and Haiti in the Age of Revolution*. New York: Cambridge University Press, 2014.

Feuillet, Nathalie, François Beauducel, and Paul Tapponnier. "Tectonic Context of Moderate to Large Historical Earthquakes in the Lesser Antilles and Mechanical Coupling with Volcanoes." *Journal of Geophysical Research* 116 (2011): B10308.

Few, Martha. *For All of Humanity: Mesoamerican and Colonial Medicine in Enlightenment Guatemala*. Tuscon: University of Arizona Press, 2015.

Few, Martha. "Killing Locusts in Colonial Guatemala." In *Centering Animals in Latin American History*, edited by Martha Few and Zeb Tortorici. Durham, NC: Duke University Press, 2013: 62–92.

Fielding, Russell. *The Wake of the Whale: Hunter Societies in the Caribbean and North Atlantic*. Cambridge, MA: Harvard University Press, 2018.

Figueredo, Alfredo E. "Manioc Dethroned and Maize Triumphant: Interpretations on the Ethnohistory and Archaeology of the Bahamas (with Sundry Notes on Relations of Production)." *Journal of Caribbean Archaeology* 15 (2015): 120–34.

Figueroa, J. P. "The HIV Epidemic in the Caribbean." *West Indian Medical Journal* 57 (2008): 195–203.

Figueroa, Luis. *Sugar, Slavery and Freedom in Nineteenth-Century Puerto Rico*. Chapel Hill: University of North Carolina Press 2005.

Finucane, Adrian. *The Temptations of Trade: Britain, Spain, and the Struggle for Empire*. Philadelphia: University of Pennsylvania Press, 2016.

Fissell, Mary. "Imagining Vermin in Early Modern England." *History Workshop Journal* 47 (1999): 1–29.

Fitz, Don. *Cuban Health Care: The Ongoing Revolution*. New York: Monthly Review Press, 2020.

Fitzpatrick, Scott M. "Seafaring Capabilities in the pre-Columbian Caribbean." *Journal of Maritime Archaeology* 8, no. 1 (2013): 101–38.

Fitzpatrick, Scott M. "The Southward Route Hypothesis." In Keegan et al. eds. *The Oxford Handbook of Caribbean Archaeology*: 198–204.

Fitzpatrick, Scott M. "Synthesizing Island Archaeology." In *Voyages of Discovery: The Archaeology of the Islands*, edited by Scott M. Fitzpatrick. Westport, CT: Praeger, 2004: 3–18.

Fitzpatrick, Scott M., M. Kappers, and C. M. Giovas. "The Southward Route Hypothesis: Examining Carriacou's Chronological Position in Antillean Prehistory." In Fitzpatrick and Ross, eds., *Island Shores, Distant Pasts*: 163–76.

Fitzpatrick, Scott M., William F. Keegan, and Katherine Sullivan Sealey. "Human Impacts on Marine Environments in the West Indies during the Middle to Late Holocene." In *Human Impacts on Ancient Marine Ecosystems: A Global Perspective*, edited by Torben.C. Rick and Jon M. Erlandson. Berkeley: University of California Press, 2008: 147–64.

Fitzpatrick, Scott M., and Ann H. Ross, eds. *Island Shores, Distant Pasts: Archaeological and Biological Approaches to the Pre-Columbian Settlement of the Caribbean*. Gainesville: University of Florida Press, 2010.

Florescano, Enrique. *Precios de maíz y crisis agrícolas en México (1708–1810)*. Mexico City: El Colegio de México, 1969.

Flores Guzmán, Ramiro Alberto. "The Feeding of Slave Population in the United States, the Caribbean, and Brazil: Some Remarks in the State of the Art." *América Latina en la Historia Económica. Revista de Investigación* 20 (2013): 16–22.

Follett, Richard. "The Demography of Slavery." In *The Routledge History of Slavery*, edited by Gad Heumann and Trevor Burnard. London: Routledge, 2012: 119–37.

Fortuné, Félix-Hilaire. *Cyclones at autres cataclysmes aux Antilles*. Fort-de-France: Masure, 1986.

Freund, Heather. "A Negotiated Possession: Law, Race, and Subjecthood in the Ceded Islands, 1763–1797." PhD diss., University of Illinois, Urbana-Champaign, 2019.

Freyre, Gilberto. *Casa-grande e senzala*. Rio de Janeiro: Editora Record, 1998 [orig. pub. 1933].

Friedman, G.C. "The Heights of Slaves in Trinidad." *Social Science History* 6 (1982): 482–515.

Fuente, Alejandro de la. *Havana and the Atlantic in the Sixteenth Century*. Chapel Hill: University of North Carolina Press, 2008.

Funes Monzote, Reinaldo. "Animal Labor and Protection in Cuba: Changes in Relationships with Animals in the Nineteenth Century," translated by A. Hidalgo. In *Centering Animals in Latin American History*, edited by Martha Few and Zeb Tortorici. Durham, NC: Duke University Press, 2013: 209–43.

Funes Monzote, Reinaldo. *From Rainforest to Cane Field in Cuba: An Environmental History since 1492*. Translated by Alex Martin. Chapel Hill: University of North Carolina Press, 2008.

Gaffield, Julia. *Haitian Connections in the Atlantic World: Recognition after Revolution*. Chapel Hill: University of North Carolina Press, 2015.

Gallant, Lauren R., et al. "A Bat Guano Deposit in Jamaica Recorded Agricultural Changes and Metal Exposure over the Last >4300 Years." *Palaeogeography, Palaeoclimatology, Palaeoecology* 538 (2020). https://doi.org/10.1016/j.palaeo.2019.109470.

Gallay, Alan. *The Indian Slave Trade: The Rise of the English Empire in the American South, 1670–1717*. New Haven, CT: Yale University Press, 2003.

Galloway, J. H. "Botany in the Service of Empire: The Barbados Cane-Breeding Program and the Revival of the Caribbean Sugar Industry, 1880s–1930s." *Annals of the Association of American Geographers* 86 (2005): 682–706.

Galloway, J. H. *The Sugar Cane Industry: An Historical Geography from Its Origins to 1914*. Cambridge: Cambridge University Press, 1989.

Gamble, Douglas. "The Neglected Climatic Hazards of the Caribbean: Overview and Prospects for a Warmer Climate." *Geography Compass* 8, no. 4 (2014): 221–34.

Gamble, Douglas, and Scott Curtis. "Caribbean Precipitation: Review, Model, Prospect." *Progress in Physical Geography* 23 (2008): 67–74.

Gamble, Douglas W., Darren B. Parnell, and Scott Curtis. "Spatial Variability of the Caribbean Mid-summer Drought and Relation to North Atlantic High Circulation." *International Journal of Climatology* 28 (2008): 343–50.

Gannon, Michael R., et al. *Bats of Puerto Rico: An Island Focus and a Caribbean Perspective*. Kingston, Jamaica: University of the West Indies, 2005.

García, Alejandro de la Fuente. "Índice de morbilidad e incidencia de enfermedades entre los esclavos en La Habana, 1580–1699." *Asclepios* 43 (1991): 7–22.

García, Guadalupe. *Beyond the Walled City: Colonial Exclusion in Havana*. Berkeley: University of California Press, 2016.

García de León, Antonio. *Tierra adentro, mar en fuera: El Puerto de Veracruz y su litoral a sotovento, 1519–1821*. Mexico City: Fondo de Cultura Económica, 2011.

Garcia-Herrera, R., L. Gimeno, P. Ribera, and E. Hernandez. "New Records of Atlantic Hurricanes from Spanish Documentary Sources." *Journal of Geophysical Research* 110 (2005): 1–7.

Garcia-Herrara, Ricardo, et al. "Identification of Caribbean Basin Hurricanes from Spanish Documentary Sources." *Climate Change* 83 (2007): 55–85.

Garmon, W. Travis, Casy Allen, and Kaelin Groom. "Geologic and Tectonic Background of the Lesser Antilles." In *Landscapes and Landforms of the Lesser Antilles*, edited by Casey Allen. Cham, Switzerland: Springer, 2017: 7–15.

Garnier, E., J. Desarthe, and D. Moncoulon. "The Historic Reality of the Cyclonic Variability in the French Antilles, 1635–2007." *Climate of the Past Discussions* 11 (2019): 1519–50.

Garrigus, John. *'Macandal Is Saved!': Disease, Conspiracy, and the Coming of the Haitian Revolution*. Forthcoming.

Garrigus, John. "'Like an epidemic one could only stop with the most violent remedies': African Poisons versus Livestock Disease in Saint Domingue, 1750–88." *William and Mary Quarterly*, 3rd Ser., 78, no. 4 (Oct. 2021): 617–50.

Gaspar, David Barry. *Bondmen and Rebels: A Study of Master-Slave Relations in Antigua*. Baltimore: Johns Hopkins University Press, 1985.

Gaspar, David Barry, and David Patrick Geggus, eds. *A Turbulent Time: the French Revolution and the Greater Caribbean*. Bloomington: University of Indiana Press, 1997.

Gay, Edwin, ed. "Letter from a Sugar Plantation in Nevis, 1723–32." *Journal of Economic and Business History* 1 (November 1928): 149–73.

Geggus, David Patrick, ed. *The Impact of the Haitian Revolution in the Atlantic World*. Columbia: University of South Carolina Press, 2001.

Geggus, David. "Indigo and Slavery in Saint Domingue." In Shepherd, ed., *Slavery without Sugar*: 19–35.

Geggus, David. "The Major Port Towns of Saint Domingue in the Later Eighteenth Century." In Knight and Liss, eds., *Atlantic Port Cities*: 87–116.

Geggus, David. "Saint-Domingue on the Eve of the Haitian Revolution." In David Patrick Geggus, and Noman Fiering, eds., *The World of the Haitian Revolution*. Bloomington: University of Indiana Press, 2009: 3–20.

Geggus, David. *Slavery, War and Revolution: The British Occupation of Saint Domingue, 1793–1798*. Oxford: Oxford University Press, 1982.

Geggus, David. "The Slaves and Free People of Color of Cap Français." In Cañizares-Esguerra, Childs, and Sidbury, eds., *The Black Urban Atlantic*: 101–21.

Geggus, David P. "Sugar and Coffee Cultivation in Saint Domingue and the Shaping of the Slave Labor Force." In Berlin and Morgan, eds., *Cultivation and Culture*: 73–98.

Geggus, David. "Urban Development in Eighteenth-Century Saint-Domingue." *Bulletin du Centre of d'Histoire des Espaces Atlantiques* 5 (1990): 197–228.

Geggus, David. "Yellow Fever in the 1790s: the British Army in Occupied St. Domingue." *Medical History* 23, no. 1 (1979): 38–58.

Genaro, Julio A., and Ana E. Tejuca. "Patterns of Endemism and Biogeography of Cuban Insects." In Woods and Sergile, eds., *Biogeography of the West Indies*: 77–81.

Gerber, Jane S., ed. *The Jews in the Caribbean*. Oxford: The Littman Library of Jewish Civilization, 2014.

Gerbi, Antonello. *Nature in the New World: From Christopher Columbus to Gonzalo Fernández de Oviedo*. Translated by Jeremy Moyle. Pittsburgh: University of Pittsburgh Press, 1985.

Gerdelan, Louis D. "The Royal Society, Port Royal, and the Great Trans-Atlantic Earthquake of 1692." *Studi Storici* 60, no. 4 (October–December 2019): 845–74.

Gergis, Joelle, and Anthony M. Fowler. "A History of ENSO Events since AD 1525: Implications for Future Climate Change." *Climatic Change* 92, nos. 3–4 (2009): 343–87.

Gherini, Claire. "'Experiment and Good Sense Must Direct You': Managing Health and Sickness in the British Plantation Enlightenment, 1756–1815." PhD diss., Johns Hopkins University, 2016.

Giffin, Karen, et al. "A Treponemal Genome from an Historic Plague Victim Supports a Recent Emergence of Yaws and Its Presence in 15th-Century Europe." *Nature: Scientific Reports* (2020). https://doi.org/10.1038/s41598-020-66012-x.

Gillespie, Rosemary G., and David A. Clague, eds. *Encyclopedia of Islands*. Berkeley: University of California Press, 2009.

Giovas, Christina M. "The Beasts at Large—Perennial Questions and New Paradigms for Caribbean Translocation Research. Parts I & II: Mammalian Introductions in Cultural Context." *Environmental Archaeology* 24, no. 2 (2019): 182–98; and 24, no. 3 (2019): 294–305.

Giovas, Christina. "Pre-Columbian Amerindian Lifeways at the Sabazan Site, Carriacou, West Indies." *The Journal of Island and Coastal Archaeology* 13, no. 2 (2018): 161–90.

Giovas, Christine M. "Though She Be But Little: Resource Resilience, Amerindian Foraging, and Long-Term Adaptive Strategies in the Grenadines, West Indies." *Journal of Island and Coastal Archaeology* 11 (2016): 238–63.

Giovas, Christina M., and Scott M. Fitzpatrick. "Prehistoric Migration in the Caribbean: Past Perspectives, New Models, and the Ideal Free Distribution of West Indian Colonization." *World Archaeology* 46, no. 4 (2014): 569–89.

Girard, Philippe. *Toussaint Louverture: A Revolutionary Life*. New York: Basic Books, 2016.

Girard, Philippe. *The Slaves Who Defeated Napoleon: Toussaint Louverture and the Haitian War of Independence, 1801–1804*. Tuscaloosa: University of Alabama Press, 2011.

Gischler, E., et al. "A 1500-Year Holocene Caribbean Climate Archive from the Blue Hole, Lighthouse Reef, Belize." *Journal of Coastal Research*, no. 246 (2008): 1495–1505.

Glen, Robert. "An Early Methodist Revival in the West Indies: Insights from a Neglected Letter in 1774." *Wesley and Methodist Studies* 9 (2017): 36–56.

Glenisson, Jean-Louis. "La défense et la mise en valeur de Saint-Domingue au lendemain du traité de Paris (1763): le rôle de la cartographie." *Le Monde des cartes* 180 (2004): 17–35.

Göbel, Erik. "The Danish West Indies, 1660s–1750s: Formative Years." In Roper, ed., *The Torrid Zone*, 118–31.

Gøbel, Erik. *The Danish Slave Trade and Its Abolition*. Leiden: Brill, 2016.

Gøbel, Erik. "Dansk slavehandel på trekantruten." *Danske Magazin* 52 (2012): 515–53.

Goddard, Robert. "Tourism, Drugs, Offshore Finance, and the Perils of Neoliberal Development." In *The Caribbean*, edited by Stephan Palmié and Francisco Scarano. Chicago: University of Chicago Press, 2011: 571–82.

Gómez, Pablo F. "Caribbean Stones and the Creation of Early-Modern Worlds." *History and Technology* 34, no. 1 (2018): 11–20.

Gómez, Pablo. "The Circulation of Bodily Knowledge in the Seventeenth-Century Black Spanish Caribbean." *Social Science Medicine* 26 (2013): 383–402.

Gómez, Pablo. *The Experiential Caribbean. Creating Knowledge and Healing in the Early Modern Atlantic*. Chapel Hill: University of North Carolina Press, 2017.

Gómez, Pablo. "Hospitals and Health in the Sixteenth-Century Spanish Caribbean." In *The Spanish Caribbean and the Atlantic World in the Long Sixteenth* Century, edited by Ida Altman and David Wheat. Lincoln: University of Nebraska Press, 2019: 211–32.

Gonzalez, Ana Rita, and Elizabeth Fee. "Anemia in Puerto Rico as the Turn of the Twentieth Century." *American Journal of Public Health* 105 (2015): 272–73.

Gonzalez, R. M. "Infant Mortality in Cuba: Myth and Reality." *Cuban Studies* 43 (2015): 19–39.

González-Herrera, Ulises M. "Food Preparation and Dietary Preferences among the Arawak Aboriginal Communities of Cuba." In Roksandic, ed., *Cuban Archaeology*: 168–84.

Goodyear, James. "The Sugar Connection: A New Perspective on the History of Yellow Fever." *Bulletin of the History of Medicine* 52 (1978): 5–21.

Gordon, A. L. "Circulation of the Caribbean Sea." *Journal of Geophysical Research* 72 (1967): 6207–23.

Gosse, Dave St. Aubyn. *Abolition and Plantation Management in Jamaica, 1807–1838*. Kingston, Jamaica: University of the West Indies Press, 2012.

Goudie, Sean X. *Creole America: The West Indies and the Formation of Literature and Culture in the New Republic*. Philadelphia: University of Pennsylvania Press, 2006.

Goveia, Elsa. *Slave Society in the British Leeward Islands at the End of the Eighteenth Century*. New Haven, CT: Yale University Press, 1965.

Gowland, R. L., and A. G. Western. "Morbidity in the Marshes: Using Spatial Epidemiology to Investigate Skeletal Evidence for Malaria in Anglo-Saxon England (AD 410–1050)." *American Journal of Physical Anthropology* 147 (2012): 301–11.

Gragg, Larry. "The Port Royal Earthquake." *History Today* 50 (September 2000): 28–34.

Graham, Aaron. "Towns, Government, Legislation and the 'Police' in Jamaica and the British Atlantic, 1770–1805." *Urban History* 47, no. 1 (2020): 41–62.

Graham, Alan. *A Natural History of the New World*. Chicago: University of Chicago Press, 2011.

Graham, Robert Cunninghame, et al. *Horses of the Conquest: A Study of the Steeds of the Spanish Conquest*. Norman: University of Oklahoma Press, 1949.

Green, Monica. "The Globalisations of Disease." In *Human Dispersal and Species Movement: From Prehistory to Present*, edited by Nicole Boivin, Rémy and Michael Petraglia. Cambridge: Cambridge University Press, 2017: 499–502.

Greene, Jack P. "Changing Identity in the British Caribbean: Barbados as a Case Study." In Nicholas Canny and Anthony Pagden, eds., *Colonial Identity in the Atlantic World, 1500–1800*. Princeton, NJ: Princeton University Press, 1987: 213–66.

Greene, Jack P. *Settler Jamaica in the 1750s: A Social Portrait*. Charlottesville: University of Virginia Press, 2016.

Greenfield, Amy Butler. *A Perfect Red: Empire, Espionage, and the Quest for the Color of Desire.* New York, 2005.

Gregorio de Souza, Jonas, et al. "Pre-Columbian Earth-Builders Settled along the Entire Southern Rim of the Amazon." *Nature Communications* 9 (2018). doi:10.1038/s41467-018-03510-7.

Gregory, B. R., et al. "Middle–Late Holocene Caribbean Aridity Inferred from for Aminifera and Elemental Data in Sediment Cores from Two Cuban Lagoons." *Palaeogeography, Palaeoclimatology, Palaeoecology* 426 (2015): 229–41.

Greer, Allan. *Property and Dispossession: Natives, Empires and Land in Early Modern North America.* New York: Cambridge University Press, 2018.

Grouard, S. "Faunal Remains Associated with Late Saladoid and Post-Saladoid Occupations at Anse a la Gourde, Guadeloupe, West Indies: Preliminary Results." *Archaeo Fauna* 10 (2001): 71–98.

Grouard, Sandrine, Sophia Perdikaris, and Karyne Debue. "Dog Burials Associated with Human Burials in the West Indies during the Early Pre-Columbian Ceramic Age (500 BC–600 AD)." *Anthropozoologica* 48, no. 2 (2013): 447–65.

Grove, Richard. "The Great El Niño of 1789–93 and Its Global Consequences: Reconstructing an Extreme Climate Event in World Environmental History." *Journal of Medieval History* 10 (2007): 75–98.

Grove, Richard H. *Green Imperialism. Colonial Expansion, Tropical Island Edens and the Origins of Environmentalism, 1600–1860.* Cambridge: Cambridge University Press, 1995.

Grupe, Gisela. "Zur Ätiologie der Cribra orbitalia: Auswirkungen auf das Aminosäureprofil im Knochenkollagen und den Eisengehalt des Knochenminerales." *Zeitschrift für Morphologie und Anthropologie*, Bd. 81, H. 1 (1995): 125–37.

Guadalupe Ortega, José. "Machines, Modernity, and Sugar: The Greater Caribbean in a Global Context, 1812–50." *Journal of Global History* 9, no. 1 (2014): 1–25.

Guerra, Francisco. "The Earliest American Epidemic: The Influenza of 1493." *Social Science History* 12 (1988): 305–25.

Guerra, Francisco. "El efecto demográfico de las epidemias tras el descrubrimiento de América." *Revista de Indias* 46 (1986): 41–58.

Guerra, Francisco. "La epidemia americana de influenza en 1493." *Revista de Indias* 45 (1985): 325–47.

Guerra, Francisco. *Epidemología americana y Filipina.* Madrid: Ministerio de Sanidad y Consumo, 1999.

Guidoboni, Emanuela, and John Ebel. *Earthquakes and Tsunamis in the Past: A Guide to Techniques in Historical Seismology.* Cambridge: Cambridge University Press, 2009.

Hall, Douglas. "Botanical and Horticultural Enterprise in Eighteenth-Century Jamaica." In *West Indies Accounts: Essays on the History of the British Caribbean and the Atlantic Economy in Honour of Richard Sheridan,* edited by Roderick A. McDonald. Kingston, Jamaica: University of West Indies Press, 1996: 101–25.

Hall, Douglas. *In Miserable Slavery: Thomas Thistlewood in Jamaica, 1750–86.* Kingston, Jamaica: University of the West Indies Press, 1989, reprint 1999.

Hall, Douglas. *Planters, Farmers and Gardeners in Eighteenth Century Jamaica.* Kingston, Jamaica: University of West Indies Press, 1987.

Hall, Neville. *Slave Society in the Danish West Indies.* Kingston, Jamaica: University of the West Indies Press, 1992.

Hamilton, Douglas J. *Scotland, the Caribbean and the Atlantic World, 1750–1820.* Manchester, UK: Manchester University Press, 2005.

Hamilton, Marcus J., Robert S. Walker, and Dylan C. Kesler. "Crash and Rebound of Indigenous Populations in Lowland South America." *Scientific Reports* 4 (2014). https://www.nature.com/articles/srep04541?message-global%3Dremove%26WT.ec_id%3DSREP-631-20140408.

Hamlin, Christopher. *Cholera: The Biography.* Oxford: Oxford University Press, 2009.

Handler, Jerome S. "Amerindians and Their Contributions to Barbadian Life in the Seventeenth Century." *Journal of Barbados Museum and Historical Society* 35, no. 3 (1977): 189–210.

Handler, Jerome S. "The Amerindian Slave Population of Barbados in the Seventeenth and Eighteenth Centuries." *Caribbean Studies* 8 (1968): 38–64.

Handler, Jerome. "Diseases and Medical Disabilities of Enslaved Barbadians from the Seventeenth Century to around 1838 (Part I)." *Journal of Caribbean History* 40 (2006): 1–38.

Handler, Jerome. "Diseases and Medical Disabilities of Enslaved Barbadians from the Seventeenth Century to around 1838 (Part II)." *Journal of Caribbean History* 40 (2006): 177–214.

Handler, Jerome. "Life Histories of Enslaved Africans in Barbados." *Slavery and Abolition* 19 (1998): 87–100.

Handler, Jerome S. "Slave Medicine and Obeah in Barbados, circa 1650–1834." *New West Indies Guide* 74 (2000): 57–90.

Handler, J., and R. S. Corruccini. "Plantation Slave Life in Barbados: A Physical Anthropological Analysis." *Journal of Interdisciplinary History* 14 (1983): 65–90.

Hanna, Jonathan A. "Camáhogne's Chronology: The Radiocarbon Settlement Sequence on Grenada, West Indies." *Journal of Anthropological Archaeology,* 55 (2019). doi.org/10.1016/j.jaa.2019.101075.

Hanna, Jonathan A., Michael P. Pateman, Lindsay Bloch, and William F. Keegan. "Human-Environment Interactions in a Bahamian Dune Landscape: A Geoarchaelogical Study of a New Lucayan Burial Site." *Geoarchaeology* (2021): 1–19. DOI: 10.1002/gea.21866.

Hansford, James, et al. "Taxonomy-Testing and the 'Goldilocks Hypothesis': Morphometric Analysis of Species Diversity in Living and Extinct Hispaniolan Hutias." *Systematics and Biodiversity* 10, no. 4 (2012): 491–507.

Hanska, Jussi. *Strategies of Sanity and Survival: Religious Responses to Natural Disasters in the Middle Ages.* Helsinki: Finnish Literature Society, 2002.

Harbitz, C. B., et al. "Tsunami Hazard in the Caribbean: Regional Exposure Derived from Credible Worst Case Scenarios." *Continental Shelf Research* 38 (2012): 1–23.

Hardt, Marah J. "Lessons from the Past: The Collapse of Jamaican Coral Reefs." *Fish and Fisheries* 10, no. 2 (2008): 143–58.

Harms, Robert. *The Diligent: A Voyage through the Worlds of the Slave Trade.* New York: Basic Books, 2002.

Harper, Kristin, et al. "The Origin and Antiquity of Syphilis Revisited: An Appraisal of Old-World Pre-Columbian Evidence of Treponemal Infection." *American Journal of Physical Anthropology* 146 (2011): 99–133.

Harrison, Mark. *Medicine in an Age of Commerce and Empire: Britain and Its Tropical Colonies, 1660–1830.* Oxford: Oxford University Press, 2010.

Harrison, Mark. "'The Tender Frame of Man': Disease, Climate, and Racial Difference in India and the West Indies, 1760–1860." *Bulletin of the History of Medicine* 70 (1996): 68–93.

Haug, Gerald. "Climate and the Collapse of Maya Civilization." *Science* 299 (March 14, 2003): 1731–35.

Hauser, Mark. *Mapping Water in Dominica: Enslavement and Environment under Colonialism.* Seattle: University of Washington Press, 2021.

Hauser, Mark William. "A Political Ecology of Water and Enslavement: Water Ways in Eighteenth-Century Caribbean Plantations." *Current Anthropology* 58, no. 2 (2017): 227–56.

Haviser, Jay B. "Archaeological Evidence and the Potential Effects of Paleotsunami Events during the Archaic Age in the Southern Caribbean." In Hofman and Antczak, eds., *Early Settlers:* 57–63.

Haviser, Jay B. "The 'Old Netherlands Style' and Seventeenth-Century Dutch Fortification of the Caribbean." In Klingelhofer, ed., *First Forts:* 167–87.

Hazareesingh, Sudhir. *Black Spartacus The Epic Life of Toussaint Louverture.* New York: Farrar, Straus, and Giroux, 2020.

Heaney, Lawrence R., and Steven M. Goodman. "Mammal Radiations." In Gillespie and Clague, eds., *Encyclopedia of Islands:* 589–91.

Hedges, Blair, Warren B. Cohen, Joel Timyan, and Zhiqiang Yang. "Haiti's Biodiversity Threatened by Nearly Complete Loss of Primary Forest." *Proceedings of the National Academy of Science, USA* 115 (2018): 11850–55.

Heinicke, M. P., W. E. Duellman, and S. B. Hedges. "Major Caribbean and Central American Frog Faunas Originated by Ancient Oceanic Dispersal." *Proceedings of the National Academy of Sciences USA* 104 (2007): 10092–97.

Helgason, A., Nicholson, G., Stefánsson, K. and Donnelly, P., "A Reassessment of Genetic Diversity in Icelanders: Strong Evidence from Multiple Loci for Relative Homogeneity Caused by Genetic Drift." *Annals of Human Genetics* 67 (2003): 281–97. doi:10.1046/j.1469-1809.2003.00046.x.

Helmus, Matthew R., et al. "Island Biogeography of the Anthropocene." *Nature* 513 (September 25, 2014): 543–46.

Henige, David. *Numbers from Nowhere: The American Indian Contact Population Debate.* Norman: University of Oklahoma Press, 1998.

Hewitt, Kenneth. *Interpretations of Calamity: From the Viewpoint of Human Ecology.* Boston: Allen and Unwin, 1983.

Hezel, F. X. "From Conversion to Conquest: The Early Spanish Mission in the Marianas." *Journal of Pacific History* 17 (1982): 115–37.

Higman, B. W. "The Chinese in Trinidad, 1806–1838." *Caribbean Studies* 12 (1972): 21–44.

Higman, Barry W. *Concise History of the Caribbean.* New York: Cambridge University Press, 2010.

Higman, Barry W. "Growth in Afro-Caribbean Slave Populations." *American Journal of Physical Anthropology* 50 (1979): 373–85.

Higman, Barry W. "Jamaican Coffee Plantations, 1780–1860: A Cartographic Analysis." *Caribbean Geography* 2 (1996): 73–91.

Higman, B. W. *Jamaican Food: History, Biology, Culture.* Kingston, Jamaica: University of the West Indies Press, 2007.

Higman, B. W. "Jamaican Port Towns in the Early Nineteenth Century." In Knight and Liss, eds., *Atlantic Port Cities:* 117–48.

Higman, B. W. *Jamaica Surveyed: Plantation Maps and Plans of the Eighteenth and Nineteenth Centuries.* Kingston: Institute of Jamaica, 1988.

Higman, B. W. "The Making of the Sugar Revolution." In *In the Shadow of the Plantation: Caribbean History and Legacy—in Honour of Professor Emeritus Woodville K. Marshall,* edited by Alvin O. Thompson. Kingston, Jamaica: Ian Randle, 2002: 40–71.

Higman, B. W. *Proslavery Priest: The Atlantic World of John Lindsay, 1729–1788.* Kingston, Jamaica: University of the West Indies Press, 2011.

Higman, Barry W. *Slave Populations of the British Caribbean, 1807–1834.* Baltimore: Johns Hopkins University Press, 1984.

Higman, B. W. "The Sugar Revolution." *Economic History Review,* 2nd Ser., 53 (May 2000): 213–38.

Higman, B. W., and B. J. Hudson. *Jamaican Place Names.* Mona: University of the West Indies Press, 2009.

Higuera-Gundy, Antonia, et al. "A 10,300 14 C Yr Record of Climate and Vegetation Change from Haiti." *Quaternary Research* 52, no. 2 (1999): 159–70.

Hirschfeld, Katherine. *Health, Politics, and Revolution in Cuba since 1898.* New Brunswick, NJ, and London: Transaction Publishers, 2007.

Hobsbawm, E. J. "Passionate Witness: Review of *Frantz Fanon: A Critical Study* by Irene L. Gendzier." *New York Review of Books,* February 22, 1973, 8.

Hofman, Corinne L., and Andrzej T. Antczak, eds. *Early Settlers of the Insular Caribbean: Dearchaizing the Archaic.* Leiden: Sidestone Press, 2019.

Hofman, Corinne L., and Anne van Duijvenbode, eds. *Communities in Contact: Essays in Archaeology, Ethnohistory & Ethnography of the Amerindian Circum-Caribbean.* Leiden: Sidestone Press, 2011.

Hofman, Corinne L., and Menno L. P. Hoogland. "Beautiful Tropical Islands in the Caribbean Sea: Human Responses to Floods and Droughts and the Indigenous Archaeological Heritage of the Caribbean." In *Water and Heritage: Material, Conceptual and Spiritual Connections,* edited by Willem J. H. Willems and Henk P. J. van Schaik. Leiden: Sidestone Press, 2015: 99–119.

Hofman, Corinne, Roberto Valcárcel Rojas, and Jorge Ulloa Hung. "Colonization, Transformations, and Indigenous Cultural Persistence in the Caribbean." In *The Global Spanish Empire: Five Hundred Years of Place Making and Pluralism*, edited by Christine Beaule and John Douglass. Tuscon: University of Arizona Press, 2020: 55–82.

Hofman, Corinne L., et al. "Island Networks: Transformations of Inter-community Social Relationships in the Lesser Antilles at the Advent of European Colonialism." *Journal of Island and Coastal Archaeology* (2020). DOI: 10.1080/15564894.2020.1748770.

Hogarth, Rana A. *Medicalizing Blackness: Making Racial Difference in the Atlantic World, 1780–1840*. Chapel Hill: University of North Carolina Press, 2017.

Hoggarth, Julie A., Matthew Restall, James W. Wood, and Douglas J. Kennett. "Drought and Its Demographic Effects in the Maya Lowlands." *Current Anthropology* 58, no. 1 (2017): 82–113.

Holland, Brendan S. "Land Snails." In Gillespie and Clague, eds., *Encyclopedia of Islands*: 537–42.

Hölldobler, Bert, and Edward Wilson. *Journey to the Ants*. Cambridge, MA: Harvard University Press, 1994.

Hoogland, Menno L. P., and Corinne L. Hofman. "Archaeological Investigations at Spanish Water, Curaçao." *Proceedings of the Twenty-Third Congress of the International Association for Caribbean Archaeology*. Antigua, 2011: 631–40.

Hopkins, Daniel. "An Extraordinary Eighteenth-Century Map of the Danish Sugar-Plantation Island St. Croix." *Imago Mundi* 41 (1989): 44–58.

Hopkins, Daniel, Philip Morgan, and Justin Roberts. "The Application of GIS to the Reconstruction of the Slave-Plantation Economy of St. Croix, Danish West Indies." *Historical Geography* 39 (2011): 85–104.

Horan, Joseph. "The Colonial Famine Plot: Slavery, Free Trade, and Empire in the French Atlantic, 1763–1791." *International Review of Social History* 55 (2010): 103–21.

Hornbach, M. J., et al. "High Tsunami Frequency as a Result of Combined Strike-Slip Faulting and Coastal Landslides." *Nature Geoscience* 3 (2010): 783–88.

Hough, Susan. *Earthshaking Science: What We Know (and Don't Know) about Earthquakes*. Princeton, NJ: Princeton University Press, 2002.

Hough, Susan. "Missing Great Earthquakes." *Journal of Geophysical Research* 118 (2013): 1098–108.

Huerga, Álvaro. *Ataques de los caribes a Puerto Rico*. San Juan: Academia Puertorriqueña de la Historia, 2006.

Hulme, Peter. *Colonial Encounters. Europe and the Native Caribbean, 1492–1797*. New York: Methuen, 1986.

Hunt, Nadine. "Expanding the Frontiers of Western Jamaica through Minor Atlantic Ports in the Eighteenth Century." *Canadian Journal of History* 45, no. 3 (Winter 2010): 485–502.

Hunter, John M. "Geophagy in Africa and the United States: A Culture Nutrition Hypothesis." *Geographical Review* 63, no. 2 (April 1973): 170–95.

Hutchinson, C. A. "The Asiatic Cholera Epidemic in 1833 in Mexico." *Bulletin of the History of Medicine* 32 (1958): 1–23.

Hutson, J. Edward, ed. *On the Treatment and Management of the More Common West-India Diseases (1750–1802)*. Kingston, Jamaica: University of the West Indies Press, 2005.

Hymes, Dell, ed. *Pidginization and Creolization of Languages* (Cambridge: Cambridge University Press, 1971.

Iannini, Christopher P. *Fatal Revolutions. Natural History, West Indian Slavery and the Routes of American Literature*. Chapel Hill: University of North Carolina Press, 2012.

Iannone, Gyles, ed. *The Great Maya Droughts in Cultural Context: Case Studies in Resilience and Vulnerability*. Boulder: University Press of Colorado, 2014.

Igler, David. "Diseased Goods: Global Exchanges in the Eastern Pacific Basin, 1770–1850." *The American Historical Review* 109, no. 3 (2014): 693–719.

Jackson, J. B. C. "Reefs since Columbus." *Coral Reefs* 16, suppl. (1997): S23–S32.

Jackson, Jeremy B. C. "What Was Natural in the Coastal Oceans?" *Proceedings of the National Academy of Sciences* 98, no. 10 (May 8, 2001): 5411–18.

Jacoby, Karl. "Slaves by Nature? Domestic Animals and Human Slaves." *Slavery & Abolition* 15 (1994): 89–99.

Jaffe, Rivke ed. *The Caribbean City*. Kingston, Jamaica: Ian Randle, 2008.

Jamku, Andrea, Gerrit Schenk, and Franz Mauelshagen, eds. *Historical Disasters in Context: Science, Religion, and Politics*. New York: Routledge, 2012.

Jarvis, Michael J. *In the Eye of All Trade: Bermuda, Bermudians, and the Maritime Atlantic World, 1680–1783*. Chapel Hill: University of North Carolina Press, 2010.

Jelly-Shapiro, Joshua. "Listen to the Storm Songs of the Caribbean." *New York Times*, September 28, 2019.

Jennings, Evelyn P. *Constructing the Spanish Empire in Havana: State Slavery in Defense and Development, 1762–1835*. Baton Rouge: Louisiana State University, 2020.

Jennings, Evelyn Powell. "State Enslavement in Colonial Havana, 1763–1790." In Shepherd, ed., *Slavery without Sugar*: 152–82.

Jensen, Niklas Thode. *For the Health of the Enslaved: Slaves, Medicine, and Power in the Danish West Indies, 1803–1848*. Copenhagen: Museum Tusculanum Press, 2012.

Jobin, William R. "Sugar and Snails: The Ecology of Bilharziasis Related to Agriculture in Puerto Rico." *The American Journal of Tropical Medicine and Hygiene* 29 (1980): 86–94.

John, A. Meredith. *The Plantation Slaves of Trinidad, 1783–1816*. Cambridge: Cambridge University Press, 1988.

Johns, William E., Tamara L. Townsend, David M. Frantanoni, and W. Douglas Wilson. "On the Atlantic Inflow to the Caribbean Sea." *Deep Sea Research Part 1* 49 (2002): 211–43.

Johnson, Matthew P. "Swampy Sugar Lands: Irrigation Dams and the Rise and Fall of Malaria in Puerto Rico, 1898–1962." *Journal of Latin American Studies* 51 (2019): 243–71.

Johnson, Sara E. "'You Should Give Them Blacks to Eat': Waging Inter-American Wars of Torture and Terror." *American Quarterly* 61, no. 1 (March 2009): 65–92.

Johnson, Sherry. *Climate and Catastrophe in Cuba and the Atlantic World in the Age of Revolution*. Chapel Hill: University of North Carolina Press, 2011.

Johnston, Katherine. "Atlantic Bodies: Health, Race, and the Environment in the Greater British Caribbean." PhD diss., Columbia University, 2016.

Johnston, Katherine. "The Constitution of Empire: Place and Bodily Health in the Eighteenth-Century Atlantic." *Atlantic Studies* 10 (2013): 443–66.

Johnston, Katherine. "Endangered Plantations: Environmental Change and Slavery in the British Caribbean, 1631–1807." *Early American Studies* 18 (Summer 2020): 259–86.

Jones, David S. "Death, Uncertainty and Rhetoric." In *Beyond Germs: Native Depopulation in North America*, edited by Catherine Cameron, Paul Kelton, and Alan Swedlund. Tuscon: University of Arizona Press, 2015: 16–49.

Jones, David S. *Rationalizing Epidemics: Meanings and Uses of American Indian Mortality Since 1600*: Cambridge, MA: Harvard University Press, 2004.

Jones, David S. "Virgin Soils Revisited." *William & Mary* Quarterly 60 (2003): 703–42.

Jones, Margaret. *Public Health in Jamaica, 1850–1940*. Mona: University of the West Indies Press, 2013.

Jopling, Carol F. *Puerto Rican Houses in Sociohistorical Perspective*. Knoxville: University of Tennessee Press, 1988.

Jordaan, Han, and To Van der Lee. "The Hurricane of 1819: Destruction and Reconstruction of Buildings on St. Martin." In *Building Up the Future from the Past: Studies in the Architecture and Historic Monuments in the Dutch Caribbean*, edited by Henry Coomans et al. Zutphen, Netherlands: De Walburg Pers, 1990: 99–108.

Jorink, Eric. *Reading the Book of Nature in the Dutch Golden Age, 1575–1715*. Leiden: Brill, 2010.

Joseph, Michael. "Military Officers, Tropical Medicine, and Racial Thought in the Formation of the West India Regiments, 1793–1802." *Journal of the History of Medicine* 72, no. 2 (2017): 142–65.

Juneja, Monica, and Franz Mauelshagen. "Disasters and Pre-industrial Societies: Historiographic Trends and Comparative Perspectives." *The Medieval History Journal* 10 (2007): 1–31.

Jury, Mark, Bjorn Malmgren, and Amos Winter. "Subregional Precipitation Climate of the Caribbean and Relationship with ENSO and NAO." *Journal of Geophysical Research* 112 (2007). https://doi.org/10.1029/2006JD007541.

Kagan, Richard L. *Urban Images of the Hispanic World, 1493–1793*. New Haven, CT: Yale University Press, 2000.

Kagan, Richard L. "A World without Walls: City and Town in Colonial Spanish America." In *City Walls: The Urban Enceinte in Global Perspective*, edited by James D. Tracy. Cambridge: Cambridge University Press, 2000: 117–52.

Kagan, Richard L., and Philip D. Morgan, eds. *Atlantic Diasporas: Jews, Conversos, and Crypto-Jews in the Age of Mercantilism, 1500–1800*. Baltimore: Johns Hopkins University Press, 2009.

Kamath, Ambika, and Jonathan B. Losos. "Does Ecological Specialization Transcend Scale? Habitat Partitioning among Individuals and Species of *Anolis* Lizards." *Evolution* 71 (2017): 541–49.

Kananoja, Kalle. *Healing Knowledge in Atlantic Africa: Medical Encounters, 1500–1850*. Cambridge: Cambridge University Press, 2021.

Kars, Marjoleine. *Blood on the River: A Chronicle of Mutiny and Freedom on the Wild Coast*. New York: Free Press, 2020.

Kashanipour, Ryan Amir. "A World of Cures: Magic and Medicine in Colonial Yucatán." PhD diss., University of Arizona, 2012.

Katona, Peter, and Judit Katone-Apte. "The Interaction between Nutrition and Infection." *Clinical Infectious Diseases* 46 (2008): 1582–88.

Kaye, Anthony. "The Second Slavery: Modernity in the Nineteenth-Century South and the Atlantic World." *Journal of Southern History* 75 (August 2009): 627–50.

Keegan, William F. "The 'Classic' Taino." In Keegan et al., eds., *Oxford Handbook of Caribbean Archaeology*: 70–83.

Keegan, William F. "The Ecology of Lucayan Arawak Fishing Practices." *American Antiquity* 51, no. 4 (October 1986): 816–25.

Keegan, William F. "Island Shores and 'Long Pauses.'" In Fitzpatrick and Ross, eds., *Island Shores, Distant Pasts*: 11–20.

Keegan, William F. "Mobility and Disdain: Columbus and Cannibals in the Land of Cotton." *Ethnohistory* 62 (2015): 1–15.

Keegan, William F. *The People Who Discovered Columbus: The Prehistory of the Bahamas*. Gainesville: University of Florida Press, 1992.

Keegan, William F. "Situating Jamaica." In Hofman and Antczak, eds., *Early Settlers*: 191–99.

Keegan, William F., and Lisabeth A. Carlson. *Talking Taíno: Essays on Caribbean Natural History from a Native Perspective*. Tuscaloosa: University of Alabama Press, 2008.

Keegan, William F., Scott M. Fitzpatrick, Kathleen Sullivan Sealey, Michelle J. LeFebvre, and Peter T. Sinelli. "The Role of Small Islands in Marine Subsistence Strategies: Case Studies from the Caribbean." *Human Ecology* 36, no. 5 (2008): 635–54.

Keegan, William F., and Corinne L. Hofman, eds. *The Caribbean before Columbus*. New York: Oxford University Press, 2017.

Keegan, William F., Corinne L. Hofman, and Reniel Rodríguez Ramos, eds. *The Oxford Handbook of Caribbean Archaeology*. Oxford: Oxford University Press, 2013.

Keegan, William F., Roger W. Portell, and John Slapcinsky. "Changes in Invertebrate Taxa at Two Pre-Columbian Sites in Southwestern Jamaica, AD 800–1500." *Journal of Archaeological Science* 30 (2003): 1607–17.

Keegan, William F., et al. "Child Labor in Saladoid St. Thomas, U.S.V.I. (300–500 CE)." *Journal of Anthropological Archaeology* 53 (2019): 222–28.

Keegan, William F., et al. "A Crab-Shell Dichotomy Encore: Visualizing Saladoid Shell Tools." *Journal of Caribbean Archaeology* 18 (2018): 1–33.

Kelman, Ilan. "Why Do Bad Ideas Stick?" *Disaster and Social Crisis Research Network Electronic Newsletter* 42 (September–November 2010): 9.

Kelly, Catherine E. *War and the Militarization of British Army Medicine, 1793–1830.* London: Routledge, 2011.

Kelton, Paul. *Epidemics and Enslavement: Biological Catastrophe in the Native Southeast, 1492–1715.* Lincoln: University of Nebraska Press, 2007.

Kemp, Melissa E., et al. "7000 Years of Turnover: Historical Contingency and Human Niche Construction Shape the Caribbean's Anthropocene Biota." *Proceedings of the Royal Society B* 287 (2020). http://dx.doi.org/10.1098/rspb.2020.0447.

Kennedy, Lisa M., Sally P. Horn, and Kenneth H. Orvis. "A 4000-Year Record of Fire and Forest History from Valle de Bao, Cordillero Central, Dominican Republic." *Palaeogeography, Palaeoclimatology, Palaeoecology* 231 (2006): 279–90.

Keuthe, Allan J. "Havana in the Eighteenth Century." In Knight and Liss, eds., *Atlantic Port Cities*: 13–39.

Kevan, Keith McE. "Mid-Eighteenth-Century Entomology and Helminthology in the West Indies: Dr. James Grainger." *Journal of the Society for the Bibliography of Natural History* 8, no. 3 (1977): 193–222.

Kilbourne, K. H., T. M. Quinn, R. Webb, T. Guilderson, J. Nyberg, and A. Winter. "Paleoclimate Proxy Perspective on Caribbean Climate since the Year 1751: Evidence of Cooler Temperatures and Multidecadal Variability." *Paleoceanography* 23 (2008): 1–14.

Killingray, David. "The Influenza Pandemic of 1918–1919 in the British Caribbean." *Social History of Medicine* 7 (1994): 59–87.

Kimber, Clarissa. *Martinique Revisited: The Changing Plant Geographies of a West Indian Island.* College Station: Texas A&M University Press, 1988.

Kimura, Birgitta K., et al. "Origins of Pre-Columbian Guinea Pigs from Caribbean Archaeological Sites." *Journal of Archaeological Science Reports* 5 (2016): 442–52.

Kincaid, Jamaica. *A Small Place.* New York: Farrar, Straus, and Giroux, 1988.

Kiple, Kenneth, ed. *The Cambridge World History of Human Disease.* New York: Cambridge University Press, 1993.

Kiple, Kenneth. *The Caribbean Slave: A Biological History.* Cambridge: Cambridge University Press, 1984.

Kiple, Kenneth. "Cholera and Race in the Caribbean." *Journal of Latin American Studies* 17 (1985): 157–77.

Kiple, Kenneth, and Brian T. Higgins. "Mortality Caused by Dehydration during the Middle Passage." *Social Science History* 13 (1989): 421–37.

Kiple, K. F., and K. C. Ornelas. "After the Encounter: Disease and Demography in the Lesser Antilles." In *The Lesser Antilles in the Age of European Expansion,* edited by Robert Paquette and Stanley Engerman. Gainesville: University of Florida Press, 1996: 51–67.

Kiple, Kenneth F., and Kriemhild Coneè Ornelas. "Race, War and Tropical Medicine in the Eighteenth-Century Caribbean." In Arnold, ed., *Warm Climates and Western Medicine*: 65–79.

Klaufus, C., and R. Jaffe. "Latin American and Caribbean Urban Development." *European Review of Latin American and Caribbean Studies / Revista Europea de Estudios Latinoamericanos y del Caribe* 100 (2015): 63–72.

Klein, Herbert S. "The First Americans: The Current Debate." *Journal of Interdisciplinary History* 46, no. 4 (2016): 543–61.

Klingberg, Frank. *Codrington Chronicle: An Experiment in Anglican Altruism on a Barbados Plantation, 1710–1834.* Berkeley: University of California Press, 1949.

Klingelhofer, Eric, ed. *First Forts: Essays on the Archaeology of Proto-colonial Fortifications.* Boston: Brill, 2010.

Klooster, Wim. "Contraband Trade by Curacao's Jews with Countries of Idolatry, 1660–1800." *Studia Rosenthaliana* 31 (1997): 58–73.

Klooster, Wim, and Gert Oostindie. *Realm Between Empires: The Second Dutch Atlantic, 1680–1815.* Ithaca, NY: Cornell University Press, 2018.

Knight, Franklin. *The Caribbean: The Genesis of a Fragmented Nationalism.* 2nd ed. New York: Oxford University Press, 1990.

Knight, Franklin W., and Peggy K. Liss, eds. *Atlantic Port Cities: Economy, Culture, and Society in the Atlantic World, 1650–1850.* Knoxville: University of Tennessee Press, 1991.

Knott, Sarah. *Sensibility and the American Revolution.* Chapel Hill: University of North Carolina Press, 2009.

Knutson, Thomas R., et al. "Climate Change Is Probably Increasing the Intensity of Tropical Cyclones." *ScienceBrief* (March 2021).

Knutson, Thomas R., et al. "Tropical Cyclones and Climate Change." *Nature Geoscience* 3 (2010): 157–63.

Koch, Alexander, et al. "Earth Systems Impacts of the European Arrival and Great Dying in the Americas after 1492." *Quaternary Science Reviews* 207 (2019): 13–36.

Koeman, C., et al. *Links with the Past: The History of Cartography of Suriname 1500–1971.* Amsterdam: Theatrum Orbis Terrarum, 1973.

Kopperman, Paul E. "The British Army in North America and the West Indies, 1755/83: A Medical Perspective." In *British Military and Naval Medicine, 1600–1830,* edited by Geoffrey L. Hudson. Amsterdam: Rodopi, 2007: 51–86.

Krichtal, Alexey. "Liverpool, Slavery, and Atlantic Cotton Frontier, 1763–1833." PhD diss., Johns Hopkins University, forthcoming.

Kris, Kay Dian. *Slavery, Sugar, and the Culture of Refinement: Picturing the British West Indies, 1700–1840.* New Haven, CT: Yale University Press, 2008.

Krise, Thomas, ed. *Caribbeana: An Anthology of English Literature of the West Indies, 1657–1777.* Chicago: University of Chicago Press, 1999.

Kumamoyo, J., et al. "Mystery of the Forbidden Fruit: Historical Epilogue on the Origin of the Grapefruit, *Citrus paradise* (Rutaceae)." *Economic Botany* 41 (1987): 97–107.

Kunitz, Stephen. "Diseases and Mortality in the Americas since 1700." In *The Cambridge World History of Human Disease,* edited by Kenneth Kiple. New York: Cambridge University Press, 1993: 328–33.

Kuppperman, Karen. "Fear of Hot Climates in the Anglo-American Cultural Experience." *William and Mary Quarterly,* 3rd. Ser., 41 (1984): 213–40.

Kurlansky, Mark. *A Continent of Islands: Searching for the Caribbean Destiny.* Cambridge, MA: Perseus Publishing, 1992.

Labelle, Kathryn. *Dispersed but Not Destroyed: A History of the Seventeenth-Century Wendat People.* Vancouver: University of British Columbia Press, 2014.

Lachiver, Marcel. *Les années de misère: La famine au temps du Grand Roi, 1680–1720.* Paris: Fayard, 1991.

Lack, David. "The Numbers and Species of Humming Birds in the West Indies." *Evolution* 27 (1973): 326–37.

Laffoon, Jason, and Bart de Vos. "Diverse Origins, Similar Diets: An Integrated Isotopic Perspective from Anse à la Gourde, Guadeloupe." In Hofman and van Diijvenbdoe, eds., *Communities in Contact:* 187–204.

Laffoon, Jason E., et al. "The Movement and Exchange of Dogs in the Prehistoric Caribbean: An Isotopic Investigation." *International Journal of Osteoarchaeology* 25 (2015): 454–65.

Laffoon, Jason E., et al. "A Multi-Isotope Investigation of Human and Dog Mobility and Diet in the Pre-colonial Antilles." *Environmental Archaeology* 24, no. 2 (2019): 132–48.

La Hausse de Lalouvière, Joseph. "Enslavement and Empire in the French Caribbean, 1793–1848" PhD diss., Harvard University, 2019.

Lalubie, Guillaume. "La perception des aléas naturels aux Petites Antilles par les Amérindiens Kalinago." Paper presented at the 24th Congress of the International Association of Caribbean Archaeologists, Martinique, July 25–29, 2011: 389–407.

Lalueza-Fox, C., et al. "MtDNA from Extinct Tainos and the Peopling of the Caribbean." *Annals of Human Genetics* 65 (2001): 137–51. doi:10.1046/j.1469-1809.2001.6520137.x.

Laluela-Fox, C., et al. "Mitochondrial DNA from Pre-Columbian Ciboneys from Cuba and the Prehistoric Colonization of the Caribbean." *American Journal of Physical Anthropology* 121 (2003): 97–108. doi:10.1002/ajpa.10236.

Lamb, Jonathan. *Scurvy: The Disease of Discovery.* Princeton, NJ: Princeton University Press, 2016.

Lambert, David. "Master-Horse-Slave: Mobility, Race and Power in the British West Indies, c.1780–1838." *Slavery & Abolition* 36 (2015): 618–41.

Lambert, David. "'[A] Mere Cloak for their Proud Contempt and Antipathy towards the African Race': Imagining Britain's West India Regiments in the Caribbean, 1795–1838." *Journal of Imperial and Commonwealth History* 46, no. 4 (2018): 627–50.

Lambert, David. "Runaways and Strays: Rethinking (Non)human Agency in Caribbean Slave Societies." In *Historical Animal Geographies,* edited by Sharon Wilcox and Stephanie Rutherford. Abingdon: Routledge, 2018: 185–98.

Lambert, David. *White Creole Culture, Politics and Identity during the Age of Abolition.* Cambridge: Cambridge University Press, 2005.

Lander, James F. "A Brief History of Tsunamis in the Caribbean Sea." *Science of Tsunami Hazards, the International Journal of the Tsunami Society* 20, no. 2 (2002): 57–94.

Landers, Jane. "The African Landscape of Seventeenth-Century Cartagena de Indias and Its Hinterlands." In Cañizares-Esguerra, Childs, and Sidbury, eds., *The Black Urban Atlantic:* 147–62.

Landers, John. *Death and the Metropolis: Studies in the Demographic History of London, 1670–1830.* Cambridge: Cambridge University Press, 1993.

Lane, Chad, Sally Horn, and Matthew Kerr. "Beyond the Mayan Lowlands: Impacts of the Terminal Classic Drought in the Caribbean Antilles." *Quaternary Science Reviews* 86 (2014): 89–98.

La Rosa Corzo, Gabino. *Runaway Slave Settlements in Cuba: Resistance and Repression.* Translated by Mary Todd. Chapel Hill: University of North Carolina Press, 2003 [orig. pub. 1988].

Larsen, Clark Spencer. "In the Wake of Columbus: Native Population Biology in the Postcontact Americas." *Yearbook of Physical Anthropology* 37 (1994): 109–54.

Leech, Roger H. "Impermanent Architecture in the English Colonies of the Eastern Caribbean: New Contexts for Innovation in the Early Modern Atlantic World." In *Building Environments: Perspectives in Vernacular Architecture 10,* edited by Kenneth Breisch and Alison Hoagland. Knoxville: University of Tennessee Press, 2006: 153–68.

Leech, Roger. "'Within Musquett Shott of Black Rock'—Johnson's Fort and the Early Defenses of Nevis, West Indies." In Klingelhofer, ed., *First Forts:* 129–40.

Leech, Roger, and Pamela Leech, eds., *The Colonial Landscape of the British Caribbean.* Woodbridge, UK: Boydell Press, 2021.

Lefebvre, Lynn W., et al. "Status and Biogeography of the West Indian Manatee." In Woods and Sergile, eds., *Biogeography of the West Indies:* 425–74.

LeFebvre, Michelle, and Susan deFrance. "Guinea Pigs in the Pre-Columbian West Indies." *Journal of Island and Coastal Archaeology* 9, no. 1 (2014): 16–44.

LeFebvre, Michelle J., and Susan D. deFrance. "Pre-Columbian Animal Management and Manipulation: A Caribbean Island Perspective." In Reid, ed., *The Archaeology of Caribbean and Circum-Caribbean Farmers:* 149–70.

LeFebvre, Michelle J., et al. "Bahamian hutia (*Geocapromys ingrahami*) in the Lucayan Realm: Pre-Columbian Exploitation and Translocation." *Environmental Archaeology* 24, no. 2 (2019): 115–31.

Lenik, Stephan. "Carib as a Colonial Category: Comparing Ethnohistorical and Archaeological Evidence from Dominica, West Indies." *Ethnohistory* 59, no. 1 (2012): 79–107.

LeRoy y Cassa, Jorge. *Estudios sobre la mortalidad de la Habana durante el siglo XIX.* Havana: Lloredo, 1913.

Leti, Geneviève. *Santé et société esclavagiste à la Martinique (1802–1848).* Paris: L'Harmattan, 1998.

Liebherr, J. K., ed. *Zoogeography of Caribbean Insects.* New York: NCROL, 1988.

Lim, Burton K., et al. "Phylogeography of Dominican Republic Bats and Implications for Systematic Relationships in the Neotropics." *Journal of Mammalogy* 98, no. 4 (2017): 986–93.

Lindo, John, Emilia Huerta-Sánchez, Shigeki Nakagome, et al. "A Time Transect of Exomes from a Native American Population before and after European Contact." *Nature Communications* (November 15, 2016). DOI: 10.1038/ncomms13175.

Lindsay, Jan, "Kick 'Em Jenny." In Gillespie and Clague, eds., *Encyclopedia of Islands*: 510–12.

Lindsay, Jan M., Richard E. A. Robertson, John B. Shepherd, and Shahiba Ali, eds. *Volcanic Hazard Atlas of the Lesser Antilles*. Trinidad and Tobago: Seismic Research Centre, 2005.

Lipschutz, Alejandro. "La despoblación de las Indias después de la Conquista." *América indígena* 26 (1966): 229–47.

Livi-Bacci, Massimo. *Conquest: The Destruction of the American Indios*. Cambridge, UK: Polity, 2008.

Lockley, Tim. *Military Medicine and the Making of Race: Lie and Death in the West India Regiments, 1795–1874*. Cambridge: Cambridge University Press, 2020.

Lokke, Carl. *France and the Colonial Question: A Study of Contemporary French Opinion, 1763–1801*. New York: Columbia University Press, 1932.

Lopez-Denis, Adrien. "Disease and Society in Colonial Cuba, 1790–1840." PhD diss., UCLA, 2007.

López-Marrero, Tania, and Ben Wisner. "Not in the Same Boat: Disasters and Differential Vulnerability in the Insular Caribbean." *Caribbean Studies* 40 (December 2012): 131.

López Sánchez, José. *Cuba: medicina y civilización, siglos XVII y XVIII*. Havana: Editorial Científico y Técnica, 1997.

Lord, E., et al. "Complete Mitogenomes of Ancient Caribbean Guinea Pigs (Cavia porcellus)." *Journal of Archaeological Science* 17 (2018): 678–88.

Losos, Jonathan B. *Lizards in an Evolutionary Tree: Ecology and Adaptive Radiation of Anoles*. Berkeley: University of California Press, 2009.

Losos, Jonathan B., and Robert E. Ricklefs, eds. *The Theory of Island Biogeography Revisited*. Princeton, NJ: Princeton University Press, 2010.

Lösch, S., et al. "Evidence for Tuberculosis in 18th/19th century Slaves in Anse Sainte-Marguerite (Guadeloupe—French Western Indies)." *Tuberculosis* 95, suppl. 1 (2015): 65–68.

Lovell, W. George. "Disease and Depopulation in Early Colonial Guatemala." In *Secret Judgments of God: Old World Disease in Colonial Spanish America*, edited by Noble David Cook and W. George Lovell. Norman: University of Oklahoma Press, 1991: 49–83.

Lowe, Henry, et al. *Poisonous Plants of Jamaica*. Kingston, Jamaica: Pelican, 2002.

Lowenthal, David. "The Range and Variation of Caribbean Societies." *Social and Cultural Pluralism in the Caribbean: Annals of the New York Academy of Sciences*, edited by Vera Rubin, 83 (1960): 786–95.

Lowenthal, David. *West Indian Societies*. London: Oxford University Press, 1972.

Lyons, S. Kathleen, Joshua H. Miller, Danielle Fraser, Felisa A. Smith, Alison Boyer, Emily Lindsey, and Alexis M. Mychajliw. "The Changing Role of Mammal Life Histories in Late Quaternary Extinction Vulnerability on Continents and Islands." *Biology Letters* 12 (2016). https://doi.org/10.1098/rsbl.2016.0342.

MacArthur, Robert H., and Edward O. Wilson. *The Theory of Island Biogeography*. Princeton, NJ: Princeton University Press, 1967.

Macdonald, R., C. J. Hawkesworth, and E. Heath. "The Lesser Antilles Volcanic Chain: A Study in Arc Magnetism." *Earth-Science Reviews* 49 (2000): 1–76.

Machling, Tessa. *The Fortifications of Nevis, West Indies, from the Seventeenth Century to the Present Day*. British Archaeological Reports 2349 (2012).

Mack, John. *The Sea: A Cultural History*. London: Reaktion Books, 2011.

MacLeod, Murdo. *Spanish Central America: A Socio-economic History, 1520–1720*. Berkeley: University of California Press, 1973.

MacPhee, Ross, ed. *Extinctions in Near Time: Causes, Contexts, and Consequences*. Berlin: Springer, 2013.

Madley, Benjamin. "The Third Vector: Pacific Pathogens, Colonial Disease Ecologies, and Native America Epidemics North of Mexico." In *Migrant Ecologies*, edited by Edward Melillo and Ryan Jones. Honolulu: University of Hawaii Press, forthcoming.

Mair, Lucille M. *A Historical Study of Women in Jamaica, 1655–1834*. Kingston, Jamaica: University of the West Indies Press, 2006.

Malaizé, B., et al. "September Hurricanes and Climate in the Caribbean during the Past 3700 Years B.P." *The Holocene* 216 (2011): 911–24.

Malmgren, Björn, Amos Winter, and Deliang Chen. "El Niño-Southern Oscillation and North Atlantic Oscillation Control of Climate in Puerto Rico." *Journal of Climate* 11 (1998): 2713–17.

Manaker, D. M., et al. "Interseismic Plate Coupling and Strain Partitioning in the Northeastern Caribbean," *Geophysical Journal International* 174 (2008): 889–903.

Mancall, Peter. *Nature and Culture in the Early Modern Atlantic.* Philadelphia: University of Pennsylvania Press, 2018.

Mandelblatt, Bertie. "Feeding the French Atlantic: Colonial Food Provisioning Networks in the Franco-Caribbean during the Ancien Régime. PhD diss., University of London, 2008.

Mandelblatt, Bertie. "How Feeding the Slaves Shaped the French Atlantic: Mercantilism and the Crisis of Food Provisioning in the Franco-Caribbean during the Seventeenth and Eighteenth Centuries." In *The Political Economy of Empire in the Early Modern World*, edited by Sophus Reinert and Pernille Røge. London: Palgrave Macmillan, 2013: 192–220.

Mandelblatt, Bertie. "'A Land Where Hunger Is in Gold and Famine Is in Opulence': Plantation Slavery, Island Ecology, and the Fear of Famine in the French Caribbean." In *Fear and the Shaping of Early American Societies*, edited by Lauric Henneton and Louis Roper. Leiden: Brill, 2016: 243–64.

Mandelblatt, Bertie. "'On the Excellence of the Vegetable Diet': Scurvy, Antoine Poissonnier-Desperrières's New Naval Diet and French Colonial Science in the Atlantic World." *Early American Studies* 19, no. 2 (Spring 2021): 322–59.

Mandelblatt, Bertie. "A Transatlantic Commodity: Irish Salt Beef in the French Atlantic World." *History Workshop Journal* 63 (2007): 18–47.

Mann, Charles. *1491: New Revelations of the Americas before Columbus.* New York: Vintage, 2006.

Mann, Michael E., Jonathan D. Woodruff, Jeffrey P. Donnelly, and Zhihua Zhang. "Atlantic Hurricanes and Climate over the Past 1,500 Years." *Nature* 460 (August 13, 2009): 880–83.

Manning, David. "Reformation and the Wickedness of Port Royal, Jamaica." In *Puritans and Catholics in the Trans-Atlantic World, 1600–1850*, edited by Crawford Gribben and Scott Spurlock. New York: Palgrave Macmillan, 2016: 131–63.

Manning, Patrick, and Daniel Rood, eds. *Global Scientific Practice in an Age of Revolutions, 1750–1850.* Pittsburgh: University of Pittsburgh Press, 2016.

Mapp, Paul W. *The Elusive West and the Contest for Empire, 1713–1763.* Chapel Hill: University of North Carolina Press, 2011.

Marciniak, Stephanie, and H. N. Poinar. "Ancient Pathogens through Human History: A Paleogenomic Perspective." In *Paleogenomics: Population Genetics*, edited by Charlotte Lindqvist and Om P. Rajora. Dordrecht: Springer, 2018: 115–38.

Marquez Morfin, Lourdes, Robert McCaa, Rebecca Storey, and Andrés del Angel. "Health and Nutrition in Prehispanic Mesoamerica." In *The Backbone of History: Health and Nutrition in the Western Hemisphere*, edited by Richard H. Steckel and Jerome C. Rose. New York: Cambridge University Press, 2002: 307–38.

Marshall, Woodville K. "Provision Ground and Plantation Labor in Four Windward Islands: Competition for Resources during Slavery." In Berlin and Morgan, eds., *Cultivation and Culture*: 203–20.

Marte, Roberto, ed. *Santo Domingo en los manuscritos de Juan Bautista Muñoz.* Santo Domingo: Fundación García Arévalo, 1981.

Martin, Debra L., and Anna J. Osterholtz. *Bodies and Lives in Ancient America: Health before Columbus.* London and New York: Routledge, 2016.

Martínez-Fernández, Luis. *Key to the New World: A History of Early Colonial Cuba.* Gainesville: University of Florida Press, 2018.

Martín-Vide, Javier, and Mariano Barriendos Vallvé. "The Use of Rogation Ceremony Records in Climatic Reconstruction." *Climatic Change* 30 (1995): 201–21.

Martis, A., G. J. van Oldenborgh, and G. Burgers. "Predicting Rainfall in the Dutch Caribbean—More than El Niño?" *International Journal of Climatology* 22 (2002): 1219–34.

Mason, Keith. "The Absentee Planter and the Key Slave: Privilege, Patriarchalism, and Exploitation in the Early Eighteenth-Century Caribbean." *William and Mary Quarterly* 70 (January 2013): 79–102.

Mason, Keith. "The World an Absentee Planters and His Slaves Made: Sir William Stapleton and His Nevis Sugar Estate, 1722–1740." *Bulletin of the John Rylands University Library* 75 (1993): 103–31.

Matthews, Gelien. *Caribbean Slave Revolts and the British Abolition Movement*. Baton Rouge: Louisiana State University Press, 2006.

Mayer, G. C., and R. M. Chipley. "Turnover in the Avifauna of Guana Island, British Virgin Islands." *Journal of Animal Ecology* 61 (1992): 561–66.

Mayer, S. V., R. B. Tesh, and N. Vasilakis. "The Emergence of Arthropod-borne Viral Diseases: A Global Perspective on Dengue, Chikungunya and Zika Fevers." *Acta Tropica* 166 (2017): 155–63.

McCaa, Robert. "Child Marriage and Complex Families among the Nahuas of Ancient Mexico." *Latin American Population History Bulletin* 26 (1994): 2–11.

McCaa, Robert. "Marriageways in Mexico and Spain, 1500–1900." *Continuity and Change* 9 (1994): 11–43.

McCandless, Peter. *Slavery, Disease, and Suffering in the Southern Lowcountry*. New York: Cambridge University Press, 2011.

McCann, William, Lawrence Feldman, and Maribel McCann. "Catalog of Felt Earthquakes for Puerto Rico and Neighboring Islands, 1493–1899, with Additional Information for some 20th Century Earthquakes." *Revista Geofísica* 62 (2010): 141–90.

McClellan, James E., III. *Colonialism and Science: Saint Domingue in the Old Regime*. Baltimore: Johns Hopkins University Press, 1992.

McClellan, James E., III. and François Regourd, *The Colonial Machine: French Science and Overseas Expansion in the Old Regime*. Turnhout, Belgium: Brepols Publishing, 2011.

McClenachan, Loren, and Andrew B. Cooper. "Extinction Rate, Historical Population Structure and Ecological Role of the Caribbean Monk Seal." *Proceedings of the Royal Society, Biological Sciences* 275 (2008): 1351–58.

McClenachan, Loren, Marah Hardt, Jeremy Jackson, and Richard Cooke. "Mounting Evidence for Historical Overfishing and Long-Term Degradation of Caribbean Marine Ecosystems: Comment on Julio Baisre's 'Setting a Baseline for Caribbean Fisheries.'" *Journal of Island and Coastal Archaeology* 5, no.1 (January 2010): 165–69.

McClenachan, Loren, Jeremy B. C. Jackson, and Marah J. H. Newman. "Conservation Implications of Historic Sea Turtle Nesting Beach Loss." *Frontiers in Ecology and the Environment* 4 (2006): 290–96.

McCook, Stuart. "Greater Caribbean: Mexico, Central America, and the West Indies." In *Modern Science in National, Transnational, and Global Context*, edited by Hugh Richard Slotten, Ronald L. Numbers, and David N. Livingstone. Cambridge: Cambridge University Press, 2020, 8: 782–98.

McCook, Stuart. "The Neo-Columbian Exchange: The Second Conquest of the Greater Caribbean, 1720–1930." *Latin American Research Review* 46 (2011): 11–31.

McCook, Stuart. *States of Nature: Science, Agriculture, and Environment in the Spanish Caribbean, 1760–1940*. Austin: University of Texas Press, 2002.

McCoy, Alfred W., and Francisco Scarano, eds. *Colonial Crucible: Empire in the Making of the Modern American State*. Madison: University of Wisconsin Press, 2009.

McGregor, Duncan. "Contemporary Caribbean Ecologies: The Weight of History." In *The Caribbean*, edited by Stephan Palmié and Francisco Scarano. Chicago: University of Chicago Press, 2011: 39–51.

McNab, Brian K. "Functional Adaptation to Island Life in the West Indies." In Woods and Sergile, eds., *Biogeography of the West Indies*: 55–62.

McNeill, J. R. *Atlantic Empires of France and Spain: Louisbourg and Havana, 1700–1763*. Chapel Hill: University of North Carolina Press, 1985.

McNeill, J. R. "The Ecological Atlantic." In Canny and Morgan, eds., *Oxford Handbook of the Atlantic World*: 289–304.

McNeill, John R. "The Ecological Basis of Warfare in the Caribbean, 1700–1804." In *Adapting to Conditions: War and Society in the Eighteenth Century*, edited by Maarten Ultee. Tuscaloosa: University of Alabama Press, 1986: 26–42.

McNeill, J. R. *Mosquito Empires. Ecology and War in the Greater Caribbean, 1620–1914*. Cambridge: Cambridge University Press, 2010.

McNeill, J. R. "Of Rats and Men: A Synoptic Environmental History of the Island Pacific." *Journal of World History* 5 (1994): 299–349.

McNeill, J. R., and Peter Engelke. *The Great Acceleration: A Global Environmental History of the Anthropocene since 1945*. Cambridge, MA: Harvard University Press, 2016.

McNeill, William. *The Global Condition: Conquerors, Catastrophes, and Community*. Princeton, NJ: Princeton University Press, 1992.

McWilliams, James. *American Pests: The Losing War on Insects from Colonial Times to DDT*. New York: Columbia University Press, 2008.

Mears, Natalie, et al. *National Prayers: Special Worship since the Reformation: Volume 1: Special Prayers, Fasts and Thanksgivings in the British Isles, 1533–1688*. Woodbridge, UK: The Boydell Press, 2013.

Meinhardt, Maren. *Alexander von Humboldt: How the Most Famous Scientist of the Romantic Age Found the Soul of Nature*. Katonah, NY: BlueBridge, 2019.

Meiri, Shai, and Pasquale Raia. "Dwarfism." In Gillespie and Clague, eds., *Encyclopedia of Islands*: 235–39.

Mena, Cesar A., and Armando F. Cobelo. *Historia de la medicina en Cuba*. 2 vols. Miami: Editorial Universal, 1992.

Mena, Miguel D. *Iglesia, espacio, y poder: Santo Domingo (1498–1521), experiencia fundacional del nuevo mundo*. Santo Domingo: Archivo General de la Nación, 2007.

Mendenhall, Emily. "Syndemics: A New Path for Global Health Research." *The Lancet* 389 (March 4, 2017): 889–91.

Mendisco, F., et al. "Where Are the Caribs? Ancient DNA from Ceramic Period Human Remains in the Lesser Antilles." *Philosophical Transactions of the Royal Society B*, 370 (2015): http://dx.doi.org/10.1098/rstb.2013.0388.

Meniketti, Marco. *Sugar Cane Capitalism and Environmental Transformation: An Archaelogy of Colonial Nevis, West Indies*. Tuscaloosa: University of Alabama Press, 2015.

Mickleburgh, Hayley. "Dental Wear and Pathology in the Precolonial Caribbean: Evidence for Dietary Change in the Ceramic Age. *International Journal of Osteoarchaeology* 26 (2014): 290–302.

Mickleburgh, Hayley. "Reading the Dental Record: A Dental Anthropological Approach to Foodways, Health and Disease, and Crafting in the pre-Columbian Caribbean." PhD diss., University of Leiden, 2013.

Millás, José Carlos. *Hurricanes of the Caribbean and Adjacent Regions, 1492–1800*. Ann Arbor, MI: Academy of the Arts and Sciences of the Americas, 1968.

Miller, Jacqueline Y., and Lee D. Miller. "The Biogeography of the West Indian Butterflies (Lepidoptera): An Application of a Vicariancce/Dispersalist Model." In Woods and Sergile, eds., *Biogeography of the West Indies*: 127–55.

Miller, Peter N., ed. *The Sea: Historiography and Thalassography*. Ann Arbor: University of Michigan Press, 2013.

Miller, Shawn William. *An Environmental History of Latin America*. New York: Cambridge University Press, 2007.

Miller, William Shaw. "Abraham Chovet: An Early Teacher of Anatomy in Philadelphia." *Anatomical Record* 5 (1911): 147–71, and extended in *Annals of Medical History* 8 (1926): 375–93.

Milne, G. A., and M. C. Peros. "Data-Model Comparison of Holocene Sea-Level Change in the Circum-Caribbean Region." *Global and Planetary Change* 107 (2013): 119–31.

Miloslavich, Patricia, et al. "Marine Biodiversity in the Caribbean: Regional Estimates and Distribution Patterns." *PloS One* 5, no. 8 (2010): e11916, 1–25.

Milroy, Gavin. "Operation and Results of Quarantine in British Ports since the Beginning of the Present Century." *Association Medical Journal* 1, no. 29 (July 22, 1853): 635–39.

Mina, Michael. "Measles, Immune Suppression and Vaccination: Direct and Indirect Nonspecific Vaccine Benefits." *Journal of Infection* 74 (2017): S10–S17.

Mina, Michael, et al. "Long-Term Measles-Induced Immunomodulation Increases Overall Childhood Infectious Disease Mortality." *Science* 348 (May 8, 2015): 694–99.

Mina, Michael, et al. "Measles Virus Infection Diminishes Preexisting Antibodies that Offer Protection from Other Pathogens." *Science* 366 (2019): 599–606.

Mintz, Sidney W. "The Caribbean as a Sociocultural Area," *Cahiers d'Histoire Mondiale* 9 (1966): 916–41. Reprinted in Michael M. Horowitz, ed., *Peoples and Cultures of the Caribbean: An Anthropological Reader*. Garden City, NY: American Museum of Natural History, 1971: 17–46.

Mintz, Sidney W. "The Caribbean Region." In *Slavery, Colonialism, and Racism*, edited by Sidney Mintz. New York: W. W. Norton, 1974: 45–72.

Mintz, Sidney W. *Caribbean Transformations*. Chicago: Aldine, 1974.

Mintz, Sidney W. *Sweetness and Power: The Place of Sugar in Modern History*. New York: Penguin, 1985.

Mintz, Sidney W., and Sally Price, eds. *Caribbean Contours*. Baltimore: Johns Hopkins University Press, 1985.

Mira Caballos, Esteban. *La Española, epicentro del Caribe en el siglo XVI*. Santo Domingo: Academia Dominica de la Historia, 2010.

Mira Caballos, Esteban. *El indio antillano: repartimiento, encomienda y esclavitud (1492–1542)*. Seville: Muñoz Moya, 1997.

Mira Caballos, Esteban. "La medicina indígena en la Española y su commercialización (1492–1550)." *Asclepio: Revista de Historia de la Medicina y de la Ciencia* 49 (1997): 185–98.

Mishra, Ashok, and Vijay Singh. "A Review of Drought Concepts." *Journal of Hydrology* 391 (2010): 202–16.

Mitchell, Piers D. "Retrospective Diagnosis and the Use of Historical Texts for Investigating Disease in the Past." *International Journal of Paleopathology* 1 (2011): 81–88.

Mock, Cary J., Michael Chenoweth, Isabel Altamarino, Matthew D. Rodgers, and Ricardo Garciá-Herrera. "The Great Louisiana Hurricane of August 1812." *Bulletin of the American Meteorological Society* 91 (December 2010): 1653–63.

Mohan, Preeya, and Eric Strobl. "The Economic Impact of Hurricanes in History: Evidence from Sugar Exports in the Caribbean from 1700–1960." *Weather, Climate, and Society* 5 (January 2013): 5–13.

Mokyr, Joel, and Cormac Ó Gráda. "Famine Disease and Famine Mortality: Lessons from the Irish Experience, 1845–50." In *Famine Demography: Perspectives in from the Past and Present*, edited by Tim Dyson and Cormac Ó Gráda. Oxford: Oxford University Press, 2002: 19–43.

Molesky, Mark. *This Gulf of Fire: The Great Lisbon Earthquake, or Apocalypse in the Age of Science and Reason*. New York: Vintage, 2015.

Monath, T. P., and Pedro F. C. Vasconcelos. "Yellow Fever." *Journal of Clinical Virology* 64 (2015): 160–73.

Monteith, Kathleen E. A. *Plantation Coffee in Jamaica, 1790–1848*. Mona: University Press of the West Indies, 2019.

Montinaro, Francisco, et al. "Unravelling the Hidden Ancestry of American Admixed Populations." *Nature Communications* 6, no. 6596 (2015): https://www.nature.com/articles/ncomms7596.

Moore, Jason. "Madeira, Sugar, and the Conquest of Nature in the 'First Sixteenth Century, Part II." *Review* 33 (2010): 1–24.

Moratelli, Ricardo, et al. "Caribbean Myotis (Chiroptera, Vespertilionidae), with description of a new species from Trinidad and Tobago." *Journal of Mammalogy* 98, no. 4 (2017): 994–1008.

Moreno-Estrada, A., et al. "Reconstructing the Population Genetic History of the Caribbean." *PLoS Genetics* 9 (2013). doi:10.1371/journal.pgen.1003925.

Moreno Fraginals, Manuel. "Africa in Cuba: A Quantitative Analysis of the African Population of the Island of Cuba." *Annals of the New York Academy of Sciences* 292 (1977): 187–201.

Moreno Fraginals, Manuel. *El ingenio: Complejo económico social cubano del azúcar*. 3 vols. Havana: Comisión Nacional Cubana de la UNESCO, 1978.

Morens, David. "Epidemic Anthrax in the Eighteenth Century, the Americas." *Emerging Infectious Diseases* 8 (October 2002): 1160–62.

Morgan, Gary S. "Patterns of Extinction in West Indian Bats." In Woods and Sergile, eds., *Biogeography of West Indies*: 369–407.

Morgan, Gary S., et al. "The Cuban Crocodile (*Crocodylus rhombifer*) from Late Quaternary Underwater Cave Deposits in the Dominican Republic." *American Museum Novitates* 3916 (December 2018): 1–56.

Morgan, Philip. "Caribbean Slavery." In *The Rise and Demise of Slavery and the Slave Trade in the Atlantic World*, edited by Philip Misevich and Kristin Mann. Rochester: University of Rochester Press, 2016: 64–99.

Morgan, Philip. "Slavery in the British Caribbean." In *The Cambridge World History of Slavery*, vol. 3, *AD 1420–AD 1804*, edited by David Eltis and Stanley Engerman. Cambridge: Cambridge University Press, 2011: 378–406.

Morgan, Philip D. "Slaves and Livestock in Eighteenth-Century Jamaica: Vineyard Pen, 1750–175. *William and Mary Quarterly*, 3rd Ser., 52 (1995): 47–76.

Morison, Samuel Eliot. *Admiral of the Ocean Sea*. Boston: Little, Brown, 1942.

Morsink, Joost. "Catalytic Environments." *Environmental Archaeology* 24, no. 2 (2019): 149–60.

Morsink, Joost. "Exchange as a Social Contract: A Perspective from the Microscale." In Keegan et al., eds., *Oxford Handbook of Caribbean Archaeology*: 312–28.

Morsink, Joost. "The Power of Salt: A Holistic Approach to Salt in the Prehistoric Circum-Caribbean Region." PhD diss., University of Florida, 2012.

Moscoso, Francisco. *El gran huracán. Las deudas y la resistencia en Puerto Rico, 1530*. San Juan, PR: Gaviota, 2013.

Motilal, Lambert, and Thayil Sreenivasan. "Revisiting 1727: Crop Failure Leads to the Birth of Trinitario Cacao." *Journal of Crop Improvement* 26 (2012): 599–626.

Mühlemann, Barbara, et al. "Diverse Variola Virus (Smallpox) Strains Were Widespread in Northern Europe in the Viking Age." *Science* 369 (July 24, 2020): DOI: 10.1126/science. aaw8977.

Muhs, Daniel R., et al. "Geochemical Evidence for African Dust Inputs to Soils of Western Atlantic Islands: Barbados, the Bahamas, and Florida." *Journal of Geophysical Research* 112 (2007): 1–26.

Mukerji, Chandra. *Territorial Ambitions and the Gardens of Versailles*. Cambridge: Cambridge University Press, 1997.

Mulcahy, Matthew. "Environmental Threats and Imperial Celebrations. Days of Fasting and Thanksgiving in the British Caribbean, 1670–1780." Paper presented at "National Worship in International Perspective" conference, Durham University, April 2010.

Mulcahy, Matthew. *Hurricanes and Society in the British Greater Caribbean, 1624–1783*. Baltimore: Johns Hopkins University Press, 2006.

Mulcahy, Matthew. "'Miserably Scorched': Drought in the Plantation Colonies of the British Greater Caribbean." In *Atlantic Environments and the American South*, edited by Thomas Blake Earle and D. Andrew Johnson. Athens: University of Georgia Press, 2020: 65–89.

Mulcahy, Matthew. "The Port-Royal Earthquake and the World of Wonders in Seventeenth-Century Jamaica." *Early American Studies* 6 (Fall 2008): 391–421.

Mulcahy, Matthew. "'That Fatall Spot': The Rise and Fall—and Rise and Fall Again—of Port Royal, Jamaica." In *Investing in the Early Modern Built Environment: Europeans, Asians, Settlers, and Indigenous Societies*, edited by Carole Shammas. Leiden: Brill, 2012: 191–218.

Mulcahy, Matthew. "Weathering the Storms: Hurricanes and Risk in the British Greater Caribbean." *Business History Review* 78 (Winter 2004): 635–53.

Mulcahy, Matthew, and Stuart Schwartz. "Nature's Battalions: Insects of Agricultural Pests in the Early Modern Caribbean." *William and Mary Quarterly* 75 (July 2018): 433–64.

Mulich, Jeppe. *In a Sea of Empires: Networks and Crossings in the Revolutionary Caribbean.* Cambridge: Cambridge University Press, 2020.

Muñoz-Sanz, Agustín. "La gripe de Cristóbal Colón: Hipótesis sobre una catástrofe ecológica." *Enfermedades Infecciosas y Microbiología Clínica* 24 (2006): 326–34.

Murphy, Kathleen S. "Collecting Slave Traders: James Petiver, Natural History, and the British Slave Trade." *William and Mary Quarterly*, 3rd Ser., 70, no. 4 (October 2013): 637–70.

Murphy, Kathleen S. "Translating the Vernacular: Indigenous and African Knowledge in the Eighteenth-Century British Atlantic." *Atlantic Studies* 8, no. 1 (March 2011): 29–48.

Murphy, Tessa. *The Creole Archipelago: Race and Colonization in the Southern Caribbean, c. 1660–1797.* Forthcoming.

Murphy, Tessa. "Kalinago Colonizers: Indigenous People and the Settlement of the Lesser Antilles." In Roper, ed., *The Torrid Zone:* 17–30.

Mustakeem, Sowande' M. *Slavery at Sea: Terror, Sex, and Sickness in the Middle Passage.* Urbana: University of Illinois Press, 2016.

Mycoo, Michelle. "Beyond 1.5°C: Vulnerabilities and Adaptation Strategies for Caribbean Small Island Developing States." *Regional Environmental Change* 18 (2017): 2341–53.

Myers, Kathleen Ann. *Fernández de Oviedo's Chronicle of America: A New History for a New World.* Translated by Nina M. Scott. Austin: University of Texas Press, 2007.

Nägele, Kathrin, et al. "Genomic Insight into the Early Peopling of the Caribbean." *Science* (June 4, 2020): 546–60.

Naipaul, V. S. *The Middle Passage: Impressions of Five Societies—British, French and Dutch—in the West Indies and South America.* Harmondsworth, UK: Penguin, 1969.

Naipaul, V. S. *The Overcrowded Barracoon.* New York: Alfred A. Knopf, 1973.

Napolitano, Matthew F., Robert J. DiNapoli, Jessica H. Stone, Maureece J. Levin, Nicholas P. Jew, Brian G. Lane, John T. O'Connor, and Scott M. Fitzpatrick. "Reevaluating Human Colonization of the Caribbean Using Chronometric Hygiene and Bayesian Modeling." *Science Advances* 5 (2019): DOI: 10.1126/sciadv.aar7806.

Nebenzahl, Kenneth. *Atlas of Columbus and The Great Discoveries.* Chicago: Rand McNally, 1990.

Neilson, G., R. M. W., Musson, and P. W. Burton. "The 'London Earthquake' of 1580." *Engineering Geology* 20 (1984): 113–41.

Nelson, Louis P. *Architecture and Empire in Jamaica.* New Haven, CT: Yale University Press, 2016.

Nelson, Louis P. "'Come Hell or High Water': Architectural Responses to Natural Disaster in the Early British Caribbean." In Leech and Leech, eds., *The Colonial Landscape:* 39–55.

Neri, Janice. *The Insect and the Image: Visualizing Nature in Early Modern Europe, 1500–1700.* Minneapolis: University of Minnesota Press, 2011.

Newfield, Timothy. "Human–Bovine Plagues in the Early Middle Ages." *Journal of Interdisciplinary History*, 46 (2015): 1–38.

Newson, Lee A., and Elizabeth S. Wing. *On Land and Sea: Native American Uses of Biological Resources in the West Indies.* Tuscaloosa: University of Alabama Press, 2004.

Newson, Linda. *Aboriginal and Spanish Colonial Trinidad: A Study in Cultural Contact.* London: Academic Press, 1976.

Newson, Linda. *Conquest and Pestilence in the Early Spanish Philippines.* Honolulu: University of Hawaii Press, 2009.

Newson, Linda. *The Cost of Conquest: Indian Decline in Honduras under Spanish Rule.* Boulder, CO: Westview Press, 1986.

Newson, Linda. "Demographic Catastrophe in Sixteenth-Century Honduras." In *Studies in Spanish American Population History*, edited by D. J. Robinson. Boulder, CO: Westview Press, 1981: 217–42.

Newson, Linda. "The Demographic Impact of Colonization." In *The Cambridge Economic History of Latin America*, edited by Victor Bulmer-Thomas, John Coatsworth, and Roberto Contés Conde. Cambridge: Cambridge University Press, 2006: 143–84.

Newson, Linda. "The Depopulation of Nicaragua in the Sixteenth Century." *Journal of Latin American Studies* 14 (1982): 253–86.

Newson, Linda. "Medical Practice in Early Colonial Spanish America: A Prospectus." *Bulletin of Latin American Research* 25 (2006): 367–39.

Nieves-Colón, M. A., et al. "Ancient DNA Reconstructs the Genetic Legacies of Pre-contact Puerto Rico Communities." *Molecular Biology and Evolution* 37 (2020): 611–26.

Norrgård, Stefan. "Practicing Historical Climatology in West Africa: A Climatic Periodisation, 1750–1800." *Climate Change* 129 (2015): 131–43.

Norton, Marcy. "The Chicken or the *Iegue*: Human-Animal Relationships and the Columbian Exchange." *American Historical Review* 120, no. 1 (February 2015): 28–60.

Norton, Marcy. "Going to the Birds: Animals as Things and Beings in Early Modernity." In *Early Modern Things: Objects and Their Histories, 1500–1800*, edited by Paula Findlen. New York: Routledge, 2013: 53–83.

Nott, Jonathan. "Paleotempestology: The Study of Prehistoric Tropical Cyclones—a Review and Implications for Hazard Assessment." *Environment International* 30, no. 3 (2004): 433–47.

Noymer, Andrew. "Population Decline in Post-Conquest America: The Role of Disease." *Population and Development Review* 37 (2011): 178–83.

Núñez, Solón. "La sanidad en Jamiaca y Puerto Rico." *Boletín de la Oficina Sanitaria Panamericana* 13 (1934): 908–17.

Nurse, Leonard, and Rawleston Moore. "Adaptation to Global Climate Change: An Urgent Requirement for Small Island Developing States." *Review of European Community and International Environmental Law* 14 (2005): 100–107.

Nurse, Leonard, and Graham Sem, et al. "Small Island States." In *TAR Climate Change 2001: Impacts, Adaptions, and Vulnerability: Third Assessment Report of the Intergovernmental Panel on Climate Change*. Edited by James J. McCarthy et al. Cambridge: Cambridge University Press, 2001: 843–75.

Nyberg, J. B., A. Malmgren, A. Winter, M. R. Jury, K. Halimdea Kilbourne, and T. M. Quinn. "Low Atlantic Hurricane Activity in the 1970s and 1980s Compared to the Past 270 Years." *Nature* 447 (June 7, 2007): 698–702.

Offen, Karl H. "Creating Mosquitia: Mapping Amerindian Spatial Practices in Eastern Central America, 1629–1779." *Journal of Historical Geography* 33, no. 2 (2007): 254–82.

Ogborn, Miles. *The Freedom of Speech: Talk and Slavery in the Anglo-Caribbean World*. Chicago: University of Chicago Press, 2019.

Ogborn, Miles. "Talking Plants: Botany and Speech in Eighteenth-Century Jamaica." *History of Science* 51 (2013): 251–82.

O'Gorman, Pamela. "Gilbert Songs." *Jamaican Journal* 22, No. 2 (May–July 1989): 2–10.

Olivarius, Kathryn. "Immunity, Capital, and Power in Antebellum New Orleans." *The American Historical Review* 124 (2019): 425–55.

Oliveira, Cristiane. "The Discourse of Sexual Excess as a Hallmark of Brazlianness: Revisiting Brazilian Social Thinking in the 1920s and 1930s." *História, Ciências, Saúde—Manguinhos* 21, no. 4 (2014): http://www.scielo.br/hcsm.

Oliver, Vere Langford. *Caribbeana: Being Miscellaneous Papers Relating to the History, Genealogy, Topography, and Antiquities of the British West Indies*. London, 1909–19.

Oliver, Vere Langford. *The History of Antigua*. London: Mitchell and Hughes, 1894.

Olmsted, J. W. "The Scientific Expedition of Jean Richer to Cayenne (1672–1673)." *Isis* 34 (1942): 117–28.

O'Loughlin, Karen Fay, and James F. Lander. *Caribbean Tsunamis: A 500-Year History from 1498–1998*. Dordrecht, Netherlands: Kluwer Academic Publishers, 2003.

Olsen, K. M., and B. A. Schaal. "Evidence on the Origin of Cassava: Phylogeography of *Manihot esculenta*." *Proceedings of the National Academy of Sciences of the United States of America* 96, no. 10 (1999): 5586–91.

O'Malley, Therese, and Amy R. W. Meyers. *The Art of Natural History: Illustrated Treatises and Botanical Paintings, 1400–1850*. Washington, DC: National Gallery of Art, 2010.

O'Neal, Michael E. "The Historical Context of Medical Practice in the British Virgin Islands." *Caribbean Perspectives* I (1991): 30–41.

Oostindie, Gert, and Alex van Stipriaan. "Slavery and Slave Cultures in a Hydraulic Society." In *Slave Cultures and the Cultures of Slavery*, edited by Stephan Palmié. Knoxville: University of Tennessee Press, 1995: 78–99.

Orgeix, Emilie d'. "French Military Engineers in the American Colonies (1635–1776)." In *Military Engineers and the Development of the Early Modern World*, edited by Bruce Lenman. Dundee, UK: Dundee University Press, 2013: 245–58.

Orr, Julie. *Scotland, Darien, and the Atlantic World, 1698–1700*. Edinburgh: Edinburgh University Press, 2018.

O'Rourke, Dennis, and Jennifer Raff. "The Human Genetic History of the Americas: The Final Frontier." *Current Biology* 20 (February 23, 2010): R202–R207. DOI: 10.1016/j.cub.2009.11.051.

Ortiz, Fernando. *El huracán. Su mitología y sus símbolos*. Mexico City: Fondo de Cultura Económica, 1947.

O'Shaughnessy, Andrew. *An Empire Divided: The American Revolution and the British Caribbean*. Philadelphia: University of Pennsylvania Press, 2000.

Ostapkowicz, Joanna. "'Made ... with Admirable Artistry': The Context, Manufacture and History of a Taíno Belt." *Antiquaries Journal* 93 (2013): 287–317.

Ostapkowicz, Joanna. "New Wealth from an Old World: Glass, Jet and Mirrors in the 16th Century Indigenous Caribbean." In *Gifts, Goods and Money: Comparing Currency and Circulation Systems in Past Societies*, edited by Dirk Brandherm et al. Oxford: Archeopress, 2018: 153–93.

Ostapkowicz, Joanna, and Lee Newsom. "'Gods Adorned with Embroiderer's Needle': The Materials, Making, and Meaning of a Taíno Cotton Reliquary." *Latin American Antiquity* 23 no. 3 (2012): 300–326.

Ostapkowicz, Joanna, et al. "Integrating the Old World into the New: an 'Idol from the West Indies.'" *Antiquity* 91, no. 359 (2017): 1314–29.

Ostapkowicz, Joanna, et al. "To Produce 'A Pleasing Effect': Taíno Shell and Stone Cibas and Spanish Cuentas in the Early Colonial Caribbean." *Beads* 30 (2018): 3–15.

Ottenwalder, Jose A. "Systematics and Biogeography of the West Indian Genus Solenodon." In Woods and Sergile, eds., *Biogeography of the West Indies*: 253–329.

Oudin-Bastide, Caroline. *L'effroi et la terreur: Esclavage, poison et sorcellerie aux Antilles*. Paris: La Découverte, Les Empêcheurs de tourner en rond, 2013.

Pagán-Jiménez, Jaime. "Human-Plant Dynamics in the Precolonial Antilles: A Synthetic Update." In Keegan et al., eds., *Oxford Handbook of Caribbean Archaeology*: 391–406.

Pagán-Jiménez, Jaime R., Reniel Rodríguez Ramos, and Corinne L. Hofman. "On the Way to the Islands: The Role of Domestic Plants in the Initial Peopling of the Antilles." In Hofman and Antczak, eds., *Early Settlers*: 89–106.

Pagán-Jiménez, Jaime R., et al. "Early Dispersals of Maize and Other Food Plants into the Southern Caribbean and Northeastern South America." *Quaternary Science Reviews* 123 (2015): 231–46.

Paravisini-Gebert, Lizabeth. "Extinctions: Chronicles of Vanishing Fauna in the Colonial and Postcolonial Caribbean." In *Oxford Handbook of Ecocriticism*, edited by Greg Garrard. New York: Oxford University Press, 2014: 341–57.

Pares, Richard. *A West-India Fortune*. London: Longmans, Green, and Co., 1950.

Parker, Geoffrey. *Global Crisis: War, Climate Change and Catastrophe in the Seventeenth Century*. New Haven, CT: Yale University Press, 2013.

Parrish, Susan Scott. *American Curiosity: Cultures of Natural History in the Colonial British Atlantic World*. Chapel Hill: University of North Carolina Press, 2006.

Parry, John H. "Plantation and Provision Ground: An Historical Sketch of the Introduction of Food Crops into Jamaica." *Revista de Historia de America* 39 (1955): 1–20.

Parry, John H. "Salt Fish and Ackee: An Historical Sketch of the Introduction of Food Crops into Jamaica." *Caribbean Quarterly* 8, no. 4 (1962): 30–36.

Parsons, James J. *The Green Turtle and Man.* Tallahassee: Florida State University Press, 1962.

Paton, Diana. *The Cultural Politics of Obeah: Religion, Colonialism and Modernity in the Caribbean World.* Cambridge: Cambridge University Press, 2015.

Paton, Diana. "Witchcraft, Poison, Law, and Atlantic Slavery," *William and Mary Quarterly*, 3rd Ser., 69, no. 2 (April 2012): 235–64.

Paton, Diana, and Maarit Forde, eds. *Obeah and Other Powers: The Politics of Caribbean Religion and Healing.* Durham, NC: Duke University Press, 2012.

Patterson, Orlando. *The Confounding Island: Jamaica and the Postcolonial Predicament* Cambridge, MA: Harvard University Press, 2019.

Patterson, Orlando. *The Sociology of Slavery: An Analysis of the Origins, Development and Structure of Negro Slave Society in Jamaica.* London: MacGibbon & Kee, 1967.

Pattullo, Polly. *Last Resorts: The Cost of Tourism in the Caribbean.* New York: Monthly Review Press, 2005.

Paugh, Katherine. *The Politics of Reproduction: Race, Medicine, and Fertility in the Age of Abolition.* Oxford: Oxford University Press, 2017.

Paugh, Katherine. "Yaws, Syphilis, Sexuality, and the Circulation of Medical Knowledge in the British Caribbean and the Atlantic World." *Bulletin of the History of Medicine* 88 (2014): 225–52.

Pauly, Philip. "Fighting the Hessian Fly: American and British Responses to Insect Invasion, 1776–1789." *Environmental History* 7 (July 2002): 377–400.

Pelletier, Monique. "La Martinique et la Guadeloupe au lendemain du traité de Paris (10 février 1763). L'oeuvre des ingénieurs géographes." *Chroniques d'histoire maritimes* 9 (1984): 22–30.

Perez, Louis. *Winds of Change: Hurricanes and the Transformation of Nineteenth Century Cuba.* Chapel Hill: University of North Carolina Press, 2001.

Pérez de la Riva, Juan. "Desaparición de la población indígena cubana." *Universidad de la Habana* 196–97 (1972): 61–84.

Pérotin-Dumon, Anne. *La Ville aux Îles, La Ville dans L'Île: Basse-Terre et Pointe-à-Pitre, Guadeloupe, 1650–1820.* Paris: Karthala, 2000.

Perri, Michael. "'Ruined and Lost': Spanish Destruction of the Pearl Coast in the Early Sixteenth Century." *Environment and History* 15 (2009): 129–61.

Perry, George H. "Parasites and Human Evolution." *Evolutionary Anthropology* 23, no. 6 (2014): 218–28.

Peters, Everson. "The 2009/10 Caribbean Drought: A Case Study." *Disasters* 39 (2015): 738–61.

Peterson, James B. "Taino, Island Carib, and Prehistoric Amerindian Economies in the West Indies: Tropical Forest Adaptations to Island Environments." In Wilson, ed., *The Indigenous People of the Caribbean*: 118–30.

Petley, Christer. *White Fury: A Jamaican Slaveholder and the Age of Revolution.* Oxford: Oxford University Press, 2018.

Picard, Jacqueline. *La Pointe-à-Pitre n'existe plus!—relations du tremblement de terre de 1843 en Guadeloupe.* Guadeloupe: Carat, 2003.

Pico, Fernando. *Puerto Rico y la sequía de 1847.* San Juan: Ediciones Huracán, 2015.

Pielke, Roger. *The Hurricane.* London: Routledge, 1999.

Pielke, Roger A., Jr., and Christopher Landsea. "La Niña, El Niño, and Atlantic Hurricane Damages in the United States." *Bulletin of the American Meteorological Society* 80 (1999): 2027–33.

Pietsch, Theodore W. "Charles Plumier (1646–1704) and His Drawings of French and American Fishes." *Archives of Natural History* 28, no. 1 (2001): 1–57.

Pitts, J. F., et al. "Manchineel Keratoconjunctivitis." *British Journal of Ophthalmology* 77 (1993): 284–88.

Plomp, E. "The Evolving Relationship between Humans and Dogs in the Circum-Caribbean." *Archaeological Review from Cambridge* 28, no. 2 (2013): 96–112.

Pluchon, Pierre. *Histoire des médecins et pharmaciens de marine et des colonies.* Toulouse: privately published, 1985.

Poëy y Aguirre, Andrés. "A Chronological Table, Comprising 400 Cyclonic Hurricanes which Have Occurred in the West Indies in the North Atlantic within 362 years, from 1493 to 1855." *Journal of the Royal Geographical Society* 25 (1855): 291–328.

Porter, Ashleigh F., et al. "Comment: Characterization of Two Historic Smallpox Specimens from a Czech Museum." *Viruses* 9 (2017): doi:10.3390/v9100276.

Portes, Alejandro, Carlos Dore-Cabral, and Patricia Landolt, eds. *The Urban Caribbean: Transition to the New Global Economy.* Baltimore: Johns Hopkins University Press, 1997.

Portuondo, María M. *Secret Science: Spanish Cosmography and the New World.* Chicago: University of Chicago Press, 2009.

Post, John. "Climatic Variability and the European Mortality Wave of the Early 1740s." *Journal of Interdisciplinary History* 15 (1984): 1–30.

Postma, Johannes. *The Dutch in the Atlantic Slave Trade, 1600–1815.* Cambridge: Cambridge University Press, 1990.

Poteate, A. S., et al. "Intensified Mollusk Exploitation on Nevis (West Indies) Reveals Six Centuries of Sustainable Exploitation." *Archaeological and Anthropological Sciences* 7 (2015): 361–74.

Potter, Robert. B. *The Urban Caribbean in an Era of Global Change.* London: Routledge, 2017 [orig. pub. 2000].

Potter, Robert, David Barker, Dennis Conway, and Thomas Klak, eds. *The Contemporary Caribbean.* New York: Pearson, 2004.

Powell, Dulcie. "The Botanic Garden, Liguanea (with a Revision of Hortus Eastensis)." *Bulletin of the Institute of Jamaica,* Science Ser., no. 15, pt. 1 (Kingston, 1972): 6–12.

Powell, Jeffrey R., Andrea Gloria-Soria, and Panayiota Kotsakiozi. "Recent History of Aedes aegypti: Vector Genomics and Epidemiology Records." *BioScience* 68, no. 11 (2018): 854–60.

Powell, J. R., and W. J. Tabachnick. "History of Domestication and Spread of Aedes aegypti." *Memorias Instituto Oswaldo Cruz* 108, suppl. (2013): 11–17.

Powell, Mary Lucas, and Della Collins Cook, eds. *The Myth of Syphilis.* Gainesville: University of Florida Press, 2005.

Price, Richard. "Caribbean Fishing and Fishermen: A Historical Sketch." *American Anthropologist* 68, no. 6 (December 1966): 1363–83.

Price, Richard. "The Concept of Creolization." In Eltis and Engerman, eds., *The Cambridge World History of Slavery,* 3: 513–37.

Price, Richard. *First-Time: The Historical Vision of an Afro-American People.* Baltimore: Johns Hopkins University Press, 1983.

Price, Richard. "The Miracle of Creolization: A Retrospective." *New West Indies Guide* 75 (2001): 35–64.

Price, T. Douglas, et al. "Home Is the Sailor: Investigating the Origins of the Inhabitants of La Isabela, the First European Settlement in the New World." *Current Anthropology* 61, no. 5 (Oct. 2020): 583–602.

Pritchard, James. *In Search of Empire: The French in the Americas, 1670–1730.* New York: Cambridge University Press, 2004.

Pulwarty, Roger S., Leonard Nurse, and Ulric O. Trotz. "Caribbean Islands in a Changing Climate." *Environment* 52 (Nov./Dec. 2010): 16–27.

Quammen, David. *The Song of the Dodo: Island Biogeography in an Age of Extinction.* New York: Scribner, 1997.

Quenet, Grégory. "Earthquakes in Early Modern France: From Old Regime to the Birth of a New Risk." In *Historical Disasters in Context: Science, Religion, and Politics,* edited by Andrea Janku et al. New York: Routledge, 2012: 94–114.

Quenet, Grégory. *Les Tremblements de terre aux dix-septième et dix-huitième siècles: La naissance d'un risque.* Seyssel, France: Champ Vallon, 2005.

Quevedo Vélez, Emilio. *Historia de la medicina en Colombia.* Bogotá: Tecnoquímicas, 2007.

Raby, Megan. *American Tropics: The Caribbean Roots of Biodiversity Science (Flows, Migrations, and Exchanges).* Chapel Hill: University of North Carolina Press, 2017.

Radell, David R. "The Indian Slave Trade and Population of Nicaragua during the Sixteenth Century." In *The Native Population of the Americas in 1492*, edited by William M. Denevan. 2nd ed. Madison: University of Wisconsin Press, 1992: 67–76.

Raff, Jennifer. "Journey into the Americas." *Scientific American* 324, no. 5 (May 2021): 26–33.

Raffaele, Herbert A., and Tracy Pederson. *A Guide to the Birds of the West Indies*. Princeton, NJ: Princeton University Press, 1998.

Raia, Pasquale. "Gigantism." In Gillespie and Clague, eds., *Encyclopedia of Islands*: 372–76.

Rallu, Jean-Louis. *Les populations océaniennes aux XIXe et XXe siècles*. Paris: Institut National d'Etudes Démographiques, 1990.

Rallu, Jean-Louis. "Pre- and Post-contact Population in Island Polynesia." In *The Growth and Collapse of Pacific Island Societies*, edited by P. V. Kirch and J. L. Rallu. Honolulu: University of Hawaii Press, 2007: 15–34.

Ramenofsky, Ann. *Vectors of Death: The Archaeology of European Contact*. Albuquerque: University of New Mexico Press, 1987.

Ramenofsky, Ann, Alicia Wilbur, and Anne Stone, "Native American Disease History: Past, Present, and Future Directions." *World Archaeology* 35 (2003): 249–51.

Rashford, John. "Arawak, Spanish, and African Contributions to Jamaica's Settlement Vegetation." *Jamaica Journal* 24, no. 3 (1993): 17–23.

Rashford, John. "Jamaica's Settlement Vegetation, Agroecology, and the Origin of Agriculture." *Caribbean Geography* 5 (1994): 32–50.

Rasmussen, Tobias N. "Macroeconomic Implications of Natural Disasters in the Caribbean." International Monetary Fund Working paper WP/04/224. Washington, DC: International Monetary Fund, 2004.

Raudzens, George. "Outfighting or Outpopulating: Main Reasons for Early Colonial Conquests." In *Technology, Disease and Colonial Conquests, Sixteenth to Eighteenth Centuries*. Leiden: Brill, 2001: 31–57.

Raudzens, George, ed. *Technology, Disease and Colonial Conquests, Sixteenth to Eighteenth Centuries*. Leiden: Brill, 2001.

Reading, Alison J., and Rory P. D. Walsh. "Tropical Cyclone Activity within the Caribbean Basin since 1500." In *Environment and Development in the Caribbean*, edited by David Barker and Duncan F. M. McGregor. Kingston, Jamaica: University of the West Indies Press, 1995: 111–23.

Réaumur, René Antoine Ferchault de. *The Natural History of Ants, from an Unpublished Manuscript* (1742). Translated by William Wheeler. New York: Knopf, 1926.

Regourd, François. "L'Expédition hydrographique de Chastenet de Puységur à Saint-Domingue (1784–1785)." In *Négoce, ports et océans XVIè - XXè siècles mélanges offerts à Paul Butel*, edited by Silvia Marzagalli and Hubert Bonin. Pessac, France: Presses universitaires de Bordeaux, 2000: 247–62.

Regourd, F. "Sciences et Colonisation sous l'ancien régime: le cas de la Guyane et des Antilles françaises, XVIIe–XVIIIe siècles." Doctoral thesis, Université de Bordeaux-III, 2000.

Reher, David S. "Reflections on the Fate of the Indigenous Populations of America." *Population and Development Review* 37 (2011): 172–77.

Reid, Basil A., ed. *Archaeology and Geoinformatics: Case Studies from the Caribbean*. Tuscaloosa: University of Alabama Press, 2008.

Reid, Basil A., ed. *The Archaeology of Caribbean and Circum-Caribbean Farmers (6000 BC–AD 1500)*. New York: Routledge, 2018.

Reitsma, Ella, with Sandrine Ulenberg. *Maria Sibylla Merian and Daughters: Women of Art and Science*. Los Angeles: J. Paul Getty Museum, 2008.

Reitz, Elizabeth J. "The Spanish Colonial Experience and Domestic Animals." *Historical Archaeology* 26, no. 1 (1992): 84–91.

Renkema, Wim. *Karten van de Nederlandse Antillen: Curaçao, Aruba, Bonair, Saba, Sint Eustatius en Sin Maarten tot 1900*. Leiden: Brill Hes & De Graaf, 2012.

Reséndez, Andrés. *The Other Slavery: The Uncovered Story of Indian Enslavement in America*. Boston: Houghton Mifflin Harcourt, 2016.

Rey, Terry. *The Priest and the Prophetess: Abbé Ouvière, Romainee Rivière, and the Revolutionary Atlantic World*. New York: Oxford University Press, 2017.

Rhiney, Kevon. "Geographies of Caribbean Vulnerability in a Changing Climate: Issues and Trends." *Geography Compass* 9 (2015): 97–114.

Richardson, Bonham C. *The Caribbean in the Wider World, 1492–1992: A Regional Geography*. Cambridge: Cambridge University Press, 1992.

Richardson, Bonham. *Economy and Environment in the Caribbean: Barbados and the Windwards in the Late 1800s*. Gainesville: University Press of Florida, 1997.

Richardson, Bonham. *Igniting the Caribbean's Past: Fire in British West Indian History*. Chapel Hill: University of North Carolina Press, 2004.

Ricklefs, Robert E. "Dynamics of Colonization and Extinction on Islands: Insights from Lesser Antillean Birds." In Losos and Ricklefs, eds., *The Theory of Island Biogeography Revisited*: 388–414.

Ricklefs, R. E., and E. Bermingham. "History and the Species–Area Relationship in Lesser Antillean Birds." *American Naturalist* 163 (2004): 227–39.

Ricklefs, Robert, and Eldredge Bermingham. "The West Indies as a Laboratory of Biogeography and Evolution." *Philosophical Transactions of the Royal Society* 363 (2008): 2393–413.

Rigau-Pérez, José. "The Introduction of Smallpox Vaccine in 1803 and the Adoption of Immunization as a Government Function in Puerto Rico." *Hispanic American Historical Review* 69 (1989): 393–423.

Rigau-Pérez, José G. "The Work of US Public Health Service Officers in Puerto Rico, 1898–1919." *Puerto Rican Health Sciences Journal* 36 (2017): 130–39.

Riley, James C. "Smallpox and American Indians Revisited." *Journal of the History of Medicine and Allied Sciences* 65 (2010): 445–77.

Rivera-Collazo, Isabel C. "Gone with the Waves: Sea-level Rise, Ancient Territories and the Socioenvironmental Context of Mid-Holocene Maritime Mobility in the Pan-Caribbean Region." In Hofman and Antczak, eds., *Early Settlers*, 47–56.

Rivera-Collazo, Isabel. "*Por el camino verde*: Long-term Tropical Socioecosystem Dynamics and the Anthropocene as Seen from Puerto Rico." *The Holocene* 25 (2015): 1604–11.

Rivera-Pagán, Luis N. "Freedom and Servitude: Indigenous Slavery and the Spanish Conquest of the Caribbean." In Sued-Badillo, ed., *General History of the Caribbean*, 1: 316–62.

Robbins, Louise E. *Elephant Slaves and Pampered Parrots: Exotic Animals in Eighteenth-Century Paris*. Baltimore: Johns Hopkins University Press, 2002.

Roberts, Charlotte, and Jane Buikstra. "The History of Tuberculosis from the Earliest Times to the Development of Drugs." In *Clinical Tuberculosis*, edited by Peter Davies, Peter Barnes, and Stephen Gordon. London: Hodder Arnold, 2008: 3–20.

Roberts, Justin. *Slavery and the Enlightenment in the British Atlantic, 1750–1807*. New York: Cambridge University Press, 2013.

Roberts, Justin. "Uncertain Business: A Case Study of Barbadian Plantation Management, 1770–1793." *Slavery & Abolition* 32, no. 3 (September 2011): 247–68.

Roberts, Justin. "Working between the Lines: Labor and Agriculture on Two Barbadian Sugar Plantations, 1796–1797." *William and Mary Quarterly* 63, no. 3 (July 2006): 551–86.

Robertson, D. Ross, and Katie L. Cramer. "Defining and Dividing the Greater Caribbean: Insights from the Biogeography of Shorefishes." *PLOS ONE*, 9, no. 7 (July 23, 2014): 1–16.

Robertson, James. *Gone Is the Ancient Glory: Spanish Town, Jamaica, 1554–2000*. Kingston, Jamaica: Ian Randle, 2005.

Robertson, James. "Island Time: Disasters in the Comprehension of Montserrat's Past." *Caribbean Quarterly* 63 (2017): 529–50.

Robertson, James. "Making Jamaica English: Priorities and Processes." In Roper, ed., *The Torrid Zone*: 104–17.

Robertson, Richard. "Antilles, Geology." In *Encyclopedia of Islands*, edited by Rosemary Gillespie and David Clague. Berkeley: University of California Press, 2009: 29–35.

Robson, G. R. "An Earthquake Catalogue for the Eastern Caribbean 1530–1960." *Bulletin of the Seismological Society of America* 54, no. 2 (April 1964): 785–832.

Rocha, Gabriel de Avilez. "The Azorean Connection: Trajectories of Slaving, Piracy, and Trade in the Early Atlantic." In Altman and Wheat, eds., *The Spanish Caribbean*: 257–78.

Rocha, Gabriel de Avilez. *Common Currents of Empire: Political Ecologies of Colonialism and Slavery in the Early Atlantic*. Chapel Hill: University of North Carolina Press, forthcoming.

Rocha, Gabriel de Avilez. "Maroons in the *Montes*: Toward a Political Ecology of Marronage in the Sixteenth-Century Caribbean." In *Early Modern Black Diaspora Studies*, edited by Cassander L. Smith, Nicholas R. Jones, and Miles P. Grier. New York: Palgrave Macmillan, 2018: 15–35.

Rocha, Gabriel de Avilez. "The Pinzones and the Coup of the *Acedares*: Fishing and Colonization in Fifteenth-Century Atlantic Africa and the Caribbean." *Colonial Latin American Review* 28, no. 4 (2019): 427–29.

Rocha, Gabriel de Avilez. "Plunder and Profit in the Name of Protection: Royal Iberian Armadas in the Early Atlantic." In *Protection and Empire: A Global History*, edited by Lauren Benton, Adam Clulow, and Bain Attwood. New York: Cambridge University Press, 2018: 72–90.

Rocha, Gabriel de Avilez. "Politics of the Hinterland: Taxing Fowl in and beyond the Ports of Terceira Island, 1550–1600." *Early American Studies* 15, no. 4 (2017): 740–68.

Rodger, J., et al. "The Transoceanic 1755 Lisbon Tsunami in Martinique." *Pure Applied Geophysics* 168 (2011): 1015–31.

Rodger, N. A. M. "Atlantic Seafaring," In Canny and Morgan, eds., *Oxford Handbook of the Atlantic World*: 71–86.

Rodríguez, M. O. Cotilla. "The Santiago de Cuba Earthquake of 11 June 1766: Some New Insights." *Geofísica Internacional* 42 (2003): 589–602.

Rodríguez Demorizi, Emilio. *Los dominicos y las encomiendas de indios de la isla Española*. Santo Domingo: Editora del Caribe, 1971.

Rodríguez-Durán, Armondo, and Thomas H. Kunz. "Biogeography of West Indian Bats: An Ecological Perspective." In Woods & Sergile, eds., *Biogeography of West Indies*: 355–68.

Rodríguez-Ferrer, Miguel. *Naturaleza y civilización de la grandiosa isla de Cuba*. Madrid: J. Noguera, 1876.

Rodríguez Morel, Genaro. "The Sugar Economy of Española in the Sixteenth Century." In Schwartz, ed., *Tropical Babylons*: 85–114.

Røge, Pernille. *Economistes and the Reinvention of Empire: France in the Americas and Africa, c. 1750–1802*. Cambridge: Cambridge University Press, 2019.

Rohland, Eleanora. *Changes in the Air: Hurricanes in New Orleans 1718 to the Present*. New York: Berghahn, 2019.

Rohland, Eleonora. "Hurricanes on the Gulf Coast: Environmental Knowledge and Science in Louisiana, the Caribbean, and the United States, 1722–1900." In Manning and Rood, eds., *Global Scientific Practice*: 38–53.

Roitman, Jessica Vance. "Dutch Colonization on the 'Wild Coast.'" In Roper, ed., *The Torrid Zone*: 61–75.

Roksandic, Ivan, ed. *Cuban Archaeology in the Caribbean*. Gainesville: University Press of Florida, 2016.

Romero, A. "Death and Taxes: The Case of the Depletion of Pearl Oyster Beds in Sixteenth-Century Venezuela." *Conservation Biology* 17 (2003): 1013–23.

Romero, A., R. Baker, J. E. Cresswell, A. Singh, A. McKie, and M. Manna. "Environmental History of Marine Mammal Exploitation in Trinidad and Tobago, WI and Its Ecological Impact." *Environment and History* 8 (2002): 255–74.

Rood, Daniel B. *The Reinvention of Atlantic Slavery: Technology, Labor, Race, and Capitalism in the Greater Caribbean*. New York: Oxford University Press, 2017.

Roper, L. H., ed. *The Torrid Zone: Caribbean Colonization and Cultural Interaction in the Long Seventeenth Century*. Columbia: University of South Carolina Press, 2018.

Rose, Paul, and Anne Laking. *Oceans: Exploring the Hidden Depths of the Underwater World*. Berkeley: University of California Press, 2008.

Rosel, Patricia E., et al. "A New Species of Baleen Whale (Balaenoptera) from the Gulf of Mexico, with a Review of Its Geographic Distribution." *Marine Mammal Science* 37 (2021): 577–610. https://doi-org.proxy1.library.jhu.edu/10.1111/mms.12776.

Rosenberg, Charles E. "Framing Disease: The Creation and Negotiation of Explanatory Schemes." *The Milbank Quarterly* 67, suppl. 1(1989): 1–15.

Rosenblat, Ángel. *La población indígena y el mestizaje en América*. 2 vols. Buenos Aires: Editorial Nova, 1954.

Rosenthal, Caitlin. *Accounting for Slavery: Masters and Management*. Cambridge, MA: Harvard University Press, 2018.

Ross, Ann H., William F. Keegan, Michael P. Pateman, and Colleen B. Young. "Faces Divulge the Origins of Caribbean Prehistoric Inhabitants." *Scientific Reports* 10, no. 1 (2020): 1–9.

Ross, Ann H., and Douglas H. Ubelaker. "A Morphometric Approach to Taino Biological Distance in the Caribbean." In Fitzpatrick and Ross, eds., *Island Shores, Distant Pasts*: 108–26.

Ross, Robert. "Smallpox and the Cape of Good Hope in the Eighteenth Century." In *African Historical Demography*, edited by C. Fyvie and D. McMasters. Edinburgh: Centre for African Studies, University of Edinburgh, 1977, I: 416–28.

Rostain, Stéphen. "Agricultural Earthworks on the French Guiana Coast." In Helaine Silverman and William Isbell, eds., *Handbook of South American Archaeology*. New York: Springer, 2008: 217–34.

Rostain, Stéphen. "Agricultural Earthworks (the Guianas)." In *Encyclopedia of Caribbean Archaeology*, edited by Basil A. Reid and R. Grant Gilmore III. Gainesville: University of Florida Press, 2014: 33–36.

Rothman, Sheila. *Living in the Shadow of Death: Tuberculosis and the Social Experience of Illness in American History*. Baltimore: Johns Hopkins University Press, 1995.

Rothschild, Bruce, F. L. Calderon., A. Copra, and C. Rothschild. "First European Exposure to Syphilis: The Dominican Republic at the Time of Columbian Contact." *Clinical Infectious Diseases* 31 (2000): 936–41.

Rothschild, Emma. "A Horrible Tragedy in the French Atlantic." *Past and Present* 192 (2006): 67–108.

Rotz, Philip. "Sweetness and Fever? Sugar Production, *Aedes agypti*, and Dengue Fever in Natal, South Africa, 1926–1927." *South African History Journal* 68 (2016): 286–303.

Rouse, Irving. *The Tainos: Rise & Decline of the People Who Greeted Columbus*. New Haven, CT: Yale University Press, 1992.

Rugeley, Terry. *The River People in Flood Time: The Civil Wars in Tabasco, Spoiler of Empires*. Stanford, CA: Stanford University Press, 2014.

Rupert, Linda M. *Creolization and Contraband: Curaçao in the Early Modern Atlantic World*. Athens: University of Georgia Press, 2012.

Rushforth, Brett. *Bonds of Alliance: Indigenous and Atlantic Slaveries in New France*. Chapel Hill: University of North Carolina Press, 2013.

Rütten, Thomas. "Early Modern Medicine." In *The Oxford Handbook of the History of Medicine*, edited by Mark Jackson. Oxford: Oxford University Press, 2011: 60–81.

Ryden, David Beck. "'One of the Finest and Most Fruitful Spots in America': An Analysis of Eighteenth-Century Carriacou." *Journal of Interdisciplinary History* 43, no. 4 (Spring 2013): 539–70.

Sachs, Aaron. *The Humboldt Current: Nineteenth-Century Exploration and the Roots of American Environmentalism*. New York: Viking, 2006.

Saenz, José Luiz. "Una carta anua de la residencia de Santo Domingo (23 Octubre 1695)." *Archivum Historicum Societatis Iesu* 62, no. 124 (1993): 281–312.

Saint-Louis, Vertus. *Système colonial et problèmes d'alimentation: Saint-Domingue au XVIIIe siècle*. Montreal: Editions du CIDIHCA, 1999.

Salisbury, Neal. "Native People and European Settlers in Eastern North America." In *The Cambridge History of the Native Peoples of the Americas*, vol. I, *North America*, edited by Bruce G. Trigger and Wilcomb E. Washburn. New York: Cambridge University Press, 1996: 399–460.

Salivia, Luis A. *Historia de los temporales de Puerto Rico y Las Antillas 1492–1970*. 2nd ed. San Juan: Editorial Edil, 1972.

Salvador-Vázquez, M., and C. Menéndez de León. "Higiene y enfermedad del esclavo en Cuba durante la primera mitad del siglo XIX." *Anuario de Estudios Americanos* 43 (1986): 419–45.

Samson, Alice V. M., and Jago Cooper. "History on Mona Island: Long-Term Human and Landscape Dynamics of an 'Uninhabited' Island." *New West Indian Guide* 89, nos. 1–2 (2015): 30–50.

Samson, Alice V. M., et al. "Artists before Columbus: A Multi-method Characterization of the Materials and Practices of Caribbean Cave Art." *Journal of Archaeological Science* 88 (2017): 24–36. https://doi.org/10.1016/j.jas.2017.09.012.

Samson, Alice V. M., et al. "European Visitors in Native Spaces: Using Palaeography to Investigate Religious Dynamics in the New World." *Latin American Antiquity* 27, no. 4 (2016): 443–61.

Sánchez-Albornoz, Nicolás. *The Population of Latin America: A History*. Berkeley: University of California Press, 1974.

Sandiford, Keith. *The Cultural Politics of Sugar: Caribbean Slavery and Narratives of Colonialism*. Cambridge: Cambridge University Press, 2000.

Santiago-Valentin, Eugenio, and Richard G. Olmstead. "Historical Biogeography of Caribbean Plants: Introduction to Current Knowledge and Possibilities from a Phylogenetic Perspective." *Taxon* 53, no. 2 (2004): 299–319.

Santos-Granero, Fernando. *Vital Enemies: Slavery, Predation, and the Amerindian Political Economy of Life*. Austin: University of Texas Press, 2009.

Sarmiento Ramírez, Ismael. "Del fun'che al ajiaco: La dieta que los amos imponen a los esclavos africanos en Cuba y la asimilación que estos hacen a la cucina criolla." *Anales del Museo de América* 16 (2009): 127–54.

Sastre, Francisco, et al. "Improving the Health Status of Caribbean People: Recommendations from the Triangulating on Health Equity Summit." *Global Health Promotion* 21 (2014): 19–28 https://doi.org/10.1177/1757975914523455.

Satchell, Veront. *Hope Transformed, A Historical Sketch of the Hope Landscape, St. Andrew, Jamaica, 1669–1960*. Kingston, Jamaica: University of the West Indies Press, 2012.

Sauer, Carl Ortwin. *The Early Spanish Main*. Berkeley: University of California Press, 1966.

Saunders, Nicholas J. "Shimmering Worlds: Brilliance, Power, and Gold in Pre-Columbian Panama." In *To Capture the Sun: Gold of Ancient Panama*, edited by Nicholas J. Saunders, John W. Hoopes, and Thomas Gilcrease. Tulsa: University of Oklahoma Press, 2011: 79–113.

Savage, John. "'Black Magic' and White Terror: Slave Poisoning and Colonial Society in Early 19th Century Martinique." *Journal of Social History* 40, no. 3 (Spring 2007): 635–62.

Scarpaci, Joseph L. "Forts and Ports." In *Mapping Latin America: A Cartographic Reader*, edited by Jordana Dym and Karl Offen. Chicago: University of Chicago Press, 2011: 98–102.

Schaffer, W. C., et al. "Lucayan-Taino Burials from Preacher's Cave, Eleuthera, Bahamas." *International Journal of Osteoarchaeology* 22, no. 1 (2012): 45–69.

Schaub, Jean-Frédéric. "Violence in the Atlantic: Sixteenth and Seventeenth Centuries." In *The Oxford Handbook of the Atlantic World, 1450–1850*, edited by Nicholas Canny and Philip Morgan. Oxford: Oxford University Press, 2011: 113–29.

Scheffers, S., et al. "Tsunamis, Hurricanes, the Demise of Coral Reefs and Shifts in Prehistoric Human Populations in the Caribbean." *Quarternary International* 195 (2009): 69–87.

Scherer, J. "Great Earthquakes in the Island of Haiti." *Bulletin of the Seismological Society of America* 2, no. 3 (1912): 161–80.

Schiebinger, Londa. *Plants and Empire: Colonial Bioprospecting in the Atlantic World*. Cambridge, MA: Harvard University Press, 2004.

Schiebinger, Londa. "Scientific Exchange in the Eighteenth-Century Atlantic World." In *Soundings in Atlantic History: Latent Structures and Intellectual Currents, 1500–1830*, edited by Bernard Bailyn and Patricia L. Denault. Cambridge, MA: Harvard University Press, 2011: 294–328.

Schiebinger, Londa. *Secret Cures of Slaves: People, Plants and Medicine in the Eighteenth-Century Atlantic World*. Stanford, CA: Stanford University Press, 2017.

Schneider, Elena. *The Occupation of Havana: War, Trade, and Slavery in the Atlantic World*. Chapel Hill: University of North Carolina Press, 2018.

Schneider, Elena. "Routes into Eighteenth-Century Cuban Slavery." In *From the Galleons to the Highlands: Slave Trade Routes in the Spanish Americas*, edited by Alex Borucki, David Eltis, and David Wheat. Albuquerque: University of New Mexico Press, 2019: 249–74.

Schoener, Thomas. "The MacArthur-Wilson Equilibrium Model: A Chronicle of What It Said and How It Was Tested." In Losos and Ricklefs, eds., *The Theory of Island Biogeography Revisited*: 52–87.

Schroeder, Hannes, et al. "Origins and Genetic Legacies of the Caribbean Taino." *Proceedings of the National Academy of Sciences* 115 (2018): 2341–46. doi.org/10.1073/pnas.1716839115.

Schroedl, Gerald F. "Enslaved Africans and the British Military at the Brimstone Hill Fortress, St. Kitts, West Indies." In DeCorse and Beier, eds., *British Forts and Their Communities*: 178–205.

Schroedl, Gerald F., and Todd M. Ahlman. "Archaeological Evidence for Enslaved African Laborers from Two Locations at the Brimstone Hill Fortress, St Kitts, West Indies." In Leech and Leech, eds., *The Colonial Landscape*: 89–130.

Schroedl, Gerald F., and Todd M. Ahlman. "The Maintenance of Cultural and Personal Identities of Enslaved Africans and British soldiers at the Brimstone Hill Fortress, St. Kitts, West Indies." *Historical Archaeology* 36, no. 4 (2002): 38–49.

Schuenemann, V. J., A. Kumar Lankapalli, R. Barquera, E. A. Nelson, D. Iraíz Hernández, V. Acuña Alonzo, et al. "Historic Treponema Pallidum Genomes from Colonial Mexico Retrieved from Archaeological Remain." *PLoS Neglected Tropical Diseases* 12 (2018): e0006447. doi. org/10.1371/journal.pntd.0006447.

Schulting, Rick J., et al. "Six Centuries of Adaptation to a Challenging Island Environment: AMS ^{14}C Dating and Stable Isotopic Analysis of Pre-Columbian Human Remains from the Bahamian Archipelago Reveal Dietary Trends." *Quaternary Science Reviews* 254 (2021): https://doi.org/10.1016/j.quascirev.2020.106780.

Schurr, Theodore, Jada Benn Torres, Miguel Vilar, Jill Gaieski, and Carlalynne Melendez. "An Emerging History of Indigenous Caribbean and Circum-Caribbean Populations: Insights from Archaeological, Ethnographic, Genetic, and Historical Studies." In *New Directions in Biocultural Anthropology*, edited by Molly Zuckerman and Debra Martin. Hoboken: Wiley Blackwell, 2016: 385–402.

Schwartz, Albert, and Robert W. Henderson. *Amphibians and Reptiles of the West Indies: Descriptions, Distributions, and Natural History*. Gainesville: University Press of Florida, 1991.

Schwartz, Marion. *A History of Dogs in the Early Americas*. New Haven, CT: Yale University Press, 1997.

Schwartz, Stuart. *Sea of Storms: A History of Hurricanes in the Greater Caribbean from Columbus to Katrina*. Princeton, NJ: Princeton University Press, 2015.

Schwartz, Stuart B. "Spaniards, *Pardos*, and the Missing Mestizos: Identities and Racial Categories in the Early Hispanic Caribbean." *New West Indies Guide* 71, no. 1/2 (1997): 5–19.

Schwartz, Stuart B., ed. *Tropical Babylons: Sugar and the Making of the Atlantic World, 1450–1680*. Chapel Hill: University of North Carolina Press, 2004,

Schwartz, Stuart, Franklin Knight, et al. "The Caribbean from the Perspective of the Social Sciences." In *Process of Unity in Caribbean Society: Ideologies and Literature*, edited by Ileana Rodríguez and Marc Zimmerman. Minneapolis, MN: Institute for the Study of Ideologies and Literature, 1983: 57–95.

Seagar, E. A. "Malaria in Barbados." *Tropical Agriculture* 5, no. 3 (1928): 48–50.

Sensbach, Jon. *Rebecca's Revival: Creating Black Christianity in the Atlantic World*. Cambridge, MA: Harvard University Press, 2006.

Serrand, Nathalie, and Dominique Bonnissent. "Interacting Pre-Columbian Amerindian Societies and Environments: Insights from Five Millennia of Archaeological Invertebrate Record on the Saint-Martin Island (French Lesser Antilles)." *Environmental Archaeology* 26, no. 16 (2018): DOI:10.1080/14614103.2018.1450463.

Seth, Suman. *Difference and Disease: Medicine, Race, and the Eighteenth-Century British Empire*. Cambridge: Cambridge University Press, 2018.

Shammas, Carole, ed. *Investing in the Early Modern Built Environment: Europeans, Asians, Settlers and Indigenous Societies*. Leiden: Brill, 2012.

Shanks, G. Dennis, et al. "Epidemiological Isolation Causing Variable Mortality in Island Populations during the 1918–1920 Influenza Pandemic." *Influenza and Other Respiratory Viruses* 6 (2019): 417–23.

Sharples, Jason. "Discovering Slave Conspiracies: New Fears of Rebellion and Old Paradigms of Plotting in Seventeenth-Century Barbados." *American Historical Review* 120 (June 2015): 811–43.

Shattuck, C. G. *The Peninsula of Yucatan: Medical, Biological, Meteorological and Sociological Studies.* Washington DC: Carnegie Institution, 1933.

Shearn, Isaac. "Canoe Societies in the Caribbean: Ethnography, Archaeology, and Ecology of Precolonial Canoe Manufacturing and Voyaging." *Journal of Anthropological Archaeology* 57 (2020): 101–40.

Shell, Richard J. "The Ladrones Population." *Journal of Pacific History* 36 (2001): 225–36.

Shell, Richard J. "The Marianas Population Decline: 17th Century Estimates." *Journal of Pacific History* 34 (1999): 291–305.

Shepherd, Verene A. *Livestock, Sugar and Slavery: Contested Terrain in Colonial Jamaica.* Kingston, Jamaica: Ian Randle, 2009.

Shepherd, Verene A., ed. *Slavery without Sugar: Diversity in Caribbean Economy and Society Since the 17th Century.* Gainesville: University Press of Florida, 2002.

Shepherd, Verene A., and G. L. Richards, eds. *Questioning Creole: Creolisation Discourses in Caribbean Culture.* Kingston, Jamaica: Ian Randle, 2002.

Sheridan, Richard. "Captain Bligh, the Breadfruit and the Botanic Gardens of Jamaica." *Journal of Caribbean History* 23, no. 1 (1989): 28–50.

Sheridan, Richard B. "The Crisis of Slave Subsistence in the British West Indies during and after the American Revolution." *William and Mary Quarterly* 33, no. 4 (1976): 615–41.

Sheridan, Richard B. *Doctors and Slaves: A Medical and Demographic History of Slavery in the British West Indies, 1680–1834.* Cambridge: Cambridge University Press, 1985.

Sheridan, Richard B. "The Jamaican Slave Insurrection Scare of 1776 and the American Revolution." *Journal of Negro History* 3 (1975): 290–308.

Sheridan, Richard, ed. "Letters from a Sugar Planter in Antigua, 1739–1758." *Agricultural History* 31 (July 1957): 3–23.

Sheridan, Richard B. *Sugar and Slavery: The Economic History of the British West Indies, 1623–1775.* Baltimore: Johns Hopkins University Press, 1973.

Sherman, William L. *Forced Native Labor in Sixteenth-Century Central America.* Lincoln: University of Nebraska Press, 1979.

Sherratt, Emma, et al. "Amber Fossils Demonstrate Deep-Time Stability of Caribbean Lizard Communities." *Proceedings of the National Academy of Sciences of the United States of America* 112 (2015): 9961–66.

Shuler, Kristin A. "Life and Death on a Barbadian Sugar Plantation." *International Journal of Osteoarchaeology* 21 (2011): 66–81.

Siegel, Peter E., ed. *Ancient Borinquen: Archaeology and Ethnohistory of Native Puerto Rico.* Tuscaloosa: University of Alabama Press 2005.

Siegel, Peter E., ed. *Island Historical Ecology: Socionatural Landscapes of the Eastern and Southern Caribbean.* New York: Berghahn Books, 2018.

Siegel, Peter E., et al. "Paleoenvironmental Evidence for First Human Colonization of the Eastern Caribbean." *Quaternary Science Reviews* 129 (2015): 275–95.

Silva, Ana Maria. "Roots in Stone and Slavery: Permanence, Mobility, and Empire in 17th-C. Cartagena de Indias." PhD diss., University of Michigan, 2018.

Simpson, M. C., et al. *Quantification and Magnitude of Losses and Damages Resulting from the Impacts of Climate Change: Modelling the Transformational Impacts and Costs of Sea Level Rise in the Caribbean.* Barbados: United Nations Development Programme, 2010.

Singer, Merrill, et al. "Syndemics and the Biosocial Conception of Health." *The Lancet* 389 (March 4, 2017): 941–50.

Sinha, Dinesh. "Changing Patterns of Food, Nutrition and Health in the Caribbean." *Nutrition Research* 15 (1995): 899–938.

Skoglund, Pontus, and Iain Mathieson. "Ancient Genomics of Modern Humans: The First Decade." *Annual Review of Genomics and Human Genetics* 19, no. 1 (2018): 381–404.

Skopyk, Bradley. *Colonial Cataclysms: Climate, Landscape, and Memory in Mexico's Little Ice Age.* Tucson: University of Arizona Press, 2020.

Slayton, Emma Ruth. *Seascape Corridors: Modeling Routes to Connect Communities across the Caribbean Sea.* Leiden: Sidestone Press, 2018.

Slud, Paul. "Geographic and Climatic Relationships of Avifaunas with Special Reference to Comparative Distribution in the Tropics." *Smithsonian Contributions to Zoology,* no. 212 (1976): 1–149.

Sluyter, Andrew. *Black Ranching Frontiers: African Cattle Herders of the Atlantic World, 1500–1900.* New Haven, CT: Yale University Press, 2012.

Smith, Jordan. "The Invention of Rum." PhD diss., Georgetown University, 2018.

Smith, Matthew J. *Liberty, Fraternity, and Exile: Haiti and Jamaica after Emancipation.* Chapel Hill: University of North Carolina Press, 2014.

Smith, Matthew J. "A Tale of Two Tragedies: Forgetting and Remembering Kingston (1907) and Port-au-Prince (2010)." *Karib-Nordic Journal for Caribbean Studies* 4 (2019): 1–14.

Smith, Michael Leonard, et al. "Caribbean Islands." In *Hotspots Revisited: Earth's Biologically Richest and most Endangered Terrestrial Ecoregions,* edited by Russell A. Mittermeier et al.. Mexico City: Agrupacion Sierra Madre, 2004: 112–18.

Smith, S. D. "Coffee and the "Poorer Sort of People' in Jamaica during the Period of African Enslavement." In Shepherd, ed., *Slavery without Sugar:* 102–28.

Smith, S. D. "Storm Hazard and Slavery: The Impact of the 1831 Great Caribbean Hurricane on St. Vincent." *Environment and History* 18 (2012): 97–123.

Smith, S. D. "Sugar's Poor Relation: Coffee Planting in the British Indies, 1720–1833." *Slavery and Abolition* 19 (December 1998): 68–89.

Smith, S. D. "Volcanic Hazard in a Slave Society: The 1812 Eruption of Mt. Soufrière in St. Vincent." *Journal of Historical Geography* 37 (2011): 55–67.

Smith, Susanna, and Anthony Oliver-Smith, eds. *Culture and Catastrophe: The Anthropology of Disaster.* Santa Fe, MN: School for Advanced Research Press, 2002.

Smith-Guzman, Nicole E. "The Skeletal Manifestation of Malaria: An Epidemiological Approach Using Documented Skeletal Collections." *American Journal of Physical Anthropology* 158 (2015): 624–35.

Snyder, N. F. R., J. W. Wiley, and C. B. Kebler. *The Parrots of Luquillo: Natural History and Conservation of the Puerto Rican Parrot.* Los Angeles: Western Foundation of Vertebrate Zoology, 1987.

Sobrevilla, Iris Montero. "The Slow Science of Swift Nature: Hummingbirds and Humans in New Spain." In Manning and Rood, eds., *Global Scientific Practice:* 127–46.

Soto, Salvador Arana. *Historia de nuestras calamidades.* San Juan, Puerto Rico: Printed by Tipografia Miguza, 1968.

Soto-Centeno, J. Angel, and David W. Steadman. "Fossils Reject Climate Change as the Cause of Extinction of Caribbean Bats." *Nature: Scientific Reports* 5, no. 7971 (2015): 1–7. DOI: 10.1038/srep07971.

Spencer-Smith, David, et al. "Biogeographical Affinities of the Butterflies of a 'Forgotten' Island: Mona (Puerto Rico)." *Bulletin of the Allyn Museum* 121 (1988): 1–35.

Spencer Smith, David, et al. *The Butterflies of the West Indies and South Florida.* Oxford: Oxford University Press, 1994.

Staflue, Frans A. *Linnaeus and the Linnaeans: The Spreading of Their Ideas in Systematic Botany, 1735–1789.* Utrecht: Oosthoek, 1971.

Stahl, Peter W. "Adventive Vertebrates and Historical Ecology in the Pre-Columbian Neotropics." *Diversity* 1 (2009): 151–65.

Stahl, Peter W. "Early Dogs and Endemic South American Canids of the Spanish Main." *Journal of Anthropological Research* 69, no. 4 (2013): 515–33.

Starr, Christopher K. "Trinidad and Tobago." In Gillespie and Clague, eds., *Encyclopedia of Islands:* 926–29.

Starks, Philip T. B., and Brittany L. Slabach. "The Scoop on Eating Dirt," *Scientific American* 306, no. 6. (June 2012): 30–33.

Staten, Clifford L. *The History of Cuba*. New York: St. Martin's Press, 2005.

Steadman, David W., and Sharyn Jones. "Long-Term Trends in Prehistoric Fishing and Hunting on Tobago, West Indies." *Latin American Antiquity* 17 (2006): 316–34.

Steadman, David W., and Anne Stokes. "Changing Exploitation of Terrestrial Vertebrates during the Past 3000 Years on Tobago, West Indies." *Human Ecology* 30, no. 3 (September 2002): 339–67.

Steadman, David W., et al. "Asynchronous Extinction of Late Quaternary Sloths on Continents and Islands." *Proceedings of the National Academy of Sciences* 102 (2005): 11763–68.

Steadman, David W., et al. "Late Holocene Historical Ecology: The Timing of Vertebrate Extirpation on Crooked Island, Commonwealth of The Bahamas." *Journal of Island and Coastal Archaeology* 12, no. 4 (2017): 572–84.

Steadman, David W., et al. "The Paleoecology and Extinction of Endemic Tortoises in the Bahamian Archipelago." *The Holocene* 30, no. 3 (2020): 420–27.

Steadman, David W., et al. "Vertebrate Community on an Ice-Age Caribbean Island." *Proceedings of the National Academy of Science, USA* 112, no. 44 (2015): E5963–71.

Stearns, Raymond. *Science in the British Colonies in America*. Urbana: University of Illinois Press, 1970.

Stearns, William T. "Grisebach's "Flora of the British West Indian Islands: A Biographical and Bibliographical Introduction." *Journal of the Arnold Arboretum* 46, no. 3 (July 1965): 243–85.

Steckel, Richard, ed. *The Backbone of History: Health and Nutrition in the Western Hemisphere*. New York: Cambridge University Press, 2002.

Steckel, Richard, and Richard Jensen. "New Evidence on the Causes of Slave and Crew Mortality in the Atlantic Slave Trade." *Journal of Economic History* 46 (1986): 57–77.

Steele, Ian K. *The English Atlantic, 1675–1740: An Exploration of Communication and Community*. Oxford: Oxford University Press, 1986.

Steffen, Will, Paul T. Crutzen, and J. R. McNeill. "The Anthropocene: Are Humans Now Overwhelming the Great Forces of Nature." *Ambio* 36 (December 2007): 614–21.

Steffensen, J. "Smallpox in Iceland." *Nordisk medicinhistorisk årsbok* 33 (1977): 41–56.

Stelten, Rudd. *From Golden Rock to Historic Gem: A Historical Archaeological Analysis of the Maritime Cultural Landscape of St. Eustatius, Dutch Caribbean*. Leiden: Sidestone Press, 2019.

Stephens, S. G. "Cotton Growing in the West Indies During the 18th and 19th Centuries," *Tropical Agriculture* 21, no. 2 (1944): 23–29.

Stephenson, Tannecia S., et al. "Changes in Extreme Temperature and Precipitation in the Caribbean Region, 1961–2010." *International Journal of Climatology* 34 (2014): 2957–71.

Stewart, Charles, ed. *Creolization: History, Ethnography, Theory*. Walnut Creek, CA: Left Coast Press, 2007.

Stipriaan, Alex van. *Surinaams contrast: Roofbouw en Overleven in een Caraïbische Plantagekolonie, 1750–1863*. Leiden: KITLV, 1993.

Stockland, Etienne. "'La Guerre aux Insectes': Pest Control and Agricultural Reform in the French Enlightenment." *Annals of Science* 70, no. 4 (2013): 435–60.

Stockland, Pierre-Etienne. "Statecraft and Insect Oeconomies in the Global French Enlightenment (1670–1815)." PhD diss., Columbia University, 2018.

Stone, Erin Woodruff. *Captives of Conquest: Slavery in the Early Modern Spanish Caribbean*. Philadelphia: University of Pennsylvania Press, 2021.

Stone, Erin Woodruff. "Chasing 'Caribs': Defining Zones of Legal Indigenous Enslavement in the Circum-Caribbean, 1493–1542." In *Slaving Zones: Cultural Identities, Ideologies, and Institutions is the Evolution of Global Slavery*, edited by Jeff Fynn-Paul and Damian Alan Pargas. Boston: Brill, 2018: 118–47.

Strang, Cameron B. *Frontiers of Science: Imperialism and Natural Knowledge in the Gulf South Borderlands, 1500–1850*. Chapel Hill: University of North Carolina Press, 2018.

Strickland, Nicola H. "My Most Unfortunate Experience: Eating a Manchineel Beach Apple.'" *British Medical Journal* 321 (August 12, 2000): 428.

Striffler, Steve, and Mark Moburg, eds. *Banana Wars: Power, Production, and History in the Americas*. Durham, NC: Duke University Press, 2003.

Stroud, James T., and Jonathan B. Losos. "Ecological Opportunity and Adaptive Radiation." *Annual Review of Ecology, Evolution and Systematics* 47 (2016): 507–32.

Sturtevant, William C. "History and Ethnography of Some West Indian Starches." In *The Domestication and Exploitation of Plants and Animals*, edited by Peter J. Ucko and G. W. Dimbleby. Chicago: Aldine, 1969: 177–99.

Sued-Balillo, Jalil, ed. *General History of the Caribbean*, vol. I, *Autochthonous Societies*. Paris: UNESCO, 2003.

Tadman, Michael. "The Demographic Cost of Sugar: Debates on Slave Societies and Natural Increase in the Americas." *American Historical Review* 105 (2000): 1534–75.

Talman, C. Fitzhugh. "Climatology of Haiti in the Eighteenth Century." *Monthly Weather Review* (February 1906): 64–73.

Tankersly, K. B., N. P. Dunning, L. A. Owen, and J. Sparks. "Geochronology and Paleoenvironmental Framework for the Oldest Archaeological Site (7800–7900 cal BP) in the West Indies, Banwari Trace, Trinidad." *Latin American Antiquity* 29 (2018): 681–95.

Tardieu, Jean-Pierre. "Cimarrón-Maroon-Marron: An Epistemological Note." *Outre-Mers: Revue d'Histoire* 94, nos. 350–51 (2006): 237–47.

Tardo-Dino, Frantz. *Le Collier de servitude: la condition sanitaire des esclaves aux Antilles françaises du XVIIe au XIVe siècle*. Paris: Editions Caribéennes, 1985.

Taylor, Dicey, Marco Biscione, and Peter G. Roe. "Epilogue: The Beaded Zemi in the Pigorini Museum." In Bercht et al., eds., *Taíno*: 158–69.

Taylor, Douglas. "Spanish Hurricane and Its Congeners." *International Journal of American Linguistics* 22 (1956): 275–76.

Taylor, Michael, et al. "Climate Change and the Caribbean: Review and Response." *Caribbean Studies* 40 (December 2012): 169–200.

Thiebaut, Claude. *Sur les ruines de la Pointe-à-Pitre: Chronique du 8 février 1843—Hommage à l'Amiral Gourbeyre*. Paris: L'Harmattan, 2008.

Thornton, Russell. *American Indian Holocaust and Survival*. Norman: University of Oklahoma Press, 1987.

Tobriner, Stephen. "Safety and Reconstruction of Noto after the Sicilian Earthquake of 1693—the Eighteenth-Century Context." In *Dreadful Visitations: Confronting Natural Catastrophe in the Age of Enlightenment*, edited by Alessa Johns. New York: Routledge, 1999: 49–77.

Todd, Kim. *Chrysalis: Maria Sibylla Merian and the Secrets of Metamorphosis*. New York: Mariner Books, 2007.

Tomblin, Judith M., and Geoffrey R. Robson. "A Catalogue of Felt Earthquakes for Jamaica, with References to Other Islands in the Greater Antilles, 1564–1971." Ministry of Mining and Natural Resources, Special Publication 2, August 1977, typescript.

Tomich, Dale. "*Une Petite Guinée*: Provision Ground and Plantation in Martinique, 1830–1848." In Berlin and Morgan, eds., *Cultivation and Culture*: 221–42.

Tomich, Dale. "World Slavery and Caribbean Capitalism: The Cuban Sugar Industry, 1760–1869." *Theory and Society* 20, no. 3 (June 1991): 297–319.

Tomich, Dale, and Michael Zeuske, "Introduction: The Second Slavery: Mass Slavery, World-Economy and Comparative Microhistories." *Review of the Fernand Braudel Center* 31, no. 2 (2008): 91–100.

Tomkins, Sandra. "The Influenza Epidemic of 1918–19 in Western Samoa." *Journal of Pacific History* 27 (1992): 181–97.

Tone, John L. *War and Genocide in Cuba, 1895–1898*. Chapel Hill: University of North Carolina Press, 2008.

Torres, Joshua M., and Reniel Rodríguez Ramos. "The Caribbean: A Continent Divided by Water." In *Archaeology and Geoinformatics: Case Studies from the Caribbean*, edited by Basil A. Reid. Tuscaloosa: University of Alabama Press, 2008: 13–29.

Trouillot, Michel-Rolph. "Coffee Planters and Coffee Slaves in the Antilles: The Impact of a Secondary Crop." In Berlin and Morgan, eds., *Cultivation and Culture*: 124–37.

Trouillot, Michel-Rolph. "Culture on the Edges: Caribbean Creolization in Historical Context." In *From the Margins: Historical Anthropology and Its Futures*, edited by Brian Keith Axel. Durham, NC: Duke University Press, 2002: 189–210.

Trouillot, Michel-Rolph. *Peasants and Capital: Dominica in the World Economy*. Baltimore: Johns Hopkins University, 1988.

Trujillo-Pagan, Nicole. "Worms as a Hook for Colonising Puerto Rico." *Social History of Medicine* 26 (2013): 611–32.

Turner, Sasha Bryson. "The Art of Power: Poison and Obeah Accusations and the Struggle for Dominance and Survival in Jamaica's Slave Society." *Caribbean Studies* 41, no. 2 (2013): 61–90.

Turner, Sasha. *Contested Bodies: Pregnancy, Childrearing, and Slavery in Jamaica*. Philadelphia: University of Pennsylvania Press, 2017.

Turvey, Nigel. *The Cane Toads: A Tale of Sugar, Politics, and Flawed Science*. Sydney, Australia: Sydney University Press, 2013.

Turvey, Samuel T. "A New Historical Record of Macaws on Jamaica." *Archives of Natural History* 37, no. 2 (2010): 348–51.

Turvey, Samuel T., et al. "The Last Survivors: Current Status and Conservation of the Non-volant Land Mammals of the Insular Caribbean." *Journal of Mammalogy* 98, no. 4 (2017): 918–36.

Tyson, George F. "On the Periphery of the Peripheries: The Cotton Plantations of St. Croix, Danish West Indies, 1735–1815." In *Bondmen and Freedmen in the Danish West Indies: Scholarly Perspectives*, edited by Tyson. St. Thomas: Virgin Islands Humanities Council, 1996: 83–107.

Udías, Augustín. "Jesuit Studies of Earthquakes and Seismological Stations." In *Geology and Religion: A History of Harmony and Hostility*, edited by M. Kölbl-Ebert. Special Publications No. 310. London: Geological Society of London, 2009.

Ulanski, Stan. *The Gulf Stream: Tiny Plankton, Giant Bluefin, and the Amazing Story of the Powerful River in the Atlantic*. Chapel Hill: University of North Carolina Press, 2008.

Upham, Nathan S. "Past and Present of Insular Caribbean Mammals: Understanding Holocene Extinctions to inform Modern Biodiversity Conservation." *Journal of Mammalogy* 98, no. 4 (2017): 913–17.

Vagene, A. J., et al. "*Salmonella enterica* Genomes Recovered from Victims of a Major 16th-Century Epidemic in Mexico." *bioRxiv* (2017): 106740. http://dx.doi.org/10.1101/106740

Valcárcel Rojas, Roberto, and Ángela Peña Obregón. "Las sociedades indígenas en Cuba." In *Historia de Cuba*, edited by José Abreu Cardet. Santo Domingo: Archivo General de la Nación, 2013: 23–73.

Valliant, Sharon. "Maria Sibylla Merian: Recovering an Eighteenth-Century Legend." *Eighteenth-Century Studies* 26 (1993): 467–79.

Van Andel, Tinde R., et al. "Local Plant Names Reveal that Enslaved Africans Recognized Substantial Parts of the New World Flora." Proceedings of the National Academy of Sciences [PNAS] (December 2014). https://doi.org/10.1073/pnas.1418836111.

Van Gijn, Annelou, and Corinne L. Hofman. "Were They Used as tools? An Exploratory Functional Study of Abraded Potsherds from Two Pre-colonial Sites on the Island of Guadeloupe, Northern Lesser Antilles." *Caribbean Journal of Science* 44, no 1 (2008): 21–35.

Varner, John Grier, and Jeannette Johnson Varner. *Dogs of the Conquest*. Norman: University of Oklahoma Press, 1983.

Vázques Cienfuegos, Sigfrido, and Antonio Santamaria Garcia. "Indio foráneos en Cuba a principios del siglo XIX: historia de un suceso en el contexto de la movilidad poblacional y la geoestrategia del imperio español." *Colonial Latin American Historical Review*, 2nd Ser., 1, no. 1 (Winter 2013): 1–34.

Vázquez, Juan Jose Ponce. "Atlantic Peripheries: Diplomacy, War, and Spanish-French Interactions in Hispaniola, 1660s–1690s." In *The Atlantic World*, edited by D'Maris Coffman et al. New York: Routledge, 2015: 300–318.

Veloz Maggioli, M. *La isla de Santo Domingo antes de Colón*. Santo Domingo: Banco Central, 2003.

Vidal, Cécile. *Caribbean New Orleans: Empire, Race, and the Making of a Slave Society*. Chapel Hill: University of North Carolina Press, 2019.

Vidal, Teodoro. *El control de la naturaleza mediante la palabra en la tradición puerorriqueña*. San Juan: Alba, 2008.

Vilar, M. G., et al. "Genetic Diversity in Puerto Rico and Its Implications for the Peopling of the Island and the West Indies." *American Journal of Physical. Anthropology* 155 (2014): 352–68.

Vilar, M., et al. "The Origins and Genetic Distinctiveness of the Chamorros of the Marianas Islands: An mtDNA Perspective." *American Journal of Human Biology* 25 (2013): 116–22.

Vila, Pablo. "La destrucción de Nueva Cádiz: Terremoto o Huracán?" *Boletín de la Academia Nacional de la Historia* 31, no. 123 (September 1948): 213–19.

Villamizar, G., and F. Cervigón. "Variability and Sustainability of the Southern Subarea of the Caribbean Sea Large Marine Ecosystem." *Environmental Development* 22 (2017): 30–41.

Vogt, Jean. "Deux séismes majeurs de Saint-Domingue au XVIIIéme siècle: Le séisme du 3 juin 1770." *Généalogie et Histoire de la Caraibe* 178 (February 2005): 4424–4434.

Vogt, Jean. "A Glimpse at Historical Seismology of the West Indies." *Annals of Geophysics* 47 (April/June 2004): 465–76.

Waff, Craig P., and Stephen Skinner. "Thomas Stevenson of Barbados and Comet Halley's 1759 Return." In *George Washington's Visit to Barbados 1751*, compiled by Richard Goddard. St. Michael, Barbados: Cole Printery, 1997.

Waldron. Lawrence. "The Caimans of Carriacou." *Proceedings of XXV Congress of the International Association for Caribbean Archaeology*. Puerto Rico, 2013: 614–32.

Waldron, Lawrence. *Handbook of Ceramic Animal Symbols in the Ancient Lesser Antilles*. Gainesville: University of Florida Press, 2016.

Waldron, Lawrence. *Pre-Columbian Art of the Caribbean*. Gainesville: University Press of Florida, 2019.

Walker, Charles. *Shaky Colonialism: The 1746 Earthquake-Tsunami in Lima, Peru, and Its Long Aftermath*. Durham, NC: Duke University Press, 2008.

Walker, Christine. "To Be My Own Mistress: Women in Jamaica, Atlantic Slavery, and the Creation of Britain's American Empire, 1660–1770." PhD diss., University of Michigan, 2014.

Walker, Robert S., Lisa Sattenspiel, and Kim R. Hill. "Mortality from Contract-Related Epidemics among Indigenous Populations in Greater Amazonia." *Scientific Reports* 5 (September 10, 2015). DOI: 10.1038/srep14032.

Wallace, Geoffrey H. "The History and Geography of Beeswax Extraction in the Northern Maya Lowlands, 1540–1700." PhD diss., McGill University, 2020.

Wallerstein, Immanuel. *The Modern World-System*, vol. 2, *Mercantilism and the Consolidation of the European World Economy, 1600–1750*. New York: Academic Press, 1974.

Wallman, Diane. "Histories and Trajectories of Socio-Ecological Landscapes in the Lesser Antilles: Implications of Colonial Period Zooarchaeological Research." *Environmental Archaeology* 23, no. 1 (2018): 13–22.

Walter, François. "Pour une histoire culturelle des risques naturels." In *Les cultures du risque (xvi-xxi siècle)*, edited by François Walter, Bernardino Fantini, and Pascal Delvaux. Geneva: Presses d'Histoire Suisse, 2009.

Walvin, James. *The Zong: A Massacre, The Law, and the End of Slavery*. New Haven, CT: Yale University Press, 2011.

Wampler, P. J., A. Tarter, R. Bailis, K. Sander, and W. Sun. "Discussion of Forest Definitions and Tree Cover Estimates for Haiti." *Proceedings of the National Academy of Science, USA* 116 (2019): 5202–3.

Wang, Sijia, et al. "Genetic Variation and Population Structure in Native Americans." *PLOS Genetics* (November 23, 2007). doi.org/10.1371/journal.pgen.0030185.

Ward, J. R. "The Amelioration of British West Indian Slavery, 1750–1834: Technical Change and the Plough." *New West Indies Guide* 63, no. 1/2 (1989): 41–58.

Ward, J. R. "The Amelioration of British West Indian Slavery: Anthropometric Evidence." *Economic History Review* 71 (2018): 1199–226.

Ward, J. R. *British West Indian Slavery, 1750–1835: The Process of Amelioration*. Oxford: Oxford University Press, 1988.

Warrick, Gary. *A Population History of the Huron-Petun, A.D. 500–1650*. New York: Cambridge University Press, 2008.

Warsh, Molly A. *American Baroque: Pearls and the Nature of Empire, 1492–1700*. Chapel Hill: University of North Carolina Press, 2018.

Warsh, Molly A. "Enslaved Pearl Divers in the Sixteenth Century Caribbean." *Slavery and Abolition* 31 (2010): 345–62.

Warsh, Molly A. "A Political Ecology in the Early Spanish Caribbean." *William and Mary Quarterly* 71, no. 4 (October 2014): 516–48.

Watanabe, Tsuyoshi, Amos Winter, and Tadamichi Oba. "Seasonal Changes in Sea Surface Temperature and Salinity during the Little Ice Age in the Caribbean Sea Deduced from Mg/Ca and $^{18}O/^{16}O$ Ratios in Corals." *Marine Geology* 173 (2001): 21–35.

Watlington, Francisco. "The Physical Environment: Biogeographical Teleconnections in Caribbean Prehistory." In *General History of the Caribbean*, vol I, *Autochthonous Socities*, edited by Jalil Sued-Badilllo. London: UNESCO, 2003: 30–92.

Watlington, Roy A., and Shirley H. Lincoln. "The Caribbean Environment and Early Settlement." In *General History of the Caribbean*, vol. II, *New Societies: The Caribbean in the Long Sixteenth Century*, edited by P. C. Emmer. London: UNESCO, 1999: 29–42.

Watlington, Roy A., and Shirley H. Lincoln. *Disaster and Disruption in 1867: Hurricane, Earthquake, and Tsunami in the Danish West Indies*. St. Thomas: Eastern Caribbean Center, University of the Virgin Islands, 1997.

Watts, David. "Cycles of Famine in Islands of Plenty: The Case of the Colonial West Indies in the Pre-Emancipation Era." In *Famine as a Geographical Phenomenon*, edited by Bruce Currey and Graeme Hugo. Dordrecht: D. Reidel, 1984: 49–70.

Watts, David. "Long-Term Environmental Influences on Development in Islands of the Lesser Antilles." *Scottish Geographical Magazine* 109, no. 3 (1993): 133–41.

Watts, David. *The West Indies: Patterns of Development, Culture, and Environmental Change Since 1492*. Cambridge: Cambridge University Press, 1987.

Watts, Sheldon. "Yellow Fever Immunities in West Africa and the Americas in the Age of Slavery and Beyond: A Reappraisal." *Journal of Social History* 34 (2001): 955–67.

Weaver, Karol. *Medical Revolutionaries: The Enslaved Healers of Eighteenth-Century Saint Domingue*. Urbana: University of Illinois Press, 2006.

Webb, James. *Humanity's Burden: A Global History of Malaria*. New York: Cambridge University Press, 2009.

Webber, Oscar. "An Intolerance of Idleness; British Disaster 'Relief' in the Caribbean, 1831–1907." *New West Indian Guide* 93 (December 2019): 201–30.

Weiss, Holger, Laura Hollsten, and Steffen Norrgård, "Cotton and Salt: Swedish Colonial Aspirations and the Transformation of St. Barthélemy in the Eighteenth Century." *Environment and History* 26 (May 2020): 261–87.

Wells, E. Christian, et al. "Agroindustrial Soilscapes in the Caribbean: A Geochemical Perspective from Betty's Hope, Antigua." *Environmental Archaeology* 22, no. 4 (2017): 381–93.

Wells, E. Christian, et al. "Plantation Soilscapes: Initial and Cumulative Impacts of Colonial Agriculture in Antigua, West Indies." *Environmental Archaeology* 23, no. 1 (2018): 23–35.

West, Robert C., and John P. Augelli. *Middle America: Its Lands and Peoples*. Englewood Cliffs, NJ: Prentice-Hall, 1966.

Westergaard, Waldemar. *The Danish West Indies under Company Rule, 1671–1754*. New York: Macmillan, 1917.

Wey Gómez, Nicolás. *The Tropics of Empire: Why Columbus Sailed South to the Indies*. Cambridge, MA: MIT Press 2008.

Wheat, David. "Afro-Portuguese Maritime World and Foundations of Spanish Caribbean Society, 1570–1640." PhD diss., Vanderbilt University, 2009.

Wheat, David. *Atlantic Africa and the Spanish Caribbean, 1657–1640*. Chapel Hill: University of North Carolina Press, 2016.

Wheat, David. "Mediterranean Slavery, New World Transformations: Galley Slaves in the Spanish Caribbean, 1578–1635." *Slavery & Abolition* 31, no. 3 (2010): 327–44.

White, Ashli. *Encountering Revolution: Haiti and the Making of the Early Republic*. Baltimore: Johns Hopkins University Press, 2010.

Whitehead, Neil L. "Indigenous Cartography in Lowland South America and the Caribbean." In *The History of Cartography*, edited by David Woodward and G. Malcolm Lewis. *Cartography in the Traditional African, American, Arctic, Australian, and Pacific Societies*. Chicago: University of Chicago Press, 1987, vol. 2, bk. 3: 301–26.

Whitehead, Neil L., ed. *Wolves from the Sea: Readings in the Anthropology of the Native Caribbean*. Leiden: Brill, 1995.

Wiecko, Cynthia. *Guam: At the Crossroads of Spanish Militarization, Ecological Change, and Identity in World History*. Washington State University, PhD diss., 2011.

Wigen, Kären. "Introduction" and "Forum: Oceans of History." *American Historical Review* 111, no. 3 (2006): 717–80.

Wiley, James W., and Joseph W. Wunderle, Jr. "The Effects of Hurricanes on Birds with Special Reference to Caribbean Islands." *Bird Conservation International* 3 (1993): 319–49.

Wilhite, D. A., and M. H. Glantz. "Understanding the Drought Phenomenon: The Role of Definitions." *Water International* 10 (1985): 111–20.

Wilkinson, R. L. "Yellow Fever: Ecology, Epidemiology, and Role in the Collapse of the Classic Lowland Maya Civilization." *Medical Anthropology* 16 (1995): 269–94.

Wille, Sheila. "Governing Insects in Britain and the Empire, 1691–1816." PhD diss., University of Chicago, 2014.

Williams, M. I., and D. W. Steadman. "The Historic and Prehistoric Distribution of Parrots (Psittacidae) in the West Indies." in Woods and Sergile, eds., *Biogeography of the West Indies*, 175–89.

Willoughby, Urmi Engineer. *Yellow Fever, Race, and Ecology in Nineteenth-Century New Orleans*. Baton Rouge: Louisiana State University Press, 2017.

Wilson, E. O. "Ant Plagues: A Centuries Old Mystery Solved." In *Nature Revealed: Selected Writings, 1949–2006*. Baltimore: Johns Hopkins University Press, 2006: 344–50.

Wilson, E. O. *The Creation: An Appeal to Save Life on Earth*. New York: W. W. Norton, 2006.

Wilson, E. O. "Early Ant Plagues in the New World." *Nature* 433 (January 6, 2005): 32.

Wilson, Samuel. *The Archaeology of the Caribbean*. Cambridge: Cambridge University Press, 2007.

Wilson, Samuel M., ed. *The Indigenous People of the Caribbean*. Gainesville: University of Florida Press, 1997.

Wing, Elizabeth S. "Native American Use of Animals in the Caribbean." In Woods and Sergile, eds., *Biogeography of the West Indies*: 418–518.

Wing, Elizabeth S. "Pets and Camp Followers in the West Indies." In *Case Studies in Environmental Archaeology*, edited by Elizabeth Reitz et al. 2nd ed. New York: Springer, 2008: 405–26.

Wing, Elizabeth S. "Zooarchaeology of West Indian Land Mammals." In *Terrestrial Mammals of the West Indies: Contributions*, edited by R. Borroto-Páez, C. A. Woods, and F. E. Sergile. Gainesville: University of Florida Press, 2012: 341–56.

Wing, S. R., and E. S. Wing. "Prehistoric Fisheries in the Caribbean." *Coral Reefs* 20 (2001): 1–8.

Winter, Amos, Hiroshi Ishioroshi, Tsuyoshi Watanabe, Tadamichi Oba, and John Christy. "Caribbean Sea Surface Temperatures: Two-to-Three Degrees Cooler than Present during the Little Ice Age." *Geophysical Research Letters* 27 (2000): 3365–68.

Wisecup, Kelly. "Communicating Disease: Medical Knowledge and Literary Forms in Colonial British America." PhD diss., University of Maryland-College Park, 2009.

Wolfe, Mikael. "'A Revolution Is a Force More Powerful than Nature': Extreme Weather and the Cuban Revolution, 1959–64." *Environmental History* 25 (2020): 469–91.

Wolfe, N. D., C. P. Dunavan, and J. Diamond. "Origins of Major Human Infectious Diseases." In *Improving Food Safety Through a One Health Approach: Workshop Summary*. Washington, DC: National Academies Press, 2012: A16.

Wood, Betty. ed. *Travel Trade, and Power in the Atlantic, 1765–1884*. Cambridge: Cambridge University Press, 2002.

Wood, G. A. R., and R. A. Lass. *Cocoa*. 4th ed. Oxford, UK: Blackwell London: Longman, 1985.

Woods, Charles A., and Florence E. Sergile. "Antilles, Biology." In Gillespie and Clague, eds., *Encyclopedia of Islands*: 20–29.

Woods, Charles A., and Florence E. Sergile, eds. *Biogeography of the West Indies: Patterns and Perspectives*. 2nd ed. Boca Raton, FL: CRC Press, 2001.

Woods, Charles A., et al. "Insular Patterns and Radiations of West Indian Rodents." In Woods and Sergile, eds., *Biogeography of the West Indies*: 335–54.

World Health Organization. "Severe Falciparum Malaria." *Transactions of the Royal Society of Tropical Medicine and Hygiene* 94, suppl. (2000): 1–90.

World Health Organization, World Food Programme, and International Fund for Agricultural Development. *The State of Food Insecurity in the World 2012. Economic Growth Is Necessary but Not Sufficient to Accelerate Reduction of Hunger and Malnutrition*. Rome: FAO, 2012.

Worth, John. *The Timucuan Chiefdoms of Spanish Florida*, vol II, *Resistance and Destruction*. Gainesville: University of Florida Press, 1998.

Wrigley, E. A. "British Population during the Long Eighteenth Century, 1680–1840." In *The Cambridge Economic History of Modern Britain*, vol. I, *Industrialisation, 1700–1860*, edited by Roderick Floud and Paul Johnson. Cambridge: Cambridge University Press, 2004: 57–95.

Wulf, Andrea. *The Invention of Nature: Alexander von Humboldt's New World*. New York: Alfred A. Knopf, 2015.

Wüst, Georg. *Stratification and Circulation in the Antillean-Caribbean Basins*. New York: Columbia University Press, 1964.

Yaremko, Jason M. "Colonial Wars and Indigenous Geopolitics: Aboriginal Agency, the Cuba-Florida-Mexico Nexus, and the Other Diaspora." *Canadian Journal of Latin American & Caribbean Studies* 35, 70 (2010): 165–96.

Young, Sera L., et al. "Why on Earth? Evaluating Hypotheses about the Physiological Functions of Human Geophagy." *Quarterly Review of Biology* 86, no. 2 (June 2011): 97–120.

Zacek, Natalie. *Settler Society in the English Leeward Islands, 1660–1776*. Cambridge: Cambridge University Press, 2010.

Zandvliet, Kees. *Mapping for Money: Maps, Plans and Topographic Paintings and Their Role in Dutch Overseas Expansion during the 16th and 17th Centuries*. Amsterdam: Batavian Lion International, 1998.

Zilberstein, Anya. "Bastard Breadfruit and Other Cheap Provisions: Early Food Science for the Welfare of the Lower Orders." *Early Science and Medicine* 21, no. 5 (2016): 492–508.

Zilberstein, Anya. *A Temperate Empire: Making Climate Change in Early America*. New York: Oxford University Press, 2016.

Zuckerman, Molly, and Kristin Harper. "Paleoepidemiological and Biocultural Approaches to Ancient Disease: The Origin and Antiquity of Syphilis." In *New Directions in Biocultural Anthropology*, edited by Molly Zuckerman and Debra Martin. Hoboken, NJ: WileyBlackwell, 2016: 317–35.

Zueske, Michael. "Alexander von Humboldt in Cuba, 1800/1801 and 1804: Traces of an Enigma." *Studies in Travel Writing* 15, no. 4 (2011): 347–58.

Zúniga, Olga Portuondo. ¡*Misericordia! Terremotos y otros calamidades en la mentalidad del santiaguero*. Santiago de Cuba: Editorial Oriente, 2014.

Websites

Acevedo-Rodríguez, Pedro, and Mark T. Strong. "Flora of the West Indies." Smithsonian National Museum of Natural History. http://botany.si.edu/antilles/WestIndies/catalog.htm

British Archives Online: West Indies, Plantations, Slavery, and Trade, Slebech Papers. https://microform.digital/boa/collections/1/the-west-indies-slavery-plantations-and-trade-1759-1832/detailed-description

"Earthquakes in Jamaica." Earthquake Unit, University of the West Indies, Mona. https://www.mona.uwi.edu/earthquake/earthquakes-jamaica.

Flores, Claudia, Uri ten Brink, and William Bakun. "Accounts of Damage from Historical Earthquakes in the Northeastern Caribbean to Aid in the Determination of Their Location and Intensity Magnitudes." U.S. Geological Survey, Open-File Report, 2011-1133, 1–190. https://pubs.usgs.gov/of/2011/1133/

Form of Prayer by the Jewish congregation as Fast-Day on Wednesday 29th Adar, 5603, or 1st March, 1843, the day specially appointed by Proclamation for General Humiliation and Thanksgiving to the Almighty, for His Bountiful Protection on 8 February, when the Earthquake, which so slightly visited this Island, did such awful damage at Guadeloupe, Antigua and the Neighbouring Islands. Barbados, 1843. Accessed August 21, 2021. https://www.kestenbaum.net/auction/lot/auction-55/055-015/.

A Form of Prayer for the General Fast to be Read in Synagogue on the 11th August in Commemoration of the Hurricane in the Year 1831. Barbados, 1835. Accessed August 21, 2021. https://www.kestenbaum.net/auction/lot/Auction-85/085-012.

Partagás, Jose Fernández. "The Deadliest Atlantic Tropical Cyclones, 1492–Present." https://www.nhc.noaa.gov/pastdeadlyapp1.shtml?

Roser, Max, Esteban Ortiz-Ospina, and Hannah Ritchie. "Life Expectancy." 2019. https://ourworldindata.org/life-expectancy.

Trans-Atlantic Slave Trade Database. http://www.slavevoyages.org

United Nations. "Population Figures." https://www.macrotrends.net/cities/21133/port-au-prince/population.

Wagner, Laura. "Chronicle of a Disaster Foretold." https://medium.com/dukeuniversity/chronicle-of-a-disaster-foretold-d560206e9a32.

World Bank. "Urban Population: Latin America and the Caribbean." https://data.worldbank.org/indicator/SP.URB.TOTL.IN.ZS?end=2019&locations=ZJ-HT&name_desc=false&start=1960&view=chart

INDEX